Contents

CHAPTER 10   **_PROPERTY MANAGEMENT AND LEASING_**   95

    Property Mangement   95
    Types of Leasehold Estates   97
    The Essentials of a Valid Lease   98
    Assignment and Subleasing   98
    Leases Classified by Method of Rent Calculation   98
    Adjustments to Rental Terms to Cope with Inflation and Value Changes   99
    Termination of Leases   100
    The Uniform Landlord-Tenant Act   101

CHAPTER 11   **_HOME OWNERSHIP_**   106

    What Motivates a Person to Purchase a House?
    Who Can Afford to Buy a House?
    How to Determine Housing Needs   107
    What to Look for in Analyzing a House   107
    Considerations in Selling a House   111
    Property Insurance   111

CHAPTER 12   **_FEDERAL FAIR HOUSING LAWS_**   116

    What Is Prohibited by the 1968 Fair Housing Act?   116
    Who is Exempt from the Provisions of the 1968 Fair Housing Act?   117
    What is Prohibited by the Civil Rights Act of 1866?   118
    Complaints and Enforcement   118

CHAPTER 13   **_DEEDS AND TRANSFER OF TITLE_**   123

    Voluntary Conveyances   123
    Transfer by Devise or Descent   129
    Transfer by Adverse Possession   130
    Transfer by Accession   130
    Transfer by Public Action or Operation of Law   130

CHAPTER 14   **_MORTGAGES AND LIENS_**   135

    The Promissory Note or Bond   135
    The Mortgage Instrument   136
    Requirements for a Valid Mortgage Instrument   139
    Rights of Third Parties   140
    Liens   141
    How are Liens Classified?   141
    Specific Liens   142
    General Liens   143
    Priority of Liens   144

CHAPTER 15 — FINANCING REAL ESTATE 148

Recent Changes Affecting Real Estate Finance 148
Reasons for Borrowing 148
The Loan Process 149
Lending Laws Affecting Real Estate Finance 151
Sources of Funds 153
Classification of Mortgages 158

CHAPTER 16 — TITLE EXAMINATION AND SETTLEMENT 170

Recordation and the Chain of Title 170
Abstract of Title 171
Title Insurance 171
Torrens System of Title Registration 173
What Is Settlement? 173
Preliminary Procedures 173
Settlement Costs 177
Documents Obtained at Closing 179
Post-Closing Procedures 180

CHAPTER 17 — RESIDENTIAL APPRAISAL 183

Value: The Heart of all Real Estate Activity 183
The Appriasal Process 184
Reconciliation of Valuation Approaches 188
The Appraisal Report 188
Ethics and Professional Practice 188

CHAPTER 18 — INCOME PROPERTY APPRAISAL AND INVESTMENT ANALYSIS 194

Income Property Appraisal 194
Estimating Net Operating Income 194
Reconstructing the Operating Statement to Find Net Operating Income 195
Selecting an Appropriate Capitalization Rate 196
Application of the Capitalization Formula to Estimate Value 197
Real Estate Investment Analysis 198
Federal Taxation 201
What Are Allowable Deductions? 202
Installment Sales and Tax-Free Exchanges 202
Securities and Syndications 203

CHAPTER 19 — ZONING AND TAXATION 207

The Planning Process 207
Police Power Regulations 207
Future Trends in Land-Use Regulation 210
The Property Tax Process 210

Contents

CHAPTER 20   **REAL ESTATE MATH**   215

            Fractions   216
            Decimals   216
            Percentages   217
            Basic Formulas Used in Solving Real Estate Problems   218
            Standards of Measurement   218
            Real Estate Applications   218

APPENDIX A   **LISTING AND SALES CONTRACTS**   230

APPENDIX B   **PREPARATION OF SETTLEMENT STATEMENT WORKSHEET**   240

APPENDIX C   **DIAGNOSTIC EXAMINATION**   258

APPENDIX D   **PRACTICE SALESPERSON'S EXAMINATION**   273

APPENDIX E   **PRACTICE BROKER'S EXAMINATION**   279

GLOSSARY OF REAL ESTATE TERMS   285

GLOSSARY OF CONSTRUCTION TERMINOLOGY AND ILLUSTRATIONS   309

SOLUTIONS AND EXPLANATIONS   314

SELECTED BIBLIOGRAPHY   329

REAL ESTATE COMMISSIONS   331

INDEX   335

Preface

Real estate sales and brokerage is more than just a business or means to a livelihood. It has become an exciting, challenging and fulfilling profession. To be a successful real estate professional, you have to become knowledgeable about a wide range of interesting subjects. This book has been designed to help you gain that knowledge.

To become a member of the brokerage profession you must first become licensed. To do this, you must pass a written licensing exam. The first chapter of this book will introduce you to the subjects that appear on the exam. The next two chapters discuss the nature of real estate and the real estate profession. The fourth chapter will show you what to look for when you are reading your state license law. By reading these four chapters carefully, you will understand what is expected of you when you enter the profession.

The book is designed to give you a systematic way to build up your knowledge in regard to important real estate subjects. A keystone to this understanding is Chapter 5, "Real Estate Contracts." Contracts are the way that people create legal obligations and transfer property interests. Contracts underlie such activities as agency relations, deeds, mortgages and leases. You should, therefore, read this chapter very carefully. A significant portion of the real estate business depends on contracts. The next chapter defines the salesperson's and broker's role as agents. Most of your activities are carred out as an agent for some client. The agent is a very special person who has certain duties that must be performed. You need to fully understand the principal-agent relationship.

Since most of your activities will involve helping sell, lease or manage real property interests, you must be able to describe what you are selling. Chapter 7 discusses how property is legally described, and Chapter 8 explains the types of rights and interests recognized in this country. Because condominiums have become such a very important part of your business, a separate chapter has been devoted to this topic.

The next three chapters are directed primarily to the consideration of leasing and the selling of housing, although other types of real estate are considered as well. Discussion is given to leases, property management, home ownership, insurance and fair housing laws.

Four chapters deal with what you need to know after you have negotiated a sale of real property. How is title transferred? Where do you go for financing? What is included in a mortgage? What happens at settlement and closing? These are questiaons that your clients ask, and these chapters provide you with some of the answers.

As you become successful in residential sales, you might want to accept the challenge of becoming involved in more complicated commercial transactions. To do this, you must be able to talk the language of investors. The next set of chapters provides a discussion of appraisal theory and investment analysis concepts. These chapters serve as a primer to this very interesting aspect of commercial brokerage activity.

Chapter 19 deals with government involvement with real estate. Discussion is given to the growth of our cities, planning theory, zoning ordinances, building codes, property taxation and similar topics. Finally, a bonus chapter is included. Chapter 20 summarizes basic math problems that are likely to appear on your exam. This can serve as a quick refresher for you if you are rusty in a particular math area.

This book contains a number of special features that you might find very helpful. There is a diagnostic exam that can help you pinpoint your subject weakness. Practice final exams are included for both salespersons and brokers. There are over 1,100 practice questions throughout the book. A careful reading of the chapters and answering the questions in this book should give you the skills, knowledge and confidence you need to enter a very exciting profession. Good luck!

1

The Real Estate Licensing Examinations

Currently, over one-half of the licensing jurisdictions in the United States use the Real Estate Licensing Examinations (RELE) administered by Educational Testing Service (ETS), Princeton, New Jersey. The guidelines for these examinations are determined by a committee consisting of one representative from each of the licensing jurisdictions presently using the RELE examinations. Any questions concerning eligibility requirements for taking either the salesperson or broker examinations should be directed to the licensing officials in the particular jurisdiction where one desires to be licensed. If you have any questions about the tests, you may write to ETS at the following address:

Real Estate Licensing Examinations
Educational Testing Service
CN 6507
Princeton, New Jersey 08541-6507

If you need to call ETS for any reason, the telephone number is (215) 750-8305.

THE TESTS

Both the salesperson and broker examinations are comprised entirely of objective, multiple-choice questions. All examination questions are contained in a test booklet, and a separate answer sheet is provided for recording answers. Since the total score on an examination is based on the percentage of questions answered correctly, it is better to guess at an answer than to leave it blank.

In all jurisdictions using the Real Estate Licensing Examinations each examination consists of two tests: (1) the uniform test and (2) the state test. The minimum passing scores are established by each licensing agency, and within two or three weeks after taking the examination the applicant is notified by ETS as to the outcome of the examination.* If an applicant successfully passes both the uniform

*Some states currently use an electronic system called keyway which permits candidates to enter their test responses on a simple miniaturized electronic Answerpad, then have their test scored and reported before they leave the testing center.

and state tests, the score report indicates *pass* and scores on individual parts of the uniform test are not given. However, if the applicant fails the examination, a separate score for each failed part will be given on a scale of 1 to 100 plus a notice of "needs improvement," "marginal," "fair," "good," or "excellent" on each subject area of the test. This is done to aid those people who fail the examination in improving weak areas.

A number of different multiple-choice formats are used on the examinations. It is important for anyone planning to take either the salesperson or broker examinations to become thoroughly familiar with these formats. By doing so, a great deal of time can be saved during the actual examination. In the sample formats below, an asterisk indicates the correct answer.

1. **Direct Question.**
   Example: Which of the following sets of terms is incorrect?
   (A) Grantor—seller (C) Grantee—buyer
   *(B) Mortgagor—lender (D) Lessor—landlord

2. **Sentence Completion.**
   Example: A husband's interest in property owned by his wife at her death is known as:
   (A) dower (C) community property
   (B) trust *(D) curtesy

3. **"Except" Format.**
   Example: According to common law, all of the following unities are required for the creation and survival of a joint tenancy EXCEPT
   (A) time (C) title
   *(B) coparcenary (D) possession

4. **The "I/II" Format.** This type of question gives a question followed by two statements or choices, labeled I and II. Four possibilities exist, but only one of the four is correct. These four choices, labeled (A), (B), (C) and (D), are as follows:
   (A) I only (C) Both I and II
   (B) II only (D) Neither I nor II

Example: A land survey should include at least
    I. a definite starting point
    II. the area in accepted units of measurement contained within the boundaries

(A) I only   *(C) Both I and II
(B) II only   (D) Neither I nor II

5. **Situational Format.** This format involves answering two or three questions from information supplied in a brief narrative. Topics such as fair housing and the handling of escrow money would be included in this type of question.
6. **Question Sets.** Questions can also be asked from information presented in graphs, tables, charts, plats, etc. If used, such visual stimuli will provide information for answering between two and three questions in one examination. A good example of this type of question would be questions based on the reading and interpretation of a subdivision plat.

SALESPERSON EXAMINATION

The salesperson examination consists of two separate tests. Depending on the particular jurisdiction, up to a total of four and one-half hours is given to answer the 80 questions on the uniform test and the 30-50 questions on the state test.

The Uniform Test (80 Questions)

These 80 questions cover information within five broadly defined subject areas. Approximately 20% of these questions concern arithmetic functions. These 20 questions appear throughout the uniform test and are not grouped as a separate examination. The five broad subject areas are as follows:

Real Estate Contracts (13% of Uniform Test)

Covered under the heading of real estate contracts are general questions and terminology regarding specific real estate contracts such as listing agreements, sales contracts, leases and options.

Financing (24% of Uniform Test)

Questions in this area cover both instruments used in financing and means of financing. Topics such as private and public sources of financing, government regulations of lenders, lending laws, types of mortgages, lending procedures, default and foreclosure appear among these 24 questions.

Real Estate Ownership (22% of Uniform Test)

This very broad area of coverage includes the following four topics:

1. Deeds: types, recordation
2. Interests in real property: estates, private rights, public powers and special interests in real property
3. Condominiums: general information, ownership of common and separate elements, duties and responsibilities of developer and homeowners' association
4. Federal Fair Housing Act: laws, practices, procedures, grievances, penalties

Real Estate Brokerage (24% of Uniform Test)

Included in this area are the following topics:

1. Law of agency: definitions, rights and duties of a principal and an agent
2. Property management: general scope and functions of property management
3. Settlement procedures: title, conveyance, settlement charges and prorations.

Real Estate Valuation (17% of Uniform Test)

The four areas included under this topic are:

1. Appraisal: definition of value, approaches to value, appraisal terminology, appraisal process
2. Planning and zoning: public land use controls, police powers, private developing and subdividing
3. Property description: types of property descriptions, plat reading and related terms and concepts
4. Taxes and assessments: real property taxes, liens, special assessments and other tax factors

The State Test (30-50 Questions)

These questions vary from one jurisdiction to another and deal specifically with the rules and regulations of a particular jurisdiction. Subjects covered include license requirements, issuance of licenses, activities of the governing agency, general operating requirements, state code of ethics, hearing procedures and refusal, suspension or revocation of licenses. The appropriate state commission can provide the applicant with information concerning this part of the examination.

BROKER EXAMINATION

The broker examination also consists of two separate tests and depending on the jurisdiction can be up to four and one-half hours long. Eighty questions are covered on the uniform test and 30-50 questions are asked on the state test.

The Uniform Test (80 Questions)

These 80 questions cover information within four subject areas. Approximately 20% of the questions require arithmetic calculations. The four subject areas are as follows:

Real Estate Brokerage (35% of Uniform Test)

Included in this area are the following topics:

1. Listing and showing property: responsibilities of a broker when contracting to list, advertise and show property for sale, lease, trade or exchange, including responsibilities under the law of agency and compliance with federal fair housing laws.

2. Settlement procedures: responsibilities of a broker in arranging settlement, including closing costs, prorations, recordation procedures and compliance with the Real Estate Procedures Act.
3. Property management: responsibilities of a broker managing property, including maintenance, rent collection, security deposits and negotiating leases.

Contracts and Other Legal Aspects
(27% of Uniform Test)

This very broad area of coverage includes the following six topics:

1. Contracts: general aspects of contract law
2. Land use controls: zoning, deed restrictions, requirements for subdividing and developing
3. Deeds: general characteristics of various types of deeds
4. Property ownership: rights and interests, characteristics of various types of ownership
5. Condominiums and cooperatives: requirements for establishment, types of ownership and aspects of property conversion
6. Other legal aspects: legal implications of public powers and special interests in real property

Pricing and Valuation (15% of Uniform Test)

Questions in this area cover principles of value, approaches to estimating value and the pricing of real estate for sale, rent or exchange in the absence of an appraisal report.

Financing and Investment (23% of Uniform Test)

The four areas included under this topic are the following:

1. Financing arrangements: costs involved in loan placement, governmental financing agencies and requirements of the Truth-in-Lending Act.
2. Financing instruments: characteristics of promissory notes, mortgages, deeds of trust, installment land contracts and other financing instruments.
3. Loans and mortgages: characteristics of different types of loans, essential elements and special clauses of mortgages, sources of junior loans and conditions and procedures involved in default and foreclosure.
4. Tax ramifications: tax consequences of home ownership and investment property, including interest and property tax deductions, depreciation, capital gains and losses and refinancing.
5. Real estate securities: basic concepts of syndications, their formation and federal laws governing securities.

The State Test (30-50 Questions)

Like the salesperson exam, these questions vary from jurisdiction to jurisdiction because they deal with specific laws, rules and regulations of a particular jurisdiction. Subjects covered include hearing proceedings, fair housing, license requirements, state code of ethics and refusal, suspension or revocation of licenses. State real estate commissions can provide applicants with information concerning the state test, and applicants are encouraged to contact their particular licensing agency.

OVERCOMING TEST ANXIETY

Are you afraid of taking tests? You are not alone. Many people are. When they face an exam situation they begin to tense up, suffer from headaches, and endure queasy stomachs. During the exam their minds sometimes go blank or they freeze. These people suffer from what is known as "test anxiety."

Test anxiety occurs for several reasons. First is the fear of the unknown. If you face a situation in which you have no knowledge of what is going to happen and the stakes or rewards are high, you are more likely to become anxious. Try to remember your first date or your first job interview. Those were tense moments. After you knew what to expect, you became more comfortable with similar situations. This book can help you cope with the unknown on state real estate licensing examinations. The material in this book is comprehensive and gives you the knowledge you need to pass the examination. The practice questions at the end of each chapter, the diagnostic exam and the practice exams at the end of the book will let you become familiar with what you can expect.

A second reason for test anxiety results from repressed feeling from having had bad test experiences in the past. If your teachers or parents have criticized you for making a bad grade when you were in school, this may have affected your attitude without you consciously realizing why. If people have told you that you do not have ability to do well on tests or if you have convinced yourself that you will not do well, this will add to your test anxiety.

One of the best ways to change your attitude is to have some successful experiences in taking tests. This book allows you to take a number of tests under no pressure. If you have carefully read the material in each chapter, you should do well in answering the review questions. At the end of the book is an explanation for each of the correct answers. The more tests you take, the better you are going to do. After you have read each chapter, you will be prepared to take the practice exam for either the salesperson or broker tests. You will discover that the exam will seem easy because of your previous work in answering the review questions at the end of each chapter.

The third reason for test anxiety results from not having developed a successful test-taking strategy. Some people with the same knowledge as you do five to ten points better on their exams. Why? Do they know some tricks that help them score better? Actually there are no tricks. What those people have is a better test-taking strategy.

SUGGESTIONS FOR TAKING STANDARDIZED EXAMINATIONS

The following suggestions are offered as aids in preparing a person for either the salesperson or broker examination. These suggestions are the basis of a successful test-taking strategy.

Before the Examination

1. Get a full night's sleep before the exam. Going to the exam well rested will help you avoid careless mistakes.
2. Do not try to memorize a large number of facts at the last minute. It is better to review over an extended period of time before taking the exam than trying to learn everything over a weekend. The day before the exam you should review your weak areas rather than trying to "cram" a great deal of information into your brain.
3. Take a watch to the exam. This will help you pace yourself.
4. Take several pencils and a calculator (if allowed) and extra batteries.
5. Before starting, read and thoroughly understand all the directions. Reading the directions can help you avoid unnecessary problems that could affect your test score.

During the Examination

1. Read each question carefully. Questions on the licensing examination are written so that you may choose one of the incorrect choices simply by not reading the stem of the question carefully.
2. Do not jump to conclusions and select the first answer that looks correct. Examine all alternative answers. All four of the possible choices on the examination questions may appear to be reasonable answers. In fact, they may be very good "incorrect" answers and generally cannot be quickly eliminated without careful thought.
3. Eliminate obvious wrong answers. You will, upon examining the alternative answers in some questions, be able to eliminate one or more of the choices as soon as you have completed reading the questions. For example, examine the following question:

    > The purpose of state real estate licensing law is to accomplish which result?
    > A. To keep down unemployment
    > B. To protect the public
    > C. To exclude retired people from the profession
    > D. To restrict competition

    Answer "C" is clearly wrong and should be eliminated. It should be obvious that discrimination against the elderly is not acceptable state policy.
4. Be aware of certain cue words such as "always," "never," "all," "only," "totally," and "without exception." As you will discover in reading the material in this text, few activities or events in real estate are "always" or "never" or "without exception." When such words appear in an examination question, the statement is more than likely a wrong choice.
5. Watch for questions that depend on words that are similar in sound or meaning and may trick the unwary reader. In your reading the material explaining the legal rights and interests in real estate, you will be introduced to the words "ownership in severalty" which sounds like it refers to ownership by several or a number of people. However, you will discover that "severalty" refers not to multiple ownership but rather ownership by an individual.
6. Do not spend too much time on any one question. After working on a question for a reasonable period of time, move on to the next question since each question counts the same. An easy question counts the same as a hard one. So that you do not run out of time answer the easy questions first and skip those that are likely to take a great deal of time to solve. Later, go back and answer the more difficult questions.
7. Make an examination budget to know how much time on the average you can take on each question. Most examinations last between three and four hours and cover between 100 and 140 questions. Thus for a 100-question exam, you should have completed 50 of the questions within one-half of the total allotted examination time.
8. Use your watch to pace yourself. Do not let your allotted test-taking time pass without maintaining a steady pace toward completion of the examination questions.
9. Stop and think. Avoid hurried answers. If you budget your time carefully, you will have adequate time to carefully read all of the questions and examine all of the alternatives. Thus, you will not have to rely on hurried answers which, as you know, usually result in incorrect choices.
10. Guess intelligently. By the time you take the licensing examination you will know a great deal about real estate. Thus, with most licensing questions you should be able to choose from the alternatives with enough knowledge of the subject to make an intelligent guess.
11. If you think none of the choices are correct, pick the closest answer. All of the licensing examination questions have been written by professionals and pretested for their accuracy and difficulty. Certain questions, no doubt, do not seem to have correct answers. However, one of the four choices given for each question is going to be graded as the correct answer and therefore, if you do not agree with any of the choices, you still need to pick the answer that you believe best answers the question.
12. Before time is up, put something down for each question since wrong answers are not subtracted from right answers in calculating final grades. Do not leave any question blank. While a guess may not give you the right answer, a guess improves your chances for a higher score.
13. Keep working until you are told to stop. Do not leave the exam early. After you have answered all of the examination questions, use the remainder of the time to rethink your unsure answers.
14. If you still have time left after you have completed the exam, go back and review each question. Do not leave early. Reviewing the exam can help you find "silly" mistakes such as mismarking an answer or having misread the question.

2

What Is Real Estate?

The term "real estate" has many meanings. One common definition is the land and all improvements on and to the land. Real estate provides the basis of shelter and privacy for the individual and the family. It is also the basis for work and commercial activities. Food and mineral resources are extracted from real estate. Cities are formed by complex and interrelated real estate decisions. How well and how wisely real estate decisions are made determines the health and prosperity of people.

Prospective brokers or salespersons should realize that real estate must be understood from at least four different perspectives. First, real estate is a physical and biological concept. It consists of surface, mineral, air, vegetation and other tangible elements. Second, real estate is an economic concept. Each surface unit has certain relationships and revenue or cost potentials which determine its function as an economic unit of production. Third, real estate is a legal concept. All land units are subject to certain property rights and limitations enforced by law. Fourth, real estate is a social and cultural concept. The way each land unit is used has an impact on the social and cultural environment.

REAL ESTATE AS A PHYSICAL CONCEPT

Each unit of real estate is comprised of three-dimensional space. This space consists of the land's surface, the space beneath, which theoretically extends to the center of the earth, and the space above, which extends to the skies. If the surface unit were square, the space would form an inverted pyramid from the center of the earth stretching into space. The various elements that the possessor of surface units controls are illustrated in Figure 2-1.

Possession of space gives access to numerous resources. For example, control of the surface gives the possessor use of the topsoil, crops, trees and other vegetation, manmade improvements, water passing on or next to the land and natural features such as hills or scenic views. Control of the subsurface gives the possessor access to various mineral rights: oil, gas, coal, geothermal energy, subsurface water and caves that are directly below the surface unit. Possession of air space permits the building of high-rise structures, gives access to solar and wind power sources, prevents others from using the space and gives the possessor various other rights enforceable by law. With the advent of air travel, the right to total control of air space has been limited to the space that the possessor could reasonably be expected to use. Space above that is shared with the public. Ownership of the surface gives the possessor control over several natural elements. Each element may be sold separately without selling the others, thereby increasing the economic worth of the real estate asset. How this may be done will be described in the legal concept section of this chapter.

There are several distinguishing *physical characteristics* of real estate. Especially significant are: (1) immobility, (2) durability and (3) heterogeneity.

Immobility

Real estate space is fixed in location; it cannot be moved. While it is true that the various elements within the space may be moved, such as the topsoil or the minerals, the space itself remains in the same geographic location. This immobility leads to several legal and economic results. From a legal standpoint only the legal rights, and not the asset itself, can be physically transferred to a purchaser. Accordingly this transference requires a description of the space which is dependent on clearly defined reference points. Without a sufficient description, courts will not recognize legal instruments purporting to convey rights in the real estate (see Chapter 7). From an economic standpoint, in order to use the real estate as part of a productive good, other factors of production must be attracted to the land; the land cannot go to the other factors of production. Likewise, the real estate is highly dependent on the surrounding environment. If someone builds a store, a factory or a house on a site nearby, this change in land use will have some effect, either positive or negative, on the subject property. The dependency of each parcel of real estate on the surrounding environment leads to a reliance on public goods such as highways, utilities, nearby schools and parks.

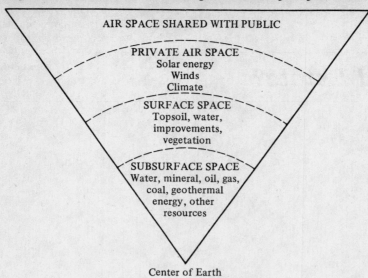

Figure 2-1. Elements Controlled by Possessors of Surface Units

The immobility also causes real estate markets to be very local in nature.

Durability

This characteristic is also described as *indestructibility*. The improvements to land are long-lived. The land itself is virtually indestructible even though certain elements of the land may be *depleted*. For example, minerals may be removed or the fertility may be diminished. Under certain circumstances if tunneling has occurred, the surface may subside. The space, however, will remain. Under unusual circumstances there are cases in which the amount of space is diminished as well. For example, if one boundary of the property is described as the center of a river, and the river gradually shifts, space could be lost. These are rare cases, and as a general rule the real estate is considered to be very durable. This feature of durability requires that a real estate development decision be carefully researched before labor and capital are committed. The results of any decision will be long-lived and have a long-term impact on the surrounding environment.

Heterogeneity

Each piece of real estate is considered to be highly differentiated: no two parcels of land are exactly the same. If nothing else, the different location makes each parcel unique and thus nonsubstitutable. Differences such as soil and subsoil conditions, zoning, availability of utilities, access, topography, market desirability and direction of prevailing winds help to differentiate each parcel of land. This characteristic of heterogeneity requires that the real estate analyst carefully inspect each parcel of land to determine its suitability to the proposed use. A failure to recognize the uniqueness of each parcel of land has led to many poor investments.

Real estate is also a biological concept. Increasing awareness has occurred since the passage of major federal and state environmental legislation that land use has an impact on the ecology. Development of land changes the drainage and absorption of water. Plant and animal life are destroyed or displaced. Noise increases. Some pollution of air and water may occur. Legal restrictions may make it necessary to limit development or change design criteria of projects. A failure to understand the ecological link of the land to the surrounding environment may lead to restraining action by public officials and the courts, or to public outcry.

REAL ESTATE AS AN ECONOMIC CONCEPT

Real estate is an economic good which satisfies human wants and needs; thus, real estate commands a price. In order for real estate or any economic good to have value, certain elements must be present. These are: (1) demand, (2) utility, (3) scarcity and (4) transferability. The first letter of each spells the word *dust*. This makes it easy to remember that in order to have value real estate must have "DUST."

Demand is a basic economic term which denotes a qualified buyer who is ready, willing and able to make the purchase. If any or all of the other three elements are missing, then no demand exists. Demand is more than just human desire; it is desire plus purchasing power. Demand for different parcels of land is different. While some parcels are quite actively demanded by potential users, other parcels are of little interest to anyone. Consequently, some real estate commands a higher price than other real estate.

Utility refers to usefulness. The more useful a parcel of real estate is, the more a user is likely to be willing to pay for it. Usefulness, by itself, is not enough to create value. For example, air and water are vital to human needs. However, air and water are ordinarily not scarce. In states where water is scarce, water rights may command a higher price than land.

Scarcity is a relative term. To speak of the scarcity of real estate is to refer to the limited supply of certain types of real estate at particular locations. For example, due to zoning restrictions industrial land may be very scarce in one city, while in another city there may be an oversupply of this type of land. In determining the scarcity of a good, it is necessary to equate supply and demand. If there is no demand, then there is no scarcity from an economic perspective.

Transferability is the ability to transfer legal rights to real estate. If legal rights could not be transferred from one person to another, no value could result.

In determining what real estate will be used and what will be produced on that real estate, it is necessary to understand the economic concept of *factors of production*. There are four factors of production: (1) labor, (2) capital, (3) entrepreneurship or management and (4) land. In the United States, where there is private ownership of these factors of production, the owner(s) must be adequately compensated in order to make the factor available for production. For example, if a particular labor skill commands $10 per hour in the marketplace, then a person (the laborer) who owns that factor of production can receive $10 for every hour he or she works. Likewise, if the interest rate being paid for the use of money or capital is 10%, then someone with $100 available to invest can expect $10 for the use of that capital. Entrepreneurship or management skills also command compensation if they are to be made available. Land as a factor of production, however, is different, due to the fact that it is immobile. Since land is immobile, it must attract the other three factors of production, and they must be compensated first. As a result, land receives its payment only after the other factors have been compensated. This means that real estate is *residual*. That is, the value of real estate or what it is worth is a function of how much compensation or income remains after the other three factors of production have been paid (see Chapter 17).

The use of land which gives the largest residual compensation is referred to as the *highest and best use* (HABU). The owner of the land will choose to employ it in such a manner as to generate the greatest possible revenue from the land. A standard definition of highest and best use is that possible and legal use which preserves the utility of the land and yields a net income stream that forms, when capitalized, the highest present value of the land.

Highest and best use does not occur if a parcel of land is underimproved or overimproved. If a parcel of land can profitably absorb more units than are currently being employed, then the land is said to be *underimproved*. This means that, given the current economic, social and political environment, more income could be generated for the land than is currently being done. However, if the landowner has combined more factor inputs with the land than can be profitably absorbed the land is *overimproved*.

Real estate also has several *economic characteristics*. These are: (1) fixed investment, (2) modification, (3) long life and high capital value, (4) economic location, (5) scarcity, and (6) divisibility. As is illustrated in Figure 2–2, these economic characteristics are influenced by the various physical characteristics of real estate.

Fixed Investment

Since a particular parcel of land cannot be moved to a more desirable location, any investment or dollar outlay on a particular site becomes somewhat fixed, or from an accounting stand point, a sunk cost. If market conditions change and suddenly there is no demand for office space at a certain location, then the present owner of an existing office building at that location cannot easily move the building to a location where demand does exist. Real estate is very susceptible to changes in the marketplace as well as changes in the surrounding physical environment. Further, real estate owners are subject to the whims of local and state government such as zoning ordinances, building codes and condemnation (see Chapter 19).

Modification

An important economic characteristic of land is how its use and its value can change as a result of modifications of other parcels. Likewise, surrounding parcels are generally influenced by changes on and to the subject property. This is often referred to as the *principle of dependency*.

Figure 2–2. Physical Characteristics Influence Economic Characteristics of Real Estate

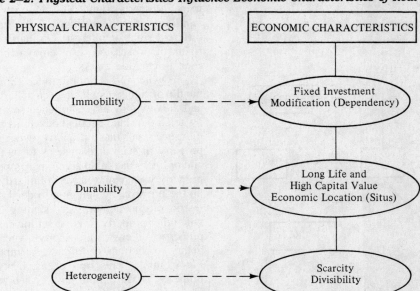

Spillover effects are most apparent in land-use changes. Such changes can be the result of both private and public expenditures. Consider, for example, the impact of building a freeway interchange next to a parcel of land, or the impact of an adjoining property owner developing a large shopping center. These modifications will in all likelihood change the highest and best use of the surrounding real estate.

Economic Location (Situs)

Economic location is an important characteristic in determining the success or failure of real estate. The importance of location is due largely to the fact that individuals need specific types of land for specific uses at specific places. A decision as to whether or not a particular parcel will be used is dependent upon how that parcel fits into the land-use pattern. For example, the success of a retail store is dependent on how near it is to where its customers live. This proximity to a supporting land use is called *linkage*. Linkage refers to the time and distance cost necessary to reach the supporting facility. If the retail store is too far away from its customers, they will be attracted to a nearer store, or a nearer store will be developed to intercept the customers.

In the case of residential real estate (see Figure 2–3) the good location (situs) typically includes proximity to work, school, church, shopping, recreation and entertainment. When asked to name the three most important factors in determining the success of a real estate project, many developers/investors respond, "*location, location* and *location.*"

Long Life and High Capital Value

Land and improvements both to and on the land have a long economic life. The development of land involves a large capital outlay, and thus the need for debt financing over a long period of time is often created (see Chapter 15).

Figure 2–3. Linkages with Single-Family Residence "Good Location"

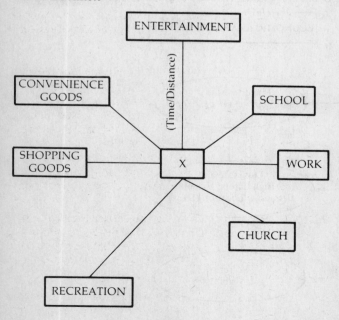

Since few buyers have large sums of money available, this economic characteristic makes real estate activity highly dependent on monetary conditions, interest rates and the availability of capital.

Scarcity

While there is no physical shortage of land in the United States, there are occasional shortages of economically useful land at particular locations. In the short term the supply of usable land is *inelastic*, which means that little if any increase in quantity can be made. Therefore, possessors of key locations may have a monopolistic advantage. Over the long term other land may be modified and brought into the effective supply. However, it should be noted that, even though there are millions of acres of land in the United States, urban land accounts for only about 2% of the total. Suppose, for example, that every man, woman and child living in the United States could all be moved to the states of Texas and Oklahoma. If this were done, then the *density* level, the number of people per square mile in the two states, would equal the current density level in Western Europe.

Divisibility

This economic characteristic is based on the idea that real estate involves legal rights and interests which may be divided and sold separately. The economic impact is that different users may utilize the real estate without being obligated to purchase the entire asset. For example, a developer leases land, constructs a building and generates rental income without having legal title to the land.

REAL ESTATE AS A LEGAL CONCEPT

The law defines rights and interests in real estate by indicating the extent of real property ownership. This ownership involves an aggregate of rights, powers and privileges which are guaranteed and protected by the government. Property rights and interests are analogous to a *bundle of sticks* (*see* Figure 2–4). Each stick represents a different right or interest. Ordinarily, the bundle includes rights of possession, use, enjoyment, disposition and the right to exclude others.

Ownership is not unlimited. Some of the sticks in the bundle of rights may have been sold or taken away. Society and the law may have shortened some of the sticks. Today ownership of land entails both rights and duties. The *law of nuisance* states that a property owner may not use his or her property in such a manner as to interfere with reasonable and ordinary use of an adjoining property owner. Further, a property owner may have voluntarily accepted limitations on the property by agreeing to deed restrictions, accepting restrictions in a mortgage, signing contractual covenants with other property owners, selling easements or leasing the property. Likewise, a property owner may have had involuntary restrictions or limitations imposed on the property. For example, prescriptive easements could exist on the property, a court could have issued an injunction prohibiting certain uses, a lien may have been placed on the property or someone could be maintaining an encroachment.

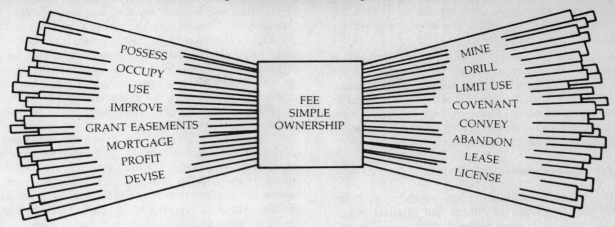

Figure 2–4. The "Bundle of Sticks"

These various concepts will be more fully discussed in Chapter 8 which deals with rights and interests in real estate. Finally, property ownership is subject to various restrictions by the public. These restrictions are: (1) police power regulations such as zoning ordinances or building codes, (2) the power of taxation, (3) the power of eminent domain and (4) the power of escheat. Public restrictions will be discussed more fully in subsequent chapters. The various limitations on real property ownership are graphically illustrated in Figure 2–5.

The law classifies property as real, personal and mixed. Property is also classified as tangible and intangible.

Real Property and Personal Property

Property may be classified as real property or personal property. *Real property, real estate* and *realty* are terms which may be used interchangeably. These terms refer to land and the improvements both on and to the land. This concept also refers to the physical aspects of real estate previously described, including surface, air and subsurface rights. Further, it refers to all man-made objects and articles permanently annexed or attached to the land. *Personal property, personalty* and *chattels* are terms which refer to moveables which are not annexed to or part of the land. Personal property also applies to objects such as trees which have been severed from the real property.

The distinction between real and personal property is important for several reasons. First, in a transfer of real estate, all objects which are classified as real property go to the purchaser and all objects classified as personal property stay in the ownership of the seller unless contractual provisions specify differently. Proof of ownership and sale is different depending on whether an object is real property or personal property. If a person dies, the law in the person's state of residence controls the disposition of personal property, but the law where the real property is located controls its disposition. Finally, the taxes levied on real and personal property differ.

Because of the different ways the law treats real versus personal property, courts have developed several tests to determine whether mixed property, which has attributes of both, is real or personal property. This is the law which deals with *fixtures*. A fixture is broadly defined as personalty which has become realty. This is also referred to as *chattel real*. A fixture is an object which has become annexed to real property. Examples of fixtures include built-in cabinets in a kitchen, bathtubs, permanent bookcases and other such objects. The tests that courts consider include the following:

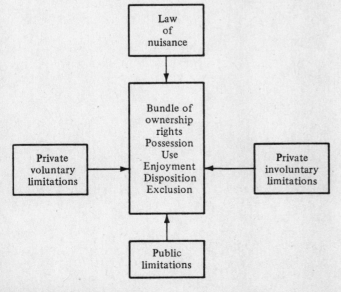

Figure 2–5. Limitations on Property Ownership

1. *Reasonable intent of the party annexing the object.* Where custom ordinarily presumes an object to be a fixture, the secret subjective intent of a party annexing an object will have little weight. However, where there is a doubt, the intent of the party will be controlling. Care should be taken with such objects as refrigerators, stoves and washers to determine whether they are locally considered to be fixtures or personal property. If a doubt arises, care should be taken to specify disposition in a contract.

2. *Adaptation of the object.* If an object has been custom-made to be used with and as part of the realty, this will lead the courts to believe that the intent was for the object to be a fixture. An example of this might be custom-made drapes or storm windows.

3. *Method of annexation.* If the removal of an article or object will cause permanent damage to the realty, it is

ordinarily considered to be a fixture. For example, wall-to-wall carpeting is often considered to be a fixture while a large rug would be considered as personalty.

4. *Relationship of parties.* In cases where property is leased to a commercial tenant, any fixtures that the tenant brings into the realty for the purpose of conducting business such as shelving and counters will not be considered as realty. These fixtures are called *trade fixtures* and retain their character as personalty unless otherwise specified in the lease contract.

Tangible and Intangible Property

This is a two-way classification of personal property. *Tangible property* refers to objects and physical things. *Intangible property* involves personal property rights which are rights the law recognizes such as patents and trademarks, contractual rights and legal claims. The law recognizes intangible property to the extent that in many cases these rights are subject to taxation by the state.

REAL ESTATE AS A SOCIAL AND CULTURAL CONCEPT

Decisions involving how real estate is used have important social and cultural impacts. The basic needs of life, food, shelter and clothing, are satisfied through the use of land. Where we live, where we work and where we play are all real estate decisions. Social services such as public schools, police and fire protection, construction and maintenance of roads, hospitals and recreational facilities are all financed at the local level primarily through the property tax. Real estate decisions such as whether or not to develop a previously undeveloped tract of land have a long-lasting and permanent impact on the physical environment of an area. A choice by an owner to abandon a building and thus add to the likelihood of the area becoming a slum is a real estate decision.

Many social scientists have argued that human behavior is influenced by both heredity and environment. The environment includes both the physical and human surroundings. The manner in which land-use decisions are made and implemented has a significant impact on the physical surroundings. Such factors as the quality of housing, the density of development, the distance from residences to places of work or the overall structure of the city are all important in forming either beneficial or detrimental environments for humans to live, work and recreate.

For example, studies have shown that the design of residential buildings can increase or decrease the crime rate in public housing projects. Cases exist of parks being designed on the basis of artistic esthetics which ignore the human element and thus fail in their primary function. A national magazine reported a city park which had to be closed at night because, although it had received design awards, it was used by muggers to hide and then attack citizens.

Failure to consider the need of the human user has often led to financial disaster on the part of real estate investors. Not considering demographics in the design of shopping centers and residential projects has led to massive investment losses. Both private and public real estate decisions have impact on the social environment. Careful design of residential neighborhood streets with well-planned curves and cul-de-sacs, neighborhood parks, sidewalks and open spaces can contribute to improved community communication and cohesiveness. Selection of proper amenities will help build good community spirit and a sense of neighborhood involvement.

As part of a profession which is in a position to influence these decisions, the real estate broker and salesperson have a major responsibility to be knowledgeable and well informed. The profession has a major public trust. One reason that professional standards and licensing requirements have become stricter is the public's growing awareness of how important real estate brokers and salespeople are to the human environment.

POINTS TO REMEMBER

1. Real estate is a study and a business which may be considered from four general perspectives: physical, economic, legal and social.
2. Real estate as a physical concept is three-dimensional space including surface, air and subsurface elements.
3. In order for real estate to have value as an economic good, demand, utility, scarcity and transferability must be present.
4. The highest and best use is that possible and legal use or employment which preserves the utility of the land and yields a net income stream that forms, when capitalized, the highest present value of the land.
5. Real estate markets and how real estate is used are highly dependent upon the physical and economic characteristics of real estate.
6. Real property ownership involves a bundle of rights, powers and privileges which are guaranteed and protected by government.
7. The bundle of real property rights includes the rights of possession, use, enjoyment, disposition and exclusion.
8. Real property ownership includes both rights and duties. Ownership is limited by nuisance law, private voluntary and involuntary limitations and public limitations.
9. Property may be classified as real and personal, tangible and intangible.
10. A fixture is personal property which has become real property. Tests for determining whether an object is a fixture include: reasonable intent of party annexing object, adaptation of object, method of annexation and relationship of parties.

KEY TERMS AND PHRASES

bundle of rights
chattel real
durability
fixtures
heterogeneity

highest and best use
immobility
law of nuisance
linkage

personal property
real property
residual
situs

QUESTIONS

1. The physical concept of real estate refers to
   I. three-dimensional space
   II. a bundle of rights in land
   A. I only
   B. II only
   C. Both I and II
   D. Neither I nor II

2. Physical characteristics of real estate include which of the following?
   A. Situs
   B. Heterogeneity
   C. Homogeneity
   D. Transferability

3. Real estate is highly dependent on the local environment because of its
   I. immobility
   II. homogeneity
   A. I only
   B. II only
   C. Both I and II
   D. Neither I nor II

4. The use of land which gives the largest residual compensation is called the
   A. extractive use
   B. land efficient
   C. highest and best use
   D. income producing use

5. Real estate interests are divisible based on
   A. modification
   B. scarcity
   C. legal rights
   D. fixed investment

6. Which of the following economic characteristics is most affected by changes in the surrounding land use pattern?
   A. Homogeneity
   B. Situs
   C. Fixity
   D. Immobility

7. Fixity of location
   I. creates the need for specialization in real estate markets
   II. causes the geographic market to be extremely volnerable to shifts in local demand
   A. I only
   B. II only
   C. Both I and II
   D. Neither I nor II

8. Ownership rights are limited by
   I. private involuntary restrictions
   II. law of nuisance
   A. I only
   B. II only
   C. Both I and II
   D. Neither I nor II

What Is Real Estate?

9. A fixture is
   A. corporeal
   B. realty
   C. intangible property
   D. incorporeal
10. A tree is ordinarily considered to be
    A. realty
    B. personalty
    C. a fixture
    D. incorporeal
11. A contract right is what kind of property?
    A. Corporeal
    B. Incorporeal
    C. Tangible
    D. Intangible
12. Determining whether or not an article is a fixture depends on
    I. the intention of the person who placed it
    II. how the article was attached
    A. I only
    B. II only
    C. Both I and II
    D. Neither I nor II
13. _____ refers to that possible and legal use or employment that will preserve the utility of the land and yield a net income flow that forms, when capitalized, the highest present value of the land.
    A. Situs
    B. Linkage
    C. Present value
    D. Highest and best use
14. What physical characteristic of land has placed it in a commodity category which entitles parties to a sales contract to the remedy of specific performance?
    A. Mobility
    B. Indestructibility
    C. Heterogeneity
    D. Scarcity
15. Which of the following is not considered to be a physical characteristic of land?
    A. Heterogeneity
    B. Indestructibility
    C. Situs
    D. Immobility

If you are not sure of your answers, see page 314 for correct answers and explanations.

3

Real Estate as a Profession

The real estate industry is a large and vital part of the American economy. Since 1971, the real estate portion of the private business sector has contributed approximately 12% to the annual gross national product. Add to that the approximately 1% to 2% that public contract construction contributes to the GNP, and the magnitude of the real estate industry is approximately 14% of the measured annual economic output. Only manufacturing (approximately 30% of GNP) and wholesale and retail trade (approximately 23% of GNP) are bigger industries than real estate.

Other measurements of the impact of the real estate industry are that it accounts for at least 10% of national employment and generates between one-sixth and one-fifth of all tax receipts collected in this country. Taxes from real estate account for more than one-third of the total revenues of state and local governments. Most significantly, real estate accounts for approximately 75% of the stored private wealth in this country. Further, real estate mortgage debt on residential and commercial properties exceeds the total federal debt by more than 30%. Certain activities such as agriculture (about 4% of GNP) and mining (about 3% of GNP) are highly dependent on real estate. Because real estate is so important to this country's welfare, more and more responsibility is being placed on the real estate professional.

At the pivot point are the real estate brokers and salespersons who put real estate transactions together that require the services of other real estate professionals (see Figure 3–1). Of course not every real estate sales transaction requires the involvement of the same participants. Likewise these participants are often employed for reasons other than to help carry out a successful sales transaction.

While not all of the indicated participants are involved in every real estate transaction, it is important to remember that each one has a specific function to perform. These various functions will be discussed in this chapter and throughout the text. It might be useful to consider the life cycle of a real estate product to understand how different participants bring real estate services to the market place (see Figure 3–2).

THE PREPARATION PHASE

Before land may be used to create real estate products such as housing, retail or office space, it must be prepared for development. One of the first steps is to either acquire good title to the property or to enter into a long-term lease. In addition, it is necessary to analyze the feasibility of potential land uses and to obtain legal permission for development of a real estate project. Among the important participants during the preparation phase are: surveyors, title examiners, real estate attorneys, syndicators, land planners and zoning and planning officials.

Surveyors

When property is conveyed from one party to another it is important to identify positively the exact boundaries of the property so that there is no doubt where the property lies in relation to all other parcels. To accomplish this task a survey is made. A surveyor physically inspects and measures the property. The precise measurements are included in the deed used to transfer ownership of the property (see Chapter 7).

Title Examiners

Ordinarily real estate is conveyed from one party to another only after the examination of the land records is made and an opinion as to what interest the seller has to convey is given. While this procedure can be done by the closing attorney or the escrow agent, it is often performed by a title company who employs specialists to search the public records and write an abstract of title. A fee is charged, usually based on the sales price of the property. In some geographic areas it is customary for the title company to also write a title insurance policy on the property (see Chapter 13).

Attorneys

Sale of real estate involves the transfer of legal rights in land. Thus, need exists for persons who have extensive

Figure 3-1. A Real Estate Sales Transaction Triggers the Services and Activities of Many Participants in the Real Estate Industry.

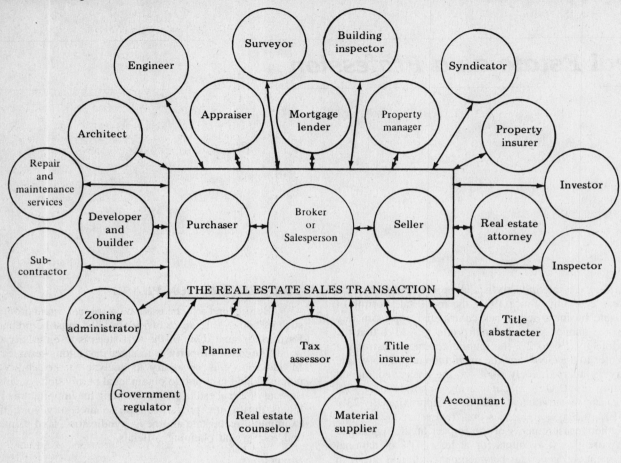

training and knowledge of real property law. Most attorneys find themselves involved in real estate transactions in the conveyance of property from one party to another, as the executor of a will or in a divorce settlement. Many real estate brokerage firms and development companies of significant size have legal counsel as part of their full-time staff. Many state bar associations are permitting attorneys to hold themselves out as real estate specialists (see Chapters 5, 8, 13, 16).

Syndicators

Syndicators have the important function of raising equity dollars for real estate investments. The syndicator receives various fees and equity interests for assembling the financial package and matching it with appropriate investments.

Planners

Land use is affected by physical, economic, social and government limitations. Planners are people trained to look objectively at a particular parcel of land and foresee how its use will affect surrounding land uses. Also with the numerous land-use controls and regulations being levied at all levels of government, developers must be certain that any proposed use they might make of a parcel of land complies with all government regulations. Planners are employed in both the private and public sectors (see Chapter 19).

THE PRODUCTION PHASE

The production phase involves clearing and preparing a site for development, doing design and engineering work

Figure 3-2. Phases in the Real Estate Project Life Cycle

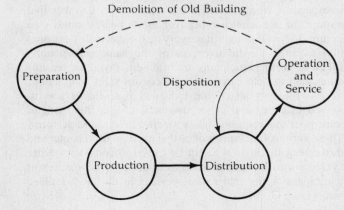

on a structure, securing financing, seeking and letting bids for construction contracts and building the real estate projects. Important participants in this phase include land developers, builders, architects, engineers, real estate consultants, lenders, mortgage brokers and bankers and inspectors or enforcement officers for various government agencies.

Land Developers

Land development involves doing whatever is necessary to convert an undeveloped tract of land into parcels ready for construction. This could mean acquiring a 100-acre tract of land from a farmer, subdividing the large parcel into one-half acre tracts, putting in roads, curbs and gutters, sewers and water mains and then selling the individual lots to either builders or private individuals who in turn construct houses on the lots. Land development can also involve commercial property such as the development of a large shopping district or industrial property such as an industrial park.

Builders

Builders construct improvements on land with the intention of selling the building to others for a profit. Real estate construction includes both custom building in which the building is constructed for a particular person to meet stated needs and speculative building in which the builder anticipates finding a buyer once the project is complete. Building is a very localized activity and the majority of construction, especially in residential real estate, is done by relatively small-scale builders.

Architects and Engineers

Normally land is purchased with the intent of adding improvements such as a house, an office building or a warehouse. Architects have the responsibility of designing the building and overseeing the proper construction. For this service a fee is paid, usually a percentage of the total cost of the structure. Engineers work with architects to design the structural and mechanical components of the project.

Real Estate Consultants

Certain real estate specialists provide consulting and counseling services to people who need specific and detailed information. Such information might involve analyzing a particular geographic area to determine whether or not adequate demand for a product exists and, if so, what site should be chosen for construction. Investment services are available that manage real estate portfolios and counsel individuals and companies on the type of real estate investments best suited to meet their investment objectives. Consultants and counselors are continually engaged in market research so as to keep abreast of what is happening in the marketplace.

Lenders

Normally, borrowed capital is a necessary part of the real estate purchase price. Money is loaned on all types of property and at various interest rates and terms. The lending officer is interested in making a financially sound loan and in return receiving an acceptable rate of return. Even though there are numerous loan opportunities for financial intermediaries, the majority of real estate loans are made locally; thus, it is necessary for the loan officer to keep up with local market activities (see Chapter 14).

Public Inspectors and Enforcement Officers

With the proliferation of local, state and federal regulations affecting the development of real estate assets, there are many individuals who work in the public sector to enforce these regulations. These participants have an important impact on the quality of the environment, the safety of workers on the job site, the protection of the public and the overall cost of real estate projects (see Chapter 19).

THE DISTRIBUTION PHASE

After a real estate product is produced, it is ordinarily placed on the market for sale to competing users. Real estate brokers and salespersons play an instrumental role. In addition, appraisers, accountants and property insurers play an important function in this phase. As was discussed previously, other participants such as mortgage lenders, title examiners and insurers, attorneys and other such professionals also perform vital services.

Real Estate Brokers and Salespersons

The key professional in the distribution phase is the real estate broker or salesperson. Although the broker and salesperson are involved in other phases as well, their primary function is in the distribution of real estate. A real estate broker is a person licensed to work on behalf of another for a fee or commission and is involved in the buying, selling, renting, leasing and exchanging of real estate. This is the area of specialization most visible to the general public since it is the real estate broker who is involved in the purchase of a home, the single most important purchase made by the average individual. Currently, there are more than 600,000 licensed real estate brokers engaged in various real estate activities. The salesperson is someone who is licensed to work on behalf of the broker (see Chapter 6).

Appraisers

An appraiser renders an opinion of value and other related services for a fee. When property is being bought or sold, an appraiser is often engaged to render an opinion or estimate of market value. Lenders employ the services of appraisers as another input into the loan decision, since loans are normally based on a certain percentage of value. Insurance companies use appraisers to determine how much to indemnify an insuree for destruction of property. Appraisers are used in condemnation procedures where just compensation must be determined. Land-use decisions such as the type and size of a particular building to construct in order to maximize net income require an opinion of value (see Chapters 17 and 18).

Accountants

A specialist well versed in tax matters is a necessary part of many successful real estate ventures. For the homeowner who is aware that property taxes and mortgage interest are legitimate tax deductions, the need for an accountant who specializes in real estate might not appear to be necessary. However, for complicated transactions, mergers, exchanges, installment land sales and other such dealings the services of an accountant are most certainly needed (see Chapter 18).

Property Insurers

All types of real estate require various forms of insurance coverage. Thus the need exists for a specialist who understands what coverage is needed and how adequate coverage can be provided at the lowest cost to the owner. Insurance agents work either as independent agents or as employees of insurance companies. The commission they receive is normally a percentage of the owner's premium. Real estate brokers often offer an insurance service as part of the brokerage business (see Chapter 11).

THE OPERATIONS AND SERVICE PHASE

Once a person acquires a finished real estate asset, consideration must be given to the operations and service phase. If the owner is not the ultimate user, the property must be managed to assure the highest net income. Consideration must be given to rental policy, repairs and maintenance. Various public officials such as tax assessors and housing or health code inspectors have important inputs into management policies of the owner. During this phase, the owner or investor must determine whether to hold on to the property, to refinance the mortgage note or to dispose of the property. Later in the project's life cycle, consideration must be given to renovation, demolition or abandonment of the asset if it cannot otherwise be disposed of. In addition to some of the parties previously described, the owner/investor, the property manager and the tax assessor have roles which should be understood.

Owners/Investors

Various purposes motivate ownership of real estate assets. A person may acquire real estate for present use or enjoyment such as the acquisition of a house as a personal residence. In addition, a person may acquire real estate for the purpose of earning an income from leasing to users or for the purpose of speculating that the asset can be resold at a profit in the future (see Chapter 11).

Property Managers

Unlike some investments, real estate requires the constant skills of someone who can oversee and direct the ongoing needs of the property. Such a role is filled by the property manager who is employed by the owner. Typically the property manager is responsible for collection of rents, full occupancy, property maintenance and other such services. For these services a fee is paid, which is normally based on the income generated by the property. Property management as a specialized field has grown in recent years due to the need for someone who knows how to incorporate sound management skills into the day-to-day operations of a real estate project (see Chapters 10 and 12).

Tax Assessors

Tax assessors play an important role in determining the tax base used to calculate total property tax revenues available to local governments. Learning how the property tax system works is important to the real property owner and manager. By knowing how to appeal a high tax assessment it is often possible to reduce the tax burden on property (see Chapter 19).

A CAREER AS A REAL ESTATE BROKER OR SALESPERSON

Not everyone is successful in real estate brokerage. As with other professions, real estate brokerage requires a great deal of work, dedication and persistence. Those who succeed discover satisfactions that are unavailable in many other careers. There are a number of steps that can be taken to increase the chances of success in this profession (see Figure 3-3).

Good Personal Attributes

It is difficult to determine exactly what personal attributes or qualities lead to success in real estate brokerage. If you were to talk to 20 different successful brokers, you would probably get 20 different sets of answers. Because each individual is different, that person's approach to success must also be different. A number of attributes seem to lead to success for many individuals. These attributes are:

1. *Motivation to succeed.* This is sometimes referred to as the "right mental attitude." It's an attitude each individual has in order to become the best at whatever he or she does.

2. *Personal organization.* A person who is not organized will find obstacles constantly blocking the road to success. One of the biggest obstacles is the problem of time. Time is very easily wasted. A well-organized individual, however, will be able to manage the limited time available each day.

3. *Ethics and integrity.* Loyalty, reliability, truthfulness and other moral factors are essential to a successful business; people almost always select "integrity" over all other attributes.

4. *Persistence.* A successful broker or salesperson must be able to overcome objections to a sale. Constant effort must be maintained to find new listings, match properties with buyers and find opportunities in the market. Real estate brokerage is not a profession for one who is easily discouraged by temporary setbacks or problems.

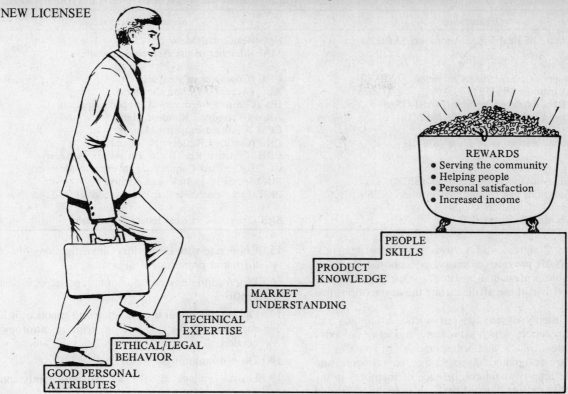

Figure 3-3. Steps to a Successful Real Estate Career

5. *Desire to help people.* Brokerage is a "people" profession. A person who enjoys helping other people will find a great deal of satisfaction in this service-oriented industry. This satisfaction will continuously reinforce a salesperson's desire to keep trying even harder.

6. *Ability to get along with people.* The more people you can work with and share information with, the more likely you are to be successful. Brokers who do a good job for their clients find these same clients coming back when they need to buy or sell real estate again. Satisfied clients can lead to referrals. It is very much like a snowball that gets bigger as it rolls down a hill. The broker's earnings will expand in direct proportion to the number of satisfied customers.

7. *Adaptability.* The real estate industry is constantly changing. A person who has the ability to learn and adapt to a new business environment is more likely to succeed than one who is not.

8. *Initiative.* Ultimately, success comes to one who is willing to take prudent risks and initiate business transactions. The broker must take the initiative to service the needs of customers.

Ethical and Legal Behavior

As discussed in the previous section, one of the most important personal attributes is a sense of ethics or integrity. Because real estate is a highly localized profession, anyone who has a reputation for unethical practices will find it very difficult to do business with other persons in the industry. Some unethical practices are also violations of state licensing laws and other laws or regulations. Violation of the law can lead to loss of license, fine or jail. In the short run, one may gain a temporary advantage from a marginal business practice. Ultimately, in most cases, the harm will outweigh the benefit.

To preserve the integrity of the profession, many real estate brokers and salespersons belong to professional organizations such as the NATIONAL ASSOCIATION OF REALTORS® (NAR) and the National Association of Real Estate Brokers (NAREB). NAREB is the nation's oldest, largest and most effective minority-oriented trade organization. The group was formed in 1947 and is represented through its national office in Washington, D.C., and through approximately 50 state associations and local boards. The designation REALTIST is awarded to its membership.

The NATIONAL ASSOCIATION OF REALTORS® (NAR), founded in 1908, is the largest and best known real estate organization in the world, with a current membership in excess of 700,000. Active brokers who maintain membership in NAR may use the term REALTOR®, and their salespersons hold membership on a REALTOR-ASSOCIATE® status. There is a recent trend for boards to provide only one class of membership to both brokers and salespersons, whereby all board members are REALTORS®, and the REALTOR-ASSOCIATE® classification is eliminated.

The organization is represented through state associations and 1,780 local boards. Of particular interest are three features of the organization. First, the NAR participates actively as a spokesman for the real estate industry and maintains a full-time staff headquartered in Washington, D.C., to provide testimony on important real-estate-related

Real Estate as a Profession

Table 3–1. Professional Institutes, Societies, and Councils Affiliated with the NATIONAL ASSOCIATION OF REALTORS®

Organization	Professional Designations
American Institute of Real Estate Appraisers (AIREA)	RM (Residential Member) MAI (Member of the Appraisal Institute)
American Society of Real Estate Counselors (ASREC)	CRE (Counselor of Real Estate)
Realtors Land Institute (RLI)	ALC (Accredited Land Consultant)
International Real Estate Federation (FIABI-USA)	IPS (Certified International Property Specialist)
Institute of Real Estate Management (IREM)	ARM (Accredited Resident Manager) CPM (Certified Property Manager)
Realtors National Marketing Institute (RNMI)	CRS (Certified Residential Specialist) CRB (Certified Real Estate Brokerage Manager) CCIM (Certified Commercial Investment Member)
Society of Industrial and Office Realtors (SIOR)	SIR (Specialist in Industrial Realty)
Real Estate Securities and Syndication Institute (RESSI)	PRE (Professional Real Estate Executive)
Women's Council of Realtors (WCR)	
Leadership Training Graduate (LTG)	SRS (Specialist in Real Estate Securities)

issues before Congress and various regulatory agencies. Second, the NAR provides extensive educational programs through its nine professional institutes, societies and councils. Table 3–1 lists these affiliates and the designations that are awarded.

Third, the NAR has passed a code of ethics and standards of practice, which serves as a model of behavior for real estate brokers and salespersons. It contains 23 articles that are designated to protect the general public and to protect the integrity and competence of members in the profession. A complete copy of the code is found at the end of this chapter. The following is a summary of what each article requires of a REALTOR®:

1. Stay informed about matters affecting real estate.
2. Be informed about laws, proposed legislation, regulations and market conditions.
3. Protect the public against fraud and other unethical practices.
4. Urge the use of exclusive listings.
5. Be loyal to the Board of REALTORS® and share your experience with other REALTORS®.
6. Be fair with other REALTORS® and avoid controversies.
7. Promote the interests of your client but treat all parties to a transaction fairly.
8. Do not accept compensation for more than one party to a transaction without full disclosure.
9. Be diligent in discovering adverse facts and avoid misrepresentation.
10. Do not unfairly discriminate in providing equal professional services.
11. Provide competent service consistent with professional standards and seek professional assistance in matters beyond your competence.
12. Disclose all interests in property for which professional service may be provided.
13. Disclose true ownership position and any potential conflicts of interest in any listings or other property bought or sold.
14. Arbitrate disputes with other REALTORS®.
15. Cooperate with disciplinary investigations of boards or affiliated professional organizations.
16. When acting as agent do not accept secret kickbacks or profits.
17. Do not engage in the unauthorized practice of law and recommend the use of a licensed attorney when needed.
18. Do not commingle funds.
19. Do not engage in false advertising or misrepresentations.
20. Have all financial commitments in writing and provide a copy of agreements to all parties in a transaction.
21. Do not undermine the agency of another REALTOR®.
22. Cooperate with other brokers and deal exclusively through the listing broker and not directly with the owner.
23. Do not publicly disparage a competitor.

Technical Expertise

The salesperson and broker must be able to handle a wide range of technical skills. These include knowledge and skill of sales techniques, financing alternatives, sources of mortgage money, appraisal and investment procedures, general marketing information, laws and regulations, construction practices and insurance.

Many brokers have learned their technical expertise by taking courses provided by the NATIONAL ASSOCIATION OF REALTORS® or affiliated institutes, societies and councils. For example, many real estate professionals have the designation of GRI after their names. GRI means that the individual is a Graduate, REALTOR'®s Institute. This is obtained by taking courses and passing tests as prescribed in each state. More specialized technical expertise is represented by such designations as MAI given by the American Institute of Real Estate Appraisers or the CPM given by the Institute of Real Estate Management.

Market Understanding

To be successful in real estate, it is essential to be familiar with the nature of the local real estate market. A real estate market is the mechanism by which rights and interests in real estate are sold, prices set, supply adjusted to demand, space allocated among competing uses and land-use patterns formed. Real estate markets have a number of significant characteristics that must be understood. These include the following:

1. *Localized*. Because real estate is fixed in location, the market is very localized. The market in one city is different from the market in another city. Further, the market in one part of the city may be very different from the market on the other side of town, or even a few miles away. It makes it difficult to generalize from one market to another. Each must be separately considered and analyzed.

2. *Segmented*. The real estate market is segmented and stratified. This means that there may be several markets operating in a single geographic area. The market may be segmented by land use (residential, commercial, industrial), by price (homes selling for $40,000-50,000 are in a different market than homes selling for $200,000-$300,00), by geography (downtown compared to suburbs).

3. *Private transactions*. The prices paid for certain properties and specific information about the transactions are often kept secret. Information is hard to obtain or verify.

4. *Inexperienced or uninformed participants*. Most people purchasing real estate only do so a few times during their lifetimes. As a result, they are often unfamiliar with the nature of the real estate market and must rely on a broker or other expert whose job it is to keep informed about changes taking place, fair market prices and sources of financing.

5. *Emotional decision making*. Many transactions in a real estate market are characterized by emotional decision making. For example, selling of a house that has been in a family for generations can be very traumatic to some people. Decisions are sometimes made on whim or fancy. A house, for instance, might sell to somebody because of the color of the wallpaper used in the master bedroom.

6. *Fixed supply in the short run*. Producers of real estate cannot respond quickly to changes in demand. It may take three to five years to obtain the correct building permits and zoning in some communities in order to increase the supply of housing. In other communities, labor and materials must be recruited or obtained from other parts of the country before a large volume of construction can take place.

7. *Volatile demand*. The demand for real estate can change overnight. Demand is the desire for a product plus the ability to pay for it. One of the most important considerations underlying real estate demand is the supply and cost of mortgage money. When money is cheap and available, the demand for real estate is likely to be high. When mortgage rates soar or money is unavailable, the demand is likely to decline or in some cases even disappear.

8. *Cyclical*. Real estate markets go through economic cycles. These cycles are a function of money supply, population shifts, oversupply and other reasons. One reason real estate is cyclical is that real estate borrowers must compete for money with other users such as businesses and government. Usually businesses and government are able to pay more for money than real estate borrowers. When other sectors in the economy are not competing heavily for money, it then becomes more available for real estate borrowers. As a result, real estate markets tend to run counter to business cycles.

Product Knowledge

Before you sell something, you should know exactly what it is that you are selling. Real estate has physical aspects, legal aspects and economic aspects. It is more than just land and buildings. To some people it is their dreams, to others it is a means of carrying out a business, to others it is merely a convenient way to store wealth. It is important, therefore, to understand what a particular user requires from the real estate. If you emphasize the wrong aspects of a real estate product or if you are unfamiliar with your product and how it can satisfy the needs of your client, then it will be more difficult for you to negotiate a sale. You will be much like a football player carrying a ball who has forgotten which goal to run towards for a touchdown.

People Skills

One of the most important people skills is the ability to listen. Before you begin to talk, you should try to find out something about your prospective purchaser or prospective seller. What do they really need? What do they really want?

Normally, what are the functions of a real estate broker or salesperson? In most cases they obtain listings, qualify potential buyers, show properties, handle buyer objections and close the sale. All of these functions require the ability to communicate. The first step to effective communication is effective listening. Other skills include use of psychology, sales techniques, good personal mannerisms, good dress and personal appearance, good attitude, self-control, enthusiasm, resourcefulness, concentration and memory.

CODE OF ETHICS AND STANDARDS OF PRACTICE

of the NATIONAL ASSOCIATION OF REALTORS®

Where the word REALTOR® is used in this Code and Preamble, it shall be deemed to include REALTOR-ASSOCIATE®. Pronouns shall be considered to include REALTORS® and REALTOR-ASSOCIATE®s of both genders.

Preamble . . .

Under all is the land. Upon its wise utilization and widely allocated ownership depend the survival and growth of free institutions and of our civilization. The REALTOR® should recognize that the interests of the nation and its citizens require the highest and best use of the land and the widest distribution of land ownership. They require the creation of adequate housing, the building of functioning cities, the development of productive industries and farms, and the preservation of a healthful environment.

Such interests impose obligations beyond those of ordinary commerce. They impose grave social responsibility and a patriotic duty to which the REALTOR® should dedicate himself, and for which he should be diligent in preparing himself. The REALTOR®, therefore, is zealous to maintain and improve the standards of his calling and shares with his fellow REALTORS® a common responsibility for its integrity and honor. The term REALTOR® has come to connote competency, fairness, and high integrity resulting from adherence to a lofty ideal of moral conduct in business relations. No inducement of profit and no instruction from clients ever can justify departure from this ideal.

In the interpretation of this obligation, a REALTOR® can take no safer guide than that which has been handed down through the centuries, embodied in the Golden Rule, "Whatsoever ye would that men should do to you, do ye even so to them."

Accepting this standard as his own, every REALTOR® pledges himself to observe its spirit in all of his activities and to conduct his business in accordance with the tenets set forth below.

Articles 1 through 5 are aspirational and establish ideals the REALTOR® should strive to attain.

Article 1

The REALTOR® should keep himself informed on matters affecting real estate in his community, the state, and nation so that he may be able to contribute responsibly to public thinking on such matters.

Article 2

In justice to those who place their interests in his care, the REALTOR® should endeavor always to be informed regarding laws, proposed legislation, governmental regulations, public policies, and current market conditions in order to be in a position to advise his clients properly.

Article 3

The REALTOR® should endeavor to eliminate in his community any practices which could be damaging to the public or bring discredit to the real estate profession. The REALTOR® should assist the governmental agency charged with regulating the practices of brokers and salesmen in his state. (Revised 11/87)

Article 4

To prevent dissension and misunderstanding and to assure better service to the owner, the REALTOR® should urge the exclusive listing of property unless contrary to the best interest of the owner. (Revised 11/87)

Article 5

In the best interests of society, of his associates, and his own business, the REALTOR® should willingly share with other REALTORS® the lessons of his experience and study for the benefit of the public, and should be loyal to the Board of REALTORS® of his community and active in its work.

Articles 6 through 23 establish specific obligations. Failure to observe these requirements subjects the REALTOR® to disciplinary action.

Article 6

The REALTOR® shall seek no unfair advantage over other REALTORS® and shall conduct his business so as to avoid controversies with other REALTORS®. (Revised 11/87)

•*Standard of Practice 6-1*

"The REALTOR® shall not misrepresent the availability of access to show or inspect a listed property. (Cross-reference article 22.)" (Revised 11/87)

Article 7

In accepting employment as an agent, the REALTOR® pledges himself to protect and promote the interests of the client. This obligation of absolute fidelity to the client's interests is primary, but it does not relieve the REALTOR® of the obligation to treat fairly all parties to the transaction.

•*Standard of Practice 7-1*

"Unless precluded by law, government rule or regulation, or agreed otherwise in writing, the REALTOR® shall submit to the seller all offers until closing. Unless the REALTOR® and the seller agree otherwise, the REALTOR® shall not be obligated to continue to market the property after an offer has been accepted. Unless the subsequent offer is contingent upon the termination of an existing contract, the REALTOR® shall recommend that the seller obtain the advice of legal counsel prior to acceptance. (Cross-reference Article 17.)"

•*Standard of Practice 7-2*

"The REALTOR®, acting as listing broker, shall submit all offers to the seller as quickly as possible."

•*Standard of Practice 7-3*

"The REALTOR®, in attempting to secure a listing, shall not deliberately mislead the owner as to market value."

•*Standard of Practice 7-4*

(Refer to Standard of Practice 22-1, which also relates to Article 7, Code of Ethics.)

•*Standard of Practice 7-5*

(Refer to Standard of Practice 22-2, which also relates to Article 7, Code of Ethics)

•*Standard of Practice 7-6*

"The REALTOR®, when acting as a principal in a real estate transaction, cannot avoid his responsibilities under the Code of Ethics."

Article 8

The REALTOR® shall not accept compensation from more than one party, even if permitted by law, without the full knowledge of all parties to the transaction.

Article 9

The REALTOR® shall avoid exaggeration, misrepresentation, or concealment of pertinent facts relating to the property or the transaction. The REALTOR® shall not, however, be obligated to discover latent defects in the property or to advise on matters outside the scope of his real estate license.

•*Standard of Practice 9-1*

"The REALTOR® shall not be a party to the naming of a false consideration in any document, unless it be the naming of an obviously nominal consideration."

•*Standard of Practice 9-2*

(Refer to Standard of Practice 21-3, which also relates to Article 9, Code of Ethics.)

•*Standard of Practice 9-3*

(Refer to Standard of Practice 7-3, which also relates to Article 9, Code of Ethics.)

•*Standard of Practice 9-4*

"The REALTOR® shall not offer a service described as 'free of charge' when the rendering of a service is contingent on the obtaining of a benefit such as a listing or commission."

•*Standard of Practice 9-5*

"The REALTOR® shall, with respect to the sub-agency of another REALTOR®, timely communicate any change of compensation for subagency services to the other REALTOR® prior to the time such REALTOR® produces a prospective buyer who has signed an offer to purchase the property for which the subagency has been offered through MLS or otherwise by the listing agency."

•*Standard of Practice 9-6*

"REALTORS® shall disclose their REALTOR® status when seeking information from another REALTOR® concerning real property for which the other REALTOR® is an agent or subagent."

•*Standard of Practice 9-7*

"The offering of premiums, prizes, merchandise discounts or other inducements to list or sell is not, in itself, unethical even if receipt of the benefit is contingent on listing or purchasing through the REALTOR® making the offer. However, the REALTOR® must exercise care and candor in any such advertising or other public or private representations so that any party interested in receiving or otherwise benefiting from the REALTOR®'s offer will have clear, thorough, advance understanding of all the terms and conditions of the offer. The offering of any inducements to do business is subject to the limitations and restrictions of state law and the ethical obligations established by Article 9, as interpreted by any applicable Standard of Practice."

•*Standard of Practice 9-8*

"The REALTOR® shall be obligated to discover and disclose adverse factors reasonably apparent to someone with expertise in only those areas required by their real estate licensing authority. Article 9 does not impose upon the REALTOR® the obligation of expertise in other professional or technical disciplines. (Cross-reference Article 11.)"

Article 10

The REALTOR® shall not deny equal professional services to any person for reasons of race, creed, sex, or country of national origin. The REALTOR® shall not be party to any plan or agreement to discriminate against a person or persons on the basis of race, creed, sex, or country of national origin.

Article 11

A REALTOR® is expected to provide a level of competent service in keeping with the standards of practice in those fields in which the REALTOR® customarily engages.

The REALTOR® shall not undertake to provide specialized professional services concerning a type of property or service that is outside his field of competence unless he engages the assistance of one who is competent on such types of property or service, or unless the facts are fully disclosed to the client. Any person engaged to provide such assistance shall be so identified to the client and his contribution to the assignment should be set forth.

The REALTOR® shall refer to the Standards of Practice of the National Association as to the degree of competence that a client has a right to expect the REALTOR® to possess, taking into consideration the complexity of the problem, the availability of expert assistance, and the opportunities for experience available to the REALTOR®.

•*Standard of Practice 11-1*

"Whenever a REALTOR® submits an oral or written opinion of the value of real property for a fee, his opinion shall be supported by a memorandum in his file or an appraisal report, either of which shall include as a minimum the following:

1. Limiting conditions
2. Any existing or contemplated interest
3. Defined value
4. Date applicable
5. The estate appraised
6. A description of the property
7. The basis of the reasoning including applicable market data and/or capitalization computation

"This report or memorandum shall be available to the Professional Standards committee for a period of at least two years (beginning subsequent to final determination of the court if the appraisal is involved in litigation) to ensure compliance with Article 11 of the Code of Ethics of the NATIONAL ASSOCIATION OF REALTORS®."

•*Standard of Practice 11-2*

"The REALTOR® shall not undertake to make an appraisal when his employment or fee is contingent upon the amount of appraisal."

•*Standard of Practice 11-3*

"REALTORS® engaged in real estate securities and syndications transactions are engaged in an activity subject to regulations beyond those governing real estate transactions generally, and therefore have the affirmative obligation to be informed of applicable federal and state laws, and rules and regulations regarding these types of transactions."

Article 12

The REALTOR® shall not undertake to provide professional services concerning a property or its value where he has a present or contemplated interest unless such interest is specifically disclosed to all affected parties.

•*Standard of Practice 12-1*

(Refer to Standards of Practice 9-4 and 16-1, which also relate to Article 12, Code of Ethics.)

Article 13

The REALTOR® shall not acquire an interest in or buy for himself, any member of his immediate family, his firm or any member thereof, or any entity in which he has a substantial ownership interest, property listed with him, without making the true position known to the listing owner. In selling property owned by himself, or in which he has any interest, the REALTOR® shall reveal the facts of his ownership or interest to the purchaser.

•*Standard of Practice 13-1*

"For the protection of all parties, the disclosures required by Article 13 shall be in writing and provided by the REALTOR® prior to the signing of any contract."

Article 14

In the event of a controversy between REALTORS® associated with different firms, arising out of their relationship as REALTORS®, the REALTORS® shall submit the dispute to arbitration in accordance with the regulations of their Board or Boards rather than litigate the matter.

•*Standard of Practice 14-1*

"The filing of litigation and refusal to withdraw from it by a REALTOR® in an arbitrable matter constitutes a refusal to arbitrate."

•*Standard of Practice 14-2*

"The obligation to arbitrate mandated by Article 14 includes arbitration requests initiated by the REALTOR®'s client."

Article 15

If a REALTOR® is charged with unethical practice or is asked to present evidence in any disciplinary proceeding or investigation, he shall place all pertinent facts before the proper tribunal of the Member Board or affiliated institute, society, or council of which he is a member.

•*Standard of Practice 15-1*

"The REALTOR® shall not be subject to disciplinary proceedings in more than one Board of REALTORS® with respect to alleged violations of the Code of Ethics relating to the same transaction."

•*Standard of Practice 15-2*

"The REALTOR® shall not make any unauthorized disclosure or dissemination of the allegations, findings, or decision developed in connection with an ethics hearing or appeal."

•*Standard of Practice 15-3*

"The REALTOR® shall not obstruct the Board's investigative or disciplinary proceedings by instituting or threatening to institute actions for libel, slander or defamation against any party to a professional standards proceeding or their witnesses." (Approved 11/87).

Article 16

When acting as agent, the REALTOR® shall not accept any commission, rebate, or profit on expenditures made for his principal-owner, without the principal's knowledge and consent.

•*Standard of Practice 16-1*

"The REALTOR® shall not recommend or suggest to a principal or a customer the use of services of another organization or business entity in which he has a direct interest without disclosing such interest at the time of the recommendation or suggestion."

Article 17

The REALTOR® shall not engage in activities that constitute the unauthorized practice of law and shall recommend that legal counsel be obtained when the interest of any party to the transaction requires it.

Article 18

The REALTOR® shall keep in a special account in an appropriate financial institution, separated from his own funds, monies coming into his possession in trust for other persons, such as escrows, trust funds, clients' monies, and other like items.

Article 19

The REALTOR® shall be careful at all times to present a true picture in his advertising and representations to the public. The REALTOR® shall also ensure that his status as a broker or a REALTOR® is clearly identifiable in any such advertising.

•*Standard of Practice 19-1*

"The REALTOR® shall not submit or advertise property without authority, and in any offering, the price quoted shall not be other than that agreed upon with the owners."

•*Standard of Practice 19-2*

(Refer to Standard of Practice 9-4, which also relates to Article 19, Code of Ethics.)

•*Standard of Practice 19-3*

"The REALTOR®, when advertising unlisted real property for sale in which he has an ownership interest, shall disclose his status as both an owner and as a REALTOR® or real estate licensee."

•*Standard of Practice 19-4*

"The REALTOR® shall not advertise nor permit any person employed by or affiliated with him to advertise listed property without disclosing the name of the firm."

•*Standard of Practice 19-5*

"The REALTOR®, when acting as listing broker, retains the exclusive right to represent that he has 'sold' the property, even if the sale resulted through the cooperative efforts of another broker. However, after the transaction has been consummated, the listing broker may not prohibit a successful cooperating broker from advertising his 'participation' or 'assistance' in the transaction, or from making similar representations provided that any such representation does not create the impression that the cooperating broker had listed or sold the property. (Cross-reference Article 21.)"

Article 20

The REALTOR®, for the protection of all parties, shall see that financial obligations and commitments regarding real estate transactions are in writing, expressing the exact agreement of the parties. A copy of each agreement shall be furnished to each party upon his signing such agreement.

•*Standard of Practice 20-1*

"At the time of signing or initialing, the REALTOR® shall furnish to the party a copy of any document signed or initialed."

•*Standard of Practice 20-2*

"For the protection of all parties, the REALTOR® shall use reasonable care to ensure that documents pertaining to the purchase and sale of real estate are kept current through the use of written extensions or amendments."

Article 21

The REALTOR® shall not engage in any practice or take any action inconsistent with the agency of another REALTOR®.

•*Standard of Practice 21-1*

"Signs giving notice of property for sale, rent, lease, or exchange shall not be placed on property without the consent of the owner."

•*Standard of Practice 21-2*

"The REALTOR® obtaining information from a listing broker about a specific property shall not convey this information to, nor invite the cooperation of a third party broker without the consent of the listing broker."

•*Standard of Practice 21-3*

"The REALTOR® shall not solicit a listing which is currently listed exclusively with another broker. However, if the listing broker, when asked by the REALTOR®, refuses to disclose the expiration date and nature of such listing; i.e., an exclusive right to sell, an exclusive agency, open listing, or other form of contractual agreement between the listing broker and his client, the REALTOR®, unless precluded by law, may contact the owner to secure such information and may discuss the terms upon which he might take a future listing or, alternatively, may take a listing to become effective upon expiration of any existing exclusive listing."

•*Standard of Practice 21-4*

"The REALTOR® shall not use information obtained by him from the listing broker, through offers to cooperate received through Multiple Listing Services or other sources authorized by the listing broker, for the purpose of creating a referral prospect to a third broker, or for creating a buyer prospect unless such use is authorized by the listing broker."

•*Standard of Practice 21-5*

"The fact that a property has been listed exclusively with a REALTOR® shall not preclude or inhibit any other

REALTOR® from soliciting such listing after its expiration.''

•*Standard of Practice 21-6*

''The fact that a property owner has retained a REALTOR® as his exclusive agent in respect of one or more past transactions creates no interest or agency which precludes or inhibits other REALTORS® from seeking such owner's future business.''

•*Standard of Practice 21-7*

''The REALTOR® shall be free to list property which is 'open listed' at any time, but shall not knowingly obligate the seller to pay more than one commission except with the seller's knowledgeable consent.'' (Revised 11/87)

•*Standard of Practice 21-8*

''When a REALTOR® is contacted by an owner regarding the sale of property that is exclusively listed with another broker, and the REALTOR® has not directly or indirectly initiated the discussion, unless precluded by law, the REALTOR® may discuss the terms upon which he might take a future listing or, alternatively, may take a listing to become effective upon expiration of any existing exclusive listing.''

•*Standard of Practice 21-9*

''In cooperative transactions a REALTOR® shall compensate the cooperating REALTOR® (principal broker) and shall not compensate nor offer to compensate, directly or indirectly, any of the sales licensees employed by or affiliated with another REALTOR® without the prior express knowledge and consent of the cooperating broker.''

•*Standard of Practice 21-10*

''Article 21 does not preclude REALTORS® from making general announcements to property owners describing their services and the terms of their availability even though some recipients may have exclusively listed their property for sale or lease with another REALTOR®. A general telephone canvass, general mailing or distribution addressed to all property owners in a given geographical area or in a given profession, business, club, or organization, or other classification or group is deemed 'general' for purposes of this standard.

Article 21 is intended to recognize as unethical two basic types of solicitation:

First, telephone or personal solicitations of property owners who have been identified by a real estate sign, multiple listing compilation, or other information service as having exclusively listed their property with another REALTOR®; and

Second, mail or other forms of written solicitations of property owners whose properties are exclusively listed with another REALTOR® when such solicitations are not part of a general mailing but are directed specifically to property owners identified through compilations of current listings, 'for sale' signs, or other sources of information required by Article 22 and Multiple Listing Service rules to be made available to other REALTORS® under offers of subagency or cooperation.''

•*Standard of Practice 21-11*

''The REALTOR®, prior to accepting a listing, has an affirmative obligation to make reasonable efforts to determine whether the property is subject to a current, valid exclusive listing agreement.''

Article 22

In the sale of property which is exclusively listed with a REALTOR®, the REALTOR® shall utilize the services of other brokers upon mutually agreed upon terms when it is in the best interests of the client.

Negotiations concerning property which is listed exclusively shall be carried on with the listing broker, not with the owner, except with the consent of the listing broker.

•*Standard of Practice 22-1*

''It is the obligation of the selling broker as subagent of the listing broker to disclose immediately all pertinent facts to the listing broker prior to as well as after the contract is executed.''

•*Standard of Practice 22-2*

''The REALTOR®, when submitting offers to the seller, shall present each in an objective and unbiased manner.''

•*Standard of Practice 22-3*

''The REALTOR® shall disclose the existence of an accepted offer to any broker seeking cooperation.''

Article 23

The REALTOR® shall not publicly disparage the business practice of a competitor nor volunteer an opinion of a competitor's transaction. If his opinion is sought and if the REALTOR® deems it appropriate to respond, such opinion shall be rendered with strict professional integrity and courtesy.

The Code of Ethics was adopted in 1913. Amended at the Annual Convention in 1924, 1928, 1950, 1951, 1952, 1955, 1956, 1961, 1962, 1974, 1982, 1986, and 1987.

POINTS TO REMEMBER

1. The real estate sector contributes approximately 14% annually to the gross national product.
2. Approximately 75% of the private wealth in this country is stored in real estate assets.
3. Real estate activities in both the public and private sector may be classified into the following phases: land preparation, real estate production, distribution and operations and service.

4. At the pivot point of much real estate activity is the real estate broker who is instrumental in putting real estate transactions together that require the services of other real estate professionals.
5. Steps to a successful real estate career include: good personal attributes, ethical and legal behavior, technical expertise, market understanding, product knowledge and people skills.
6. The NATIONAL ASSOCIATION OF REALTORS® (NAR) is the largest and best known real estate professional organization in the world.
7. The NATIONAL ASSOCIATION OF REALTORS® has passed a code of ethics containing 23 articles which are intended to promote ethical behavior by REALTORS® with respect to the public, clients and other REALTORS®.
8. There are nine professional institutes, societies, and councils affiliated with the NAR. Many of these groups give professional designations to qualified members.
9. Real estate markets are localized, segmented and private; contain inexperienced or uninformed participants; are subject to emotional decision making; have fixed supply in the short run; volatile demand; and are cyclical.

KEY TERMS AND PHRASES

Appraiser
Broker
Code of Ethics
CPM
GRI

MAI
NAR
NAREB
Property Manager

REALTIST
REALTOR®
Salesperson
Syndicator

QUESTIONS

1. The term REALTOR® is a registered trademark of what group?
   A. NAREB
   B. NAR
   C. AIREA
   D. RESSI

2. Real estate markets
   A. are efficient in adjusting supply to demand
   B. are a mechanism by which prices are set
   C. are very elastic
   D. coincide with business cycles.

3. The real estate market behaves in a cyclical fashion because
   I. there is a high dependence on the fluctuations in the money supply
   II. real estate deals with a bundle of rights
   A. I only
   B. II only
   C. Both I and II
   D. Neither I nor II

4. A person who raises equity dollars for real estate investments is called a (an)
   A. speculator
   B. investor
   C. mortgage banker
   D. syndicator

5. A property manager is likely to hold what designation?
   A. CRE
   B. CPA
   C. CPM
   D. CMB

6. The real estate industry accounts for approximately what percent of the national employment?
   A. 10%
   B. 20%
   C. 25%
   D. 30%

7. If a REALTOR® has a business dispute with another REALTOR®, how should one proceed to settle the dispute?
   A. File a complaint with the local Board of REALTORS.®
   B. File a grievance with the state real estate commission.
   C. File a court suit.
   D. Seek arbitration.

8. What should the REALTOR® do to promote the best interest of a client?
   I. Commingle funds.
   II. Urge the use of exclusive listings.
   A. I only
   B. II only
   C. Both I and II
   D. Neither I nor II

9. As a REALTOR,® if you have a buyer who wishes to make an immediate offer on a house listed with another broker, you should
   A. urge the buyer to look at other houses
   B. contact the owner and present the offer
   C. contact the listing broker
   D. turn your buyer over to the listing broker

10. If you are asked to represent both a seller and a buyer in the same transaction, you should
    A. represent neither
    B. represent the seller
    C. represent the buyer
    D. disclose the dual representation to both

If you are not sure of your answers, see page 314 for correct answers and explanations.

Real Estate as a Profession

4
State License Laws and Statutes

Early in the 20th century various states began to recognize the need for regulating the activities of certain participants engaged in real estate. In 1913 the National Association of real Estate Boards, predecessor to the NATIONAL ASSOCIATION OF REALTORS®, took a strong position encouraging each state to enact statutes for the regulation of certain real estate activities. States began enacting real estate license laws, and today every state has some form of regulation. Anyone desiring to become a real estate licensee must be familiar with the license laws in his or her particular state. For those practitioners involved in real estate activities in other states or jurisdictions, an understanding of the laws and statutes in those locations is also important.

The Real Estate Licensing Examination for both broker and salesperson is divided into two separate tests—the uniform test and the state test. The 30-50 questions on the state test vary from jurisdiction to jurisdiction and deal specifically with the rules and regulations of a particular jurisdiction. Subjects covered include license requirements, issuance of licenses, activities of the governing agency, general operating requirements, state code of ethics, hearing procedures, and refusal, suspension or revocation of licenses. Thus, a license applicant must have a basic understanding of state license laws and statutes prior to taking the uniform licensing examination.

PURPOSE

The power to enact and enforce real estate license laws is provided for under the police power reserved by implication to each state by the Constitution of the United States. (See Chapter 19 for a discussion of police power.) While laws and statutes differ from jurisdiction to jurisdiction, the purpose of the real estate license law is the same—*to protect the public* rather than to merely produce revenue. The licensee must know what is required in protecting the public in real estate transactions. A first step in this direction is to acquire a copy of the real estate laws from the appropriate real estate regulatory body. (See end of text for addresses.)

LOOK THIS UP:
State Real Estate Commission Mailing Address:

_____

_____

_____

For the most part it is the information provided in these rules and regulations which serves as the basis for the 30-50 questions on the state test.

LICENSE LAW PROVISIONS

In a textbook such as this it would be impossible to list and discuss all of the specific points of law appropriate in each particular state. However, since many states have structured their rules and regulations after a model real estate license law published by the License Law Committee of the NATIONAL ASSOCIATION OF REALTORS® in cooperation with the National Association of Real Estate License Law Officials (NARELLO), certain uniformity from state to state does exist.

The more common provisions in the real estate laws cover such topics as: (1) definitions, (2) who must be licensed, (3) real estate commission, (4) issuance of license, (5) refusal, suspension or revocation of license, (6) hearing procedures and (7) numerous additional provisions.

Each of these topics is discussed below in somewhat general terms. Please note that space is provided following each topic for the reader to write the definitions, rules and regulations appropriate in his or her particular jurisdiction. Little can be learned from these general provisions unless the reader takes the time and makes the effort to find out how each particular provision is treated in the appropriate state real estate law. Filling in the blanks in the following paragraphs will give the reader an intensive review of the state provisions in the jurisdiction where the applicant hopes to become licensed.

Definitions

A basic part of the real estate law is the definition of certain terms. Typically found in the first part of the law is the definition of such words as real estate, real estate commission, broker, associate broker and salesperson.

Real Estate

Real estate is normally defined as land and all man-made improvements both on and to the land, plus all tangible interests in the real property (see Chapter 2).

(Your State) _____
_____
_____

Real Estate Commission

A real estate commission or department of real estate refers to the particular state regulatory body whose duty it is to enforce the real estate license laws in a particular state.

(Your State) _____
_____
_____

Real Estate Broker

Real estate broker normally refers to any person, association, copartnership or corporation, foreign or domestic, *who for another* and for a *fee, commission or other valuable consideration* lists, sells, purchases, exchanges, leases, rents or collects rent for the use of real estate or who *attempts* or who *offers to perform* any such functions or who *advertises or holds himself out as engaged* in any of these activities.

A real estate broker can be a corporation or other legal entity. If a corporation's name is used, a natural person will also be named on the license. The definition normally includes the words "who for another" (see Chapter 6) and "for a fee, commission, or other valuable consideration." Note also that to be defined as a real estate broker, one does not have to actually accomplish the task; rather, if one engages in certain activities, attempts to engage, or offers to perform these activities, he or she will be defined as a real estate broker.

(Your State) _____
_____
_____

Real Estate Associate Broker

An associate broker is any person who has the qualifications necessary for a broker's license but is *employed by another broker*.

(Your State) _____
_____
_____

Real Estate Salesperson

A real estate salesperson (salesman in some states) is any *person licensed to perform on behalf* of any licensed real estate broker any act or acts authorized to be performed by the real estate broker. This is the person often carelessly or casually referred to as an "agent," although the reader is cautioned against using the term "agent" to describe the real estate salesperson (see Chapter 6).

(Your State) _____
_____
_____

Who Must be Licensed?

Anyone defined as a real estate broker, associate broker or real estate salesperson must be licensed. In addition, certain states also require persons engaged in related activities to be licensed. These related activities include such things as:

(Your State)

_____ (1) auctioneers of real estate

_____ (2) sellers of cemetery lots

_____ (3) people dealing in mineral, oil and gas rights

_____ (4) mortgage brokers

_____ (5) appraisers

_____ (6) subdividers and developers

_____ (7) property managers

_____ (8) others _____
_____

Exceptions

Persons involved in particular real estate activities are often exempt from having to acquire a real estate license. Among the more common exceptions are:

(Your State)

_____ (1) Persons such as receivers, trustees, administrators, guardians, executors or others appointed by a court or acting under court order to oversee the property of others.

State License Laws and Statutes

_____ (2) Public officers while performing their official duties.

_____ (3) A financial intermediary involved in managing or selling property acquired through mortgage foreclosure.

_____ (4) Owners of property who wish to sell their own property unless their principal business is the purchase, sale, lease or exchange of real estate.

_____ (5) Home builders selling or renting houses constructed by them.

_____ (6) Attorneys at law who are not regularly engaged in the real estate business and who do not advertise as performing the services performed by a real estate broker.

_____ (7) A person holding a power of attorney from someone who has authorized him or her to sell, convey or lease property in a single transaction.

_____ (8) Property managers in the management of property belonging to others.

(Your State) _____
_____
_____
_____
_____
_____

Real Estate Commission

Included in state license laws are provisions for the creation of real estate commissions. It is the duty of a commission to administer the real estate laws of a particular state. Under certain conditions real estate commissions also have the authority to refuse, suspend or revoke licenses for just cause provided constitutional due process is afforded the applicant or licensee.

In a few states the commission is created as a separate department of real estate. However, in most states the real estate commission is part of some centralized licensing body such as the Department of Licensing and Regulation. The real estate commission is comprised of persons called *commissioners* normally appointed by the governor for specific terms who act as a governing or policymaking body of the commission. The actual number of commissioners varies from state to state. Some states require the commissioners to be licensed as either real estate brokers or real estate salespersons; other states require a certain number of the commissioners specifically not to be engaged either directly or indirectly in the real estate business. Quite often the state is divided into areas or districts, and the commissioner representing a particular area must have been and continue to be a resident of that area. In some states the commissioners are paid an annual salary while in others they receive expenses incurred in traveling to meetings, etc. The commissioners annually elect from among their group a chairperson who serves as such for that year.

A chief administrative officer, referred to as an executive director, director, executive secretary, secretary or administrator, is employed to do all other things deemed necessary to carry out the duties of the real estate commission. This person will be someone who possesses a broad knowledge of the generally accepted practices in the real estate business and will be well informed as to the real estate license laws in that state. The chief administrator's staff will include assistants, investigators, education directors, clerical staff and others.

The commission or department of real estate meets periodically in public session, and anyone has the right to appear and be heard. Accurate accounting records of fees collected and expenses incurred must be kept; funds collected by the commission are normally deposited into the state treasury.

(Your State)

Name of regulatory body _____

Number of members _____

Geographic representation _____

How members are selected _____

Qualifications of members _____

Length of term _____

Can members be reappointed _____

How vacancies are filled _____

Compensation _____

How chairperson is selected _____

Other officers _____

Title of chief administrative officer _____

Other information _____
_____
_____
_____
_____

Issuance of License

Although jurisdictional qualifications for acquiring a real estate license may vary, some of the more common requirements include:

(Your State)

_____ (1) application form

_____ (2) age

_____ (3) education

_____ (4) examination

_____ (5) sponsor

_____ (6) fees

_____ (7) photograph

_____ (8) fingerprints

_____ (9) bond, recovery fund or guaranty fund

_____ (10) credit report

_____ (11) minimum experience

_____ (12) Other _____

Application Form

An applicant for a license must apply in writing on forms prepared by the real estate commission or department of real estate. These forms are available at the commission and once completed are returned as described in the application. Normally, different forms are used for a broker's license, an associate broker's license and a salesperson's license.

(Your State) _____

Age

Most states have a minimum age requirement for both the broker applicant and the salesperson applicant. In the majority of states this minimum is 18 years, although in some states the applicant must be 19 or 21 years of age.

(Your State) Broker _____

Salesperson _____

Education

The minimum education requirements for an applicant vary from no requirement in some states up to approved college credit courses in real estate or other comparable educational qualifications in other states. Certain states require additional college courses or approved courses such as those offered by Graduate Realtors Institute (GRI) for anyone applying for a broker's license. This additional work is over and above what was required when the applicant acquired a salesperson's license. Subject matter covered in these courses includes such topics as principles of real property, contracts, principal-agent relationships, listings, transfer of title, estates, forms of ownership, leases, landlord-tenant relationships, closings, finance, appraisal, investment, federal fair housing, license law and basic math.

More and more states have enacted continuing education programs, and in order to renew a license a licensee must attend a prescribed number of these courses. The idea of this requirement is to upgrade the profession and to provide the licensee with an ongoing opportunity to increase knowledge of the subject matter.

(Your State)
Salesperson:

Education requirement at time of application _____

Education requirement after licensure _____

Broker:

Education requirement at time of application _____

Education requirement after licensure _____

Examination

The need for an applicant to have a basic understanding of real estate principles and practices is important. Accordingly, real estate commissions have devised various means of testing the applicant's knowledge of the subject matter. An examination is given prior to the issuance of a license, and a minimum passing score is required.

The Real Estate Licensing Examinations prepared by the Educational Testing Service are used by more states than any other type examination. A few states use the ACT National Real Estate Examination, while others employ real estate examination specialists within their own state or from colleges and universities to write the examination questions. The examinations are given periodically. State requirements vary as to how often the examination can be taken by someone who has previously failed all or part of the examination.

(Your State)

Examination used _____

Minimum score _____

Exam sessions _____

Writing time _____

How often exam can be taken _____

Sponsor

Most states require all persons applying for a salesperson's license to have a licensed broker who agrees to hold the license of the salesperson. (Note: the standard definition of a real estate salesperson is any person licensed to perform on behalf of any licensed real estate broker.) Therefore, the broker is responsible for the activities of persons licensed under him or her (see Chapter 6).

(Your State) _____

Fees

Various fees are charged by and paid to the commission by applicants and licensees. These charges include original license, renewal license, recovery funds, examinations, transfer of license, duplicate license and other fees. In some states the fee for taking the examination is paid directly to the testing service while in other states the payment is made to the commission.

(Your State)

	Broker:	Salesperson:
Original license	_____	_____
Renewal license	_____	_____
Examination	_____	_____
Re-examination	_____	_____
Recovery fund	_____	_____
Change of address	_____	_____
Duplicate license	_____	_____
Others	_____	_____

Photograph

The majority of states require a photograph of the applicant which must be included with the original application.

(Your State) _____

Fingerprints

Some states require the applicant to submit a fingerprint card, which becomes part of a permanent file.

(Your State) _____

Bond, Recovery Fund or Guaranty Fund

As part of the application, some states require the filing of a bond. Other jurisdictions require a payment into a recovery fund or guaranty fund. Any person injured by any action of a licensee arising out of a real estate transaction may recover compensation from the fund. The normal procedure would be for the complaint to be filed with the commission, followed by an investigation, hearing and, possibly, the awarding of compensation in the amount of the actual loss.

(Your State) _____

_____

Credit Report

Certain states require an applicant to submit a credit report from an approved credit reporting agency. This report would include a statement of the applicant's personal background with respect to law suits, judgments and moral character.

(Your State) _____

Minimum Experience

Normally there is no minimum experience requirement for a salesperson applicant. However, it is common for states to include experience requirements for broker applicants. This requirement normally includes a certain number of years (one, two or three is quite common) as a licensed salesperson in that state. In some instances, substitutions such as a certain number of transactions or a certain amount of education are allowed.

(Your State)
Broker:

   Minimum experience _____

   Substitution _____

Salesperson:

   Minimum experience _____

   Substitution _____

Other Requirements

The requirements discussed above are the more common ones required for licensure. Not all of these apply in every state. The applicant is advised to consult the appropriate real estate commission regarding specific requirements in that jurisdiction.

(Your State) _____

_____

_____

_____

_____

_____

_____

_____

Refusal, Suspension or Revocation of License

A real estate commission may refuse to issue a license to an applicant who has not met the necessary requirements or acceptable substitutes. Anyone refused a license is notified by the commission and can request a hearing before the commission or regulatory body.

Most real estate commissions also have the authority to suspend or revoke the license of any licensee who violates the rules and regulations of that state. Since this is of such serious nature, all licensees should be aware of what practices either performed or attempted can result in suspension or revocation.

The more common acts mentioned in license laws which can result in suspension or revocation include the following:

(Your State)

_____ (1) Willful misrepresentation or knowingly making a false promise (see Chapter 5).

_____ (2) Using a contract form or any advertising matter which includes the name of any association or organization of which the licensee is not a member.

_____ (3) Employing a person on a single-deal basis as a means of evading the law regarding payment of commissions to nonlicensed persons.

_____ (4) Acting for more than one party in a transaction without the knowledge of all parties for whom the salesperson or broker is acting.

_____ (5) Accepting a commission or valuable consideration as a real estate salesperson from any person except the employing broker.

_____ (6) Representing or attempting to represent any other real estate broker as a real estate salesperson without the express knowledge and consent of the broker named in the license.

_____ (7) Failing to account for and remit as soon as possible any monies belonging to others.

_____ (8) Failing to promptly furnish a duplicate copy of all listing contracts or contracts of sale to all parties to any such contract, or failure by the licensee to retain a copy of such contract.

_____ (9) Any misleading or untruthful advertising including advertising property or offering to buy property as a broker or salesperson without disclosing in such advertising the name of the advertiser and the fact that the person is a broker or salesperson. Where such advertising is published over the name of the salesperson, the name of the broker whom the salesperson is licensed to represent must also be disclosed.

_____ (10) Paying or receiving any undisclosed rebate, profit, compensation or commission on expenditures made for a principal.

_____ (11) Soliciting or inducing any party to a contract to break the contract for the purpose of substituting a new contract which would result in personal gain for the licensee.

_____ (12) Forgery, embezzlement, obtaining money under false pretenses, larceny, extortion, conspiracy to defraud or other like offenses.

_____ (13) Guaranteeing, authorizing or permitting any person to guarantee future profits which may result from the resale of real estate.

_____ (14) Soliciting, selling or offering for sale real property by offering "free lots" or offering prizes for the purpose of influencing a purchaser or prospective purchaser. Offering "free appraisals" unless the advertiser stands ready to appraise for any person requesting such an appraisal free of charge regardless of the purpose for which such appraisal is requested.

_____ (15) Accepting a listing contract unless such contract provides for a definite termination date without notice from either party.

_____ (16) Accepting a listing contract which provides for a "net" return to seller leaving the licensee free to sell the property at any price and retain the full amount of the excess as compensation.

_____ (17) Negligence or failure to disclose or to ascertain and disclose to any person with whom the licensee is dealing any material fact, data or information concerning or relating to the property which such licensee knew or should have known.

_____ (18) Discriminating against any prospect or client on the basis of race, color, sex, religion or national origin (see Chapter 12).

_____ (19) Acting as both principal and agent in the same transaction without the consent of all parties concerned (see Chapter 6).

_____

_____

_____

_____

_____

_____

_____

Hearing Procedures

Before denying a real estate license to an applicant or suspending or revoking the license of a licensee, the conditions which could result in denial, suspension or revocation are reviewed by the real estate commission or a real estate hearing board. Included in the rules and regulations will be the procedure to be followed if indeed an investigation takes place. These procedures normally involve:

(Your State)

_____ (1) Formation of hearing board.

_____ (2) How charges or complaints are to be referred to the hearing board.

_____ (3) Notification, normally in writing, to applicant or licensee of the charges made.

_____ (4) Provisions for how applicant or licensee is to respond to the charges and the procedure to be followed, such as the opportunity to be heard in person or by legal counsel.

_____ (5) When a decision by the hearing board will be made and when it will take effect.

_____ (6) The appeals process available to the applicant or licensee.

(Your State) _____

_____

_____
_____
_____
_____
_____

Additional Provisions

License laws also contain a number of general regulations. Among the more common additional provisions would be the following.

Penalties for Violation of Law

In addition to having his or her license suspended or revoked, a licensee can also be fined, imprisoned or both.

(Your State) _____
_____
_____
_____
_____

Reciprocity

Certain states have full reciprocity agreements with other states; some states have partial reciprocity agreements. This provision in the license law provides the means by which a licensee can be involved in real estate transactions in other states. Jurisdictions allowing reciprocity have strict requirements as to place of business, maintaining an active license, splitting of fees and other regulations.

(Your State)

Full reciprocity _____
_____

Partial reciprocity _____
_____

Requirements _____
_____

License Renewal

Licenses remain in effect for a definite time period and must, if the licensee wishes to remain licensed, be renewed. In some states the only requirement for renewal is the payment of a fee whereas in other states the license will be renewed only if certain additional requirements have been met since the previous license was issued.

(Your State)

Broker _____
_____

Salesperson _____
_____

License Transfer

A licensed salesperson or associate broker might for a number of reasons desire to transfer a license to another broker. License laws provide for this transfer although certain conditions must ordinarily be met.

(Your State) _____
_____
_____

Inactive Status

For various reasons a licensee might wish to have his or her license placed in inactive status. These reasons could include moving to another jurisdiction for a short period of time, military service or change in occupation. Provisions are included for meeting this request. During the time a license is deemed to be inactive, a person cannot be engaged in any of the activities requiring a real estate license.

(Your State) _____
_____
_____

Lending License

It is unlawful for a broker licensee to lend his or her license to a salesperson or to permit a salesperson to operate as a broker. A salesperson is not allowed to lend his or her license to another person.

(Your State) _____
_____
_____

Settlement Conditions

A licensee cannot require as a condition of settlement that a buyer employ a particular title insurance, settlement, escrow company or title attorney. Some license laws require that each real estate contract submitted by a real estate broker or salesperson contain in boldface type an offer to the buyer to select a particular title insurance, escrow company or title attorney.

(Your State) _____
_____
_____

Code of Ethics

Included in the license laws of most states is a code of ethics which is regarded as the standard of conduct required by the commission of all persons licensed in that state. The code of ethics, designed to protect the public, includes articles dealing with the licensee's relations to the public, relations to the client and relations to fellow licensees.

(Your State) _____

_____
_____
_____
_____
_____

Handling of funds

Brokers are normally required to maintain an escrow or special account. Deposits or monies collected by the broker or salespersons licensed to work on his or her behalf cannot be *commingled* with the broker's or salesperson's personal accounts.

(Your State) _____

_____

Additional Provisions in Your State

_____
_____
_____
_____
_____
_____
_____
_____
_____
_____
_____
_____
_____
_____
_____
_____
_____
_____
_____

POINTS TO REMEMBER

1. The license law is a measure of a state's police power and is intended to protect the public.
2. All states have enacted various rules and regulations and require a license of anyone engaged in certain real estate activities.
3. A real estate broker is someone who for another and for a fee, commission, or other valuable consideration does, attempts to do, or offers to perform certain real estate functions.
4. A real estate salesperson is anyone who has been licensed to perform on behalf of a real estate broker any act or acts authorized to be performed by the broker.
5. In most jurisdictions persons involved in certain activities are exempt from having to acquire a real estate license.
6. Real estate commissions are established to carry out the real estate laws of a particular state.
7. Before an applicant is issued a license, certain minimum qualifications must be met. These include age, education, examination, fees, photograph and others.
8. A license can be refused, suspended or revoked for the violation of certain rules and regulations. However, a hearing will take place which will allow the applicant or licensee an opportunity to respond to any charges made.
9. All states have numerous additional provisions in their license law with which an applicant should become familiar prior to taking a licensing examination.

KEY TERMS AND PHRASES

associate broker	escrow	NARELLO
broker	guaranty fund	reciprocity
code of ethics	inactive status	recovery fund
commingling funds	licensee	salesperson
commission		

State License Laws and Statutes

QUESTIONS

1. The main purpose of real estate license law is to
   A. limit competition
   B. protect the public
   C. protect the licensee
   D. add professionalism to the real estate field

2. If the license of a salesperson has expired and he or she becomes the procuring cause of a real estate sale, the commission would be payable to whom?
   A. Broker only
   B. Buyer
   C. Salesperson
   D. No one

3. Which of the following would not need to be licensed?
   A. A person selling industrial real estate
   B. A person selling houses on a part-time basis
   C. A trustee appointed by a court to sell property
   D. A person selling vacant land

4. A license issued June 30 will expire
   A. one year from the date of issue
   B. on the licensee's birthday
   C. January 1 of the following year
   D. at the end of the license period

5. For a broker to act for more than one party in a real estate transaction without full knowledge and consent of all parties in the transaction is
   A. an acceptable practice
   B. acceptable if no party in the contract suffers financially
   C. grounds for suspension of license
   D. an ethical practice in certain states

6. The license issued to a salesperson must be
   A. carried by the salesperson at all times
   B. displayed by the broker in his or her place of business
   C. retained by the real estate commission
   D. displayed by the salesperson in his or her home

7. Monies collected by a salesperson as deposits on properties must be
   A. turned over to the real estate commission
   B. deposited in the salesperson's business account
   C. turned over to the broker holding the salesperson's license
   D. held by the salesperson until settlement

8. Who is the broker in a license issued to ABC Realty, Inc.?
   A. The president of the corporation
   B. Any member of the board of directors
   C. The person named in the license
   D. There is no broker of record for a corporation

9. If a broker discharges a salesperson, the license of the salesperson should be
   A. returned to the real estate commission by the broker
   B. returned to the real estate commission by the salesperson
   C. removed from the wall but retained by the broker
   D. returned to the salesperson

10. A nonexempt person who receives a salary for working full time selling real estate but does not charge a commission
    I. does not have to be licensed
    II. must accept a reasonable commission or else is in violation of state licensing law
    A. I only
    B. II only
    C. Both I and II
    D. Neither I nor II

11. Which of the following could not be licensed as a real estate salesperson?
    I. Corporation
    II. Copartnership
    A. I only
    B. II only
    C. Both I and II
    D. Neither I nor II

12. Which of the following is exempt from having to acquire a real estate license?
    A. Executors
    B. Part-time salespersons
    C. People who list real estate but do not sell it
    D. Attorneys who sell real estate on a part-time basis

13. If a broker has his or her license suspended by the real estate commission,
    I. salespersons employed by the broker may never be licensed again
    II. the commission has the final word and no appeal is possible
    A. I only
    B. II only
    C. Both I and II
    D. Neither I nor II

14. Broker "A" has his license revoked. His salespersons may
    A. continue to engage in real estate activities until their current licenses expire
    B. under certain conditions transfer to another broker
    C. automatically lose their licenses for one year
    D. take over the operation of the brokerage business

15. A commission paid to a broker may be shared directly with
    I. any person who supplied the name of the principal
    II. another licensed broker
    A. I only
    B. II only
    C. Both I and II
    D. Neither I nor II

16. Violation of a state real estate regulation by a broker or salesperson can result in

  I. fine
  II. imprisonment
  A. I only   C. Both I and II
  B. II only   D. Neither I nor II

17. Before obtaining a license as a real estate salesperson, most states require
  I. minimum education requirements
  II. minimum experience
  A. I only   C. Both I and II
  B. II only   D. Neither I nor II

18. An associate broker
  I. has met the qualifications of a broker
  II. is the name commonly given to a salesperson who "associates" with a broker
  A. I only   C. Both I and II
  B. II only   D. Neither I nor II

19. A licensed salesperson can only receive a commission from
  I. the seller successfully represented
  II. any licensed broker
  A. I only   C. Both I and II
  B. II only   D. Neither I nor II

20. Which of the following statements is false?
  I. Violating license law rules and regulations is grounds for suspension but not revocation.
  II. A person selling his or her own home must be licensed as a broker or salesperson.
  A. I only   C. Both I and II
  B. II only   D. Neither I nor II

21. A licensee can have his or her license revoked for
  I. acting for more than one party without the knowledge of all parties in a transaction.
  II. representing or attempting to represent a real estate broker as a real estate salesperson without the knowledge and consent of the broker named in his or her license.
  A. I only   C. Both I and II
  B. II only   D. Neither I nor II

22. Provided he or she is properly licensed, a salesperson may
  I. leave the employment of one broker and become associated with another broker without reporting the change to the Real Estate Commission.
  II. act as an agent for a seller without the broker's knowledge.
  A. I only   C. Both I and II
  B. II only   D. Neither I nor II

23. A licensed real estate broker must
  I. keep a separate escrow account for each client's money.
  II. never act for more than one party in a transaction without the knowledge of all parties to the transaction.
  A. I only   C. Both I and II
  B. II only   D. Neither I nor II

24. A nonlicensed person who collects a real estate commission is generally guilty of:
  A. coercion   C. reciprocity
  B. a misdemeanor   D. duress

25. The real estate licensing rules and regulations are an expression of
  A. the police power of the state   B. the power of escheat
  C. the right of eminent domain   D. gubernatorial authority

If you are not sure of your answers, see page 315 for correct answers and explanations.

State License Laws and Statutes

5

Real Estate Contracts

Contract law is the hub of real estate transactions (see Figure 5–1). Ordinarily, a broker and salesperson are involved with contracts on two levels of business activity. The first level involves the broker's employment through a listing contract. This contract defines the broker's right to a commission upon fulfilling the obligations agreed to in the listing (see Chapter 6). The second level involves the negotiation of some kind of contract between two or more other parties. This contract may be a sales agreement, a lease or some other agreement involving the disposition of real estate rights and interests.

WHAT IS A CONTRACT?

A contract is essentially an agreement based on a promise or set of promises which results in some legally enforceable obligations between two or more parties. The purpose of contract law is to make sure that the *reasonable expectations* of the parties to the contract are fulfilled. For example, a promise to sell a house in exchange for $100,000 is a contract. An agreement to try to find a buyer for an office building in exchange for a promise to pay a commission if the building is sold is another contract. Contracts are based on bargains where one person is willing to give up a right, object or service in exchange for something of value.

For a contract to be valid and enforceable, the following essential elements must be present:

1. There must be an *offer* and an *acceptance*.
2. There must be *consideration*.
3. Contracting parties must have *legal capacity*.
4. There must be *reality of consent* on the part of the contracting parties.
5. The object or the subject matter of the contract must be *legal*.
6. The agreement must be in proper *legal form*.

FORMATION OF CONTRACTS

To form a contract there must be an *offer* and an *acceptance* supported by legally sufficient consideration. Together offer and acceptance are referred to as *mutual assent*.

Offer

An offer is a promise conditioned upon some requested or asked for act or promise. In order to be effective, an offer must contain three essential elements:

1. An offer must be an expression of *present contractual intent*. This means that an advertisement or any other preliminary negotiation could not, as a general rule, be an offer.

   Example:
   John writes the following words to Bob: "I might be interested in selling my house for $53,000." Is this an offer which Bob can accept? No. John has merely expressed a desire to sell his house. He did not express intent to be presently bound. Contrast with these words: "I will sell you my house for $53,000." This phrasing suggests present contractual intent.

2. An offer must be *definite and certain* in terms. Ordinarily an offer must include, either expressly or by implication, the following:

   A. Identification of the parties to the contract
   B. Description of the subject matter
   C. Time for performance
   D. Price

It should be noted that the law will allow a reasonable time for performance unless the phrase "time is of the essence" is used in the contract. "Time is of the essence" requires strict performance of all time obligations. The reader must also be aware of *illusory offers*. Illusory offers are those which do not really bind the offeror to any real commitment.

Figure 5–1. Contract Law is the Hub of Real Estate Transactions.

Example:
"I offer to purchase your house for $100,000 subject to my finding acceptable financing." Since the offeror may personally determine what is or is not "acceptable" financing and this is not measured by any objective standard, there is no effective way to bind the offeror.

3. An offer must be *communicated* to the offeree. An offer ordinarily can only be effective when the offeror volitionally (voluntarily) communicates the offer.

Example:
Gene signs a written offer to purchase Tom's house for $74,000. Gene has not determined whether or not to make the offer and leaves it on his own desk. If Tom were to come into the office while Gene was out to lunch, Tom could not accept the offer if he happened to see it lying on the desk. However, if Gene inadvertently included the offer with a number of other documents he mailed to Tom, his mailing would be considered volitional, and a man receiving the offer would be reasonably entitled to accept it. It should be noted that only Tom or an authorized agent of Tom's could accept the offer.

The rule is that only the person (or persons) to whom an offer is made is empowered to accept the offer. However, if an offer is made to the public, as in a reward offer, then anyone who performs as requested by the offer may accept.

As noted in Figure 5–2, when an offer is communicated to the offeree, this creates a power to bind the offeror to a contract. The offeree exercises this power through a timely and appropriate acceptance.

Acceptance

An acceptance is a voluntary expression by the offeree to be bound by the exact terms of the offer in the manner requested or authorized by the offeror. Occasionally a problem occurs in a case of cross offers where two offers are made between parties which have substantially the same terms. In cases of cross offers, no contract is deemed to exist because no real acceptance is present.

Example:
Tom sends a letter to Ken which reads: "I will pay you $40,000 cash for Blackacre, which you own." On the same day and at the same time Ken independently sends a letter to Tom which reads: "I will sell you Blackacre for $40,000 cash." No contract exists because there are two offers instead of an offer and an acceptance.

An acceptance must be *unequivocal and unconditional*. Any qualified acceptance which adds new conditions is an implied rejection of the offer. This implied rejection, called a *counteroffer*, has the legal effect of reversing the position of the original parties. The original offeror is now the new offeree and may accept or reject the counteroffer. This rule of implied rejection does not operate if the condition requested was already in the original offer by implication.

Example:
Jay offers to sell his house to Barbara. Barbara replies: "I accept if you provide me with good title." Unless Jay specifically limited the quality of the title in his original offer, his offer is considered to have implied good title. This means that Barbara's acceptance was unconditional and a binding contract would result. If, however, Barbara replies: "I accept if you provide me with financing," this is a counteroffer and the original offer is rejected.

Once an offer is expressly or impliedly rejected, it is extinguished, and the offeree may no longer make a valid acceptance unless the offeror revives the original offer or in some way indicates that a counteroffer would not extinguish the original offer.

The offer must be accepted in the manner requested or authorized by the offeror. In the case of a bilateral contract, the offer ordinarily requires that a return promise be communicated to the offeror. A *bilateral contract* is one in which a promise is given for the promise of another. A bilateral contract involves reciprocal obligations and becomes binding when mutual promises are communicated. An example would be a promise to pay $10,000 for a house at closing if the owner promises to sell the house and convey a warranty deed at the same time.

A *unilateral contract* is one for which a promise is given for the act or performance of another. Acceptance occurs generally by the performance of the required act. A unilateral contract is not binding until the act has been performed. A common example of a unilateral contract is a listing contract where the seller agrees to pay a commission

Figure 5–2. Legal Effect of Offer

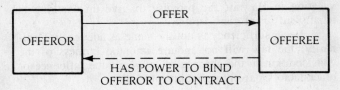

Real Estate Contracts

to a broker if the broker finds a suitable buyer. Most modern listing contracts are written in a bilateral form in which the broker promises to use due diligence to find a buyer. The more modern rule is that the unilateral offer is accepted when the offeree has substantially started the performance of the act. Unilateral offers or contracts are, however, an important part of the Multiple Listing Service (MLS) agreement among real estate brokers. This will be discussed in the next chapter.

As a general rule, in bilateral contract situations an acceptance is effective immediately when properly dispatched by an authorized means of communication. An authorized means of communication can be implied. For example, if someone sends you an offer in the mail and you mail back an acceptance, when is the acceptance effective? Is it effective when you place the letter in the mailbox, or is it effective when the offeror actually receives it? Since you received the offer in the mail, return of the acceptance by mail is authorized by implication. Because of this, the law states that the acceptance is effective when mailed. However, the original offer may state that the acceptance must actually be received, or the offer may even specify the exact manner that acceptance must be made.

Example:
Farmer Brown states: "You must accept by bringing an earnest money deposit of $1,000 in a brown paper bag and delivering it to me by sundown tomorrow while I am working in my cornfield." The only manner that the offeree may accept is by performing the requested act.

With auctions being used frequently as merchandising techniques for acreage property and surplus property in oversupplied market areas, the reader should be aware of special rules regarding offers and acceptances in auction sales. When an auctioneer places a property for sale, he or she is not making an offer but is merely soliciting offers. The auctioneer accepts bid offers when he or she slams down a gavel or says "Sold!" Auctions may be *with reserve* or *without reserve*. Unless it is stated to the contrary, an auction is considered to be with reserve. This means that the seller reserves the right to accept or reject bids and to withdraw the property from sale. Until actual acceptance, the bidder may withdraw a bid at any time.

Duration of Offers

While an offer is in existence, the offeree has the power to accept and create a contract. The duration of the offer, however, is limited and may be terminated by the provisions of the offer itself, by acts of the parties or by operation of law.

Provisions in Offer

The offer may specify a time limit within which the offeree must accept. Further, the offer may indicate certain conditions which, if they occur, will terminate the offer. For example, an offer could contain a provision that the offeree could purchase the property unless someone else purchased it first.

Acts of Parties

Normally the offeror may *revoke* the offer at any time unless the offer is an option. A revocation is effective only when it is communicated to the offeree. The revocation must be communicated before there has been a proper acceptance in order to be effective. If the offeree learns of the revocation from *any* source, it is considered effective. In public offers such as rewards, revocation is effective when advertised in the same medium of communication as the original offer was made.

An *option* is an offer which, because it is secured by consideration, cannot be revoked. An option is defined as a right which is given for consideration to purchase or lease property within a specified time at a specified price and terms. An option may be assigned to another person who may exercise the option. This is an exception to the rule that only the offeree may accept an offer. Assignment is not effective if the option itself prohibits the assignment or if the terms are dependent on the personal credit of the original option holder. The holder of the option is known as the *optionee* and the seller of the option is known as the *optionor*.

The offeree may *reject* the offer. When rejection takes place the offer is terminated. Rejection may be expressed or implied. A rejection is expressed when the offeree specifically refuses the offer. A rejection is implied when a counteroffer is made or a conditional acceptance is attempted. A conditional acceptance is treated by law the same as if it were a counteroffer. A rejection is communicated when actually received by the offeror or agent of the offeror.

Operation of Law Where the contract does not specify the time, the contract will lapse after the passage of a *reasonable time*. Death or insanity of either the offeror or offeree will cause the offer to terminate by operation of law. Destruction or material change in the subject matter will terminate the offer. For example, if an offer for the sale of a house is made and the house burns down before acceptance or if oil is discovered on the land before acceptance, the offer is deemed to have terminated. Supervening illegality will also cause an offer to cease. For example, if Tom offers to lend money to Nancy at 9% interest and before acceptance, a usury law is passed setting the ceiling at 8.75%, the offer terminates. The courts will not remake the contract at 8.75%.

Consideration

In order to have a valid informal contract, there must be *legally sufficient* consideration which was *presently bargained for* by each promisor in exchange for his promise to the other. A legally sufficient consideration may consist of a promise, an act, or a forebearance to act. Legal consideration does not have to be money. For example, if a person agrees to give up smoking for one year in exchange for a vacation in Hawaii, the promise to give up smoking is legally sufficient consideration.

Legal sufficiency is not the same as adequacy. Ordinarily, the law will not inquire into the fairness of the consideration in the absence of fraud, undue influence or other factors preventing reality of consent.

Example:
A widow sells her house for $50,000. Later she learns that the market value of the house was $60,000. She claims that she was ignorant of the fair market price and that because the consideration was inadequate she may rescind the contract. The widow has no valid case and will lose if this issue were litigated. While the price she bargained for was economically inadequate, it was legally sufficient; the courts will not assist persons who make bad business judgments.

A legally sufficient consideration may be a *legal detriment* suffered by the promisor or a *legal benefit* gained by the promisee. A legal detriment occurs when one does something that one is not obligated to do or gives up a legal right.

Example:
A contractor agrees to build a house for $75,000. He finds out later that he miscalculated the difficulty of the design and that he will lose money on the contract. The contractor refuses to complete the job unless the landowner agrees to pay an extra $10,000. Because the contractor owed a pre-existing duty to build the house for $75,000, the premise for the extra $10,000 is not supported by a legally sufficient consideration.

Some people think that consideration is money or property. However, this is not always the case. Some examples of consideration include:

1. Promise to do something. *Example:* I promise to mow the lawn.
2. Promise *not* to do something. *Example:* I promise not to smoke for one year.
3. An act. *Example:* A person paints a house in response to an offer to pay him or her to paint the house.
4. A cancellation of an obligation. *Example:* A mutual rescission of a contract.
5. Giving up a legal right. *Example:* Cancellation of all rights to an existing easement.

FACTORS AFFECTING VALIDITY OR ENFORCEABILITY

Factors which involve capacity of contracting parties, reality of consent, legality of object and the legality of form can operate to make a contract void, voidable or unenforceable. (See Table 5–1).

A *void contract* is an agreement which is totally absent of legal effect. The law will give neither remedy nor otherwise recognize a duty in a case where a void contract is involved, except to prevent a gross injustice. Ordinarily a void contract is a contract which is missing an essential element of a valid contract or involves some kind of illegality.

A *voidable contract* is an agreement in which one or more of the parties may elect to avoid or to ratify the legal obligations created by the contract. Many contracts are voidable on the part of one party and valid on the part of the other party. Contracts may be avoided on the basis of fraud, limited legal capacity of one party, or other such reasons for which the law will give relief to one party but not to the other.

An *unenforceable contract* is an agreement to which a legal bar prevents courts from hearing disputes regarding the enforceability of the agreement. Unenforceable contracts include oral contracts which fall under the statute of frauds, contracts barred by bankruptcy or the statute of limitations or those that may be barred for some other reason. A contract may be valid but will not be enforced because of the bar. It should be noted that this rule generally applies only to executory contracts. An *executory* contract is one in which obligation to perform exists on one or both sides of a contract. An *executed contract* is one in which the obligations have been performed on both sides of the contract, and nothing is left to be completed. A contract may be executed on one side and executory on the other side.

Capacity of Parties

Both parties to a contract must have legal capacity in order for the contract to be binding on both parties. *Legal capacity* is the recognition which the law gives that a person has the ability to incur legal liability or acquire legal rights. Some of the following classes of people are in some fashion protected or limited by the law.

Infants (minors)

Infants are those persons who are below a state's statutorily prescribed age. In some states this age is 21, whereas in others it is as low as 18. Most contracts entered

Table 5–1. Contracts Classified by Legal Effect

Category	Legal Effect	Illustration
Valid	Binding on all Parties	Agreement between two adults who freely consent to a legal transaction. *Example:* Purchase and sale of a house
Void	Binding on no party	Agreement to pay a bribe to influence a zoning decision; or a contract that lacks mutual consideration or any other essential element.
Voidable	Valid contract that one or all of the parties may choose not to be bound by	Contract with a child; or a contract signed under threat of violence or one signed due to fraud.
Unenforceable	Valid contract that is barred from being enforced in court	Oral contract for the sale of real estate that has not been fully executed; a contract by a person in bankruptcy; or a contract barred by state statute of limitations.

into by an infant (or minor) are voidable at the infant's option. An infant may choose to *ratify* a contract after achieving majority. An infant is bound to pay the reasonable value of necessities. Necessities include food, shelter and clothing which are appropriate for a person in the infant's station of life.

LOOK THIS UP:
What is the age of majority in your state?
_____ Years

If possible, an infant must restore any money or property before he or she disaffirms the contract. However, if nothing is left, the infant will nevertheless be permitted to rescind.

Example:
Maudie buys 10 acres of land from Peggy, who is a minor. Maudie hires an architect and builds an expensive home on the land. When Peggy achieves her majority, she disaffirms the sale and tenders the full purchase price for the land back to Maudie. Who receives the home and the land? While some courts may be sympathetic toward Maudie's plight, the general rule is that Peggy would win. The reason is that the contract for sale of land with an infant is voidable on the part of the infant. After the infant attains adulthood, he or she may ratify or disaffirm the contract. The contract is binding on the adult. The adult may not, however, use the infant's legal incapacity in order to disaffirm the contract.

Insane Persons

If a person is insane but has not been so adjudicated, any contract that person enters into is voidable just as if he or she were an infant. The person is still liable for the reasonable value of necessities provided. A person who has been judged insane and is under guardianship enters into void contracts; only the guardian can act.

Intoxicated Persons

Generally, most states do not give relief for contracts entered into by a person under intoxication unless it can be shown that the person was incapable of understanding the effects of actions in entering into a contract. This rule applies to people under the influence of various drugs and narcotics.

The fact that many intoxicated people enter into valid contracts may be a surprise. The reason for law cases that have decided that such contracts are generally valid is the idea that each person is responsible for his or her actions. If a person voluntarily becomes drunk, the law is not going to be very sympathetic if that person enters into a bad business deal. An exception to this rule is if the person became so drunk that he or she was totally unaware of reality and the other party intentionally took advantage of the drunken state, then the law might decide that the contract is invalid.

Corporations

The power of a corporation to enter into certain transactions is defined by the corporation's charter and by the laws in the state where the entity was incorporated. Contracts entered into by the corporation which exceed its authority will not be enforced. Care should be taken that the agent dealing for the corporation is properly authorized to act. In the sale and purchase of real estate, it is ordinarily advisable to require a corporate resolution by the board of directors. The rules applying to corporations also apply to trusts and other artificial legal entities.

Reality of Consent (Meeting of the Minds)

Contract law deals with the fulfillment of reasonable expectations of the contracting parties. A person who is forced or tricked into a contract cannot normally achieve reasonable expectations. The law will give relief to an innocent party in cases where fraud, misrepresentation, certain kinds of mistakes, duress, menace or undue influence caused one or more of the parties to a contract not to freely give consent. Contracts induced without reality of consent are normally voidable at the option of the innocent party but valid as to the wrongdoer.

Misrepresentation and Fraud

Misrepresentation is an innocent or negligent misstatement of a material fact detrimentally relied upon by the other party. If a person makes a misrepresentation and later learns of the mistake, a duty then arises to inform the person who is detrimentally relying on the misrepresentation. Failure to do so is fraud.

Example:
Don is planning to sell a house which has a flooded basement whenever it rains. He paints the basement in such a manner that all water marks are removed. Shirley inspects the house and makes no inquiry as to whether there is a leaky basement. She buys the house. One week after closing, the basement floods after a thunderstorm, and she wishes to rescind the contract. Many courts will find fraud in Don's concealing the water marks and then failing to advise Shirley of the flooding problem.

Fraud is defined as a misrepresentation of a material fact which is made with knowledge of its falsity and with intent to deceive a party who in fact relies on the misrepresentation to his or her detriment and injury. Fraud can result from words spoken or written, acts or nondisclosure where there is a duty to inform. Fraud is a defense against the enforcement of a contract. It is grounds for damages in a separate tort action and in many circumstances a criminal violation.

While ordinarily the doctrine of *caveat emptor* or "let the buyer beware" is used to justify that the purchaser is responsible for observing defects in a house, this doctrine does not apply in situations of concealment or hidden defects. It should also be noted that courts are moving away from the doctrine of *caveat emptor* as more states adopt consumer-oriented policies.

Mistakes

Certain kinds of mistakes are grounds for rescinding a contract; others are not. Mistakes are classified as *unilateral* or *mutual*. A unilateral mistake is a mistake of a material fact involving a contract made by just one of the parties. If only one of the parties is mistaken as to a material fact, the mistake is *not* a defense unless the other party is chargeable with knowledge of the mistake. Whether or not the mistake is chargeable is judged by a reasonable man standard; that is, whether a reasonable man would believe that the other party made a mistake.

Example:
Seale sends a bid of $11,000 to construct a warehouse for Chap. He meant to send a bid of $110,000. Chap, who received other bids ranging from $90,000 to $120,000, would have to reasonably believe that a mistake had been made. If, however, Seale had sent a bid of $100,000 instead of $110,000, Chap could not be chargeable with the knowledge of the mistake.

A mutual mistake occurs when both parties in a contract are mistaken as to the same material fact. This is grounds for rescission. For example, Kathy and Hilda enter into a contract for the purchase of Kathy's office building not knowing at the time that the building had been destroyed in a fire. Both made a mistake as to the existence of the subject matter.

Duress, Menace or Undue Influence

Duress involves the use of force or improper actions against a person or property in order to induce a party to enter into a contract. Examples of duress include blackmail, extortion, unlawful retention of property, a threat to bring a criminal action, or threats against family. *Menace* involves the threat of duress. *Undue influence* occurs when a person in a fiduciary capacity or in a position of authority misuses the trust or power in order to unfairly induce a party to enter into a contract. The essence of undue influence is mental coercion by one person over another. Contracts induced by duress, menace or undue influence are voidable at the option of the innocent party.

Legality of Object

The law will not enforce a contract in which either the consideration or object is illegal or against public policy. If a contract contains independent components, some legal and some illegal, the law may enforce the legal components.

Example:
Karen pays a member of the city council $1,000 to "fix" a zoning hearing so that her property is zoned commercial. The council member takes the money but then refuses to help her with the rezoning matter. Karen brings a suit to recover the $1,000 she paid. The court refuses her recovery because the money was paid for an illegal purpose.

Example:
John, who is not a licensed broker, enters into a listing contract to find a buyer for Ann's house. For this service John and Ann agree that John will earn a 10% commission. John finds a buyer who purchases the house for $75,000. Ann refuses to pay a commission because John was not licensed. In a court case, John would lose because without a license the listing provisions regarding his commission are void.

Many contracts or contract stipulations are treated as though they were illegal on the basis of morality or public policy. Contracts which contain unreasonable penalty clauses or forfeiture clauses may have the oppressive clauses held unenforceable. *Exculpatory clauses* in which a person attempts to excuse his or her negligence will as a general rule not be enforced. Also, many states do not enforce certain contracts made on a Sunday but do enforce them if they were actually signed or ratified on a weekday.

LOOK THIS UP:
Are real estate contracts signed on a Sunday legal in your state?

Yes _____ No _____

Legality of Form

Certain classes of contracts must be in writing and contain certain essential elements in order to be enforceable. This requirement is called the *statute of frauds*. A statute of frauds has been adopted in some form by every state. The original statute of frauds was passed by the British Parliament in 1677 in order to prevent fraud and perjuries. Certain types of transactions are so important to human activities that many people have incentive to lie, or these transactions are for such a long period that people forget. In order for courts to enforce these categories of contracts a sufficient memorandum must be present. The statute applies only to executory oral agreements. Fully executed contracts are not within the statute. Where there has been performance on one side which would lead to injustice or fraud if the other side did not perform, the courts may nevertheless compel performance. While the provisions of the statute of frauds differ somewhat from state to state, the following three types of contracts are important from the viewpoint of real estate transactions.

1. Contracts for the sale of an *interest in land*. Ordinarily contracts involving land sales, leases, mineral rights, air rights, easements and similar rights must be in writing. In some states oral contracts for leases of a certain duration are enforceable. Where there has been partial performance in a real estate sales agreement, the courts will ordinarily enforce an oral contract where the purchaser has gone into possession, paid part of the purchase price and made improvements to the property.

2. Contracts which *cannot* be performed *within one year*. A contract for a lifetime employment would be enforceable in most states because the employee could conceivably die within one year. Some states, however, include lifetime contracts specifically within their statutes of frauds.

    Example:
    Neil orally agrees on December 1, 1983, to lease his farm to Bonnie on December 15, 1984, for the period of thirty days. This contract is not enforceable because, although the lease is for only thirty days, the commencement of the lease is more than one year away.

3. Contracts for the *sale of goods* in excess of a statutory amount, typically $500. This provision does not, how-

ever, apply to contracts for services even if the service involves providing materials worth more than the statutory amount.

Example:
Dick orally agrees to build a house on Dudley's land for $70,000. This oral agreement is enforceable since it is for services rather than for the sale of goods.

In order to satisfy the statute of frauds, a writing or memorandum must contain the following essential elements:

1. Identity of the contracting parties
2. Description of the subject matter
3. The terms and conditions of the contract
4. The consideration
5. The signature of the party to be charged or an authorized agent. Some states may require both parties to sign the contract in order for it to be enforceable.

It is essential that all oral promises related to the real estate transaction be reduced to writing. The *parol evidence rule* states that testimony will be inadmissible to show oral agreements which modify the subject matter of a written contract which is objectively intended to be a complete integration of the agreement of the parties. This rule does not relate to matters involving fraud, mistake and ambiguities (see Figure 5–3).

In many states a *deposit receipt* or *binder* is used when a broker receives an earnest money deposit from a prospective purchaser. Many people may be surprised to learn that such a document is a valid and enforceable contract if accepted by the seller. Care should be taken to include all intended agreements when this instrument is used.

When a real estate sales contract is signed which is not subject to any unfulfilled contingencies, under common law *equitable conversion* occurs and equitable title passes to the purchaser. The result of this is that the risk of loss also passes to the purchaser. If the subject matter is destroyed before closing, the purchaser suffers the loss. This is the rule in many states. A number of states have modified the common law rule by passing the *Uniform Vendor and Purchaser Risk Act*. This act provides for risk of loss to shift only if either legal title or possession has been transferred. Either under common law or statute, the purchaser and seller may specify in the contract who has the risk of loss.

CONDITIONS AND CONTINGENCY CLAUSES

It is common to include various conditions and contingency clauses in real estate contracts. These give the parties an opportunity to limit their liability if certain events occur or fail to occur and provide sufficient flexibility to truly express their contractual intent. Care should be taken to specify with definiteness and certainty the conditions and contingency so that a reasonable man could know precisely what was intended. Poor drafting may cause the obligations to become illusory or too vague for enforcement.

A condition may be defined as any fact or event which, if it occurs or fails to occur, creates or extinguishes a contractual obligation. Conditions may be written so that they will void the entire contract or merely part of the contract.

Example:
Jack agrees to buy a house from Pam subject to receiving a loan of $50,000 at 8 ¾% for 30 years from First National Bank. If First National Bank refuses a loan or offers a loan which is less attractive, such as a loan for $50,000 at 8 ¾% for 25 years, then Jack is excused from performance. If the bank gives a more attractive loan, such as a loan for $50,000 at 8 ½% for 30 years, then Jack is bound to perform.

The reader must be aware of the differences between a covenant and a condition. A *condition*, upon the occurrence of the specified event, will automatically create or extinguish a legal obligation. A *covenant* is a promise. If a person fails to adhere to a covenant, this will result in a cause of action for damages, but it will not automatically create or extinguish legal obligations.

Example:
Darren agrees to sell his house to Vicki for $400,000. He also agrees to include three sets of keys at closing. Each set of keys

Figure 5–3. Parol Evidence Rule: When a written contract exists all oral agreements are merged and have no separate legal existence.

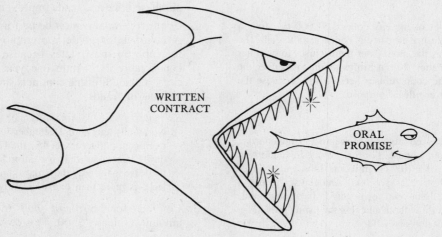

is worth $25. When time for settlement arrives, he only delivers two sets of keys. May Vicki cancel the contract?

The answer to this question is whether the promise to deliver three sets of keys was a condition. If it is a condition, Vicki can cancel the contract. Since the example does not specifically state that this promise is a condition, most courts would interpret the promise as a covenant. The only way breaching a covenant will allow Vicki to cancel the contract is if the covenant is very important in comparison to the size and nature of the total transaction. In this example, the value of the missing set of keys is $25 in comparison to a total transaction amount of $400,000. It should be clear that Vicki is bound to fulfill her obligations to buy the house although she may sue for $25 in damages.

RIGHTS OF THIRD PERSONS

Rights under contracts are valuable property rights which may be sold or otherwise transferred to third persons. The law has developed a number of principles which guide persons who wish to transfer contractual rights and obligations to third persons and which specify the legal relationship between the new set of obligors and obligees. An *obligor* is one who owes a duty, while an *obligee* is the one for whom the duty is to be performed.

A person transfers contract rights by *assignment*. Normally all contract rights may be assigned; the exceptions will be described later in this section. The person transferring a contractual right or benefit is called an *assignor*, and the person receiving the benefit or right is called the *assignee*. The legal effect of an assignment is to substitute the assignee for the assignor in the contractual relationship with the other original contracting party. All rights are considered terminated in the assignor after he or she makes the transfer. The assignee takes the contract subject to all defenses which existed prior to the assignment.

Contract rights which may not be assigned include those rights which would materially change duties. Personal service contracts, therefore, are ordinarily not assignable. Rights which would materially vary the risk of a return performance are also not assignable. This means that contracts involving the personal credit of a party or a contract for insurance coverage may not be assigned. The parties may stipulate that a contract is not assignable, or they may agree that some rights which are ordinarily not assignable may in fact be assigned.

Obligations under a contract may be *delegated*. Unlike an assignment of rights, the person making the delegation of duties remains liable for performing the obligations. An example of a delegation of duties occurs in the assumption of a mortgage. The original mortgagor remains liable on the note. An exception occurs when the person to whom the duty was owed expressly agrees to substitute the delegatee or new obligor for a consideration and agrees to discharge the old obligor from the obligations under the contract. This is called a *novation*.

A contract often contains both rights and obligations. An example of such a contract is an option which is sold to a third person. The third person may now exercise the option by tendering the purchase price within the time specified and receive in return the title to the property.

BREACH OF CONTRACT AND REMEDIES

Each party to a contract has a duty to perform as promised. A failure to do so is called a *breach* of contract. If the breach is only incidental, it is called *minor*, and the remedy is the actual damage sustained by the innocent party; if the breach is serious, it is called *major*. In the latter case, the innocent party has a number of alternative remedies to choose from.

First, a material breach gives grounds for *rescission*. The innocent party is excused from performance and is entitled to a return of any consideration he or she may have rendered to the other party.

Second, an injured party is entitled to collect any *actual damages* suffered. The rule that courts apply is that the injured party is entitled to be placed as nearly as possible in the same monetary position as if the contract had been performed. Punitive damages are normally not awarded in contract cases. Indirect damages called *consequential damages*, such as lost profits or lost business opportunities, are also ordinarily not awarded unless the breaching party could have reasonably foreseen them.

An injured party has a general duty to *mitigate* (lessen) damages whenever reasonable. If a tenant breaks a lease, the landlord may not refuse to rent the premise to credit-worthy prospects in order to run up the damages against the breaching tenant.

Third, if the contract is for the sale of unique goods or property, an alternative remedy called *specific performance* is available. Since by definition all real estate is considered unique, this remedy is available to both the purchaser and seller. Specific performance is an equitable remedy in which the court orders the contract to be performed as agreed to by the parties.

In many cases, the contracting parties may have agreed in advance that, if the contract were breached, the injured party would be entitled to *liquidated damages*. Liquidated damages are an agreed upon sum which will be paid if the contract is breached. The courts will enforce the liquidated damages stipulation only if the agreed upon sum is reasonable. If the sum is unreasonably high, the courts will consider the sum to be a penalty and will refuse enforcement. Liquidated damages are common in real estate sales agreements. Typically, a provision exists that, if a purchaser defaults on the contract, the earnest money that he or she may have paid will be kept by the seller or seller and broker as liquidated damages. Where a liquidated damages provision exists, other remedies are precluded, and the innocent party may not seek actual damages or specific performance.

DISCHARGE OF CONTRACTS

Most contracts are discharged by full performance on the part of all of the parties to the contract. Contracts may also be discharged by acts of parties and by operation of law.

Acts of Parties

Acts of parties include: alteration, written release, mutual rescission, novation and accord and satisfaction.

Alteration is an unauthorized modification of the contract by one of the parties. If the alteration is intentional and material, it will be treated as fraud, and the innocent party may avoid the contract at his or her option. *Written release* occurs when one party agrees to discharge an obligation of the other party. Ordinarily, to be effective the release must be supported by new consideration. *Mutual rescission* is a kind of mutual release. Each party agrees to release the other party in exchange for his or her own release. *Novation* is a substitution of a new obligor and an agreement by the obligee to discharge the old obligor. Novation normally requires consideration. *Accord and satisfaction* is an agreed upon substitution of a different performance for the original obligation. In order to be effective, the different performance must actually be accepted by the obligee.

Operation of Law

Discharge by operation of law includes an occurrence of an event which triggers a condition subsequent to discharging an obligation in the contract, impossibility of performance such as destruction of the subject matter or the death of a party in a non-assignable contract, frustration of purpose, bankruptcy, statute of limitations and merger. Discussion is restricted to those items which have not been previously covered in this chapter.

Supervening illegality occurs when either the subject matter or object of the transaction is declared illegal by law prior to performance.

Example:
Jake agrees to purchase equipment from Minnie for the purpose of making cigarettes. Prior to the delivery of the goods, the U.S. Congress makes the manufacturing of cigarettes illegal in this country. The obligation to purchase the equipment would be discharged.

Frustration of purpose occurs when the object of the contract is frustrated by some supervening event. In order for this reason to be operative in discharging obligations, both parties must have known the object of the contract and the supervening event could not have been reasonably foreseeable.

A contract is discharged by *merger* when a superior legal instrument covering the same subject matter is issued. For example, when a deed is delivered at closing, many of the obligations under the contract are merged into the deed. Provisions may be made to avoid merger by specifically stating so in the contract.

POINTS TO REMEMBER

1. A contract is an agreement resulting from the *objective* expression of mutual assent by competent parties, which the law recognizes in some way as a duty, and the breach of which the law gives a remedy. The purpose of contract law is to carry out the *reasonable expectations* of the parties which were induced by the contract.

2. In order to have a valid and enforceable informal contract, the following elements must be present:
   A. Mutual assent (offer and acceptance)
   B. Consideration or substitute
   C. Legal capacity of parties
   D. Reality of consent
   E. Legality of object
   F. Legal form

3. An offer is a promise conditioned upon some requested or asked for act or promise. An offer must show present intent, be definite and certain in terms and must be communicated to the offeree.

4. An acceptance is a voluntary expression of unconditional and absolute assent by the offeree to be bound by the terms of the offer in the manner requested or authorized by the offeror.

5. An offeror may revoke an offer at any time prior to acceptance even if he or she stated the offer would be open for a specified time period. This rule does not apply if the offer is held open by consideration given by the offeree as in an *option*.

6. An offer is *communicated* when received by the offeree. An acceptance for a bilateral contract is communicated when dispatched through an authorized medium. An acceptance for a unilateral contract is effective when the requested act is performed.

7. In order to have a valid informal contract, there must be *legally sufficient* consideration which was *presently bargained for* by each promisor in exchange for the promise or act to the other.

8. Infants, insane persons and other persons of limited legal capacity may disaffirm most contracts except those for necessities, at any time before or at any reasonable time after achieving full legal capacity. Parties dealing with these persons, however, are validly bound if the protected person fails to disaffirm.

9. Contracts induced without reality of consent are normally voidable at the option of the innocent party, but are valid as to the wrong-doer. Included are contracts induced by fraud, misrepresentation, duress, menace or undue influence.

10. A unilateral mistake is ordinarily not a defense in a contract unless the other party is chargeable with the mistake. Mutual mistakes prevent reality of consent.

11. The law will not enforce a contract in which either the consideration or the object is illegal or against public policy. Ordinarily, the law will not aid either party to an illegal contract but will leave them where it finds them.

12. On the basis of the *statute of frauds*, certain kinds of contracts must be in writing to be enforceable. In most states the following classes of contracts are covered by the statute:
    A. Contracts for the sale of interests in land

B. Contracts which *cannot* be performed within one year

C. Contracts for the sale of goods in excess of the statutory amount

13. The *parol evidence rule* makes testimony or oral agreements inadmissible to modify fully integrated written contracts.

14. When a real estate sales contract is signed which is not subject to any unfulfilled contingencies, *equitable conversion* occurs and the risk of loss shifts to the purchaser before the closing.

15. A *condition* is a provision in a contract which may create or extinguish absolute obligations.

KEY TERMS AND PHRASES

acceptance	executory contract	option
assignment	fraud	parol evidence rule
breach of contract	infant (minor)	reality of consent
capacity of parties	legal capacity	reject
caveat emptor	legality of form	rescission
communicated	legality of object	revoke
competent	legally sufficient consideration	specific performance
consideration	misrepresentation	statute of frauds
equitable conversion	mutual assent	valid
exculpatory clause	mutual mistake	void
executed contract	offer	voidable

QUESTIONS

1. Which of the following is always required for a valid real estate contract?
   I. Witnesses
   II. Date of closing
   A. I only
   B. II only
   C. Both I and II
   D. Neither I nor II

2. Holly makes an offer to purchase Tom's property. In her offer she states that the purchase price offered is $48,700. She had intended to offer $47,800. Tom accepts her offer. Which of the following is most correct?
   A. No contract exists because there was no "meeting of the minds."
   B. No contract exists because there was a mutual mistake.
   C. No contract exists because there was a unilateral mistake.
   D. A contract exists.

3. Bob and Kathy enter into a contract in which Kathy promises orally that she will pay the first year's dues in a country club if Bob purchases her property. A written agreement is signed for the sale of the property but this provision is left out. Which of the following is true?
   I. Bob cannot recover because of the statute of frauds.
   II. Bob cannot recover because of the parol evidence rule.
   A. I only
   B. II only
   C. Both I and II
   D. Neither I nor II

4. Greg is an auctioneer who is accepting the bids on a tract of land. Lisa bids $40,000. Greg refuses to sell the property at that price and withdraws the property from the auction block. Lisa's bid was the highest. Which of the following is true?
   I. Lisa is entitled to specific performance.
   II. Lisa may sue for damages.
   A. I only
   B. II only
   C. Both I and II
   D. Neither I nor II

5. Dick sends Louie a letter which states: "I will sell you my house for $65,000." Simultaneously, Louie sends a letter which states: "I will purchase your house for $65,000." Which of the following is true?
   A. A contract exists because the terms are identical and there has been a meeting of the minds.
   B. Louie has sent a counteroffer.
   C. Dick and Louie have sent cross offers and no contract exists.
   D. Objectively a contract exists and subjective intent is not essential in this case.

6. Randy and Ruth enter into a written contract in which Randy agrees to purchase Ruth's house subject to "finding acceptable financing." Which of the following is true?
   A. Acceptable financing is the prevailing market rate of interest.
   B. Randy's offer is illusory because he cannot be held to any objective standard.

Real Estate Contracts

C. Acceptable financing means financing which would be acceptable to a reasonable man.

D. Ruth can enforce this contract if she finances the house herself at the market interest rate.

7. Lester makes an offer to sell his house for $90,000. Jimmy writes back: "I accept on the condition you provide good title." Which of the following is true?

    A. This is a valid acceptance.

    B. This is a counteroffer and the original offer is void.

    C. This agreement is unenforceable because the statute of frauds states that contracts involving the sale of interests in land must be in a single formal contract.

    D. This is a voidable contract.

8. Under common law an acceptance for a unilateral contract takes place

    A. when a written contract is signed

    B. at the completion of the requested act

    C. when the completion of the act is communicated to the offeror

    D. when the offeree communicates a promise to do the requested act

9. Mark offers orally to sell his office building to Pam. Pam accepts by handing Mark the full price of $500,000 in cash. Mark takes the money.

    I. This is a valid contract.

    II. Since there was nothing in writing, the money can be considered a gift.

    A. I only   C. Both I and II
    B. II only   D. Neither I nor II

10. Joe offers to sell his warehouse to the XYZ Investment Company. The company deposits an acceptance in the mail.

    A. A valid contract exists.

    B. The acceptance must be personally received by Joe before it is valid.

    C. If the letter is lost in the mail no contract exists.

    D. A voidable contract exists which Joe may elect to enforce or avoid before receiving the letter.

11. A property owner agrees to indemnify a building contractor for any damage that may occur due to the negligence of the contractor or his employees.

    I. This is an exculpatory clause.

    II. Ordinarily this kind of provision is not enforceable as a matter of public policy.

    A. I only   C. Both I and II
    B. II only   D. Neither I nor II

12. Dudley agrees to lend Richard $10,000 at 9%. After the contract is signed, the state legislature passes a usury ceiling of 10%. Previously the ceiling had been 8%.

    I. The contract is void because it was illegal at the time it was made.

    II. A contract to pay a debt must be in writing in order to be enforced.

    A. I only   C. Both I and II
    B. II only   D. Neither I nor II

13. Martin sends Fred an offer to sell his land. Martin writes: "This offer will be irrevocable for ten days." Two days later Martin revokes the offer. Which of the following is true?

    A. Martin is in breach of contract.

    B. Fred may still accept the offer until the ten days is up.

    C. Fred is entitled to damages of $10,000.

    D. Martin may revoke the offer.

14. Which of the following is true about a counteroffer?

    I. It reverses the legal position of the offeror and offeree.

    II. It terminates the original offer.

    A. I only   C. Both I and II
    B. II only   D. Neither I nor II

15. Gary bids $100,000 for a contract to build a house. After he is awarded the bid he threatens to walk off the job if the landowner does not agree to pay an extra $20,000 for the job. Gary did this because he learned that the next lowest bid was $30,000 higher than his. Which of the following is true?

    I. The new agreement is enforceable because of commercial necessity.

    II. No consideration exists for the promise of $20,000.

    A. I only   C. Both I and II
    B. II only   D. Neither I nor II

16. Jonathan offers $400 for two acres of land valued at $2,000. Harvey, who lives out of state, accepts the offer. Later Harvey learns that the land was worth $2,000 and refuses to go through with the deal. Which of the following is true?

    I. The $400 offer was legally sufficient consideration.

    II. Jonathan is entitled to specific performance of the contract.

    A. I only   C. Both I and II
    B. II only   D. Neither I nor II

17. A note on the back of an envelope stated the following:
    To: Tony Palaigos
        As per our oral conversation I agree to sell you my two acres of land in Carroll County. Legal description affixed to this note, for $10,000 cash.
    A long legal description was stapled to the envelope. John Hentschel, who was the owner of the property, had signed the legal description. If Tony Palaigos signs the envelope, who, if anybody, has enforceable rights under this memorandum?

    I. Tony Palaigos
    II. John Hentschel

    A. I only   C. Both I and II
    B. II only   D. Neither I nor II

18. Nancy, who is a minor, offers Sam a commission of 10% if he will sell for her 10 acres of land she inherited from her mother. Sam is able to sell the property for

$100,000, which is above the market value of the property. Nancy cancels the entire transaction and thus refuses to honor her contract to pay Sam the commission. Which of the following is true?

I. Nancy must pay Sam $10,000.

II. Nancy must pay Sam the reasonable value of his services.

A. I only
B. II only
C. Both I and II
D. Neither I nor II

19. Joe and Jim are drinking heavily at a local tavern. During their conversation they agree that Jim will sell Joe a house for $20,000, which is the fair market value. They write a contract on a soggy napkin and affix their signatures. The next day Jim remembers selling the house. Which of the following is true?

A. This is a voidable contract.
B. This is a void contract.
C. This is a valid contract.
D. This is an unenforceable contract.

20. George and Wendy enter into a sales contract. George agrees to pay $77,000 in 10 days for Wendy's house. Before closing, the house is destroyed by fire. Under common law which of the following is true?

A. George suffers the risk of loss because he had legal title.
B. George suffers the risk of loss because he had equitable title.
C. Wendy suffers the risk of loss because she had legal title.
D. Wendy suffers the risk of loss because she had equitable title.

21. In the event of a fire or other disaster which destroys the subject matter of a contract between the sales date and the date that closing occurs, which is most correct?

A. The loss is borne by the seller.
B. The loss is borne by the buyer.
C. The loss is borne as defined by the Uniform Vendor and Purchase Risk Act.
D. The loss is borne in accordance to contract terms despite any presumptions under common law or state statute.

22. If the phrase "time is of the essence" is used in a real estate sales contract, which of the following is most correct?

A. A reasonable time is presumed for the performance of all obligations in the contract.
B. All performances will be rendered as soon as possible.
C. All performances will occur within the time periods specified in the contract.
D. All performances must be rendered within 30 days.

23. Assuming the contract is silent on the issue of death, which of the following will terminate an executory real estate sales contract?

I. Death of the purchaser or seller

II. Death of the broker

A. I only
B. II only
C. Both I and II
D. Neither I nor II

24. Which of the following statements is true about the provisions of the statute of frauds?

I. Contracts involving the sale of interests in land are void unless they are in writing.

II. Fraud and perjury are forbidden in real estate contracts.

A. I only
B. II only
C. Both I and II
D. Neither I nor II

25. Restoring one party in a contract to where he or she was before a contract was breached is called

A. estoppel
B. specific performance
C. rescission
D. arbitration

26. Deeds and sales agreements must be in writing to satisfy the requirements of

A. constructive notice
B. actual notice
C. the statute of frauds
D. the parol evidence rule

27. Don sells a house to Shirley for $250,000. He has made a covenant to paint the front door green before settlement. When the date of settlement arrives, the door is not painted. Shirley may

A. rescind the contract
B. sue for specific performance
C. sue for damages
D. seek statutory redemption

28. Which of the following is *not* an excuse for nonperformance of a contract?

A. Destruction of subject matter
B. Mutual mistake
C. Death of a party to the contract
D. Misrepresentation

29. A contract where a promise is exchanged for a promise is referred to as what type of contract?

A. Unilateral
B. Executory
C. Bilateral
D. Express

30. Most real estate contracts are "express" in that

A. the agreement is evidenced by acts and conduct
B. the parties to the contract declare terms, conditions and their intent by written or oral statements.
C. a promise is exchanged for a promise
D. a promise is exchanged for an act

If you are not sure of your answers see page 315 for correct answers and explanations.

Real Estate Contracts

6

The Principal-Agent Relationship

Most of the activities a broker undertakes in real estate transactions are undertaken as an agent working for a client, who is known as a principal. As a result, the broker's exposure to legal liability for contracts and torts (civil injuries) is often defined by the law of agency. Legal liability extends not only to the broker's own actions or inactions in regards to principals and third persons but to the activities of the broker's employees.

THE NATURE OF THE AGENCY RELATIONSHIP

What is Agency?

The law of agency deals with the imposition of legal consequences upon a person, called a *principal*, for acts carried out for him or her by a person called an *agent*. An agent is defined as one who acts for and in the place of a principal for the purpose of affecting the principal's legal relations with third persons. The power of an agent to affect the principal's legal relations for lawful purposes is called *authority*. The principal is bound by the acts of the agent when the latter is operating within the scope of the agent's authority. Agency law generally involves rights and liabilities among three parties: the principal, the agent and the third person. The relationship of these three parties is illustrated in Figure 6–1.

Agency Distinguished from Other Relationships

It is important to consider the differences among several types of relationships that the law recognizes. These relationships impose certain legal liabilities and duties upon the parties involved. Ordinarily an agent only has authority to bind the principal in contractual relationships with third parties. Under certain circumstances, however, an agent may damage a third person and impose *tort* liability on the principal. A tort is a civil wrong for which the law will allow an injured party to recover damages from a wrongdoer. Torts include intentional or negligent injury to a person, property or legally protected relationships. Additionally, the law classifies torts in nuisance and in strict liability.

The test to determine if a principal will be liable in tort for the actions of an agent is whether the agent is a *servant* or an *independent contractor*. If the principal and agent are also in a master-servant relationship, the law will impose vicarious liability on the master for torts committed by the servant while in the scope of the master's employment. *Vicarious liability* means that the master will be civilly liable to injured third persons even though the master did not personally commit the tort. The doctrine which allows a third person to recover is called *respondeat superior* or "let the master answer." An employer, however, is not generally liable for torts committed by an independent contractor. An independent contractor, unlike a servant, is not subject to the control of the person with whom the contract is made. A master has the right to control the physical activities of a servant in the performance of the duties of employment, whereas an independent contractor contracts for particular results and retains control and discretion over how such results will be accomplished. The distinction between servant and independent contractor is also important from the perspective of who is responsible for paying federal withholding taxes and social security. Independent contractors are responsible for paying their own taxes. The distinction is also important in the application of state workmen's compensation laws. A real estate broker working for a principal is considered to be acting as an independent contractor. A typist or clerk in a broker's office is generally considered to be a servant of the broker. The test to be applied is whether the employer has the right to control the method and mode of service.

Salespeople working for a broker can be either servants or independent contractors. Which status a salesperson has depends on the method of compensation and the agreement between the broker and salesperson as to the broker's right to control activities. Some state licensing laws specify that a salesperson is essentially a servant under the control of the broker.

Figure 6-1.

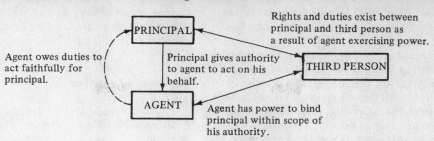

Kinds of Agents

Agents may be classified either on the basis of the manner that the agency was created or on the basis of the agent's authority. If the agency occurred on the basis of consentual agreement of the principal and agent, the relationship is called *actual agency*. If the agency occurred because of reasonable reliance on the part of a third party, the relationship is called *ostensible agency*. An ostensible agency may result from the principal's express, implied or negligent representation that an agency exists.

Agents classified on the basis of authority include universal, general and special agents. *Universal agents* have the authority to do all acts that can be lawfully delegated to a representative. Ordinarily, a universal agent is created by a *power of attorney*. Anyone of legal capacity may be an attorney-in-fact, a position created by the power of attorney. Care should be taken not to confuse this status with an attorney-at-law, a person who must be admitted to an appropriate bar. Power of attorney is useful when a principal wishes to empower a broker to sell a house while the principal must be out of the country and thus is unable to personally sign appropriate documents to convey title. It should be noted that power of attorney may be limited in authority so that a universal agency is not necessarily created.

A *general agent* is authorized to transact all of the principal's affairs within the context of a broad commercial or other kind of endeavor. A general agent is deemed to have broad discretionary powers. When a person is held out to be a general agent, the general duty of a third person to inquire as to the scope of the agent's actual authority may be mitigated. An example of a general agent is a general manager of a store who has been delegated broad discretion to operate the business. A *special agent* is generally limited in authority to transacting a single business affair or a specific series of business affairs or to perform restricted acts for the principal. Ordinarily a real estate broker is construed to be a special agent. A person dealing with a special agent must inquire as to the scope of the agent's actual authority.

Kinds of Principals

Principals may be disclosed, partially disclosed or undisclosed. The distinction is important because it defines the liability of the agent to the third person with whom the agent enters into contractual relationships on behalf of the principal. A *disclosed principal* is one whose identity is known to the third person before the third person enters into contractual relationships negotiated by the agent. The agent is not considered liable under the contract in the absence of personal wrongdoing. A *partially disclosed principal* is one whose identity is not known to the third person, but the third person knows that he or she is dealing with an agent. When an agent is representing a partially disclosed principal, the agent is considered to be liable under the contract. However, the third person and the agent may agree to limit the agent's personal liability. When the third person is not advised of the existence of an agency relationship, the agent is considered to be working for an *undisclosed principal*. The agent is personally liable under the contract.

The Agency Role of the Real Estate Broker

A real estate broker is considered to be a professional agent. Because the broker is usually employed to conduct a single transaction, he or she is also considered to be a special agent. Ordinarily the primary function of a broker is to act as an intermediary between two parties, seller-buyer or lessor-lessee. Generally, the broker is limited in authority to bringing the parties together and assisting in the negotiation but generally not to binding the principal contractually. Because the broker is dealing with subject matter affecting the public interest, many of his or her duties and liabilities are defined to some extent by state licensing statutes. The broker is held to a strict code of ethics not just to the principal but also to the public at large. He or she offers the skills and services of a professional and is expected to be knowledgeable of local market conditions and real estate values. The broker owes a duty to the principal to properly advise on all matters related to the real estate transaction where such matters are ordinarily within the scope of services provided by other brokers in the community.

Problems often occur when a broker is acting on his or her own account as a principal in a real estate transaction when another party is led to believe that the broker is acting as an agent. The broker must give full disclosure when he or she is acting as a principal and not as an agent. Ambiguities will be construed against the broker. Difficulties also occur when a broker begins a relationship as an agent and later switches status to that of a principal. Situations occur when a prospective principal asks a broker to list a property at a certain price and the broker, who has superior knowledge of the market, knows that the price is unrealistically low. It is considered improper not to disclose that the price is too low. Because of the broker's status as a professional agent, the public is reasonably entitled to expect good-faith dealing.

Brokers and Salespersons

A salesperson is deemed to be an agent of the broker. This means that the salesperson owes fiduciary duties to the broker and is obligated to follow all lawful instructions. A salesperson is considered to be an agent of the broker, not of the broker's principal. As a result, a salesperson may not bring a suit against the broker's principal for a commission owed. Many people inappropriately refer to salespeople as subagents. Strictly speaking a subagent has a contractual and fiduciary relationship with the original agent's principal. The subagent may sue the original agent's principal in the subagent's own right, and the original agent is not liable for the acts of the subagent unless the original agent was negligent in the appointment. Cooperating brokers may often be construed to be subagents. Since a broker is always liable for the civil acts of his or her salespeople, salespersons are not considered to be subagents when they act within the scope of employment.

However, a salesperson may be held personally liable to the broker's principal for torts, misrepresentations and breach of implied warranties of authority. A broker must fulfill contractual agreements with his or her salespeople. A broker is obligated to compensate the salesperson for sales made as agreed to in the employment contract. He or she is also obligated not to collude with buyers or sellers in order to deprive salespeople of properly earned shares of commissions in cases where they are paid on a commission basis.

CREATION OF THE AGENCY RELATIONSHIP

No agency relationship is ever created without some action or conduct, whether intentional or negligent, on the part of the principal. The exception to this rule is the special situation of an agency being established by operation of law. A purported agent cannot establish an agency by conduct or statements alone. Generally, a third person is under a duty to inquire as to the scope of an agent's authority. To rely on the agent's statements of the authority given by the principal is to act at one's own risk. A principal is not bound by acts of nonagents or agents who act beyond the scope of their actual or ostensible authority.

There are several ways an agency relationship may be created to give an agent power to obligate the principal to third persons: by necessity, estoppel or ratification, or by agreement, either express or implied. In order to be entitled to a commission, the relationship is conventionally only created by express contract. It is essential, however, for the reader to understand the different methods by which agency relationships are formed. On occasion, a real estate broker may create or assume legal liabilities by inadvertently becoming involved in an agency relationship. Such a relationship may impose duties on the broker to perform, while not necessarily entitling the broker to a commission (See Figure 6–2).

Capacity of Parties

Any persons who are legally able to effect their legal relations with others are deemed to have the capacity to delegate to agents the authority to act on their behalf. A principal, however, may not empower an agent to do what the principal does not have the power to do. Thus a legal nonentity such as an unincorporated club may not create powers in agents to enter into contracts on its behalf.

Special problems occur when a person acts for minors and other parties of limited legal capacity. The contracts of minors, people adjudged insane and other people of limited capacity are voidable at their election unless the contracts are for the reasonable value of necessities such as food, clothing and shelter. Therefore, a contract made for a minor by an agent is voidable at the election of the minor. An agent for a disclosed principal is generally not considered to be liable under any contract negotiated on behalf of the principal with a third party. This protection does not apply if the agent warrants that the principal has full capacity or if the agent knows that the third person is unaware of the principal's limited capacity and the agent fails to disclose this material fact. Under such circumstances, the agent would be found personally liable under the contract if the principal should choose to disaffirm it.

Generally, any person may be an agent subject to mental and physical limitations. Obviously a person unaware of surrounding environment and without any mental capacity could not be an agent. However, a person does not have to have legal capacity to bind himself legally to be an agent for another. The reason for this is that generally an agent is not a party to a contract between the principal and the third party. His or her legal capacity is therefore not generally relevant in the contract between the principal and third person. It is clear that a minor or other party of limited capacity may fully bind a principal to a valid contract and the principal may not use the agent's lack of capacity as a defense so long as the agent was acting within the scope of the agent's authority. In other words, an agent may do for a principal what the agent is unable to do for himself.

Figure 6–2. How a Principal Creates an Agency Relationship

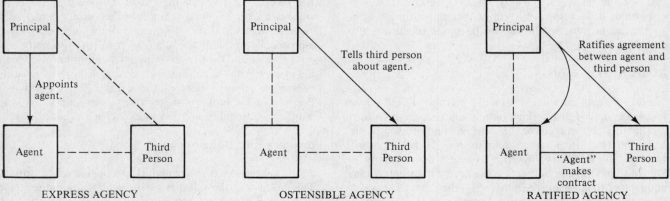

Purpose

In order for an agency relationship to be valid, it must be for a legal purpose. The law will not provide remedies for breach of agency contract or breach of agency duties if the agency is for an unlawful purpose. As in other illegal contracts, this kind of contract is void, and the law will generally leave the parties as it found them.

Express Agency (Appointment)

Agency is a consensual relationship ordinarily formed by the express agreement of the principal and agent. Express agency may be created orally or in writing. The reader should examine the licensing law in his or her state to determine whether oral agreements for a listing by a broker are valid for the purpose of the broker's entitlement to receive a commission if a buyer is found.

LOOK THIS UP:
Are oral listing contracts binding in your state?
Yes_____ No_____

There are circumstances when an appointment for an express agency must be in writing as a result of the requirements of the statute of frauds which was discussed in Chapter 5. Typically, if the agency cannot be completed within one year, the appointment must be in writing. Also, if the principal wishes to empower the agent to enter into a contract on the principal's behalf, and the contract falls within the requirements of the statute of frauds, the appointment must also be in writing. This is the *equal dignities rule*.

Example:
Pete orally gives Andy authority to sell his farm to Tom for $100,000. Tom and Andy sign a written contract. Tom may not enforce the contract against Pete because Andy's appointment was not in writing. Contracts for the sale of real estate must be in writing. It should be noted that the contract is enforceable against Tom because he signed it but not against Andy who was acting for a disclosed principal. If Pete wishes to go through with the transaction he may ratify the contract in writing.

Implied Agency

An agency relationship may be implied by the acts and conduct of the parties involved.

Example:
Pam advertises her lot for sale with the words: "7% commission paid to licensed brokers finding a buyer accepted by purchaser." If Bob, a licensed broker, brings a purchaser and this purchaser is accepted, Bob will be entitled to a commission in most states even though no actual listing contract was signed and no words were exchanged between Pam and Bob.

Agency by Necessity

During emergencies it is generally unnecessary to gain consent from a principal in order for a person to act to protect property or person. This agency is created by operation of law.

Example:
While a broker is showing a prospect her principal's property, a large tree limb falls, breaking a plate glass picture window. If the broker is unable to contact the principal for instructions, she may by implication act to repair the window in order to prevent vandals or vermin from entering the house or to prevent the elements from causing damage to the interior of the dwelling.

Agency by Estoppel (Ostensible Agency)

Generally an agency is created by consent between the principal and agent. Agency by estoppel occurs when the principal leads a third person to believe that somebody is an agent. The principal may create the impression of agency either intentionally or negligently. If the third person relies on the principal's manifestations and enters into a contract with the ostensible agent, the principal will be "estopped" from denying the agency. The agency may not be created solely by the purported agent's conduct or assertions, but where the principal has a duty to talk and remains silent the agency may nevertheless be created.

Example:
Patty's brother-in-law, Abel, tells Terry that Patty has authorized him to sell her house for $50,000. Terry calls Patty on the telephone to inquire about Abel's authority to act. Patty tells Terry that she is planning to get rid of her house but fails to deny Abel's authority as an agent. Terry pays Abel $50,000 on the basis of the conversation. Patty refuses to deliver the deed saying that Abel was not appointed her agent. Some courts will hold that Patty is bound because she led Terry to believe that Abel was her agent. She is estopped from denying the agency. It should be observed that the statute of frauds may prevent any recovery because the contract was not in writing.

Agency by Ratification

A principal may agree to be bound by the acts of a person purporting to act as an agent, even though the person was not in fact an agent. The principal may also be bound if there are acts of an agent who acted beyond the scope of authority. This agreement, called ratification, may be done by express affirmation or by implication.

Ratification may also be implied if the principal attempts to accept the benefits or attempts to affirm only part of the transaction. However, if part of the transaction is accepted, then all of it is accepted. Once a transaction is ratified, the principal is bound by the duties and the liabilities as well as being entitled to the rights.

The principal must have knowledge of all material facts or waive rights to knowing these facts by negligently ratifying without proper inquiry as to the circumstances of the transaction. Where a principal, with the knowledge of all material facts, ratifies a transaction, the principal becomes liable for all misrepresentations on the part of the agent.

THE REAL ESTATE BROKER AS AN AGENT

Custom, case law and licensing legislation have altered traditional agency law principles in the creation of the real estate brokerage agency relationship. Ordinarily a broker represents a property owner who desires to sell, lease or exchange real estate or the broker represents a prospective purchaser who wishes to find a property to purchase. When the broker provides the professional services contracted for, the commission is earned. A prerequisite to compensation, however, is a proper license recognized by the state in which the transaction or property is situated. In the ordinary situation where the broker represents an owner seeking to sell a property, the broker is entitled to a commission if it can be proven that the broker was licensed, employed and the efficient and procuring cause of the sale.

Licensing Law Considerations

Generally, the license must be valid *at the time* the broker provides that particular service which entitles him or her to compensation. A lack of a license is fatal to the ability to recover the commission. In many states if the broker was not licensed at the time the listing was obtained, no recovery for commission would be permitted. A broker, therefore, would not be entitled to a commission if his license or the license of the broker's sales employee, who was the broker's instrument in a transaction, has lapsed. Even if a license is obtained before closing, this would generally not be enough to cure the defect. Further, most state license laws make it illegal for a broker to share a commission with a nonlicensed person or to pay a finder's fee to a nonlicensed person. Some states even make it illegal to pay a fee or split a commission with a nonresident broker licensed in another state.

LOOK THIS UP:

Is it illegal in your state to split a commission with a nonresident broker licensed in another state?

Yes _____ No _____

How a Broker is Employed

Conventionally, a broker shows employment by producing a written listing contract, although in some states the broker may be employed by oral agreement. If the broker cannot show employment, his or her right to a commission is defeated despite the fact that the broker provided a service or helped bring a buyer and seller together.

Example:
> Betty Broker brings Tim Client to see Pat Owner's house. Betty has no listing agreement with Pat. Betty introduces herself as a licensed broker and indicates that Tim, who is not paying her a commission, is interested in purchasing the house. A deal is consummated and Betty sues Pat for a commission. Betty will lose. The court would view her as a volunteer. Even though Betty may have hinted that she expected a commission from the seller when she made the introduction, she will not recover. Betty should have entered into a definite understanding that she would be paid a commission if she found a buyer for Pat.

The Listing Contract

Even in states which permit oral listing agreements, it is nevertheless a good idea to enter into a written contract. This precaution may help prevent misunderstanding, disagreements, and litigation in the future. Further, written listing contracts help define duties and rights on the part of both the broker and owner and may be entered into evidence to prove these obligations in a court of law.

In states which require written listing contracts, the following elements should generally be included: the name of the parties; description of the property; sales price; terms of sale if other than cash; duration of the listing; type of listing—open, exclusive agency or exclusive right to sell; amount of commission and how and when it will be paid; special stipulations concerning earnest money deposits; multiple listing arrangements and other special conditions or covenants. Some states have specific elements which must be included in order to permit the broker to receive the commission. For example, many states require that a definite expiration date be specified on the listing contract. If a date is not specified, the broker will not be permitted to recover a commission.

LOOK THIS UP:

Does your state require a definite expiration date specified on a listing contract?

Yes _____ No _____

Since generally it is the broker who prepares the contract, any ambiguity will be construed against the broker in a dispute. It is important, therefore, that the listing contract be carefully and precisely prepared. If the broker has any question as to the proper wording or a provision, a competent real estate lawyer should be consulted. Since the broker is a party to the listing agreement, preparation of a prepared form would not be deemed as practicing law without a license. This rule does not apply to sales contracts. A broker is generally restricted to mechanically filling out blanks in a prepared form. Any other work should be delegated to a licensed attorney. Appendix A provides the reader with some training in the interpretation of listing contracts.

Types of Listing Contracts

Listing contracts may be classified into the following categories: (1) open listing, (2) exclusive agency listing, (3) exclusive right to sell listing, (4) net listing or (5) multiple listing.

Open Listing

This listing is also known as a simple listing or a general listing. Under this contract the property owner will pay a commission only to the broker who is the efficient and procuring cause of the sale. More than one broker may be employed, and the owner is not obligated to pay anyone a commission if the owner personally sells the property.

Exclusive Agency Listing

In this type of listing the owner employs only one broker but retains the right to personally sell the property and thereby not pay a commission. If any other broker negotiates a sale, the listing broker is nevertheless entitled to the full commission unless the listing broker had agreed otherwise with the procuring broker. Thus, if a procuring broker has a prospect who is interested in a house that another broker has under an exclusive listing, the listing broker should first be contacted and arrangement for a cooperation agreement should be made.

Exclusive Right to Sell Listing

When a broker is hired under this listing arrangement, there is entitlement to a commission no matter who sells the property during the listing period. This is true whether another broker or the owner sells the property. It may be noted that general rules of law may be modified by specific agreement.

One modification which occasionally appears in listing contracts is an exclusion by the owner from the contract of people the owner has been negotiating with prior to the listing. If the owner sells the property to one of these excluded people, he or she would not be liable to the broker for a commission, despite the general exclusive right to sell provision. Another problem often occurs when a house is sold after the expiration of the listing period to a purchaser procured by the broker during the stipulated period. Normally, unless the sale was imminent and effectively completed during the period or if the buyer and the seller acted in bad faith to conspire to deprive the broker of the justly earned commission, no commission is owed. The broker can be protected with an *extender* or *carryover* provision in the original listing contract. This clause provides that the broker will be entitled for a specified period after the expiration date of the listing to receive a commission if the property is sold to any prospect to whom he had shown the property during the listing period.

Net Listing

A net listing may be an open, an exclusive agency or an exclusive right to sell listing. The feature which distinguishes this listing is the method of compensation to the listing broker. A broker agrees to sell the property in order to achieve a minimum net price to the owner. Anything which is received above the net price is the broker's compensation. For example, if a property has a net listing for $25,000 and it is sold for $35,000, the broker is entitled to a $10,000 commission. If, however, the property sells for $25,000, the broker is entitled to nothing. Because of the potential for conflicts of interest, many state licensing laws prohibit a true "net" listing contract.

LOOK THIS UP:

Are net listings legal in your state?

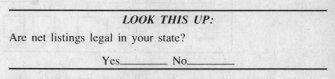

Multiple Listing

A multiple listing is an agreement joined into by brokers to pool all of their listings and establish procedures for sharing commissions. Multiple Listing Services (MLS) are often administered by local real estate boards.

To help understand how a multiple listing service works, consider the problem that would occur if no MLS arrangement were available. Consider Figure 6–3. In this figure there are three brokers, each with five listings. A buyer who was interested in seeing houses would approach a broker and ask to see what was available. Without a prior arrangement with other brokers, this broker would only be able to show the houses he or she had listed with the firm. The houses listed by the other brokers would not be available. If the buyer did not find anything suitable with the first broker, then it would be necessary to approach another broker to see additional houses. In a large city this process might have to be repeated many times before a suitable house would be found by the buyer. Brokers who did not have a listing on the house that was sold would earn no commission, and the buyer would be frustrated because a single broker could not show all houses available. Under MLS the buyer could approach a single broker and see a much larger selection of houses (see Figure 6–4). All houses listed by brokers participating in MLS would be potentially available by going through just one broker. If the

Figure 6–3. No Multiple Listing Service Available

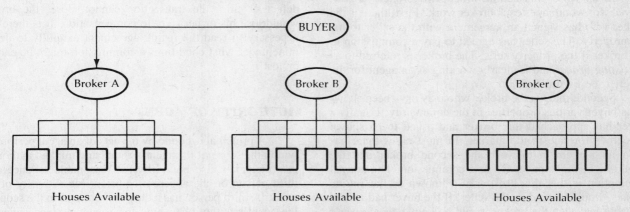

Only Houses Listed With Broker A Available To Buyer

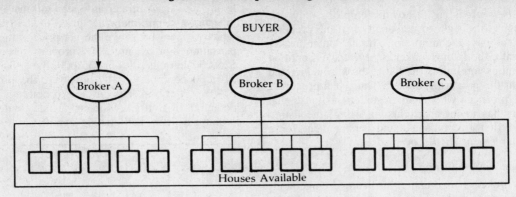

Figure 6–4. Multiple Listing Service

buyer agreed to purchase a house that was listed by another broker, there would be no problem. By prior arrangement, the two brokers involved would have agreed to share the commission. The broker who showed the house to the buyer is known as the *selling broker*. The broker who had the listing on the house would be known as the *listing broker*. To illustrate how the commission might be split, consider the following example.

Example:

An MLS arrangement in Anytown gives a selling broker 60% of a commission and the listing broker 40%. Assume that Ann, a salesperson for the selling broker, has agreed to split commissions fifty-fifty with her broker. She has successfully sold a house for $80,000 which was listed with another broker. If there is a 6% commission, how much did she earn? To solve this problem find the commission involved. This is $4,800 ($80,000 × .06 = $4,800). Next find the selling broker's share of the commission. This is $2,880 ($4,800 × .6 = $2,880). Finally, find Ann's share of the commission. This is $1,440 ($2,880 × .5 = $1,440).

In order to market the MLS system effectively many MLS organizations require a property owner to sign an exclusive agency or an exclusive right to sell before a house can be included in the marketing pool. Because an MLS is a local arrangement among cooperating brokers, there is likely to be a difference in local procedures on splitting commissions and participation.

In an MLS transaction, when two brokers are involved, for whom does each broker work? First, there is the broker who has signed an agreement with the seller to list the property. The seller has agreed to pay a commission to the broker if the property sells. The broker is referred to as the *listing broker* and is clearly working as an agent for the seller. (See Figure 6–5.)

Second, there is the broker who may have been showing a buyer various properties in the community. Usually a buyer has approached this broker and asked to be shown properties for sale in the market. In most cases there has been no agreement between the second broker and the would-be buyer to pay a fee or a commission. The normal assumption is that this broker, also known as the *selling broker*, would be paid by the seller. If the buyer had agreed to pay a fee, then the broker would be known as a *buyer's broker* and would therefore be an agent for the buyer. However, since the seller is paying the fee, the selling broker does *not* work for the buyer. He or she is, in fact, a subagent of the seller.

How does the selling broker become a subagent of the seller? Remember, this broker may never even have met the seller. In most MLS agreements, brokers who place a property on the MLS also make a unilateral offer of subagency to any broker who shows the property. This offer is accepted by the mere act of showing the property to a buyer. In order not to accept this unilateral offer, the selling broker must make it clear at the first reasonable opportunity, usually the first contact with the listing broker, that the offer of subagency is being rejected. However, in this case, since the act of showing the property is an acceptance of the offer, silence means that the offer has been accepted by implication.

A Note on Commissions

Unless there is agreement to the contrary, a broker is usually entitled to a commission when a buyer is found *ready*, *willing* and *able* to purchase the listed property on the terms specified by the seller. The right to the commission is not defeated by some subsequent events such as the inability of the seller to convey good title or an agreement between the seller and buyer to cancel the sale.

In many states it has become common for a listing agreement to specify that a broker is entitled to a commission only if the transaction actually goes to settlement. In other words, if for some unavoidable reason, such as a defect of title, the transaction cannot close, the broker would lose his or her right to compensation. It is therefore necessary to read the listing agreement carefully to determine under what conditions a commission might be earned or lost.

AUTHORITY OF AGENT

A principal is bound by the acts of an agent performed within the scope of the agent's actual and implied authority. A principal is also bound by the reasonable reliance of a third person on the apparent or ostensible authority of the agent. A third person has a duty to inquire as to the scope of the agent's authority to bind the principal since generally the principal cannot be bound by unauthorized acts.

When a broker receives a listing from one who is not

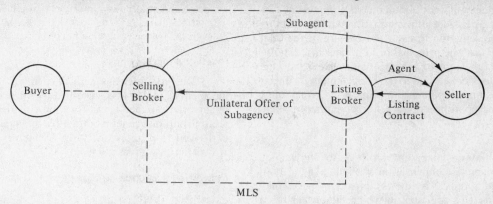

Figure 6–5. How a "Selling Broker" Becomes a Subagent Under MLS

the owner of a property or if a co-owner such as a spouse is involved, the broker should be assured that the listing was authorized. It should be noted that familial relationship does not necessarily make one member of a household an agent for the others. If a broker negligently fails to inquire as to the authority of such a member to list the property, the broker may find it difficult to recover the commission.

When acting without authority or behind the scope of authority, the agent may be liable to third persons for a breach of an *implied warranty of authority*. This is the warranty that the law will hold to be implied by the agent's actions in representing him- or herself as having authority which the agent in fact does not have.

RELATIONS OF PRINCIPAL AND AGENT

Agent's Duties to Principal

Agents are considered by law to be *fiduciaries*. A fiduciary is a person who essentially holds the character of trustee. Thus, an agent has a duty to act primarily for the principal's benefit and not his or her own. The agent must act with the highest degree of care and good faith in relations with the principal and on the principal's business. The penalties for failing in fiduciary duties may be quite severe. For example, a broker generally loses the right to a commission if the following duties are breached: loyalty, fidelity, obedience of legitimate instructions, due care, accounting and the giving of notice of material facts affecting the subject matter of the agency. The extent of the penalty depends on the seriousness of the breach and the damages sustained by the principal. There are cases where the penalty was a loss of the brokerage license and even criminal sanctions.

Perform with Due Care and Skill

An agent has a duty to perform the acts that were contracted for with reasonable care and diligence. The standard of performance that a real estate broker must meet is that of a professional agent holding out skills and knowledge customary in the profession. The broker must not be negligent and must actively seek to promote the interests of the principal. The broker has a duty to advertise and merchandise the property in a manner that is customary in the market area. A broker should also take care not to make negligent misrepresentations about the subject matter of the agency which could be binding on the principal. If the broker attempts to fill out the blanks in a standard sales contract on behalf of the principal, it is a duty to do so accurately, completely and unambiguously.

Perform Personally

An agent must personally perform the contracted-for acts. He or she may only delegate mechanical tasks, activities permitted by usages of the trade, expressly authorized acts, or acts improper and illegal for the agent to do personally, such as the practice of law. By custom, brokers work through sales employees under their supervision. A salesperson employed by a broker is an agent of the broker and not directly an agent of the broker's clients. This is true even if the salesperson is an independent contractor. The broker is therefore personally liable for negligence or wrongdoing that salespersons perform in the scope of their employment. Tasks which clearly involve the practice of law must be delegated to an attorney.

Obey Legitimate Instructions

An agent must obey all legitimate instructions related to the subject of the agency. Any material deviation from instructions which results in damage or injury is at the risk of the agent. Instructions which are contrary to the agency contract or are illegal do not fall within the scope of this rule.

Loyalty

An agent must be loyal. The agent is not permitted to compete with the principal nor to take advantage of confidential information to the detriment of the principal. If a broker is employed to sell a property, the broker may not purchase the property without *disclosure* to the principal. This rule cannot be circumvented by selling to relatives, straw men, or nominee corporations. The broker must disclose all facts which may affect the interests or actions of the principal. If the broker is selling to a relative or business associate, this fact must also be disclosed even if the broker gains no personal profit or proprietary interest in the real estate. The duty of loyalty also extends to situations in which a broker is employed to purchase a property. The broker may not buy the property himself without disclosure of this fact to the principal.

An agent must disclose all conflicts of interest to the principal. An agent may not simultaneously represent two principals on opposite sides of a transaction without disclosing the dual representation to each. Disclosure of the dual representation to just one principal or to neither is a defense against the broker's right to a commission. However, the duty of loyalty does not extend to the concealment of illegal or dishonest acts on the part of the principal. Crimes must be reported to the appropriate law enforcement authorities.

Fidelity

An agent may not make any profit out of the agency beyond the stipulated compensation without a good-faith disclosure to and approval by the principal. A broker may not sell a property to a principal in which the broker has a direct or indirect interest without disclosing this interest. Indirect interests include ownership of the subject property by business associates and relatives. The broker may not accept any gratuities, kickbacks or finder's fees from third persons which are in any way related to the subject matter of the agency. The rule is that the broker must be faithful to the interests of the principal.

Accounting

An agent must account for money and property belonging to the principal and entrusted to the agent's care. Funds belonging to the principal should be kept separate from the personal funds of the agent. The agent must be careful not to *commingle* funds by placing the principal's money in the broker's personal savings account. A separate trust account must be established for the principal's funds. This is usually required by state licensing law.

A problem often occurs with the disposition of earnest money deposits when the buyer defaults. Once the broker has accepted the earnest money as authorized by the principal, then, in the absence of contractual provisions to the contrary, earnest money deposits belong absolutely to the principal. The broker may not retain the deposit for a commission which the principal may owe. The broker must turn over the deposit money to the principal and then bring a separate lawsuit for the money owed.

Notice of Material Facts

An agent is under a duty to give notice to the principal of all material facts which affect the subject matter of the agency. Knowledge gained by the agent is imputed to the principal even though the agent never communicates the information to the principal. A fact is material if the knowledge of the fact might reasonably be expected to affect the judgment or decisions of the principal.

Example:

Dudley, a broker retained by Elbert to sell a house, receives two offers for the house. One offer is for $50,000 and the other offer is for $40,000. Dudley wishes to know if he must submit both offers to the principal or whether he should just submit the higher. He reasons that since the commission he receives is based on a percentage of the sales price, the principal must always accept the highest offer. What Dudley thinks is not relevant. Dudley must turn over both offers to the principal for him to make the choice. This is true even though one offer was significantly lower. Both offers are considered to be material facts. The reader may infer what would happen if the high bidder defaulted and, the low bidder, because he had not heard from the owner, withdrew his offer.

Indemnification

The principal has a right to indemnification against the agent as to any loss sustained by the principal as a result of any tortious act or any act in violation of the agency relationship or agency contract by the agent. A tortious act is derived from the word "tort" which is a civil wrong to which the law gives remedy.

Principal's Duties to Agent

In general, the duties that a principal owes to an agent may be classified as: (1) compensation, (2) cooperation, (3) due care and (4) reimbursement and indemnification.

Compensation

Generally, in a sale of real estate, a broker earns a commission when he or she finds a *qualified* buyer who is *ready, willing* and *able* to purchase a property on the terms set by the seller. A qualified buyer is a solvent purchaser of legal capacity. A minor, for example, would not ordinarily be a qualified buyer. The term "ready" indicates the buyer is prepared to meet the time stipulated in the listing by the seller. The term "willing" indicates that the purchaser agrees to the stated terms and conditions of the sale offer. The term "able" means that the buyer has the financial resources to purchase at the price indicated.

A broker and principal could agree that a broker's commission was conditioned on the transaction actually being consummated. This would mean that more than just finding a ready, willing and able buyer would be required in order to earn a commission. For example, a common condition in a sales contract is that the sale is contingent on the buyer being able to secure adequate financing. If the buyer is unable to receive financing, the broker has no right to a commission.

Cooperation

Unless there is agreement to the contrary, there is usually an implied covenant that the principal will cooperate and do nothing to hinder the agent from carrying out the performance of the agency contract. A principal is not permitted to attempt secretly to undermine the performance of the agent in order to avoid paying the agreed upon compensation. It should be noted that a principal may retain the right to compete with the agent if this right is specified in the contract or if this right is customary in the usage of the trade. For example, the right to compete is specified in an open listing.

Due Care

The principal owes the duty to act as an ordinary prudent man to avoid negligently injuring or damaging the agent. Where the agent's work involves entry on the principal's property, the agent is owed the same duty of care that would be owed to anyone else entitled to enter upon the property.

Reimbursement and Indemnification

Unless there is contrary agreement or contrary custom in the usage of the trade, the agent is entitled to reimbursement for all authorized and necessary expenditures made on the principal's behalf. Further, in a situation where an agent is working for an undisclosed or partially disclosed principal and as a result suffers losses from contractual liabilities undertaken on behalf of the principal, the agent is entitled to indemnification. In real estate, a broker is not customarily entitled to reimbursement for advertising a listed property, but an agreement may be made for this provision.

RELATIONS OF PRINCIPALS AND AGENTS WITH THIRD PARTIES

Liabilities of Real Estate Brokers Under Licensing Laws

Licensing laws impose greater burdens and liabilities on brokers than conventional agency law imposes on agents. Brokers have certain responsibilities for fair dealing with the public which are regulated through various state licensing commissions. Many states have real estate recovery funds to compensate members of the public who are financially damaged by dishonest or negligent dealings of real estate brokers.

Salespersons

It is well settled that a salesperson does not have a right against third persons for services rendered. A salesperson works for a broker and is under the broker's control. Any lawsuits against third persons related to commissions or other such matters must be undertaken by and through the broker.

Making Representations

An area of activity which is very carefully scrutinized by real estate disciplinary boards deals with liability imposed on brokers for misrepresentation. A broker is responsible for careless mistakes and intentional misrepresentations. A misrepresentation of fact or failure to disclose a fact by silence where there is a duty to do so will impose liability on a broker where the fact was material, false and detrimentally relied upon by the third person. It must be determined whether the misrepresentation was innocent, negligent or intentional fraud. Where the misrepresentation is innocent, and the broker was representing the seller, the buyer will be permitted to rescind the contract but generally no further liability will be incurred. Negligent statements will lead to civil liability. Recovery will depend on the extent of the negligence and of the damages.

It might be noted that misrepresentation applies to material facts and not to opinions. For example, the broker in showing a house to a prospective buyer might say, "This is the prettiest kitchen in the neighborhood." This statement is the broker's opinion and is referred to as "puffing the goods." This little exaggeration appears to be a normal practice and would be understood by most people to be nothing more than the broker's opinion.

Fraud will lead to civil, disciplinary and criminal liability; the penalty will depend on the seriousness of the offense and the damages actually sustained. A broker may be protected from this type of problem by assembling data on the property in the listing contract and having the property owner certify the accuracy of the summary. Further, when the broker is asked questions about the condition of the property or other such matters of which he or she is uncertain, the broker should direct the buyer to the owner for the answer.

Brokers' Third Party Liability

The law makes a distinction between patent defects and latent defects. *Patent defects* are those that are obvious to a person who makes a reasonable inspection of a property. *Latent defects* are those that are hidden and not obvious from an inspection. What are the broker's responsibilities to a buyer for latent defects? Consider the following:

Example:
John owns a house that was constructed over a landfill. Joan, a real estate broker, shows the house to Mr. and Mrs. Smith who are impressed with its construction quality. They buy the house. Joan never disclosed the fact that the house was constructed on a landfill. Three years later the foundation of the house cracks. Mr. and Mrs. Smith file a lawsuit against Joan the real estate broker for failing to advise them about the defect. Who wins?

The traditional rule had been that, unless Joan knew about the landfill, she was not obligated for resulting damage. However, in similar cases, in some states (such as California) the courts have held that, if the broker *should have known* about the defect, he or she can be held liable to third party purchasers. Obviously a similar situation exists with regard to toxic waste dumps and other problems. This rule puts the burden on the broker to try to discover any latent defects that may exist in or on a listed property.

Rights of Agents Against Wrongs by Third Persons

Generally, a broker is working for a principal and is not a party to a contract which would give enforceable rights against the third person. There are situations, however, in which a broker does have a good cause of action against a third party. Where a broker, for example, shows a prospect a house and the prospect pretends to have no interest in the house, but later secretly approaches the buyer and purchases the house, a broker may have the right to collect a commission from the third person. Also, where a buyer and seller collude to avoid paying a broker the commission, the broker may be able to bring an action for the commission against either.

TERMINATION OF AGENCY RELATIONSHIP

An agency relationship or an agent's authority may be terminated by acts of parties, by stipulated events or by operation of law.

Acts of Parties

Acts of parties include performance, mutual agreement, discharge, resignation, abandonment or breach of agency duties.

Performance

An agency relationship will ordinarily be terminated when the purpose of the relationship has been completed. Thus, when a broker has been employed to sell a house, the agency would normally expire when the broker procured a qualified buyer. In an open listing where several brokers are employed, the agency relationships and authority of all brokers are extinguished when one of the brokers finds a buyer who signs a contract or if the owner sells the property.

Mutual Agreement

Both parties may agree to rescind the agency contract.

Discharge

An agency relationship may be terminated at any time by the principal (unless it is an agency coupled with an interest). The broker's only recourse for a wrongful termination is to sue for breach of contract. This rule is true even if the parties had agreed that the agency would be "irrevocable" for a specific period of time. In a case of wrongful discharge, the general rule is that the broker will only be entitled to recover for damages actually sustained, such as the cost of advertising and promoting the property. In some jurisdictions, the measure of damages is the commission which might have been earned, but most jurisdictions will not award anything in excess of actual damages except as a punitive measure. In order to limit the damages, the discharge must be made in good faith. If a broker is discharged when a sale is imminent, the broker will be entitled to the full commission.

Unilateral act of the principal or the principal's death may not terminate an agency coupled with an interest. This kind of agency occurs when a person is given powers to secure the performance of a duty owed or to protect some proprietary interest. It must be supported by consideration.

Example:
Alan lends Ellwood $100,000 to help purchase 25 acres of lake-front property in the mountains. At the same time, Alan is given an exclusive right to sell lots which will be subdivided from the tract of land. Alan is also given a 20% equity interest in the development and is told that his loan will be repaid from the proceeds of the sales. In this case, Alan has an agency coupled with an interest. His interest is both a debt and an equity interest in the subject matter of the agency.

Resignation

An agent may resign at any time. If the resignation is wrongful, the agent will be liable for breach of contract. When the agent resigns he or she no longer has authority to bind the principal.

Abandonment

The agent may abandon the agency without explicitly resigning. Inactivity for a prolonged or unreasonably long period of time would suggest abandonment and thereby termination of the agent's authority.

Breach of Agency Duties

While not all breaches of an agency contract necessarily terminate an agency relationship, there are circumstances where the agent's authority is suspended or even terminated. Such breaches generally involve loyalty or fidelity. An unfaithful and disloyal agent cannot be acting with actual authority to bind the principal. A contract entered into for the principal would not be valid unless the agent is also exercising apparent authority in relation to innocent third parties.

Operation of Law

Termination by operation of law includes expiration of term, death of parties, insanity, bankruptcy, change in law, destruction of subject matter or material change in circumstances.

Expiration of Term

The agency relationship expires at the end of a specified term. If no term is specified, it expires at the end of a reasonable period.

Death of Parties

Death of either the principal or agent automatically terminates the agency relationship. The reader is advised to beware of situations in which a complicated transaction is involved which includes a death of either the principal or agent without notice to parties to the transaction. The entire transaction may also be terminated. The exception to the rule of automatic termination is an agency coupled with an interest.

Insanity or Bankruptcy

Insanity or bankruptcy of either party will automatically terminate the agency relationship as a general rule. In the former case the party would not have mental responsibility, whereas in the latter case the party would not have financial responsibility. It should be noted that the bankruptcy of the agent does not always terminate the relationship when the subject matter of the agency is in no way related to the agent's financial responsibility or if the parties established the relationship in contemplation of the agent's bankruptcy.

Change in Law

Where the purpose or consideration of the agency contract becomes illegal because of a change in the law, the agency is terminated.

Destruction of the Subject Matter

If the subject matter of the agency is destroyed, the relationship is also terminated. For example, if a listed house burns down before a buyer is procured, the brokerage agency is terminated. However, it should be noted that if the broker's right to a commission was vested by the broker's having previously performed as stipulated in his employment contract, the agent would still be entitled to a commission even if the house had burned down before closing. This rule would not apply if the commission was contingent on the closing actually occurring.

Material Change in Circumstances

If the subject matter of the agency changes materially or is affected by a material change, the authority of the agent may be cancelled. For example, if after a property had been listed at a certain price, gold was discovered on the land causing the property value to change dramatically, this would be construed as a material change in circumstances. The authority of the broker to find a buyer at the listed price would be cancelled.

Requirement of Notice

When an agency is terminated by acts of parties, the principal has a duty to inform and give notice to third persons reasonably relying on the continuance of the agency. Termination by the unilateral act of the principal must be communicated reasonably to the agent. When an agency relationship is terminated by operation of law, it is unnecessary to give notice in order to cancel the agent's authority; the termination is automatic.

POINTS TO REMEMBER

1. No agency is ever created without some action or conduct, whether intentional or negligent, on the part of the principal. A purported agent cannot establish an agency relationship by conduct or statement alone. A third person acts at his or her own risk in relying solely on the manifestation of a so-called agent as to the agent's authority. This rule does not operate when the agency is created by operation of law.

2. A principal is bound by the acts of an agent performed within the scope of the agent's actual and implied authority.

3. A broker is generally entitled to a commission if it can be proven that he or she was licensed, employed and was the efficient and procuring cause of the sale. (Note: the license must be valid *at the time* the broker engages in any real estate negotiations. Conventionally, the broker shows employment by producing a listing contract, although in some states the broker may be employed by oral agreement.)

4. Unless there is agreement to the contrary, a broker is usually entitled to a commission when a qualified buyer is found *ready, willing* and *able* to purchase the listed property on the terms specified by the seller. The right to the commission is not defeated by some subsequent event such as the inability of the seller to convey good title or an agreement between the seller and buyer to cancel the sale.

5. An agency relationship may be terminated at any time by the principal (unless it is an agency coupled with an interest). The broker's only recourse for a wrongful termination is to sue for breach of contract.

6. When an agent acts without authority or beyond the scope of authority, he or she may be liable to third persons for a breach of an implied warranty of authority.

7. An agent is always liable to third persons for the agent's personal torts. The principal is also bound for the agent's torts if the agent is a servant under the principal's right to control; the principal is generally not bound if the agent is an independent contractor.

8. A broker generally loses the right to a commission if he or she breaches duties of loyalty, fidelity, obedience of legitimate instructions, due care, accounting and notice of material facts affecting the subject matter of the agency. In some cases, a breach of these duties may also lead to a loss of a real estate license.

9. An agent may not make any profit out of the agency beyond the stipulated compensation.

10. An agent must disclose all conflicts of interest to the principal. An agent may not simultaneously represent principals on opposite sides of a transaction without disclosing the dual representation in advance.

11. An agent is under a duty to give notice to the principal of all material facts coming to his or her attention which affect the subject matter of the agency. Knowledge gained by the agent is imputed to the principal even though the agent never communicates the information to the principal.

12. The principal has a right to indemnification against the agent as to any loss sustained by the principal as a result of any tortious act or any act in violation of the agency relationship by the agent.

13. A salesperson employed by a broker is an agent of the broker and not of the broker's principal.

KEY TERMS AND PHRASES

actual agency	exclusive right to sell (listing)	open listing
agency by estoppel	fiduciaries	partially disclosed principal
agency by ratification	general agent	power of attorney
agent	independent contractor	principal
authority	loyalty	special agent
commingle	multiple listing	undisclosed principal
disclosed principal	net listing	universal agent
exclusive agency (listing)		

QUESTIONS

1. Generally, in the absence of agreement to the contrary, a licensed real estate broker has earned a commission when
   A. the property is listed
   B. the purchaser hands the broker an earnest money deposit
   C. a purchaser is found who is ready, willing and able to buy the property on the seller's terms
   D. title to the property is transferred at closing

2. Your mother-in-law, who is not licensed to sell real estate, finds a prospect to buy a house listed with your brokerage firm. Before she introduces the prospect to you, she insists that you agree in writing to give her a 3% finder's fee. Which of the following is true?
   A. Legally, you may not agree to pay her a finder's fee.
   B. You may agree to pay her a finder's fee.
   C. You must tell her that withholding the name of the prospect is illegal because it is a restraint of trade.
   D. You may not, under most licensing laws, pay her a finder's fee, but you are permitted to buy her an expensive ring.

3. A homeowner wishes to list a house with you for $40,000. On the previous day a prospect came into your office and indicated that he wanted to buy a similar house for $60,000. You tell the homeowner that instead of listing the house you will be happy to take an option for $40,000. He agrees. You exercise the option and sell the house to the prospect for $60,000. Which of the following is true?
   A. Because of your status as a licensed broker you had the duty to reveal the true value of the house. You earn no commission.
   B. You may agree to pay him a finder's fee.
   C. You are entitled to the $20,000 profit which you made.
   D. You are only entitled to a reasonable commission on the sale of the house, and thus you may keep only 7% of the sale price. The rest you must turn over to the original homeowner.

4. John Cline comes to your brokerage office and agrees to pay you a fee of 5% if you locate and negotiate the purchase of a warehouse for him which meets his specifications and does not exceed $100,000. At this time you have David Knox's warehouse listed for $100,000 which meets these exact specifications. If you sell this property you are entitled to a 7% commission. Without disclosing the fact that you have been hired by both parties, because you respect the confidentiality of the broker-client relationship, you bring the two parties together and close the deal. Which of the following is true?
   I. John Cline owes you $5,000.
   II. David Knox owes you $7,000.
   A. I only   C. Both I and II
   B. II only   D. Neither I nor II

5. You are a broker who is showing Mr. and Mrs. Fite several houses in a fine residential neighborhood. You pass a lovely house which has a sign "For Sale By Owner." Because the Fites express enthusiasm over the appearance of the house, you stop and meet the owner. You introduce yourself as a real estate broker and the owner agrees to let the Fites see the house; however, the owner refuses to employ you. You are able to get the Fites and the homeowner to agree to a contract for the sale of the house. Which of the following is true?
   I. The homeowner owes you a reasonable commission for your professional services as a broker.
   II. The Fites owe you a commission since they knew the house was not listed and yet they still benefited from your services.
   A. I only   C. Both I and II
   B. II only   D. Neither I nor II

6. You have an open listing contract on Mr. Thomas' house. You are showing Mr. Adams houses in a neighborhood in which Mr. Thomas' house is located. As you drive by Mr. Thomas' house you tell Mr. Adams that you have an open listing on the house and ask him if he is interested in seeing the house. Even though Mr. Thomas is not at home, you show the house to Mr. Adams. The next day Mr. Adams contacts Mr. Thomas and the parties agree on a sales price which is lower

than the listed price because of the savings on not having to pay a real estate commission. Mr. Adams does not tell Mr. Thomas that you are involved. Which of the following is true?

　I. Mr. Thomas owes you a commission.

　II. Mr. Adams owes you a commission.

　A. I only　　　　　C. Both I and II
　B. II only　　　　　D. Neither I nor II

7. You have a salesperson who has been inactive for three years. His license has been allowed to lapse. One day the salesperson calls your office and tells you that he has procured a listing. The salesperson negotiates a sale and a contract is signed. Before closing, it is discovered that the salesperson's license has lapsed. You quickly fill out the appropriate forms and are able to reactivate the license before closing. Which of the following is true?

　I. The broker is entitled to a commission.

　II. The salesperson is entitled to his agreed upon share of the commission.

　A. I only　　　　　C. Both I and II
　B. II only　　　　　D. Neither I nor II

8. A real estate broker personally inspects a house he has listed and discovers that the house has termites. He later is able to successfully negotiate a sale of the property. He prepares a standard form contract which contains a representation that the house is free of termites. He brings this contract to the seller to sign. Which of the following is *not* true?

　A. An agent is required to bring to the attention of the principal any material facts which may affect the subject matter of the agency.

　B. A principal is bound by the negligent or intentional misrepresentations of the agent who is acting within the scope of his authority.

　C. It is the duty of the seller to read and understand a contract before it is signed.

　D. The broker is entitled to the commission on this sale.

9. James Hooley hires you to sell his house. You find a purchaser who is ready, willing and able to buy the house on the terms specified in the listing contract. The contract is silent as to whether or not closing needs to take place. A contract of sale is entered into by both parties. During the title search, it is discovered that there is a defect in title which prevents Hooley from being able to give a warranty deed. As a result the deal cannot be consummated. Which of the following is true?

　A. You are entitled to a commission from Hooley.

　B. You are not entitled to a commission from Hooley.

　C. You are entitled to any expenses that you may have had in advertising and selling the house.

　D. You are entitled to the escrow deposit.

10. You are showing a house to a prospect. In your sales talk you state that the house is considered to be in the most beautiful and desirable part of town and in your opinion only the most important people in town live in the neighborhood. Relying on your statements the prospect buys the house. Later he discovers that another neighborhood is more desirable. Which of the following is true?

　A. You are guilty of a fraudulent misrepresentation.

　B. You were negligent in choosing your words and must pay damages to the home purchaser.

　C. You were merely "puffing the goods" and thus not liable.

　D. You are guilty of violating most state licensing laws regulating real estate brokers.

11. Generally, a real estate broker acts as a (an)

　A. universal agent
　B. general agent
　C. special agent
　D. ostensible agent

12. On behalf of the principal, a broker accepts an earnest money deposit in cash. Because he has an appointment on the other side of town, the broker does not have time to deposit the money in a bank. The broker carefully places the money in a safe in his office. Overnight the office is robbed and the money is stolen. The broker's principal had insisted on cash. The purchaser did not get a receipt. Which of the following is true?

　A. The risk of loss is on the part of the purchaser. He should have required a receipt.

　B. The risk of loss is on the part of the seller. He should have required a check.

　C. The broker must replace the money and bear the loss.

　D. This is the kind of loss which the broker may seek compensation for from a state real estate recovery fund.

13. James Spence, an infant of 17 years of age, hires Kathy Morris to sell a house he has inherited. The listing contract is an exclusive right to sell. Spence voids the listing, finds a buyer and sells the house himself to Ken Drucker. Which of the following is true?

　I. Morris is entitled to a real estate commission.

　II. Spence may refuse to sell the house to Drucker if he decides to change his mind.

　A. I only　　　　　C. Both I and II
　B. II only　　　　　D. Neither I nor II

14. Sharon Nicholson signs a listing contract with Doug Wedgworth. The contract is silent as to whether or not closing needs to take place. Wedgworth finds a buyer for the house, Karen Adams. Nicholson and Adams enter into a sales agreement. Before closing, Adams learns that her company has decided to transfer her to another state. Adams and Nicholson agree to mutually rescind the contract and instruct the real estate broker to return the earnest money deposit. The sales contract did not indicate that the commission would be paid out of the earnest deposit. Which of the following is true?

The Principal-Agent Relationship

I. Wedgworth may keep the earnest deposit as liquidated damages from Adams for backing out of the deal.

II. Wedgworth is entitled to a commission from Nicholson.

A. I only
B. II only
C. Both I and II
D. Neither I nor II

15. State law makes net listings illegal in the state that George Fox, broker, and Jerry Segal, homeowner, are in when they enter into a listing contract to sell Segal's house. The contract states that Segal will net at least $50,000 and that Fox is entitled to a commission up to 7% of the sales price. If the house sells for $50,100, how much will Fox receive as his sales commission?

A. Nothing. Net listing contracts are illegal in the state.
B. $3,507.00. This is 7% of the total purchase price since the net listing limitation is illegal.
C. $100.00
D. $7.00

16. Broker Jones has a house listed for $50,000. His daughter sees it and decides that she would like to purchase it. The broker convinces the seller to accept $45,000 from ''the young married couple who are buying their first house.''He does not reveal his relationship as the father of one of the purchasers. Before closing, the seller discovers the relationship and refuses to pay the broker his commission. Which of the following is true?

A. The broker is entitled to his commission.
B. The broker is not entitled to his commission.
C. The contract for the sale of the house is void.
D. The broker's daughter and son-in-law must pay $50,000 for the house.

17. Johnson, a broker, receives three legitimate offers for a house that he has listed. His client advised Johnson that he did not wish to sell to minority groups. One offer is from a minority group member. The broker must

A. submit the highest offer
B. submit the offer which he believes is in the best interest of his client
C. submit all offers
D. submit only those offers which are not from minority group members

18. If an agent exceeds his authority and enters into a contract on behalf of a principal, the principal may become bound if the principal

I. ratifies the contract
II. fails to dismiss the agent

A. I only
B. II only
C. Both I and II
D. Neither I nor II

19. An agent for an undisclosed principal is

A. personally liable for any contracts entered into on behalf of the principal
B. not liable if the principal is disclosed before the contract is executed
C. only liable on contracts which are entered into beyond the scope of the agent's authority
D. only liable on contracts which are in writing

20. In a state where net listings are legal, Bob Brown, a broker, is given power of attorney to sell Harry Bennett's store while Bennett is out of the country for a two-month vacation. Brown is instructed to sell the store for $150,000 net to Bennett. Brown is further personally instructed that he may sell the store to anyone except Fred Roe, who has been a bitter rival of Bennett's for 30 years. While Bennett is out of the country, Brown advertises the store for sale. Roe submits the highest offer by $10,000. Brown sells the store to Roe. Which of the following is true?

I. Bennett can rescind the contract with Roe.
II. Bennett can sue Brown for failing to follow instructions and for breaching his fiduciary duty.

A. I only
B. II only
C. Both I and II
D. Neither I nor II

21. A real estate broker is hired to negotiate the purchase of a unique Victorian mansion for Sam Patton. After examining the house, the broker buys it for himself. Which of the following is true?

A. The broker may purchase the house for himself unless he has a written contract with Sam Patton.
B. Sam Patton may sue the broker and be able to require the broker to reconvey the house to him.
C. The broker may purchase the house if he is able to find a similar house for Sam Patton.
D. The broker may purchase the house if he is willing to pay more than Sam Patton.

22. If Abe tells Betty that Caine is authorized to act on Abe's behalf, insofar as Betty is concerned, Caine is an

A. actual agent
B. express agent
C. ostensible agent
D. implied agent

23. Dick tells Tom that he is an agent for Seale to sell Seale's house for $10,000. Tom pays Dick $10,000 and Seale refuses to convey the property, explaining that Dick was not authorized to sell the house. What are Tom's rights against Dick? Dick explains that it was a mistake and returns the money.

A. None. A third person has the duty to inquire into an agent's scope of authority.
B. Tom may sue Dick for a breach of his warranty of authority.
C. Tom may sue Dick for fraud and deceit.
D. Tom may sue Dick for specific performance.

24. Bryan is given an exclusive right to sell Millie's property for $50,000. Bryan is told three days later that oil has been discovered on the property and that the value of the property has increased tenfold. Bryan finds a

buyer ready, willing and able to purchase the property for $50,000. Which of the following is true?

I. Bryan is entitled to his commission.

II. Bryan must advise Millie that oil has been discovered on her property.

A. I only
B. II only
C. Both I and II
D. Neither I nor II

25. Peter agrees with Betty, a real estate broker, that if she lends him $50,000 to buy a coal mine, that she will have irrevocable authority to sell the coal mine one year later, receive a commission and have her loan repaid from the proceeds of the sale. Peter and Betty hold the mine as tenants in common. Peter dies. Which of the following is true?

A. Betty has an agency coupled with an interest and the principal's death does not terminate her authority to sell the coal mine.

B. Betty's authority is terminated.

C. Betty is a real estate broker and her $50,000 loan which would be paid from the proceeds of the sale was a conflict of interest. She may not receive a real estate commission on the sale of the coal mine.

D. Betty gains sole title to the coal mine by right of survivorship.

26. Brokers must submit offers which are

I. above the listing price

II. below the listing price

A. I only
B. II only
C. Both I and II
D. Neither I nor II

27. The three classifications of agencies created between principal and agent are

A. universal, principal and special
B. listing, principal and universal
C. universal, general and special
D. general, listing and special

28. Salesperson "A" shows a property owned by Seller "B" and listed with Broker "B." Which of the following is the most true?

I. Broker "B" is the agent of Seller "B."

II. Salesperson "A's" broker is responsible to Seller "B."

A. I only
B. II only
C. Both I and II
D. Neither I nor II

29. When a broker enters into a listing agreement with a seller, which of the following statements is (are) correct?

I. The seller is the agent of the broker.

II. The broker is the agent of the seller.

A. I only
B. II only
C. Both I and II
D. Neither I nor II

30. An agent who has authority to perform all lawful acts for a principal is referred to as a (an)

A. special agent
B. general agent
C. universal agent
D. implied agent

If you are not sure of your answers, see page 316 for correct answers and explanations.

The Principal-Agent Relationship

7

Legal Descriptions

Deeds and other real estate documents must contain a legally sufficient description. In legal cases involving disputes as to exactly what land was being conveyed from one person to another, courts have interpreted this to mean that property is sufficiently described if a competent civil engineer or surveyor could locate the exact boundaries of the subject property given the legal description included in the conveyance. Thus, the need exists for correctly identifying the property being conveyed as well as the physical boundaries of that property. A deed which does not have a legally sufficient description is void and not enforceable.

In addition to the inclusion of a proper legal description in a deed, numerous other real estate documents need to have a property description as part of their wording. Listing agreements, sales contracts, leases, promissory notes and mortgages contain wording or phrases that identify the property which is the subject of the contract. In some instances, such as a listing agreement, the legal description may be less than precise. At other times, when for example a lender wishes to place a lien against the property of a debtor and record that lien in the public records, two or three different methods of describing the property may be included, any one of which could be used to properly locate and accurately describe the subject property.

As noted in Figure 7-1, there are a number of different methods used to describe land. The primary methods include: (1) street address, (2) metes and bounds, (3) monuments and (4) rectangular survey. A secondary method is the lot and block description, used extensively in urban areas with both residential and commercial property.

STREET ADDRESS

The name of a street and a particular number on that street is certainly the easiest and quickest way to identify a parcel of land. To have mail delivered or to find a house that has been advertised as being "For Sale" normally require no more exact legal description than this method. However, this is not a formal method since it does not identify the exact boundaries of the subject land, nor does it indicate the quantity of land being described. This method should only be used to give the location of the land rather than as a precise legal description.

In addition to being an informal method, street names and addresses can be unclear or confusing, particularly in large urban areas. "House For Sale-1520 Washington." Is that the house on Washington Avenue or the one on Washington Street? Is that 1520 North Washington or 1520 South Washington? Furthermore, streets are sometimes renamed and renumbered.

This method is best used as an additional means of locating property. For example, the wording ". . . and more commonly known as 1738 Aberdeen Road," or ". . . the improvements being known as No. 1149 Kirkland Avenue" often appear in a sales contract or deed following the use of a more formal method.

METES AND BOUNDS

This method involves identifying distances and directions and makes use of both the physical boundaries and measurements of the land. Legally describing land by means of metes (distances) and bounds (directions) is the oldest method of land description in the United States and is the primary method of land description in some 20 states. Even in those states where another method is the primary means of describing property, the metes and bounds method is often used.

To correctly use this method, there must be a definite starting point. This starting point must be one that can be located by future surveyors; thus, it is necessary that it be as precise as possible. Physical evidence of this point, referred to as a *monument*, is often an iron pipe set in concrete which in turn can be and often is referenced to a permanent reference point such as a *bench mark*. Bench marks are bronze disks permanently placed and precisely identified by government survey teams. Monuments, both natural and artificial, also include fences, rivers and streams, trees,

Figure 7–1. Basic Methods of Property Description

INFORMAL DESCRIPTION Street Address FORMAL DESCRIPTION Metes and Bounds (Monuments) Rectangular Survey	Lot and Block
PRIMARY METHODS	SECONDARY METHODS

wooden stakes and road intersections. However, none of these is as precise as bench marks.

Once the point of beginning (POB) on the property has been established, *boundary lines* are identified and described until the land being surveyed has been *completely enclosed*. Boundary lines measure *distance* and *direction*. Where two boundary lines cross, referred to as a *corner*, a monument is often used to identify the intersection. Distance is stated in terms of feet, normally to the nearest hundredth (for example, 212.65′). Direction is given by its *bearing* (angle) which shows the direction of one object with respect to another object. The bearing of a boundary line is the *acute angle* (an angle of less than 90°) the line makes with a *meridian* (an imaginary line running north to south extending from the North Pole to the South Pole).

In land description, the bearings are identified with reference to the *quadrants* on a compass and are expressed in terms of *degrees, minutes* and *seconds*. A circle contains 360 degrees, 1 degree contains 60 minutes and each minute contains 60 seconds. The circle is divided into four quadrants, each containing 90 degrees. The quadrants are identified by their boundary lines, namely Northeast (NE), Northwest (NW), Southeast (SE), and Southwest (SW) (see Figure 7–2). All bearings begin in either a north or south direction, which identifies whether the angle is measured from due north or due south. The direction following the degrees, minutes, and seconds identifies whether or not the angle is east or west of due north or due south.

The normal way to record a bearing is as follows:

1. The first letter of the quadrant (N or S)

Figure 7–2. Metes and Bounds Directions

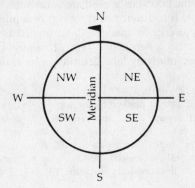

2. The value of the acute angle
3. The second letter of the quadrant (E or W)

Examine Figure 7–3 and read each of the three bearings. The bearings are:

N45°W   S30°E   N80°E

Examine Figure 7–4 and try to read the bearings of the four-sided tract. (The four corners have been labeled to assist in identifying the corners).

In Figure 7–5 imaginary lines (meridians) have been drawn through each of the four corners so as to help identify the correct quadrant of each angle.

The four angles would be read as follows:

Line ab	N15°10′12″E
Line bc	N82°54′38″E
Line cd	S08°02′39″E
Line da	S85°08′16″W

For each boundary line used in a metes and bounds description, the distance of the line, the direction of the line and the monument used to mark the end of the distance

Figure 7–3.

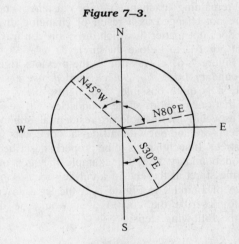

Figure 7–4.

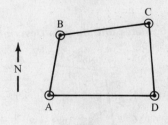

Figure 7–5.

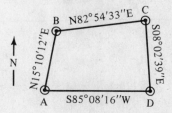

Legal Descriptions

should be clearly and precisely stated in the legal description. Study Figure 7–6 as you read the following metes and bounds description:

> Beginning for the same at a pipe set on the north side of Charles Street, distance South 85°08'16"East 430.50 feet measured along the north side of said Charles Street from the east side of Mt. Royal Avenue and running thence for new lines of division through the property now or formerly owned by John Smith the three following courses and distances; namely, North 15°10'12"East 224.60 feet to a pipe set, North 82°54'38"East 315.00 feet to a pipe set and South 08°02'39"East 286.65 feet to a pipe set on the north side of said Charles street and thence binding on the north side of said Charles Street South 85°08'16"West 332.45 feet to the place of beginning. Containing 80,313.23 square feet or 1.8437 acres of land, more or less. All courses and distances in the above descriptions are referred to the true meridian as adopted by the Orange County Survey Control System.

    This particular description was based on "walking" around the property in a clockwise direction. While it is common to describe land this way, the description would be perfectly acceptable had the direction been counterclockwise. In Figure 7–6 a description based on a counterclockwise direction would result in changing the "N" directions to "S," the "E" to "W" with the degrees, minutes and seconds remaining unchanged. The distances between points are not changed as a result of changing direction. While it does not matter in which direction you travel, the important point is to "close the circle."

    In Figure 7–6, as was true in the previous figure, all of the boundary lines, *ab, bc, cd,* and *da* were straight. However, it is quite possible, and highly likely in some terrains, that one or more of the boundaries will be curved. This is especially noticeable in residential subdivisions where streets are laid out with cul-de-sacs or courts with no through street. If such land is to be properly described, then the curved boundary line, for example the area of a lot fronting the street at the end of a cul-de-sac, is shown by using *arcs* of a circle. In Figure 7–7, the legal description needed to describe the curved area would be derived through the following steps:

- *Step 1:* Draw an imaginary circle upon which the *arc* rests.

Figure 7–6. Metes and Bounds Description

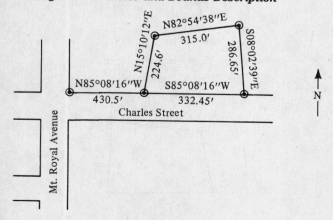

Figure 7–7. Mapping a Curve

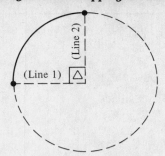

- *Step 2:* Mark the center of the circle.
- *Step 3:* Draw a dotted line (radius) from each end point of the arc (see Line 1 and Line 2). This is the *radius*, which is the distance from the center of the circle to its perimeter.
- *Step 4:* Measure the angle formed by the intersection of Line 1 and Line 2. This angle is referred to as *delta* (Δ).
- *Step 5:* Measure the length of the arc, referred to as "A."

Thus the legal description used to describe a parcel of land which contained this curved boundary would include the following wording: ". . . thence along the curve of Broadmoor Court for a distance of 300', Radius 180' to a point . . . ."

MONUMENTS

    As noted above, in the metes and bounds description the physical evidence of the starting point is known as a *monument*. From that point to the next boundary marker, the direction is stated in terms of compass quadrants. However, with certain types of property, particularly rural agricultural land, monuments are used not only as the starting point but as each boundary marker. Furthermore, the direction between any two monuments is stated in much less exact terms than are used in the metes and bounds method. Rather than stating ". . . North 80°54'16"East 305.45 feet to an iron pipe. . . . ," a monuments description might say ". . . about 300 feet in a northeasterly direction to an oak tree. . . ."

    This method, while quite common in older descriptions in rural areas, relies on the use of both natural and artificial monuments. Land description by monuments is considered less exact than a description by metes and bounds since the boundaries used are sometimes something not permanent, for instance, a river bed or a pile of rocks. Oftentimes reference is made to land owned by someone else, for instance, a neighbor's farm. Examine Figure 7–8 as you read the following land description (note direction of arrow):

> Beginning at a point marked by an iron pipe on the south side of State Highway 31E, approximately 8 miles west of Dycusburg and at the beginning of a fence row marking the land of John Smith; then along the fence line in a southerly direction for 935' to an oak tree marking the land of Elbert Jones; thence in a westerly direction for 1,750' to Mansker

Figure 7–8. Description by Monuments

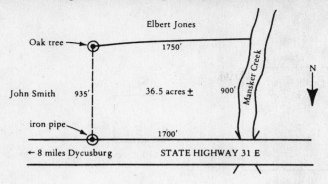

Creek; thence along the creek bed of Mansker Creek in a northerly direction for 900′ to the right-of-way of State Highway 31E; thence easterly along the right-of-way line of State Highway 31E for approximately 1,700′ to the point of beginning, containing 36.5 acres more or less.

RECTANGULAR SURVEY

Also referred to as the *U.S. government survey system*, this method of land description was established in 1785 and is used in some 30 states. As can be seen in Figure 7–9, this system is based on imaginary lines of longitude (north-south and referred to as *meridians*) and latitude (east-west and referred to as *base lines*). There are 36 principal meridians, some designated by names, others by numbers. Each principal meridian has an intercepting base line. This system is based on the idea of progressively dividing an area into a number of smaller and smaller areas (see Figure 7–10).

Guide meridians are located every 24 miles east and west of a principal meridian and *parallels* or *correction lines* are located every 24 miles north and south of a base line. These 24-by-24 mile areas formed by this checkerboard pattern are the basic *quadrangles* called *checks*. Checks are only approximately 24 miles square; since the earth is not perfectly flat, the meridian lines move closer together as they approach the North and South Poles. (Although this results in the checks, townships and sections being something less than true squares, for purposes of illustration the following figures assume straight lines.)

LOOK THIS UP:

Is the rectangular survey method used in your state?

Yes_____ No_____

Ranges are located every 6 miles east and west of each principal meridian. These are imaginary lines numbered Range 1 East (R1E), Range 2 East (R2E), Range 1 West (R1W), etc. Imaginary township lines are drawn every 6 miles north and south of a base line. Where they intersect with the range lines a 6-by-6 *township* is formed. Each tier or row of townships is numbered according to its proximity to a base line. For example, Township 1 South (T1S), Township 2 South (T2S) and Township 7 South (T7S) lie south of the base line. T3S, R3E would identify the township lying in the third tier south of the base line and third range east of the principal meridian (see shaded township in Figure 7–11). Figure 7–11 identifies a principal

Figure 7–9. Principal Meridians of the Federal System of Rectangular Surveys

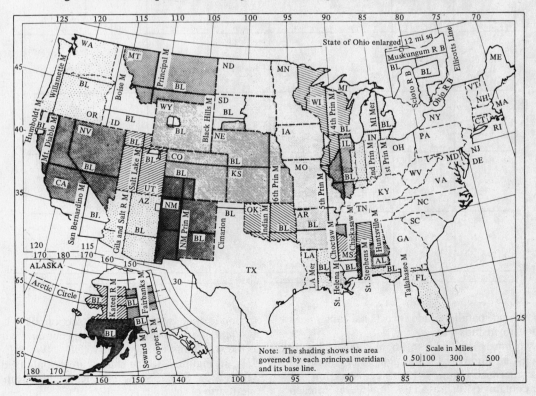

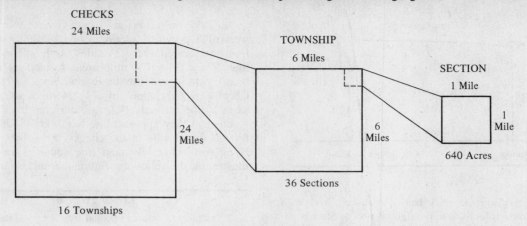

Figure 7–10 Progressive Division of Rectangular Survey System

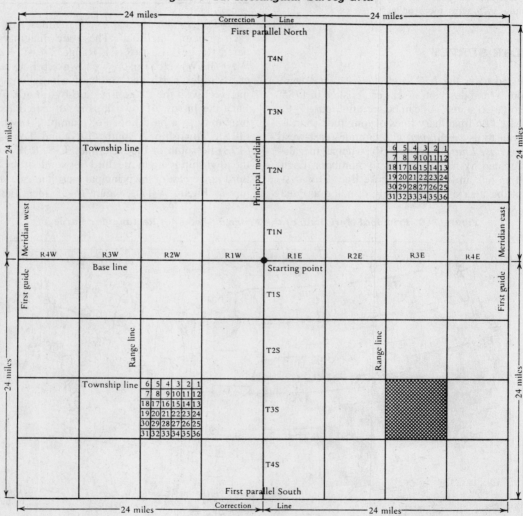

Figure 7–11. Rectangular Survey Grid

meridian, a base line, parallel guide meridians, range lines (R), checks and townships (T).

Each township is divided into 36 *sections* of 1 mile square. Sections are numbered 1 through 36 beginning in the northeast corner (see Figure 7–12). Since a section is 1 square mile it contains 640 acres. The subdividing of each section is done by quartering the section. This is referred to as *aliquot parts*, and the quartering continues with reference to the quadrants of a compass (NE, NW, SE, SW).

In Figure 7–13 the shaded area would be described as SE ¼, S ½, SE ¼, S.18, T3S, R3E which is the Southeast one-fourth of the South one-half of the Southeast one-fourth

Figure 7-12. Map of a Township with Adjoining Sections

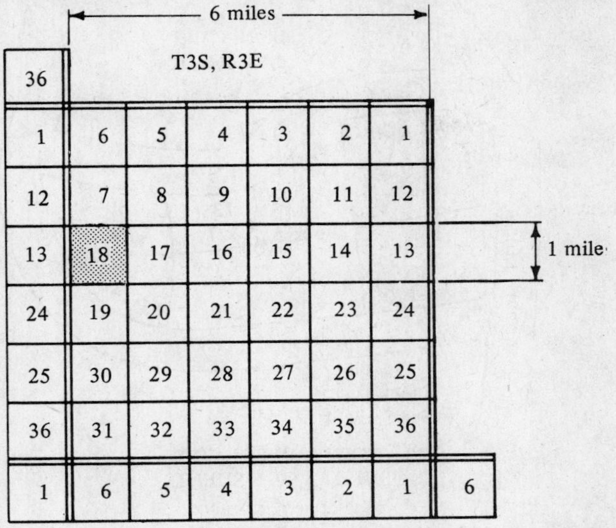

of Section 18 of Township 3 South, Range 3 East. This particular parcel of land could be located in the rectangular survey system by tracking the above description in reverse; that is, starting with the range, then the township and section, part of a section and part of that section.

In order to calculate the area contained in a part of a section, the fractional part is multiplied by the area contained in a section.

Example:
One section contains 640 acres
SW ¼ contains ¼ × 640 = 160 acres
SE ¼ of SW ¼ contains ¼ × ¼ × 640 = 40 acres
and for the shaded area of Figure 7–13:
SE ¼ of the S ½ of the SE ¼ = ¼ × ½ × ¼ × 640 = 20 acres

LOT AND BLOCK

Also referred to as the *recorded plat* method, this method of property description is frequently used after land has been subdivided into building lots. If you have ever looked at building lots in a subdivision, more than likely the property was identified using this approach.

When a land developer subdivides a tract of land, a surveyor's plat map is recorded in the public records of the jurisdiction where the land is located. The subdivision plat contains a great deal of information regarding the intended use of the land being subdivided. Included in the plat map are the boundaries of each parcel of land (this boundary description is normally by metes and bounds or by rectangular survey). Each parcel of land is assigned a *lot number* and each group of contiguous lots is given a *block number*.

Figure 7-13. Division of a Section Section 18, T.3S, R.3E

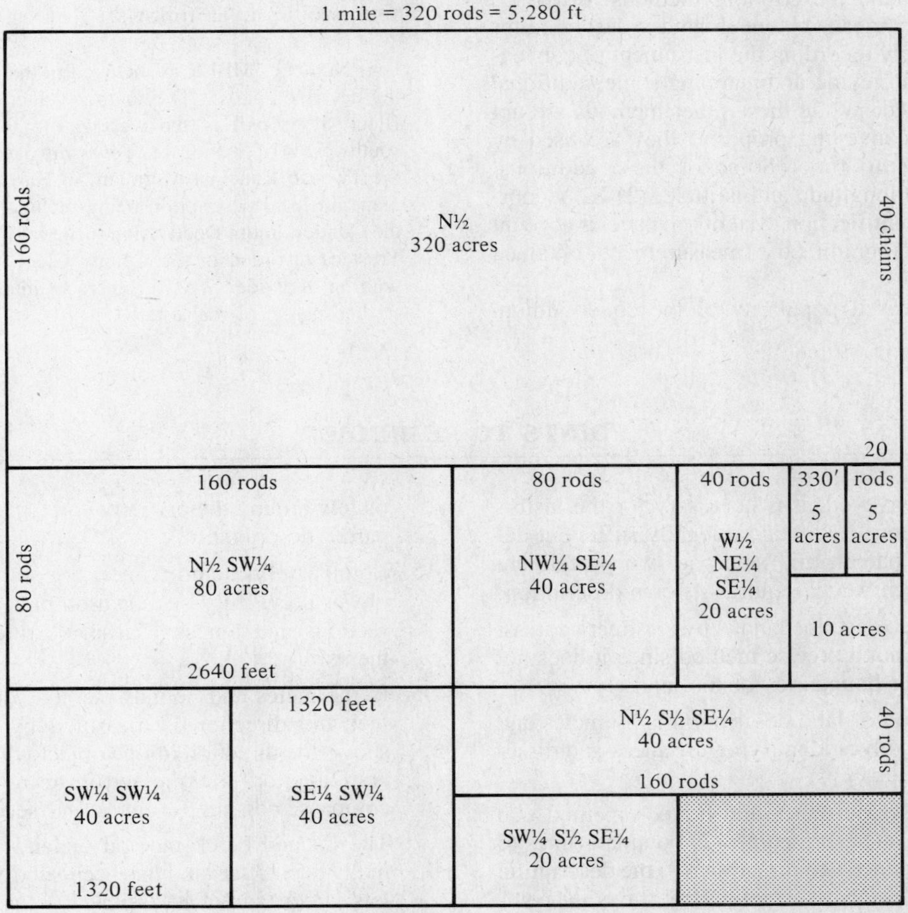

Legal Descriptions

Streets in the subdivision are identified and the tract itself is given a name. A directional arrow and scale will also be included. Easements (see Chapter 8) will also be identified. If an easement lies completely within one lot, it is normally shown by dotted lines; if the easement lies along the boundary of a lot, the boundary line appears as a solid line.

Once the plat is recorded in the public records, any future reference to a particular lot within the subdivision will be by lot and block description. Consider the following lot and block description in a deed:

> Being known and designated as Lot No. 24 as shown on Subdivision Plat of Block 1, of "Loch Raven Village," which Plat is recorded among the Land Records of Carroll County in Liber C.H.K. No. 13, Folio 122. The improvements thereon being known as No. 1738 Aberdeen Road.

By referring to this particular book and page number in the land records (Book 13, page 122), a copy of the surveyor's plat map could be examined and Lot 24 of Block 1 could be identified. As this particular piece of property is conveyed from one party to another, reference to the plat will be made in the same way.

Figure 7–14 illustrates a plat showing lots and blocks in a subdivision. (Note the easements on Lots 1, 5, 6 and 10.)

OTHER METHODS

The various land description methods discussed above are the primary means by which land is described for the purpose of publicly recording the instrument of conveyance. However, in surveying and mapping some additional methods are employed. While these other methods are not commonly used in conveying property, they are used by surveyors from time to time. Some of these additional methods include: (1) longitude and latitude, (2) X, Y coordinates, (3) parcel identification system (taxpayer's account number) and (4) photogrammetry (measurements obtained by photographs).

With the increased popularity of the condominium

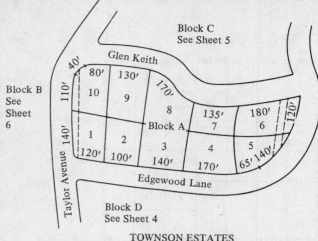

Figure 7–14. Subdivision Plat

TOWNSON ESTATES
SHEET 3 OF 8 SHEETS

form of property ownership in the United States, more and more purchasers are seeing the use of a legal description in the condominium plan or plat (see Chapter 9) when they receive title to their unit. Typically such a legal description is a graphical three-dimensional description of the various units and common areas included in the development. If the condominium project is a multistory structure, a separate plat is prepared for each floor of the structure. An example of a legal description used in the conveyance of a condominium would be as follows:

> Unit Number 3MBLR as included in the survey of the following described parcel: The south 200 feet of the northeast ¼ of Block 8, as part of the west ½ of the southeast ¼ of the southwest ¼ of Section 18, Township 3 South, Range 3 East of the Twelfth Principal Meridian, in Harrison County, California; said legal description being included as Attachment 6 to the Condominium Declaration made by First National Bank as Trustee, recorded in the County Clerk's Folio 122; together with an undivided 3-MBLR percent interest in the above described parcel of real estate.

POINTS TO REMEMBER

1. When land is conveyed, it is necessary for the instrument of conveyance to contain a legally sufficient description of the parcel, and since no two parcels are exactly alike, each parcel requires its own description.

2. The easiest way to describe land is by its street address; however, this is not a precise method since it does not identify the exact boundaries of the land.

3. The oldest method of land description is by metes and bounds which involves identifying distances and directions.

4. To accurately use the metes and bounds method one should have: (1) a starting point, (2) boundary lines to measure both distance and direction, (3) the description returning to the point of beginning by traveling completely around the property and (4) the total area of the parcel described.

5. Boundary lines and corners are sometimes marked by physical evidence such as iron pipes, trees, road intersections and fences. These are referred to as monuments.

6. In the metes and bounds method, distance is stated in feet and direction is measured by its bearing which shows the direction of one object with respect to another. Direction is expressed in terms of quadrants of a compass, degrees, minutes and seconds.

7. The lot and block method of land description is normally used after land has been subdivided into building lots. Each parcel is assigned a lot number and each

group of contiguous lots is given a block number. The plat is then recorded.
8. An easement is normally identified on a plat by dotted lines.
9. Land is sometimes described by the monuments method which identifies the boundaries of the subject parcel.
10. The rectangular survey method of land description is based on imaginary lines of longitude (meridians) and latitude (base lines). There are 36 principal meridians in the United States.
11. Ranges are located every 6 miles east and west of each principal meridian. Where the imaginary lines that are drawn every 6 miles north and south cross the ranges, 6-by-6 townships are formed.
12. Each township is divided into 36 sections. A section contains 640 acres or one square mile and is subdivided into quarters, parts of a quarter and so forth until the exact parcel has been described.

KEY TERMS AND PHRASES

acre
base lines
bearing
bench mark
block
boundary line
checks
degrees
guide meridians

legally sufficient description
meridians
metes and bounds
minutes
monument
plat book
quadrangles
quadrant

range
rectangular survey system
seconds
section
starting point
subdivision
township
U.S. government survey system

QUESTIONS

1. "Beginning at a point marked by an iron pipe at the foot of Highway 6 bridge; thence along the creek bed to an oak tree; thence easterly along a fence row; thence along Farmer Brown's property line to the right-of-way line of Highway 6 and back to the point of beginning." The above property description is an example of which method of land description?
   A. Lot and block
   B. Rectangular survey
   C. Government survey
   D. Monuments

2. The smallest unit of measure in the rectangular survey method is a
   A. township   C. check
   B. section   D. monument

3. The land description method based on surveying lines running north and south, and east and west is known as
   I. rectangular survey method
   II. U.S. government survey system
   A. I only   C. Both I and II
   B. II only   D. Neither I nor II

4. The land description method not commonly found in urban areas is
   A. lot and block   C. metes and bounds
   B. recorded plat   D. monuments

5. Reference would be made to a plat map in which land description method?
   A. Lot and block   C. Metes and bounds
   B. Monuments   D. Street address

6. If the price of land is $2,000 per acre what is the price of the S ½ of SW ¼ of SE ¼ in a section?
   A. $40,000   C. $80,000
   B. $64,000   D. $128,000

7. An area 6-by-6 miles is called a
   A. section   C. check
   B. township   D. quadrant

8. In the rectangular survey method, correction lines are added in order to
   I. allow for curvature of the earth's surface
   II. allow for errors due to faulty surveying equipment
   A. I only   C. Both I and II
   B. II only   D. Neither I nor II

9. If the metes and bounds method is being used to describe land
   I. the starting point must be a benchmark
   II. monuments cannot be used in the description
   A. I only   C. Both I and II
   B. II only   D. Neither I nor II

10. A range line is parallel to a
    A. base line   C. principal meridian
    B. township line   D. standard line

11. The township immediately to the west of T.1N, R.2W is identified as

Legal Descriptions

A. T.1N, R.1W C. T.1N, R3W
B. T.2N, R2W D. T.1S, R2W

For questions 12 through 14 refer to the following plat:

Subdivision Plat

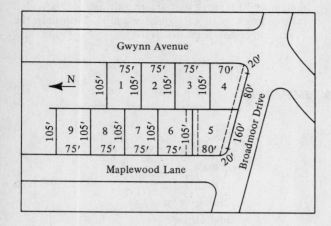

12. A house built on Lot 3 would face which direction?
    A. North C. East
    B. South D. West
13. How many lots have easements?
    A. None C. 2
    B. 1 D. 3
14. If the combined costs of Lots 6 & 7 is $3,000, what is the cost per acre?
    A. $3,000 C. $8,300
    B. $6,000 D. $16,600

For questions 15 through 17 refer to the following Section 18:

Section 18

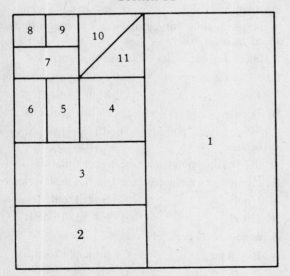

15. The area designated as "5" would be described in a rectangular survey method as
    A. E ½ of SW ¼ of NW ¼, S.18
    B. S ½ of SW ¼ of NW ¼, S.18
    C. E ½ of SW ¼ of SW ¼, S.18
    D. E ½ of S ½ of NW ¼, S.18
16. The parcel of land marked "9" contains how many acres?
    A. 5 C. 20
    B. 10 D. 40
17. The description SW ¼ of NW ¼, S.18 refers to the area marked
    A. 2 & 3 C. 4
    B. 7 & 8 & 9 D. 5 & 6
18. The N ½ of NW ¼ of SW ¼ of a section contains how many acres?
    A. 10 C. 30
    B. 20 D. 40
19. In the rectangular survey method, a check would contain at least
    I. 500 square miles
    II. 500 sections
    A. I only C. Both I and II
    B. II only D. Neither I nor II
20. Which of the following statements concerning the metes and bounds description is the *least* accurate?
    A. A permanent reference point such as a bench mark is often used.
    B. The description is always recited in a clockwise direction.
    C. To correctly use this method, there must be a definite point of beginning.
    D. Boundary lines measure both distance and direction.
21. Which of the following statements is false?
    A. There are 43,650 square feet in an acre.
    B. There are 640 acres in a square mile.
    C. There are 640 acres in a section.
    D. There are 36 sections to a township.
22. A plat is a
    A. legal device used to record the subdivision of land
    B. process whereby variances to required development standards may be obtained
    C. diagram showing how structures are to be placed on a lot
    D. surveying instrument used in determining angles
23. Each 24 × 24 mile area created by guide meridians and correction lines is called a
    A. township C. parallel
    B. range D. check

24. In the metes and bounds land description method, the angle between two intersecting points is known as a (an)

A. radius C. arc
B. delta D. monument

25. "Being known and designated as Lot # 3, Block 2, Country Club Subdivision." The above property description is an example of which method of land description?

A. Metes and bounds
B. Rectangular survey
C. Government survey
D. Recorded plat

If you are not sure of your answers, see page 317 for correct answers and explanations.

Legal Descriptions

8

Rights and Interests in Real Estate

The system of property ownership in America today is called the allodial system. The term *allodial* means free from the tenurial rights of a feudal overlord. In other words, in this country, a person may own full property rights in land subject only to the various restrictions described in Chapter 2. Full ownership or less than full ownership may be transferred. For example, a landowner may transfer property rights in the land which are restricted by use. Likewise the landowner may restrict the time of enjoyment that the person to whom the property has been transferred may possess the property. Property owners may do such things since the law treats the rights and interests in land separately from the land itself. The roots of this separation are found in the feudal system of land ownership. When the American colonies broke away from England, some of the principles and terminology of the feudal system were retained.

This chapter discusses: (1) the estate concept of real property which evolved directly from feudal system of ownership, (2) the future interests and other property interests which are recognized by modern American law and (3) the major various forms of property ownership recognized by law in different states.

THE ESTATE CONCEPT IN REAL PROPERTY

An *estate* is a legally recognized interest in the use, possession, control and disposition that a person has in land. It defines the nature, degree, extent and duration of a person's ownership of land. Estate relates to the degree of interest that a person has in land. The degree of interest may be classified: (1) by the quantity and quality of the interest, (2) by the time of enjoyment and (3) by the number of individuals connected with the ownership.

One important characteristic of the estate concept is that ownership is divisible. The original owner may separate his or her full ownership into different interests which may be granted to several persons. These interests may change over time as different contingent events occur or fail to occur. Further, one estate may be divided into two or more estates, all of which can exist simultaneously. This is the key to understanding estates—the idea that many individuals can own various interests in the same land simultaneously.

Figure 8–1 illustrates the conventional ways interests in land may be classified. In general, this classification is: (1) estates in possession, (2) future interests and (3) other interests.

ESTATES IN POSSESSION

Estates in possession are immediate possessory interests in land and are classified as *freehold* and *less than freehold* estates. A freehold estate is one which continues for an indefinite period of time. Freehold estates may be inheritable or not inheritable. Inheritable estates include the fee simple absolute, the qualified fee, and the fee tail. Noninheritable estates include various life estates which are created by acts of parties or by operation of law.

Less than freehold estates are estates in possession and are generally referred to as leaseholds. These estates are considered to exist for a definite period of time or successive periods of time until terminated by notice. Conventionally, nonfreehold estates may be classified as follows: (1) estate for years, (2) estate from period to period or periodic tenancy, (3) tenancy at will and (4) tenancy at sufferance. Some states make a distinction between leasehold estates and tenancies. A leasehold estate severs any relationship between the grantor and grantee. It is a real property interest in the grantee and a revision in the grantor. A tenancy involves the holding of another's land and the continuing relationship of landlord and tenant. The legal and economic principles of leaseholds will be discussed in Chapter 10.

Inheritable

Fee Simple Absolute

The fee simple absolute is also referred to as the "fee simple" or the "fee." It represents the largest amount of

Figure 8-1. Estates and Interests in Realty

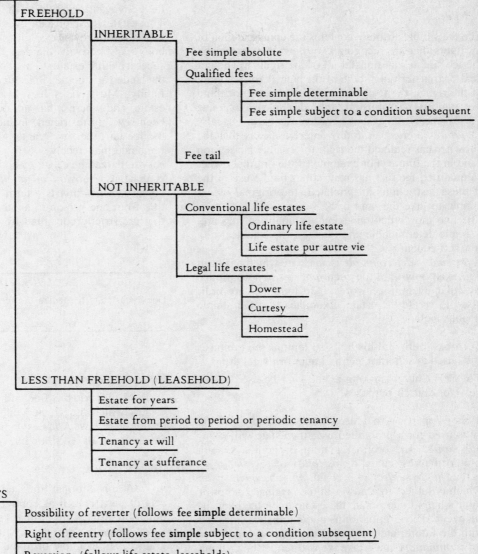

ownership recognized by the law. The owner of the fee simple has unlimited power to dispose of the interest during his or her lifetime, and upon death the property is automatically passed on to the owner's heirs and devisees either by will or by descent. Ownership in this country is ordinarily in the fee simple form. The only restrictions on use are those restrictions defined by the law of nuisance or those necessarily imposed by law in order to protect the interests of society (see Chapter 2). A fee simple owner may convey lesser estates, sell easements, mortgage the property or do whatever else he or she wishes with the property so long as others are not harmed by the improper use of the property.

The fee simple absolute is created by using the words "to (name) and his heirs and assigns forever."

Qualified Fees

The fee simple absolute contains the complete total of property rights that are recognized by law. A person who owns the fee simple can transfer all of the rights to another individual or transfer only some of the rights. By retaining some of the rights, the fee simple is split into two or more estates or interests. To illustrate this idea, please examine Figure 8–2. The rights that the owner retains are usually called a *future interest*. A future interest means that the original owner has retained the right to possible possession of the land in the future. For example, if the original owner passes a qualified fee that has restrictions on the use of the land, if these restrictions are violated, the original owner may be able to take the land back.

The two most important kinds of qualified fees are: (1) fee simple determinable and (2) fee simple subject to a condition subsequent.

A *fee simple determinable* is an estate which has been created to exist only until the occurrence or nonoccurrence of a particular event. The words, "so long as" are ordinarily used to create the estate. Examples of a fee simple determinable include:

1. "To John Smith and his heirs so long as the premises not be used to sell intoxicating liquor or illegal drugs."
2. "To XYZ Church so long as the land be used exclusively for church purposes."

If the property is not used as designated or if the property is used for a prohibited use, the estate will *automatically expire*. The original grantor or grantor's heirs have a future interest called a *possibility of reverter*.

A *fee simple subject to a condition subsequent* is an estate which is subject to a power in the original grantor or the grantor's heirs to terminate the estate upon the happening of an event. The termination is not automatic, since the party with the future interest, called the *right of reentry or power of termination*, must take steps to either enter upon the property or to bring a court action to recover the land. Examples of a fee simple subject to a condition subsequent include:

1. "To Mary Jones on the condition that the property be used as a camp for parentless children.
2. "To James Smith on the condition that he remain single until he is thirty years of age."

Figure 8–2. The Fee Simple Can Be Split into Two or More Simultaneously Existing Estates or Interests.

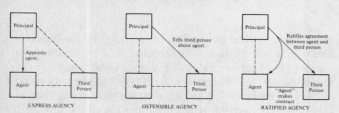

Fee Tail

A fee tail is an estate which was designed to restrict the conveyance of title to the descendents of the grantee. This estate is established by a grant in which the following words of conveyance are used, "to X and the heirs of his body." Effectively the fee tail created a long series of successive life estates. This estate was designed to promote the landed aristocracy in England by keeping property in the family. Most states in this country have abolished this estate, and where it has not been abolished, the estate has been severely restricted. In those states that still recognize the fee tail, the first grantee is given a life estate, but the remainderman receives a fee simple. It is also ordinarily easy to defeat the estate by court action. The reason for this is that any *restraint on alienation* is not favored in this country. *Alienation* is a term which means the transfer of title from one person to another. Any restraints on alienation are strictly construed by the courts.

LOOK THIS UP:

Does your state recognize the fee tail estate?

Yes _____ No _____

Not Inheritable

Noninheritable freehold estates include various life estates which are created either by acts of parties or by operation of law. A *life estate* is an interest which lasts only for the term of a life or lives of one or more persons.

Conventional Life Estates

A conventional life estate may be created by various acts of parties such as contracts, wills or deeds. Conventional life estates are ordinarily of two types. The first type is an *ordinary life estate* which lasts for the life of the grantee. An example of this is: "X," the owner of Blackacre, grants the property to "B" for life; when "B" dies the interest is automatically terminated. The second type of conventional life estate is one in which the term is measured by the life or lives of one or more third persons. This type of estate is called a *life estate pur autre vie*. An example of this is: "X" grants Blackacre to "B" for the life of "C"; when "C" dies, "B's" life estate is terminated. It might be noted that "B's" death would not terminate the estate so long as "C" were alive. The estate in that case would belong to "B's" heirs.

The life tenant may do nothing which will impair the value of the property to the owner of the future interest unless permitted to do so explicitly or implicitly in the grant. Impairment of the property is called *waste*. Examples of waste include the cutting of trees, mining, the failure to pay property taxes, and the failure to make reasonable repairs. However, if the property were originally a tree farm or a mine, the life tenant could continue in these operations without being considered to have committed waste. The life tenant is not obligated to make major repairs, restore destroyed buildings or keep the premises insured.

If the life tenant should happen to get ownership of the reversion or the remainder, the doctrine of *merger* would change the life estate into a fee simple absolute.

Legal Life Estates

Legal life estates include dower, curtesy and homestead. These life estates exist by operation of law when certain status such as marriage is achieved. Some states also define ownership rights of married persons for property acquired by either spouse during the period of marriage. These are community property states.

Under common law *dower* referred to the rights that a wife acquired in her husband's fee simple property. Conventionally, this right was a life estate in one-third of all the property that the husband owned *at any time* during the marriage. While the husband was alive this right was *inchoate* or an expectancy. This expectancy could not be defeated by the husband by sale or mortgage. In order to convey property which was freed from the dower interest, the wife had to sign a *release*. When the husband died, the wife's interest was called *consummate*, and she was entitled to one-third of the property to be held in life estate, despite any will provisions which sought to dispose of the property otherwise. Many states have abolished dower because of the uncertainty this right has placed on title assurance. Other states have created substitutes such as community property or a statutory share in lieu of dower. Some states give the widow a one year's support which could conceivably tie up all of the husband's estate until the right was exercised. Other states give the widow 25 to 50% of the estate. However, if the husband sells his property before his death, then there will be nothing for the wife to receive under the statutory share. In some states, the husband as well as the wife is entitled to dower rights.

LOOK THIS UP:

Does your state recognize dower rights?

Yes_____ No_____

If your state does not recognize dower, does it have a substitute?

Yes_____ No_____

If yes, what is the substitute? _____

Under common law, *curtesy* referred to the rights that a husband acquired in the wife's property. After a wife's death, the husband acquired a life estate in *all* of the wife's property. In order for this right to exist, however, a child had to have been born of the marriage. If a child had not been born, the husband's rights would terminate upon the wife's death.

Normally divorce cuts off all dower, curtesy and similar statutory rights. However, in some states if the court decides that one of the parties was at fault, the innocent spouse may still retain the marital property rights.

LOOK THIS UP:

Does your state recognize curtesy?

Yes_____ No_____

A *homestead exemption* is a statutory or constitutional right which gives a person who is defined as the head of a household protection from creditors for property known as the homestead. The homestead is ordinarily defined as the primary dwelling and surrounding land, and usually there must be a family which owns and occupies the dwelling. This exemption does not normally apply to rented premises. Many states define this exemption in terms of money. Some states include both real and personal property. This right exists during the lifetime of the head of the household, and not all debts are subject to the homestead exemption. While states differ in the application of the exemption, ordinarily any recorded debts which existed before the declaration of the exemption are not affected. In some states, homestead exists automatically by operation of law, while in other states the head of the household must file a declaration of homestead with the appropriate public official in the jurisdiction. Debts incurred to finance and to repair the homestead may or may not be affected by the exemption. The exemption may be waived; each state has its own requirements for what constitutes a waiver. Upon the death of the head of the household, the surviving spouse may be entitled to the exemption.

In some states the homestead is also important in calculating property taxes. A certain statutory amount may be subtracted from the assessment of the homestead before the tax rate is applied.

LOOK THIS UP:

Does your state recognize homestead?

Yes_____ No_____

Who may file a homestead in your state? _____

How is a homestead declared? _____

How may one waive homestead? _____

Does homestead lower property taxes?

Yes_____ No_____

FUTURE INTERESTS

A future interest is a present ownership interest or possibility of ownership in land with the right of possession postponed into the future. Essentially a future interest is a present nonpossessory right which will or may become a possessory right at some future date. Future interest may be classified as follows:

1. Possibility of reverter
2. Right of reentry of power of termination
3. Reversions
4. Remainders

The first three future interests are vested rights which are retained by the original grantor. The *possibility of reverter* is the right retained when a fee simple determinable is granted. The *right of reentry* or the *power of termination* is the right retained when a fee simple subject to a condition subsequent exists. These rights will ripen to rights of present possession upon the happening or nonhappening of a specified event. A *reversion* occurs whenever the owner of real estate conveys an estate of lesser duration than the owner has. A reversion is the right that the original owner, or heirs, has in the future possession of land after the estate of the present possessors ends. For example, when land is rented to a tenant, at the end of the lease the land and its improvements revert back to the landlord. The landlord's right is called a reversion.

A *remainder* is a future interest which is created simultaneously with the granting of an estate of limited or potentially limited duration. A remainder is like a reversion except that someone other than the original owner(s) or heir(s) will receive the land upon the expiration of the present estate. This individual is called the *remainderman*. For example, John Brown gives a life estate to Mary Smith and then upon her death, he directs that the land go to Sally Jones. In this case Sally Jones is the remainderman.

OTHER INTERESTS IN REAL ESTATE

Persons may own rights which are nonpossessory interests in the property of others. Consideration will be given to easements, licenses, encroachments, profits, emblements and other nonpossessory interests.

Easements

An *easement* is a right to limited use or enjoyment by one or more persons in the land of another. An easement is a nonpossessory and intangible interest. The right to use land does not include with it the right to remove any part of the land. A right to remove part of the land such as trees, soil and minerals is called a *profit à prendre*, normally called a *profit*. Examples of easements include such rights as the permission of passage across one's land to reach a fishing pond, right-of-way access roads, telephone lines, pipelines, drainage and flooding rights, support of adjoining buildings and support for pillars used in air-space construction.

Easements may be affirmative or negative. An affirmative easement permits one to use another's property. A negative easement is used to prevent a landowner from using his or her property in some manner. One example of a negative easement is an easement for light and air. This easement prevents a landowner from erecting a structure so high that it would cast shadows or restrict light and air from the property of the owner of the easement. Another common negative easement is one which prevents the impairment of a scenic view or prevents any construction. Such an easement is called a *scenic easement*. The extent of the rights or limitations created by the easement is a matter of contract or grant.

Easements may be appurtenant or in gross. The term "appurtenance" refers to any right or privilege which belongs and passes with land. *Easements appurtenant* involve easements which are created to benefit a particular tract of land. In order to create an easement appurtenant, there must be at least two tracts of land. One tract is called the *dominant estate*, the tract which benefits from the easement. The other tract is called the *servient estate*, the tract which is burdened by the easement. An easement appurtenant "runs with the land." This means that when the land is sold or otherwise conveyed, the easement is also one of the rights which is conveyed, even if the instrument conveying the land is silent about the easement. Unless there is a specified limitation on the time of the easement it is considered to exist indefinitely. An *easement in gross* is a personal right to use the land of another. No dominant estate exists, only a servient estate. Ordinarily this personal right may not be conveyed or assigned. Modern commercial necessity has caused the creation of commercial easements in gross which may be transferred. Such easements include pipelines, telephone lines and billboards. Figure 8–3 illustrates the dominant and servient estates formed when a right of way easement is created.

An easement may be created by *express agreement* between parties. Since an easement is considered to be an interest in land, it falls under the statue of frauds and the agreement must be in writing (see Chapter 5). A deed is usually used to convey an easement. An easement may also be created by reservation or exception by the grantor when the land is conveyed to another by retaining in the conveyance the right to use the land in some particular fashion. An easement may also be created by implication. *Easements by implication* may occur because of necessity, such as the conveyance of a landlocked property. The grantor by implication must give the purchaser the right to pass over his or her property in order to access the road. An easement by implication may also be created because the purchaser had reasonably believed that an easement would be conveyed with the grant.

Example:
> Ann owns two adjoining houses with a common driveway. Mary purchases one of the houses, but nothing is stated about the common driveway which is totally on the adjoining lot. At the time that Mary was examining the property, Ann had indicated that the drive had been used by both properties. In this situation Mary would have an implied easement to use the common driveway unless it was clear at the time of the transaction that this would not be the case.

An easement may be created by *prescription*. If a person uses another's land for a sufficient period of time, the owner of the land may not be able to prevent further continued use. The rules of prescription and adverse possession are discussed in Chapter 13. Finally, easements may be created by the government's *power of eminent domain*.

Easements may be terminated by written release, by merger when the dominant and servient estates come under one ownership, by the cessation of the necessity, by pre-

Figure 8–3. Illustration of Easement Appurtenant

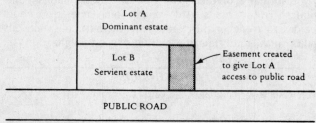

scription when the owner of the servient estate adversely to the owner of the dominant estate for a sufficient period of time, by abandonment or by destruction of the purpose for the existence for the servient or dominant estates. An example of the latter is the destruction of two buildings where there was a mutual easement for support. Easements may be recorded. If a person purchases a servient estate without actual or constructive notice of the easement, the unrecorded easement will be extinguished by operation of law. Rules on actual and constructive notice are discussed in Chapter 14.

License

A *license* is a personal privilege to go upon the land of another. A license is a personal property right and may be created orally. An attempt to create an easement orally would be treated as the creation of a license. A license does not run with the land and unlike an easement, which is more or less a permanent right, a license is mere authority to enter upon land for a particular purpose and is usually temporary. Without a license a person who enters upon land without authority would be considered a trespasser and would be liable in damages to the landowner. The owner of the land who grants the license is called the *licensor* and the recipient of the privilege is called the *licensee*. The licensor may revoke the license at will. Examples of licenses include: tickets to theaters, ball games and concerts; the right to hunt, fish or ski on someone's land; the rental of a parking space; and the rental of camp sites.

Encroachments

Encroachments are the extension of some improvement or object across the boundary of an adjoining tract. Examples of encroachments include walls, fences, cornices or buildings. If an encroachment exists and appropriate and timely steps are not taken to secure the removal of the encroaching object, an easement may be formed by prescription or the boundary of the property may change in favor of the encroaching party. The innocent landowner may seek removal or damages of trespass. The court will weigh the cost of removal with the benefits to be derived. In some cases, if the cost is excessive, the remedy will be restricted to damages. If the court finds gross negligence or wrongful intent, the remedy may be very harsh. Cases have been decided in which a person has constructed a house on someone else's property and has lost the house. The landowner, in effect, has received a free gift. An encroachment may affect the marketability of title. A purchaser might be freed of the obligation to buy the property where an encroachment prevents the title from being marketable (see Chapter 16).

Profits

A *profit* is a right to remove something from the land of another. Rights to remove gravel, water, minerals, coal, gas, oil, timber and game are considered to be profits. Ordinarily a profit is created and terminated the same way as an easement. A profit is considered to be a real property right.

Emblements

Emblements refer to the crops which require annual planting. This is considered to be a form of personal property, unlike other vegetation, which is considered real property. In cases of indefinite leases and other indefinite estates, if notice is given to terminate the estate, the tenant is entitled to harvest the crops even after the end of the term. However, if a fee owner sells unencumbered real estate, the emblements pass with the realty unless an express reservation excepts the crops from the sale.

Other Nonpossessory Interests

One of the nonpossessory rights which is recognized by law is the right of *lateral and subadjacent support* of the soil in its natural state by adjoining landowners. This means that a landowner may not excavate on his or her land in such a manner as to cause an adjoining property owner's land to subside or collapse.

Other property interests include various rights in water. There are two major systems of water law in this country with peculiar differences. The first system, which is primarily used on the East Coast where there is relatively abundant water, is the riparian system. The *riparian system* gives a landowner who owns land next to a natural watercourse reasonable use of whatever water flows past his or her property. The landowner may not deprive other landowners downstream from their fair share of the water. Thus, the landowner may not materially reduce the flow of water or pollute the water so as to materially change its purity (see Figure 8–4). Land that borders a stream is referred to as *riparian land*. Land that borders on the ocean shore is referred to as *littoral land*. Owners of littoral land usually own up to the mean tide mark. The beach or land on the other side of the mean tide mark is owned by the state. In some states that boundary is the vegetation line.

Figure 8–4. Riparian Rights. Properties B and C have riparian rights; Property A does not. Owner B cannot interfere with the rights of Owner C.

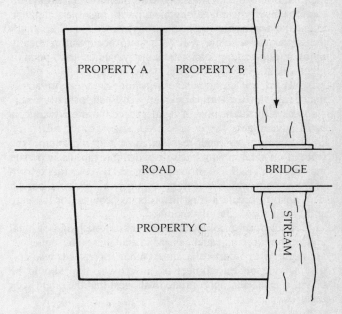

The second major system of water law is the *prior appropriation system*. This is the system of water law which is used in most of the western states and is based on water scarcity. Under this system, a water right is a separate property right and is apart from the ownership of land. It is determined on a hierarchy which is based on the priority of the time a claim was established. The first claim has priority over all other subsequent claims. If any water remains after the first claimant or appropriator has received his or her share, the second appropriator receives his or her share and so on until the water supply is exhausted. This system is subject to administrative control by state agencies and by the federal government where federal water is involved.

Property rights may also be created by *covenants and conditions in deeds*. For example, when a subdivision is platted, the subdivider may restrict the use of the lots by the permissible architectural style of the housing, by minimum square footage or by setback and sideyard requirements.

FORMS OF PROPERTY OWNERSHIP

Property may be owned directly by one individual or by a group of individuals in some form of concurrent ownership, or property may be owned indirectly through a legally recognized entity such as a corporation or a trust. Creation of the form of ownership that property is held by may occur by the act of parties or by operation of law. The real estate professional must be familiar with the different ways that property may be owned for several reasons. Among these reasons are the following.

First, transfer of title may require more than one signature. For example, in many states both the husband and wife must sign a deed to effectively convey property. In other cases, such as those involving property held in a trust or property in probate, the sale may require confirmation by the court. Property which is owned by a corporation may require a resolution by the corporation's board of directors in order to make an effective conveyance.

Second, some forms of ownership must be created at the time title is transferred. For example, in order to create a joint tenancy or a tenancy by the entirety in some states, the intent must be specified in the conveyance. In other states the form of ownership will be held to occur automatically by operation of law unless the conveyance clearly specifies otherwise.

Third, different business or investment motivations may determine the form of ownership. Each form of ownership has a different mix of legal and economic advantages or disadvantages.

Finally, personal reasons may help determine the form of ownership which is selected. For example, a person may wish to minimize probate problems by selecting a form of ownership which has right of survivorship, or a person may wish to create a trust in order to provide for the care and welfare of a family member.

Each form of ownership has its unique blend of legal and economic consequences. Many of these consequences are peculiar to a particular state. When a broker is asked to give advice on the subject of how ownership should be taken, it is usually appropriate to suggest that the client seek legal counsel.

Individual Ownership

Individual ownership is referred to as *ownership in severalty*. The word "severalty" or "several" in property law means separate or severed. It should not be confused with the normal usage of the word "several" which means many. Owning land in severalty means owning an estate or other interest in the land by separate or individual right. An individual who is the sole owner of property has exclusive right to the estate without sharing the ownership of the estate with another. The person who owns the estate in severalty is the only one required to sign a deed to convey title, unless an additional signature is required to release some curtesy, dower or homestead right which might be recognized in a particular state. It is also possible for an estate to be owned in some type of concurrent or multiple ownership.

Concurrent Ownership

The concurrent forms of ownership which were recognized under common law and which have relevance today include: (1) tenancy in common, (2) joint tenancy and (3) tenancy by the entirety. Not every concurrent form of ownership is recognized in every state. In addition, each state may have peculiar rules which affect the creation, termination and rights associated with the concurrent form of ownership. A few states have enacted community property laws which is a form of concurrent ownership not recognized under common law. The four forms of concurrent ownership are illustrated in Figure 8–5.

Tenancy in Common

A *tenancy in common* occurs when two or more persons hold separate titles in the same estate. This form of ownership is recognized in all states except for Louisiana, which recognizes a statutory estate with essentially the same legal effect. In a tenancy in common, each co-owner has an undivided fractional interest in the land and a right to use the whole property. No tenant may exclude a co-owner from any portion of the property. Each co-owner may own a different fractional interest. For example, Beth, Sally and Janet may own Greenacres as tenants in common with Beth having a 60% interest, Sally a 30% interest and Janet a 10% interest. Each co-owner may transfer his or her interest to a third party without the consent of the other co-owners. Upon death of one of the co-owners or co-tenants, that person's interest is passed on to his or her heirs or devisees. In those states that have dower or curtesy, these rights attach to the deceased co-tenant's interest. If there is any doubt what kind of co-ownership was intended, states today favor the creation of a tenancy in common unless the grantees are husband and wife. In the latter case, those states recognizing tenancy by the entirety would presume the co-ownership to be a tenancy by the entirety unless the deed or will specified otherwise.

Joint Tenancy

A *joint tenancy* occurs when two or more persons own a single estate in land. This is a form of ownership which is recognized by all but a small handful of states. The distinguishing feature of this form of ownership is the *right*

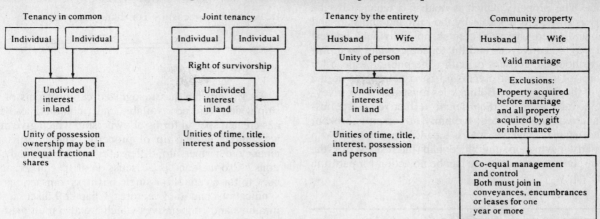

Figure 8–5. Concurrent Forms of Ownership

of survivorship. Upon the death of a joint tenant, the interest does not pass to the joint tenant's heirs or devisees but to the other joint tenants. Effectively, when a joint tenant dies, his or her interest is automatically extinguished. As a result of this, no interest exists which may be passed on after death by will. Likewise, no dower or curtesy can attach. Further, all unforeclosed liens one joint tenant placed on the land are extinguished. The same result occurs to any easements or leases which were granted by one of the joint tenants without the conveyance by the other joint tenants. Because no interest passes after death, there is no need for probate; the surviving tenants retain the property. If two or more tenants die simultaneously, who receives the property if no joint tenants survive? These rights are controlled by state law. Most states have passed the Uniform Simultaneous Death Act which defines how the property interests would be allocated.

This form of co-ownership is not favored by the courts. In order to create such an ownership form, the conveying deed must be clear and specific and ordinarily must specify the right of survivorship. Also, in order to create this form of ownership, four *unities* were required under common law and still are essential in many states. These are the unities of time, title, interest and possession.

The *unity of time* states that all interests of the joint tenants must have been acquired at the same moment.

Example:

Jay owns Blackvalley in severalty. He married Barbara and wishes to hold Blackvalley as joint tenants with his wife. In order to do this, Jay must convey the property to some third party known as a *straw man* or nominee who in turn reconveys the property "to Jay and Barbara as joint tenants with right of survivorship and not as tenants in common." Some states have modified the rule that a person cannot grant property to himself and would allow Jay to directly create the joint tenancy without the process of using a nominee.

The *unity of title* states that the joint tenancy interests were created in a single conveying instrument. This means that if a joint tenant sells his or her interest to a third party, the joint tenancy is terminated in relation to the third party. If originally two joint tenants owned the property and one of these conveyed his or her interest to a third party, a tenancy in common would be created. If there are more than two joint tenants, the conveyance by one tenant of his or her interest would not terminate the right of survivorship among the remaining tenants as to their interests but would create a tenancy in common only insofar as the purchaser was concerned.

Example:

Mary, Kris and Fred own Hillystreet as joint tenants. Kris sells an undivided one-third in Hillystreet to Sam. Mary and Fred remain joint tenants in two-thirds of Hillystreet while Sam holds one-third interest as a tenant in common. If Sam were to die, his interest would pass on to his heirs or devisees. If he left no heirs or devisees the interest would pass to the state by escheat. If either Mary or Fred were to die, the survivor would automatically acquire the deceased's interest.

The *unity of interest* states that each joint tenant must have the same estate and an equal fractional share in the property.

Example:

Jim conveys Prettyshore to Jack and Pam in joint tenancy. Jim specifies Jack is to have 60% interest in the property and Pam is to have 40% interest. Despite Jim's attempt to create a joint tenancy, all he was able to create would be a tenancy in common.

The *unity of possession* is the right of each tenant to the possession and use of the whole property. A tenancy in common has only the unity of possession. If one of the four required unities is destroyed, the joint tenancy is terminated as described above, unless state law specifies otherwise. A joint tenant may sell his or her share without the consent or permission of the other joint tenants. If a creditor forecloses on a lien, this would terminate the joint tenancy except as described above when more than two joint tenants are involved. In some states which recognize title theory mortgages, a conveyance of a mortgage would terminate the joint tenancy unless all of the joint tenants joined in the conveyance. This rule would not apply in most lien theory states. A difference between between title theory and lien theory states is discussed in Chapter 14.

Tenancy by the Entirety

A *tenancy by the entirety* may only be created in cases of a husband and wife. In addition to the four unities required for the creation of a joint tenancy, there must also be the *unity of person* which is created by the marriage contract. The property which is held in a tenancy by the entirety is owned as a whole by the husband and wife and not in undivided shares. There is no individual interest which may be conveyed, and the tenancy cannot be terminated without the consent of both. The public purpose for this form of concurrent ownership is to help preserve the assets of the family unit. Both parties must sign any conveyances in order to make them legally effective. If the husband and wife are divorced, the unity of person is broken, and the tenancy changes into a tenancy in common with each party having an undivided half interest. While the unity of person is intact, there can be no action for partition by one party.

LOOK THIS UP:
Does your state recognize joint tenancy?

Yes_____ No_____

Does your state recognize tenancy by the entirety?

Yes_____ No_____

All three of the common law concurrent forms of ownership share the unity of possession. Occasionally the co-tenants may find this arrangement to be cumbersome and may wish to divide the property. They may do this by joining in a conveyance to a third party who could subdivide the land and reconvey it in separate deeds to the former co-tenants. A second method is to file a suit for *partition*. It should be noted that this remedy is not available in tenancy by the entirety situations without consent of both parties. If a physical division of the real estate is equitable and feasible, the judge will order this be done; otherwise the property will be ordered sold and the proceeds divided.

Community Property

Property acquired by a husband and wife during marriage in those states which recognize *community property* is owned in equal, undivided interests no matter how much either spouse contributed to the acquisition. In these states, dower and curtesy do not exist. Any property acquired by purchase or as compensation by either spouse is considered to be owned in an undivided half-interest by each, and how much either contributed in acquiring the property is not relevant. This rule does not apply to property with each spouse owned prior to marriage or to property received as gifts or inheritance; this type of property is owned individually.

To sell or otherwise convey community property, both wife and husband must join in the conveyance. Husband and wife share the unity of possession but no right of survivorship exists in community property; so if one spouse dies, that spouse's interest will go to his or her heirs. If the property interest passes by will to a third person, the surviving spouse and the third person are considered to be tenants in common. Community property should not be confused with separate property, which is that property acquired before marriage or received by gift or inheritance after marriage.

LOOK THIS UP:
Does your state recognize community property?

Yes _____ No _____

Multiple Ownership

Modern law has recognized certain forms of ownership which were not available under common law. The law has created special forms of ownership which give individuals indirect ownership of property. These forms include tenancy in partnership, different types of trusts and corporations. Also included is a discussion of special arrangements used to raise capital for single business transactions such as syndications and joint ventures. Chapter 9 discusses condominiums and cooperatives which are also multiple forms of ownership.

Tenancy in Partnership

Under common law, a partnership was not considered to be an entity which could own property. Title was held in each of the partner's individual names. Most states have passed the Uniform Partnership Act which permits a partnership to own property in its own name. No individual partner owns a direct specified interest in property so held. The property is limited to use for partnership business, and the partner's property right is in a fractional share of the partnership which is specified in the partnership agreement. No partner may sell his or her partnership interest without consent of the other partners. If a partner dies or goes bankrupt, title to real property passes to the other partners who have a duty to pass the value of the partner's interest to the heirs or devisees of the deceased.

A disadvantage of a general partnership is that each general partner is jointly and severally liable for the expenses and claims against the partnership. Unless care is taken by providing appropriate provisions to the contrary in the partnership agreement, the death or bankruptcy of one of the general partners will terminate the partnership. Further, many states apply a usury ceiling to the borrowings of the partnership.

One method whereby the problem of personal liability may be solved is by creating a limited partnership. A limited partnership consists of at least one general partner, who may under certain circumstances be a corporation, and at least one limited partner. A limited partner has no control over the day-to-day management of the partnership and is essentially a passive investor. The limited partner's liability is restricted only to the money which he or she has invested in the partnership.

Corporation

As indicated in the section on cooperatives, a corporation may own real estate. A corporation is organized by receiving a charter from the state where the entity is created. The corporation is authorized to carry out those acts which are specified in the corporate charter or by the state enabling legislation. In dealing with a corporation, it is ordinarily advisable to assure that the officer with whom a real estate transaction is being negotiated is in fact authorized to act for the corporation. Ordinarily this is done by requesting that the board of directors pass a resolution.

A corporation has certain advantages and disadvantages. The advantages include continuity of life, limitation on personal liability of the shareholders, freedom from many usury laws if the entity needs to borrow money, well-organized markets to transfer ownership interests in the corporation and access to financial markets in issuing bonds, warrants and various types of debentures. The disadvantages include an inability to pass through operation losses and other deductions and double taxation of income—once on the corporate level and then again when dividends are distributed to the shareholders.

Trust

A trust is a legal relationship under which title to property is transferred to a person called a *trustee* who has control over the property and must manage it for some other person, called a *beneficiary*. The trustee is called a fiduciary and must act in the best interests of the beneficiary in managing the property. The trustee is controlled by the instructions given by the person who created the trust, called a *settlor* or *trustor*. The trustee has legal title to the property while the beneficiary has equitable or beneficial title. There are several different kinds of trusts which can be created for different legal or economic reasons. Two kinds of trusts that are of particular interest to the reader are the land trust and the real estate investment trust (REIT).

The land trust is a device whereby property is transferred to a trustee under a trust agreement. The trust agreement provides that the trustee will have authority to deal with the property under written instructions of the beneficiary. The beneficiary may retain possession and control of the property. One advantage of the land trust is that it conceals the name of the true owner. The beneficiary is considered to have personal property. This makes it convenient to convey this property interest to others and may simplify probate.

The real estate investment trust, or REIT, is a creature of both state and federal tax law. A REIT is created in the form of a business trust. If the tax requirements are met, it provides for a pass through of income without double taxation. Further, it has the added advantage of limited liability to the investor and ease in the transfer of shares. However, the value of an REIT share is based on the capability of the management and the quality of the investments. Many people suffered significant financial losses during the 1973-1975 recession because of incompetent management, poor investments and a bad real estate climate. Some REITs fared well and were able to weather the economic downturn.

In order to qualify for a pass through of income, the trust must have at least 100 investors, no five persons may own more than 50% of the beneficial title, 90% of the income received must be from passive sources such as mortgage interest or rentals, 75% of the income must be from real estate investments and the trust must distribute 95% of its annual income to the beneficiaries. Significant disadvantages to the REIT includes no pass through of capital losses or net operating losses and the requirement that assets be managed by an independent contractor.

Syndications and Joint Ventures

A syndication is an arrangement to raise equity capital for real estate purchases or for other types of investments. A syndication is usually arranged in the form of a limited partnership.

A joint venture is an agreement by two or more individuals or entities to engage in a single project or undertaking. Joint ventures are means of raising capital and spreading risk. For all practical purposes, a joint venture is similar to a general partnership. However, once the purpose of the joint venture has been accomplished, the entity ceases to exist.

POINTS TO REMEMBER

1. The system of ownership in America today is called the allodial system.
2. The law treats rights and interests in land separately from the land itself.
3. An estate is a legally recognized interest in the use, possession, control, and disposition that a person has in land. It defines the nature, degree, extent and duration of a person's ownership in land.
4. An estate can be divided into two or more concurrent estates.
5. Estates in possession are classified as freehold and less than freehold. A freehold estate is one which continues for an indefinite period of time; less than freehold estates are considered to exist for a definite period of time or successive periods of time until terminated by notice.
6. The fee simple absolute represents an estate which contains the highest or largest quantum of ownership rights recognized by the law.
7. Life estates may be created either by acts of parties or by operation of law. A life estate is an indefinite interest which lasts only for the term of a life or lives of one or more persons.
8. Life estates may be sold, mortgaged, leased or otherwise conveyed but will automatically cease upon the death of the person who is the measuring life.
9. Legal life estates include dower, curtesy and homestead. Dower is the rights that a wife has in a husband's estate at his death; curtesy is the rights that a husband has in a wife's estate at her death; homestead is a statutory or constitutional exception which gives a person defined as the head of a household certain limited protection against creditors.
10. An easement is a right to a limited use or enjoyment by one or more persons in the land of another. An easement is a nonpossessory and intangible property interest in land.
11. Easements may be appurtenant or in gross. Easements appurtenant involve easements which are created to benefit a particular tract of land called a dominant

estate by burdening a tract of land called a servient estate. Easements appurtenant run with the land, while easements in gross are considered to be personal.

12. A license is a personal privilege to go upon the land of another and is revocable at the will of the licensor.

13. A profit is the right to remove something from the land of another.

14. Property may be owned directly by one individual or by a group of individuals in some form of concurrent ownership, or property may be owned indirectly through a legally recognized entity such as a corporation or a trust.

15. Individual ownership is also known as ownership in severalty.

16. A tenancy in common occurs when two or more persons hold separate titles in the same estate. A tenancy in common has the unity of possession. If a co-tenant should die, his or her interest will pass by will to the heirs or to the descendents specified in the state's law of intestacy.

17. A joint tenancy occurs when two or more persons own a single estate in land. The distinguishing feature of this form of ownership is the right to survivorship.

18. In order to create a joint tenancy there must be four unities present. These unities are time, title, interest, and possession.

19. A tenancy by the entirety may only be created in cases of husbands and wives. The property held in a tenancy by the entirety is owned as a whole by the husband and wife and not in undivided shares. There is no individual interest which may be conveyed.

KEY TERMS AND PHRASES

alienation	freehold	remainder
allodial	future interest	reversion
community property	homestead exemption	right of survivorship
curtesy	inheritable	servient estate
dominant estate	joint tenancy	tenancy by the entirety
dower	less than freehold	tenancy in common
easement	license	unity of interest
easement appurtenant	life estate	unity of person
easement in gross	ordinary life estate	unity of possession
encroachment	ownership in severalty	unity of time
estate	partition	unity of title
fee simple	profit	waste
fee tail	qualified fee	

QUESTIONS

1. One important characteristic about the "estate" concept which adds to the economic value of land is its
   A. immobility
   B. stability
   C. divisibility
   D. revertibility

2. Which of the following is a freehold estate?
   A. Estate *cestui que vie*
   B. Estate for years
   C. Fee tail
   D. Reversion

3. As a result of the occurrence of an event specified in the grant of an estate, the estate was *automatically* terminated. This estate was a
   A. fee simple determinable
   B. fee simple subject to condition subsequent
   C. fee tail
   D. fee simple absolute

4. A power of termination is a future interest which exists concurrently with which of the following estates?
   A. Fee simple absolute
   B. Fee simple determinable
   C. Fee simple subject to condition subsequent
   D. Fee simple subject to an executory limitation

5. The estate which contains the highest quantum of ownership rights recognized by law is
   I. fee simple absolute
   II. fee
   A. I only   C. Both I and II
   B. II only   D. Neither I nor II

6. If "Y" conveys to "Z" for the life of "X" and then to "Z," this creates
   A. a life estate in "Z"
   B. a life estate in "X"
   C. because of merger, a fee simple in "Z"
   D. a legal life estate for "Z"

7. If "A" conveys Greensprings to "X" for life, this creates a
   I. life estate
   II. freehold
   A. I only
   B. II only
   C. Both I and II
   D. Neither I nor II

8. Which of the following is not true about a life estate?
   A. It may be sold to a third person.
   B. It is inheritable.
   C. It may be mortgaged.
   D. It may be leased.

9. A life tenant who allows a house to deteriorate
   I. commits waste
   II. injures the interest of the remainderman
   A. I only
   B. II only
   C. Both I and II
   D. Neither I nor II

10. The life estate which under *common law* a husband owned in his wife's property at her death is called
    A. dower
    B. severalty
    C. community property
    D. curtesy

11. If John conveys Greenhills to Ann for life and then to Sally, Sally has a (an)
    I. estate in land
    II. future interest
    A. I only
    B. II only
    C. Both I and II
    D. Neither I nor II

12. A reversion can follow which of the following estates?
    I. Life estate
    II. Leasehold
    A. I only
    B. II only
    C. Both I and II
    D. Neither I nor II

13. The right to remove topsoil and minerals from the land of another is called a (an)
    A. easement
    B. license
    C. emblement
    D. profit

14. A tract of land benefited by an easement is called a (an)
    A. appurtenant estate
    B. estate in gross
    C. servient estate
    D. dominant estate

15. In which of the following interests does the benefit "run with the land"?
    A. License
    B. Easement appurtenant
    C. Easement in gross
    D. Easement in net

16. Ann grants Yellowvalley to Betty for life and the remainder to Charlene. Betty has
    I. ownership in severalty
    II. a life estate
    A. I only
    B. II only
    C. Both I and II
    D. Neither I nor II

17. Alfred grants Pink Hills to Jeffrey Smith and Mary Jones. What form of ownership do they possess?
    A. Trust
    B. Tenancy in common
    C. Tenancy by the entirety
    D. Community property

18. Betty and Lyndon who are married to other people are tenants in common. When Betty dies, what happens to the property which is owned in common?
    A. Betty's interest goes to Betty's heirs.
    B. Betty's interest passes to Lyndon.
    C. Betty's interest passes to the state by escheat.
    D. Both Betty's and Lyndon's interest terminate.

19. Denise owns Deepgorge and Parks owns Shady Hills. When Denise and Parks are married in a state that recognizes community property, what happens to Shady Hills and Deepgorge?
    A. The properties are owned in severalty and as separate property.
    B. The properties are owned in community property.
    C. The properties are owned in tenancy by the entirety.
    D. The properties are owned in tenancy in common.

20. The chief advantages of owning property in joint tenancy include
    I. simplification of probate
    II. avoidance of federal inheritance taxes
    A. I only
    B. II only
    C. Both I and II
    D. Neither I nor II

21. Under common law, which unity differentiates joint tenancy from tenancy by the entirety?
    A. Interest
    B. Person
    C. Possession
    D. Time

22. Under common law, which unity is not critical in order to create a joint tenancy?
    A. Interest
    B. Person
    C. Possession
    D. Time

23. Under common law, which unity is present in a tenancy in common?
    A. Interest
    B. Person
    C. Possession
    D. Time

24. Ann, Betty and Charlene own Shallowcreek as joint tenants. If Charlene transfers her interest to Jenny, which of the following is the most correct?
    A. Ann and Betty are joint tenants in an undivided two-thirds of Shallowcreek and tenants in common with Jenny, who has an undivided one-third of Shallowcreek.

Rights and Interests in Real Estate

B. Ann, Betty and Jenny are tenants in common.

C. Ann, Betty and Jenny are joint tenants.

D. Charlene may not convey her interest in Shallowcreek without consent of her joint tenants.

25. In community property states, ordinarily which type of property is classified as community property?
    I. Property which is owned by the husband in severalty before the marriage
    II. Property which is owned by the wife in severalty before the marriage
    A. I only
    B. II only
    C. Both I and II
    D. Neither I nor II

26. If Avery, Clyde and Beatrice wish to maximize their tax deductions of owning an apartment project together, how would you advise them to hold the property?
    A. In a corporation
    B. In a REIT
    C. As tenants in common
    D. In a trust which is revocable upon the sale of the property.

27. If George owns Silversprings in sole ownership, he owns the property
    A. by the entirety
    B. in severalty
    C. by tenancy in common
    D. by concurrent ownership

28. If Jan and Carol own property in tenancy by the entirety, which of the following is true?
    I. The concurrent owners must be husband and wife.
    II. If Jan dies the property goes to Jan's heirs.
    A. I only
    B. II only
    C. Both I and II
    D. Neither I nor II

29. If an entity's earnings are subject to double taxation, this entity could be a
    I. corporation that distributes its earnings to stockholders
    II. REIT which only distributes 50% of its earnings in any one year
    A. I only
    B. II only
    C. Both I and II
    D. Neither I nor II

30. Concurrent ownership in which there is right of survivorship is a
    A. cooperative
    B. trust
    C. partnership
    C. joint tenancy

31. A form of ownership which separates title into legal and equitable ownership interests is a
    I. condominium
    II. trust
    A. I only
    B. II only
    C. Both I and II
    D. Neither I nor II

32. A form of ownership which limits an investor's personal liability is a
    A. general partnership
    B. severalty
    C. joint tenancy
    D. real estate investment trust

33. Which of the following forms of ownership must have at least 100 owners in order to be afforded federal income tax advantages?
    A. Corporation
    B. REIT
    C. Land trust
    D. RESPA

34. In a limited partnership, who has unlimited liability for the debts of the entity?
    I. Limited partners
    II. General partners
    A. I only
    B. II only
    C. Both I and II
    D. Neither I nor II

35. If a husband and wife wish to divide a specific portion of land which is owned by tenancy by the entirety, the conventional way to do this is by
    A. petition
    B. partition
    C. arbitration
    D. use of a straw man

36. The right to use the land of another without the existence or necessity of an adjacent or dominant estate is referred to as a (an)
    A. easement in gross
    B. easement appurtenant
    C. prescriptive easement
    D. encroachment

37. A right acquired by a dominant estate to benefit from a servient estate is called an
    A. easement appurtenant
    B. easement in gross
    C. encroachment
    D. emblement

38. A life estate is granted by "A" to "X" for the life of "Y." "X" dies. Which of the following is the most true?
    I. "X" had a life estate *pur autre vie*.
    II. "X's" heirs take a life estate interest in the property.
    A. I only
    B. II only
    C. Both I and II
    D. Neither I nor II

39. Which of the following is not a function of a homestead?
    A. Provide for a reduction in property taxes
    B. Prevent a bank from foreclosing on a family's home
    C. Protect a family from claims by unsecured creditors
    D. Protect a renter from eviction

40. There are no survivorship rights associated with
    A. tenancy by the entirety
    B. joint tenancy

C. tenancy in common
D. curtesy

41. An easement
    I. must be in writing
    II. may be terminated when its purpose no longer exists
    A. I only
    B. II only
    C. Both I and II
    D. Neither I nor II

42. Which of the following is not a form of ownership?
    A. Community property
    B. Syndication
    C. Corporation
    D. Partnership

43. Which system of water law predominates in the Eastern part of the United States?
    A. Prior appropriation
    B. Reliction
    C. Accession
    D. Riparian

44. Which statement concerning joint tenancy is true?
    A. No right of survivorship exists.
    B. Each co-owner holds separate title.
    C. In case of death, a co-owner's interest goes to his heirs.
    D. In ase of death, a co-owner's interest goes to the remaining co-owners.

45. What is the basis for the system of property ownership in the United States?
    A. Allodial
    B. Prescription
    C. Feudal
    D. Civil law

If you are not sure of your answers, see page 318 for correct answers and explanations.

Rights and Interests in Real Estate

9
Condominiums and Cooperatives

As a result of increasing land and energy costs, condominiums and cooperatives are becoming important forms of multiple ownership. This chapter will explain the similarities and differences in the two forms of ownership.

A *condominium* is a form of property ownership which involves a separation of property into individual ownership elements and common ownership elements. Condominium refers to a legal form of ownership and not to a specific land use. Many readers may associate the term solely with residential housing. While much residential housing is in the condominium form of ownership, commercial, industrial and mixed land uses are also being structured as condominiums. The popularity of the condominium form of ownership is a recent phenomenon in the United States. Before 1960 no state had enacted condominium legislation, while today every state has some form of condominium legislation. The titles of these acts differ; for example, some states call their enabling legislation "Horizontal Property Acts."

Cooperatives are an indirect form of property ownership. Individuals own shares of a corporation which in turn owns the real estate. Because of the complexity of this form of ownership it is not as common as the condominium form (see Figure 9-1).

LEGAL CONSIDERATIONS OF A CONDOMINIUM

A condominium form of ownership or *condominium regime* involves the creation of complicated legal relationships which are established when individual property ownership is separated into severalty (individual ownership) and ownership in common. A condominium buyer owns an individual unit outright, but he also owns jointly with other unit owners common grounds and facilities in the development. The word "condominium" comes from the Latin words "dominium" meaning "control" and "con" meaning "with others." Thus, condominium means control of property with others.

Ownership elements in a condominium may be separated into: (1) individual unit elements, (2) common elements and (3) limited common elements. *Individual units* are owned as separate fees by each individual owner. The *unit* refers to that portion of the condominium which is intended for the exclusive use and possession of the unit owner. The owner arranges for separate financing for the unit and is responsible for property taxes on the unit, plus taxes on a pro rata share of the common and limited common elements. *Common elements* relate to property which is jointly owned on a pro rata basis with other unit owners. Typically this may include the land, exterior walls, the roof, club houses, swimming pools, parking lots and other amenities on the property. Ownership of the common elements is analogous to ownership by tenants in common described in Chapter 8. Each unit owner has an undivided interest on a pro rata basis in the common elements; however, unlike a tenancy in common, no right of partition exists while the condominium regime is in existence. *Limited common elements* are those portions of a condominium which are jointly owned by all unit owners but under the exclusive control or possession of only some of the owners. Limited common elements may include enclosed courtyards, balconies, shutters and other features which may lie outside the description of an individual unit but are under the exclusive control of a percentage of the owners.

An individual is responsible for the cost of operating and maintaining the individual unit. The common areas are the responsibility of a *home-owner's association* of which each unit owner is a member. The unit owner is obligated to pay a *maintenance fee*, ordinarily collected monthly, to the association. On occasion, the unit owner may also be charged a *special assessment* to pay for unusual costs which have not been adequately provided for in a reserve fund. Failure to pay maintenance fees or special assessments can lead to liens being placed on the individual unit, attachment and foreclosure. These risks do not exist for individual property owners owning a fee in land and improvements. The difference between individual ownership (severalty) and condominium ownership is illustrated in Figure 9-2.

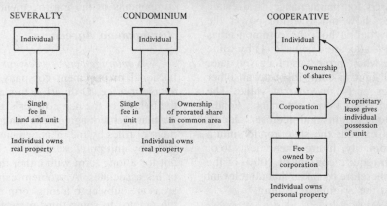

Figure 9-1. Common Types of Property Ownership

LEGAL DOCUMENTATION

The establishment of a condominium regime requires the drafting and recording of several legal documents. These documents include: (1) public offering statements, (2) condominium declaration, (3) condominium plan, (4) bylaws, (5) operating budget, (6) management agreement, (7) subscription and purchase agreement and (8) unit deed.

Public Offering Statement

Many states require that a public offering statement be filed with state authorities and made available to prospective purchasers before a condominium may be marketed. The offering statement is intended to protect the public by disclosing pertinent facts to the purchasing public. Further, if the condominium mortgages are to qualify for FHA insurance under Section 234 of the National Housing Act of 1961, a disclosure bulletin must be provided. Under certain circumstances, a condominium may also fall under the disclosure requirements of the Securities and Exchange Commission (SEC) or of individual state securities laws. This is likely to occur in recreational condominiums or time-sharing condominiums which provide for a rent pooling arrangement. A time-sharing condominium is becoming increasingly popular in resort condominiums. Property is separated by space and by time. Normally a unit is broken into 52 one-week time intervals. A purchaser may buy as many intervals as he or she wishes. Each time share gives the owner exclusive possession of the condominium unit for the same week out of every year. Some time-sharing condominiums are tied to rent pooling arrangements with other projects. A rent pooling arrangement allows a condominium owner to rent out a condominium unit while he or she is not using it by making it available to a management company for rent to prospective tenants. The management company has several other units available in the rental pool as well, and at the end of the accounting period, the unit owner will receive profits based on a percentage of how long the unit was available in the pool.

Example:
Assume that three units are placed in a rental pool. Unit 1 is in the pool for 120 days; unit No. 2 for 150 days and Unit No. 3 for 300 days. If the profit from the rents after expenses and management fees is $3,000, how much is each unit owner entitled to?
Answer: The denominator is 570 days, the total time the three units were available for rental.

Unit No. 1 : 120/570 × $3,000 = $ 631.58
Unit No. 2 : 150/570 × $3,000 = $ 789.47
Unit No. 3 : 300/570 × $3,000 = $1,578.95

If this rent pooling arrangement is part of the original sales offering, the unit is defined as a security and unless otherwise exempt, must be registered before any sales are made to the public. A *security* is defined as any investment by which one expects to make a profit primarily through the efforts of others.

Condominium Declaration

The condominium declaration is also referred to as the *master deed*. This is the document which legally establishes the condominium regime. The condominium declaration is prepared by a *grantor* or *declarant* who previously had the property under individual ownership. The declaration describes the individual units and authorizes the formation of the homeowner's association; also, the common areas are defined and described. The common areas and limited common areas are allocated in an undivided interest

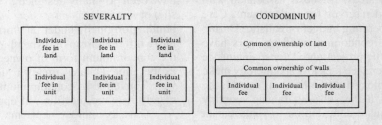

Figure 9-2. Difference Between Severalty and Condominium Forms of Ownership

percentage to each unit. This determines the amount each unit owner will be assessed for maintenance, real estate taxes and, in some cases, how much voting power the owner has. State law may define how the common areas will be allocated. Typically, allocation is made (1) by value of unit in proportion to the whole project as of a given date, (2) by living area of each unit in comparison to all other units, (3) by equal shares or (4) by market value. The declaration also states the restrictions, covenants, conditions, right of access and other rights and interests. Once a declaration is recorded, it extends the state condominium laws to the real estate. Ordinarily, future amendments to or changes in the declaration require consent of 100% of the unit owners. Care should therefore by taken that all relevant provisions are included in the original recording.

Condominium Plan

The condominium plan, also called the *plat of the condominium subdivision* or the *record plat*, is normally included as part of the declaration. This is a graphic three-dimensional description of the various units and common areas in the condominium regime.

Bylaws

The *bylaws* contain provisions for the administration and management of the condominium. Bylaws provide for the establishment of the homeowner's association, enumerate the powers and authority given to the board of directors and indicate various rights and responsibilities of the unit owners. Provisions are ordinarily included which define the use and maintenance of the common areas, establish the operating budget, give notice to lenders of unpaid assessments, provide for property management, fire and hazard insurance and general liability insurance. The board of directors may also be empowered to pass rules and regulations which regulate the use of common areas by unit owners and guests. Detailed provisions for meetings by the homeowner's association, election of officers and amendments to the declaration are also included. Ordinarily the bylaws may be amended by a simple majority of all the owners, although provisions may be made more stringent for important matters. Provisions are also included for the enforcement of liens and other matters necessary to assure that maintenance fees and special assessments will be paid.

Operating Budget

This is a financial statement which provides a projection of revenues and cost of the condominium regime. Revenues are normally in the form of maintenance fees paid by the unit owners. Expenses are disbursements for the operation of the common areas, the costs associated with maintenance contracts and reserves for replacement. Care should be taken that the operating budget is realistic. During the marketing phase of a condominium, developers have been known to subsidize the project and defer maintenance to keep the monthly maintenance fees low and thereby make the project more marketable. After the last unit is sold, the developers have withdrawn the subsidy, raising monthly fees dramatically. Inadequate contribution to replacement reserves results in high special assessments when major components of the improvements need replacing.

Management Agreement

A *management agreement* is established with a professional management company to maintain the common areas for a fee. Ordinarily, this agreement is authorized by the bylaws of the homeowner's association. In many cases, the management agreement contains provisions for enforcement of rules by the management company. Care should be taken by unit purchasers that the management agreement is not for a long term with either the developer of the project or his associates. A problem can occur when the common areas are subject to a long-term recreational lease given by the grantor to some third-party investor or retained by the declarant for his or her own investment. A long-term lease allows the lessee to charge user fees to the unit owners without adequate service in return. The user charges are usually mandatory and enforced by placing a lien on units which fail to pay the fees required. Many states have restricted this kind of practice to protect the public.

Subscription and Purchase Agreement

The subscription and purchase agreement, the sales contract for each condominium unit, must fulfill all of the elements of a real estate contract (see Chapter 5). Many states provide for a 10- to 15-day "cooling-off" period which allow a purchaser to change his or her mind and rescind the purchase agreement.

Unit Deed

The condominium property interest is conveyed to the unit owner through the legal instrument known as the *unit deed*. The deed conveys both the individual and the undivided common property elements to the grantee. All of the legal elements of deeds described in Chapter 13 must be met. The legal description is usually made by reference to the record plat.

MANAGEMENT OF CONDOMINIUMS

Management of condominiums occurs in three phases: control of management by the developer, a period of transition and control by the homeowner's association.

Developer Control

At the inception of a condominium, the project is under the control of the grantor or developer. A project may have been originally designed to be in condominium ownership or it may be a *conversion*. A conversion occurs when a building originally under one form of ownership is changed into a different form of ownership. During the periods when the condominium form of ownership was first popularized in the United States, many residential apartment projects were converted to condominium projects. The conversion merely required the filing of appropriate legal documents.

Just as improvements may be constructed on leaseholds, so can improvements in condominium ownership be constructed on leaseholds. These are called *leasehold condominiums* and at the expiration of the lease the condominium is dissolved. Normally these leaseholds are 99-year ground leases. Both conversions and leasehold condominiums provide unique marketing problems to the broker given a listing.

While the developer controls the condominium, the unit owners have little power to influence factors affecting the value of the units. While the developer wishes to sell out as soon as possible, marketing conditions may be such that he or she may decide to rent units until the likelihood of sales improves. Unless there are covenants in the declaration prohibiting this, the developer has the legal right to do so.

Transition

The declaration provides for the time when the control of the project will shift to the homeowner's association. Ordinarily, the declaration specifies a certain time or an event such as the sale of a certain percentage of the units in the project. Problems may occur in cases of *expandable or incremental condominiums*. These are projects in which the developer reserves the right to add additional units to the project and to change the pro rata interest of each unit owner in the common elements. Problems occur from the viewpoint of the consumer when new units are added without the amenity package being expanded as well. One swimming pool for 100 units may be adequate, but if 400 additional units are added, this amenity may become overcrowded for the project.

Control by the Homeowner's Association

The homeowner's association has the authority and responsibility to manage the common elements of the project after the original grantor gives up control. This, however, does not imply ownership. Each individual unit owner has an undivided interest in the common elements which leads to certain legal consequences. The individual homeowner is responsible for property taxes in the pro rata share; the association is not. A loan must be co-signed by all of the owners since they, not the homeowner's association, own the property. Condominium ownership also involves certain risks for liability which should be insured. Each unit owner is jointly and severally liable for negligence in the condition and management of common areas. If a third party were injured, any unit owner could be sued if the injury was due to negligence of the association in maintaining the property. Ordinarily, a package insurance policy is carried to cover the liability of each unit owner as a co-owner in the common areas, while a separate policy is carried by the unit owner for liability coverage within the unit itself (see Chapter 11). The package policy also provides coverage for the board of directors. In addition to liability coverage, a blanket policy is usually carried for fire and hazard insurance. If the improvements are destroyed, many state condominium statutes provide for a termination of the condominium regime if the improvements are not replaced within a specified time. The insurance proceeds are therefore paid to the directors as agents or trustees for the unit owners for the purpose of replacing the destroyed improvements. Because a condominium involves the creation of a community with each member of the community having responsibilities to the other members, provisions in the declaration often provide for a *first right of refusal* by the association. This provision requires a unit owner seeking to sell his or her unit to notify the association and allow them to purchase the unit as a fair market price. As indicated in Chapter 12, this device may not be used to discriminate on the basis of race, color, creed, national origin or sex.

Condominium Conversion

In modern real estate terms, "conversion" has become known as a process of changing property from one form of ownership to another. Normally, the conversion is to some form of condominium ownership. While most conversions involve residential properties, some conversions have included office buildings and other commercial properties.

In many states, condominium conversions have proven to be very profitable to the original property owner. This has been especially true in residential rental properties. This is partly a result of rentals not increasing as quickly as other real estate prices. With some communities imposing rent controls or rent rollbacks, the economic pressures for conversion have intensified. In addition, due to the nature of federal income tax rules, many projects need to be sold after being fully depreciated in order to avoid adverse tax consequences.

Several communities have restricted or considered restricting residential condominium conversions. Typical restrictions include approval of a certain percentage of existing tenants or the payment of moving expenses to tenants who are displaced due to a conversion. Whether all of these types of restrictions are constitutionally justified is still open to debate and will need to be resolved by the courts. The social argument raised is that condominium conversion reduces the amount of rental housing in a community. This forces persons to purchase housing, pay higher rentals because of a shrinking supply or move out.

TIME SHARING

A form of ownership which has become popular in recent years is the time-share condominium. Time sharing has become very common in selling off ownership units in recreational properties. It involves a separation of individual units from common areas just like the conventional condominium regime. However, the time share adds an additional fragmentation. It allows an individual to own a certain specified time interval.

The attractiveness of the time-share unit depends on the location of the property, the level of amenities offered and the season. Consider a family who wishes to take a vacation in the same location and at the same time each year. This family may find a time-share unit or *interval ownership* a very useful idea. A promoter usually divides the right to use a time-share unit into 52 weekly time intervals. A purchaser may buy as many time intervals as desired. Normally the intervals are priced according to the season. For example, a time-share condominium in a ski resort may cost more for a week during the winter than during the summer.

The purchaser will pay a fixed price for the time-share unit, which can be financed by the developer or another lender. In addition, there is usually an annual maintenance fee that is assessed for each time interval purchased. By purchasing such an interval the owner will have the right to occupy the space for the same week each year for as long as the time share was purchased. Some time-share units are purchased in fee simple, and the right to use these units will continue indefinitely. In other instances, the purchaser buys a *right to use* for a set time period. Many rights to use last no longer than 25 years, after which time the property reverts back to the original developer.

To make the time interval more attractive, some promoters have joined a vacation pooling arrangement with developers of other time-share projects. A purchaser in one project can decide to use a time interval in another project by paying a registration fee and making his or her time interval available for the use of someone else. For example, a person who owns a time-share interval in Hawaii may decide not to use the unit that year and instead use someone else's time interval in Paris, France or in Houston, Texas.

Landed Homes

The condominium concept has influenced other forms of ownership. The *landed homes* association (LHA) ownership is a concept which allows for fee ownership in a single-family detached house and the land surrounding the house. In addition, the owner voluntarily or mandatorily owns an interest called a *participation membership* in a homeowner's association which owns a package of amenities such as a club house, swimming pool, golf course or other property. The LHA concept is a hybrid ownership form which takes elements of condominium ownership, cooperative ownership and ownership in severalty. The homeowner's association is generally a separate corporation.

Association and Townhouses

Some states recognize the townhouse form of ownership. This is a form comprised of ownership of both an attached dwelling and some land. As in the LHA there may be common areas shared by all townhouse owners.

ADVANTAGES AND DISADVANTAGES OF CONDOMINIUM OWNERSHIP

The condominium form of ownership provides several advantages and disadvantages over other forms of ownership. Each of these should be carefully reviewed by anyone considering the purchase of a condominium.

To consider residential condominiums as an example, unit owners are generally able to acquire more living space for the dollars spent on housing than they would get from acquiring a detached house. Likewise, these owners get a better amenity package than they might be able to afford as individuals. By cluster design, unit owners have access and ownership in more open space. There are fewer worries about maintenance and lawn care, since these tasks are handled by professional property managers. Unlike tenants leasing their housing, the unit owners are able to deduct interest on mortgage and property taxes. If the units appreciate, the benefits accrue to the unit owners; likewise, unit owners are protected against rent increases caused by undersupply of rental housing or inflation.

Condominium ownership, however, also entails certain disadvantages. For example, in residential condominiums, the unit owners do not have the same degree of personal freedom to control the environment as an individual property owner does. Many condominiums have architectural controls on the exterior of buildings, and any modifications such as patios or gardens might have to be approved by the association. Pets may be prohibited. Unit owners need to participate in frequent meetings of the homeowner's association to protect their property rights. In poorly constructed projects, unit owners may be annoyed by noise coming through thin walls from the adjoining unit. If repairs are needed, responsibility has to be determined, and if the interior of a unit needs repair, the individual unit owner is solely responsible unless the declaration specified otherwise. It may be difficult to approve major expenditures; thus, the project may be allowed to deteriorate.

COOPERATIVES

A cooperative or co-op is a form of property ownership in which a corporation is established to hold title in property and to lease the property to shareholders in the corporation. Cooperatives have been established primarily for housing purposes. A corporation is set up by filing articles of incorporation as specified in each state. The corporation bylaws define how the corporation will function. Persons wishing to occupy units which are owned by the corporation sign a *subscription agreement* for stock and enter into an *occupancy agreement* or proprietary lease.

In the subscription agreement and in the lease, the member agrees to pay a proportional share of expenses incurred by the corporation for maintenance, property taxes and debt service. Federal income tax law allows the tenant to deduct the portion of each payment which represents property taxes and interest just as in ownership in severalty. The tenant right or interest in the cooperative is considered to be personal property. Much like a tenant in a lease, the occupant is restricted in the use to which he or she may put the property. If the tenant fails to pay monthly assessments the lease agreement may provide for the termination of the tenants' rights. Certain difficulties arise when the tenant wishes to sell an ownership interest in the cooperative. The corporation may retain the right of first refusal and may require that the occupant sell the shares for the original price paid.

POINTS TO REMEMBER

1. A condominium is a form of property ownership which involves a separation of property into individual ownership elements and common ownership elements.
2. The term "condominium" relates to a form of ownership and not a type of use. Residential, commercial, industrial and mixed uses may all be held in condominium ownership.
3. A condominium *unit* refers to that portion of the condominium which is intended for the exclusive use and possession of the unit owner.
4. *Common elements* in a condominium refer to property which is owned pro rata on an undivided basis by all owners of the units in common.
5. Governance of the condominium and responsibility for maintenance of the common areas are in the *homeowner's association* as specified in the *bylaws*.
6. The instrument by which a condominium regime is established is referred to as the *declaration* or the *master deed*.
7. Allocation of a pro rata share in the common areas may be specified by a state's condominium law, or if the law is silent, by value as of a given date, by living areas, by equal shares or by market value.
8. The contract to purchase a condominium is called the *subscription and purchase agreement*.
9. When a property such as an apartment building which is in severalty ownership is changed to condominium ownership, this is referred to as *conversion*.
10. An individual unit owner is responsible for the payment of taxes on the individual unit plus a pro rata share of the common areas; each unit owner is jointly and severally liable for negligence in maintaining the property in the common areas.

KEY TERMS AND PHRASES

bylaws
common elements
condominium declaration
condominium plan
cooperative

first right of refusal
homeowner's association
individual unit elements
maintenance fee
management agreement

master deed
right to use
unit
unit deed

QUESTIONS

1. Property in a condominium which is owned in severalty is called a
   A. unit
   B. common element
   C. limited common element
   D. condominium regime

2. The legal instrument which establishes a condominium is called the
   I. master deed
   II. enabling declaration
   A. I only
   B. II only
   C. Both I and II
   D. Neither I nor II

3. A condominium homeowner's association is ordinarily responsible for paying
   I. property taxes for the common areas
   II. premiums on a package insurance policy
   A. I only
   B. II only
   C. Both I and II
   D. Neither I nor II

4. Unless otherwise exempt, a condominium offering must be registered with the SEC when it
   I. provides for a rental pooling arrangement
   II. seeks to qualify under Section 234 of the National Housing Act of 1961
   A. I only
   B. II only
   C. Both I and II
   D. Neither I nor II

5. An individual's unit may have a lien placed on it if the unit owner fails to pay
   I. special assessments
   II. insurance premiums
   A. I only
   B. II only
   C. Both I and II
   D. Neither I nor II

6. A condominium declaration may be amended by what percentage of the unit owners after it has been recorded?
   A. 100%
   B. 66⅔%
   C. A majority of all of the owners
   D. A majority of all owners present and voting at an association meeting

7. Who owns the common areas in a condominium?
   I. The homeowner's association
   II. The declarant

Condominiums and Cooperatives

A. I only
   B. II only
   C. Both I and II
   D. Neither I nor II

8. A purchaser buys a _____ in a landed homes association.
   A. leasehold
   B. participation
   C. unit
   D. fee

9. The normal cause of special assessments in condominiums is ordinarily due to
   I. inadequate contribution to replacement reserves
   II. refusal of unit owners to make mortgage payments
   A. I only
   B. II only
   C. Both I and II
   D. Neither I nor II

10. Many states provide for a _____ in subscription and purchase agreements.
    A. cooling-off period
    B. right of first refusal
    C. rental pooling arrangement
    D. filing fee

11. Which of the following land uses may be a condominium?
    I. Residential use
    II. Commercial use
    A. I only
    B. II only
    C. Both I and II
    D. Neither I nor II

12. Ordinarily, how is collection of maintenance fees legally enforced by the homeowner's association?
    A. Placing a lien on delinquent units
    B. Condemnation
    C. Agreement with the lender to raise the monthly debt service
    D. Referral to a debt collection agency

13. The condominium declaration is also referred to as the
    A. bylaws
    B. master deed
    C. management agreement
    D. subscription and purchase agreement

14. Which document primarily provides for the administration of the condominium?
    A. Bylaws
    B. Master deed
    C. Management agreement
    D. Subscription and purchase agreement

15. Which of the following is most true of a condominium?
    I. It is a legal form of property ownership.
    II. It provides unit owners with proprietary leases.
    A. I only
    B. II only
    C. Both I and II
    D. Neither I nor II

If you are not sure of your answers, see page 318 for correct answers and explanations.

10

Property Management and Leasing

This chapter briefly examines property management as a specialized field of real estate and explains the functions of property managers. In addition, this chapter discusses the landlord-tenant relationship, the types of leasehold estates, the essentials of a valid lease and how leases may be terminated.

PROPERTY MANAGEMENT

Property management as a specialized field of real estate has grown rapidly in recent years. Reasons for employing a professional manager to manage property have been the growth in multi-ownership forms, the increase in absentee ownership and in size of projects, the proliferation of housing laws and regulations, the requirements of lending institutions and the more competitive real estate market. Property management has become a highly specialized field, and owners of property find that the cost of employing a property manager is more than offset by total dollars saved by efficient management.

Scope

Each property has unique features that require both knowledge and expertise if the property is to be managed correctly. The demand for office space has continued to increase in most urban areas. As more and more office buildings are added to the supply, an owner needs someone who can market space and at the same time maintain good owner-tenant relationships. Industrial properties, either warehouses or manufacturing facilities, have unique management problems which need to be solved by someone familiar with this type of property. Shopping centers, small retail stores and residential properties also need efficient property management.

Objectives

There are two primary objectives of property management, which are interrelated. The first objective is to generate for the owner the highest net operating income over the economic life of the property. Thus, potential income, vacancy allowances and operating expenses are of great concern since they determine what the net operating income will be. Secondly, the property manager strives to maintain, and, if possible, enhance the owner's capital investment in the property.

Neither objective can be met without considering the effect of one objective on the other. Net income can possibly be increased in the short run by cutting back on maintenance and repair. However, over the long run such an approach will result in both a decrease in net income and a lessening of the property's value. Likewise, more than an adequate amount can be spent on operating expenses through poor management. This can also result in a decrease in net income.

Types of Managers

There are three levels on which the managers of property can be involved.

The Property Manager

This person can be a member of a real estate brokerage office who oversees the management of a number of different properties for various owners. However, in large urban areas it has become quite common for persons to establish property management firms specializing only in the management of property.

The Building Manager

This person can be either employed by a property management firm or, as often is the case, directly by the owner of a building. Such a person is involved in the management of only one building and is generally hired on a straight salary basis.

The Resident Manager

The resident manager is an employee of the property management firm and is its representative on the premises.

Such a person could be the building superintendent or the manager of an apartment complex. If the latter, the resident manager normally lives on the premises. This person is also normally employed on a straight salary basis.

Employment

As is true in any business agreement, the property manager or management firm and the owner of the property should enter into a normal contract. The management contract should include the responsibilities and obligations of both parties. Responsibilities specified in the employment agreement should include the term and period of the contract, the management policies to be followed, the power and authority of the property manager and the compensation for the management services. Normally, a property manager's compensation is an agreed-upon percentage of gross income. The range can vary from a very small amount, perhaps 1% on a large structure, to as much as 10 or 15% percent on a single-unit house.

Functions

There are a number of functions required of a good property manager. For purposes of discussion, the more important ones are classified as follows: (1) management plan, (2) budget preparation, (3) leasing space, (4) collecting rent, (5) keeping accurate records, (6) maintenance and (7) tenant-owner-manager relations.

Management Plan

Before assuming the management of a piece of property, a long-range plan should be developed. Such a plan should include what the management company hopes to accomplish and how it intends to do so. Before the plan can be developed, an analysis has to be made of the owner's objectives. Certainly the property manager has to be confident that these objectives can be met. A physical inspection of the property itself has to be made, and the property manager needs to understand existing market conditions regarding competition, rental structures and operating expenses.

Budget Preparation

Once a definite management plan has been established, a budget for each property must be carefully prepared. The budget should contain an estimate of the total income and expenses to be incurred in the operation of the project. For the property manager the budget can serve as a guide in how successful the management plan is being carried out. The owner will want to know the projected budget to see if the return on investment desired can be obtained and, if not, what can be done to obtain it.

Leasing Space

An important function of the property manager involves attracting and selecting tenants. It is usually the responsibility of the property manager to select those tenants who fit into the overall management plan. For residential real estate, such as an apartment complex, the lease agreement normally follows a standard form and typically does not provide for *concessions* to be made. A concession is a service offered by the owner to a tenant that results in the actual rent paid being less than the rent specified in the lease.

Example:
An office 100 × 75 feet rents for $6.00 per square foot. If a tenant will sign a five-year lease, rent will only be charged for the first four years.
Rent Calculation: 100 × 75 × $6.00 = $45,000 per year or $3,750 per month.
With Concession: $45,000.00 × 4 = $180,000/5 = $36,000 per year or $3,000 per month.

Reasons for offering concessions to tenants might include the desire to attract anchor tenants such as a national chain store or the desire to "rent up" a certain amount of available space prior to the actual completion of the building. Even though less common than with commercial buildings, apartment complexes sometimes offer concessions. Examples would include such things as free membership in a private club or a 12-month lease for 11 months' rent.

Collecting Rent

If tenants have been properly selected and the lease agreements clearly worded, the collection of rents is a much easier task. If not stated in the lease, rent payments are due on the last day of the leasing period. However, both the amount of rent and the due date are normally stated very clearly in the lease agreement. Rent payments are typically stated as being due on the first of the month, payable in advance. It is important for the property manager not to let tenants become delinquent in the payments since a steady gross income is needed both to meet the expenses of the building and to return a positive net income to the owner.

Keeping Accurate Records

The means by which records are kept vary from manager to manager and from property to property. The most important thing is that the records kept should be accurate, precise, easy to understand and complete. They should present to the owner a clear picture of what happened and both income and expenses during the particular accounting period. A common practice is to present a monthly statement to the owner.

Maintenance

Neither of the two objectives of property management can be met without proper physical maintenance. Included in the maintenance function will be a certain amount of repair work such as fixing doors and repairing air conditioners. Also included will be preventive maintenance which involves the periodic inspection of both the building and the equipment. The property manager's maintenance responsibility also encompasses purchasing supplies, managing maintenance personnel and overseeing any service contracts such as pool cleaning or window washing services.

Tenant-Owner-Manager Relations

The property manager is employed by the owner and as such is a representative or agent of the owner in dealing with third parties. Thus, the property manager has certain duties to the owner. At the same time, the property manager must also deal with tenants who are expecting to receive the services called for in the lease agreements. To many tenants, especially in residential complexes, the property manager is the only contact the tenant has with the owner. In fact, the tenant may not even know who owns the building. Therefore, the property manager must form a good business relationship with both the owner and the tenants to meet the objectives of property management.

A landlord-tenant relationship is created by *lease*. A lease is an agreement by which a landlord (lessor) gives the right to a tenant (lessee) to use and to have exclusive possession, but not ownership, of realty for a specified period of time in consideration for the payment of rent. The interest that the tenant has is a nonfreehold estate, also known as a *leasehold*. The landlord's interest is referred to as a *leased fee*. A leased fee interest includes both the right to receive the contract rent and the *reversion*, the right to repossession of the realty at the end of the term. A leasehold and a leased fee are valuable property rights which may under certain circumstances be sold, assigned or mortgaged.

A lease creates rights and liabilities between the landlord and tenant. A lease operates both as a conveyance of a property interest and as a contract between the landlord and tenant. As a result, rights and liabilities between the parties are defined by both property law and contract law principles.

When a lessor conveys property by a lease, he is said to do so by *demise*. The leasehold estate conveyed is ordinarily considered to be personalty, even though it involves a real property interest. The technical term for this type of personal property is *chattel real*. Some states distinguish between lease-hold which are chattel real and those which are real property on the basis of the length of the lease term. A lease term which exceeds a statutory minimum creates a real property interest. Figure 10-1 illustrates the fact that, in addition to negotiations between landlord and tenant, a lease is also influenced by real property rules, personal property rules and contract rules.

TYPES OF LEASEHOLD ESTATES

Leasehold estates may be grouped into four general classifications: (1) estate for years, (2) estate from year to year, or periodic tenancy, (3) tenancy at will and (4) tenancy at sufferance.

Estate for Years

This is the most common type of leasehold. This estate or tenancy is a conveyance of realty for a definite stated period of time. This type of leasehold has a specified beginning and ending to the term. Although the leasehold is called an estate for years, it may in fact be for a shorter time. The term may be one month, one week or even one day. In most states if the term is less than one year, it may be created by oral agreement. Some states permit leaseholds for less than three years to be created orally. During the term of this lease, a tenant has a right to possess, control, enjoy and dispose of the property rights. If the tenant were to die during the term of the leasehold, the property interest would pass to the tenant's estate. If the tenant retains possession of the property after the expiration of the term, this is referred to as *holding over*. The landlord has the option to treat the holdover tenant as a trespasser and proceed to dispossess him or her from the property, or he may elect to treat the term of the lease as renewed, thereby converting the leasehold into a periodic tenancy, or in some states into a tenancy at will.

Estate from Year to Year

This type of leasehold is also referred to as a periodic tenancy or an estate from period to period. It is a leasehold which is automatically renewed for the same term as in the original lease. If the lease term is for more than one year, the term upon renewal is considered by most states to be for one year.

Example:
> If Jan signs a lease for a five-year period with an automatic renewal provision, then at the end of the term, if Jan has failed to give proper notice to terminate the lease, the tenancy will automatically renew for an additional term of one year.

Where no term is specified, the manner and time that the rent is paid establishes the term by implication. For example, if the rent is paid quarterly, the implication is that the term is from quarter to quarter.

What is proper notice to prevent renewal of the term? Ordinarily, this is specified by the lease itself, or where the

Figure 10-1. Legal Rules Affecting Leases

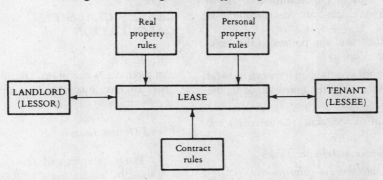

Property Management and Leasing

lease is silent, by statute. Under common law, where a lease term was for less than one year, notice had to be given at least one period in advance. If the lease was for one year or more, six months' advance notice was considered sufficient. Despite notice, if the tenant held over by even one day past the expiration of the term, the courts under common law construed this as a renewal of the lease for another term. As with the estate for years, death of either the lessor or lessee does not terminate a periodic tenancy.

Tenancy at Will

Under common law, a tenancy at will was for an indefinite period which could be terminated by either the lessor or lessee at any time. No advance notice was required. This has been modified by statute in most states today. A tenant has no right to dispose of the leasehold, and the death of either will terminate the tenancy. In those agricultural leases which are tenancies at will, if the lease is terminated unexpectedly, the tenant may enter on the land after the expiration of the term to harvest the crops. This is referred to as recovering the *emblements*.

Tenancy at Sufferance

A tenancy at sufferance occurs when one is in wrongful possession of realty, even though the original possession may have been legal. Under common law no notice was required by the landlord to dispossess the tenant. A tenant at sufferance is treated as a bear licensee. He or she is not a trespasser and the landlord has a duty not to injure that person. However, if the landlord accepts rent, this converts the tenancy to either a periodic tenancy or a tenancy at will, depending on the circumstances. A tenancy at sufferance may occur when a tenant holds over from an estate for years. Such a tenancy may also be created when a mortgagor continues to possess realty after foreclosure, or if a spouse or a deceased life tenant continues to occupy the property after the realty has passed to a remainderman. In some states, advance notice is required to dispossess a tenant at sufferance if the original possession was legal.

THE ESSENTIALS OF A VALID LEASE

Because a lease is both a conveyance of an interest in land and a contract, it must meet certain minimum legal essentials in order to be valid. These essentials depend on whether the lease is oral or whether it falls within the ambit of the state's statute of frauds and therefore must be in writing. The essentials of a valid lease are described below:

1. In order to have a valid lease, the parties to the lease must have *contractual capacity*.
2. A valid written lease should contain an *agreement to let and take*. This agreement states the conveyance by the landlord to the tenant.
3. A *sufficient* description of the realty demised by the lease is essential.
4. The *term* of the lease should be specified.
5. The lease should indicate the *consideration*.

6. If the *purpose* or consideration of the lease is illegal, the lease is considered to be void.
7. A *statement of the rights and duties* of the respective parties should be included in the written lease.
8. The *signature* of the landlord is essential to a valid written lease.
9. Where required to be valid, the lease should be *executed and acknowledged*.
10. If a lease exceeds a statutory term as it does in some states, the instrument must also be *recorded* in order to be valid.

LOOK THIS UP:

Do leases exceeding a certain term have to be recorded in your state in order to be valid?

Yes _____ No _____

If yes, what is the term? _____ years

What effect does nonrecording have? _____

ASSIGNMENT AND SUBLEASING

Normally, both the lessor and lessee may transfer their respective interests in a lease to a third person, unless prohibited by the terms of the lease. The lessor may sell, assign or mortgage the leased fee interest. Conveyance is taken subject to the rights of the lessee, unless the lessee has agreed to subordinate the rights. The lessee may transfer the leasehold interest either by assignment or by sublease. In a few states the law now requires that the tenant receive permission from the landlord before an assignment or sublease can take place. If the lessee parts with the entire estate, retaining no interest, the transfer is called an *assignment*. If the lessee retains a reversion, the transfer is called a *sublease*.

In a sublease, the sublessor has a *sandwich lease* and no direct legal relationship is created between the landlord and the sublessee. A sublease is really an estate within an estate. The lessee becomes a sublessor and a landlord-tenant relationship is established between the sublessor and the sublessee. Since the sublessor can only convey the rights which he or she has, the sublessee is effectively bound by any limitations in the main or underlying lease. The sublessor remains primarily liable to the landlord for rent and the performance of all covenants. (See Figure 10-2.)

LEASES CLASSIFIED BY METHOD OF RENT CALCULATION

Leases may be classified in the manner in which the rent payment is calculated. Rentals may be based on a fixed gross amount, a net amount, a percentage amount or some combination.

Fixed Gross Lease

When payment of rent in a lease is a fixed gross amount, the lessee gives the lessor a straight rental amount

Figure 10-2. Obligation for Rent Under an Assignment or a Sublease

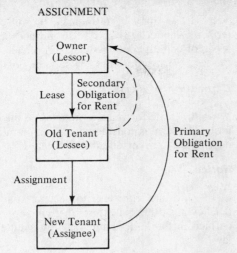
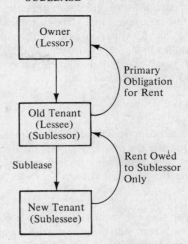

over the term of the lease. The essence of the gross lease is that the lessor pays most costs incidental to the leasehold: property taxes, insurance, maintenance costs and many of the operating costs. The fixed gross lease is typically used in short-term leases. Commercial leases are often expressed on an annual dollar per square foot basis. Even if the rent is collected more frequently, care should be taken to specify for which areas rent is being charged. Unless a tenant is leasing the entire floor, the common hallway areas are not included in the net leasable space. The charge for leasable space should therefore include indirect costs.

Example:
Assume that Mildred is leasing 3,000 square feet at $8.00/square foot. What is the monthly rental? 8.00/square foot is an annual charge. The calculation would be as follows: 3,000 × $8.00 ÷ 12 = $2,000 per month.

Net Lease

A net lease imposes on the lessee an obligation to pay such costs as the real estate taxes, special assessments, insurance premiums, insurance, cost of repairs, maintenance and operating costs as agreed to between the parties. A net lease does not ordinarily include the cost of debt service which was placed on the property by the lessor. The lessor receives a fixed amount which may be treated as an annuity because, in a pure net lease, the lessor is not encumbered by an expense associated with the property. The terms "net," "net, net" and "net, net, net" are often used in real estate markets. The number of "nets" indicates that the lessee is assuming more and more of the expenses. For example the "net" lease may include only an obligation by the tenant to pay increases in property taxes, insurance and maintenance while the lessor pays all other costs from the rental payment received. A "net, net, net" lease may include an obligation by the tenant to pay all expenses except a debt service. The degree of "netness" is subject to negotiation by the parties.

Percentage Lease

A percentage lease allows the lessor to receive the benefit of the locational value of a particular property. Percentage leases are commonly used in shopping centers and merchandising activity uses. In a percentage lease, the lessor receives a percentage of the gross sales or net profits as the rental for the property. The percentage lease may also include a fixed guaranteed minimum. Normally, percentage leases are based on gross sales because the term "profits" is ambiguous and often leads to dispute and litigation. A lessor ordinarily requires that a provision be included in the lease to allow for an inspection of the lessee's books in order to ensure that the correct rent amount is paid. Percentage leases often include a restriction as to the type of activity which must or must not be carried out on the premises. In some cases, the percentage lease contains a *recapture* clause which allows the lessor to take back the realty if the property does not generate a certain minimum of gross receipts.

Example:
Mark agrees to pay a rent of 6% of the gross sales with a guaranteed minimum of $400 rent each month for the rent of a key store. If the key store receives $7,500 in sales in May, what is the rent owed? The answer is $7,500 × .06 = $450.

ADJUSTMENTS TO RENTAL TERMS TO COPE WITH INFLATION AND VALUE CHANGES

There are several ways that a lessor may maintain flexibility to adjust the rentals received from the property to cope with inflation and changes in the market value of the property. One strategy is to enter only into short-term leases of three to five years. At the end of each term, the lessor may reset the rental payments to whatever the market will pay. This approach calls for close management on the part of the lessor and takes the chance of high vacancy rates in periods of oversupply in the market place. The lessee might be reluctant to make significant improvements or to risk loss of good will in short-term leases. Another strategy is to provide for automatic adjustment by a provision in the lease itself. Leases which provide for flexibility within the lease provisions may be classified into the following categories: (1) graduated leases, (2) reappraisal leases and (3) index leases.

Graduated Leases

Graduated leases call for periodic step increases in the rental payments. For example, in a five-year graduated lease, the rental may be $500 per month for the first two years, $550 per month for the next two years and $625 per month for the last year. The rentals can be gross or net payments as agreed to by the lessor and lessee.

Reappraisal Leases

A reappraisal lease or reevaluation lease includes a provision that periodically the property will be revalued and the rent will be set at a percentage of the appraised fair market value, or the tax assessed value.

Example:
If Joe agrees to pay Nancy 12% of the fair market value of Nancy's property each year, with the property being appraised every three years, and if the property is worth $100,000 at the beginning of the term and found to be valued at $250,000 three years later, how much will Joe owe for the first three years? He will owe $100,000 × .12 or $12,000 per year. How much will he owe the second three years? $250,000 × .12 or $30,000 per year.

Disputes often occur over the fair market value of the real estate involved with a reappraisal lease. Provisions are often made for an appraisal by professional appraisers and if a dispute occurs, the matter is to be resolved in *arbitration*. Arbitration is a procedure for resolving disputes out of court.

Index Leases

An index lease has rentals tied to some commonly agreed to price index such as the Consumer Price Index or the Wholesale Price Index. The clause which connects the rent to this index is called an *escalation clause*, and an index lease is often referred to as an escalation lease. An escalation clause may also include factors other than inflation. For example, an escalation clause may provide increases in the tenant's gross rents if the landlord's property taxes go up or if the cost of heating oil increases. Through escalation clauses, a lessor may build in some of the same financial safety features of a net lease. Ordinarily, the index is used to adjust the rent on an annual basis. The application of the index is, however, as mutually agreed to by the lessor and lessee.

Example:
If the rent for office space is $8.00/square foot and the rent is tied to a commonly agreed to index which is 1.87, what will the rent per square foot be if the index goes to 2.03 at the time the rental terms are reassessed? The reader must first determine the percentage rate that the index has increased. This calculation is as follows:

$$2.03/1.87 = 1.0856$$

This factor will then be multiplied by the per square foot rate to get the new rate. This calculation is as follows:

$$\$8.00 \times 1.0856 = \$8.68/\text{square foot}$$

TERMINATION OF LEASES

Leases may be terminated by (1) expiration of the term, (2) notice, (3) surrender and acceptance, (4) occurrence of certain contingencies, (5) breach of covenant, (6) merger, (7) eviction and (8) suit for possession.

Expiration of Term

An estate for years terminates on the expiration of the term. The term is considered expired on midnight of the last day of the term specified in the lease.

Notice

An estate from year to year, a tenancy at will and a tenancy at sufferance expire by giving appropriate notice as defined in the lease agreement, by statute or by common law.

Surrender and Acceptance

Surrender and acceptance terminates a lease either by mutual agreement or by operation of law. Surrender and acceptance occurs by mutual agreement if the lessee offers to terminate the lease, which is the "surrender," and the lessor agrees to the offer, which is the "acceptance." Surrender is distinguished from mere *abandonment*. A lessee may not just walk away from a lease and hope to escape legal liability. A lessor does not show acceptance by entering on the realty in order to protect it after abandonment. The landlord may attempt to lease the property for the best terms that he or she can get in order to mitigate damages and to sue the breaching lessee for the actual injury suffered. Surrender and acceptance, however, will occur by operation of law if the landlord takes unqualified possession of the property and gives a new lease without reservation.

Occurrence of Certain Contingencies

The lease may specify several contingencies which serve to terminate the lease. Other events beyond the control of either party may also serve to terminate the lease. For example, destruction of the premises, if no covenant to repair by the lessee exists, would serve to terminate the lease. Likewise if a mortgage which was recorded prior to the lease is foreclosed, the lease is terminated. It should be noted that the foreclosure of mortgages on the leased fee recorded subsequent to the lease have no effect on the lease. The lessee merely gets a new landlord. Provisions may also be included to terminate the lease upon sale of the leased fee to a third person or by bankruptcy of either party. Some courts recognize the doctrine of *commercial frustration*. Commercial frustration occurs if the purpose of the leasehold cannot be effectuated. For example, if the purpose of the leasehold were to sell liquor, and the tenant is unable to procure a license, some courts may allow this lease to be terminated for hardship. This approach, however, is in the minority.

Breach of Covenant

Breaches of implied or express covenants may terminate the lease. While there is no implied warranty as to the condition of the premises, as an ordinary rule, some exceptions exist which would allow the lessee to terminate the lease. If a new building is being constructed and is not finished when the lease is signed, or if the building is not fit for occupancy when it is completed, the lessee may terminate the lease. Likewise, if the landlord allows the condition of the premises to materially change after the lease is signed but before deliver of possession, the tenant may terminate the lease.

If the tenant uses the property for unauthorized purposes or breaches other covenants which are expressed in the lease, the landlord may call for a *forfeiture* and declare the lease to be terminated. Courts construe forfeiture strictly. A landlord must be acting in good faith when using this power in enforcing covenants and conditions in the lease.

Merger

If the lessee acquires the leased fee interest, the leasehold and the leased fee interest are merged and the lease is terminated. This is also true if the lessor somehow acquires the leasehold. The doctrine of merger states that when two estates or two legal instruments are brought together under one ownership, the inferior right or interest merges into the superior right or interest.

Eviction

When most people think of "eviction" they think of the poor tenant who has been physically expelled out of an apartment. They can envision a picture of the tenant sitting on a pile of possessions that have been placed on the sidewalk by the sheriff. Actually, the word "eviction" is a much broader legal concept. It includes physical dispossession that is properly administered by the law, but it also includes wrongful interference by a landlord of a tenant's right to possess and use the property. The following definition helps clarify this concept.

Eviction is any action by the landlord which interferes with the tenant's possession or use of the leased premises in whole or in part. Sometimes suits for dispossession or acts in ejectment are referred to as evictions. The reader should be aware of this ambiguity, because sometimes the uniform examinations use the term "eviction" in a question meaning lawful dispossession, while, in another question the term is used in its more technically correct definition of wrongful interference with the lessee's beneficial enjoyment of the leased premises.

The reader should distinguish between actual eviction, partial eviction and constructive eviction. *Actual eviction* is a material breach by the landlord of any covenants or any other act which wrongfully deprives the tenant of the possession of the premises. A *partial eviction* occurs when the tenant loses possession of part of the premises. If an actual eviction occurs, the tenant may bring a suit to recover possession or for damages. Where a partial eviction occurs, the tenant is freed from the obligation to pay rent until he or she regains full possession of the premises. *Constructive eviction* occurs when the tenant's use of the premises is substantially disturbed or interfered with by the landlord's actions or failure to act where there is a duty to act. For example, if the premises become unfit for occupancy because of the landlord's failure to maintain heat in the winter or to repair elevator service in a high-rise building or to exterminate insects and vermin, the tenant may vacate the premises within a reasonable time and be freed from any further obligations to pay rent. In order to have constructive eviction, the tenant must give up possession.

Suit for Possession

A suit for possession is sometimes referred to as an *actual eviction by law*. When a tenant unjustifiably retains possession of land, this is called *unlawful detainer*. A suit for possession is a court suit to regain lawful possession of the leased premises. After a hearing, the judge issues a writ of possession which is executed by the sheriff. Procedure and terminology differ slightly form jurisdiction to jurisdiction.

Possession of the premises may not be a sufficient remedy if the tenant still owes rent. Common law provides remedies called *distress* or *distraint* which allowed the landlord to seize the tenant's property on the premises and to sell or hold the property to satisfy a claim for rent. Today, a court action is required. Many states give the landlord a lien on the personal property. Often, in the lease, a *cognovit* or confess judgment clause is included. This clause authorizes the landlord's lawyer to appear in the name of the tenant and to confess judgment to the court allowing the landlord to recover delinquent rent, court costs and attorney's fees. In many cases several tenants seek to lease one housing unit, common office or commercial space. A clause for *joint and several liability* is often included. This allows the landlord to sue any and all of the tenants in the case of a default on the lease.

THE UNIFORM LANDLORD-TENANT ACT

Many of the principles discussed in this chapter will be modified by those states which adopt the American Bar Association's Uniform Residential Landlord and Tenant Act. This act will modify the duality of property law and contract law that presently determine the rights and obligations under a lease. The shift is toward more adherence to contract law. Substantive provisions of the act include disposition of security deposits by landlords, ensuring the habitability of the dwelling and restricting the landlord's remedies. The act establishes the requirement on the landlord's part to mitigate damages in cases of tenant abandonment, abolishes distraint for rent, provides for a grace period for late payment of rent, prohibits exculpatory clauses and prohibits retaliatory conduct on the part of the landlord after a tenant seeks to assert legal rights by complaining or by joining tenants' rights organizations. As the reader will note, the uniform act is very pro-tenant. It is an attempt to remove the old feudal principles which define the relationships of landlords and tenants. The uniform law has no legal effect until passed by a state's legislature.

POINTS TO REMEMBER

1. The objective of property management would include the highest net income possible to the owner and the maintenance of the owner's investment in the property.
2. So as to be clear as to responsibilities and duties, the property management firm should enter into a contract with the owner of the property.
3. A lease is an agreement by which a landlord (lessor) gives the right to a tenant (lessee) to use and to have exclusive possession, but not ownership, of realty for a specified period of time in consideration for the payment of rent.
4. The tenant's interest is known as the leasehold; the landlord's interest is known as the leased fee.
5. The leased fee interest includes a right to receive contract rent and the reversion.
6. A lease is both a conveyance and a contract.
7. An estate for years is for a definite stated period of time.
8. An estate from year to year (periodic tenancy) is a leasehold which is automatically renewed at the end of each term for successive periods until it is terminated by proper notice.
9. A tenancy at will, under common law, is for an indefinite period which may be terminated by notice of either the lessor or lessee at any time.
10. Leases for more than one year must normally be in writing sufficient to meet the requirements of the statute of frauds in order to be enforceable. Some states require recordation in order for the lease to be valid.
11. The tenant has exclusive possession of the realty, the right to make reasonable use of the property and the right to quiet enjoyment.
12. Waste, a violation of the landlord-tenant relationship, is anything which the tenant does or fails to do which injures or changes the essential character of the landlord's reversion.
13. Both the lessor and lessee may transfer their respective interests in a lease by assignment or sublease to a third person, unless prohibited by the lease. Restraints against alienation are not favored by the courts and will be strictly construed.
14. Rents may be calculated on a gross, a net, a percentage or some combination basis.
15. Leases may provide for adjustments to rental terms to cope with inflation and value changes. Three common methods are graduated leases, reappraisal leases and index leases.
16. Leases may be terminated by expiration of term, notice, surrender, and acceptance, the occurrence of certain contingencies, breach of covenant, merger, eviction and a court judgment in a suit for possession.
17. Eviction is any action by the landlord which interferes with the tenant's possession or use of the leased premises in whole or in part.

KEY TERMS AND PHRASES

actual eviction
commercial frustration
concessions
constructive eviction
demise
distress
escalation clause
estate for years
estate from year to year

eviction
fixed gross lease
graduated lease
holding over
landlord
lease
leased fee
leasehold
lessee

lessor
net lease
partial eviction
percentage lease
periodic tenancy
sublease
tenancy at sufferance
tenancy at will
tenant

QUESTIONS

1. Jack leases Greenacre to Ann for 10 years. The next day he sells Greenacre to Millie. Which of the following is true?
   I. Ann's leasehold is terminated by operation of law.
   II. Millie has an option as to whether she wishes to accept Ann as a tenant or not.
   A. I only
   B. II only
   C. Both I and II
   D. Neither I nor II

2. John stumbles and falls on a scatter rug in Fred's apartment and injures himself. The rug was carelessly placed on the floor. Whom may John successfully sue?
   I. Fred
   II. Fred's landlord
   A. I only
   B. II only
   C. Both I and II
   D. Neither I nor II

3. Mary signs a lease for five years. At the end of the term she fails to notify the landlord that she would like to terminate the periodic tenancy. Mary pays her rent at the beginning of each month. This lease is
   A. terminated by operation of law
   B. renewed for five years
   C. renewed for one year
   D. renewed for one month at a time

4. Ariel is the manager of Deluxe Apartments in a northern state. One winter she fails to provide heating to Gene's apartment unit for two weeks. When the rent becomes due Gene refuses to pay his rent. What is the legal basis of his argument?
   A. Constructive eviction
   B. Actual eviction
   C. Partial eviction
   D. Since he did not give up possession there is no legal basis for his argument.

5. Martha signs a lease for three years for an apartment from XYZ rental company. Two months after she moves in she has a heart attack and dies. Alice is her sole heir. She continues paying the rent. Which of the following is true?
   A. The lease is terminated by operation of law.
   B. Alice will take over the lease.
   C. XYZ rental company has the option as to whether or not to accept Alice as a tenant.
   D. The disposition of the lease will be decided by a suit to quiet title.

6. The plumbing in Richard's bathroom breaks. Under common law, who is responsible for the repair? The lease is silent on this matter.
   A. Richard
   B. Richard's landlord
   C. The insurance company of either party
   D. Both must share in the expense unless Richard has covenanted to make repairs.

7. Harry and Tonto enter into a lease agreement whereby Harry agrees to pay Tonto $250 per month to lease an apartment. If the lease is silent as to when the rent is due, then it is due
   A. at the beginning of each month
   B. At the end of each month
   C. the lease is too vague to be enforceable
   D. at the option of Tonto

8. The leased fee interest is held by the
   A. lessor
   B. lessee
   C. mortgagor
   D. mortgagee

9. Maureen has a life estate in Green Springs. Eugene has the remainder interest. Maureen leases Green Springs to Bill for 10 years. Which of the following is true?
   A. Bill's lease is invalid.
   B. Maureen has committed waste.
   C. Bill has a tenancy pur autre vie which terminates on Maureen's death.
   D. Bill has a tenancy in coparcenary which terminates on Maureen's death.

10. George leases a vacant lot to Herman. Herman uses the lot to store lumber. One day George uses a portion of the lot to store some of his own lumber. Herman has not given permission to George to do this. The vacant lot is large and has a great deal of excessive space. George does not interfere with Herman's lumber. Which of the following is true?
    I. Herman has been partially evicted.
    II. Herman owes no more rent until George removes his lumber.
    A. I only   B. II only
    C. Both I and II D. Neither I nor II

11. Mike has a leasehold for three years. He assigns the right to possess the premises to Alfred for one year. This is called a (an)
    A. assignment   B. sublease
    C. cognovit   D. writ of possession

12. John and James enter into a tenancy at will whereby John agrees to pay a monthly rent to James for an apartment. The death of which party will terminate the lease?
    I. John
    II. James
    A. II only   B. II only
    C. Both I and II D. Neither I nor II

13. Sally Landlord and Beth Tenant mutually agree to cancel a lease. This is called
    A. surrender and acceptance
    B. merger
    C. recission
    D. detainer

14. A lessee has a
    A. leasehold
    B. leased fee interest
    C. remainder interest
    D. reversion

15. In an agricultural lease which is unexpectedly terminated, the lessee may
    A. recover the emblements
    B. seek attornment
    C. recover the encumbrances at harvest time
    D. receive a ground rent

16. A lessor may collect delinquent rent by
    A. demise   B. distress
    C. devise   D. a writ of possession

17. Harold leases a building to Carne for a retail store. Harold learns later that Carne is using the building illegally as a house of gambling. Which of the following is true?

Property Management and Leasing

A. Carne's action has no effect on the lease.

B. Harold may terminate the lease.

C. Harold may bring a suit to abate the activity.

D. Harold is no longer entitled to rents unless he agrees to allow Carne to continue with the activity under a new lease.

18. Karen signs a lease to rent Worthington Valley from Jerome for five years. Later Jerome mortgages his interest in the land to XYZ bank. XYZ forecloses on the mortgage. Which of the following is true?

    A. Karen's lease is terminated.

    B. The foreclosure has no effect on Karen's rights.

    C. Karen is freed from paying rents during the remainder of the term.

    D. Karen may be constructively evicted.

19. A leasehold is a

    I. chattel real
    II. nonfreehold estate

    A. I only   B. II only
    C. Both I and II   D. Neither I nor II

20. In a sublease, the sublessee owes rents to the

    I. lessor
    II. lessee

    A. I only   B. II only
    C. Both I and II   D. Neither I nor II

21. What the property management company hopes to accomplish and how it intends to reach these objectives should be stated in the

    A. lease agreement

    B. monthly accounting statement

    C. management plan

    D. contingency agreement

22. When a tenant sublets, the

    I. sublessee becomes liable to the original landlord for rent
    II. sublessor transfers only a part of the remaining term of the lease

    A. I only   B. II only
    C. Both I and II   D. Neither I nor II

23. Which of the following leases does *not* provide at least some protection against inflation?

    A. Graduated lease

    B. Reappraisal lease

    C. Index lease

    D. Flat lease

24. Ordinarily, which of the following interests may be mortgaged?

    I. Leased fee
    II. Leasehold

    A. I only   B. II only
    C. Both I and II   D. Neither I nor II

25. Ordinarily, whose interest in a leased property should be insured?

    I. Lessor's
    II. Lessee's

    A. I only   B. II only
    C. Both I and II   D. Neither I nor II

26. In a transaction where the owner of land gives a ground lease to a developer, what clause should be included to give a lender financing the improvements a first lien on the entire property?

    A. Subordination clause

    B. Contingency clause

    C. Acceleration clause

    D. Exculpatory clause

27. A lease for a store in a shopping center should include which method of calculating the rent in order to give the owner of the leased fee the full benefit of the locational value which contributes to the merchandise sales in the shopping center?

    A. New lease

    B. Escalated lease

    C. Percentage lease

    D. Proprietary lease

28. In what kind of lease does the lessee agree to pay rent and bear certain costs of operation in order to provide a guaranteed annuity to the lessor?

    A. Sandwich lease

    B. Graduated lease

    C. Percentage lease

    D. Net lease

29. The rent in reappraisal leases is calculated on which basis?

    A. Wholesale Price Index

    B. Consumer Price Index

    C. Market reevaluation at specified time intervals

    D. Sales price with an adjustment periodically for inflation

30. An office 150 × 70 feet normally rents for $5.75 per square foot. If the tenant signs a three-year lease, no rent is due for the first three months. Under these conditions, what is the average rent paid per month over the full term of the lease if the tenant signs the lease?

    A. $4,612   B. $5,031
    C. $4,528   D. $5,534

31. In a sublease, the sublessor holds a

    A. sandwich lease

    B. security lease

    C. subordinated lease

    D. special assignment lease

32. Anything offered by the owner to a tenant that results in a lower actual rent than specified in the lease is referred to as a (an)

A. rebate B. escalator
C. contingency D. concession

33. A professional property manager is normally compensated by a
    A. straight salary
    B. percentage of gross income
    C. percentage of net income
    D. percentage of potential income

34. A rest schedule which is periodically reassessed due to changes in the Consumer Price Index is in what kind of lease?
    A. Variable rate lease
    B. Reappraisal lease
    C. Graduated lease
    D. Index lease

35. A net lease ordinarily does not include payment by the lessee for
    A. mortgage debt service
    B. property tax
    C. maintenance
    D. insurance premiums

36. The conveyance of an estate by a lease is by
    A. devise B. demise
    C. escheat D. exculpatory

37. The word "tenancy" as used in nonfreehold interests generally relates to
    A. for whom
    B. how the property will be used
    C. when signed
    D. how long

38. In a leasehold estate, the owner with reversionary interest is the
    A. reversionor B. lessee
    C. dower D. lessor

39. A lease agreement in which the lessor pays all of the expenses incurred is referred to as a
    A. net lease B. gross lease
    C. percentage lease D. portion lease

40. A commercial space leases for $5.50 per square foot. The first floor is 60 × 100 feet and the second floor is 48 × 100 feet. What is the annual rent?
    A. $59,400 B. $4,950
    C. $49,500 D. $64,900

If you are not sure of your answers, see page 319 for correct answers and explanations.

11

Home Ownership

One of the successes of the American economic system has been its ability to provide a decent home to a broad number of households. Approximately 65% of all occupied housing in the United States is owner occupied. The real estate brokerage profession has been instrumental in distributing housing to the public through the free market system. Figure 11-1, which was prepared by the President's Committee on Urban Housing, illustrates the vital role of real estate brokerage in the marketing and transfer of housing.

If the broker or salesperson is to be successful in residential sales, he or she must understand what factors motivate a prospective home buyer. One who is able to give intelligent assistance to a home purchaser will maximize the opportunity of finding the right house for the right person. A broker or salesperson must also be able to secure listings from prospective sellers. There are many services that a brokerage firm may provide to a seller in marketing a house. Brokers and salespersons who are able to help the seller properly prepare the house for sale and assist in showing the house only to qualified prospects will instill confidence and thereby will increase the probability of a successful sale at a fair price. Good service based on product knowledge and on an appreciation of the needs of both the buyer and seller builds a solid reputation in the community and leads to repeat business.

WHAT MOTIVATES A PERSON TO PURCHASE A HOME

Everyone must make a basic choice of where to live. Should a person rent or buy? A number of considerations influence this choice including: the need for space, the availability of housing in the community, the amount of flexibility desired, the family size and life cycle, life styles and personal finances.

Homeownership offers several advantages to an individual. It provides a sense of security and belonging to a community. There is a certain pride and satisfaction in controlling one's own territory without being restricted by rules established by a landlord or having one's privacy intruded upon by strangers. In a privately owned home, there is generally more living space, more rooms, more storage space and more privately controlled outdoor space for the dollar spent. This is particularly important for large families with young children. Homeownership often gives a person more social status and a better credit rating. In addition, there are certain financial benefits; monthly payments for a mortgage include a build-up of equity and tax deductible interest. There are often tax advantages as well. Property taxes are deductible, and capital gains on the sale may be deferred if a person reinvests in another house of same or greater price. Except for certain types of variable rate mortgages, the mortgage debt service remains constant, providing protection against inflation while the asset generally appreciates in value.

Homeownership, however, is not for everyone. It may lead to constraints on one's ability to relocate. For example, in housing markets which are overbuilt or in times of tight mortgage money, it may be very difficult to arrange a quick sale at a reasonable price. Howeownership also entails certain responsibilities that not everyone is willing to accept. The yard must be maintained, taxes and mortgage payments must be paid, risks must be insured against. This means there is generally less leisure time and during the early years of homeownership, a person often has less discretionary income. Owning a home ties up capital and in some situations causes a drain on savings. For example, a home may suffer damage from an uninsured peril or the local government may unexpectedly raise property taxes. In addition, if the homeowner fails to make mortgage payments, all invested equity could be wiped out in foreclosure.

WHO CAN AFFORD TO BUY A HOUSE

One of the valuable services that a broker or salesperson can provide is to offer counseling on how the purchaser can finance the house. The real estate professional must be familiar with local sources of mortgage money and the restrictions that each lender places on loans (see Chapter

Figure 11-1. Role of Real Estate Brokerage in the Marketing and Transfer of Housing (Source: The President's Committee on Urban Housing, A Decent Home, p. 193.)

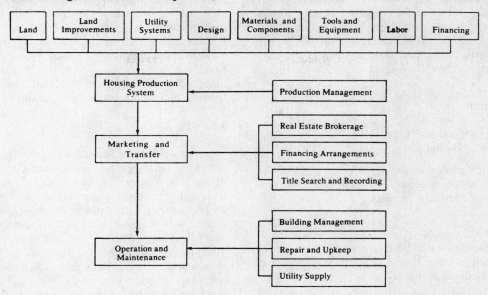

15). A broker or salesperson should be able to assist the purchaser in securing a loan by advising on conventional, FHA and VA loans. In addition, it may be helpful to suggest second mortgage financing or a purchase-money mortgage. If a purchaser is able to assume or take subject to a mortgage, the financing problem may be considerably easier to solve. A lender is usually reluctant to lend mortgage money if the monthly mortgage expense including taxes, property insurance, PMI premium and any assessments exceed 28% of the monthly gross income earned by the borrower. In addition, all long-term installment contracts, such as car payments, plus the monthly mortgage expenses should not exceed 38%. A broker or salesperson may wish to suggest that the purchaser defer a new car purchase until after the house purchase. Lenders are also concerned with the length of employment, the sources of income and the credit history of the purchaser. Some lenders use a rule of thumb that the total mortgage loan should not exceed two to two and one-half times the purchaser's annual income. If a couple in which both spouses are working wishes to apply for a loan, both sources of income will be included. Federal regulations makes it illegal to discriminate on the basis on sex (see Chapter 15).

A broker or salesperson may wish to demonstrate the financial benefits of the home purchase as compared to rental. Many software computer programs exist which allow the purchaser to input mortgage payments, housing expenses, income tax considerations, and expected appreciation of the house and compare the total of these costs and benefits with the costs and benefits of renting.

HOW TO DETERMINE HOUSING NEEDS

Sociologists have discovered that the average family goes through several distinct phases in a life cycle. Housing needs are ordinarily different in each phase. In the early years, a young family has very limited housing needs; a small two-bedroom house, a small apartment or trailer might be sufficient. This phase might last two to five years. As the family begins to increase with the birth of children, housing needs will also increase. This phase might last from 5 to 15 years. After the fifteenth year until about the twenty-fifth year, the family is in a stable period as the children are growing up. After the twenty-fifth year, the children begin to leave, and the need for housing begins to decline. Around the fortieth year, the household may be down to one or two persons. At this point in time, there may be a need for specialized housing in a community designed for the elderly.

Each home purchaser has different tastes and needs. A broker or salesperson should sit down with the client and discuss the type of housing that will best suit the client's needs. The real estate professional may wish to develop a checklist which identifies key factors that a purchaser might consider important. A determination should be made of the number of bedrooms and bathrooms desired. A family may have special interests which may require a study, workshop, sewing room, game room, music room or other specialized space. Storage considerations may include a need for a boat, sports gear or other such possessions. The broker or salesperson should inquire whether the purchaser has needs for indoor or outdoor entertaining. Outdoor entertaining may mean the purchaser will be interested in a house with a patio or large porch. A key consideration is the location of the house. Certain neighborhoods have more prestige than others. A primary concern is usually the time needed to get from the home to the place of work. Other considerations may include distance to schools, churches, shopping and similar land uses. The broker and salesperson should be careful, however, not to make any representations that would violate federal and state fair housing laws (see Chapter 12).

WHAT TO LOOK FOR IN ANALYZING A HOUSE

A purchaser should not restrict research and investigation just to the house. Consideration should be given to the neighborhood, the homesite and to the improvements to and on the site, including the house. A broker or salesperson can give useful advice to the consumer as to important factors and features which should be studied before a purchase is made. Care should be taken not to violate any duties that the broker may have to the seller in the case where the broker is the seller's agent (see Chapter 6).

The Neighborhood

A purchaser should check the following points in the analysis of the neighborhood.

Examine the location of the neighborhood. How accessible is it from shopping areas, schools, churches, place of work and other facilities important to the home purchaser?

Examine the accessibility of the neighborhood. How easy is it to reach major arteries? Examine this during rush hour traffic as well as other times. Is public transportation available? How frequent is it?

Examine the design of the neighborhood. What is the physical layout of the streets? Curved streets and cul-de-sacs are preferable to straight grid design streets for residences with children since such designs slow traffic down. Is there adequate off-street parking? Are there any neighborhood parks? Are the houses well balanced and homogeneous? Are there adequate shade trees and landscaping?

Examine the condition of the neighborhood. Is the neighborhood clean, and do neighbors take pride in maintaining their houses? How old are the buildings? Are they well maintained?

Estimate the future trend of the neighborhood's life cycle. Is the neighborhood stable, transitional or in a state of decline? Check the number of "for sale" signs, abandoned houses, percentage of owner-occupied houses. If the neighborhood is old, is there any sign of rehabilitation or restoration activity? If the neighborhood is a new subdivision, what do older subdivisions built by the same developer look like?

Examine the services and costs of utilities. Are all utilities provided? Are they public or private? What are the costs? Is there adequate police and fire protection? What is the crime rate? What are the fire insurance ratings? Is there a hospital nearby? Are storm drains and fire hydrants in place? What are the property taxes? Are the streets or other public spaces in need of major repair? If so, this could result in a large tax assessment being levied on the property being considered.

Examine the quality of the schools. Where are your children likely to go to school? What is the reputation of these schools?

Examine the reputation of the neighborhood and type of neighbors. What kind of people will you be living next to? Are they friendly? Is there an abnormal turnover of people in the neighborhood? What is the general reputation of the neighborhood?

Determine what kind of nuisance exists and whether there is adequate protection from other nuisances. How close are industries and other potentially blighting uses? Is there pollution being emitted? Are there sufficient buffers? Is there noise from nearby railroads? What are the traffic patterns from airports? Are there problems of drainage or flooding? Is there too much traffic friction from automobiles? How is the neighborhood zoned? Are building, housing and health codes being enforced?

The Site

The purchaser should carefully examine the site to determine whether it has any problems of a physical or legal nature. The soil and subsoil should be checked to determine their ability to absorb water and permit construction without unnecessary excavation or blasting. Some soils shrink and expand with changes in the weather and thus require expensive foundations. Drainage should be checked and attention given to flooding problems. The site should be of adequate size to permit the use intended and guarantee privacy. The purchaser should examine the view and also determine if there are any off-street nuisances or hazards. The site should be properly supplied with utilities or provision should be made for acquiring them. If the site is developed, an examination should be made of the vegetation and trees to determine if resodding is needed or if any of the trees are affected with disease and must be removed. Ease of access from the site to the street should be checked. Are there any blind turns or other problems? Is the site properly zoned? Is the zoning compatible with the building? There might be a problem involving a nonconforming use (see Chapter 19). An examination should be made of the site to check the boundaries for encroachments and other deficiencies. Worn paths or roads or wires may indicate an unrecorded easement. These should be noted and turned over to the title examiner for investigation.

Improvements Analysis—New Houses

A new house is an untested product, and it is difficult to determine if there are any construction defects even with expert inspection (see Figure 11-2.) There are, however, some legal protections available to safeguard the purchaser from defects which are hidden from view. When HUD approves a subdivision for FHA financing, the houses must be inspected three times during construction whereas if a *Home Owners Warranty* (HOW) policy is provided, inspection is required only once, at completion. *The Home Owners Warranty* is a 10-year warranty program, which is administered by a subsidiary of the National Association of Home Builders (NAHB). In order for a builder to qualify for the HOW program, the constructed house must meet HOW's strict building standards. The builder gives a one-year warranty against defects in workmanship and a two-year warranty against limited defects in electrical and mechanical systems and major structural or unsanitary defects. For an additional eight years, a national insurer provides protection for major structural defects. The warranty is transferable, and provision is made for arbitration in case of disputes. Even with the warranty, the purchaser should

Figure 11-2. Schematic Diagram of a Home

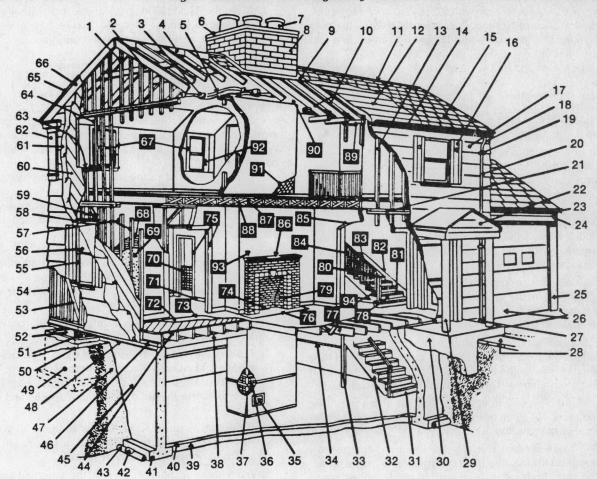

1. Gable stud	25. Door jamb	49. Window well wall	73. Finish floor
2. Collar beam	26. Garage door	50. Grade line	74. Ash dump
3. Ceiling joist	27. Downspout shoe	51. Basement sash	75. Door trim-casing
4. Ridge board	28. Sidewalk	52. Window well	76. Fireplace hearth
5. Insulation	29. Entrance post	53. Corner brace	77. Floor joists
6. Chimney cap	30. Entrance platform	54. Corner stud	78. Stair riser
7. Chimney flues	31. Stair riser	55. Window frame	79. Fire brick
8. Chimney	32. Stair stringer	56. Window light	80. Newel cap
9. Chimney flashing	33. Girder post	57. Wall studs	81. Stair tread
10. Rafters	34. Chair rail	58. Header	82. Finish stringer
11. Ridge	35. Cleanout door	59. Window cripple	83. Stair rail
12. Roof boards	36. Furring strips	60. Wall sheathing	84. Balusters
13. Stud	37. Corner stud	61. Building paper	85. Plaster arch
14. Eave gutter	38. Girder	62. Pilaster	86. Mantel
15. Roofing	39. Gravel fill	63. Rough header	87. Floor joists
16. Blind or shutter	40. Concrete floor	64. Window stud	88. Bridging
17. Bevel siding	41. Foundation footing	65. Cornice moulding	89. Lookout
18. Downspout gooseneck	42. Paper strip	66. Facia board	90. Attic space
19. Downspout strap	43. Drain tile	67. Window casing	91. Metal lath
20. Downspout leader	44. Diagonal subfloor	68. Lath	92. Window sash
21. Double plate	45. Foundation wall	69. Insulation	93. Chimney breast
22. Entrance canopy	46. Sill plate	70. Wainscoting	94. Newel
23. Garage cornice	47. Backfill	71. Baseboard	
24. Facia	48. Termite shield	72. Building paper	

Home Ownership

examine carefully for design defects, quality of construction and types of equipment provided. The size of the house should be sufficient to meet the various needs of the purchaser. Special attention should be given to insulation and the cost of utilities.

HUD gives the following advice to purchasers of new homes:

If, after weighing all the factors, you decide that a new home will best meet your needs, make certain that you make the best buy by following these helpful rules.

The reliability of the builder is an important consideration in choosing a new home. A reputable builder is in business for life. Arrange to talk with people who are living in houses constructed by the builder you are considering. When you've decided on the builder, consider these points:

1. Don't be overwhelmed by the appearance of a glittering model home. Pin down exactly which features are provided with your new house and which are "extras" displayed in the model.
2. Be sure the contract is complete and that there is agreement on all the details of the transaction. Don't assume an item is included and later discover you've misunderstood.
3. If the community is to have new street paving, water and sewer lines and sidewalks, make sure you know whether you or the builder will assume the costs. Find out about charges for water and trash collection.
4. Check the lot size in advance. Is it the size and setting you want for your home? After the bulldozer has arrived it may be too late.
5. Don't take anyone else's word about the zoning uses permitted for the area in which you plan to buy a home. The neighborhood may be strictly residential or zoned for certain commercial uses. This information could affect future property values. The city, county or township clerk's office can tell you where to inquire about zoning.
6. The contract with the builder should set forth the total sales price. If possible, try to locate a lender who will allow you to take advantage of lower interest rates which may apply at the time of closing. In any event, avoid an arrangement which would allow the lender to increase the mortgage interest rate if market conditions change between the date of mortgage commitment and closing date.
7. Be sure your contact with the builder definitely stipulates the completion date of your new home.
8. Don't be afraid to check construction progress regularly while the house is being built.
9. Any extra features to be included in the finished house should be described in writing.
10. The day before you take title to the house (closing day) make a thorough inspection trip. Check all equipment, windows and doors. This is your last chance to request changes.
11. Insist on these papers when you take possession: (a) warranties from all manufacturers for equipment in the house; (b) certificate of occupancy and (c) certificates from the Health Department clearing plumbing and sewer installations. It would also be best to obtain all applicable certificates of code compliance.

Improvement Analysis—Old Houses

Many brokers are offering one- and two-year warranties to cover certain defects in older houses. In addition, certain home inspection services inspect a house, provide a written report to the purchaser and issue a one-year warranty for those elements that the inspectors find to be in sound condition.

HUD gives the following advice to purchasers of old homes:

Older houses deserve special attention in nine areas before a prospective buyer signs on the dotted line. So check these items carefully:

1. *Termite infestation and wood rot*. The importance of a check by a termite specialist cannot be overemphasized, particularly in those areas of the country that have a history of infestation.
2. *Sagging structure*. Look carefully at squareness of exterior walls.
3. *Inadequate wiring*. Be sure that there is sufficient amperage and enough electric outlets. Request inspection by the local government for code compliance to make sure the wiring is not dilapidated, exposed and dangerous.
4. *Run-down heating plant*. Check the general condition of the heating system. What kind of repairs are needed and how long will the system last?
5. *Inadequate insulation*. Ask if the attic and the space between interior and exterior walls has been filled with an insulating material. What material was used, and how was it installed?
6. *Faulty plumbing*. Choose a home that is connected to a public sewer system in preference to one served by a septic tank or a cesspool. Check with the plumber who last serviced the house to determine condition of the plumbing and ask him to test for water pressure.
7. *Hot-water heater*. Check the type and capacity of the tank to determine if there will be sufficient hot water for family needs. Look for any signs of rust or leaks. Obtain any guarantee held by the present owner, if it is still in effect.
8. *Roof and gutters*. What kind of roofing material was used and how old is it? Check inside the attic for water stains and discolorations. Ask the owner for a guarantee if one exists.
9. *Wet basements*. A basement that looks dry in summer may be four inches under in the spring. Are there any signs around the foundation walls of water penetration?

Energy Efficiency

There are four important ways to reduce energy costs in the construction characteristics of a home:

1. Avoid heat loss or gain because of improper amounts of insulation or loss through windows. The energy efficiency of elements in a structure is measured by its "R" value. Minimum FHA standards require walls to have insulation sufficient to be rated R11 and the attic to be rated R19. Storm windows or treated glass on conventional windows can be effective energy saving devices. Most utility companies will provide a free energy analysis and suggest the necessary R value ratings for their service areas.
2. In most homes, 65 to 70% of energy usage goes for cooling, heating and water heating. Efficient washers, dryers, furnaces and other mechanical equipment can save significant energy dollars.
3. Attic ventilation systems can prevent heat build-up in the attic that causes hotter interiors as the heat is transferred. Ventilation also prevents moisture build-up.
4. Air leakage can cause significant energy loss. Caulking and weather stripping are important ways to prevent this kind of energy loss.

CONSIDERATIONS IN SELLING A HOUSE

Two very important considerations in selling a house are the price set by the seller and how the house is shown to the purchaser. A price should be fair and reasonable given the particular market. If the price is set too high, this reduces the probability that it will be sold. Purchasers will find substitutes to purchase instead. A high price will usually result in the house remaining on the market for a long time. Even if the price is ultimately reduced, many people will shy away from it because they might assume that something was wrong with the house which caused it to remain on the market for such a long time. If the price is set too low, this will unfairly deprive the seller of equity to which he or she is entitled. If later the seller discovers that the house was greatly underpriced, this will cause ill feeling toward the broker or salesperson, causing damage to the brokerage firm's reputation.

Showing a house involves two phases: preparation and the actual showing. The seller should make sure that the house is clean and the lawn is well manicured before the showing. All clutter and excess furniture should be removed. It may be appropriate to paint the house and fix all minor defects. Dogs and cats which may leave hair or odor should be temporarily boarded elsewhere. All light fixtures should be in good working condition and all leaks in plumbing should be repaired. Special attention should be given to the kitchen and bathroom areas. In the actual showing, the presentation of the house should be left to the broker. The seller may remain on the premises but only to answer questions if they should be asked.

PROPERTY INSURANCE

Insurance is a means by which one party shifts the risk of a certain loss or disastrous event to another party. This is done through a contract called a *policy* and with a certain payment called a *premium*. The party assuming the risk, an insurance company, normally insures many parties against the same risk and is therefore able to predict the number of losses likely to occur. The individual being insured needs this service because he or she cannot accurately predict the probability of loss.

This idea is based on the law of large numbers. If one has a large enough number of people, it is possible to estimate that a certain percentage of these people will suffer from accidents. Although no one knows if a specific individual will suffer from an accident, an insurance company can usually calculate within a very close degree of accuracy how many accidents and the total money loss that will result when a large group of people are involved. By charging each person a small premium, the insurance company is able to assemble a large amount of money that can be used to pay individuals who suffer from losses. In other words, each individual is able to shift his or her risk of loss to the insurance company, and the company is able to spread the loss among a large number of people.

Brokers and salespersons need to be familiar with the kinds of insurance coverage available for protecting property owners against a multitude of risks. Often a purchaser will seek the broker's or salesperson's advice as to how much insurance is needed and what type to purchase.

When to Insure

In order to collect payment from an insurance policy, one must have an *insurable interest* in the subject matter. Insurable interest means that in case of some event, such as a fire, the insured suffers some injury or loss. The interest could be either a legal or an equitable interest.

Quite often the purchaser of real estate has little choice concerning insurance. If there is a third party providing any part of the financing, the funds will not be made available until the borrower can show that adequate insurance coverage has been obtained. The same is generally true for someone leasing property. A common covenant in the lease agreement calls for the lessee to maintain a certain amount of insurance on the property.

Property Insurance for the Homeowner

It is quite common for a homeowner to purchase and maintain insurance coverage for his or her residence. For a relatively small and certain amount of money, the homeowner buys protection against a potentially large and unpredictable loss.

Numerous types of policies are available. The homeowner can buy a standard fire insurance policy which insures only against fire and lightning, whereas for an additional premium, the coverage is broadened to include damage from wind, hail, smoke, explosion, riot, vehicles and falling aircraft. Or one can purchase protection against burglary, injuries suffered by parties while on the property and damages the policyholder causes to the property of others. Besides being able to purchase any number of separate policies, one can also purchase a package policy called a *homeowner's policy* that includes all of the above-mentioned risks.

A homeowner's policy can be purchased by anyone who owns and occupies either a one- or two-family residence. The advantages of purchasing such a policy are numerous: (1) only one policy is purchased, (2) only one premium has to be paid, (3) the coverage is for a wide variety of perils and (4) the cost is considerably less than if the same perils were covered through individual policies.

What Properties Are Covered?

First, the house or *dwelling* is covered. In addition to the living quarters, this includes such structures as garages or other additions. Other structures, referred to as *appurtenant structures*, are covered such as tool shed or a detached garage. However, buildings located on property that are either rented to others or used for commercial purpose are not covered. *Personal property* including all household contents and personal belongings is covered. This would include losses both at home or away from home. Pets are not protected, nor are automobiles, which have their own special insurance. Another added feature of a homeowner's policy is the coverage of *additional living expense*, which is intended to cover the increase in living expenses incurred while a house cannot be occupied because of damages caused by an insured peril.

What Perils Are Insured Against?

The number of perils insured against under a homeowner's policy depends upon what form is purchased. As can be seen in Figure 11-3, three forms are available: (1) the Basic Form (HO-1), (2) the Broad Form (HO-2) or (3) the Comprehensive Form (HO-5). The Broad Form, which is the most common, insures against 18 different perils. The Basic Form insures only against the first 11, whereas the Comprehensive Form covers the 18 perils, plus additional coverage. While the (HO-5) is often referred to as an *all-risk* policy, it still has certain exceptions listed in the policy.

A Policy for Renters

For those who rent, the Tenant's Form (HO-4) of the homeowner's policy is available. It insures contents and personal property against the same perils included in the Broad Form. However, since a renter does not own either the dwelling or other private structures on the property, the dwellings are not insured. Such a policy does, however, provide coverage for additional living expense.

Other Forms

Some homeowners would like the extended coverage on their dwelling provided in the Comprehensive Form but do not need such extensive coverage on their personal property. They can purchase a Special Form (HO-3) which provides (HO-5) dwelling coverage and (HO-4) personal property coverage. Form (HO-6) is available for condominium and co-operative owners.

Property Insurance for the Business

A business package policy is available for the owner of an apartment building, office building or store. Such a policy offers the same type of advantages to the business

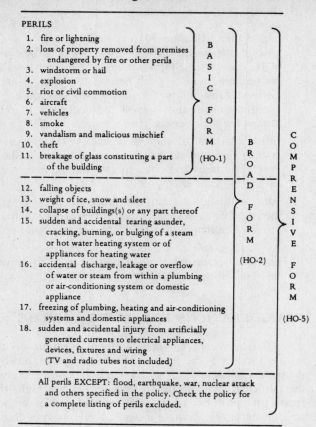

Figure 11-3.

owner as the homeowner's policy offers to the homeowner. This policy is cheaper than separate policies and can be adapted to the particular needs of the individual.

Coinsurance

Most losses due to fire or some other peril do not result in 100% loss. Since the cost of a policy is based on a certain amount per $100 of coverage, the owner of a building might decide to insure for only a small amount of the building's total value and gamble that in case of damage there will only be a partial loss. If a policy has a *coinsurance clause*, and there is a loss, then the amount recovered from the insurance company will be derived as follows:

$$\frac{\text{amount of insurance carried}}{\text{amount of insurance required}} \times \text{amount of loss} = \text{recovery}$$

Example:

The value of a building is $500,000, and the insurance policy has an 80% coinsurance clause. The owner has the property insured for $200,000. There is a loss due to fire of $90,000. Will the insured collect the full $90,000?

$$\frac{\$200,000 \text{ [amount of insurance carried]}}{\$400,000 \text{ [amount of insurance required]}} \times \text{[amount of loss]}$$
$$\$90,000 = \$45,000 \text{ [recovery]}$$

The insured will only receive $45,000 even though the actual loss was less than the amount of insurance carried.

How Much Insurance?

Many property owners find that, even though they had adequate coverage when the policy was initially purchased, as a result of inflation their property is seriously underinsured. This can be true even through the owner has the property insured for the amount of its current market value. It is the *replacement cost*, not the market value, that should determine how much insurance coverage is carried. Most homeowners' policies contain a clause which states that if damage occurs, be it full or partial loss, the *total* replacement cost will be paid by the insurance company, provided that the property is insured for a certain percentage of the replacement cost, usually 80%. If the house is insured for less than the stated minimum, then in case of damage, the insurance company will pay the larger amount of either (1) the cash value of the damaged property (replacement cost minus depreciation) or (2) a percentage of the replacement cost (a ratio of the insurance carried to 80% of the current replacement cost).

Example:
A house is insured for $60,000, but its current replacement cost is $100,000. If the owner suffers a $40,000 loss, the insurance company will normally pay only 75% (the $60,000 carried is 75% of what should be carried) or any loss, up to a maximum of $60,000 for a total loss.

Particularly for an older home, the owner might find little relationship between the replacement cost and the fair market value. Insurance companies provide a general formula for deriving the replacement cost of a home, derived by multiplying the total base cost by a location multiplier.

Full Replacement Coverage

Most insurance policies will make an adjustment for any depreciation that has reduced the value of a property. This applies to both real and personal property. For example, assume that a homeowner purchased a television set, with an expected life of seven years, five years ago for $1,000. If the homeowner's policy covers theft, and the television set is stolen, how much will the homeowner recover from the insurance company? Unless the policy contains full replacement coverage, the insurance company will subtract depreciation of five-sevenths of the value, or the homeowner will recover only about $286. If full replacement coverage is carried, the homeowner would receive $1,000 or a new television set of similar type, whichever cost less. Full replacement coverage can be purchased for a relatively small additional premium by adding an endorsement to the homeowner's policy.

Apportionment (Pro rata clause)

An apportionment or pro rata clause is normally included in standard insurance policies to prevent financial gain by the insured as a result of insuring the same property with two or more companies and hoping to collect more than the loss.

Example:
A building valued at $200,000 is insured with Company A for $160,000 and with Company B for $200,000. An $80,000 loss is incurred. Company A is liable for only $35,200 of the loss and Company B is liable for $44,800.

Solution:
$160,000 + $200,000 = $360,000

Company A's liability $= \dfrac{160,000}{360,000} = 44\%$ of loss

Company B's liability $= \dfrac{200,000}{360,000} = 56\%$ of loss

$80,000 \times .44 = $35,200 for Company A
$80,000 \times .56 = $44,800 for Company B

Cancellation

The insured has the right to cancel a policy at any time. Written or oral notice must be received by the insurance company, and any unused part of the premium is refunded. However, the refund is normally less than the straight pro rata charge since upon cancellation insurance companies calculate the used portion based on *short rates*. Short rates are higher than pro rata charges.

Subrogation

In case of an actual loss, this clause prevents the insured from collecting both from the insurance company and from the third party who actually caused the damage. When the insurance company pays the insured, any rights the insured may have to sue the party at fault will be assigned to the insurance company. The insurance company may then, if it so chooses, take legal action against the third party to collect what was paid to the insured.

Cost of Insurance

In most states, insurance companies who desire to adjust their rates must submit a request supported with data to the state department of insurance or the insurance commissioner. State insurance laws typically require that rates be adequate, not excessive or unfairly discriminatory. This does not mean that every insurance company must offer the same coverage and charge exactly the same rates.

Many factors enter into how much a certain amount of coverage will cost. One thing is the *loss experience* of the insurance company. This refers to how much money the insurance company has paid out for damages to property and people. If this loss experience is increasing, then the company will want to charge more to provide that type of coverage. The material used to construct the improvements is also important. Rates for an all-brick house will normally be less than for an all-wood house. Further, the fire rating or classification of the jurisdiction is important. This rating is based on the amount of fire protection available in the jurisdiction. Obviously, the more perils insured against, the higher the cost. The amount of coverage purchased also affects the cost. It would stand to reason that a person insuring a house for $30,000 would not pay as much as someone purchasing $90,000 coverage. The cost of insurance is also affected by the *deductible* clause. If the insured chooses $100 deductible, for example, the insured is responsible for all losses up to that amount.

POINTS TO REMEMBER

1. If one is to be successful in residential sales, a clear understanding of what motivates a prospective home buyer is necessary. Good service based on product knowledge and on an appreciation of the needs of both the buyer and seller builds a solid reputation in the community and leads to repeat business.

2. Homeownership has both advantages and disadvantages. Advantages include: a sense of security, pride, freedom from landlord control, more space, privacy, financial and tax advantages. Disadvantages include: loss of mobility, house and yard maintenance, losses from uninsured perils and possible risk of equity invested through foreclosure.

3. A lender is reluctant to lend money if mortgage and other home ownership expenses exceed 25% of gross pay or if all long-term loan expenses exceed 35% of gross pay.

4. Housing needs are usually tied to the family life cycle, financial capability, life style and availability of alternative housing.

5. A purchaser should investigate the neighborhood, the site and the improvements before committing himself or herself to a particular home purchase.

6. Insurance is a means by which one party shifts the risk of a certain loss or disastrous event to another party. This is done through a contract called a policy and with a certain payment called a premium.

7. In order to collect payment from an insurance policy, one must have an insurable interest in the subject matter. Insurable interest means that in case of some event, such as a fire, the insured suffers some injury or less.

8. A homeowner's policy can be purchased by anyone who owns and occupies either a one- or two-family residence. This all-inclusive policy is normally cheaper than purchasing a number of separate policies. The Broad Form (HO-2), which is the most common, insures against 18 different perils.

9. Special homeowners's policies are also available for apartment dwellers and condominium and cooperative owners.

10. It is the replacement cost, and not the market value, that should determine how much insurance coverage to carry.

11. Insurance policies contain numerous clauses that need to be fully understood by the insured. Among the most common are: (1) coinsurance, (2) apportionment, (3) cancellation and (4) subrogation.

KEY TERMS AND PHRASES

apportionment
appurtenant structures
cancellation
coinsurance

homeowner's policy
Home owners Warranty Program (How)
insurable interest

perils
R value
replacement cost
subrogation

QUESTIONS

1. Reasons why people would rather buy a house than rent include which of the following?
   I. Tax deductions
   II. Protection against inflation
   A. I only
   B. II only
   C. Both I and II
   D. Neither I nor II

2. What consideration(s) would cause a lender to refuse a mortgage loan to a home purchaser?
   I. Mortgage debt service costs exceed 25% of net income.
   II. Mortgage exceeds two and one-half times annual salary.
   A. I only
   B. II only
   C. Both I and II
   D. Neither I nor II

3. Which of the following statements is a characteristic of housing.
   A. Housing needs are usually tied to phases in the family life cycle.
   B. Housing needs remain constant over time.
   C. Housing should always be purchased by those in lower tax brackets.
   D. If one is single, it is always better to own a house rather than rent a house.

4. Which of the following statements is (are) a characteristic of neighborhood stability?
   I. Large number of "for sale" signs
   II. High percentage of owner occupied houses
   A. I only
   B. II only
   C. Both I and II
   D. Neither I nor II

5. Which of the following can protect a neighborhood from nuisances and hazards?
   I. Buffers
   II. Building and health code enforcement
   A. I only
   B. II only
   C. Both I and II
   D. Neither I nor II

6. In examining a site, a worn trail is important because it is a sign of a (an)
   I. possible unrecorded easement
   II. encroachment
   A. I only
   B. II only
   C. Both I and II
   D. Neither I nor II

7. What best describes HOW?
   A. Subagency of HUD
   B. Warranty program sponsored by FHA
   C. Warranty program sponsored by a subsidiary of NAR
   D. Warranty program sponsored by a subsidiary of NAHB

8. What is covered by the HOW program?
   I. All defects of workmanship for 10 years
   II. All major structural defects for 10 years
   A. I only
   B. II only
   C. Both I and II
   D. Neither I nor II

9. In order to encourage policyholders to keep an adequate amount of insurance, insurance policies have a (an) _____ clause.
   A. coinsurance
   B. endorsement
   C. liability
   D. indemnity

10. If a neighborhood has a need to construct a new sewage treatment facility, this might be a sign of
    A. a forthcoming special tax assessment
    B. a neighborhood with a small number of tenants
    C. a need for road repairs
    D. a transitional neighborhood

11. The clause in an insurance policy which prevents financial gain by the insured as a result of insuring the property with two or more companies is referred to as
    A. apportionment
    B. coinsurance
    C. subrogation
    D. pro forma

12. A building's value is $150,000. If the insurance coverage is for $90,000 and the policy has an 80% coinsurance clause, how much will the insured recover if there is a $40,000 loss?
    A. $0
    B. $24,000
    C. $30,000
    D. $40,000

13. In case of an actual loss, the clause in an insurance policy preventing the insured from collecting both from the insurance policy and the third person who actually caused the damage is the
    A. short release clause
    B. apportionment clause
    C. coinsurance clause
    D. subrogation clause

14. A building valued at $500,000 is insured with Company A for $400,000 and with Company B for $500,000. A $300,000 loss is incurred. What is the liability of Company A?
    A. $133,000
    B. $167,000
    C. $240,000
    D. $400,000

15. The widely purchased homeowner's Broad Form (HO-2) would not insure against which of the following perils?
    A. Earthquake
    B. Aircraft
    C. Riot or civil commotion
    D. Weight of ice

If you are not sure of your answers, see page 320 for correct answers and explanations.

12

Federal Fair Housing Laws

Every real estate broker and salesperson must be familiar with the scope and coverage of federal fair housing legislation and other federal laws which relate to the sale of real estate. The penalties for violation of these federal laws can be very expensive and quite severe. This chapter outlines the major federal legislation which affects brokers in the areas of civil rights and fair housing. It is the responsibility of every person to know not only these laws, which are constantly changing due to acts of Congress, but also regulations of federal agencies and decisions of courts. A practicing broker is advised to stay current with changes in the laws by reading literature and reports provided by professional organizations such as the NATIONAL ASSOCIATION OF REALTORS® and by attending continuing education seminars sponsored by various groups and universities.

It is the stated policy of the federal government to eradicate discrimination in real estate markets. In recent years the federal government has shown its concern about housing discrimination. Two actions were taken that signified this concern. President John F. Kennedy issued *Executive Order No. 11063*, which prohibited discrimination in housing financed by the Federal Housing Administration (FHA) or the Veterans Administration (VA). This was followed by the *Civil Rights Act of 1964*, which extended this prohibition to housing programs receiving federal money. Of broader general impact was the enforcement of two major fair housing laws. These two major laws which were enacted by Congress are of particular concern to real estate brokers, and questions based on these laws appear on uniform licensing examinations. The first law is the *Federal Fair Housing Act of 1968* which was passed as Title VIII of the Civil Rights Act of 1968. As originally passed, the act prohibited discrimination in the sale or rental of residential dwelling units or vacant land intended to be used as such on the basis of race, color, religion or national origin. Discrimination on the basis of sex was prohibited by an amendment in the Housing and Community Development Act of 1974. The Fair Housing Amendment Act of 1988, which became effective March 13, 1989, adds two new protected classes, the handicapped and the "familial" status, or those with children under 18. The second law is the *Civil Rights Act of 1866*. This law passed after the Civil War provided that "all citizens of the United States shall have the same right, in every State and Territory, as is enjoyed by white citizens thereof to inherit, purchase, lease, sell, hold, and convey real and personal property." This law prohibits discrimination in all real estate transactions based on race. In 1968, this law was revived and given substance by the U.S. Supreme Court in the case of *Jones v. Alfred H. Mayer Co.*, 392 U.S. 409 (1968). In this case, the court prohibited any racially motivated refusal to sell or rent property. The case involved a refusal of a builder to sell a house to a black person in 1965. Three years later, the builder was ordered to sell a house to the injured party at 1965 prices and to absorb the price difference.

In other cases, the Supreme Court ruled that the two laws are to be given very broad construction in order to accomplish the national goal of fair housing for everyone. This interpretation is important because it makes it more difficult to disprove allegations that a broker has violated the provisions of the laws. So the broker must use extreme care not to give even the appearance of violating the intent of the laws. A broker may not defend on the basis that his or her principal instructed the discriminatory action or that it was the principal who was practicing the discrimination. Further, a principal cannot defend for discriminatory acts performed by a broker on the basis that the broker was an independent contractor.

WHAT IS PROHIBITED BY THE 1968 FAIR HOUSING ACT?

This law prohibits the following discriminatory acts if the discrimination is based on race, color, religion, national origin or sex in all instances except where otherwise specified:

1. It is unlawful to refuse to sell or rent, or to refuse to negotiate to sell or rent, or otherwise make unavailable

or deny a dwelling to any person in the protective classification.

Example:
Joan is an apartment manager for Frosty Pines Apartments which are rented by many people who originally came from Pakistan. A prospective tenant who came from India seeks to rent an apartment. Because of trouble between the countries of Pakistan and India, Joan's tenants tell her that if she rents to an Indian, they will move out. Joan refuses to rent to the Indian. She has violated the law.

It should be noted that under this provision the practice of *steering* would be considered illegal. Steering is defined as a real estate broker or salesperson channeling prospective home purchasers or renters into homogeneous neighborhoods and actively discouraging them away from neighborhoods of different racial or ethnic composition. Thus, if a broker intentionally fails to make a house available to a prospect because of the prospect's race, sex, religion, color or national origin, the broker is in violation of the law. The prospect, not the broker, is entitled to choose which neighborhoods are suitable.

2. It is unlawful to modify terms, conditions, or privileges of sale or rental or change the provisions of services or facilities in connection with the sale or rental of a dwelling on the basis of race, color, sex, religion, national origin, handicapped persons and families with children.

Example:
John Developer is selling houses in a subdivision he has completed. When a purchaser buys a house he is automatically given a free membership in a club which is part of the subdivision. Harry Gold, a member of the Jewish faith, buys a house but is told by John that the club is for Gentiles only. John offers to give Harry a rebate on the purchase price. John is in violation of the law.

3. It is unlawful to make any statement or advertise that sale or rental is limited to certain groups or that certain groups are preferred.

Example:
Jan tells a white couple that the project is restricted to whites and that no blacks will ever be welcome so long as she is manager. This statement is illegal.

It might be noted that the U.S. Supreme Court in *Trafficante v. Metropolitan Life Insurance Company*, 409 U.S. 205 (1972) permitted a white plaintiff to recover against an owner of an apartment project because the plaintiff was denied the social benefits of associating with black due to the owner's discriminatory practices.

4. It is unlawful to represent to a person in a protected classification that any dwelling is not available for inspection, sale or rental when such dwelling is in fact so available.

Example:
Mike and Janet, an interracial married couple, answer an advertisement for an apartment. The manager of the apartment shows the couple the apartment. When the couple seeks to place a deposit on the apartment, the manager tells them that unfortunately he cannot accept the deposit because someone has previously made a deposit on the apartment. The manager's statement is false. The statement violates the law.

5. It is unlawful to make representations that a person or person of any classification are entering into a neighborhood to induce sales for the purpose of profiting from the sale or rent of any dwelling.

Example:
Mary and Joe are concerned that their neighborhood may be racially transitional. They ask their broker, Ann Smith, if there is any danger of minorities or foreigners moving into their neighborhood. Ann Smith urges them to list their house because Vietnamese refugees are moving into the neighborhood and will undoubtedly drive prices down. Ann Smith is acting illegally by blockbustting.

Any activity which attempts to drive prices down for the purpose of causing transition from one ethnic group to another is illegal. It should be noted that blockbusting does not occur from selling a house to a member of a minority group, but from attempting to drive out existing owners. Thus, courts have construed even broad statements such as "this is a changing neighborhood" as falling within his provision.

6. It is unlawful for any bank, building and loan association, insurance company or other lender to modify the terms or conditions on a loan as the basis of discrimination where the purpose of this loan is to buy, build or repair a dwelling.

Example:
The Friendly Finance Company of Anystate tells Mary Jones, who is seeking to borrow money to paint her house, that because she is likely to become pregnant they will require that she pay back the loan within nine months. This kind of restriction on the terms of the loan is illegal.

7. It is unlawful to deny or to impose on any person discriminatory conditions because of the person's race or other protected classes in order to participate in any multiple listing service or any other real estate business organization.

Example:
Anytown Listing Association refuses to list any house in a neighborhood which is racially transitional. This restriction would be illegal.

WHO IS EXEMPT FROM THE PROVISIONS OF THE 1968 FAIR HOUSING ACT?

There are four exemptions noted in the law. The reader is advised that these exemptions *do not* apply to the provisions of the 1866 law where discrimination is on the basis of race.

1. The sale or rental of single-family homes rented by an owner is exempt provided that the following conditions are met:

A. Only one sale within any 24-month period is permitted if the owner was not residing in the home at the time of the sale or was not the most recent resident of the home prior to the sale.

B. The owner cannot own any more than three homes at one time.

C. A broker or salesperson or the services of any person in the business of selling or renting dwellings cannot be used.

D. Discriminatory advertising cannot be used.

The reader should note that if a person who is in the business of selling or renting dwellings assists in the sale, the exemption does not apply. Such a person is anyone who has participated as a principal in three or more rental or sales transactions within the preceding 12 months, or if the person has acted as an agent in two or more rental or sales transactions within the preceding 12 months, or if the person is the owner of any dwelling designed for five or more families.

2. Rentals of dwellings designed for four or fewer families are exempt if the owner occupies one of the units.

3. Religious organizations may give preference to members of their own religion in sales and rentals so long as the groups do not discriminate on the basis of color, race sex, national origin, handicapped persons and families with children.

WHAT IS PROHIBITED BY THE CIVIL RIGHTS ACT OF 1866?

All racial discrimination in the sale or rental of real estate, whether public or private, is prohibited by this law. The reader should note that this refers to all real estate, unlike the 1968 Fair Housing Act, which just covers dwellings. Further, the reader should note that there are no exceptions.

COMPLAINTS AND ENFORCEMENT

Under the 1968 Fair Housing Act, a civil complaint may be handled in three ways:

1. *A complaint may be filed with HUD.* HUD must promptly investigate complaints, unless state or local law provides rights and remedies which are substantially equivalent. If the latter is the case, then the complaint must be referred to the appropriate state or local agency. While HUD has broad investigatory and subpoena powers, it is not empowered to issue cease and desist orders. HUD is restricted to *informal conciliation* to seek a resolution to complaints. While this process is time consuming, the advantage to the complainant is that HUD bears the cost of investigation and discovery. This information may be used as evidence in a private civil suit for damages and for injunctive relief. If HUD or the state agency is unable to cure the discriminatory practice or correct the damage, the injured party may then bring a civil suit in the federal district court.

2. *A civil suit may be filed in federal district court.* A civil suit must be filed in federal district court within 180 days of the discriminatory act. The 180-day rule does not apply where the complaint is first filed with HUD. The federal district court may give injunctive relief and award actual damages and up to $1,000 in punitive damages. It might also be noted a complaint to HUD and a separate civil suit may take place simultaneously.

3. *Action may be taken by the Attorney General.* The Attorney General of the United States may file a civil suit where there exists a pattern or practice of discrimination or if a number of persons have been injured by such practices. This avenue of enforcement is ordinarily restricted to cases of general public importance.

Example:

A large brokerage firm makes it a practice to have white agents show houses to white prospects, while black agents show houses to black prospects. The Attorney General could become involved in a case such as this to correct this type of pattern of discrimination.

Where there are criminal complaints, these should be directed to the Federal Bureau of Investigation (FBI) or to the local police. The 1968 law is also designed to protect individuals from acts or threats of violence and intimidation.

The 1866 Civil Rights Act may be enforced by bringing a civil suit in the federal district court. Proceedings under the 1866 law give certain advantages to the plaintiff. The courts are not restricted to $1,000 punitive damages, nor must the suit be brought within 180 days of the injury. The time period for bringing a suit would be the appropriate state statute of limitations for tort actions.

LOOK THIS UP:

What is the statute of limitations in your state for tort actions?

_____Years

A technique used by plaintiffs or government investigators to gather evidence of discrimination is that of "testing" or "checking." A typical example of this technique is described. Assume that a broker is suspected of not treating whites and blacks in the same manner. A complaint has been filed that the broker has discouraged blacks from purchasing homes. The following sequence of events might take place to investigate the complaint. First, a white couple of a certain socio-economic status would approach a house that the suspected broker was showing. They would ask certain questions and give certain facts about themselves to the broker. After the first couple left, a black couple of the same socio-economic status would come and ask the same essential questions and give the same essential facts about themselves. After the black couple left, another white couple would repeat the same procedure. A comparison would be made to determine if the attitude and representations made were different in the treatment of the black couple than with the two white couples. The findings of this checking would be admissible in court.

The two federal laws discussed in this chapter have been very broadly construed. Violations which have been recognized as actionable have included, among others, the following: agents neglecting to provide listings in certain neighborhoods to black couples, the recordation of racially restrictive covenants, newspapers printing discriminatory advertisements, credit checks which primarily screen out

Figure 12–1. Equal Housing Opportunity Poster

EQUAL HOUSING OPPORTUNITY

We Do Business in Accordance With the Federal Fair Housing Law

(Title VIII of the Civil Rights Act of 1968, as Amended by
the Housing and Community Development Act of 1974)

IT IS ILLEGAL TO DISCRIMINATE AGAINST ANY PERSON BECAUSE OF RACE, COLOR, RELIGION, SEX, OR NATIONAL ORIGIN

- In the sale or rental of housing or residential lots
- In advertising the sale or rental of housing
- In the financing of housing
- In the provision of real estate brokerage services

Blockbusting is also illegal

An aggrieved person may file a complaint of a housing discrimination act with the:
U.S. DEPARTMENT OF HOUSING AND URBAN DEVELOPMENT
Assistant Secretary for Fair Housing and Equal Opportunity
Washington, D.C. 20410

HUD-928.1 (7-75) Previous editions are obsolete

Federal Fair Housing Laws

minority groups, discrimination as to membership in a community swimming pool, blockbusting, reprisal against white tenants who have black guests visit, appraisal reports that state population transitions affect value and eviction of tenants because of an interracial marriage.

The reader should also be aware that many states have passed individual civil rights and fair housing legislation. Often the state provisions provide for more extensive penalties and enforcement than do the federal laws. Such provisions are often included in the state licensing laws for brokers and salespersons.

When a state or local law has been deemed *substantially equivalent* to the federal fair housing law, enforcement can be in the hands of local authorities. In such a situation, all complaints should be filed through the appropriate state or local agency. The local office of HUD can advise individuals as to the appropriate place to file complaints.

LOOK THIS UP:

Does your state have a fair housing provision in the licensing law?

Yes _____ No _____

If yes, make the following notations:

Who enforces it? _____

What are the penalties? _____

What is the time period complaints must be brought? _____

Who is exempt? _____

In order to implement Title VIII (1968 Fair Housing Law), HUD has attempted to seek voluntary compliance from industry, government and private citizens. In addition, HUD has required *Affirmative Fair Housing Marketing Plans* from all subdivisions, multi-family projects and mobile home parks or five or more units before these projects are eligible for participation in various federal programs, including home mortgage programs.

Affirmative marketing programs involve two aspects. (1) An initial sales or rental phase which involves "efforts to reach those persons who traditionally would not have been expected to apply for housing." HUD regulations specify the need for attracting minorities to predominantly white areas and whites to predominantly minority areas. (2) HUD regulations require continuing marketing activity to accomplish affirmative action goals whenever vacancies occur. Further, HUD requires nondiscriminatory hiring of sales and rental personnel and the prominent displaying of HUD's fair housing logo or statements on equal opportunity (see Figure 12–1).

Coinciding with federal and state efforts to prohibit housing discrimination have been efforts by professional organizations to encourage their members to act accordingly. For example, Article 10 of the National Association of Realtors' *Code of Ethics* states that Realtors should neither discriminate in providing professional services nor participate in any plan or agreement to discriminate (see "Code of Ethics" in Chapter 3). The National Association of Realtors has also adopted a *Code of Equal Opportunity*, which emphasizes that Realtors who violate the spirit of the intent not to discriminate "shall be subject to disciplinary action."

POINTS TO REMEMBER

1. Under the Air Housing Act of 1968, as amended it is illegal to discriminate in the area of housing and the marketing of housing on the basis of race, color, religion, national origin, sex, handicapped persons and families with children.

2. The only exemptions from the 1968 Housing Act are individual owners of three houses or less who are not using the services of a real estate broker or doing discriminatory advertising, owners of owner-occupied dwellings designed for no more than four families, religious organizations who restrict rentals to church members but do not discriminate for any other prohibited reasons and private clubs who rent dwellings to their own membership and do not rent on a commercial basis.

3. Complaints under the 1968 Housing Act may be handled three ways: (1) by filing a complaint with HUD or appropriate state or local agency, (2) by bringing a civil suit within 180 days of the last alleged complaint or (3) by a civil suit being filed by the U.S. Attorney General in cases involving a pattern or practice of discrimination. Punitive damages are restricted to $1,000 but actual damages and injunctive relief are available.

4. The 1866 Civil Rights Act prohibits all discrimination on the basis of race in real estate transaction. Enforcement of the law takes place through a civil suit in federal court. There is no restriction on punitive damages, and suit may be filed within any time specified by individual state statutes of limitation.

KEY TERMS AND PHRASES

Affirmative Fair Housing Marketing Plans

blockbusting

Civil Rights Act of 1866

Fair Housing Amendment Act of 1988

Federal Fair Housing Act of 1968

steering

QUESTIONS

1. Elizabeth, a student at XYZ State College, sought to rent an apartment from Badspot Rental Company. She was advised that the company did not rent to students, who they believed to be bad risks. Elizabeth has remedies under which of the following acts:

   I. Federal Fair Housing Act of 1968

   II. Civil Rights Act of 1866

   A. I only B. II only
   C. Both I and II D. Neither I nor II

2. John Smith refuses to rent to Mary Jones, who is black. Smith owns only one duplex and he personally occupies the other unit. He tells Jones that he has nothing personally against her but he just does not want to rent to blacks. Jones has remedies under which of the following acts?

   I. Federal Fair Housing Act of 1968

   II. Civil Rights Act of 1866

   A. I only B. II only
   C. Both I and II D. Neither I nor II

3. If you have a complaint under the 1968 Federal Fair Housing Act, what can you do?

   I. File a complaint with HUD

   II. File a civil suit in the federal district court

   A. I only B. II only
   C. Both I and II D. Neither I nor II

4. If you have a complaint under the Civil Rights Act of 1866, what can you do?

   I. File a complaint with HUD

   II. File a civil suit in the federal district court

   A. I only B. II only
   C. Both I and II D. Neither I nor II

5. Dick paints a sign which says, "Rooms for rent—Available only to Christians and people who are not attorneys." Which of the following is true under both the 1968 Federal Fair Housing Law and the Civil Rights Act of 1866?

   A. Dick may restrict the rooms he rents by occupation and religion.
   B. Dick may restrict rooms to people by occupation.
   C. Dick may restrict rooms to Christians.
   D. Dick may advertise as he pleases, but he must rent the rooms to anyone who is able to pay the room rent.

6. An all-black Baptist Church builds an apartment project for its membership. Fred Roe, a white civil rights lawyer, wishes to move into the project because he is fully committed to integration. Roe is a Roman Catholic. Which of the following is true?

   I. Roe may be barred because he is white.

   II. Roe may be barred because he is Roman Catholic.

   A. I only B. II only
   C. Both I and II C. Neither I nor II

7. In which way is HUD authorized to enforce the Fair Housing Act of 1968?

   A. Seek informal conciliation
   B. Issue "cease and desist" orders
   C. File action directly through the Justice Department
   D. Bring a civil suit in the federal district court

8. Jan is the sole owner of a house which she is selling. She tells her broker that she refuses to sell the house to anyone of German origin. The broker brings a prospect named Kurt Wagner, a recent immigrant from Germany. Jan refuses to sell to Kurt. Which of the following is true?

   A. Jan may not under any circumstances discriminate on the basis of national origin.
   B. Jan must sell to Kurt because she used the services of a broker.
   C. Jan is not required to sell because the broker exceeded his authority.
   D. Jan, who is the owner of only one house, is exempt from the 1968 Federal Fair Housing Act in the situation described.

9. X publicly embarrasses Mr. and Mrs. Ted, a well-educated black couple, when they seek to buy a condominium at a public auction. X tells a group of 150 people present that blacks like the Teds are useless and may never buy a dwelling he is selling. If Mr. and Mrs. Ted wish to seek $100,000 punitive damages, they should proceed under which acts?

   A. Civil Rights Act of 1866
   B. Federal Fair Housing Act of 1968
   C. Housing and Community Development Act of 1974
   D. Interstate Land Sales Act of 1968

10. The Federal Fair Housing Act of 1968, as amended, prohibits

    I. favoring one sex over another in renting apartments to the public

    II. discriminating on the basis of race in extending credit terms for the purpose of home improvements.

    A. I only B. II only
    C. Both I and II D. Neither I nor II

11. The unlawful act of directing a prospective buyer away from or to a particular area is known as

    I. blockbusting II. steering

    A. I only B. II only
    C. Both I and II D. Neither I nor II

12. Federal fair housing laws are administered by which federal agency?

    A. NAR
    B. Attorney General
    C. HUD
    D. FRS

13. Which federal law specifically prohibits sex discrimination in housing sales?
    A. Civil Rights Act of 1866
    B. Housing and Community Development Act of 1974
    C. Civil Rights Act of 1866
    D. Equal Rights Amendment of 1968
14. Does the 1968 Federal Fair Housing Act prohibit steering?
    A. Yes.
    B. Yes, but only if the services of a real estate broker are used.
    C. No.
    D. Steering is not mentioned in the act.
15. Mr. Smith leases units in his apartment units to the families of Johnson, Smith, Jones, and Browne. A discriminatory complaint is made against him. Mr. Smith says, "I'm exempt from the 1968 Federal Fair Housing Act because I, too, occupy a unit in my apartment complex."
    I. Mr. Smith is in violation of the 1968 Federal Fair Housing Act.
    II. Mr. Smith may not be sued in civil court for damages.
    A. I only
    B. II only
    C. Both I and II
    D. Neither I nor II

If you are not sure of your answers, see page 320 for correct answers and explanations.

13

Deeds and Transfer of Title

The ways in which title to real property is transferred may be classified as: (1) voluntary conveyance, (2) transfer by devise or descent, (3) transfer by adverse possession, (4) transfer by accession and (5) transfer by public action or by operation of law. *Title* is the legally recognized evidence of a person's right to possess property. By being able to transfer title, real property gains economic value and permits land to be used efficiently as a factor of production.

A detailed description is provided of the major kinds of deeds which are recognized by various states. The sections of deeds are analyzed, and a brief discussion is given to important legal principles which affect the enforceability of deeds. Consideration is given to the other means by which title may be transferred. Because of the legal complexity of title transfer and assurance in this country and because each state has its own peculiarities, care should be taken to consult an attorney in most property conveyances. It may also be noted that if someone other than the grantor or an attorney-at-law prepared the deed for another, it would be considered the unauthorized practice of law in many states.

VOLUNTARY CONVEYANCES

A *deed* is defined as a written instrument, usually under seal, conveying some property interest from a grantor to a grantee. A *grantor* is the person who conveys the property interest; the *grantee* is the person to whom the grant is made.

In order for a deed to be effective in transferring title, it must be in proper legal form and executed as specified by the law in the state in which the property is located. The title is actually transferred the moment the deed is properly delivered to and accepted by the grantee. In order to protect the validity of the title from subsequent innocent third parties purchasing the same property from the original grantor, the deed must be recorded as required by the particular state's recording statute. This also gives assurance to third parties that no one else has good title, unless the title has been recorded. This gives *constructive notice* to third parties (see Chapter 14). When a deed is delivered, all prior oral and written agreements are *merged* into the deed unless these obligations do not contradict the deed and are collateral. This means that when a deed is delivered and accepted all prior agreements which are inconsistent with the deed are superseded and have no legal effect. An exception to this rule occurs in cases of fraud and mutual mistake. Another exception exists when the contract specifically provides that the obligations will survive the closing.

Example:
> Jeff and Jane entered into a written sales contract in which Jeff agreed to convey Blackshear by a general warranty deed. He then delivers a quitclaim deed which Jane accepts. Jane cannot later bring a suit to require Jeff to give a general warranty deed.

Deeds contain much information which is of value to a real estate broker and salesperson. Since deeds are kept in the public records, this information is readily available to the public. Deeds vary in content because of state law provisions and the purpose of the deed.

General Warranty Deeds

A general warranty deed contains covenants in which the grantor formally guarantees that *good and marketable title* is being conveyed. In some states, this type of deed is called a *full covenant and warranty deed*. *Good title* is one which is free from encumbrances such as liens, pending litigation and other such defects (see Chapter 14). *Marketable* or *merchantable title* is one which is free from reasonable doubts or objections and which the courts would compel a purchaser to accept under the terms of a sales contract. A general warranty deed gives the grantee legal recourse against the seller in the event that the title is not as represented. This deed provides the purchaser with the greatest number of assurances and is considered the most desirable type of deed which can be received. In order for the purchaser to be legally entitled to receive such a deed, a provision must be inserted in the original sales contract; otherwise, the seller is only required to give a quitclaim deed, which contains no guarantees or assurances.

A general warranty deed normally contains three *present covenants* (in praesenti) and three *future covenants* (in futuro). The present covenants include: (1) covenant of seizin, (2) covenant of right to convey and (3) covenant against encumbrances. The future covenants include: (1) covenant of quiet enjoyment, (2) covenant of further assurances and (3) covenant of warranty of title. In addition, some states, such as New York, have added an additional statutory covenant of trust.

Covenant of Seizin (or Seisin)

This covenant gives the assurance that the grantor has the exact estate in the quantity and quality which in fact is being conveyed. For example, if the grantor is attempting to convey a fee simple absolute and in fact only has a fee simple determinable, this covenant would be violated (see Chapter 8). This is important because a grantor may legally convey only that title which is possessed and no better.

Covenant of Right to Convey

This is very similar to the covenant of seizin, and in some states both covenants are treated as one under the covenant of seizin. The covenant of right to convey is the assurance that the grantor has the right, power and authority to convey the title being granted. For example, in the case of a joint tenant or a tenant by the entirety, this covenant would be violated if an attempt was made to convey the entire estate without the other co-owners joining in the conveyance (see Chapter 8).

Covenant Against Encumbrances

This covenant provides the assurance that no encumbrances other than those specified in the deed exist. For example, if it is later discovered that an unrecorded prescriptive easement exists or that dower rights still cloud the title, the grantee may bring a suit for damages to the extent that the value of the estate has been diminished. Because of this covenant, care should be taken to specify all encumbrances in the drafting of the deed.

Covenant of Further Assurances

This covenant is a promise that the grantor will perform further acts reasonably necessary to correct any defects in the title or in the deed instrument. For example, if a cloud on title exists because the deed was improperly signed or contains other mistakes, the grantor has agreed by this covenant to give the grantee or the grantee's successor any legal document necessary to perfect the title.

Covenant of Quiet Enjoyment

This is a promise that no one has superior or paramount title to that of the grantor and assures the grantee of peaceful possession without fear of being ousted by a person with a superior claim to the property. For example, if the grantee is evicted because an outstanding mortgage given by the grantor has been foreclosed, the grantee would be able to collect damages for breach of this covenant. Quiet enjoyment refers to right of peaceful possession free of hostile title and not to noise or loud neighbors (see Chapter 2).

Covenant of Warranty of Title

Sometimes called "warranty forever" this covenant is the assurance that the grantor will underwrite the legal expenses if any person establishes a claim superior to the title given by the grantor. However, this does not mean that the grantor agrees to indemnify the costs for all court suits involving title, but only for those prior claims which actually put the grantee out of possession. This warranty applies to all claims which existed prior to as well as those which occurred during the grantor's possession.

Covenant of Trust

A covenant of trust has been established by statute in several states to protect the purchaser from unrecorded liens. This covenant makes the seller a trustee of the purchase price funds for the benefit of the buyer until the time for recording mechanic and materialman liens has expired. If the grantor has failed to pay off contractors and other workers who have performed work on the transferred property, the grantor would be obligated under state penal laws to satisfy any subsequently recorded liens (see Chapter 14).

LOOK THIS UP:

Is a covenant of trust used in your state?

Yes _____ No _____

Special Warranty Deeds

Because sellers are often reluctant to assume the risk of a title defect which may have occurred prior to their acquisition of the title, they will limit their liability by giving a *special warranty deed* rather than the general warranty deed. The special warranty deed does *not* contain the covenant of warranty of title. Instead, the grantor will warrant against defects that have occurred *after* the grantor acquired title (see Figure 13–1). Language is usually used that the grantor warrants only against lawful claims on the title which occurred "by, from, through or under" the grantor. The grantor is warranting that he or she did not encumber the property but makes no representations as to what may have happened prior to the time of his or her ownership. In both categories of warranty deeds, if the grantor has conveyed defective title and later acquires good title, this good title passes to the grantee automatically by operation of law.

Example:

John gives Harry a general warranty deed to convey title to Green Valley under the mistaken notion that he had good title when in fact the title resided in his sister Mary. Later Mary dies leaving the property to John. By operation of law, this newly acquired title is passed to Harry.

Figure 13–1. A Cloud on Title Resulting from a Defect before Grantor Acquired Title Is Covered by a General Warranty Deed But Not a Special Warranty Deed.

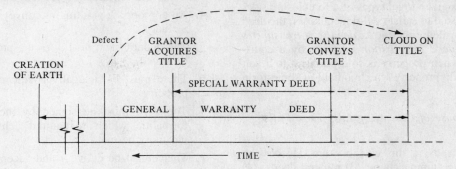

Grant Deeds

Like the special warranty deed, the *grant deed* limits the responsibility of the grantor to the period of time that the grantor actually possessed the property. The grant deed conveys any title and any after-acquired title that the grantor has, unless intent is clearly expressed otherwise. By implication of law the grantor warrants that title has not been conveyed to another person and that the property is free of encumbrances such as unpaid taxes, assessments and liens except as is noted otherwise in the deed.

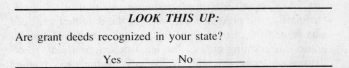

Bargain and Sale Deeds

Bargain and sale deeds may be with or without covenants. These are deeds which recite a valuable consideration and commonly use the words "bargain and sell" or words of similar import. A deed with covenants is like a special warranty deed in which the grantor covenants that the property has not been encumbered during the time that the grantor possessed the estate. A deed without covenants is similar to a quitclaim deed. There is an implication in both types of bargain and sale deeds that the grantor has possession and has some ownership interest, usually substantial, in the property.

Quitclaim Deeds

A *quitclaim deed* only conveys what present interest a person may have in a particular property and makes no representations or warranties of title. This deed is useful in clearing up doubtful claims such as possible dower rights or disputed liens. A person giving a quitclaim deed releases and waives all present rights, and if the grantor has good and merchantable title, this is what is conveyed. If the grantor actually has no interest in the property, no interest is conveyed. However, if the grantor later acquires good title to the property previously conveyed by a quitclaim deed, the grantor keeps it; it is not automatically passed on to the grantee.

Special Purpose Deeds

Because a number of transactions occur on a frequent basis, several *special purpose deeds* have been developed in many states. These deeds may be given by fiduciaries or pursuant to court orders involving persons other than the true owners. As a result, many of these deeds are either quitclaim deeds or special warranty deeds. In all fiduciary deeds, the actual consideration should be stated and usually the transaction should be confirmed by the courts. These special purpose deeds may be classified by purpose.

Deeds for Carrying Out Fiduciary Purposes

Among the deeds which may be placed in this category are: (1) administrator's deeds, (2) executor's deeds, (3) committee deeds, (4) guardian deeds and (5) deeds in trust. When a person dies *intestate* (without a will) the court appoints an administrator to pay the debts of the estate and to dispose of the property in a manner consistent with each state's statutes of descent and distribution. In conveying property, an *administrator's deed* is issued to grantees who purchase property from the estate. When a person dies *testate* (with a will), the will specifies the appointment of an executor or executrix. This is a person who carries out the intent of the will in supervising the disposition of the estate. The executor would issue an *executor's deed* in conveying real property. A *committee deed* is issued by a group of people who are appointed by the court to administer the property of someone who has been adjudged legally incompetent. A similar type of deed is issued by the guardian of a minor or insane person. This is called a *guardian's deed*. A *deed in trust* is used to convey property to a trustee in a land trust.

Deeds for Carrying out Judicial Purposes

Among the deeds which may be placed in this category are: (1) commissioner's deeds, (2) sheriff's deeds, (3) referee's deeds in foreclosure, (4) tax or treasurer's deeds and (5) referee's deed in partition. Various mortgage instruments require title to be conveyed to a purchaser after a foreclosure. Depending on the type of instrument used and the foreclosure procedure in a particular state, these deeds are variously named. They include a *commissioner's deed*, which is given to foreclose a deed of trust in lieu of a trustee's sale; a *sheriff's deed*, which is given when property is sold by a court order to satisfy a judgment for money or for foreclosure of a mortgage; and a *referee's deed in foreclosure* which is given in all types of a foreclosure sale. When a property is sold to satisfy delinquent taxes, the deed which is issued is called either a *tax deed* or a *treasurer's deed*. A *referee's deed in partition* is given by a court-appointed official when property is sold pursuant to a suit for partition to divide property which is held in some form of co-ownership.

Deeds for the Purpose of Conveying Less Than Full Interest in Property

Among the deeds in this category are: (1) cession deeds, (2) deeds to a mining claim, (3) mineral deeds, (4) security deeds and (5) trust deeds. A *cession deed* is used to transfer a portion of an individual's property to a local government for street or sidewalks. A *deed to a mining claim* is drafted to convey rights to a mine. A similar deed is a *mineral deed* which conveys only the mineral rights while reserving the surface and air rights to the property. *Security deeds* and *trust deeds* are actually types of mortgage instruments and will be discussed in Chapter 14.

Deeds for Personal Purposes

A *gift deed* is used to convey property which is given without valuable consideration. The deed is supported by *good consideration* which is "love and affection." *Valuable consideration* is the price paid for property, and if valuable consideration is used to support a deed, general creditors may not set the transaction aside, in the absence of an intent to defraud the creditors, because something of worth has been used to replace the land. A *support deed* is conveyed by a grantor in consideration for an agreement to take care of the grantor for life.

Deeds Created for Technical Purposes

Among the deeds in this category are: (1) deeds in lieu of foreclosure, (2) deeds of release, (3) reconveyance deeds, (4) deeds of surrender and (5) correction deeds. A *deed in lieu of foreclosure* is used by the mortgagor (borrower) who is in default to convey the property to the mortgagee (lender) in order to eliminate the need for a foreclosure. A *deed of release* is given by lien holders, remaindermen or mortgagees to relinquish their claims on the property. A *reconveyance deed* is one given by a trustee when he or she wishes to reconvey the property of the trust to the trustor. The trustor is the person who originally set up the trust. A *deed of surrender* is used to merge a life estate with a reversion or remainder. A *correction deed*, also known as a *deed of confirmation*, is used to correct errors or defects in a previous deed.

Deed Requirements

In order for a conveyance to have legal effect, the deed must be in *proper legal form* and meet other requirements specified by law in the state in which the land is located. The basic requirements for a valid deed is most states include the following:

1. The grantor and grantee must be named.
2. Both grantor and grantee must have legal capacity.
3. Consideration must be recited.
4. An appropriate granting or conveyance clause must be included.
5. The quantity and quality of the property interest must be stated.
6. There must be a legally adequate description of the property.
7. The deed must be signed by the grantor and other formalities which are required such as a seal or witnessing must be met.
8. There must be delivery and acceptance.
9. In most states in order to be legally effective against innocent third parties, the deed must be recorded.

Deed Contents

For the purpose of analysis, a deed may be divided into three sections: (1) the premises, (2) the habendum and (3) the testimonium. In Figure 13–2, a general warranty deed is illustrated. (Note: The circled numbers correspond to the numbers listed below.)

The Premises

The *premises* is the introductory section of the deed. Ordinarily, the premises will contain the date that the deed was signed, identification of the parties, a recital of consideration, a granting clause, the legal description, any reservations or exceptions, the recital, any "subject to" clauses and the conveyance of the appurtenances.

1. *Date*. The date on the deed is the *date of execution* and does not necessarily indicate when title passes. Title is transferred only when the deed is actually delivered and accepted. In some states, "Sunday" laws exist which prohibit transactions on the Sabbath. A deed which is dated on a Sunday will nevertheless be valid if it is delivered on a weekday.
2. *Grantor*. The grantor must be identified with the same name that was used when the title was received as grantee. For example, if the title was received as "George S. Hinds, grantee" it would not be proper to convey property from "G. Sims Hinds, grantor." This might cause a cloud on title since the title examiner could not be certain that "George S. Hinds" and "G. Sims Hinds" are the same person. If the name has been changed because of marriage or other reason, both the new name and old name should be indicated.

Example:
Fanny Hart Brice, Formerly Fanny Hart

The grantor should be identified according to marital status. In states that recognize curtesy, dower, homestead or community property, both spouses should join in the grant.

Other state requirements may specify that the grantor's name be followed by the address of the grantor's residence. If the property is in some form of co-ownership, all co-tenants should be indicated and join

Figure 13-2.

GENERAL WARRANTY DEED

PREMISES {

THIS WARRANTY DEED made on the ① day of _____ 19 ____ by ② _____

_____ , herein called the GRANTOR, residing at _____ to ③ _____

herein called the GRANTEE, residing at _____ . WITNESSETH that in consideration for the sum of ④ _____ and other consideration, paid by the grantee, the grantor hereby ⑤ grants, bargains, sells, and conveys unto the grantee the following described land:

    A. Legal Description ⑥
    B. Reservations or exceptions ⑦
    C. Restrictions ⑧
    D. Recital ⑨
    E. Subject to clause ⑩

Together with all of the ⑪ tenements, herediments, and appurtenances thereto belonging or in other wise appertaining.

HABENDUM {

⑫ TO HAVE AND TO HOLD, the same in fee simple forever.
⑬ AND the grantor hereby covenants that the grantor is lawfully seized of said land in fee simple and has good right and lawful authority to sell and convey said land; that the grantor hereby fully warrants the title to said land and will forever warrant and defend title to said land, and that said land is free of all encumbrances, except taxes accruing subsequent to December 31, 19 ___.

TESTIMONIUM {

IN WITNESS WHEREOF, the Grantor has duly executed this deed the day and year first written above

_____⑭_____ L.S.
_____⑮_____

Witness: _____

Witness: _____

State of _____

County of _____

On this ____ day of _____ 19 ____ before me; an officer duly authorized in the state aforesaid to take acknowledgement, personally appeared

_____ known to me to be the person whose name is subscribed within the foregoing instrument and acknowledged before me that he(she) executed the same.

⑯
Notary Public
My Commission Expires: _____

SEAL _____

---

in the conveyance. The grantor must be of legal capacity. If the grantor is a guardian, or some other representative, the authority to act should be indicated in the deed. When the deed is recorded, the written authority to act, such as the power of attorney, should also be recorded.

3. *Grantee*. The grantee must be identified and be legally capable of receiving title. A conveyance to a fictitious person, a nonexistent person or an entity which is not recognized by law is a void conveyance. For example, a conveyance to an unincorporated association or to a deceased person could not take place. The grantee may use a fictitious name so long as he or she exists. However, if the deed is ambiguous as to the identity of the grantee, the deed will be void on account of vagueness.

4. *Consideration*. Except in some states, such as Nebraska and Maryland, the actual consideration does not need to be stated if the stated consideration is clearly nominal, e.g., "$10.00 and other valuable considerations." Deeds which are given by fiduciaries, such as trustees or executors, should state the actual amount of consideration involved.

5. *Granting clause*. The granting clause contains the operative words of conveyance. Without these words there can be no effective transfer of title through the deed. Care should be taken to use the appropriate words which convey the quantity and quality of title intended. State law generally specifies the words of conveyance that create a certain type of deed such as a warranty deed or a quitclaim deed. Examples of operative words:

    A. *Warranty deed:* "Grant, bargain, sell and convey"

    B. *Bargain and sale deed:* "Grant, release, bargain and sell"

    C. *Quitclaim deed:* "Release, remise, convey and quitclaim"

6. *Legal Description*. A deed that does not sufficiently identify the property to be conveyed is void. The description should be a formal legal description and not just a street address (see Chapter 7).

7. *Reservations or Exceptions*. The grantor may wish to limit the estate to be conveyed. A *reservation* creates a right which is retained by the grantor. For example, the grantor might wish to keep a life estate or an easement in the property. This could be done by including a reservation at this point in the deed. An *exception* is an exclusion of a specified portion of the land previously described in the deed. Example: Tom grants a 500-acre farm to Christine except for a quarter-acre family graveyard. (Legal description of the graveyard is included.)

8. *Deed Restrictions*. A deed restriction is a clause which limits the future use of the property granted in some manner. The restriction may be in the nature of a *condition* or a *covenant*. As was described in Chapter 8, a condition creates a conditional fee such as a fee simple determinable. The breach of a condition can lead to the forfeiture of the estate. In cases of ambiguity, the courts will attempt to interpret a deed restriction as a

covenant. A covenant is a contractual promise on the part of the grantee to restrict the use of the granted property in some manner. If a *restricted covenant* is breached, remedy is restricted to a suit for money damages or injunctive relief. Through restrictive covenants or restrictive conditions, it is possible to limit the land-use activities that are permitted, to limit height and density of structure, to require minimum floor area ratios and other such restrictions. Deed restrictions accomplish the same things for the individual that zoning and subdivision regulations accomplish for local government. If there is a conflict between the application of a zoning restriction and a deed restriction, the more restrictive of the two applies.

Example:
Jane grants Hillyvalley which is zoned R-3 to Anne with the restrictive covenant that the land be used for a single-family house. R-3 zoning permits duplexes. Anne may *not* construct a duplex permitted by the zoning ordinance.

Certain covenants which discriminate against persons on the basis of race or other reasons will not be enforced by the courts because they violate the U.S. Constitution. In order to be enforced, deed restrictions must be clearly specified. These restrictions may be included directly in the deed or cited by reference to a previously recorded plat. In addition, the restriction must be reasonable and usually must be limited in time. Many states limit deed restrictions to 20, 30, or 50 years.

9. *Recital*. The recital is not mandatory, but is included to give information useful in title examinations. The recital may be used to explain the reason for the transaction or to indicate how the grantor acquired the title.

10. *"Subject to" Clause*. In a warranty deed, title is assumed to be free and clear of all encumbrances except for those which are specifically stated in the deed. All existing encumbrances and clouds on title would be noted in this portion of the deed. This includes all unrecorded prescriptive easements, encroachments, unpaid tax assessments and any other specific liens (see Chapter 14).

11. *Appurtenances*. The premises normally end with the words, "Together with all tenements, hereditaments and appurtenances thereto belonging or in anywise appertaining." The purpose of this clause is to convey all of the property rights associated with the land. A *tenement* refers to houses, improvements an other permanent things that go with the land. *Hereditaments* refers to real and personal property which would pass to heirs by inheritance. This is to distinguish chattel real from items which are clearly personal property. *Appurtenances* refers to all incidental rights such as riparian rights or easements which belong with the land.

The Habendum

The *habendum* refers to the formal words which define the extent of ownership which is granted.

12. *Habendum*. This is a term which comes from the Latin phrase "habendum et tenendum" which means "to have and to hold." Today a habendum begins with these same words.

13. *Covenants of title*. The covenants of title, which follow the habendum, should be carefully examined to determine the quality of deed which is actually being delivered.

The Testimonium

The *testimonium* contains the execution, attestation and acknowledgment of the deed. In addition, some states may have additional requirements such as provisions for release of a spouse's interest.

14. *Execution*. The execution refers to the signing of the deed by the grantor. Originally, the signature of the grantor had to be under *seal*. A seal was an impression in hot wax which was affixed to the document in order to give it the necessary formality. Today the need for wax is no longer present. Seals are impressed on wafers of paper affixed to the deed. Many states recognize the initials L.S. which mean "in place of the seal," or the word, "seal" as a substitute. Others have no requirement for a seal unless a corporation is the grantor. While as a general rule the owner of the property personally signs a deed, certain circumstances may require a representative to sign on the owner's behalf. Such a representative is called an *attorney-in-fact* and derives authority from a *power of attorney*. A power of attorney is a formal statement of authority which is drafted with all of the formalities of a deed. The instrument should clearly specify the extent of authority being given and contain a legal description of the property which the attorney-in-fact is authorized to convey. An example of how the agent would sign a deed follows:

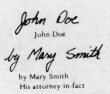

John Doe

by Mary Smith
His attorney-in-fact

15. *Attestation*. Some states require that the deed be witnessed by at least two witnesses, one of whom may need to be an official witness such as a notary. The process of witnessing is called *attestation*. Without the attestation, the deed is void in those states that have this requirement. Some deeds may require a witnessing in cases involving grantors who have not learned to write or are paralyzed. Such a handicapped grantor would be required to make a mark or at least a thumbprint which manifests intent to sign. Both the marking and the statement or declaration of intent by the grantor would need to be witnessed.

Example: John Doe
X (SEAL)
HIS MARK

Example: His
John X Doe (SEAL)
Mark

LOOK THIS UP:

Does your state require deeds to be witnessed?

Yes _____ No _____

If yes, how many? _____ witnesses

If witnesses are required, does one have to be an official witness?

Yes _____ No _____

---

16. *Acknowledgment.* An acknowledgment is necessary to permit recording of important documents such as deeds in the public records. Acknowledgment is required to ensure the authenticity of documents filed. An acknowledgment is a formal witnessing of the grantor's signature by a competent officer such as a notary public or a justice of the peace. The grantor must declare that the deed is a voluntary act; it is the legal obligation of the official to become assured of the true identity of the signer in order to prevent forgeries.

LOOK THIS UP:

Who is authorized to take an acknowledgment in your state?

_____

_____

_____

Delivery and Acceptance

In order to be legally effective, a deed must be delivered within the lifetime of the grantor. The deed may be delivered directly to the grantee or placed into escrow. There must be an objective intent to give up present control of the deed. A deed cannot pass title after the grantor's death unless it also meets the state's formalities of a will.

Example:

George prepared a deed conveying title to his niece, Frances. He intended that the deed be given to Frances upon his death. After George died, the deed was found among his personal possessions. Because the delivery had not taken place within his lifetime the deed was void and Frances received nothing. It might be noted that George could have achieved a different result by conveying his land to Frances while he was still alive and reserving a life estate for himself.

In order to complete the delivery, the grantee must accept the deed. However, acceptance is ordinarily presumed if the grantee is silent.

Recording and Taxation

Recording is not necessary in order to make an effective conveyance of title. However, if the grantee wishes to have good title against a subsequent third-party purchaser to whom the grantor fraudulently conveys the same property, recording is usually essential. Prior to January 1, 1968, there was a requirement for U.S. revenue stamps on deeds at the rate of $.55 per $500. Since the end of this requirement, some states have passed their own requirements for revenue stamps. In order to record a deed, these stamps must be attached to the instrument.

LOOK THIS UP:

Does your state levy a tax on real estate deeds and conveyances?

Yes _____ No _____

If yes,

Documentary stamps rate _____

Transfer tax rate _____

TRANSFER BY DEVISE OR DESCENT

Death is an event which results in property of the *decedent* being transferred into different ownership. A person may direct the disposition of property by leaving a will. In such case the person is said to have died *testate*. A person who has made a will is called a *testator* (male) or a *testatrix* (female). A *devise* refers to a testamentary disposition of land or real property. If a person dies without a will, the person is said to have died *intestate*. *Descent* refers to any passage of title to property upon intestacy to those heirs who are related by blood or marriage whom the law designates.

Devise (Dying With a Will)

In order to make a valid *formal will*, a person must be of statutory age, generally 18 or 21 in most states, although some states set the age as low as 14. In addition, the person must be of "sound mind" at the time of the execution of the will. A formal will must be in writing, which may be typed, printed or handwritten. Real estate must be described with sufficient certainty, but it is not required that a complete legal description be included. A formal will must be signed.

Descent (Dying Without a Will)

If a person dies intestate, the disposition of the person's property will pass as defined by state laws called *statutes of descent and distribution*. Real estate will pass directly to person's heirs as defined by the state law in which the real estate is located subject to the debts of the decedent. A court in the state where the decedent lived will appoint a person called an *administrator* to dispose of the property of the estate. The administrator will collect the assets of the estate, pay debts and distribute the remainder. The administrator is usually required to put up a bond and may sell that real property which is necessary to pay off the estate's debts if the sale of personal property produces insufficient proceeds. The real estate remains charged with debts of the estate until the state's statute of limitations has run. States have different rules as to who receives property of the decedent. For example, depending on the state, a wife might receive half the property, the same share as the children, a dower's share or the entire property.

Escheat

If a person dies without a will and leaves no heirs, the property will pass to the state. This reversion of property is called *escheat*. The state is thought of as analogous to a feudal lord who was entitled to enter upon land which became vacant because no competent tenant was left.

TRANSFER BY ADVERSE POSSESSION

Adverse possession, which is also referred to as *title by prescription* in some jurisdictions, is a method of acquiring original title to property by possession for a statutory period of time. In order to acquire such title, certain conditions must be fulfilled:

1. There must be *actual* possession which is *open* and *visible*. This means that the property must be openly used in a manner which could be readily observed. Such possession might be evidenced by the construction of improvements, the enclosure by fences or walls, the cultivation of fields or physical occupancy. Something like a hidden underground drainage pipe would not be considered sufficient.

2. The possession must be *hostile* to the true owner's title. Hostile means denial or opposition to the true owner's title. Such hostility might be evidenced by *color of title*. Color of title is any claim to title which for some reason is defective. For example, a deed which has been granted but is void because it contains a vaguely worded legal description may be used to support color of title. In cases where the claimant has color of title, many states shorten the required time period for possession. This claim to title must be *notorious*, which means that the claim must be made public.

3. Possession must be *exclusive*. This means that the claimant must claim right to the possession against the whole world; the claimant cannot share ownership in joint tenancy or tenancy in common with the true owner. Likewise, allowing the public to use the property would remove the exclusivity of possession.

4. The possession must be *continuous* and *uninterrupted* for a sufficient statutory period. If the claimant gives up occupancy, the time period must begin again. If the true owner is out of the country in the military or is a minor, the period will not begin until the disability is removed. It should be noted that a person cannot claim adversely against the state or federal government. Is the period interrupted if the claimant sells his or her interest to a purchaser? The law permits the original claimant's possession to be *tacked* to a person in privity with the claimant. Privity relates to succession of title by purchase, devise or other bond between the parties.

5. Some states require that property taxes be paid by the claimant during the time of possession.

Adverse possession is useful in clearing up title and in settling boundary disputes. Less than a possessory property interest can be conveyed by prescription. For example, use of property for a sufficient time period can ripen into an easement, that is, an easement by prescription.

LOOK THIS UP:

What is the statutory time period for adverse possession in your state?

_____ years.

If the claim is based on color of title, is the statutory period shortened?

Yes _____ No _____ If yes, how long is it?

_____ years.

Does a claimant have to pay property taxes in order to receive title by adverse possession?

Yes _____ No _____

TRANSFER BY ACCESSION

Accession refers to the idea that the owner of land is entitled to all that the soil produces or all that is added to the land either intentionally or by mistake. Consideration should be given to accretion, addition of improvements and addition to improvements.

Accretion

This refers to land which is accumulated by the gradual washing or motion of water. Title may be given by nature through accretion to owners who have land adjoining rivers, lakes or oceans. A similar process of acquiring new land is *reliction* or *dereliction*. This is a process by which water gradually recedes, leaving dry land where water was previously. Both concepts must be contrasted with *avulsion*, a sudden change in the bed of a river which had been used as a boundary by property owners. Such a sudden change conveys no new land; the dry bed remains as the boundary.

Addition of Improvements

If a person builds a house or makes other improvement on the land of another by mistake, under common law that person loses the improvement to the owner of the land. Some states have modified the harshness of this rule by statutes which permit the improvements to be moved after paying damages to the property owner.

Addition to Improvements

Any additions of fixtures other than trade fixtures by a tenant which are added without permission or agreement by the landlord, belong to the landlord on the termination of the lease (see Chapter 10).

TRANSFER BY PUBLIC ACTION OR OPERATION OF LAW

Title to property may be transferred by government action, by court judgments and by operation of law.

Government Action

Most title in land stems from grants given by the government of this country and before territory was acquired by this government from governments such as England, France, Spain or Mexico. A government grant is called a *patent*. Because of the necessity to build public improvements such as roads, airports or other public purposes, government may require the conveyance of private property through its power of eminent domain. The use of eminent domain requires just compensation at the time of the taking. This power may be delegated to private corporations that are engaged in a quasi-public activity such as power and utility companies. The process of acquiring property is called *condemnation*. Compensation is calculated on the basis of the fair market value of the property at the time of the taking. In a partial taking, a person is compensated for the loss of value to the remainder. However, in some states compensation is calculated only on the market value of the taken piece. Such losses as goodwill, loss of business during the move, personal inconvenience and certain moving costs are not normally compensated. Under some circumstances, title to property may be transferred due to forfeiture. *Forfeiture* is loss of property to the state when it is used in the commission of crime. Likewise, property may be conveyed by gift to a government. This process is called *dedication* (see Chapter 19).

Court Judgments

Courts are often involved in establishing title or causing title to be transferred as an incident to settling disputes. For example, when a mortgage is in default, the procedure for transferring title is a court remedy called *foreclosure* (see Chapter 14). Where there is a dispute among co-owners, the property may be divided or sold pursuant to a suit for *partition* (see Chapter 8). Where title is clouded or someone has acquired title by adverse possession, a *suit to quiet title* may be used to acquire good and marketable title. In cases that various parties claim disputed rights in the same property, these rights can be defined in a *declaratory judgment*. Also, the court may cause the title to transfer by ordering *specific performance* of a contract.

Operation of Law

Various transfers of property may take place by operation of law. For example, if a condition in a conditional fee is broken, the estate is forfeited, and the owner of the future interest becomes entitled to the property. In states that recognize various marital rights, property may automatically pass to both spouses when the property is acquired by one.

POINTS TO REMEMBER

1. Title transfers may be classified as (1) voluntary conveyances, (2) transfer by devise or descent, (3) transfer by adverse possession, (4) transfer by accession and (5) transfer by public action or by operation of law.

2. Title is the legally recognized evidence of a person's right to possess property.

3. A deed is a written instrument, usually under seal, conveying some property interest from a grantor to a grantee.

4. A grantor is the person who conveys the property interest; the grantee is the person to whom the grant is made.

5. A voluntary conveyance may occur by purchase or by gift; a gift of real property to the public is called a dedication.

6. Title is actually conveyed the moment that the deed is properly delivered to and accepted by the grantee.

7. When a deed is delivered, all prior oral and written agreements are merged into the deed, unless these obligations do not contradict the deed and are collateral or unless specific provisions are included in the contract which state the obligations will service the passage of title.

8. A general warranty deed, also known as a full covenant and warranty deed, formally guarantees that good and marketable title is being conveyed. The covenants which are included are seizin, right to convey, against encumbrances, quiet enjoyment, further assurances and warranty of title. In addition, some states add the covenant of trust.

9. Good title is one which is free of encumbrances; marketable title is one which is free from reasonable doubts or objections and which the courts would compel a purchaser to accept under the terms of a sales contract.

10. In a special warranty deed, the grantor does not give a covenant of warranty of title. Instead, the grantor warrants against defects that have occurred *after* the grantor acquired title.

11. A bargain and sale deed contains the covenant that the property has not been encumbered during the grantor's possession. There is an implication that the grantor has possession and has some ownership interest, usually substantial.

12. A quitclaim deed conveys whatever present interest the grantor may have in a particular property, but makes no representations or warranties of title.

13. A person who dies with a will is said to have died testate; one who dies without a will is said to have died intestate.

14. Property may pass through adverse possession if possession is actual, open, visible, hostile, notorious, exclusive and continuous and uninterrupted for a statutory period of time.

15. Accession refers to the idea that the owner of land is entitled to the products of the land and any additions to it by intention or mistake.

KEY TERMS AND PHRASES

accession	covenant of seizin	grantee
accretion	covenant of trust	grantor
acknowledgment	covenant of warranty of title	intestate
adverse possession	deed	merger
bargain and sale deed	delivery and acceptance	premises
condemnation	descent	prescription
conveyance	devise	quitclaim deed
covenant	escheat	special warranty deed
covenant against encumbrances	full covenant and warranty deed	testate
covenant of further assurance	general warranty deed	testimonium
covenant of quiet enjoyment	grant deed	title
covenant of right to convey		

QUESTIONS

1. In most states, a deed must be recorded in order to
   I. convey title from the grantor
   II. give constructive notice
   A. I only
   B. II only
   C. Both I and II
   D. Neither I nor II

2. When a warranty deed is accepted
   I. prior oral agreements are merged
   II. prior written agreements are merged
   A. I only
   B. II only
   C. Both I and II
   D. Neither I nor II

3. Under what kind of deed(s) does a grantor guarantee that good and marketable title is being conveyed?
   I. General warranty deed
   II. Quitclaim deed
   A. I only
   B. II only
   C. Both I and II
   D. Neither I nor II

4. Which kind of deed is the most desirable from the viewpoint of the grantee?
   A. General warranty deed
   B. Special warranty deed
   C. Bargain and sale deed
   D. Quitclaim deed

5. Which covenant is violated if a person attempts to grant an entire estate held in joint tenancy without concurrence of the other co-tenants?
   A. Covenant of seizin
   B. Covenant of further assurances
   C. Covenant of quiet enjoyment
   D. Covenant of warranty of title

6. Which covenant is a promise that no one has title superior to that of the grantor?
   A. Covenant against encumbrances
   B. Covenant of trust
   C. Covenant of further assurances
   D. Covenant of quiet enjoyment

7. What covenant assures the grantee that unrecorded mechanic liens will be paid from purchase price funds?
   A. Covenant of seizin
   B. Covenant of further assurances
   C. Covenant of quiet enjoyment
   D. Covenant of trust

8. What type of deed(s) warrants title *only* against defects which have occurred after the grantor acquired title?
   I. Special warranty deed
   II. Grant deed
   A. I only
   B. II only
   C. Both I and II
   D. Neither I nor II

9. If a grantor has conveyed defective title and later acquires good title, which type of deed(s) will pass the title to the grantee automatically by operation of law?
   I. Special warranty deed
   II. Quitclaim deed
   A. I only
   B. II only
   C. Both I and II
   D. Neither I nor II

10. In most states, which element(s) is essential to convey title by warranty deed?
    I. Actual consideration recited
    II. Delivery and acceptance
    A. I only
    B. II only
    C. Both I and II
    D. Neither I nor II

11. If property is sold to satisfy the debts of a person who has died testate, what kind of deed is issued?
    A. Executor's deed
    B. Administrator's deed
    C. Committee deed
    D. Deed in trust

12. Which kind of deed is given for "good" consideration?
    A. Sheriff's deed
    B. Guardian's deed
    C. Gift deed
    D. Cession deed

13. Which kind of deed is used to merge a life estate with a reversion or remainder?
    A. Deed of release
    B. Reconveyance deed
    C. Deed of surrender
    D. Correction deed

14. What is used to correct a previously delivered defective deed?
    A. Deficiency judgment
    B. Reconveyance deed
    C. Deed of release
    D. Deed of confirmation

15. Which is the most accurate about a deed granted to an unincorporated association?
    A. It is void.
    B. It must be acknowledged.
    C. It must be signed under seal.
    D. It must be confirmed by a court.

16. In most states, when does title pass under a deed?
    A. When it is dated
    B. When it is executed
    C. When it is delivered and accepted
    D. When it is acknowledged

17. If a grantor wishes to keep a life interest and convey the remainder to a relative, how can this best be accomplished?
    A. Execute a deed but do not have it delivered until death.
    B. Execute and deliver the deed reserving a life estate.
    C. Execute and deliver the deed excepting a life estate.
    D. Execute and deliver the deed restricting a life estate.

18. A breach of a _____ will lead to the forfeiture of an estate.
    I. condition
    II. covenant
    A. I only
    B. II only
    C. Both I and II
    D. Neither I nor II

19. In order to convey property encumbered with an unpaid tax assessment, how should the grantor proceed when issuing a warranty deed?
    A. Grant the property "subject to" the tax assessment.
    B. Indicate the tax assessment in the recital clause.
    C. Include the tax assessment in the appurtenances.
    D. Instruct the broker to pay the assessment from the earnest money deposit.

20. Which clause means "to have and to hold"?
    A. Hereditament
    B. Habendum
    C. Recital
    D. Tenement

21. When a deed is witnessed, this is called
    A. execution
    B. attestation
    C. recital
    D. recording

22. _____ refers to a testamentary disposition of land or other real property.
    A. Bequest
    B. Devise
    C. Descent
    D. Testate

23. The right of the state to receive your property if you die without either a will or heirs is known as
    A. dedication
    B. eminent domain
    C. escheat
    D. patent

24. A method by which title to property may be taken by actual, open, hostile and exclusive possession which is continuous and uninterrupted for a statutory period of time is called
    A. adverse possession
    B. succession
    C. reliction
    D. accession

25. A government grant of land is called a (an)
    A. addendum
    B. copyright
    C. patent
    D. statutory conveyance

26. A squatter may be able to cause a transfer of title under which theory?
    A. Voluntary alienation
    B. Succession
    C. Accession
    D. Prescription

27. Generally when does constructive notice of the transfer of legal title become effective?
    A. When a sales contract that is absolute and unconditional is signed
    B. When the deed is signed and attested
    C. When the deed is delivered and accepted
    D. When the deed is recorded

28. The covenant of quiet enjoyment means
    A. freedom from distressing noise from an adjoining property owner
    B. the seller must quietly relinquish possession
    C. the purchaser shall not be disturbed in the peaceful possession of property
    D. there are no unrecorded encumbrances on the property title

29. A deed that conveys only the present interest a person may have in a particular property is known as a

Deeds and Transfer of Title

I. general warranty deed
   II. special warranty deed
   A. I only
   B. II only
   C. Both I and II
   D. Neither I nor II
30. The difference between a general warranty deed and a special warranty deed is the
   A. covenant against encumbrances
   B. covenant of warranty forever
   C. covenant of seizin
   D. fact that the general warranty deed has present covenants, while the special warranty deed has future covenants
31. One who dies intestate is said to pass title to real property by
   A. devise
   B. descent
   C. involuntary alienation
   D. will
32. Which of the following refers to a sudden change in a river that has been set as a boundary?
   A. Accession
   B. Alluvion
   C. Avulsion
   D. Accretion
33. When only a portion of a parcel of land is being taken, _____ damages may be awarded in addition to payment for the land actually being taken.
   A. inverse condemnation
   B. severance
   C. consequential
   D. condemnation
34. What action will cause a court to order land to be sold and divide the proceeds among the co-owners?
   A. Partition
   B. Declaratory judgment
   C. Specific performance
   D. Suit to quiet title
35. Which part of the deed contains the legal description?
   A. Premises
   B. Habendum
   C. Apiladium
   D. Testimonium

If you are not sure of your answers, see page 320 for correct answers and explanations.

14

Mortgages and Liens

Before a lender is willing to lend money to a borrower there must be some assurance that the money will be paid back. One way to create such assurance is by requiring the borrower to pledge property through a mortgage to secure the debt. A borrower who gives a mortgage is called a *mortgagor* and the lender who receives the pledge is called the *mortgagee*. It is important to realize that the mortgage is given by the borrower, not the lender. The term "mortgage" is derived from the Old French term "mort" meaning dead and "gage" meaning pledge. Thus, when a mortgage note is paid off, the pledge is cancelled or becomes dead.

Real estate financing involves two separate obligations, one represented by the *promissory note* or the *bond*, the other by the mortgage or some similar security instrument. The promissory note is the primary financing obligation in which the borrower promises to pay back a sum of money borrowed. This is the main evidence of the actual debt and is a personal obligation of the borrower. The mortgage is the secondary financing obligation in which the borrower or mortgagor agrees to pledge property to secure the debt represented by the note. This chapter describes the legal aspects of the promissory note and the mortgage instrument. A discussion is given to essential elements and clauses necessary to protect the rights and interests of the parties involved in the financing transaction. Legal considerations involving other instruments are discussed as well. In addition, some thought is given to legal problems involving foreclosure and redemption. Liens are classified and the priority of liens is explained. An analysis of the economic and financial aspects of real estate financing is reserved for the next chapter.

THE PROMISSORY NOTE OR BOND

The primary evidence of a debt is the promissory note or bond. A *promissory note* is defined as a written promise to pay back a specified sum of money at specified terms and at a specified time. The primary distinction between a promissory note and a bond is that the bond is under seal. Without a valid promissory note or bond giving evidence to a debt, a mortgage is no good. A mortgage is only good so long as a debt exists. If the note is paid off or in some other fashion cancelled, the mortgage will also be cancelled. However, it should be noted that, in some areas of the country, a common practice is to incorporate both the promissory note and the mortgage into one legal document. Conceptually, these are legally two different instruments. The borrower is a person who has an obligation to pay a debt; thus the borrower is also referred to as the *obligor*. The lender is referred to as the *obligee*. If an obligor defaults on the obligation, the lender may bring a personal suit against the borrower. If insufficient money exists to pay off the judgment, the lender may move against the security pledged by the mortgage. The mortgage is usually referenced in the promissory note or bond. In order for a promissory note or bond to be valid, it must meet certain requirements:

1. There must be a *written* instrument.
2. Both the obligor and obligee must have *contractual capacity*.
3. There must be a *promise* or covenant to pay a *sum certain* by the obligor.
4. The *terms of payment* as well as the interest rate must be specified. There is ordinarily no right to prepay a promissory note unless this privilege is specified in the note itself or in the mortgage. A lender has a contractual right to expect that the money lent will be fully invested for the time specified. A *prepayment privilege clause* may provide for a small penalty if the privilege is exercised.
5. A clause providing for what constitutes *default* must be specified. It is advisable to include an *acceleration clause* in either the note or in the mortgage. An acceleration clause states that upon default all of the principal installments come due immediately. If an acceleration clause is not included, then the obligee must bring a

separate suit each time another installment is due. In a 30-year mortgage note payable in monthly installments, conceivably 360 separate suits would be required to collect all of the installments.

6. The note or bond must be properly *executed*.
7. The instrument must be voluntarily *delivered* by the obligor and *accepted* by the obligee.

LOOK THIS UP:

Which instrument is used as the primary evidence of a debt in your state?

Promissory Note _____ Bond _____

THE MORTGAGE INSTRUMENT

A *mortgage* may be defined as an interest created by a person in regards to a particular property to secure the payment of a debt or performance of some other obligation. This interest may be a lien or a conditional title interest subject to defeasance when the debt is paid or obligation fulfilled.

There exist several devices which are used to provide assurance to the lender that a loan is secured. In addition to the mortgage instrument, the reader should also be familiar with the *trust deed* and the *land contract*. These instruments are discussed in the following paragraphs.

Many of the principles used to define mortgage rights and liabilities are a result of historic development. Under early common law, when a person wished to borrow money, the lender would receive a deed upon the condition that if the loan would be paid off by a day known as *law day* the property title would be reconveyed. The English were not permitted to charge interest on their loans because any interest was considered to be usury. The lender was compensated by taking possession of the property and keeping all rents and profits. If the borrower failed to pay the debt, the property would be lost.

The king could give relief from the harshness of the forfeiture where justice required it. Sometime in the fifteenth century the king began to delegate the responsibility of hearing such cases to the king's chancellor. Later a special court called the chancery court or equity court was set up to standardize the procedure in hearing the cases. The court began to take the position in the seventeenth century that the mortgage forfeiture was unjust unless the mortgagor had waited an unreasonably long time to seek relief from the court. The right to redeem the property became almost automatic. By paying the debt owed, interest and court costs, the defaulting mortgagor could get back the property. This right is still known as the right of *equitable redemption* or *equity of redemption*.

The right of equitable redemption caused a great deal of uncertainty as to when the mortgagor would choose to exercise the right. This made land transaction more difficult and led to the development of the *foreclosure suit*. Foreclosure was a suit to bar the mortgagor's right of equitable redemption. After a mortgagor defaulted on the mortgage, the mortgagee would file a petition with the court to foreclose. The court would issue a decree which gave the mortgagor a certain time, usually about six months, to make good on the debt. If the mortgagor was unable to make good, he would be forever barred from asserting rights in the property. The title to the property would go to the mortgagee. This was known as *strict foreclosure*. This kind of foreclosure is not favored in this country because the mortgagor loses all equity invested in the property. Most states have *foreclosure by sale* in which the pledged property is sold at public auction with the proceeds used to pay off the debt and any remainder being returned to the mortgagor after a deduction of costs.

In many states, legislatures have passed a law recognizing a statutory period of redemption, usually six months to two years. This is the right to redeem property after foreclosure within the specified time period by paying the debt, interest and costs. The equity of redemption is the right to redeem up to the foreclosure sale. This is illustrated in Figure 14-1. Rules differ as to who is entitled to possession of the property during the statutory period of redemption. Most states permit the original mortgagor to continue in possession while some states give possession to the purchaser at the foreclosure sale. If the mortgagor remains in possession, very little incentive may exist to conserve and maintain the property. To correct this potential problem many mortgages provide that the mortgagee may have a *receiver* appointed to protect the property from *waste* after the date of default. A receiver is a court-appointed person who is charged with preserving a property, collecting rents and doing anything necessary to maintain the property's condition. The term *waste* refers to any impairment of the property. If the property is the mortgagor's personal residence, the receiver will ordinarily not ask the mortgagor to vacate the home but will determine a reasonable rent and treat the mortgagor like a tenant.

Figure 14-1. Equity of Redemption and Statutory Redemption

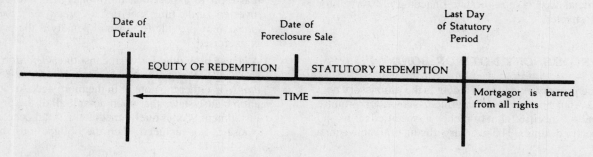

LOOK THIS UP:

Is the right to statutory redemption recognized in your state?

Yes _____ No _____

For how long a period does the statutory redemption last?

_____ (months; years)

Who is entitled to possession during the period of statutory redemption?

Mortgagor _____ Purchaser _____

The most common type of foreclosure in most states is foreclosure by sale. Foreclosure by sale takes two general forms: (1) *foreclosure by judicial sale* and (2) *foreclosure by power of sale* (also known as foreclosure by advertisement). While procedures differ from state to state, under a foreclosure by judicial sale, a petition is usually filed with the court against the defaulting mortgagor and all persons having junior lien interests in the property. The petition states the nature of the default, the amount due and the property involved. A person who has a junior lien position and is not included in the foreclosure suit is unaffected by the court decree. In order to prevent new liens from attaching while the property is being foreclosed, it is customary to file a *notice of pendency* which gives constructive notice to the world that the property is in litigation. A person who has a junior position is able to foreclose the rights of all persons in a junior position but not persons in a senior position. However, the junior lienholder may take the property subject to the senior position or redeem the senior interest. Once all parties have been notified according to state procedure, the court will make a determination whether there has been a default. If a default is declared and the mortgagor is unable to make good, the court will order the property sold at auction. Depending on local rules, a person such as a sheriff or referee will place the property for sale. After the sale is made, the court will be asked to *confirm* the price. In the process of *confirmation*, the court will determine whether the foreclosure sale was fairly held. If the price achieved is unreasonably low, the court has power to set the sale aside. If there is a surplus, the lienholders will be paid off in the order of their priority according to state rules. The mortgagor will receive any remaining amount. In situations where the proceeds from the foreclosure sale are insufficient to pay off the mortgage note, the note holder may seek a *deficiency judgment* from the court, a personal claim against the debtor.

Foreclosure under a power of sale is permitted in many states as a substitute for a foreclosure by judicial sale. A provision is included in the mortgage which gives the mortgagee the right to sell property upon default by giving proper statutory notice. There are both advantages and disadvantages to such a foreclosure. The advantages include speed and efficiency in disposing of the property. As in the judicial sale, the foreclosure under power of sale is held at a public auction with the property going to the highest bidder. Some states severely limit the right to a deficiency judgment, and there may also be some question as to the marketability of title acquired pursuant to such a sale.

Rather than going through the process of a foreclosure the mortgagor may be willing to give a *deed in lieu of foreclosure*. When a mortgagee accepts a deed in satisfaction of the mortgage debt, the mortgagor's redemption rights are terminated in the absence of any fraud. One disadvantage to the mortgagee, however, is that the property is taken subject to all of the junior liens on the property. These liens would have been terminated if the property had undergone a foreclosure sale.

A few states recognize *foreclosure by entry and possession*. This is peaceful possession or possession by a court order called a *writ of entry* by the mortgagee upon the default by the mortgagor. Some states such as Pennsylvania recognize a special type of foreclosure procedure called a *foreclosure by scire facias*. This is essentially the same as a sale by judicial sale but cannot take place until one year after default. Other peculiarities exist, and the reader should become familiar with local and state requirements.

After default but prior to foreclosure, the mortgagee may find it desirable to be able to take immediate possession of the property. In the absence of a receiver's clause in the mortgage, the mortgagee's right to possession will depend on whether a state is a *title theory, lien theory* or *intermediate theory* state. Especially in income-producing properties or ongoing businesses the right of a lender to become a *mortgagee in possession* is particularly important. By taking possession, the lender will be able to apply rents or revenues to the payment of interest and reduction of the mortgage. In addition, the lender will be able to maintain the property and preserve the goodwill of an operating business. This right exists in a title theory state but not in a lien theory state. A *title theory* state holds that a mortgage actually conveys title subject to a condition. This type of mortgage contains a *defeasance clause* which states that, when the condition is met, the debt is satisfied; title will automatically pass back to the borrower. In *lien theory* states, a mortgage merely creates a lien right in the mortgagee with the mortgagor retaining the title. *Intermediate theory* states are similar to title theory states in that title is said to pass to the mortgagee upon default. Due to problems involving possession and foreclosure, a borrower and lender may choose to use a trust deed as a substitute for the mortgage instrument. One state, Georgia, recognizes a lien theory mortgage, but most parties in the state substitute a *security deed* which has the advantage of a title theory instrument. Today it is not necessary for the borrower to give up possession when a mortgage is given. When one pledges property without giving up possession, the person is said to *hypothecate* the property.

LOOK THIS UP:

Are foreclosures by power of sale recognized in your state?

Yes _____ No _____

Are strict foreclosures recognized in your state?

Yes _____ No _____

Are foreclosures by entry and possession recognized in your state?

Yes _____ No _____

What mortgage theory does your state recognize?

Title _____ Lien _____ Intermediate _____

Trust Deeds

Unlike a mortgage, which involves only two parties, a trust deed involves three parties. States which permit this type of security instrument have passed trust deed acts specifying the various requirements in the state. The borrower under a note secured by a trust deed or *deed of trust* is called the *trustor* or in some states the *grantor*. The lender is called the *beneficiary*. When a loan is made, the borrower conveys *naked title* to a third party called the *trustee*, who holds the title for the benefit of the lender although the instrument itself may remain in the lender's possession. A state's trust deed act specifies who may act as a trustee. Some states have created the office of public trustee, while others allow individuals such as attorneys or brokers or entities such as title insurance companies or savings and loan associations to serve in that capacity. As with mortgages, states have title theory and lien theory trust deeds (see Figure 14–2).

If a note is in default, the trustee may hold a *trustee's sale* or use a court-ordered foreclosure. As procedures differ slightly from state to state, care should be taken to consult the local law. A foreclosure based on a trustee's sale takes the following steps:

1. Lender notifies the trustee of the borrower's default in a document called a *beneficiary's notice of default and election to sell*.
2. The trustee files a notice of default in the public records and notifies the borrower of this fact.
3. For a statutory period of time (90 to 180 days depending on the particular state law) the borrower may make good on the default, and this will terminate the proceedings. This right is analogous to equitable redemption in the mortgage.
4. Once the statutory waiting period has passed, the trustee may begin advertising the sale for a statutory period. After the advertising is placed but before the actual sale, the borrower may pay off the note plus any accrued interest and expenses incurred by the trustee.
5. After proper advertising, the property is put up for bid at public auction in the jurisdiction where the property is located.
6. The successful bidder receives a trustee's deed with whatever title the original borrower has possessed. In many states, the bidder must be able to produce cash at the sale.

LOOK THIS UP:

Does your state recognize trust deeds?

Yes _____ No _____

Who may serve as a trustee in your state?

As with mortgages, state rules on statutory redemption differ. One advantage of the trust deed may be the cutting off or limitation on the statutory redemption period. Foreclosure of a trust deed by a trustee's sale may be speedier than the process needed to foreclose a mortgage. Care should be taken, however, because some states do not permit deficiency judgments unless there is a judicial foreclosure.

When a note or bond is paid off, the lender will deliver the note or bond and the trust deed to the trustee for cancellation. The trustee then will issue a *trustee's deed of reconveyance* to the borrower. This has the same effect as a mortgage release or satisfaction piece. To clear any clouds on title created by the recording of the trust deed, the deed of reconveyance may also be recorded.

Land Contracts

A land contract is also referred to as a *land sales contract*, an *installment land contract*, an *agreement for purchase and sale*, or a *contract for a deed*. The terminology depends on the local custom. This is a type of financing agreement between a seller of property and a purchaser. The seller passes possession but retains title to the property until the total or a substantial portion of the purchase price is paid. It is essentially an agreement to deliver a deed at a certain time provided that the purchaser meets all of the conditions of the contract. If the purchaser defaults, the seller can normally cancel the contract and keep all payments as rent. This type of agreement is not favored by courts in many states because the failure to meet an installment payment date could cause a purchaser to lose all invested equity without the benefit of a foreclosure hearing and other protections such as the equity of redemption or statutory redemption. In order to protect the purchaser from unfair and unscrupulous sellers, many states require a foreclosure proceeding if the purchaser has substantial equity invested.

Land contracts are often used for the sale of unimproved lots and for recreation property. People who cannot qualify for long-term financing because of a poor credit

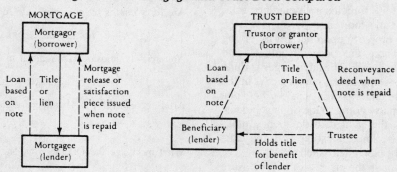

Figure 14–2. Mortgage and Trust Deed Compared

rating may be able to purchase property through the use of this device. It is not uncommon for a land contract to require a low downpayment and a term of seven or more years to pay off the obligation (see Chapter 15). Land contracts are seldom recorded, even though it is advisable to do so. Therefore, if the seller incurs debts which are reduced to a court judgment, it is possible or a lien to attach on the land since the title is still in the seller's name.

REQUIREMENTS FOR A VALID MORTGAGE INSTRUMENT

The requirements for a valid mortgage or deed of trust are very similar to the requirements of a valid deed since both instruments convey an interest in land and must stipulate requirements necessary to permit recordation. Both mortgages and deeds of trust will be referred to as mortgage instruments for the purpose of subsequent discussion. A valid mortgage (deed of trust) instrument should provide for the following:

1. There must be a written instrument involving a mortgagor and mortgagee, each having contractual capacity. These parties must be identified in the instrument. Where the mortgagor is a co-owner of the property to be pledged, or where curtesy or dower rights are recognized, the co-owners or spouse should also be identified and join in the mortgage.
2. The property interest being pledged must be specified. For example, if the mortgagor only possesses a leasehold, this leasehold must be described.
3. A legal description of the property must be included.
4. Words of conveyance should be used which are compatible with either the title theory or lien theory which prevails in the state where the property is located. These words are often referred to as the mortgaging clause.
5. A statement of the obligation should be included. This can be done by referring to the obligation in the promissory note or bond. In order to preserve the confidentiality of the transaction, financial information such as the interest rate is seldom included on the mortgage instrument, but it is included on the note, which is ordinarily not recorded. It should be made clear that the mortgage is being given to secure payment of a debt or some other obligation. Without a debt or some other obligation there can be no mortgage.
6. Any promises or covenants must be included. As described in a previous section, such covenants might include a prepayment clause and an acceleration clause. In addition, a mortgage instrument may contain several other kinds of clauses. Some of the more common are described in the following paragraphs. These clauses may be classified into four general categories according to the purposes they are intended to serve. The categories are: (1) clauses to facilitate foreclosure, (2) clauses to define or add to rights of mortgagee, (3) clauses to preserve asset from impairment or liens and (4) clauses to define or add to rights of mortgagor.

Clauses to Facilitate Foreclosure

When a mortgage is given, a promise is made in a *covenant to pay indebtedness* that the mortgagor will pay back money borrowed under the note. A failure to fulfill this covenant will permit the lender to foreclose on the property. If a lender wishes to have a receiver appointed to manage the property after a default and before foreclosure, this right may be granted by including a *receiver clause*. A similar right is agreed to in a *clause providing for assignment of rents upon default*. This clause permits the mortgagee to enter the premises after default and collect rents, manage the property and use the net proceeds to pay interest and amortization of the principal. Some mortgages include a provision called a *cognovit* or *confess judgment clause* which empowers the mortgagee's attorney to confess default by the mortgagor to a court. In states that recognize foreclosure by power of sale, a *statutory power of sale clause* is included in the mortgage or deed of trust to permit this kind of foreclosure action. After default of a mortgage, the lender may wish to be able to treat the borrower as a tenant and collect rents for the use of the premises. This power can be agreed to in an *owner rental clause*.

Clauses to Define or Add to Rights of Mortgagee

As in a deed, the mortgagor gives various covenants warranting the quality of title in states that recognize the title theory of mortgages. The lender may find it desirable to include provisions which will increase the interest rate to the market rate upon the default of the mortgagor. In inflationary times, the mortgagee may wish to cause the interest rate on the note to increase if an agreed to national index also increases (see variable rate mortgages in Chapter 15). Both of these goals can be accomplished by including an *escalation clause* permitting the lender to raise the interest rate upon the occurrence of certain stipulated conditions. If the mortgage covers real property and personal property, the personal property should be specified in a *personal property clause* (see package mortgages in Chapter 15). Similar to this clause is the *afteracquired personal property clause* which states that any personal property which is attached to the real property becomes added to the original security pledged by the mortgage. A *condemnation clause* may be included to require that the borrower apply any condemnation award received in a whole or partial taking by government to pay off the mortgage principal. If the borrower is tardy in making installments, a *late payment clause* can be used to assess a penalty for the delay. Care should be taken not to make the late payment unreasonable or to violate the state usury law. If a lender wishes to sell or assign the mortgage and note to another investor, it is necessary to determine what amount still remains on the principal. The borrower can be required to issue an *estoppel certificate* which states how much is owed if the mortgage contains an *estoppel certificate clause*. In some jurisdictions, the estoppel certificate is known as the *certificate of no defense* and, when issued, bars any defenses the borrower may have that the principal amount stated is not the true amount.

Clauses to Preserve Asset from Impairment or Liens

The lender may wish to provide that if the property is not kept insured for the benefit of the lender or if property taxes or special assessments are not paid, this will cause the mortgage to go into default. Such clauses are commonly called the *insurance covenant* and the *tax covenant*. If a senior lienholder forecloses on a defaulted senior mortgage or trust deed, a junior lienholder's security may disappear. If the borrower has been making payments and met other conditions, no default would exist in regards to the junior mortgage unless a *default in prior mortgage clause* was also included. A *covenant against removal* would prevent the destruction or removal of any improvements on the land. If the lender wished the borrower to keep the property in good repair and constantly maintained, a *covenant against waste* could be included. This clause would be very important in those jurisdictions which have strict housing code enforcement. Violation of the housing code could result in repairs being made by the local government and a senior lien being placed on the property or even the removal of the entire building for reasons of health and public safety. As in the deed, some states would recognize a *trust clause* which would require the borrower to pay all prior unrecorded mechanic liens which might impair the lender's priority. Some states impose a tax on the lender holding a mortgage. If this tax were raised, the lender's yield might be severely impaired. A *Brundage clause* would permit the lender to call a mortgage note due upon the event of a rise in the mortgage tax.

Clauses to Define or Add to Rights of Mortgagor

For various commercial reasons, a borrower may wish to include some rights which are not included unless provisions exist to the contrary in the mortgage instrument. One such clause is the *partial release clause* which permits the sale of individual lots when one blanket mortgage covers an entire tract of land. Without a partial release clause the borrower would have to pay off the entire mortgage note before a small portion of the tract could be sold.

Example:
Joe borrows $150,000 from the XYZ bank to purchase and develop 30 acres of land into 60 one-half acre lots. The bank will release a lot under the mortgage if Joe pays them 4% of the original principal amount due. When this amount is paid, Joe may have two lots released, one designated by Joe and one by the bank. By requiring two lots to be released and by requiring more than a proportionate share of the principal to be paid off, the bank protects itself from releasing all of the choice lots and being left with inferior lots as security.

A second such clause is the *subordination clause*, used to change the priority of a senior lien to a junior position. Such a clause is often included in a purchase money mortgage which is used in the acquisition of acreage property requiring a later construction and development loan. A commercial bank or insurance company may be legally prohibited from lending large amounts of money unless it has a first-lien priority.

Example:
Alice agrees to purchase 100 acres from Farmer Brown for $50,000 down and a purchase money mortgage of $250,000 for the remainder of the price. Alice has paid a price slightly higher than the prevailing market price in order to induce Farmer Brown to subordinate his position to a $1 million loan secured by a mortgage being issued by Greensprings Commercial Bank. If the bank issues a $2 million loan, what happens? Farmer Brown will be subordinated to a $1 million mortgage, his mortgage of $250,000 will be in second position, and the remaining $1 million of the bank will be in third-lien position.

A third kind of clause is a provision which limits the borrower's personal liability to the equity invested in the mortgaged property. This is a type of exculpatory clause, variously called in different parts of the country a *sole security clause* or a *hold-harmless clause*. Such a clause is often included in a purchase money mortgage used to acquire acreage in a speculative land market. If the market turns sour, such a mortgagor can walk away without fear of personal liability and deficiency judgments.

7. The mortgage must be properly executed according to state law. Execution requires a voluntary signature by the mortgagor. If there are co-owners or dower and curtesy rights involved, the co-owner or spouse must also join in the execution. Some states may require attestation by witnesses and a seal.

8. The instrument must be voluntarily delivered by the mortgagor and accepted by the mortgagee.

9. In order to give constructive notice to the world that there is a lien or a conditional title held by the mortgagee, the instrument must be recorded. In order to record, the instrument must be acknowledged in the same way as was the deed, and in some states a recordation tax or filing fee must be paid. In addition, some states may require the mortgagee to pay a yearly intangible tax to keep the instrument enforceable in a court.

RIGHTS OF THIRD PARTIES

Third persons to the mortgage can acquire rights and liabilities when either the mortgage or mortgagee transfers these rights or liabilities. For example, if there is an existing mortgage on a property and the mortgagor wishes to sell the property, the new purchaser can take the property *subject to* the mortgage or the purchaser may *assume* the mortgage. When a purchaser takes subject to a mortgage, no personal liability is undertaken to the lender. The purchaser could theoretically walk away from the mortgage and lose nothing but the equity already invested. If the purchaser assumes the mortgage, he or she becomes personally liable on any deficiencies occurring in a foreclosure sale (see Figure 14–3). In both situations, the original borrower is liable to the lender unless specifically released in a *novation* (see Chapter 5). A mortgage may contain a *nonassumption* clause or *due on sale* clause which prohibits an assumption without consent of the lender. Such consent is normally given for a fee and a possible jump in the interest rate if the contract rate is below the prevailing market rate. In a situation when a person is taking subject to or assuming a mortgage, it is useful to find out how much remains unpaid on the principal

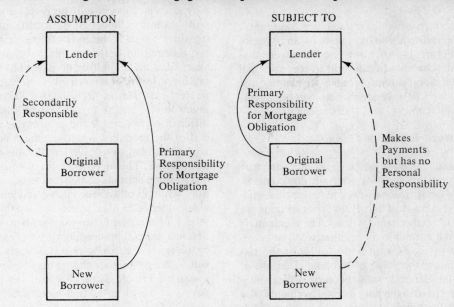

Figure 14–3. Mortgage Assumption Versus Subject To

balance. The mortgagee may be requested to furnish a *certificate of reduction of mortgage*. Like the estoppel certificate which is given by the mortgagor, the certificate of reduction bars the issuer from pleading any subsequent defenses that the principal stated is incorrect.

A mortgage may be assigned to a new mortgagee by the original mortgagee. A form called an *assignment of mortgage* is used to make the transfer. Often included in this assignment is a provision called a *no recourse clause* which prevents the original mortgagee from being held personally liable in the event that the mortgagor defaults.

LIENS

Consider a hypothetical situation in which Janet and Bobby Harrison purchase a newly constructed house from XYZ Development Company. Due to financial problems, the company goes into bankruptcy soon after Janet and Bobby have closed on the house by paying their life savings of $50,000 cash. Two months after closing they receive a registered letter in the mail advising them that Angus Wicker, a subcontractor, has recorded a mechanic's lien of $20,000 for work performed in building the house and unless he is paid, Angus intends to bring a court action to foreclose on the house to satisfy the debt. Janet and Bobby also discover that there is an unpaid special assessment of $2,500 and an unpaid property tax bill of $900 owed to the county. They consult an attorney and are advised that they must pay off all three liens or face losing the house in a foreclosure action or a tax sale. Janet and Bobby have no title insurance to indemnify them for the loss, and there is no legal action they can take against XYZ Development Company, which is protected by federal bankruptcy laws. They feel they have been ill-served by the real estate broker who negotiated the sale of the house for failing to advise them about the possibility of liens. They advise all of their friends to avoid the broker in the future.

A *lien* is a legally recognized right to enforce a claim or charge on the property of another for payment of some debt, duty or obligation. A lien may be created voluntarily, such as by the giving of a mortgage, or it may be created involuntarily, such as by the imposition of a mechanic's lien. The lien may be *specific* (*in rem*) in that it attaches to a particular property or it may be *general* (*in personam*) in that it attaches to all property owned by an individual. This right may be enforced by the judicial sale of a person's property if the claim or charge which the property secures is not satisfied. A lien is a type of *encumbrance* on property. An encumbrance is any interest in the land of another which in some manner burdens or diminishes the value of property. Because liens diminish the use of land or quality of title, where they exist there may be problems with the marketability and insurability of title.

HOW ARE LIENS CLASSIFIED?

There are three classifications of liens which indicate the legal basis of their creation: (1) contractual liens, (2) statutory liens and (3) equitable liens. *Contractual liens* are created by agreement of parties. A common example of a contractual lien is a mortgage which is given to secure the debt represented by a promissory note. A *statutory lien* is created when requirements specified in state law are fulfilled. For example, when a judgment is issued by a court against a person, a lien attaches over all of that person's property which is the legal effect specified by state statute. An *equitable lien* is created when justice and fairness would require a court of equity to declare that such a lien exists or when conduct of parties would imply that a lien was intended. For example, if a tenant in common made necessary repairs to a house which was in danger of collapse and in violation of the housing code, an equitable lien would attach to the other co-tenants' undivided interest for a proportionate share of the expenses. The person who owns the lien is called the *lienor* while the person whose property is burdened by the lien is called the *lienee*.

SPECIFIC LIENS

The principal kinds of specific liens are mortgages, mechanic's and materialman's liens, tax liens and special assessments. (See Figure 14–4.) Mortgage liens were discussed earlier in this chapter. In addition to the principal kinds of liens, the reader should be able to identify the following liens: vendor's lien, vendee's lien, bail bond lien, judgments in rem, attachment, and lis pendens.

Mechanic's and Materialman's Liens

Mechanic's and materialman's liens are statutory liens levied on property by persons who are not compensated after providing labor (mechanic) or material (materialman) for the improvements to land. Both types of liens are commonly referred to as mechanic's liens. The mechanic's lien is justified on the equitable theory that work or materials provided by contractors add to the value of the improvements and increase the value of the land. Because of this theory, work and materials must become permanently attached or incorporated into the land or improvements. For example, if a materialman provides lumber which is merely stored in a warehouse, no specific lien would attach to the land on which the warehouse stands. Likewise, if a property owner hires workmen to build a fence on only one of his two lots, the workmen may not levy a lien on both lots, but only on the lot that they built the fence on. Some states permit those who rent out construction equipment used on the property to levy a lien, others do not.

Tax Liens and Special Assessments

As will be discussed in Chapter 19, local governments have the right to assess and collect taxes on real property located within the taxing jurisdiction. A failure to pay these taxes can result in the levying of a tax lien which, in most states, is prior and senior to all other liens, even those which pre-existed the tax lien. If the lien is not satisfied within the time period specified at law, the taxed property may be sold at a tax sale. The defaulting taxpayer will be sent a tax sale notice advising of the impending sale. This gives the taxpayer an opportunity to appeal and state a defense or to pay the tax. If the tax is still not paid, the property will be put up for sale at a public sale. The purchaser at auction will be given a *tax certificate* which will entitle the holder of the certificate to a tax deed or a treasurer's deed at the end of the tax redemption period. The tax redemption period is the time, usually two to seven years, that the defaulting taxpayer has to make good on the tax owed to the purchaser plus interest and legal fees. The interest may run as high as 18%, although generally it is much lower, and is usually payable semi-annually. Rules differ in each state. If the property is not redeemed by the end of the redemption period, the holder of the certificate will be entitled to receive a quitclaim deed from the taxing jurisdiction. This deed is in the nature of a quitclaim deed and in some states is considered to be very weak evidence of title, while in other states it is considered to be very acceptable evidence of title. Instead of just taking such a deed, the holder of the certificate may wish to foreclose on the tax lien in a judicial proceeding to cut off all other claims on the property. Where a city provides water and other utilities, a *water charge* or other charge may be levied on the property. The legal effect, if the charge is not satisfied by the taxpayer, is the same as if it were a tax lien.

LOOK THIS UP:
How long is the tax redemption period in your jurisiction?

When a property receives a special benefit which differs significantly from the benefit that the public at large receives from a government improvement, the property may be charged with a *special assessment*. For example, if a government widens a road adjoining the property, or builds sewers, sidewalks or a nearby neighborhood park, the owners of property benefiting from this action may be required to pay a special assessment. The assessment will ordinarily be levied on the proportionate benefit to the property and not as a percentage of the value of the property.

Example:
The city constructs a sidewalk costing $1,500 in front of three lots of similar size. The lots have houses costing $50,000, $80,000 and $120,000, respectively. How much will each lot

Figure 14–4. Difference Between General Lien and Specific Lien

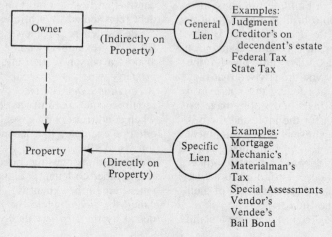

be assessed? Since each lot benefited equally from the sidewalk, each lot would have a $500 special assessment imposed.

Vendor's Lien

A vendor's lien is one which originated in equity and arose when a seller of land financed the purchase without taking back a mortgage to secure the payment of a promissory note. The seller has a lien on the unpaid balance. This lien has been codified as a statutory lien in most states.

Vendee's Lien

This is an equitable lien on the land of a seller after the purchase price has been paid or after expenditures were made to improve the property on the understanding that a deed would be delivered. If the seller defaults on the delivery of the deed, a vendee's lien can be placed on the land. The lien is for the money actually given to the seller and for some additional expenditures made in anticipation of the sale.

Bail Bond Lien

When a person is arrested, a bail bond may be set permitting release from imprisonment until the time of the trial. The bond will be forfeited if the accused fails to appear. This bail bond can be arranged by paying a fee to a professional bail bondsman, by putting up the money in cash, or by pledging real property located in the jurisdiction. If real property is pledged, the amount of the bond constitutes a bail bond lien on the property.

Judgments in Rem

A judgment in rem is an adjudication as to the status of a particular property. The term is often used interchangeably with the term "specific lien," but is in fact a much broader concept.

Attachment

Attachment is the process of taking a person's property into legal custody by a court order called a *writ of attachment*. A writ of attachment may be issued upon the commencement of a lawsuit. A writ may be issued out of fear that the defendant is planning to dispose of property and flee the state, or, if the defendant is outside the state, as a way to bring the defendant within the court's jurisdiction. The attachment will remain on the property until the lawsuit is concluded or if the defendant posts a bond equal to the amount in dispute plus court costs or other amount specified by law. By attachment, a plaintiff is assured of the existence of property to levy upon in the case that the lawsuit is successful.

Lis Pendens

Lis pendens is notice filed for the purpose of serving constructive notice that title or some matter involving particular real property is in litigation. Any person who acquires land under a notice of lis pendens will take it subject to any adverse judgment which may result.

GENERAL LIENS

The principal kinds of general liens are judgment liens, liens of creditors on decedent's estate and federal and state tax liens.

Judgment Liens

A judgment is the final legal determination of rights between disputants by a court of competent jurisdiction. The effect is the same whether it is a state or federal court. When the judgment is for a money award, the party who gains under the judgment is called the *judgment creditor* and the person burdened by the judgment is called the *judgment debtor*. Once a certified abstract of the court judgment is recorded it becomes a lien upon all of the judgment debtor's real and personal property within the jurisdiction. The lien may be suspended by posting a bond until the time for final appeal has expired or an appeal has been turned down by the appellate court. This abstract is recorded in a judgment docket kept by the county clerk or other public official which is arranged alphabetically according to the names of judgment debtors. This places a cloud on title of all real property owned by the judgment debtor for the statutory time of the judgment lien or until the lien is satisfied. When a judgment is a lien on all property of the judgment debtor, it is called a *judgment in personam* as contrasted to a *judgment in rem*, which applies only to a specific property. The statutory time period is set by state law, in most states 10 years.

Liens of Creditors on Decedent's Estate

When a person dies, creditors have a lien on all real and personal property of the decedent. This lien is superior to any rights that heirs may have irrespective of whether the decedent dies testate or intestate, except for the order that property will be sold to satisfy debts. Where there is a will, the executor will first sell undesignated personal property, then designated personal property, called bequests, then, if the debts are still not satisfied, real property. When a person dies intestate, the administrator will first sell personal property; if this is insufficient, then real property may be sold. Creditors also have a general equitable claim on all real property which a person owns while alive. This claim has no effect unless the debtor attempts to convey real property as a gift. Such a conveyance may be viewed as an attempt to defraud creditors and will be set aside by the court.

Federal and State Tax Liens

When a person dies, his or her estate is subject to a state inheritance tax and a federal estate tax. These taxes cause a lien to attach on all real and personal property in the estate for a statutory period or until the tax is paid. The statutory period for federal tax liens is 10 years; each state defines its own time period. If a person fails to pay federal income taxes, the government may issue a tax warrant which, when recorded in the federal tax docket in the county records, attaches a federal tax lien. Similar provisions exist as to state income taxes in the many states.

PRIORITY OF LIENS

What happens when two or more liens attach to the same property? Which lien has priority in a foreclosure action? This is important when insufficient proceeds are generated in a foreclosure sale to satisfy all liens. If a senior lienholder is the party bringing the foreclosure action, all junior liens are extinguished at the sale. But when a junior lienholder brings a foreclosure action, the property is sold subject to all existing senior liens. In order to determine the priority of liens, the reader should be familiar with the treatment of three basic rules in each state.

Rule One

What is the priority of tax liens and special assessments in a state? In most states, specific liens and special assessments take priority over all private liens no matter when the private liens have attached. This helps explain why many mortgage lenders require that property taxes be paid in advance into an escrow account or that some mortgages make nonpayment of property taxes and special assessments a default of the mortgage.

Rule Two

Priority of all other liens, except for specific statutory exceptions such as mechanic's liens, are defined by the state's recording statute. The general rule is that the lien which is first recorded is superior to all subsequent liens. This is usually true unless the lienholder recording first had actual or constructive notice of a prior claim. The reader should be familiar with the distinction between actual notice and constructive notice. *Actual notice* is the actual knowledge that a person has about the existence of a particular fact. For example, Sally tells Ken that she sold her house to David. Ken has actual notice of the sale to David. *Constructive notice* is the knowledge that the law presumes a person has about a particular fact, irrespective of whether the person knows about the fact or not. Any information which is recorded properly in the public records or announced in an official legal newspaper is constructive notice on every person in the world. (See Figure 14–5.)

Rule Three

Irrespective of the rule of priorities established by the state's recording statute, in some states subsequent recorded mechanic's liens may nevertheless still have priority.

In addition to the three rules which have been described, the reader should note that priority liens can be reordered by contract, that is, a subordination agreement by a senior lienholder, or by operation of law, that is, order by a court in bankruptcy for certain kinds of priorities.

Figure 14–5. Actual Versus Constructive Notice

Actual Notice	Constructive Notice
Any information of which a person has direct knowledge	Any information a person is presumed by law to know, even if the information is not actually known.
Examples: 　Anything seen 　Anything heard 　Anything read 　Anything felt	*Examples:* 　All official laws 　Publicly recorded documents 　Legal notices 　People in possession 　Information available by inspection

POINTS TO REMEMBER

1. Real estate financing involves two separate obligations. The primary obligation to pay back borrowed money is represented by a promissory note or bond. The secondary obligation which is a pledge of property to secure the debt is represented by a mortgage or a trust deed.

2. Under a promissory note or bond the borrower is called an obligor and the lender is called the obligee.

3. A mortgage instrument creates an interest in a person in regards to a particular property to secure the payment of a debt or the performance of some other obligation. This interest may be a lien or a conditional title interest subject to defeasance when the debt is paid or the obligation fulfilled. The borrower is known as the mortgagor and the lender on the note called the mortgagee.

4. Equity of redemption is the time period that a mortgagor has to satisfy a default prior to foreclosure. Statutory redemption is the time period that a person may redeem a property after foreclosure by paying the debt, interest and costs.

5. If the proceeds from the foreclosure sale are insufficient to pay off the mortgage note, the noteholder may seek a deficiency judgment from the court which is a personal claim against the debtor.

6. When a mortgagee accepts a deed in satisfaction of the mortgage debt, the mortgagor's rights of redemption are terminated, but the property is taken subject to the existence of all liens.

7. Three mortgage theories prevail in this country: the title theory, the lien theory and the intermediate theory. In a title theory state, a mortgage conveys title subject to a condition which is defeased when the debt is satisfied. In a lien theory state, a mortgage merely creates a lien right in the mortgagee with the mortgagor retaining title. In an intermediate theory state, title will pass to the mortgagee upon default. A borrower who mortgages property is said to hypothecate it. Hypothecation involves pledging property without actually giving up possession.

8. A trust deed is used as a substitute for a mortgage in many states. A trust deed involves three parties: the trustor or borrower under a note, a beneficiary who is

the lender and a trustee who is a statutorily approved fiduciary who holds naked title to the property until the note is satisfied or until the property must be foreclosed because of a default. Foreclosure of a trust deed may take place by a trustee's sale or by judicial foreclosure.

9. A land contract is a financing arrangement in which actual title to land does not pass until the total or a substantial portion of the purchase price is paid.

10. A purchaser of property with an existing mortgage may either assume the mortgage or take subject to the mortgage in the absence of a prohibition in the mortgage instrument. A person who assumes a mortgage becomes personally liable to the mortgagee; this does not occur when the purchaser takes subject to the mortgage. In both cases, the original mortgagor is liable for deficiencies unless the lender has agreed to a novation.

11. A lien is a legally recognized right to enforce a claim or charge on the property of another for payment of some debt, duty or obligation.

12. A lien may be specific (in rem) in that it attaches to a particular property or it may be general (in personam) in that it attaches to all property owned by an individual.

13. The principal kinds of specific liens are mortgages, mechanic's lien, tax liens and special assessments.

14. A mechanic's lien is a statutory lien levied on property by persons who are not compensated after providing labor or supplying materials for the improvements to land.

15. Actual notice is the actual knowledge that a person has about the existence of a particular fact; constructive notice is the knowledge that the law presumes a person has about a particular fact, irrespective of whether the person knows about the fact or not.

16. In most states, specific tax liens and special assessments take priority over all private liens, no matter when the private liens have attached.

KEY TERMS AND PHRASES

actual notice
assumption
beneficiary
bond
confirmation of sale
constructive notice
contract for a deed
default
defeasance clause
deficiency judgment
due on sale clause
equitable redemption
encumbrance
escalation clause
estoppel certificate

foreclosure
general lien
hypothecation
installment land contract
intermediate theory mortgage state
land contract
lien
lien theory mortgage state
lis pendens
mechanic's lien
mortgage
mortgagee
mortgagor
obligor

obligee
partial release clause
prepayment privilege
promissory note
special assessment
specific lien
statutory redemption
subordination clause
subject to mortgage
tax certificate
title theory mortgage state
trust deed (deed of trust)
trustee
trustor

QUESTIONS

1. In a mortgage and promissory note, who is commonly known as the lender?
   I. Obligee
   II. Mortgagee
   A. I only
   B. II only
   C. Both I and II
   D. Neither I nor II

2. In a deed of trust, who is the person making the pledge of property as security of a debt?
   A. Trustor
   B. Mortgagor
   C. Trustee
   D. Beneficiary

3. In a real estate financing transaction, which instrument represents the primary obligation to repay a debt?
   A. Mortgage
   B. Deed
   C. Promissory deed
   D. Promissory note

4. A clause which causes all future installments of a mortgage note to become due at the option of the lender upon the default of the borrower is referred to as the
   A. extension agreement
   B. defeasance clause
   C. escalation clause
   D. acceleration clause

5. The right of a borrower who has defaulted on a mortgage to pay off the debt plus any accrued costs and interest after foreclosure is based on a right called

A. statutory redemption
B. equity of redemption
C. prepayment privilege
D. novation

6. What kind of foreclosure causes the borrower to lose all equity in a mortgaged property?
   A. Strict foreclosure
   B. Foreclosure by judicial seal
   C. Foreclosure by power of sale
   D. Trustee's sale

7. A court may turn aside a sale made during a foreclosure by power of sale if the court finds irregularities or a clear miscarriage of justice during what process?
   A. Pendency
   B. Confirmation
   C. Deficiency judgment
   D. Defeasance

8. When a lender takes a deed in lieu of foreclosure after a mortgage is in default, which of the following statements is true?
   I. The lender may seek a deficiency judgment if the market value of the property is insufficient to cover the debt.
   II. The property is taken subject to all junior liens.
   A. I only
   B. II only
   C. Both I and II
   D. Neither I nor II

9. When a trust deed is cancelled, what is used to clear the lien created in the public records?
   A. Estoppel certificate
   B. Certificate of reduction
   C. Deed of reconveyance
   D. Brundage clause

10. A financing arrangement in which the seller does not convey title until the debt has been satisfied is called a
    A. purchase money mortgage
    B. land contract
    C. promissory note
    D. deed of reconveyance

11. When a mortgage is cancelled, what document is given to the mortgagor?
    A. Estoppel certificate
    B. Deed of reconveyance
    C. Defeasance certificate
    D. Satisfaction piece

12. When a person pledges property without giving up possession, this is known as
    A. defeasance
    B. novation
    C. brundage
    D. hypothecation

13. A clause in a mortgage in which the mortgagor promises to maintain the property and keep it in good repair is called
    A. covenant against removal
    B. trust clause
    C. covenant against waste
    D. cognovit clause

14. In a blanket mortgage, what clause gives the developer the right to sell an individual lot without paying off the entire principal amount secured by the mortgage?
    A. Partial release clause
    B. Prepayment privilege clause
    C. Subordination clause
    D. Exculpatory clause

15. What frees a mortgagor of personal liability under a mortgage?
    A. When a new purchaser takes subject to the mortgage
    B. When a new purchaser assumes the mortgage
    C. When a new purchaser assumes the mortgage and there is a novation
    D. When the mortgage is assigned by the lender

16. In order to determine the amount that is owed on the principal secured by a mortgage, which of the following is true?
    I. The mortgagee may furnish a certificate of reduction of mortgage.
    II. The mortgagor may furnish an estoppel certificate.
    A. I only
    B. II only
    C. Both I and II
    D. Neither I nor II

17. An agreement between two lenders to join in the financing of a project is called a
    A. spreading agreement
    B. participation agreement
    C. consolidation agreement
    D. collective mortgage agreement

18. When a lender enters upon property which is secured by a mortgage defaulted by the borrower, and the lender collects rents and maintains the property until foreclosure, the lender is referred to as a
    A. mortgagee in possession
    B. receiver
    C. trustor
    D. collection agent

19. A lien which is attached to a particular property is a
    I. judgment in rem
    II. judgment in personam
    A. I only
    B. II only
    C. Both I and II
    D. Neither I nor II

20. What do a lien and an easement share in common?
    A. They are both encumbrances.
    B. They both must be recorded to be valid.
    C. They can only be created by statute in order to be authorized in a state.
    D. They cannot be involuntarily imposed on the property without the consent of the owner.

21. A statutory lien which permits a laborer to levy upon property on which work was done without compensation is referred to as a
    A. mechanic's lien
    B. performance bond lien
    C. vendor's lien
    D. vendee's lien

22. When a person purchases property at a tax sale, what will ordinarily be given the purchaser by the sheriff before the redemption period has expired?
    A. Writ of execution
    B. Tax certificate
    C. Tax deed
    D. Writ of attachment

23. When a person receives a special benefit which differs significantly from the benefit the public at large receives from a government improvement, the property may be charged with a
    A. writ of attachment
    B. writ of execution
    C. payment bond
    D. special assessment

24. What is filed for the purpose of serving constructive notice on the world that title or some matter involving a particular real property is in litigation?
    A. Lis pendens
    B. Attachment
    C. Judgment in personam
    D. Performance bond

25. When a path crosses someone's backyard, what legal doctrine requires a purchaser to take note of the possibility of an unrecorded prescriptive easement, even if the purchaser were unaware of the path?
    A. Actual notice
    B. Constructive notice
    C. Marshalling
    D. Lis pendens

26. The mortgagor is the
    A. borrower
    B. broker
    C. lender
    D. agent or a mortgage broker

27. What prevents the buyer of a house from "assuming" or taking "subject to" an existing mortgage?
    A. Due on sale clause
    B. Brundage clause
    C. Escalator clause
    D. Forfeiture clause

28. The obligor on a mortgage note is the
    A. borrower
    B. lender
    C. nominee
    D. seller

29. Priorities of mortgages can be changed by a (an)
    A. estoppel certificate
    B. release of mortgage
    C. subordination agreement
    D. collateral bond

30. In most states, in cases dealing with more than one recorded mortgage, the mortgage having priority is
    A. the one that has the earliest date of execution
    B. a subordinated mortgage
    C. the one with the earliest recorded date
    D. the one with the highest monetary value

31. The right given by law to a creditor to have a debt or charge satisfied out of the property belonging to the debtor is referred to as a (an)
    A. attachment
    B. lien
    C. encroachment
    D. security

32. What type of lien arises by operation of law when the seller conveys a piece of property to the purchaser and does not receive the entire purchase price at closing?
    A. Mechanic's lien
    B. Vendee's lien
    C. Purchase money mortgage lien
    D. Vendor's lien

33. Which of the following allows the mortgagee to proceed to a foreclosure sale without first going to court?
    A. Hypothecation
    B. Statutory foreclosure
    C. Waiver of right of redemption
    D. Power of sale

34. When personal property is used as a pledge for a mortgage, this is known as a (an)
    A. equitable mortgage
    B. regular mortgage
    C. chattel mortgage
    D. title mortgage

35. After a borrower pays off a loan, the borrower should require the lender to issue a
    A. partial release
    B. foreclosure release
    C. notice of lis pendens
    D. satisfaction of mortgage

If you are not sure of your answers, see page 321 for correct answers and explanations.

Mortgages and Liens

15

Financing Real Estate

Licensing examinations cover numerous aspects of real estate financing:

1. Mortgages and mortgage clauses.
2. Lending agencies.
3. Government mortgage institutions.
4. Federal lending legislation.
5. Mathematics of financial practice.

In Chapter 14, mortgages and other legal instruments were discussed. The mathematics of financial practice is covered in Chapter 20. This chapter examines the financial side of the lending process. The primary reasons for borrowing are identified and the typical steps in the loan process are explained. Pertinent lending laws are described. Both primary and secondary sources of funds are identified. Finally, the common types of loans are classified, and the ever more common, innovative financing techniques are examined.

RECENT CHANGES AFFECTING REAL ESTATE FINANCE

During the 1980s a number of changes occurred that have resulted in a significant difference in the way both borrowers and lenders approach the financing of real estate. While all of the changes have not had the same effect on the industry, each in its own way has played a role in the rethinking, as well as the restructuring, of real estate financing.

The overall deregulation of lenders has had a profound effect on the credit markets. Today, housing financing does not receive the favored treatment over other capital markets as was the case prior to deregulation. The end result has been less monies for residential financing. A changing attitude on the part of lenders toward inflation has meant that numerous alternative mortgage instruments are used today that were not readily available a decade ago. Whereas the level-payment, fixed-rate mortgage was the mainstay of financing from the 1950s through the end of the 1970s, today both lenders and borrowers are searching for financing techniques that better fit their particular needs. Changes in the secondary mortgage market have meant more uniformity in the way lenders do business. Today, in terms of underwriting guidelines, the fact that most loans are made with the possibility of being sold in the secondary mortgage market means there is a great deal of uniformity from lender to lender. Thus, the loan requirements in one region of the country are not that much different from the requirements in another region.

REASONS FOR BORROWING

So much borrowed capital is used to finance real estate purchases for a number of reasons. While specific reasons vary from individual to individual and from situation to situation, a few of the more general ones include:

1. *Dollar amount of the purchase*: Real estate is a high-cost item. This purchase will normally be the largest single expenditure made during the average homebuyer's lifetime. Add to this the fact that approximately two-thirds of all households in the United States currently have purchased and will continue to purchase a home means there is a need for a tremendous amount of capital. For commercial and income-producing property, the need to borrow some or all of the purchase price is even greater than in the case of income-producing or commercial property, with its steep prices.
2. *Income tax incentives*: Recent changes in federal tax laws have significantly altered the ability to deduct certain expenditures in deriving one's income tax liability. However, the interest deduction on money borrowed to purchase real estate still remains. Thus, the financial impact of the tax deduction means a decrease in the effective cost of borrowing. Add to this the fact

that property taxes are also a legitimate tax deduction, and the total effect is a very real and measurable incentive that encourages one to purchase rather than rent.

3. *Possible hedge against inflation*: Historically, real estate values have increased at a faster rate than the general price level. Thus, real estate has been considered a good hedge against inflation. In addition, for may years the majority of real estate loans had fixed interest rates. Therefore, an increase in value as a result of inflation or changes in demand in the marketplace did not mean, in turn, an increase in the mortgage payment(s). While the percentage of loans made with a long-term fixed rate of interest has decreased in recent years, loans with fixed interest rates are still available. In addition, some of the consumer safeguards built into many of today's adjustable interest rate mortgages often still provide the purchase of real estate as a hedge against inflation. Many people feel that, as we move into the next century, real estate will continue to be a good hedge against inflation.

4. *Leverage (using other people's money)*: Real estate has historically offered the purchaser/investor an opportunity to legally borrow a significantly higher percentage of the purchase price than is typically possible with other purchases and investments. A person buying a residence can legally borrow up to 100% of the sales price and in fact the average loan-to-value ratio for the first homebuyer in this country approaches 80%. For commercial property, the expected ability of a property to generate enough income after operating expenses to more than pay the monthly mortgage payment means the lender may be willing to lend all or nearly all of the purchase price. In addition, the purchaser/investor does not normally have to share any increase in the value of the property with the lender, even though as much as 100% of the purchase price may have come from the lender. However, it should be noted that, in some instances (particularly in the financing of income-producing property), the lender does share or participate in the equity buildup of the property. But this practice is the exception rather than the rule.

THE LOAN PROCESS

While no two real estate loans are exactly alike in every detail, the normal loan process used in real estate financing follows a somewhat systematic approach. The uniformity that exist with most residential loans means that the steps followed with one loan are basically followed with the next one. There is some variation when different types of loans are made, such as FHA loans versus VA loans or residential loans versus commercial loans.

The normal loan process involves a number of steps, which are explained in the following section.

Qualifying the Borrower

The loan process begins when a potential borrower approaches either the lender or a representative of the lender with the intention of securing a certain amount of money. Historically, loan-to-value ratios were much lower than they are today and subsequently in case of default the lender was in a low risk position. However, as loan-to-value ratios have increased, it has become necessary for the lender to look beyond the property and thus qualify both the credit and the financial ability of the borrower to repay the loan. This involves the filling out of a loan application which asks for employment, credit history, assets, liabilities and other personal information. Once this information is obtained the lender then verifies it. When it is verified, the lender can make a credit evaluation that becomes an important input into the final loan decision.

The loan application used for residential real estate is a uniform statement. Thus, the questions asked one borrower are basically the same asked of all borrowers. For commercial property, there is no standard or uniform loan application. What is often required for a loan to finance income-producing real estate is a great deal of specific information in regard to the property. Specifically, the lender wants to be assured the property has the ability to generate enough income to cover the debt payment each period. Secondly, the lender wants to be certain the financial position of the borrower is strong enough to warrant making the loan. Thus, a financial statement is normally required of a potential borrower attempting to finance income-producing property. If two or more people will be involved in the ownership of the property, then each of these people will have to provide individual financial statements to the lender.

Qualifying the Property

Lenders are not in business to foreclose on property; rather, they are in business to lend money, charge interest on that money, and receive payment of both interest and principal. However, under certain conditions, both within and beyond the control of the borrower, the lender may find it necessary to foreclose on the property used to secure the debt. The property being used to secure the debt will be qualified in a number of ways.

Economically (Appraisal)

As was discussed in the previous chapter, a lender requires the borrower to secure a loan with the very property being purchased with the borrowed dollars. Thus, as was explained in that chapter, if the borrower either cannot or for whatever reason chooses not to make the periodic mortgage payment(s), the lender has legal recourse against the property through foreclosure. While a lender would never make a loan with the belief that foreclosure was certain to occur, a lender does need some assurance as to the value of the property if indeed foreclosure does occur. Thus, prior to a final decision with regard to a loan, the property will be appraised. The appraisal process, as explained in Chapter 17, will normally be conducted by an independent appraiser, someone who has no financial or legal interest in the property. The overall purpose of the appraisal is to render an opinion as to the value of the property. With this information the lender can then compare the estimated appraised value of the property with the loan request of the borrower. Generally, if a loan is actually made, the amount of the loan is based on the sales price of the property or the appraised value, whichever is less.

Example:
> A potential borrower approaches a lender with regard to a loan on a house. The contract price is $100,000 and the lender decides an 80% loan can be made. If the property appraises for $110,000, the loan will be for $80,000 (80% of the $100,000), which in this case is the sales price. However, if the property appraises for only $90,000, then the loan will, in this instance, only be for $72,000 which represents 80% of the appraised value. In either instance, the amount of the loan is based on the lower of the sales price or the appraised value.

The necessity of having an appraisal performed on the property is also due to regulations of various federal agencies. Any government-insured or government-guaranteed loan, such as an FHA or a VA loan, will need an appraisal done on the property as part of the loan documentation package. In addition, if the lender decides to sell the loan in the secondary mortgage market, the loan documentation package will have to include an acceptable appraisal of the property. Thus, it is standard operating procedure for any and all property to be appraised as part of the general loan process. In addition, the fee for having the property appraised is often collected by the lender at the time of loan application, the rationale being that the property will have to be appraised regardless of whether the loan is made or not. Thus, the borrower is charged for the appraisal even though the loan may not actually be made.

Physically (Survey)

As was explained in Chapter 7, deeds and other real estate documents such as the promissory note the borrower signs with the lender must contain a legally sufficient description of the property. Thus, the need exists for correctly identifying the property being conveyed as well as the physical boundaries of that property. As part of the steps taken during the loan process, the lender will require that the property be surveyed. The actual work will be done by an approved civil engineer or surveyor and will be charged to the borrower as part of the closing costs. Ordinarily, unless the property has been surveyed within the previous six months, the borrower can expect to have to pay for a survey. Property just recently surveyed may have to be resurveyed to meet the specific requirements set by the lender. However, this decision will be made by the lender and not by the borrower.

Legally (Title Search and Opinion)

To determine the legal rights and interests that currently exist on the property being financed, the lender will seek to qualify the title to the property by examining the public land records and tracing the legal history of the property (see Chapter 16). Normally, the lender desires a first lien position, and the ability of the lender to be in such a legal position can only be determined by an abstract of title. Often this legal work is performed by the same individual who will conduct the actual closing of the loan. Such a person may be someone used by the lending institution to do all of its real estate closings or someone that is qualified and that has been chosen by the borrower. In such a case the lender would have to approve the qualifications of the person chosen and would have to agree to accept his or her work. While the borrower is not legally required to use someone suggested by the lender, borrowers often do not know whom to seek to do the legal work, and thus borrowers often accept the suggestion of the lender as to whom will be used.

In urban areas title abstract and title insurance companies do much of the legal work in terms of examining titles and closing loans. Such companies employ specialists to conduct the title search and write the opinion of title. In small towns and rural areas, the task is often performed by a local attorney who performs real estate closings as part of a general law practice. The fee for having the title search performed is normally charged to the borrower and, if so, appears on his or her closing statement as a debit entry. The actual cost of a title search and abstract of title may be based on a flat fee, an hourly charge, or (as is the case in many parts of the country) a percentage of the loan amount. In those areas where the amount of the charge is based on the amount of the loan, a 1% fee to conduct the search and closing is quite common.

Closing the Loan Transaction

Once the buyer and the property have been qualified and after the lender is confident that title to the subject property is free and clear, the final step in the loan process involves closing the loan transaction. The lender notifies the applicant that the loan will be made and states when and where closing will take place. Normally, the loan transaction takes place at the same time title is conveyed to the buyer (see Chapter 16). Quite possibly the closing will occur at the lender's office or at the attorney's office representing the lender.

At such time the required legal documents are exchanged, the closing statement is explained, title to the property is delivered and accepted, and the funds are distributed. Following the loan closing, certain legal instruments will be recorded in the land records of the jurisdiction where the property is located. Such recordation gives constructive notice to the world that title to the property has transferred. In addition, any documents recorded by the lender in regard to the lien that now exist on the property to secure the debt also serve to give proper notice to any interested party as to the legal position of the lender. In addition to recording certain information, the lender will also set up a procedure to establish the means and time of repayment of the debt by the borrower. While it is possible for the actual closing to occur on any date during a particular month, lenders like to have all loans due and payable on the first day of each month. Normal procedure is that the lender will, at the time of closing the loan, charge prepaid interest on the total amount of the loan from the date of closing until the first day of the next month.

Example:
> A closing takes place on September 20 and the loan amount is $50,000 with an annual interest rate of 12%. Daily interest of $16.67 ($50,000 × .12 ÷ 12) times the number of days remaining in the month would be charged: $16.67 × 10 = $166.67. The $166.67 would appear on the borrower's closing statement as a debit to be paid at closing along with the other closing costs. Thus the loan is now set up to be repaid on the first day of each month. However, on the first day of the month

following the closing, October 1 in this example, no payment will be made by the borrower since if a payment was made on October 1st, the borrower would be paying interest in advance. The actual first payment will be due on November 1 and the interest due will be based on the outstanding balance for the last period which in this case is the month of October. From November 1st and for the remaining months, the payment will be due and payable on the first day of each month.

Servicing the Loan

Once the loan has been closed and either sold to an investor or retained by the lender, the loan must be serviced. Servicing involves all of the activities necessary to keep the loan in good standing. This includes collecting the loan repayment, seeing that property taxes and special assessments are paid and making sure sufficient property insurance is maintained. If the lender has sold the loan as part of a package to an investor, the lender normally continues to service the loan. For this service, a servicing fee is charged, which is typically a specified percentage of the outstanding balance. While the amount of the servicing fee is relatively small on any particular loan, the total servicing fees collected by a lender on a large portfolio can be significant. In today's financial climate, many lenders sell all of the mortgages they originate and rely on the servicing fees as a continuous source of revenue.

LENDING LAWS AFFECTING REAL ESTATE FINANCE

A number of significant laws have been enacted in regard to the financing of real estate. Since the majority of these are directly related to protection for the consumer, the legislation is normally at the federal level rather than at the state level. For this reason, there is a great deal of uniformity in real estate lending since all lenders must adhere to the requirements of these federal laws. Among the pertinent lending laws are those affecting

- Usury
- Truth-in-lending
- Equal credit opportunity
- Fair credit reporting
- Community reinvestment
- National flood insurance

Usury

Historically, states enacted legislation to limit the interest rate that could be charged to individuals borrowing money in those states. Such laws were not limited to the financing of real estate and included consumer purchases such as automobiles, other durable goods, and consumer goods charged on revolving charge accounts. Usury laws, once enacted, affect all lenders in a state regardless of what federal or state agency issued the lender's charter.

While usury laws are intended to protect the borrower, these laws can, in times of rising interest rates, result in there being less money available than if there were no such laws. If a state sets a certain interest rate ceiling and the effective rate necessary to induce a loan to be made is greater than this ceiling, the result can easily be: (1) no loans made, (2) lenders charging applicants certain fees which in effect raises the effective yield or (3) funds normally available in that state flowing to other parts of the country where interest rate ceilings are higher. This latter can result in fewer dollars being available in the state with low usury ceilings.

In addition to usury laws, little or no money may be available in a certain location due to the impact of *disintermediation*. Disintermediation refers to the withdrawing of funds from the financial institutions by the depositors, generally for the purpose of investing in instruments that pay higher interest rates. Quite often these higher paying instruments may be offered by financial institutions or brokerage houses outside the state. However, at this time, an investor can easily transfer funds from one location to another, and the fact that the source of the higher interest rate is not geographically convenient may be insignificant. The result of such action can easily mean less mortgage money being available for loans in those states that have enacted ceilings on the amount of interest that can legally be paid. In recent years, many states have taken action to either raise the legally allowed rate of interest or as is true in some jurisdictions, the rate is allowed to float or change as other rates change.

Truth-in-Lending Law (Regulation Z)

The National Consumer Credit Protection Act, referred to as the Truth-in-Lending Act, became effective July 1, 1969. Regulation Z, published by the Federal Reserve System to implement this law, requires lenders to make meaningful credit disclosures to *individual borrowers* for certain types of consumer loans. The regulation also applies to all advertising seeking to promote credit. This advertising is required to include specific credit information. Consumers are given information on credit costs both in total dollar amounts and in percentage terms. The intent of Congress was to assist consumers (residential, noninvestment customers) with their credit decisions by providing them with specific information. It should be noted that the law merely requires disclosure and does not attempt to establish minimum or maximum interest rates or other charges.

To Whom Does Regulation Z Apply?

Regulation Z applies to a person (or business) who is classified as a "creditor." A creditor is one who regularly extends consumer credit that is either subject to a finance charge or is payable in more than four installments. The phrase "regularly extends" means that a person or firm has been engaged in five or more transactions in the past calendar year. Regulation Z also requires that the note signed by the consumer be payable on its face to the creditor. In other words, Regulation Z applies only to actual extenders of credit and not arrangers of credit. Thus, if a real estate broker or salesperson helps arrange creative financing to sell a house, the broker or salesperson would not have to comply with Regulation Z disclosure requirements.

What Transactions Are Covered?

All real estate lending transactions involving consumers are covered by Regulation Z. Except for real estate transactions, all credit extended in five or more installments and not in excess of $25,000 for personal, family, household or agricultural purposes is covered by the regulation. The regulation does not apply to credit extended to non-natural persons such as corporations or governments, to credit extended for business and commercial purposes or for credit transactions with an SEC-registered broker for trading in securities and commodities. The regulation applies to new loans, refinancing or consolidation of loans. However, an assumption of a loan by a new borrower is exempt.

Notice that Regulation Z applies to consumer real estate transactions. Would a loan to renovate an apartment building be covered by the regulation? Since an apartment building is normally a business to collect rents from tenants, this would not be deemed a consumer transaction. Thus, the loan would be exempt from Regulation Z reporting requirements.

What Information Must be Disclosed?

The law requires a lender to make several types of credit information disclosures. Two important disclosures include the *finance charge* and the *annual percentage rate (APR)*. The finance charge includes a disclosure of the following: interest, finder and origination fees, discount points, service charges, credit report fees and other charges paid by the consumer directly or indirectly which are imposed as an incident to the extension of credit. Certain fees which are not in fact additional finance charges are exempt. These charges may include various title examination fees, escrow requirements and appraisal fees. To determine the charges which are covered or exempt, Regulation Z should be examined by anyone extending credit to consumers. (Note: this includes brokers, professionals and craftsmen as well as financial intermediaries unless exempt.)

The APR is the yearly cost of credit stated to the nearest one-eighth of 1 percentage point in regular transactions and the nearest one-fourth of 1 percentage point in irregular transactions. A transaction is irregular if repayment is in uneven amounts or the loan is made in multiple advances. The APR is usually different from the contract or nominal rate of interest and includes the impact on the effective rate from discount points and other charges. The calculation of the APR is complex and involves the use of actuarial tables which are available from the Federal Reserve and member banks.

Example:

Tom borrows $1,000 from Holly which is repayable in one payment at the end of the year. The loan is to finance a real estate purchase. They agree to a contract rate of 10% plus four discount points. What is the APR?

Actual amount borrowed:
$1,000 − $40 [discount points] = $960
Amount to be paid back:
$1,000 + $100 [contract interest] = $1,100
Actual interest: $1,100 − $960 = $140
APR: $140 / $960 = 14.58%

This calculation would differ depending on the term of the loan and the amortization period. If the interest is collected in the beginning, the APR could be twice the contract rate.

If the loan involves variable payments, then the creditor must disclose how the payments may change, including the index that is being used, limitations on increases and an example illustrating how payments would change in a given increase.

In addition to the finance charge and the APR, anyone extending credit must also disclose such information as the number, amount and time that the installments are due, description of the penalties and charges for prepayment and the description of the security which is used as collateral. If a personal dwelling is used as collateral, as in refinancing or using a second mortgage to obtain equity, a consumer has three business days to rescind (cancel) the credit transaction. This right of rescission does not apply to credit which was used to purchase the home originally.

Effect of Violations

Violation of Regulation Z provisions can lead to both civil and criminal penalties. Civil penalties include a penalty of up to $1,000 paid to the borrower, actual damages plus attorney's fees. Criminal penalties include a fine of up to $5,000, up to one year in jail, or both.

Equal Credit Opportunity Act

As originally passed, the Equal Credit Opportunity Act prohibits discrimination by lenders on the basis of sex or marital status in any aspect of a credit transaction. As of 1977, the act was extended to cover additional protected groups of borrowers. These include individuals who are discriminated against on the basis of race, color, religion, national origin, age, receipt of income from a public assistance program and good faith exercise of rights under the Consumer Protection Act. Exceptions to the protection of the law are individuals who do not have contractual capacity (minors) and individuals who are noncitizens and whose status might affect a creditor's rights and remedies in the case of a default.

The purpose of this law and Regulation B, which was issued by the Board of Governors of the Federal Reserve System, was to assure that lenders would not treat one group of applicants more favorably than other groups except for reasonable and justifiable business reasons. Strict rules have been established to require fair dealing in all aspects of a credit transaction.

A creditor failing to comply with the law is subject to civil liability for damages in individual or class actions. These damages can be actual or punitive. Punitive damages are intended to punish a wrongdoer. These are limited to $10,000 in individual actions or the lesser of $500,000 or one percent of a creditor's net worth in class actions. A class action occurs when a specific group of individuals has been harmed from a violation of the law. In general, lawsuits must be filed within two years of a violation.

The law is very broadly worded and covers all phases of a credit transaction. The following is a lender's lists of "do's" and "don'ts":

1. *Do not* ask about a person's birth control practices or intentions to bear children; however, a neutral question such as whether the applicant expects his or her income to be interrupted in the future is considered proper.
2. *Do* tell the applicant that income from alimony or child support need not be disclosed unless the applicant wishes this source of income considered.
3. *Do* tell the applicant that the federal government needs certain information for monitoring purposes, but that this information will not be used as a means of discrimination. Note that the applicant may decline to furnish this information.
4. *Do not* require a spouse to co-sign a credit instrument except where state laws, such as California's community property law, require a signature to create a proper lien on property serving as security for a loan.
5. *Do not* use age in evaluating an applicant's creditworthiness. One exception to this rule is if the applicant is considered "elderly" (age 62 or over), and the age is being considered to *favor* the applicant.
6. *Do not* require the applicant to reveal marital status. This extends to the use of courtesy titles (Ms., Mr., Mrs., Miss) unless requested by the applicant.
7. *Do* furnish credit information in the names of both spouses for the purpose of establishing a credit history in each name if both are participating in the loan.
8. *Do* notify the applicant within 30 days whether you are approving the loan or taking an adverse action.
9. *Do* give a specific reason for an adverse action. Specific reasons could include: no credit file, insufficient credit references, law suits, liens, excessive obligations, delinquent credit obligations, unable to verify employment or income, denial by FHA or other government program, inadequate collateral.
10. *Do* retain records for at least 25 months after notifying applicant of action taken.

Fair Credit Reporting Act

This act, which became effective April, 1971, attempts to regulate the actions of credit bureaus that give out erroneous information regarding consumers. First, banks and credit companies must make a customer's credit file available to the person in question. Further, the consumer upon examining the file, has the right to correct any errors that may appear in the credit reports. Secondly, if a creditor denies a loan to an applicant, the applicant must be given the name and address of the credit bureau that supplied the credit information to the creditor. Upon request, the credit bureau must supply the consumer with the pertinent information contained in the applicant's credit file. Finally, the act limits the access of the consumer's credit records to people who: (1) evaluate an applicant for insurance, credit or employment; (2) secure the consumer's permission; or (3) secure court permission.

Community Reinvestment Act

In order to prevent the practice of redlining and disinvestment in central city areas, Congress passed the Community Reinvestment Act. "Redlining" is a practice whereby lenders refuse to make loans in certain geographic areas of a city. It is as if someone had taken a red pencil and drawn a line around the boundary of a neighborhood and said that no loans would be made in that neighborhood.

To comply with the act, lenders must prepare Community Reinvestment Statements. These statements contain up to four basic elements:

1. The lender delineates a "community" in which its lending activities take place. The lender may use political boundaries, designate an "effective lending territory" in which a "substantial portion" of its loans are made, or any other "reasonably delineated local area." Care must be taken that such designations do not unreasonably exclude territory occupied by persons of low or moderate incomes (see also requirements in Federal Fair Housing Laws, Chapter 15).
2. The lender must make available a listing of the types of credit it offers in each community.
3. Appropriate notice and information regarding lending activity by territory must be given or made available for public inspection. The specific language of the notice is dictated by the government.
4. The lender has the option to disclose affirmative programs designed to meet the credit needs of the community.

National Flood Insurance

In 1968, Congress enacted the National Flood Insurance Program. The intent of this legislation is to provide insurance coverage for those people suffering both real and personal losses as a result of floods. As of 1975, people seeking to finance property located in such areas must obtain flood damage insurance if the property is to be financed by mortgages obtained from federal agencies or from federally insured or regulated lending institutions. Owners of property located in areas not covered by flood insurance because the local jurisdiction does not participate in the program cannot obtain federally related assistance.

SOURCES OF FUNDS

Since the purchase of real estate normally involves the use of borrowed funds, anyone desiring to buy real estate needs to fully understand the sources of funds, how these lenders operate, and the type of loans they generally make. As noted in the introductory comments in this chapter, changes during recent years have meant that lenders often make the same type of loans. While in years past a clear distinction could be made from one source of financing to another, such is not always the case today. However, for purposes of discussion, the more common sources have been divided into four groups:

1. Primary sources
2. Financial middlemen
3. Other sources
4. The secondary mortgage market

Primary Sources

Savings and loan associations

While savings and loan associations (S&Ls) are not the largest financial intermediary in terms of total assets, they are one of the most important sources of funds in terms of the dollars made available for financing real estate. Traditionally, the 3,000 associations have been the largest supplier of single-family, owner-occupied residential permanent financing although in recent years their percentage of the total has continued to decrease. Today, primarily as a result of the Depository Institutions Deregulation and Monetary Control Act of 1980, savings and loan associations make home improvement loans and loans to investors for apartments, industrial property, and commercial real estate. In addition, S&Ls offer interest-earning checking (NOW) accounts.

An S&L is either federally or state chartered. Less than one-half of the S&Ls are federally chartered. If federal, the association must be a member of the *Federal Home Loan Bank System* (FHLBS), and its funds must be insured by the *Federal Savings and Loan Insurance Corporation* (FSLIC). All federally chartered S&Ls are mutually owned (owned by depositors) and the word "federal" must appear in their title.

State chartered S&Ls can be either mutually owned or stock associations. (In a stock association, individuals buy stock, which provides the equity capital.) They have optional membership in both the FHLBS and the FSLIC. In some states, these lenders are known as *building and loan associations*, or *cooperative banks*.

Commercial Banks

In terms of total assets, the more than 14,000 commercial banks are the largest financial intermediary directly involved in the financing of real estate. Commercial banks act as lenders for a multitude of loans. While they occasionally provide financing for permanent residential purchases, commercial banks' primary real estate activity involves short-term loans, particularly construction loans (typically six months to three years) and to a lesser extent home-improvement loans. Most large commercial banks have a real estate loan department; their involvement in real estate is through this department. Some of the largest commercial banks are also directly involved in real estate financing through their trust departments, mortgage banking operations and real estate investment trusts. Today, in some areas of the country commercial banks play a significant role in residential financing, particularly in regard to FHA and VA loans.

All commercial banks are either federally (nationally) chartered or state chartered. National banks are chartered and supervised by the U.S. Comptroller of the Currency. The word "national" appears in their title, and they are members of the *Federal Reserve System* (FRS). However, only one-third of all commercial banks are members of the FRS, even though the member banks control the majority of total banks assets. Nationally chartered banks are also required to maintain membership in the *Federal Deposit Insurance Corporation* (FDIC). Federally chartered banks can make insured real estate residential loans up to 95% of the appraised value with a maturity of not more than 30 years. However, any government insured or guaranteed loans are exempt from these limitations.

State chartered banks are regulated by various agencies in their particular state, and membership in both the FDIC and the FRS is optional. Banks not members of the FDIC are normally required to maintain membership in a state insurance corporation.

Life Insurance Companies

Insurance companies play an important role as providers of capital for real estate both from a mortgagee's (lender) standpoint and from an equity (owner) standpoint. Unlike the savings and loan association or the bank, which normally deal directly with the borrower, the 2,000 insurance companies typically do their lending through local correspondents, either mortgage brokers or mortgage bankers. Insurance companies normally specialize in large-scale projects and mortgage packages. Historically, between 25 and 30% of their assets have been invested in mortgages.

Insurance companies receive their money through the payment of premiums by their policyholders and since both the inflow of premiums and the outflow of claim payments can be predicted with reasonable accuracy, insurance companies are able to invest in those assets yielding higher returns but less liquidity than is available to either banks or associations. For their real estate investments, this normally means long-term commercial and industrial financing. While insurance companies have historically invested in residential mortgages, this form of investment has continued to become a smaller and smaller percentage of their portfolio. Few insurance companies presently originate residential mortgages.

All insurance companies are state chartered since there is no federal agency which issues charters. The result is less regulation in most states than is true for either S&Ls or banks. Less regulation generally results in liberal lending patterns which leads to the funding of a wide variety of real estate projects. Over 90% of the insurance companies are stock companies; however, the majority of the industry's assets are held by mutual companies.

Mutual Savings Banks

Located primarily in northeastern states, the 500 mutual savings banks are an important supplier of real estate financing. As their name indicates, these banks are owned by their depositors, who receive interest on their deposits.

All mutual savings banks are state chartered and typically are less regulated than their closest financing relative, the savings and loan association. The percentage of their assets invested in real estate mortgages is less than the average S&L, although a higher percentage of their total mortgage portfolio is FHA and VA loans. Most mutual banks have a relatively larger percentage of their mortgage loan portfolio invested in multi-family mortgages. Mutual banks also make personal loans and, unlike S&Ls, make interstate loans which can result in capital being moved from surplus areas to deficit areas.

Over two-thirds of the mutual banks maintain membership in the FDIC. The remaining ones are insured by state savings insurance agencies. These state agencies exercise authority over both the type of investments and the amount of their assets mutual banks can invest in particular types of real estate.

LOOK THIS UP:
Are there mutual savings banks in your state?

Yes _____ No _____

Financial Middlemen

In today's economy the flow of funds, as well as the availability of credit, has clearly moved beyond the local sources traditionally turned to for the financing of real estate. Funds flow not only from state to state but from country to country. Thus the need exists for lenders to establish a working relationship with a loan correspondent to take advantage of the correspondent's knowledge and expertise of local conditions, financing programs available, and general economic conditions that exist. Loan correspondents are normally classified as either mortgage brokers or mortgage bankers.

Mortgage Brokers

Mortgage brokers are not direct or primary suppliers of capital. However, they do play an important and necessary role in the financing process. A mortgage broker is a person who serves to bring together the user of capital (borrower or mortgagor) and the supplier of capital (lender or mortgagee). For this service, a *finder's fee* equal to one percent or so of the amount borrowed is normally paid by the borrower. The financial success of the mortgage brokerage firm depends upon the ability to locate available funds and to match these funds with creditworthy borrowers.

Certain sources of funds, particularly insurance companies and the secondary sources discussed below, do not always deal directly with the person looking for capital; rather, they work through a mortgage broker. Thus, if you wish to borrow from certain lenders you would need to go through a mortgage broker. Normally, the mortgage broker is not involved in servicing the loan once it is made and the transaction is closed.

Mortgage Bankers

The mortgage banker is also a financial middleman; however, the services offered include more than simply bringing borrower and lender together.

In some geographic areas, mortgage bankers are the primary source for financing real estate. All mortgage bankers try to stay in constant touch with investors and are aware of changing market conditions and lender requirements. Quite often the loan origination fee or finder's fee charged the borrower is more than offset by a lower interest rate from a lender not directly accessible to the borrower. Mortgage bankers are involved in both commercial and residential financing and also carry out related activities such as writing hazard insurance policies, appraising and investment counseling. As with mortgage brokers, mortgage bankers are regulated by state law.

Mortgage bankers generally follow certain steps, which include the following:

Loan Origination: The first step necessary in order for a mortgage banker, and for that matter any lender, to be successful is to originate loans, or to put it another way, "go out and get the business." Obviously, if mortgage bankers do not have anyone interested in borrowing money, then they will not be in business very long. Mortgage bankers begin the loan process by working with correspondent accounts, such as commercial banks and savings and loan associations, as well as with real estate brokers and salespersons. The various financial programs available, in addition to interest rates and terms are made available by the mortgage banker. In turn, the mortgage banker hopes that as property is sold, these contacts will turn to the mortgage banker as the source of funding for the property.

Loan Processing: Once a loan has been originated the next step is the processing of the loan—doing what is necessary to complete the loan transaction once the application has been approved. For real estate loans, the steps would include such things as a credit report, verification of employment and gross income, appraisal report, survey, title examination, and various other documentation.

Loan Underwriting: After the loan has been processed, final decisions will have to be made as to the completion of the loan documentation and whether or not a loan will be made. Such decisions are normally made by a person referred to as an *underwriter*. An underwriter reviews all of the documentation and makes a recommendation to the loan committee as to the desirability and risk of making the loan. Underwriting, an integral part of the lending process, is normally performed by someone who has had a great deal of experience in processing loans.

Loan Closing: As noted earlier in this chapter, the closing of the loan will take place following the loan decision. Mortgage bankers often are correspondents with local lenders and may actually close the loan by using an officer or employee of the local lending institution. For example, a mortgage lender in one city may be underwriting the loan on a property located in another state. In this instance, the buyer and seller will meet at the office of the lender in their particular location. The documentation, closing statement, and other documentation may have been physically completed by that lender, or it could have been completed by the mortgage banker and forwarded to the lender for the purpose of closing the loan.

Loan Warehousing: To be successful, a mortgage banker must make numerous loans. The lapse of time between when loans are made becomes a factor since obviously the loans are closed at different times. As will be noted, the end result of making these various loans will be selling them rather than merely maintaining them in a portfolio held by the mortgage banker. Therefore the need exists for "warehousing" the loans as they are made. *Warehousing* simply refers to the step taken by a mortgage banker in which the loans are assembled and held by the mortgage banker between the time a loan has been closed and the time it will be sold to an investor. Warehousing may and often does require the establishment of a line of credit with a financial institution. The purpose of this line of credit is to provide the funds necessary to close the loan(s). Since the mortgage banker may not have the necessary capital or perhaps has loaned all of its working capital available, funds are borrowed over a short period of time from a financial institution, and the mortgages being funded with the proceeds of this line of credit are warehoused with the lender. As such, these mortgages serve as collateral from when the loans are closed to when the next step in the mortgage banking process takes place.

Packaging and Shipping: Since the objective of the mortgage banker involved in a loan is normally not to hold the loan until maturity, the loan will be sold. The selling of the loan(s) simply means that an investor will be found who desires to purchase the loan for the purpose of receiving some expected rate of return on the purchase price. To deliver the loan(s) purchased by the investor, the mortgage banker will take a group of mortgages he or she has made (or perhaps ones that have been purchased from someone else) and then package these mortgages and ship (deliver) them to the investor. This step may occur either very soon after the closing of the loan(s) or after some period of time. Once the loans are delivered, the final step in the loan process begins.

Loan Servicing: Normally, the mortgage banker continues to service the loan (collect the mortgage payment, pay property taxes and insurance, handle delinquent accounts, etc.) even after the loan has been packaged and sold. For this service a small percentage of the amount collected is retained by the mortgage banker before forwarding the balance to whoever purchased the loan(s). Obviously, the more loans a mortgage banker is originating and thus servicing, the greater the total amount of servicing fees generated. For this reason the long-term success of a mortgage banker depends upon the ability to generate new loans, sell them, service the loans, and take the proceeds from the sale and originate new loans.

LOOK THIS UP:

Are mortgage bankers required to be licensed or registered in your state?

Yes _____ No _____

Other Sources

Besides the four primary sources of funds, a number of other sources are available and each plays an important role in financing real estate. Most of these sources rely on mortgage brokers and mortgage bankers to assemble loan packages for them since they normally do not provide funds directly to the ultimate user.

Pension funds

Pension funds are one of the newer sources available for financing real estate. Whereas these funds historically were invested in stocks and bonds, the recent growth of pension funds has meant new outlets have had to be found for their investments. This growth, plus the favorable yield available through real estate investments, has resulted in active participation in financing real estate projects. Besides making mortgage loans, pension funds also own real estate. The majority of all their real estate activity is done through mortgage bankers and mortgage brokers.

Finance companies

Traditionally, finance companies have provided consumer loans for the purchase of both durable and nondurable goods. However, as commercial banks have become more and more involved in personal loans, finance companies have turned to other forms of investment including real estate mortgages. In residential real estate, finance companies are actively engaged in second mortgages. This type of mortgage is usually made at an interest rate four or more percentage points above the rate on first mortgages and is amortized over a much shorter time period. Some of the larger finance companies—such as those owned by the automobile manufacturers—finance land development, provide commercial gap financing, acquire land leasebacks and enter into joint ventures with real estate developers.

Real estate investment trusts

Federal legislation passed in 1961 created Real Estate Investment Trusts. REITs may be divided into *mortgage trusts* and *equity trusts* (see Chapter 8). These trusts invest in all types of real estate both from a mortgagee position and an equity position. Their loans include all aspects of financing from construction to permanent, both residential and commercial, and although much of their financing activity is done directly, trusts use mortgage brokers to locate outlets for their funds.

Credit unions

While the majority of loans made by credit unions are consumer loans some of the more than 22,000 credit unions provide mortgage money for both residential and nonresidential financing. In addition to permanent loans, credit unions also make home-improvement loans directly to depositors. Credit unions normally use mortgage brokers to locate real estate investments for their portfolios.

Individual investors

There are a number of large investors located throughout the United States who constantly lend money on real estate. These investors include individuals with available funds, groups of investors seeking mortgage ownership and large investment companies desiring to hold a diversified portfolio. They deal both direct and through mortgage brokers. Additionally, many of these investors seek to take an equity position in real estate. It is thus possible to raise equity capital through syndication instead of relying solely on mortgage funds.

Foreign funds

Over the past decade, a substantial sum of foreign capital has flowed into the United States and much of it has taken the form of real estate equity capital. The relatively high return offered through real estate ownership in this country coupled with a stable economic system means a financially attractive alternative for foreign investors.

Farmers Home Administration

The Farmers Home Administration (FmHA) is an agency of the U.S. Department of Agriculture. In addition to making loans for the ownership and operation of family farms, FmHA also provides loans to low- and moderate-income families for both the purchasing and improving of single-family homes. FmHA administers two loan programs for rural housing: (1) a direct loan program and (2) a guaranteed loan program. Properties securing such loans are generally located in rural areas of 10,000 people or less, although some FmHA programs are available in communities up to 50,000 people. As is true with both FHA and VA, the Farmers Home Administration requires that the property meet certain minimum requirements. Legally, a FmHA loan can be up to 100% of the appraised value of the property, and the interest rate charged can be as low as 1% depending on the borrower's income. Information on loan programs is available from any office of the Farmers Home Administration.

Federal Land Bank

The Federal Land Bank was established in 1919 for the purpose of making loans to farmers. The program has evolved into a rural housing program, as well as a program that makes direct loans to people for the purpose of buying and maintaining land to be used for farming. As is true with the FmHA program, borrowers under the Federal Land Bank program must meet certain income and credit guidelines in order to qualify for such loans. The program is coordinated through the twelve regional Federal Land Banks located throughout the United States.

State finance programs

A number of states have enacted state housing finance agencies (SHFAs) for the purpose of providing direct loans at a preferred interest rate to citizens of that state who, for various reasons, have been unable to obtain financing from private institutions. Typically the state funds such a program by selling tax-exempt bonds secured either by the mortgages that will be made or by the full faith and credit of the state issuing the bonds. Thus the interest rate made available to the borrower is normally below the rate the borrower could obtain in the marketplace. Normally, to qualify for such a program, the applicant must have been a resident of the state for a specified period of time and under most programs the applicant may not own other real property. In recent years, cities and counties have also established mortgage funds to meet the needs of the housing market in their political jurisdictions. Such programs have become extremely important when interest rates in the marketplace increase and low- and middle-income persons are unable to qualify for a loan.

The Secondary Mortgage Market

The availability of funds for financing real estate is affected by economic conditions, both local and national. The result is that at certain times or in certain geographic locations little or no capital is available for mortgages; consequently, few if any loans are made. From the viewpoint of the lender, another problem is that real estate loans can be highly illiquid; thus, the supplier of funds can have a difficult time converting loans into cash. For these reasons, the need exists for some means by which a lender can sell a loan prior to its maturity date (see Figure 15–1).

The secondary mortgage market attempts to meet these needs. Capital can be made available during times of tight money and at capital-deficit locations. By selling mortgages in the secondary mortgage market, a lender can convert existing mortgages into cash which can in turn be used to fund new mortgages. Likewise, an investor in the secondary mortgage market can buy existing mortgages, pay the seller a small servicing fee and avoid the time and expense of originating and servicing the loans.

Federal National Mortgage Association

The largest and best known buyer of existing mortgages is the Federal National Mortgage Association (FNMA), known to many as "Fannie Mae." The FNMA was originally organized by the federal government in 1938 to purchase FHA-insured mortgages. The association was reorganized in 1968 as a quasi-private corporation whose entire ownership is private. Fannie Mae raises capital by issuing corporate stock which is actively traded on the New York Stock Exchange and by selling mortgages out of its portfolio to various investors. Over the past 20 years, Fannie Mae has purchased many times more than it has sold. At the beginning of 1990, current mortgage holdings exceeded $100 billion, the majority being conventional mortgages.

Figure 15–1. Secondary Mortgage Market

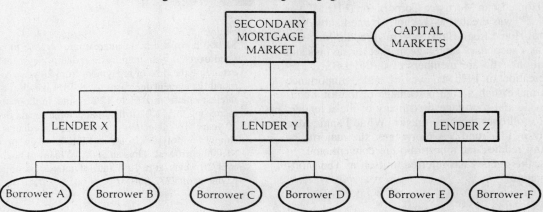

Financing Real Estate

The mortgage purchase procedure used by FNMA is conducted through an auction process referred to as the *Free Market System Auction*. Periodically, the association accepts bids from approved lenders as the amount, price and terms of existing mortgages that these lenders wish to sell to Fannie Mae. Upon deciding how much money it will spend during a given time period, FNMA notifies the successful bidders (determined by those mortgages offered for sale that will generate the highest yield to FNMA), and these bidders have a certain time period in which they can choose to deliver the mortgages. Once the mortgage has been delivered to Fannie Mae, the originator of the mortgage continues to service the loan (collect monthly payments, escrow property taxes, etc.) and for this service the originator receives a servicing fee.

By selling to Fannie Mae, a lender is allowed to *roll over* its money. That is, by selling $1,000,000 worth of mortgages to FNMA, a savings and loan association now has $1,000,000 that can be used to originate new mortgages. Thus funds are provided that would not have been available had Fannie Mae not purchased the mortgages.

Government National Mortgage Association

When the Federal National Mortgage Association reorganized in 1968, the Government National Mortgage Association (GNMA) was completely separated as a legal entity. Referred to as "Ginnie Mae," this participant in the secondary mortgage market is a wholly-owned government corporation under the office of the U.S. Department of Housing and Urban Development. While FNMA is involved with the selling and purchasing of existing mortgages, Ginnie Mae is responsible for the liquidation and special assistance functions previously carried out by FNMA. Ginnie Mae is also involved with the mortgage securities pool plan and the tandem plan. The tandem plan provides that Fannie Mae may purchase high-risk and low-yielding mortgages at the full market rate or price, with Ginnie Mae in turn guaranteeing the payment of these mortgages and absorbing the difference between the current market rate of interest and the low yield expected on the mortgages. GNMA also makes financing available to certain urban renewal projects, elderly housing, and other high-risk mortgages.

Federal Home Loan Mortgage Corporation

In 1970, under the Emergency Home Finance Act, the Federal Home Loan Mortgage Corporation (FHLMC) or "Freddie Mac" was created as a wholly owned subsidiary of the Federal Home Loan Bank System. Freddie Mac was established as a secondary mortgage market for savings and loan associations who are members of the FHLBS.

The creation of FHLMC was of added importance since S&Ls make such a high percentage of the total conventional residential mortgages and many of these lenders would like to roll over their mortgages. While Fannie Mae deals heavily in FHA and VA mortgages, the majority of mortgages in Freddie Mac's portfolio are conventional. In recent years, this agency has referred to itself as The Mortgage Corporation.

CLASSIFICATION OF MORTGAGES

In no area of real estate terminology is there more diverse classification of terms than with real estate mortgages. The following classification is offered as an aid in explaining the more common types of mortgages used in financing real estate.

Method of Payment

Straight-Term Mortgages

Prior to the Great Depression of the 1930s, the straight-term or term mortgage was the common means of financing residential real estate. Under this method of payment, interest only is paid periodically (monthly, quarterly, annually) and the initial amount borrowed, the principal, is not paid until the last day of the loan period. Typically, term mortgages covered short periods of time—three to five years—and there was normally little intent by either the borrower to repay the principal or the lender to demand payment of the principal. The original amount borrowed was either extended for another term at an agreed upon interest rate or the borrower would negotiate with a new lender and pay off the old loan. However, as a result of financial conditions during the Depression and the National Housing Act of 1934, which among other things established the Federal Housing Administration, term mortgages became less popular. Borrowers during the Depression were unable to pay the principal when it became due. Because of the tightness in the money supply, lenders were unable to roll these loans over, and thus had to foreclose. Over a million families lost their homes during this time. The failure of the money market led to the creation of the Federal Housing Administration and increased usage of the amortized mortgage. Today, term mortgages are generally used only in the financing of land and construction.

Fully Amortized Mortgages

Unlike the term mortgage where none of the principal is repaid during the life of the mortgage, a fully-amortized mortgage requires periodic (typically monthly) payment of both interest and principal. As can be seen in Table 15–1, given a specific interest rate, the total periodic payment decreases as the length of the loan increases. Likewise, holding the length of the loan constant while increasing the interest rate causes the periodic payment, in turn, to increase.

Example:

$1,000 borrowed at an interest rate of 10% to be fully amortized over 20 years requires a monthly payment of $9.66. By extending the time of repayment from 20 years to 30 years, the monthly payment decreases to $8.78. Likewise, a change in the interest rate from 10% to 12% results in the monthly payment increasing to $11.02 if the loan is to be repaid over a period of 20 years. To calculate the amount of a particular loan amount, simply multiply the factor in Table 15–1 by the increments of $1,000 borrowed. Thus an $80,000 loan, to be fully amortized over 20 years at a 10% rate of interest, requires a monthly payment of $772.80 (80 × 9.66).

Table 15–1. Amortization Table
Monthly Payment Per $1,000

Length of the Loan (years)	Interest Rate per Year				
	8%	10%	12%	14%	16%
5	20.28	21.25	22.25	23.27	24.32
15	9.56	10.75	12.01	13.32	14.69
20	8.37	9.66	11.02	12.44	13.92
25	7.72	9.09	10.53	12.04	13.59
30	7.34	8.78	10.29	11.85	13.45

The first part of the payment covers interest on the outstanding debt as of the payment date, and the remainder of the payment reduces the outstanding debt. At the maturity date, the balance has been reduced to zero. The initial payments will consist of more interest than principal reduction; however, the percentage of the periodic payment reducing the outstanding balance will continue to increase as each subsequent payment is made. Table 15–2 illustrates the remaining (outstanding) balance on a $1,000, 12%, fully amortized loan at various stages over the life of the loan. Some people are quite surprised when they realize just how little of each month's payment goes toward the reduction of principal. As is shown in Table 15–2, $1,000 borrowed over 25 years results in an outstanding balance of $952 at the end of five years. The same loan, financed over 25 years, still has a remaining balance of $460 at the end of twenty years.

Fully amortized mortgages have in recent decades been the normal means of securing permanent financing. The maturity date is usually much longer than with a term mortgage. For residential property, this type of mortgage usually covers 25 to 30 years, and for commercial property the time period is normally 10 to 15 years.

Two important concepts you are likely to face in discussions about mortgages are the "debt service" and the "mortgage constant." Debt service is the periodic payment (usually monthly in residential loans) that covers both the amortization and the interest payment. In other words, if you have to pay $500 each month to the lender to pay off a mortgage loan, this amount is referred to as the *debt service*.

The *mortgage constant* is the percentage relationship (rate) between the debt service and the original loan amount, usually expressed on an annual basis, although it can be expressed on a monthly or other period of time basis.

Table 15–2. Remaining Balance—12% $1,000 Fully Amortized Loan

Age of Loan (years)	Original Term (years)				
	5	15	20	25	30
1	843	973	986	993	996
5	—	830	912	952	974
10	—	529	756	868	927
15	—	—	483	720	846
20	—	—	—	460	701
25	—	—	—	—	380
30	—	—	—	—	—

Example:

The $500 each month is being used to pay off a $50,000 loan. What is the annual mortgage constant? First, convert the monthly payment to an annual payment ($500 × 12 = $6,000). Second, divided the annual debt service by the amount of the original loan ($6,000 ÷ $50,000 = .12 or 12%). This means that you have a 12% mortgage constant. Sometimes this is simply referred to as a mortgage constant of 12.

If you have a 12% mortgage constant, what does this tell you about the interest rate being charged on the loan? In a level-payment, fully amortized mortgage, the mortgage constant includes both interest and amortization of principal. You therefore know that the interest rate is *lower* than the rate expressed by the mortgage constant.

Partially Amortized Mortgages

The partially-amortized mortgage also requires periodic repayment of principal. However, unlike the fully-amortized mortgage, the balance at maturity under a partially-amortized mortgage is *not* zero; rather, the principal has been only partially reduced. The remaining balance is referred to as a *balloon payment*.

As a result of higher interest rates and inflation during the early part of this decade, this type of mortgage has become more common in residential financing. Today, some lenders make loans based on, for example, a 30-year amortization schedule but with a five-year term. Thus, at the end of five years, the outstanding balance is due. Figure 15–2 illustrates repayment patterns for these three types of mortgages.

Budget Mortgages

Besides paying interest and principal each period, a borrower can also be required to pay a certain percentage of annual property taxes and property insurance. For a residential mortgage this means one-twelfth of the property taxes and one-twelfth of the property insurance each month. The advantage to the borrower is that a budget mortgage allows the spreading out of these annual expenses into 12 equal payments. For the lender, who normally places these funds into an escrow or reserve account, the advantage is the assurance that these expenses will be paid when due.

LOOK THIS UP:

Are lenders in your state required to pay interest on escrow or reserve accounts?

Yes _____ No _____

Time Period

Construction loans

These are also referred to as *interim* financing. A construction mortgage provides the funds necessary for the building or construction of a real estate project. The project can be a residential subdivision, a shopping center, an industrial park or any other type of property requiring financing during the time required to complete construction.

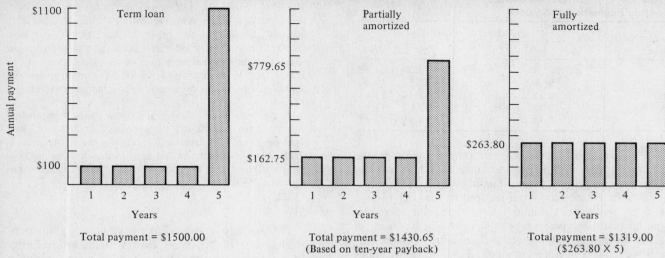

Figure 15–2. Repayment of Five-Year $1,000 Loan Carrying 10% Interest per Year

Normally, the full amount to be loaned is committed by the lender, but the actual disbursement is dependent upon the progress of the construction. Funds are sometimes distributed to the borrower in a series of draws, depending upon work required by the lender. Another method used is for the developer to submit all bills to the lender, who in turn pays the bills. In either case, interest is paid on what has been distributed and not on the total amount to be borrowed. Typically, the interest rate charged is tied to the lender's *prime rate*, which is the interest rate charged to the lender's AAA customers. In addition to interest, the borrower is normally charged a 1 or 2% origination fee. Since construction mortgages are considered high-risk loans, a lender often requires a *standby* or *take-out commitment* from a permanent lender. A standby or take-out commitment means that another lender will provide permanent financing when a certain event, generally the completion of the project occurs. Sometimes, permanent lenders require a certain percentage of a project to be rented before the financing is provided. This assures the construction lender that permanent financing will be available to repay the construction loan if the project is completed and other conditions are met.

Permanent Loans

The permanent loan is used to repay the construction loan. Whereas a construction loan is typically short term, permanent financing normally covers 10 years or more. Permanent financing will either be fully- or partially-amortized through periodic mortgage payments. Since the payment will be paid from the income generated from the project, the lender can make the amount borrowed contingent upon a certain amount of the available space being leased prior to closing the loan transaction. For instance, the developer of a shopping center might be able to borrow $2,000,000 if 80% of the available space is leased but only $1,600,000 if 70% of the space is leased. This could result in a *gap* in the capital needed for financing.

Gap Financing

Gap financing often covers a shorter period of time than permanent financing and usually at a substantially higher interest rate. First of all, it is a junior mortgage, which means the lender does not have the same lien position as the permanent lender; second, there is more risk involved. Normally, different lenders will be involved with these different types of financing. For instance, a commercial bank might provide the construction financing and a real estate investment trust the gap financing. Quite often all of this is arranged through a mortgage broker. Gap financing may also be needed if the conditions set by the permanent lender have not been met and the construction financing has expired. In this case, the gap financing would be senior financing.

Priority

Senior Instruments (First Mortgages)

To hold the first mortgage on real estate means that the lender's rights are superior to the rights of subsequent lenders. This means less risk to the lender, which normally results in a lower interest rate charged to the borrower than charged on second or junior mortgages. Certain lenders only make first mortgages due to regulatory requirements; others limit mortgages to these senior instruments due to company policy.

Conventional mortgages. The majority of permanent residential financing provided in this country is through the fully-amortized conventional mortgage. The term "conventional" refers to a mortgage that is not FHA-insured or VA-guaranteed. Since there is no third party to insure or guarantee the mortgage, the lender assumes full risk of default by the borrower. A lender's decision to make a conventional loan is usually dependent upon: (1) the value of the property being used to secure the debt and (2) the credit and income position of the borrower. As more and more conventional loans have been made, the *loan-to-value ratio* (relationship between amount borrowed and the appraised value or sales price of the property) has continued to increase, even though most lenders still limit the amount they will lend to no more than 80% of value unless private mortgage insurance is carried. This downpayment requirement is higher than with either FHA or VA loans. As the market price or residential real estate has continued to increase, more cash downpayment has been required of the borrower, and thus many people have been eliminated from financing with a conventional mortgage. With both insured and guaranteed mortgages, people have been able to purchase real estate with a smaller cash downpayment.

Federal Housing Administration Insured Mortgages (FHA). In 1934, Congress passed the National Housing Act, thus establishing the Federal Housing Administration (FHA) which immediately resulted in more construction jobs for the unemployed. This in turn helped to stimulate the depressed economy. In order to provide the means by which these new homes could be purchased, FHA established an insurance program to safeguard the lender against the risk of nonpayment by people purchasing these homes. The result was that the majority of homes financed were FHA insured. Even though the percentage of homes insured under FHA coverage has continued to decrease, the standards and requirements under FHA programs have been credited with influencing lending policies and techniques in financing residential real estate.

Under an FHA-insured mortgage, both the property and the borrower must meet certain minimum standards. FHA insures not the property, but rather the lender against loss. Prior to 1983 the borrower was charged an insurance fee of .5% on the unpaid balance and could under certain conditions receive up to 97% financing on the appraised value of the property. However, in 1983 FHA changed to a one-time *mortgage insurance premium (MIP)* of 3.8% of the loan amount, which is either paid in cash at closing or added to the amount of the loan and thus repaid as part of the monthly debt service. The property must be appraised prior to the loan being made by an approved FHA appraiser. If the purchase price exceeds the FHA-appraised value, the buyer may pay the difference in cash as part of the down payment. The loan amount insured by FHA is 97% on the first $25,000 borrowed and 95% on the remainder up to a maximum insured by FHA. FHA sets the maximum loan amounts for various regions of the country, and the local or regional office of FHA can give the current amount being insured. Since 1983, FHA has permitted the lender to charge points in addition to the 1% loan origination fee. Thus, the low closing costs, the relatively low down payment, and the long amortization period permitted under FHA have all aided in providing residential financing for millions of people who otherwise would not have been able to purchase property. As is true with conventional loans, the interest rates on FHA loans are set by the lender involved. Historically, interest rates on FHA mortgages have been slightly below conventional mortgage interest rates since FHA loans are insured. In recent years FHA has expanded its operation; currently, the agency administers a number of programs dealing with housing. The most popular program is Title II, Section 203(b), which covers loans on one-to-four family residences. Other programs include home improvement loans, loans for the purchase of condominiums, and various graduated payment mortgage loans.

Veterans Administration Loan Guarantee Program (VA). Included in the Servicemen's Readjustment Act of 1944 were provisions covering the compensation to lenders for losses they might sustain in providing financing to approved veterans. The VA-guarantee program covers both the purchase of homes and the construction of new homes for eligible veterans. VA also guarantees loans for the purchase of mobile homes and plots on which to place them. There is no limit on the amount of the loan; the limit is determined by the lender. VA does, however, set a limit on the amount of the loan it will guarantee. Currently that limit is 60% or $36,000, whichever is less. The maximum limit is the amount of the guarantee, which is the amount the lender will receive from VA in case of default if the foreclosure sale does not bring enough to cover the outstanding balance. Quite often it is common for an approved veteran to receive 100% VA financing. It should be noted, however, that some lenders set limits on how much they will finance using VA financing. VA guarantees loans up to 30 years.

To qualify for VA financing, the veteran applies for a *certificate of eligibility*. The property as well as the borrower must qualify. If the property is approved a *certificate of reasonable value* (CRV) is issued stating the property's current market value based on a VA-approved appraisal. The CRV places a ceiling on the amount of the VA loan allowed and, if the purchase price is greater than the amount cited in the CRV, the veteran must pay the difference in cash.

Coverage also extends to the financing of mobile homes, condominiums and nonreal estate purchases such as farm equipment and business loans. A VA loan is assumable; however, unless released by the lender, the veteran who borrowed the funds initially remains liable to the lender (see Chapter 14). Lenders cannot insert prepayment penalties under either VA or FHA loans. A mortgage without a prepayment penalty is commonly referred to as an *open mortgage* while one that cannot be prepaid is a *closed mortgage*. VA limits the points charged to the buyer to one. Any other points must be paid by the seller.

LOOK THIS UP:

Current FHA interest rate _____%

Current VA interest rate _____%

Current VA guarantee $_____

Insured Conventional Loans. An insured conventional loan is one which is insured by a private (nongovernmental) insurance company. The establishment of FHA-insured loans and VA-guaranteed loans resulted in higher loan-to-value ratios and longer amortization periods than lenders were willing to offer under conventional financing. As the costs of housing continued to increase year after year, some means of providing protection against loss of high loan-to-value conventional mortgages was needed. Thus, in 1957, the Mortgage Guaranty Insurance Corporation (MGIC) or "Magic" as it is normally referred to, established a private mortgage insurance program (PMI) for approved lenders. MGIC offered the lender quicker service and less red tape than FHA. Today private mortgage insurance companies insure more loans than both FHA and VA. Unlike FHA which insures the whole loan, PMI insures only the top 20 or 25% of the loan, and the insurer normally relies on the lender to appraise the property. While the majority of PMI loans are for 90% loan-to-value, coverage

Table 15–3. Financing Programs

General Regulation	FHA	VA	Conventional	Insured Conventional
Loan approval process	FHA guidelines	VA guidelines	In house staff	In house staff
Guaranteed or insured	Insured—mortgage insurance premium	Guaranteed—60% of loan up to $36,000	None—credit of borrower	Insured—premium at closing plus percent of loan
Downpayment required	3–5% varies with programs	None—up to amount set by lender	20–25% or more as set by lender	5–10%—the balance to 20% is insured
Origination fee	Set by lender	Reasonable costs—1% maximum	Set by lender	Set by lender
Appraisal	FHA issues conditional property value	VA issues Certificate of Reasonable Value (CRV)	Lender decision	Lender decision
Period of loan	Up to 30 years	Up to 30 years	Established by lender	Established by lender
Assumption	Assumable by anyone	Assumable by anyone	Determined by lender	Determined by lender
Prepayment penalty	None	None	Discretion of lender	Discretion of lender

does extend to a maximum of 95%. On a 90% loan, the borrower is normally charged one-half of 1% at closing and one-fourth of 1% of the outstanding balance each year thereafter. With a 95% loan, the rate is normally 1% of the loan at closing plus ¼% of the outstanding balance each year the insurance is carried. Since only the top portion of the loan is covered, once the loan-to-value drops below a certain percentage, the lender may terminate the coverage, and thus, the insurance premium is no longer charged to the customer. In case of default, the insurance company can either pay off the loan or let the lender foreclose and pay the loss up to the amount of insurance coverage.

A summary of the general regulations under conventional, FHA, VA and insured conventional loans is presented in Table 15–3.

Junior Instruments (Second Mortgages)

A junior mortgage is one which has a lower priority or lien position than a first mortgage. A third or even a fourth mortgage is also classified as a junior mortgage. What establishes a mortgage as being a junior mortgage is that it was recorded after the first mortgage was recorded and thus its lien position is inferior to the first mortgage.

Purchase Money Mortgages (PMM). The term *purchase money mortgage* has a dual meaning in real estate financing. All mortgage loans for real estate purchases are designated purchase money mortgages by lenders, and thus all the different types of mortgages explained in this chapter could be classified as purchase money mortgages. The second meaning of the term explains what happens when the buyer does not have the necessary cash and the seller agrees to *take back* a part of the selling price in the form of a purchase money mortgage. Such a mortgage is ordinarily subordinated to take a second-lien position since the primary lender will require a first lien position before making the loan. For the purchaser, this means less cash and possibly an interest rate on the PMM less than if those same dollars were borrowed from a primary lender. The seller can possibly induce a sale not otherwise possible by agreeing to take back a purchase money mortgage. The seller is protected in that a PMM places a lien on the property the same as any other second mortgage.

Home-improvement (equity) loans. In recent years, one result of increased housing costs and higher market prices has been the relatively fast equity build-up for owners of real estate. To an owner, this equity can become a source of capital that can be drawn out of the home for home improvements, personal or business reasons. Numerous commercial banks and finance companies make short-term (three to five years) junior mortgages based on a percentage of the homeowner's equity. Since they are junior mortgages, such loans normally carry an interest rate three or four percentage points above that charged on senior instruments. As a result of changes in the Tax Reform Act of 1986, the popularity of home equity loans continues to increase. Under certain conditions the interest paid on such loans is fully deductible in determining personal taxable income whereas with certain interest expenses, the deduction is either not allowed or severely limited. Thus in recent years consumers have turned to the equity in their property as a source of collateral for purchasing various consumer products, such as automobiles and other durable goods. Today, numerous lending institutions make such loans available, based often on a floating rate of interest tied to the prime rate and with a total loan-to-value ratio not to exceed 75% or 80% of the value of the property.

Wraparound Mortgages. As its name implies, a wraparound mortgage is a junior mortgage that wraps around an existing first mortgage. This method of obtaining additional capital is often used with commercial property where there is substantial equity in the property and where the existing first mortgage has an attractive low interest rate. By obtaining a wraparound, the borrower receives dollars based on the difference between current market value of the property and the outstanding balance on the first mortgage. The borrower amortizes the wraparound mortgage which now includes the balance of the first mortgage, and the wraparound lender forwards the necessary periodic debt service to the holder of the first mortgage. Thus, the borrower reduces the equity and at the same time obtains an interest rate lower than would be possible through a normal second mortgage. The lender receives the leverage resulting from an interest rate on the wraparound greater than the interest paid to the holder of the first mortgage.

Type of Property Pledged

Package Mortgages

Quite often the sale of real property includes certain items and equipment as part of the sales price. Rather than acquiring separate mortgages on each of these items, the buyer can, through the use of a package mortgage, finance both the real property and the personal property. In residential real estate, a builder might include a stove, refrigerator, dishwasher or air conditioning in the sales price. For commercial real estate, certain equipment or furniture is often included in the sales price. The advantage to the purchaser is that these items can be financed over a much longer period and at a much lower interest rate than if a separate financial instrument was used. For the builder or seller, these items often serve as inducements used in finalizing the sale.

Blanket (Land Development) Mortgages

A blanket mortgage is often used by a developer to cover more than one parcel of land under the same mortgage. For example, a developer buys a large tract of land and plans to subdivide the land into 100 lots and then build homes on the lots. Rather than going to the expense and time of obtaining 100 separate mortgages, one blanket mortgage covering all the lots is obtained. Since the developer will probably be developing a few lots at a time, the mortgage will include a *partial release clause* which means that as the debt is paid, individual lots will be released from the mortgage. Thus, the developer can pay off part of the mortgage, have a certain number of lots released, build on the lots and then sell them free and clear from the lien that still exists on the unreleased lots.

Mobile Home Loans

Certain lenders, although not all, make loans on mobile homes. Typically, the amount financed is for much less than the average residential loan, and the amortization period is much shorter, perhaps seven to 10 years, even though longer terms are available under both FHA and VA financing. The amortization period is usually shorter since, unlike a permanent home, a mobile home normally depreciates in value, and thus, the lender wants to be repaid over a shorter period of time. A fear of some lenders is that since mobile homes are not permanently affixed to the land, the security for the loan, the mobile home, can be moved by a dishonest borrower. Thus, not all lenders make mobile home loans.

Land Contracts

Also referred to as an *installment sales contract*, a land contract involves the seller's accepting a down payment on a parcel of land and a series of periodic payments of principal and interest. However, unlike other types of financing, title to the property does not pass until the last payment has been received. Although called a land contract, this means of financing can also be used to purchase improved land. Rules relating to land contracts differ from state to state. For instance, some states require that title be passed when a certain percentage of the loan has been paid by the borrower.

Leasehold Mortgages

Sale-leasebacks are used by owners of commercial property as a means of raising capital. The process involves the simultaneous selling and leasing back of the property usually through a net lease (see Chapter 10). The advantages to the seller include the freeing of capital previously tied up in the project and the inclusion of the rental payment as a legitimate operating expense for income tax purposes. For the investor, the rental payment represents a return on investment and any depreciation for tax purposes or increases in value due to market conditions accrue to the investor.

Land Leases (Ground Leases)

A ground lease is ordinarily a long-term lease for a parcel of unimproved land. The tenant pays what is known as a *ground rental* and pays all taxes and other charges associated with ownership. The landlord receives a net amount which may have an escalation clause to periodically adjust the ground rental so that the property reflects the changing values of the land.

Normally, a ground lease contains a *subordination* clause. A subordination clause is an agreement that the first lienholder will agree to take a junior position to another lienholder. Without a subordination clause, it may be more difficult to construct improvements on the land. A lender, without a subordination agreement by the lessor of the land, will only consider the value of the leasehold in making a loan, while with a subordination will consider the full value of the property.

In certain parts of the country, most notably Baltimore, Maryland, the land under residential real estate is leased through a long-term lease agreement whereby the owner of the land receives periodic rent for the use of the land. Such an agreement covers an extended period of time, possibly 99 years, renewal at the lessee's option and results in a lower purchase price of the home, since the land is not owned in fee simple. Thus, less money has to be borrowed. The owner of the ground rent has a superior lien position to that of the lender, and therefore the lender normally requires the borrower to include the ground rent as part of the monthly debt service. State statutes regulate land leases.

Flexible Financing Techniques

As conditions and needs change, new and more flexible financing techniques have been introduced by lenders. The switch from term mortgages to fully-amortized mortgages and the increase in the loan-to-value ratio are examples of such action. While no one is sure as to exactly what lies ahead, a number of different types of financing techniques are currently being used in certain parts of the country and under certain economic conditions.

Graduated Payment Mortgages (GPM)

Under the level annuity, fully-amortized mortgage, each month's payment is exactly the same. The obvious advantage is that when securing a mortgage the borrower is assured of a level or constant mortgage payment. However, for some purchasers the required monthly payment is so high that a lender will not make the loan simply because the borrower's income is insufficient. With a GPM, monthly mortgage payments start at an amount less than would be required under a level annuity payment and increase periodically over the life of the mortgage. Therefore, the borrower can finance a larger purchase than if the monthly payment were level throughout the life of the mortgage. FHA has a number of GPM programs currently available.

Flexible Loan Insurance Program (FLIP)

This is a graduated payment mortgage developed to overcome the negative amortization aspects of the GPM. The key to the FLIP mortgage is the use of the buyer's downpayment. Instead of being used as a downpayment, the cash is deposited in a pledged, interest-bearing savings account where it serves as both a cash collateral for the lender and as a source of supplemental payments for the borrower during the first few years of the loan. During the early years of the mortgage, each month the lender withdraws predetermined amounts from the savings account and adds them to the borrower's reduced payment to make a full normal mortgage payment. The supplemental payment decreases each month and vanishes at the end of a predetermined period (usually five years). By using this type of program, a borrower is likely to qualify for a larger loan than with a conventional fully-amortized mortgage.

Reverse Annuity Mortgages (RAM)

This is a good financing technique for older people who have little or no debt on their property. Under this arrangement, the lender pays the borrower a fixed annuity based on a percentage of the property's value. The loan is not repaid until sale of the property or the death of the borrower when it is settled through normal probate procedures.

Variable Interest Rate Mortgages (VRM)

Under a variable rate mortgage, the interest rate charged by the lender can vary according to some reference index not controlled by the lender, such as the interest rate on three- to five-year United States government securities. For the lender, this means that as the cost of money increases, the interest being charged on the existing mortgage can be increased, thus maintaining the gap between the cost of money and return. Either the monthly payment, the maturity date or both can be changed to reflect the difference in interest rates. In addition, the mortgage usually stipulates a maximum annual charge and a maximum total increase in the interest the lender may charge. Under current regulations established by the FHLBB, the interest rate may not be raised more than 2½ percentage points above the initial rate. The rate can be changed only once a year, with no more than ½–1% change per year. In addition, borrowers must be allowed to pay off the loan within 90 days of notification of a rate increase.

Renegotiable Rate Mortgages (RRM)

The RRM, following guidelines set by the Federal Home Loan Bank Board, is actually a series of short-term loans issued for terms of 3–5 years each but secured by a long-term 30-year mortgage and carries a mortgage rate that is adjusted every 3–5 years in accordance with a national index. The interest rate can change by only half a percentage point per year for each short term with a maximum increase or decrease of five percentage points. A loan with an original rate of 15%, for example, could go as high as 20% or as low as 10%. The lender cannot refuse to renew the loan at the end of one of the loan periods. However, after the end of the first renewal term, there is no prepayment penalty, and the homeowner can pay off the loan and seek another lender. There are also no penalties for partial prepayment on mortgages.

Adjustable-Rate Mortgage (ARM)

Under this type mortgage, the interest rate can be changed every six months, but the increase cannot be greater than 1%. The interest rate is based on an index tied to U.S. treasury rates or FHLBB mortgage contract rates, neither of which are directly controlled by the lender. Many lenders offer an *interest rate cap* with adjustable rate mortgages which sets a maximum on the amount the interest rate can increase over the life of the loan.

A major drawback in consumer acceptance of the ARM has been the possibility of *negative amortization* during the early years of the loan. Under certain conditions, a rise in interest rates with no increase in monthly payments can result in an increase in the outstanding balance and thus negative amortization. To prevent such from happening, most lenders adjust monthly payments upward when interest rates increase under an adjustable rate mortgage.

Growing Equity Mortgage (GEM)

A growing equity mortgage is a fixed-rate, long-term mortgage that requires periodic increases in the amount of the mortgage payment. The increase in monthly payments is intended to reflect the borrower's ability to repay more debt service over the life of the loan as a result of his or her own financial position. As a result of higher monthly mortgage payments, the borrower is amortizing or repaying the debt much quicker than would normally be the case and thus is able to completely repay the original amount borrowed relatively quickly, perhaps in as little as 12 to 15 years.

Buydown Mortgages

During the late 1970s, builders found it increasingly difficult to locate buyers who could qualify for permanent home loans given the high market interest rates being charged by lenders. In an attempt to qualify more would-be purchasers for loans and in turn find buyers to purchase their homes that were going unsold, some builders began what became known as *buydown* programs or *builder's buydowns*.

Example:
With the current market interest rate at 12% a builder knows a particular purchaser can qualify for a 9% loan and thus could, with the lower interest rate, buy one of the builder's homes. The builder pays the lender the present value difference between what the monthly payments would be with a 12% loan (the market rate of interest) and what they will be if the borrower is only charged a 9% rate (the buydown rate). The length of time over which the buydown rate will apply deter-

mines the actual number of dollars the builder owes the lender. The term of the buydown may cover only 1 or 2 years, or as much as 5 to 7 years. Obviously, the longer the time over which the builder is willing to buy down the interest rate, the more attractive such a loan is to a potential purchaser. In recent years such financing has extended into *for sale by owner* resales as well as new home sales by builders.

Shared Appreciation Mortgage (SAM)

A shared appreciation mortgage is a type of equity participation loan in that in exchange for charging a below-market interest rate, the lender receives a predetermined percentage of any increase in value of the property over a specified period of time. For the lender, the money received from the appreciation of the property increases the effective yield on the investment. The borrower, by agreeing to share the increase in value with the lender, receives a lower interest rate which in turn reduces the monthly mortgage payment. A SAM is normally written so that at the end of the shared appreciation period, the property will be appraised and the amount due to the lender through appreciation is due at that time. The amount due the lender is often referred to as a *piece of the action*, denoting his or her equity involvement in the transaction.

Deferred Interest Mortgages

This financing technique is aimed at those people who plan to live in a house for only a short period of time. Under this mortgage, a lower interest rate and thus a lower monthly mortgage payment is charged. Upon the selling of the house, the lender receives the deferred interest plus a fee for postponing the interest that would normally have been paid each month.

Participation Mortgages

This term, when used to classify types of mortgages, has numerous meanings. One common type of participation mortgage is when more than one mortgagee lends on a real estate project, such as with a large commercial project. A second type of participation mortgage involves more than one borrower being responsible for a mortgage, such as with a co-operative apartment. Finally, a participation mortgage also represents an agreement between a mortgagee and a mortgagor which provides for the lender having a certain percentage ownership in the project once the lender makes the loan.

Sale-Leaseback

A sale-leaseback is a situation in which an owner of property sells the property to an investor and then leases the property back, usually for a twenty- or 30-year term.

Example:
John sells Greencroft to Peggy for $500,000 and agrees to lease it at a net rental to give her a 10% return on her investment. John will receive $500,000 in cash and will keep the property, paying Peggy a net amount of $50,000 each year. At the end of the term, the property will revert to Peggy.

POINTS TO REMEMBER

1. While there are numerous reasons why borrowed capital is used in the purchase or real estate, the more important ones are: (1) size of the capital investment, (2) price increase, (3) leverage and (4) tax incentives.

2. Numerous sources of funds are available for financing real estate purchases. The four primary sources are: (1) savings and loan associations, (2) commercial banks, (3) life insurance companies and (4) mutual savings banks.

3. Savings and loan associations have historically been the most important source of funds for financing real estate in terms of the dollars made available. They are the largest supplier of single-family, owner-occupied, residential permanent financing.

4. Commercial banks are the largest financial intermediary directly involved in financing real estate. Their primary real estate activity involves short-term construction loans.

5. Mortgage brokers and mortgage bankers are financial middlemen who bring together the borrower and the lender. For this service, a finder's fee is paid by the borrower.

6. The secondary mortgage market provides a means by which lenders can convert existing mortgages into cash, which can in turn be used to fund new mortgages. This term should not be confused with a second mortgage, which is a mortgage with a subordinated lien position.

7. The major participants in the secondary mortgage market include: (1) Federal National Mortgage Association, (2) Government National Mortgage Association and (3) Federal Home Loan Mortgage Corporation.

8. Mortgages can be classified a number of different ways. Common classifications include: (1) method of payment, (2) time period, (3) priority and (4) type of property pledged.

9. The FHA usually insures mortgages; the VA usually guarantees mortgages.

10. Regulation Z was published by the Federal Reserve System to implement the regulations covered under the National Consumer Credit Protection Act (Truth-in-Lending Act). The act requires lenders to make credit disclosures to individual borrowers for certain types of loans. Two important disclosures include the finance charge and the annual percentage rate (APR). All real estate lending transactions involving consumers are covered by Regulation Z.

11. As originally passed, the Equal Credit Opportunity Act prohibits discrimination by lenders on the basis of sex or marital status. The Act has been extended to cover additional protected groups of borrowers.

12. In order to prevent the practice of redlining and disinvestment in central city areas, Congress passed the Community Reinvestment Act. Redlining is a practice whereby lenders refuse to make loans in certain geographic areas of a city.

KEY TERMS AND PHRASES

adjustable rate mortgage (ARM)
annual percentage rate (APR)
balloon payment
blanket mortgage
buydown mortgage
closed mortgage
conventional mortgage
Equal Credit Opportunity Act
equity
Fair Credit Reporting Act
Federal Deposit Insurance Corporation (FDIC)
Federal Home Loan Bank System (FHLBS)
Federal Home Loan Mortgage Corporation
Federal National Mortgage Association (FNMA)

Federal Reserve System (FRS)
Federal Savings & Loan Insurance Corporation (FSLIC)
FHA-insured mortgage
flexible loan insurance program (FLIP)
fully-amortized mortgage
Government National Mortgage Association (GNMA)
graduated payment mortgage (GPM)
growing equity mortgage (GEM)
loan-to-value ratio
mortgage banker
mortgage broker
National Flood Insurance
open mortgage
package mortgage
partial release clause

partially-amortized mortgage
permanent mortgage
purchase money mortgage
redlining
Regulation Z
renegotiable rate mortgage (RRM)
reverse annuity mortgage (RAM)
savings and loan associations
second mortgage
secondary mortgage market
shared appreciation mortgage (SAM)
straight-term mortgage
Truth-in-Lending Act
usury
VA-guaranteed mortgage
variable interest rate mortgage (VRM)
wraparound mortgage

QUESTIONS

1. Which of the following can FHA mortgages be used to finance?
   I. Single-family homes
   II. Mobile homes
   A. I only
   B. II only
   C. Both I and II
   D. Neither I nor II

2. If the buyer gives a note or bond and a mortgage to the seller as part of the purchase price, the resulting mortgage is commonly referred to as a (an)
   A. purchase money mortgage
   B. package mortgage
   C. security mortgage
   D. open-end mortgage

3. If the buyer of a home wanted to include in the terms of a mortgage the financing of such items as a stove, refrigerator and air-conditioning, the mortgage used would be a (an)
   A. open mortgage
   B. wrap-around mortgage
   C. package mortgage
   D. blanket mortgage

4. An annual insurance fee of ¼% of the unpaid balance would normally be found with which of the following types of mortgages?
   A. VA
   B. FHA
   C. Conventional
   D. Conventional with private mortgage insurance

5. The home buyer who pays a lump sum insurance fee at closing known as a mortgage insurance premium in addition to the mortgage payment is probably suing a (an)
   A. VA mortgage
   B. FHA mortgage
   C. conventional mortgage
   D. privately insured conventional mortgage

6. A mortgage without a prepayment penalty is commonly referred to as a (an)
   A. closed mortgage
   B. open-end mortgage
   C. balloon mortgage
   D. open mortgage

7. Which of the following is *most* correct about Regulation Z?
   I. It requires full disclosure of all closing costs.
   II. It is referred to as the Truth-in-Lending Act.
   A. I only
   B. II only
   C. Both I and II
   D. Neither I nor II

8. A mortgage loan which gives the mortgagee a fixed interest return plus a percentage of gross sales is called a (an)
   A. blanket mortgage
   B. wrap-around mortgage
   C. participation mortgage
   D. insured mortgage

9. All federally chartered savings and loan associations must be members of the
   I. Federal Home Loan Bank
   II. Federal Deposit Insurance Corporation
   A. I only
   B. II only
   C. Both I and II
   D. Neither I nor II

10. Which of the following is a buyer in the secondary mortgage market?
    A. Federal Reserve System
    B. Veterans Administration
    C. Federal Housing Administration
    D. Federal National Mortgage Association

11. Which of the following statements is true?
    I. VA insures mortgages.
    II. FHA guarantees mortgages.
    A. I only
    B. II only
    C. Both I and II
    D. Neither I nor II

12. The fee received by a mortgage broker who brings a lender and a borrower together is known as a (an):
    A. underwriter's fee
    B. servicing fee
    C. finder's fee
    D. estoppel fee

13. The fee for the appraisal of the property is part of the loan origination fee and is paid by the
    A. mortgagor
    B. mortgagee
    C. broker
    D. trustee

14. Regulation Z requires disclosure of credit information regarding
    I. finance charges
    II. APR
    A. I only
    B. II only
    C. Both I and II
    D. Neither I nor II

15. The body which establishes basic policies to be followed by nationally chartered banks is the
    A. FHLBB
    B. FHA
    C. FSLIC
    D. FRS

16. As a hedge against inflation, a long-term commercial lender often requires the borrower to accept a (an)
    A. prepayment penalty
    B. defeasance clause
    C. equity participation mortgage
    D. balloon payment

17. In a construction loan mortgage,
    A. the funds are advanced before construction begins
    B. the funds are not advanced until construction is completely finished
    C. the loan is advanced in installments at various stages of construction
    D. interest on the total loan begins at the beginning of construction

18. Where two or more properties are covered by one mortgage and one property is to be freed from the mortgage, the instrument used is a
    A. partial release of mortgage
    B. satisfaction of mortgage
    C. certificate of reduction of mortgage
    D. assignment of mortgage

19. VA-guaranteed mortgages may *not* exceed
    A. $27,500
    B. $55,000
    C. $100,000
    D. No limit has been set by Congress

20. The mortgage purchase procedure used by the FNMA is conducted through an auction process referred to as a (an)
    A. tandem plan
    B. open market operation
    C. Free Market System Auction
    D. straight pass-through auction

21. What types of credit transactions does Regulation Z cover?
    I. Credit in excess of $25,000
    II. All real estate transactions involving consumers
    A. I only
    B. II only
    C. Both I and II
    D. Neither I nor II

22. Usury occurs when the lender
    A. collects more than the maximum legal rate of interest
    B. charges less than the maximum legal rate of interest
    C. loans more than 95% of the appraised value of the property
    D. defaults

23. The difference between the price of a parcel of land and the balance owed on the existing mortgage is known as
    A. equality
    B. fee
    C. equity
    D. profit

24. Loans are usually based on the
    A. sales price
    B. appraised value
    C. appraised value or sales price, whichever is less
    D. amount of the assessed value

25. The mortgage which covers two or more pieces of property pledged as security is a
    A. second mortgage
    B. blanket mortgage
    C. package mortgage
    D. participation mortgage

26. An open-end residential mortgage permits
    I. the borrower to borrow additional funds for home improvements from the current lender
    II. fluctuations in the interest rate charged the borrower

Financing Real Estate

A. I only   C. Both I and II
B. II only   D. Neither I nor II

27. When using the fully-amortized level payment mortgage
    A. the amount of payment on the principal stays the same
    B. the interest payment is always greater than the principal payment
    C. each payment remains the same
    D. a lump sum payment is made at the end of the mortgage

28. Who is protected by Regulation Z?
    A. Consumers
    B. Businesses
    C. Governments
    D. Lenders

29. Historically, approximately one-half of all single-family real estate mortgages in the United States have been financed through
    A. savings and loan associations
    B. Federal National Mortgage Association
    C. life insurance companies
    D. governmental agencies

30. The penalty for prepaying an FHA mortgage is
    A. $100
    B. 1% of the balance at time of prepayment
    C. 1% of the original amount borrowed
    D. There is no prepayment penalty for FHA mortgages.

31. Mortgage bankers often operate through take-out commitments which are
    A. binding letters of agreement from a permanent lender to purchase a group of mortgages for a stated time at a given price
    B. agreements by the mortgage banker to finance a given number of mortgages for a builder
    C. written agreements by commercial banks to lend working capital to the mortgage banker
    D. agreements for the Federal National Mortgage Association to buy a given number of mortgages from the mortgage banker

32. A mortgage lender's practice of refusing to make mortgage loans in certain neighborhoods because of high risk or lack of profit potential is called
    A. blacklisting   C. redlining
    B. mortgage screening   D. black-balling

33. Which of the following must be disclosed as a finance charge under Regulation Z?
    A. Discount points
    B. Title examination fees
    C. Appraisal fees
    D. Survey fees

Questions 34 and 35 refer to the following information:
"A" wishes to purchase a home with the help of a loan from a savings and loan association. The purchase price is $40,000. The S&L is willing to make an 80% loan and will charge "A" three discount points. "A's" attorney advises him that there will be $1,000 in closing costs over and above the discount points.

34. What is the amount of the discount points?
    A. $960   C. $8,000
    B. $1,200   D. $240

35. How much cash will "A" need to close?
    A. $8,000   C. $9,960
    B. $9,240   D. $10,200

36. The annual percentage rate (APR) is the annual cost of credit and is
    A. the same as the contract rate in a note
    B. a rate that includes any adjustments for service charges and discount rates
    C. an estimate of the nominal interest rate on the mortgage
    D. the same as the debt service

37. Usury laws fix which of the following?
    A. Minimum interest rates
    B. Maximum interest rates
    C. Length of time for repayment of a loan
    D. Loan-to-value ratio

38. In the case of the privately insured conventional loan, the interest rate is
    A. set by the federal government
    B. set by the private mortgage insurance company
    C. negotiated with the lender by the borrower
    D. negotiated with the lender by the private mortgage insurance company

39. A borrower who in addition to the monthly interest and principal payment also pays one-twelfth of the annual property tax and property insurance is using a (an)
    A. purchase money mortgage
    B. open-end mortgage
    C. package mortgage
    D. budget mortgage

40. The person in the loan process who reviews all the documentation and makes a recommendation on the loan is known as the
    A. originator
    B. servicer
    C. underwriter
    D. warehouser

41. Which of the following type of loans is insured by the Mortgage Guaranty Insurance Corporation?
    A. FHA   C. FNMA
    B. VA   D. conventional

42. In regard to discount points, which of the following statements is (are) correct?
    I. Discount points serve as a substitute to raising mortgage interest rates.
    II. Lenders charge discount points on federally insured and guaranteed loans when the yield on these loans falls below current market interest rates.
    A. I only
    B. II only
    C. Both I and II
    D. Neither I nor II

43. The term lenders use to describe the relative amount of money they will loan on a given piece of property is the
    A. debt-to-equity ratio
    B. times interest earned
    C. loan-to-value ratio
    D. gross income multiplier

44. The money for an FHA loan is secured from
    A. any governmental agency
    B. the Federal Housing Authority
    C. a qualified lending institution
    D. the Federal Deposit Insurance Corporation

45. The _____ was created in 1934 by an act of Congress to encourage the construction and ownership of homes, especially those in the lower price ranges.
    A. Federal Housing Administration
    B. Federal National Mortgage Association
    C. Federal Savings and Loan Insurance Corporation
    D. Department of Housing and Urban Development

If you are not sure of your answers, see page 322 for correct answers and explanations.

Financing Real Estate

16

Title Examination and Settlement

Title defects can result in serious consequences. A purchaser of land may lose all or partial use of the property due to bad title, adverse possession, liens or other encumbrances. A lender may lose the security represented by the pledged property. A lienholder may lose priority of lien. For these reasons, as well as others, a very elaborate system of title assurance has been developed in this country.

RECORDATION AND THE CHAIN OF TITLE

In order to determine whether title contains any defects or encumbrances which would mar its marketability, it is necessary to trace the chain of title in the public records. The *chain of title* is merely a successive series of title transfers from grantors to grantees. Since as a general rule a person can acquire no better title than that held by the previous grantor, it is necessary to trace the chain back to the origins of title in some government patent. Because this is time consuming, many states have passed laws which establish a statutory presumption that if the chain is unbroken for some period of time, such as 50 years, the title is presumed to be valid.

The key to title examination is the recordation system in each state. State recording acts are designed to provide a means of protecting persons who acquire an interest in real estate by permitting them to give constructive notice to the whole world as to the existence of that interest. This also gives subsequent purchasers protection from secret, unrecorded claims on the property by cutting off those claims when the land is acquired by a bona fide purchaser who pays value without notice of these adverse claims. Thus, in most cases a person who wishes to preserve a claim or interest in property must record or file an appropriate instrument as required by state law. This rule does not apply to persons in possession of property such as a tenant under a short-term lease. Any evidence of possession which can be determined by reasonable physical inspection of property also serves as constructive notice. It is therefore always advisable to inspect land before purchase to determine if such unrecorded interests as prescriptive easements burden the property.

Title records are normally indexed one of two ways: (1) the grantor-grantee or cross index, and (2) the tract index. Under the *grantor-grantee or cross index* system two sets of indexes exist, one for each party to an instrument. These indexes are kept in alphabetical order for each year. If for example, John Doe grants Hillydale to Mary Jones, the deed would be referenced in the grantor index under John Doe's name and in the grantee index under Mary Jones' name. Depending on the sophistication of the records, this index is computerized or is handwritten in a book by the clerk or recorder. Sometimes all of the names beginning with a particular letter are only indexed chronologically by when the instrument was filed, requiring a title examiner to check all of the names under that letter; sometimes the index is refined enough for all names to be in alphabetical order. Under the *tract index* a separate page is kept for each tract of land in a particular jurisdiction. All instruments involving a particular tract are indexed on the page for that tract. Because each jurisdiction has its own peculiarities in keeping and indexing records, the job of title examination is often left to professionals who are called *title examiners* or *abstractors*.

In order for an instrument to have the legal effect of constructive notice, it must be within the chain of title. For example, John Brown on March 1 grants Yellow Valley by deed to Elma Fudd who promptly records on the same day. On March 15 John Brown grants the same property to Mary Smith, who also records. Mary Smith's recordation would have no legal effect—it is not in the chain of title since John Brown had earlier passed title to Elma Fudd. What happens when there is a mistake in the recording of an instrument by the clerk? In most states the document is binding just as if it had been properly recorded. This is an exception to the rule that an instrument not in the chain of title is not binding. However, in some states it is the obligation of the party seeking the recording to make sure that the instrument is properly recorded.

ABSTRACT OF TITLE

An *abstract of title* is a condensed chronological history of all recorded instruments in the chain of title which affect the title. An abstract of title is prepared by an abstractor who may be an attorney, a public official or an employee of an abstract company. The abstractor examines the records and condenses relevant information on each instrument affecting title. No opinion as to the quality of the title is normally given.

A typical examination would begin by the abstractor examining the grantee index for each preceding year until the name of the current owner of the examined property is found. The same procedure is followed to find the source of title of the current owner's grantor. This is repeated as many times as is necessary until a satisfactory grantor is found, usually a government patent. The next step is to examine the grantor index and check to determine for each subsequent year whether the original grantor conveyed or in some manner encumbered title to property prior to the conveyance to the grantee found in the first search. This procedure is repeated for each grantor in the chain of title. Occasionally, a break in the chain occurs, and this break must be satisfactorily explained. For example, the abstractor may find that George Harris granted Greensprings to Karen Harper in 1936. Later the examiner discovers that Greensprings was granted by Karen Adams to Fred French in 1942. The examiner has to determine if Karen Harper and Karen Adams are actually the same person. Other problems occur when there is a death or a mortgage foreclosure sale. The abstractor will need to examine other records to determine if the transfer was valid and confirmed by a court. Examination is normally made of proceedings of a probate court to determine if an executor's or administrator's deed was issued pursuant to proper authority. If a mortgage has been given, the examiner must determine whether it has been released or a satisfaction piece recorded. Judgment and lis pendens dockets must be examined to determine whether the property has any liens burdening it. Property tax liens, special assessments, mechanic's liens, federal tax liens and other such encumbrances should be checked for in the appropriate records by the title examiner. Normally an abstractor will not examine records outside the jurisdiction or physically inspect the property.

After the title examination, the abstractor prepares the abstract of title and issues a certificate. The abstract of title contains a caption which includes a legal description of the property of which the title was examined. Following the caption is a condensation for each instrument examined. A typical condensation might look as follows:

IRVING BERLIN to JACK LONDON	Special Warranty Deed Dated May 15, 1945 Acknowledged May 17, 1945 Recorded May 25, 1945 in Deed Book 503, Page 87 Consideration: $25,000.00 Revenue Stamps: $27.50 Attested by: Sam Tracy Garry Ford

Conveys caption property with easement to cross land to reach fishing hole reserved to grantor

This certificate issued by the abstractor states what records were examined and for what period of time the search was made. The certificate limits the liability of the abstractor to omissions in the search due to negligence. In some states the abstractor is liable for negligence only to those who paid for the search. No liability is accepted for unrecorded instruments such as mechanic's liens, or those instruments that were outside the chain of title or recorded outside the jurisdiction.

If a person wishes to have the quality of title evaluated, the abstract is given to a qualified attorney. After examining the abstract, the attorney then renders an opinion based on the written abstract. This is referred to as *opinion of title*. Alternatively, the title attorney or title examiner issues a *certificate of title* which is an opinion of the quality of the title. The opinion or certificate will point out any defects which are revealed by an examination of the record. The opinion is not a guarantee that the title has no defects but only that the record reveals no defects as of a given date.

There are a number of defects that may exist which cannot be discovered by an examination of the record. Examples include delivery of a deed after the death of a grantor or grantee; deeds issued by persons who are legally incapacitated by virtue of insanity, minority or other reasons; and deeds issued without release of dower, curtesy or other marital rights. In addition, the record may contain forged deeds, satisfaction pieces and others. The purpose for acknowledgment is to screen out such defective instruments, but this is not always successful. There may be errors in the indexing of instruments or other mistakes in the recordation process. When a person dies, there may be an invalid will or missing heirs. Other technical problems might include a deed given under an invalid power of attorney or failure of a co-owner to join in a conveyance. These types of title defects may be covered by commercial title insurance.

TITLE INSURANCE

Title insurance provides protection to a named insured for loss sustained from title defects not excepted in the policy. This type of protection extends not only to negligent errors and omissions by the title examiner but also to hidden or unknown defects in title prior to the date of the title policy. In addition to indemnification of losses, the title insurance company also promises to pay the cost of defending a lawsuit brought about because of alleged defects in title insured by the policy.

Title insurance involves the payment of a single premium at the time that the coverage is purchased. Premiums vary from company to company but usually range between $3.50 to $5.00 per $1,000 of coverage. This premium is in addition to the costs of the title examination itself. The protection is for the face amount of the policy or the insured's interest, whichever is the lesser sum. In general there are two types of title insurance policies: (1) the *owner's policy* and (2) the *mortgagee's policy*. Many lenders require a borrower to take out a title policy in favor of the lender at the time a loan is made for the principal amount of the loan. As the principal is amortized, the maximum coverage on the policy is also reduced. Even though the owner may pay the premium on the mortgagee's policy, in the event of loss due to a title defect, the owner's equity interest is not protected. In addition, after indemnification is made to the mortgagee, the insurance company, by right of subrogation, may be able to place a lien on the property unless the owner also has title insurance coverage with the same company. This coverage can be acquired under an owner's policy for a small additional premium which is paid at the same time the mortgagee's policy is purchased. This protection is personal to the named insured and subsequent heirs, and the policy is not transferable. The mortgagee's policy, however, may be transferred by assignment.

As with other contracts, care should be taken to read a title insurance policy to determine exactly what kind of coverage is being purchased. A title insurance policy is usually divisible into five section, discussed below. (See Figure 16–1.)

Agreement to Insure

The agreement to insure specifies what the title insurance company agrees to do in case of loss sustained due to defects in title. This agreement is entered into after the company has examined title and has satisfied itself that the risk of loss is minimal. The company is under no obligation to insure title which it deems to be uninsurable due to unexplained breaks in the chain or due to other serious clouds on title. After the search, the company issues a *preliminary binder* which indicates the company's willingness to insure subject to stated exceptions. These exceptions may be due to defects which can be cleared prior to issuing the final policy.

Description of the Subject Matter

This section describes the estate or interest being insured. For example, the policy may be issued to protect the interests of a lessee having a long-term leasehold which will be improved with a costly building. A sufficient legal description of the land is included plus identification of any improvements on the land. This section of the policy is sometimes referred to as "Schedule A."

Exceptions

This section, sometimes referred to as "Schedule B," lists all discovered defects and encumbrances against which the company will not insure. If these defects are satisfactorily corrected by obtaining proper releases, the company may remove the exception from this schedule. The process of removing defects is called *perfecting title*. In addition, each policy contains standard exceptions. Included are any facts that a survey would disclose, rights of parties in possession, facts that physical inspection of the property would reveal, any unrecorded tax liens and special assessments, any unrecorded mechanic's liens and any losses sustained by planned government action such as zoning restrictions or actions taken pursuant to the power of eminent domain. Some of these exceptions may be left out by agreement of the insured and the insurer. For example, if the company is provided with a survey taken by a licensed surveyor, the company may broaden the coverage to include protection against encroachments or other such defects that a survey would be expected to reveal.

Conditions

This is a set of stipulations which must be met before the company is required to pay indemnification. Conditions may include the right of the company to step in and defend a lawsuit and the requirement that they reach final adjudication. Another requirement may be the company's right of subrogation, a right to step into the legal position of the insured. Any waiver of a person's rights against those persons responsible for the loss by signing releases could damage the company's right to subrogation and acts as a defense against the company being required to pay indemnification. Another condition might be the right of the company to take over the property at a fair appraised price if it pays out money exceeding a certain amount to cover a loss.

Endorsements

In addition to the standard coverage, an insured may wish to purchase additional coverage for an extra premium. The amount and cost of this additional coverage is subject to negotiation and agreement between the insurer and the insured. For example, a mortgagee may wish to have an endorsement which will extend coverage for any subsequent loss of priority of lien by any unrecorded mechanic's lien which is later properly filed.

Figure 16–1. Title Insurance—Owner's Policy

Schedule A (Coverage)
Negligent Errors or Omissions
  —errors in indexing
  —other mistakes in recordation

Hidden or Unknown Defects Prior to Date of Policy
  —forged deeds or documents
  —failure of co-owner to join in conveyance
  —failure to release dower or other marital rights
  —deeds issued by incapacitated persons (insane, minors)
  —invalid power of attorney
  —delivery of deed after death of grantor or grantee
  —invalid will
  —missing heirs

Schedule B (Exceptions)
  —facts that a survey would disclose
  —rights of parties in possession
  —facts that physical inspection of property would reveal
  —unrecorded tax liens/special assessments
  —unrecorded mechanic's liens
  —government actions such as zoning or eminent domain

Endorsements (Additional Coverage)
Subject to negotiation and agreement with insurance company
  —mechanic's liens
  —other unrecorded liens
  —adjustments for appreciation in property

TORRENS SYSTEM OF TITLE REGISTRATION

Many states recognize a system of title registration called the *Torrens System*, named after Sir Robert Torrens who developed the system in Australia in 1857. This system operates parallel to the more conventional system of title transfer and recordation. The Torrens System is very similar to the system of registering automobile titles, in that the person who owns title to land registers the title and the title is represented by a certificate of registration called a *Torrens Certificate*. For any liens or encumbrances to have validity, they must appear on an original certificate of title kept by the registrar of titles in the jurisdiction.

In states that recognize the Torrens System a property owner initially has the option to record title conventionally or to register title under the Torrens System. Once the option is taken to register the title, only a court order can remove the title from registration. All subsequent transfers and other dealings involving the title must take place through the registrar's office, or the transaction will have no validity against innocent third parties. Under the Torrens System, title does not pass until it is properly registered and a new original certificate issued to replace the cancelled old one; thus, a deed is not effective in passing title when it is delivered and accepted as it is under the conventional system. Once title is registered, all prior liens are cancelled and all title defects removed. Title becomes absolute in the name of the registered owner. Because of this serious legal consequence, each state has developed an elaborate procedure for the initial title registration.

LOOK THIS UP:
Does your state recognize a Torrens System of title registration?
Yes_____ No _____

WHAT IS SETTLEMENT?

As was discussed in Chapter 13, legal title to property is transferred from seller to buyer when the instrument of conveyance is delivered. Normally this takes place at a meeting after various preliminary procedures having been performed. This meeting, commonly called *closing* or *settlement*, will normally be attended by seller and buyer, or their representatives; attorneys representing various parties; representatives of the lending institution; and some representative of the broker of record. At this meeting certain documents are delivered by each party, papers are signed, the closing statement is reviewed, the parties obtain certain documents and funds are disbursed.

Normally, the sales contract specifies where settlement is to occur. Depending on where the buyer and seller reside in the United States, settlement can take place at the lender's office, the closing attorney's office or at the title company. Also stated in the sales contract is the time and date of the settlement. Enough time should be allowed for the necessary requirements of closing such as inspection, title search, drawing of instruments and survey. If the time of closing is not stated in the sales contract, a court will allow a reasonable period of time to complete the necessary requirements. Provision is often made in a sales contract to permit the seller a reasonable period of time to correct any defects reported by the title examiner. If the phrase "time is of the essence" is included in the sales contract, then the closing date must take place as specified in the sales agreement.

In some parts of the country, the actual settlement does not involve a buyer, seller, attorneys and brokers assembling at a meeting; rather, the transaction is closed by an *escrow agent*. This procedure is referred to as closing in escrow, and the person acting for all the parties is a neutral third party. The deed is delivered by the seller to the escrow agent and the money necessary to purchase the property is delivered from the buyer to the escrow agent. The escrow agent will hold all papers until the occurrence or nonoccurrence of some event or act. Normally, once an examination of title is completed and the escrow agent is satisfied that the seller has clear title, the money collected passes to the seller and the deed is delivered to the buyer.

PRELIMINARY PROCEDURES

For illustrative purposes a hypothetical residential purchase transaction is used here to explain what happens before, during and after closing. While no two closings are ever exactly alike, the procedures and requirements discussed below cover the normal course of events in a real estate transaction.

The Listing Contract

Before a buyer and seller enter into a sales agreement, the seller has ordinarily entered into a binding agreement with a real estate broker. Included in this agreement are the rights and responsibilities of the parties to the listing contract. In the vast majority of residential transactions the listing contract is a preprinted form and is completed by either the broker or a salesperson licensed to act on behalf of the broker. The terms of the agreement should be specified so that each party knows exactly what he or she agreed to do.

The Preliminary Negotiations

Once the listing contract has been signed, the broker begins showing the subject property to potential buyers. Normally, negotiations between at least one of the persons who inspects the property and the seller will begin. When this happens, the broker normally acts as the intermediary, although the buyer should remember that the broker, if employed by the seller, is legally bound to act on behalf of the seller (see Chapter 6). As the negotiations continue, such things as sales price, closing costs, financing and items included in the sale are negotiated. Offers and counteroffers will perhaps be made until both parties agree to the specific conditions of sale and are ready to enter into a sales agreement.

The Sales Contract

Once both parties have agreed to all the conditions of sale, a formal sales contract will be entered into by buyer and seller. In some jurisdictions it is customary for the broker to also be a party to the contract. If he or she is not, provisions should be made in the contract to define the rights of the broker.

As is true with the listing agreement, the sales contract is often a standardized form provided by the broker. Each transaction, however, has certain conditions of sale unique to it which should be included in the contract. Common conditions of sale include financing arrangements, service fees, amenities included in the sales price and date of possession and disposition of the earnest money deposit made by the buyer. Each party receives a copy of the contract, and state licensing laws normally require the broker to retain a copy of all contracts.

Financing Commitment

As was fully discussed in Chapter 15, most real estate transactions require the borrowing of money in order to pay for the property. Thus, it is necessary for the buyer to find someone who is willing to advance the necessary funds. The broker should know who is making loans and the type of loans being made. In order to protect himself or herself against possible default or having to accept undesirable financing terms, the buyer should insert a "subject to financing" clause in the sales contract. This clause will state the amount to be financed, the type of loan, the interest rate and term. Then, if this financing cannot be found, the buyer will not have to default on the contract and the contract will not be enforceable.

Since lenders will be required to spend both time and money in determining whether or not the requested funds should be provided, a common practice is to require a prospective borrower to present a signed contract of sale *prior to* the borrower's taking the loan application. The signed contract provides such pertinent information to the lender as sales price, location of the property and conditions of sale. At the same time the signed contract is presented to the lender, other information is also supplied by the buyer such as an employment record, current financial holdings, additional sources of income and other personal data. Both sorts of information are used by the lender in evaluating the borrower so as to reach a loan decision.

Real Estate Settlement Procedures Act (RESPA)

In 1974, Congress passed the Real Estate Settlement Procedures Act which took effect in June, 1975. This act covers most mortgage loans made for one to four unit *residential* property. While RESPA does not set limits on the charges lenders can levy in closing a loan, it does require the lender to provide the loan applicant with pertinent information so that the borrower can make informed decisions as to which lender to use in financing the purchase.

Information Booklet

When a person submits an application or when a lender prepares a written application, RESPA requires the lender to give the applicant a copy of a booklet prepared by the U.S. Department of Housing and Urban Development (HUD) entitled "Settlement Costs And You." If the booklet is not made available by the lender on the day of the application, it must be mailed to the applicant within three business days after the application is filed.

Part One of the booklet describes the settlement procedures, the various services the buyer needs and information on the borrower's rights under RESPA. *Part Two* explains each item in the settlement statement and gives sample forms for the borrower to use in making cost comparisons.

Good-Faith Estimates

When someone applies for a loan, the lender must also provide good-faith estimates of the settlement costs that will likely be incurred in financing the property. If this estimate is not provided at the time of application, it must be mailed within three business days.

The estimates given are supposed to be based on the lender's experience in making such loans, but they may change due to changing market conditions. The final costs incurred at closing may not be exactly the same since the lender's good-faith estimate is not a guarantee.

Lender Designation of Settlement-Service Providers

Some lenders use particular closing attorneys, title examination companies, title insurers and other settlement-service providers. Where this occurs, RESPA requires the lender to provide the borrower with the name, address and telephone number of each provider, the specific service each firm provides and an estimate of charges the borrower can expect to pay. Also, the lender must specify if the provider has a business relationship with the lender. The lender is prohibited from receiving secret kickbacks from a provider of a service.

Disclosure of Settlement Costs

One day before the scheduled closing the borrower has the right under RESPA to inspect the Uniform Settlement Statement which gives an itemized account of all fees charged by the lender. While some of the fees to be incurred at closing might not be known, the lender must make available those charges he or she knows will be levied. Even though the borrower might choose to waive the right to examine the settlement statement, it must be mailed at the earliest practical date. A Uniform Settlement Statement form is presented in Figure 16–2.

Truth-in-Lending

At the time the loan is actually consummated, which is normally the same time as settlement, the lender must disclose the effective interest rate or annual percentage rate (APR) being charged the borrower. The APR is likely to be higher than the contract interest rate quoted by the lender when the commitment to provide the financing was made. This is true since the effective interest rate includes not only the contract interest rate but also any discount points, fees and financial charges to be paid at the time of settlement. Also, any charges made by the lender if the borrower decides to prepay the loan must also be included in the Truth-in-Lending statement (see Chapter 15).

Figure 16–2. Uniform Settlement Statement

A. Settlement Statement

U.S. Department of Housing and Urban Development

OMB No. 2502-0265 (Exp. 12-31-86)

B. Type of Loan

1. ☐ FHA 2. ☐ FmHA 3. ☐ Conv. Unins.
4. ☐ VA   5. ☐ Conv. Ins.

6. File Number | 7. Loan Number | 8. Mortgage Insurance Case Number

C. Note: This form is furnished to give you a statement of actual settlement costs. Amounts paid to and by the settlement agent are shown. Items marked "(p.o.c.)" were paid outside the closing; they are shown here for informational purposes and are not included in the totals.

D. Name and Address of Borrower | E. Name and Address of Seller | F. Name and Address of Lender

G. Property Location

H. Settlement Agent

Place of Settlement | I. Settlement Date

J. Summary of Borrower's Transaction		K. Summary of Seller's Transaction	
100. Gross Amount Due From Borrower		400. Gross Amount Due To Seller	
101. Contract sales price		401. Contract sales price	
102. Personal property		402. Personal property	
103. Settlement charges to borrower (line 1400)		403.	
104.		404.	
105.		405.	
Adjustments for items paid by seller in advance		*Adjustments for items paid by seller in advance*	
106. City/town taxes to		406. City/town taxes to	
107. County taxes to		407. County taxes to	
108. Assessments to		408. Assessments to	
109.		409.	
110.		410.	
111.		411.	
112.		412.	
120. Gross Amount Due From Borrower		420. Gross Amount Due To Seller	
200. Amounts Paid By Or In Behalf Of Borrower		500. Reductions In Amount Due To Seller	
201. Deposit or earnest money		501. Excess deposit (see instructions)	
202. Principal amount of new loan(s)		502. Settlement charges to seller (line 1400)	
203. Existing loan(s) taken subject to		503. Existing loan(s) taken subject to	
204.		504. Payoff of first mortgage loan	
205.		505. Payoff of second mortgage loan	
206.		506.	
207.		507.	
208.		508.	
209.		509.	
Adjustments for items unpaid by seller		*Adjustments for items unpaid by seller*	
210. City/town taxes to		510. City/town taxes to	
211. County taxes to		511. County taxes to	
212. Assessments to		512. Assessments to	
213.		513.	
214.		514.	
215.		515.	
216.		516.	
217.		517.	
218.		518.	
219.		519.	
220. Total Paid By/For Borrower		520. Total Reduction Amount Due Seller	
300. Cash At Settlement From/To Borrower		600. Cash At Settlement To/From Seller	
301. Gross Amount due from borrower (line 120)		601. Gross amount due to seller (line 420)	
302. Less amounts paid by/for borrower (line 220)	( )	602. Less reductions in amt. due seller (line 520)	( )
303. Cash ☐ From ☐ To Borrower		603. Cash ☐ To ☐ From Seller	

Previous Edition Is Obsolete

HUD 1 (3-86)

Figure 16–2. con't.

L. Settlement Charges			
700. Total Sales/Broker's Commission based on price $ @ % =		Paid From Borrower's Funds at Settlement	Paid From Seller's Funds at Settlement
Division of Commission (line 700) as follows:			
701. $ to			
702. $ to			
703. Commission paid at Settlement			
704.			
800. Items Payable In Connection With Loan			
801. Loan Origination Fee %			
802. Loan Discount %			
803. Appraisal Fee to			
804. Credit Report to			
805. Lender's Inspection Fee			
806. Mortgage Insurance Application Fee to			
807. Assumption Fee			
808.			
809.			
810.			
811.			
900. Items Required By Lender To Be Paid In Advance			
901. Interest from to @$ /day			
902. Mortgage Insurance Premium for months to			
903. Hazard Insurance Premium for years to			
904. years to			
905.			
1000. Reserves Deposited With Lender			
1001. Hazard insurance months@$ per month			
1002. Mortgage insurance months@$ per month			
1003. City property taxes months@$ per month			
1004. County property taxes months@$ per month			
1005. Annual assessments months@$ per month			
1006. months@$ per month			
1007. months@$ per month			
1008. months@$ per month			
1100. Title Charges			
1101. Settlement or closing fee to			
1102. Abstract or title search to			
1103. Title examination to			
1104. Title insurance binder to			
1105. Document preparation to			
1106. Notary fees to			
1107. Attorney's fees to			
(includes above items numbers:)			
1108. Title insurance to			
(includes above items numbers:)			
1109. Lender's coverage $			
1110. Owner's coverage $			
1111.			
1112.			
1113.			
1200. Government Recording and Transfer Charges			
1201. Recording fees: Deed $; Mortgage $; Releases $			
1202. City/county tax/stamps: Deed $; Mortgage $			
1203. State tax/stamps: Deed $; Mortgage $			
1204.			
1205.			
1300. Additional Settlement Charges			
1301. Survey to			
1302. Pest inspection to			
1303.			
1304.			
1305.			
1400. Total Settlement Charges (enter on lines 103, Section J and 502, Section K)			

I have carefully reviewed the HUD-1 Settlement Statement and to the best of my knowledge and belief, it is a true and accurate statement of all receipts and disbursements made on my account or by me in this transaction. I further certify that I have recieved a copy of HUD-1 Settlement Statement.

Borrowers   Sellers

The HUD-1 Settlement Statement which I have prepared is a true and accurate account of this transaction. I have caused or will cause the funds to be disbursed in accordance with this statement.

Settlement Agent   Date

WARNING: It is a crime to knowingly make false statements to the United States on this or any other similar form. Penalties upon conviction can include a fine or imprisonment. For details see: Title 18 U.S. Code Section 1001 and Section 1010.

The Right to File Complaints

Normally, any complaints the borrower might have are satisfied by discussing the problem with the lender rather than taking civil action. However, if a person believes he or she has been damaged under the Real Estate Settlement Procedures Act, he or she may be entitled to civil action in U.S. District Court. A suit must be filed within one year of the alleged violation. Certain acts may also be in violation of other federal and state laws.

Complaints and inquiries can be made to:

Assistant Secretary for Consumer Affairs and Regulatory Functions
Attention: RESPA Office
U.S. Department of Housing and Urban Development
451 7th Street, S.W.
Room 4100
Washington, D.C. 20410

SETTLEMENT COSTS

There are no requirements in RESPA as to who can close the transaction. Since procedures vary from jurisdiction to jurisdiction, settlement is conducted by different people: the lending institution or its attorney, the title company, the broker or an escrow agent. Regardless of who actually closes the transaction, certain costs will be incurred. Some of the more common ones are discussed below (also see Appendix B).

Broker's Commission

This is the sales commission due the broker for finding the qualified buyer who was ready, willing and able to purchase the property. Usually paid by the seller, this fee will normally have been stated in the listing contract and is usually a percentage of the selling price.

Loan Fees

Certain fees will be charged by the lender in connection with the loan.

Loan Origination

This charge covers the administrative costs incurred by the lender and is typically stated as a percentage of the loan. For example, the lender might charge a 1% fee. On a $50,000 loan this charge would be $500. Generally, the buyer pays this fee.

Loan Discount or Points

A discount point is 1% of a loan amount. It is normally paid by someone other than the borrower. Examine Figure 16–3.

The reason discount points are paid is that lenders require minimum interest rates in order to make loans. This interest rate is normally the prevailing market rate. Often

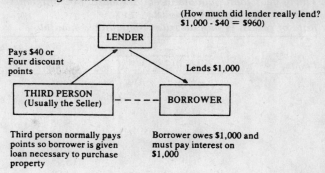

Figure 16–3. How Discount Points Are Normally Paid in a Lending Transaction

state usury laws will set an interest rate ceiling lower than the market rate of interest. A similar ceiling may also exist on VA or FHA mortgages. In these situations, the law is designed to prevent a lender from charging more than the ceiling to the borrower. However, without discount points a lender could not make loans because not enough interest could be charged. Thus, to increase the yield, someone other than the borrower must pay the bank to make a loan.

Why would third persons want to pay discount points if the loan is actually being given to the borrower and not to themselves? The third person usually stands to benefit from the loan indirectly. The third person might be a seller, and the borrower might be a purchaser of a house. Without the loan, the transaction might not take place.

How do discount points increase the effective yield to the lender? First, consider what would happen without discount points. Assume a lender makes a loan of $1,000 at 11%. Over the term of the loan, the lender would receive interest at 11% effective yield plus repayment of the original principal of $1,000. With discount points the following would happen.

Example:
Assume the third person must pay four (4) discount points in order for the lender to make the same $1,000 loan. The lender would give $1,000 to the borrower but would receive $40 back from the third person. How much did the lender actually lend?

Answer: $1,000 − $40 = $960.

How much must the borrower pay back?

Answer: $1,000

This means the bank receives 11% interest on $1,000 even though it only lent $960. Further, since it will receive back $1,000 instead of $960, it makes an additional $40 over the life of the loan. If the loan is paid off over a period of 30 years, this will increase the effective yield of the loan from the nominal rate of 11% to an effective rate of 11.5%. In other words, as a rule of thumb, each discount point paid will increase the effective yield by ⅛ of 1% over the full term of the loan. Or in order to increase the yield by ½ of 1%, four (4) discount points should be charged; or to increase the yield by one full percent, eight (8) discount points should be charged.

What happens if the loan is paid off early? In that case, the lender's yield increases. Table 16–1 shows what happens to the lender's yield if a loan is paid off early. You

Table 16–1. Internal Rate of Return
Thirty year loan payable in equal monthly installments
Interest rate on original loan = 11%
Rate of return is annual rate compounded monthly

Points	Payout Time From Origination				
	6 Months	12 Months	36 Months	60 Months	360 Months
1	13.08	12.07	11.40	11.27	11.13
2	15.18	13.15	11.80	11.53	11.26
3	17.31	14.24	12.21	11.81	11.39
4	19.47	15.35	12.62	12.08	11.52
5	21.65	16.47	13.04	12.36	11.66
6	23.86	17.60	13.46	12.64	11.80
7	26.10	18.75	13.88	12.93	11.94
8	28.36	19.91	14.32	13.22	12.08
9	30.67	21.08	14.75	13.51	12.23
10	32.99	22.27	15.20	13.81	12.38

will notice the rule of thumb does not work with short loan terms.

Appraisal Fee

Since the property being purchased is used by the borrower to secure the loan, the lender wants some idea as to the worth or value of the subject property. Thus, either someone on the lender's staff or an independent fee appraiser will be employed to appraise the subject property. The appraisal report supplied to the lender will include supportive information used by the appraiser in reaching an estimate of value. This charge is normally paid by the borrower.

Credit Report Fee

Since the borrower signs a personal note for the loan, the lender is interested in the credit history of the borrower and wants to know how the borrower has handled other credit transactions. This fee is also normally paid by the borrower.

Assumption Fee

If the buyer is assuming an existing mortgage on the property, the lender might charge a certain fee for the processing of the necessary papers (see Chapter 14).

Items Paid in Advance

At the time of settlement the lender will require certain items to be paid in advance by the borrower.

Interest

Mortgages are normally written so that payment is due on the first day of the month. Since settlement can occur on any date, the lender will require the borrower to prepay interest on the amount borrowed from the date of settlement until the beginning of the mortgage period covered by the first full loan payment. For example, if closing takes place September 22, the first monthly payment will be due November 1 which will cover the interest due for the month of October. In this case, the borrower would prepay on the amount borrowed from September 22 until October 1 at an interest rate established at settlement.

Mortgage Insurance Premium

If the loan is insured, the borrower might be required to pay the first premium in advance. (Private mortgage insurance is discussed in Chapter 15.)

Hazard Insurance Premium

Insurance to cover loss due to fire, floods, wind and natural hazards plus additional risks such as personal liability and theft will be required of the borrower. Normally, the lender will require the borrower to show proof at settlement that a prescribed minimum amount of insurance coverage has been purchased. The coverage required is ordinarily for a minimum of one year.

Escrow Accounts

Escrow or reserve accounts are held by the lender to meet future payments incurred in connection with the property. To assure that these payments will indeed be made, the lender establishes escrow accounts at closing by requiring an initial payment and then adding a certain amount of each month's total payment to these accounts.

Property Tax

Local governments levy taxes on property, which if unpaid can result in the property being sold at public auction. The lender may require a monthly payment into this account, and when the borrower receives the annual tax bill, payment is made out of this reserve account.

Hazard Insurance

At some point the hazard insurance policy required at closing will expire. In order to have adequate funds to renew the policy, the lender determines how much must be escrowed each month for insurance.

Mortgage Insurance

If the mortgage is insured and future premiums are due, the lender can require funds to be escrowed to cover this charge.

Annual Assessments

Annual assessments are levied by some municipalities for improvements such as sidewalks, roads and parks. Also, homeowner's association fees are levied against property. The lender could require these charges to be escrowed.

Title Charges

Certain charges are incurred in connection with the examination of title. These expenses cover a wide range of services and vary greatly from jurisdiction to jurisdiction. In some instances all of the fees associated with the title search are included in one charge; in other cases they are itemized.

Title Examination

This charge covers the costs of searching the land records and determining whether the owner has clear title to the property. The abstract of title gives the history of the ownership and any liens or encumbrances that presently exist.

Title Insurance

In many jurisdictions it is customary for the lender to require the borrower to purchase title insurance. This one-time charge covers the mortgagee's interest against loss due to defects of title. For an additional fee, the borrower can also insure his or her own interest against title defects.

Attorney's Fees

A charge is sometimes made for legal services provided in the settlement procedures. This fee would be in connection with services provided the lender but charged to the borrower. Any charges made by an attorney representing the buyer or seller would be an additional expense.

Notary Fee

Various documents must be notarized to authenticate the execution by the parties involved.

Preparation of Documents

A fee may be charged for the preparation of certain documents presented at closing. These documents include deeds, mortgages, liens and leases.

Government Recording and Transfer Charges

These fees are collected when the property changes hands and are paid when the deed is recorded in the land records. They can be paid by either buyer, seller or both depending upon the terms of the sales contract. The recording fees are normally a certain amount per page, whereas transfer taxes and document stamps are based on a certain percentage of sales price.

Additional Settlement Charges

Survey

The lender or title insurance company may require a survey, conducted by a registered surveyor, to show the boundaries of the property and any encroachments.

Termite Inspection

A common condition in the sales contract is for the seller to pay for an inspection of the house for termites and other pest infestation. A termite certificate is normally required at closing.

Structural Inspection

An inspection of the property for structural soundness may also be a condition of the contract. With older property the lender might require all mechanical equipment to be inspected prior to consummating the loan.

Bill of Sale

The deed conveys the real property from seller to buyer. If any personal property is sold, a bill of sale needs to be prepared and delivered at settlement. Examples of personal property sold in residential transactions include items such as washers, dryers, window air conditioners, yard equipment and area rugs. If there is any doubt as to whether or not these items are personal property, a bill of sale should be prepared.

Deed

A deed is prepared prior to closing by the party conducting settlement and is read for delivery to the buyer. The cost of drawing this instrument can either be a specific charge or part of the attorney's fee. Who is to pay this fee should be stated in the sales contract.

DOCUMENTS OBTAINED AT CLOSING

At settlement the various charges, fees and adjustments will be entered on the settlement statement. When completed the settlement statement will reflect the total credits and debits made to each party.

Seller

In most cases the total of the seller's credits exceeds the debits and the seller receives the balance, normally in the form of a check. If personal property were sold and the total charge not included on the settlement statement, the seller would also receive this amount from the buyer. If the seller has received a purchase money mortgage (see Chapter 15), he or she would receive a mortgage note. The seller also receives a copy of the settlement statement.

Buyer

The buyer will leave settlement with many more documents than the seller. These documents include a title policy, a copy of the settlement statement, bill of sale, survey, a copy of the insurance policy, receipts for property tax, water, gas and special assessments, a copy of the mortgage note and a receipt for the balance paid to close the transaction. The deed is often kept for recording by the settlement officer and mailed to the buyer after recordation.

POST-CLOSING PROCEDURES

Immediately after closing, the buyer should record the deed and pay the necessary government recording and transfer charges. This action gives constructive notice of the buyer's ownership and is normally conducted by the closing attorney or escrow agent. In the near future, the buyer receives the deed stamped with the time of recording plus where in the land records the deed is recorded. Public services such as gas, electricity and water should be turned on and charged in the buyer's name.

POINTS TO REMEMBER

1. In order to determine whether title contains any defects or encumbrances which would mar its marketability, it is necessary to trace the chain of title in the public records. The chain of title is a series of successive title transfers from grantors to grantees, ordinarily stemming from some government patent.

2. State recording acts are designed to provide a means of protecting persons who acquire an interest in real estate by permitting them by recordation to give constructive notice to the whole world as to the existence of that interest; this also gives subsequent bona fide purchasers protection from secret unrecorded claims, except for those interests that do not require recordation.

3. An abstract of title is a condensed chronological history of all recorded instruments in the chain of title which affect the title in some way.

4. Title insurance provides protection to a named insured for loss sustained from title defects not excepted in the policy. In general, there are two types of title insurance policies: (1) the owner's policy and (2) the mortgagee's policy.

5. Some states recognize a system of title registration called the Torrens System, which is similar to the system of registering automobile titles in that title to land is registered and represented by a registration certificate. Under the Torrens System, title does not pass until it is properly registered; thus a deed by itself is not effective in conveying title when it is delivered and accepted as it is under the conventional system.

6. Legal title to property is transferred from seller to buyer when the instrument of conveyance is delivered. This normally takes place at a meeting called settlement, or closing.

7. In some parts of the country, the transaction is closed by an escrow agent, so there is no meeting of buyer and seller. The deed is delivered to the escrow agent, who after determining title and receiving payment from the buyer, delivers title to the buyer.

8. If the property being conveyed is residential and the buyer is acquiring a loan to purchase the property, the lender falls under the requirements of the Real Estate Settlement Procedures Act (RESPA).

9. RESPA places certain requirements on the lender as to what and when certain information concerning the loan and the costs of closing the loan must be made available to the buyer.

10. Specific settlement costs are charged to both buyer and seller. These costs include such items as broker's commission, loan fees, items paid in advance, escrow accounts and title charges.

11. Immediately after closing, the buyer or someone representing the buyer should record the deed. This action gives constructive notice of the buyer's ownership.

KEY TERMS AND PHRASES

abstract of title
APR
assumption fee
certificate of title
chain of title
closing
cross index system
defect in title

disclosure statement
discount points
escrow accounts
good-faith estimate
loan origination fee
mortgagee's title policy
opinion of title
owner's title policy

preliminary binder
Real Estate Settlement Procedures Act (RESPA)
settlement
title insurance
Torrens Certificate
tract index
Truth-in-Lending

QUESTIONS

1. Constructive notice consists of which of the following?
   I. All recorded instruments in the chain of title
   II. All facts that physical inspection of a property might reveal

   A. I only
   B. II only
   C. Both I and II
   D. Neither I nor II

2. When all transactions affecting a particular property are indicated on one page, what kind of index is being used in the title records?

A. Cross index
B. Reverse index
C. Grantor-grantee index
D. Tract index

3. A chronological history of all recorded instruments in the chain of title is called a (an)
   A. abstract of title
   B. opinion of title
   C. Torrens Certificate
   D. tract index

4. A break or gap in the chain of title is a (an)
   A. cloud on title   C. encroachment
   B. encumbrance   D. lis pendens

5. Which of the following kinds of defects will ordinarily be revealed by an examination of the record?
   A. Lis pendens
   B. Deed delivered after death of grantor
   C. Forged satisfaction piece
   D. Missing heir

6. Title insurance provides what kind of protection in a mortgagee's policy?
   I. Any defects in title which result in loss of the owner's equity
   II. The amount of unpaid principal owed to a lender in case of a total loss from a pre-existing title defect
   A. I only   C. Both I and II
   B. II only   D. Neither I nor II

7. The right of an insurance company to step into the shoes of an indemnified insured and assert all of the insured's legal rights against a wrongdoer is called
   A. subordination   C. special endorsement
   B. subrogation   D. exception

8. Title insurance provides what kind of protection under an owner's policy?
   I. Indemnification for all defects which arise after the date of the policy
   II. Costs of defending a lawsuit brought about because of alleged defects in the title insured by the policy
   A. I only   C. Both I and II
   B. II only   D. Neither I nor II

9. When a title is registered under the Torrens System of title registration, which of the following is true?
   A. Title is transferred when a deed is delivered and accepted.
   B. Title is transferred when a new Torrens Certificate is issued.
   C. Title is insured against defects by a fund which is accumulated from title examination fees.
   D. Title is guaranteed by the full faith and credit of the state.

10. In which of the following systems of title assurance will the costs of defending title defects be borne by someone other than the owner?
    I. Torrens System
    II. Title insurance system
    A. I only   C. Both I and II
    B. II only   D. Neither I nor II

11. The Real Estate Settlement Procedures Act regulates
    I. land recording methods
    II. disclosures in title closing
    A. I only   C. Both I and II
    B. II only   D. Neither I nor II

12. If the closing date is not specified in the sales contract, then it will occur within
    A. three business days
    B. one year from the date of the sales contract
    C. a reasonable period of time
    D. the time period specified by the seller

13. An escrow agent acts only on behalf of the
    I. mortgagee
    II. broker
    A. I only   C. Both I and II
    B. II only   D. Neither I nor II

14. A purchaser wanting to make sure that correct public notice has been given as to his or her property rights would use a (an)
    A. title examination
    B. title search
    C. acknowledgment
    D. recording procedure

15. Which of the following statements is correct?
    I. In most jurisdictions closing costs are set by law.
    II. RESPA sets limits on financial fees charged by the lender.
    A. I only   C. Both I and II
    B. II only   D. Neither I nor II

16. Prorations are used to determine the
    A. broker's commission
    B. title insurance premium
    C. purchaser's share of property taxes
    D. cost of survey

17. When an escrow settlement is conducted
    I. only the buyer, seller and escrow agent meet together
    II. the procedure can be conducted by mail
    A. I only   C. Both I and II
    B. II only   D. Neither I nor II

18. At the settlement meeting, the deed to the property is normally signed by the
    I. seller
    II. buyer
    A. I only   C. Both I and II
    B. II only   D. Neither I nor II

Title Examination and Settlement

19. An advantage of the escrow closing method is that it eliminates the need for
    I. buyer and seller to meet together
    II. an attorney to represent either buyer or seller
    A. I only   C. Both I and II
    B. II only   D. Neither I nor II

20. RESPA prohibits
    I. a buyer's using his or her own attorney to represent him or her at closing
    II. a lender receiving a secret kickback from a provider of a service
    A. I only   C. Both I and II
    B. II only   D. Neither I nor II

21. The sales contract is normally signed
    I. prior to the financing commitment
    II. after the lender has agreed to make the loan
    A. I only   C. Both I and II
    B. II only   D. Neither I nor II

22. RESPA covers all
    I. real estate loans
    II. real estate loans involving government guarantee or insurance
    A. I only   C. Both I and II
    B. II only   D. Neither I nor II

23. The "good-faith estimates" provided by the lender at the time of application for the loan
    I. are based on the lender's experience in making such loans
    II. may change because of changing market conditions
    A. I only   C. Both I and II
    B. II only   D. Neither I nor II

24. According to RESPA
    I. a lender cannot use a particular settlement-service provider
    II. a borrower can choose any settlement-service provider and those chosen must be used by the lender
    A. I only   C. Both I and II
    B. II only   D. Neither I nor II

25. A 2% loan origination fee on a $60,000 loan would be
    I. 2% of the amount borrowed
    II. $1200
    A. I only   C. Both I and II
    B. II only   D. Neither I nor II

26. An owner's policy of title insurance is good as long as the
    A. mortgage debt is outstanding
    B. owner pays the annual insurance premium
    C. owner or the owner's heirs have any interest in the property
    D. owner is alive

27. A home selling for $60,000 is purchased with an 80% loan. The lender charges a 1% loan origination fee payable at closing. The loan origination fee is
    I. $600
    II. .01 of the loan amount
    A. I only   C. Both I and II
    B. II only   D. Neither I nor II

28. RESPA prohibits
    I. the use of an escrow agent
    II. a lender requiring the borrower to pay for a mortgagee's title insurance policy
    A. I only   C. Both I and II
    B. II only   D. Neither I nor II

29. Normally, prorations are used to calculate the buyer's share of the
    I. title examination expenses
    II. property taxes
    A. I only   C. Both I and II
    B. II only   D. Neither I nor II

30. An escrow agent acts on behalf of whom?
    A. Buyer   C. Lender
    B. Seller   D. All parties to the transaction

If you are not sure of your answers, see page 322 for correct answers and explanations.

17

Residential Appraisal

Numerous types of real estate activities require an appraisal. To appraise means to estimate the value of a particular asset. When property is being bought or sold, a specialist known as an appraiser is often employed to render an estimate of value. Lenders employ the services of appraisers in making a loan decision since loans are normally based on a certain percentage of value. Appraisers are used in condemnation procedures where just compensation must be determined. Land-use decisions such as the type and size of a particular building to construct in order to maximize net income require an opinion of value and, therefore, the skills of an appraiser.

The purpose of this chapter is to introduce the reader to the concept of value, which serves as the foundation of all appraisal techniques. Basic value principles are defined, and the appraisal process is explained. In this chapter, emphasis is placed on residential appraisal techniques. The income approach, normally used in the appraisal of income-producing property, is explained in detail in Chapter 18.

VALUE: THE HEART OF ALL REAL ESTATE ACTIVITY

At the heart of all real estate activity lies the economic concept of value. Understanding the meaning of value and how land or real estate has value requires aligning the principles and practices of real estate with the broader principles of economics.

Meaning of Value

The word *value* has different meanings to different people. Value is normally defined as the ability of a good or service to command other goods or services. Historically, this definition of value has been termed *value in exchange* and denotes how one good exchanges in the marketplace for other goods. For the potential real estate investor another type of value, namely *value in use,* enters into the analysis. This type of value is defined as the present worth of the future rights to income and involves calculating the income generated from a particular use in determining the worth or value of the real estate. Value in use is discussed in Chapter 18.

Basic Value Principles

The basic concepts of land use are built on certain economic principles. These principles influence the value of the real estate being appraised. The more important basic principles are briefly explained below.

Highest and Best Use

The highest and best use of a parcel of land is that legal use which will generate, when capitalized, the greatest net present value of income. An existing use of a parcel of land may not be the highest and best use. Quite often an interim use, for example, a parking lot in a downtown area, might be made until a more profitable use, such as an office building, can be made.

Substitution

The value of a parcel of real estate is normally equal to the cost of acquiring an equally desirable substitute. A vacant lot would not sell for $50,000 if equally desirable substitutes were available, with no costly delay, for $30,000.

Conformity

According to this economic principle, a piece of land must be used in such a way as to conform to surrounding land uses if maximum value is to be achieved. Zoning regulations and deed restrictions are both intended to maintain conformity.

Competition

Competition is a function of supply and demand and ordinarily results from excess profits which attract an increase in supply. For example, if only one fully leased apartment complex exists in a growing area of a city, normally competitors will construct additional apartments to take advantage of the anticipated demand. The fully leased project will be able to temporarily charge higher than normal rental rates, giving the owner excess profits.

Contribution

The value of a component part of a piece of property is equal to what that component part adds to total value, less any costs incurred. For example, an old apartment building would not be remodeled unless the rent schedule could be increased enough to pay for the expense of remodeling. This idea of contribution is very important in the adjustment process described in the sales comparison approach. If a bedroom costs $5,000, a house with six bedrooms would not necessarily be worth $5,000 more than a house with five bedrooms because the value contribution of one additional bedroom might not equal the cost.

Increasing and Decreasing Returns

This basic principle of economics states that the addition of more factors of production (land, labor, capital and management) adds higher and higher amounts to net income (additional revenue minus additional cost) up to a certain point. Once this point has been reached (highest and best use), the maximum value is reached.

Change

Change is constantly affecting land use which in turn changes in value. Most real estate passes through certain life stages: (1) a period of growth, (2) a period of stability, (3) a period of decline and, in many cases, (4) renewal or restoration. If real estate goes through the fourth stage, the cycle can repeat itself.

Anticipation

Value changes in expectation of some future benefit or detriment affecting the property. For example, the value of a vacant parcel of land can increase if an office building is constructed next to it; likewise, use of land as an open dump results in decreased values of surrounding residential properties.

Supply and Demand

If supply increases and demand either remains constant or decreases, the value of the good or service decreases. Likewise, an increase in demand and a constant supply results in a higher value. The last remaining vacant lot in a desirable subdivision will probably cost more to purchase than the first lot.

Value, Cost and Price

While the terms *value*, *cost* and *price* are sometimes used synonymously, the three do not mean the same thing and, in fact, can be quite different. Value is an estimate of future rights to income, whereas cost is a quantitative measure of previous expenditures. While the two can be equal (assuming the improvements are new and the use is the highest and best use), typically value and cost are not equal. Consider the situation where houses are located in an undesirable part of the city because of traffic patterns, public services or tax rates. In this instance, the value of these homes will possibly be much less than the cost of constructing the same house on another lot in a more desirable location.

Price is the amount of money actually paid for a piece of property, and while it may be equal to value and/or cost, this is not always the case. Consider the family moving to another city who must sell their home. They might be forced to accept a price much lower than what a comparable property is selling for. Or consider the buyer who is able to finance 100% of the purchase price with borrowed capital and is therefore willing to pay more than if the purchase were made entirely with cash. For anyone involved with appraising, a clear distinction must be made among value, cost and price.

Market Value

While the term *value* has numerous meanings, its use in the appraisal of real estate normally refers to market value. Market value can be defined as the price at which a willing buyer and willing seller will agree upon where neither is under any undue pressure and both are negotiating at arm's length with complete knowledge of the market. This definition assumes that there is sufficient activity in the marketplace to generate enough buyers and sellers so that no one of them controls the price. Each party is also acting in his or her own best interest and is informed as to market conditions. Finally, individual financing and taxation possibilities are not considered, the property is exposed on the market for a reasonable period of time and the seller is capable of conveying marketable title. Market value is an ideal standard which is very seldom achieved in real-world real estate markets. Nevertheless, this is ordinarily the objective of most appraisals.

THE APPRAISAL PROCESS

Regardless of the approach chosen in estimating value, the appraiser must follow a systematic step-by-step analysis to estimate value accurately. While each appraisal varies according to the purpose of the appraisal and the approach(es) used, a well-done estimate of value will follow some procedure similar to that presented in Figure 17–1.

Define Assignment

The first step in any appraisal process is to define the assignment and to state the problem. This involves identifying the purpose of the appraisal and defining what value is to be estimated. Also, the exact real estate to be appraised and the property rights of the parcel must be known. The appraiser should also know how much time is available for the completion of the appraisal and the fee being paid. Also, at this initial step, the approach(es) to be used should be determined. In short, if the assignment is correctly and accurately defined, the remaining steps will be much easier.

Figure 17-1. The Appraisal Process

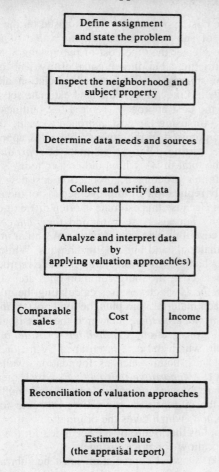

Inspection

Before determining data needs and sources, the appraiser should personally inspect both the neighborhood and the subject property. This will provide the appraiser an opportunity to inspect visually what is to be appraised before actually beginning to collect data.

Determine Data Needs and Sources

Numerous data sources are available for use by the appraiser. While not all of these will be used for each and every appraisal, those pertinent to a particular appraisal need to be identified. The following is a partial list of some of the more common sources of information used by appraisers:

Recorded deeds	Transportation companies
Assessor's office	Government agencies
Newspapers	Title reports
Accountants	Cost manuals
Plats	Personal inspection
Brokers	Attorneys
Utility companies	Seller
Libraries	Buyer
Financial statements	Builders
Chamber of Commerce	Labor organizations
Property managers	Other appraisers
Veterans Administration	Federal Housing Administration
National Association of Home Builders	Professional journals
City hall	Multiple Listing Services
Financial lenders	Local real estate boards
Planning departments	Local material suppliers

Collect and Verify Data

Once these numerous data sources have been identified, the next step is for the appraiser to collect and verify the appropriate data. The data collected will, of course, depend on which factors appear to be important. While no single list can include all factors, the following are normally applicable to all types of appraisals:

Economic	*Government related*
Availability of insurance	Budgets
Construction	Housing programs
Costs	Land-use controls
Economic base	Lending requirements
Employment	Public services
Income taxes	
Population	

Physical	*Social*
Area	Attitudes
Climate	Behaviors
Topography	Cultural facilities
	Stability

Apply Valuation Approach(es)

General data collected will be used to analyze the influence of national, regional, city and neighborhood forces, while specific data will address the site and improvements on the site. The means of analyzing and interpreting the data collected will be through the application of one or more of the three valuation approaches: (1) comparable sales approach, (2) cost approach and (3) income approach. While all three approaches may be appropriate for a particular piece of real estate, often only two of the three will be relevant. Thus, it is up to the appraiser to pick the appropriate approach(es). In this chapter, the comparable sales and cost approach will be explained. The income approach is the subject of the next chapter.

Comparable Sales Approach

This approach assumes the value of the subject property can be accurately estimated by comparing similar properties. The comparable sales approach is used when there is an active market and comparables can be identified. It is most often used in the appraising of single-family residential real estate.

The comparable properties selected should be substantially similar to the subject property and should be arms-length transactions. However, since each comparable will

Residential Appraisal

probably be different from the subject property in terms of location, condition of sale, amenities, time of sale, etc., adjustments must be made in the comparison process in order to derive a value for the subject property. The principal factors for which adjustments will normally be made can be divided into four categories: (1) date of sale, (2) location, (3) physical condition and features and (4) terms or conditions of sale. This adjustment process involves the adding and subtracting of dollars for those items where the comparable properties differ from the subject property. The dollar value of a feature present in the subject property but not present in the comparables is *added,* while the dollar value of a feature present in the comparables but not present in the subject property is *subtracted.* The total adjustment for each factor when either added or subtracted will provide for an adjusted sales price for each comparable. The adjusted sales price of each comparable represents a value range of the subject property.

A weighted average or straight average is often used to derive the indicated value of the subject property. It should be noted that an appraiser must use his or her judgment and experience to determine how much weight to place on each adjusted comparable.

Table 17–1 presents an example of how this approach is used to derive value for a residential property. For this particular piece of property, three comparables were chosen. The sales price as well as other vital information was known for each. Adjustments were made in the sales prices for such variables as time of sale, condition of sale and house size. For each comparable, an adjustment in the market price had to be made. The adjusted sales prices are then given a weighted average to arrive at the indicated value of $78,031 for the subject property. Note that Comparable A was given a weighted average of 50% which indicates the appraiser believed this particular comparable was closest to the subject property in terms of the items used for the comparison. The indicated appraised value of $78,031 was rounded to $78,000.

Cost Approach

The cost approach to value is based on the economic principle of substitution, that is, the value of a building cannot be greater than the cost of purchasing a similar site and constructing a building of equal utility. This new reproduction cost, taken before any depreciation allowances, when added to the value of the land estimate sets the upper limit for the cost approach. Table 17–2 outlines the basic procedure for using the cost approach to value the subject property appraised in the comparable sales approach.

The starting point, an estimate of *reproduction cost new,* is the total of what it would cost in today's dollars to build a similar structure. Reproduction cost new is the cost of actually replicating an improvement as of the date of the appraisal. Because this estimate is often difficult or impractical, many appraisers seek to find the *replacement cost new,* the cost of producing a structure of similar utility using modern materials and building techniques. While there are numerous techniques available to estimate reproduction or replacement cost, the more common ones are: (1) *quantity survey method,* which requires calculating the quantity and cost of each material item plus the total cost of installation; (2) *unit-in-place method,* in which the cost is grouped by stages of construction; (3) *builder's (trade breakdown) method,* in which the cost is grouped by major functional parts of the structure such as foundation, walls, heating system; (4) *comparative unit method,* which measures the total square footage or cubic footage and multiplies this total by the current cost per square or cubic foot; or (5) *index method,* which takes the original cost of construction and multiplies that figure by a price index for the geographic area to allow for price changes.

Next, accrued depreciation must be subtracted from this replacement cost to derive an estimate of building value. Accrued depreciation is considered to be any diminishment of utility or value from the reproduction cost new. Depreciation is divided into three types: (1) physical deteri-

Table 17–1. Comparable Sales Property Comparison

Item	Comparable A		Comparable B		Comparable C	
Address of comparable	1738 Aberdeen		1601 Deveron		208 Edgewood	
Sales price of comparable		$76,000		$74,500		$80,000
Time of sale	3 months ago (+3%)	+2280	6 months ago (+6%)	+4470	Last week	0
Terms or conditions of sale	Normal	0	Normal	0	Hurried	+1500
House size	Same	0	1 bedroom smaller	+3500	1 bedroom larger	−3500
Overall condition	Worse	+2000	Same	0	Better	−1000
Physical characteristics (kitchen, baths, etc.)	New kitchen	−3000	New patio Screened porch	−2000	Same	0
Location	Next door	0	1 block	0	Worse	+1500
Lot size	Same	0	Larger	−1500	Same	0
Total adjustments		+1280		+4470		−1500
Adjusted sales price		$77,280		$78,970		$78,500
Weighted average: Comparable A Comparable B Comparable C	$77,280 × .5 = $38,640 $78,970 × .3 = $23,691 $78,500 × .2 = $15,700 Indicated value $78,031 Rounded to $78,000					

Table 17–2. Cost Approach to Value

Value of building: Reproduction Cost		
1,600 sq. ft. @ $50 per sq. ft.		$80,000
Less Depreciation:		
Physical deterioration		
curable (deferred maintenance, painting, etc.)	$3,500	
incurable (structural damages)	2,000	
Functional obsolescence	3,000	
Economic obsolescence	-0-	
Total Depreciation		−8,500
Building Value Estimate		$71,500
Value of Land: Size 60 × 180 @ $170 per front foot		10,200
Total Property Value		$81,700

oration, (2) functional obsolescence and (3) economic obsolescence. *Physical deterioration*, which allows for actual wear and tear or the action of natural elements, can be either *curable* or *incurable*. Depreciation is considered curable if the cost of the repair would not exceed the contribution to value. For example, if a house valued at $60,000 had a leaky roof which would cost $5,000 to repair, and if the house would be valued at $68,000 after the repair, this defect would be considered curable. Curable physical deterioration estimates deferred maintenance, such as repairing the roof, while incurable physical deterioration estimates elements of the structure which are not economically feasible to correct. *Functional obsolescence* allows for conditions within the structure which make the building outdated compared with a new building. For example, inadequate loading facilities in a warehouse or a single bathroom in a five-bedroom house each subtract from the value of the structures. Functional obsolescence also includes features which are not fully valued by the market. For example, if a house had a marble sink with 24-karat gold faucets, the market might not add the cost of the sink to the value of the home. This sink would be called a *superadequacy*. Finally, *economic obsolescence* considers factors outside the subject property such as changes in competition, desirability of the neighborhood or surrounding land use. While all three types of accrued depreciation are difficult to measure, each must be estimated and subtracted to estimate the present value of the building. It should be noted that cost of improvements includes the cost in the marketplace, not the cost to an individual builder. This means that costs include materials, labor, indirect costs and a reasonable builder's profit.

A second general approach to depreciation often used by appraisers is referred to as the *theoretical* method. The theoretical method of depreciation is a charge which is related to the expired economic life of an improvement. Each improvement is assumed to have a theoretical *economic life*. This economic life is a function of materials used, construction quality and methods of engineering and architectural design and various environmental or climatic factors. Under the principle of anticipation, an investor is willing to pay a price equal to the value of all future benefits, minus the cost of all future expenses, discounted to a present value. The longer an improvement is useable, the more the investor is generally willing to pay. The remaining years that a real estate improvement is productive is referred to as the *remaining economic life*. The difference between the economic life and the remaining economic life is the *effective age*. The effective age is not the chronological age, but the age that is indicated by the condition and utility of the improvement. It should be clear that the amount of maintenance and care given to a building helps determine its effective age. A 10-year-old building might have an effective age of 25 years because of poor or deferred maintenance. After the appraiser has determined the effective age, accrued depreciation is then ordinarily determined by a straight-line method of depreciation which considers the proportional loss in value by relating effective age to economic life without considering the effect of compound interest, or by a sinking-fund method which does consider compound interest.

Example:
> Assume a building would cost $100,000 if new. If the building had a theoretical economic life of 40 years and an effective age of 10 years, what would be the accrued depreciation using straight-line depreciation?
>
> $\frac{100\% \text{ [Value when new]}}{40 \text{ [Years of economic life]}} = 2\frac{1}{2}\%$ [Straight-line depreciation per year]
>
> $2\frac{1}{2}\%$ per year × 10 years [Effective age]
>   = 25% Loss of value
>
> 25% × $100,000 [Value if new]
>   = $25,000 [Accrued depreciation]

The value of the land is appraised as if the land were vacant and available for construction at its highest and best use. This is done by using the same basic techniques discussed in the sales comparison approach, namely, analyzing current market conditions. By adding the land value estimate to the building value estimate, the total property value as indicated by the cost approach can be stated. While this approach can be used with all types of property, it is most applicable in appraising new buildings or nonincome-producing property, such as schools and churches.

Gross Rent Multiplier

While the market comparison approach is normally considered the most reliable appraisal method for residential real estate, data generated via the market can also be used in appraising income property. Income properties can be valued by comparing their gross rent multipliers (GRM). Such a comparison converts the gross annual or monthly income of a piece of property (for instance, an apartment complex) into a value estimate. By taking the sale prices of other properties and dividing each one by its gross annual or monthly rent, a gross rent multiplier for each comparable is derived. The average GRM of the group can then be multiplied by the gross annual or monthly rent of the subject property to set a value. This popular method is a quick and easy means of comparing properties based on what the market is paying for similar properties.

Example:
Assume the three properties used as comparables in the comparables sales approach are currently rented. The monthly rental of each house can be used to derive a correlated GRM.

	Sales Price	Monthly Rental	GRM
Comparable A	$76,000	$600	127
Comparable B	$74,500	$575	130
Comparable C	$80,000	$600	133
Correlated Gross Rent Multiplier			130

Note that in this example the correlated GRM of 130 is the same as the average GRM of the three comparables. Anytime the GRM approach is used, it is up to the appraiser to pick the monthly or annual rentals that best reflect the value of the subject property.

Assume the subject property appraised in Table 17–1 is renting for $575 per month. An estimate of its value based on the gross rent multiplier approach would derive a value of $74,750 ($575 × 130). In inflationary times such as today, it is not uncommon for the value derived by the GRM to be less than the value based on the other approaches. Consequently, this technique for deriving value is generally not given the same weight as the market and cost approaches.

RECONCILIATION OF VALUATION APPROACHES

Assuming the appraiser has used two or more of the approaches, the next step is to weigh the approaches used in such a way as to reach a rational conclusion regarding the value of the property. This is referred to as *reconciliation* or *correlation*. Whatever means used, the intent to accurately measure value is the same.

Example:
For the subject property used throughout this chapter, the values derived were as follows:

Comparable Sales	$78,000
Cost	$81,700
Gross Rent Multipliers	$74,750

In the reconciliation process, every important fact, trend and observation noted by the appraiser should have been analyzed and interpreted. At this point, the appraiser is rendering a professional opinion of the value of the property. If, in the opinion of the appraiser analyzing the subject property used in this chapter, the sales comparison approach is the most accurate indicator of value, the value derived would be $78,000. The estimate would be somewhat higher if the cost approach was used and somewhat lower if the GRM was considered. In this example, an overall average using all three derived values would be $78,150.

THE APPRAISAL REPORT

Normally, the opinion of value as determined by the appraiser is in the form of a written report. The form can be a letter of valuation, a single-page standard form or a more elaborate report. In appraising single-family dwellings, a form appraisal is normally used which provides space for recording neighborhood, site and building data. Figure 17–2 is a copy of the FNMA appraisal report used in appraising residential property. Income-producing property normally requires a more detailed *narrative report* which not only gives the appraiser's opinion of value but also provides supportive evidence to substantiate the opinion. The documentation necessary with the narrative report is much greater than with the standard form. Professional standards of what is expected in a narrative appraisal report are available from the American Institute of Real Estate Appraisers, the Society of Real Estate Appraisers or the American Society of Appraisers.

ETHICS AND PROFESSIONAL PRACTICE

During the late seventies and early eighties, the need to improve appraisal practices throughout North America has become evident. The difficulties of may lending institutions underscore the need to ensure that appraisals are based upon viable standards, free from outside pressures. Moreover, they demonstrate the need to have persons qualified by education and experience in the appraisal profession nationwide. In 1986, instability in the real estate and mortgage lending industries, which depend upon accurate, professional appraisal services, led eight leading U.S. professional appraisal organizations, along with the Appraisal Institute of Canada, to form the Ad Hoc Committee on Uniform Standards of Professional Appraisal Practice. In 1987, agreeing upon a viable set of standards, the U.S. committee members adopted them and established the Appraisal Foundation to implement them.

The Appraisal Foundation is a nonprofit, educational corporation established by the appraisal profession. It benefits appraisers, developers, investors, financial institutions, homeowners, real estate brokers, issuers of securities, government agencies and the American public. The Foundation fosters professionalism by helping to ensure that appraisers are qualified to offer their services and by promoting the Uniform Standards of Professional Appraisal Practice and the Uniform Code of Ethics. The work of the Foundation is vital to the integrity of the American appraisal profession, financial institutions and real estate industry, as well as to the financial well-being and confidence of the American public and every user of appraisal services.

To address the two principal concerns of the industry, the Appraisal Foundation created an Appraisal Standards Board and an Appraiser Qualifications Board. Members of these boards, selected by the Foundation's trustees, are appraisers of outstanding competence and integrity. The

Figure 17-2. Residential Appraisal Report

UNIFORM RESIDENTIAL APPRAISAL REPORT

Property Description & Analysis — File No. _____

SUBJECT
- Property Address
- Census Tract
- LENDER DISCRETIONARY USE
- City / County / State / Zip Code
- Sale Price $
- Legal Description
- Date
- Owner/Occupant / Map Reference
- Mortgage Amount $
- Sale Price $ / Date of Sale
- PROPERTY RIGHTS APPRAISED
- Mortgage Type
- Loan charges/concessions to be paid by seller $
  - ☐ Fee Simple
- Discount Points and Other Concessions
- R.E. Taxes $ / Tax Year / HOA $/Mo.
  - ☐ Leasehold
- Paid by Seller $
- Lender/Client
  - ☐ Condominium (HUD/VA)
  - ☐ De Minimis PUD
- Source

NEIGHBORHOOD

	Urban	Suburban	Rural	NEIGHBORHOOD ANALYSIS	Good	Avg.	Fair	Poor
LOCATION	☐	☐	☐	Employment Stability	☐	☐	☐	☐
BUILT UP	Over 75% ☐	25-75% ☐	Under 25% ☐	Convenience to Employment	☐	☐	☐	☐
GROWTH RATE	Rapid ☐	Stable ☐	Slow ☐	Convenience to Shopping	☐	☐	☐	☐
PROPERTY VALUES	Increasing ☐	Stable ☐	Declining ☐	Convenience to Schools	☐	☐	☐	☐
DEMAND/SUPPLY	Shortage ☐	In Balance ☐	Over Supply ☐	Adequacy of Public Transportation	☐	☐	☐	☐
MARKETING TIME	Under 3 Mos. ☐	3-6 Mos. ☐	Over 6 Mos. ☐	Recreation Facilities	☐	☐	☐	☐

PRESENT LAND USE	%	LAND USE CHANGE	PREDOMINANT OCCUPANCY	SINGLE FAMILY HOUSING		
Single Family	___	Not Likely ☐	Owner ☐	PRICE $ (000)	AGE (yrs)	Adequacy of Utilities
2-4 Family	___	Likely ☐	Tenant ☐			Property Compatibility
Multi-family	___	In process ☐	Vacant (0-5%) ☐	Low		Protection from Detrimental Cond.
Commercial	___	To: ___	Vacant (over 5%) ☐	High		Police & Fire Protection
Industrial	___			Predominant		General Appearance of Properties
Vacant	___			—		Appeal to Market

Note: Race or the racial composition of the neighborhood are not considered reliable appraisal factors.

COMMENTS: _____

SITE
- Dimensions _____ / Topography _____
- Site Area _____ / Corner Lot _____ / Size _____
- Zoning Classification _____ / Zoning Compliance _____ / Shape _____
- HIGHEST & BEST USE: Present Use _____ Other Use _____ / Drainage _____

UTILITIES	Public	Other	SITE IMPROVEMENTS	Type	Public	Private	View
Electricity	☐		Street		☐	☐	Landscaping
Gas	☐		Curb/Gutter		☐	☐	Driveway
Water	☐		Sidewalk		☐	☐	Apparent Easements
Sanitary Sewer	☐		Street Lights		☐	☐	FEMA Flood Hazard Yes ___ No ___
Storm Sewer	☐		Alley		☐	☐	FEMA* Map/Zone

COMMENTS (Apparent adverse easements, encroachments, special assessments, slide areas, etc.): _____

IMPROVEMENTS

GENERAL DESCRIPTION	EXTERIOR DESCRIPTION	FOUNDATION	BASEMENT	INSULATION
Units	Foundation	Slab	Area Sq. Ft.	Roof ☐
Stories	Exterior Walls	Crawl Space	% Finished	Ceiling ☐
Type (Det./Att.)	Roof Surface	Basement	Ceiling	Walls ☐
Design (Style)	Gutters & Dwnspts.	Sump Pump	Walls	Floor ☐
Existing	Window Type	Dampness	Floor	None ☐
Proposed	Storm Sash	Settlement	Outside Entry	Adequacy ☐
Under Construction	Screens	Infestation		Energy Efficient Items
Age (Yrs.)	Manufactured House			
Effective Age (Yrs.)				

ROOM LIST

ROOMS	Foyer	Living	Dining	Kitchen	Den	Family Rm	Rec Rm	Bedrooms	# Baths	Laundry	Other	Area Sq Ft
Basement												
Level 1												
Level 2												

Finished area above grade contains: _____ Rooms; _____ Bedroom(s); _____ Bath(s); _____ Square Feet of Gross Living Area

INTERIOR

SURFACES	Materials/Condition	HEATING	KITCHEN EQUIP	ATTIC	IMPROVEMENT ANALYSIS	Good	Avg	Fair	Poor
Floors		Type	Refrigerator ☐	None	Quality of Construction	☐	☐	☐	☐
Walls		Fuel	Range/Oven ☐	Stairs	Condition of Improvements	☐	☐	☐	☐
Trim/Finish		Condition	Disposal ☐	Drop Stair	Room Sizes/Layout	☐	☐	☐	☐
Bath Floor		Adequacy	Dishwasher ☐	Scuttle	Closets and Storage	☐	☐	☐	☐
Bath Wainscot		COOLING	Fan/Hood ☐	Floor	Energy Efficiency	☐	☐	☐	☐
Doors		Central	Compactor ☐	Heated	Plumbing-Adequacy & Condition	☐	☐	☐	☐
		Other	Washer/Dryer ☐	Finished	Electrical-Adequacy & Condition	☐	☐	☐	☐
		Condition	Microwave ☐		Kitchen Cabinets-Adequacy & Cond	☐	☐	☐	☐
Fireplace(s) #		Adequacy	Intercom ☐		Compatibility to Neighborhood	☐	☐	☐	☐

AUTOS

CAR STORAGE:	Garage ☐	Attached ☐	Adequate	House Entry	Appeal & Marketability				
No. Cars ___	Carport ☐	Detached ☐	Inadequate	Outside Entry	Estimated Remaining Economic Life ___ Yrs
Condition ___	None ☐	Built-In ☐	Electric Door	Basement Entry	Estimated Remaining Physical Life ___ Yrs

COMMENTS
Additional features: _____

Depreciation (Physical, functional and external inadequacies, repairs needed, modernization, etc.): _____

General market conditions and prevalence and impact in subject/market area regarding loan discounts, interest buydowns and concessions: _____

Freddie Mac Form 70 10/86

Residential Appraisal

Figure 17–2. cont'd.

UNIFORM RESIDENTIAL APPRAISAL REPORT

Valuation Section — File No. _____

Purpose of Appraisal is to estimate Market Value as defined in the Certification & Statement of Limiting Conditions.

COST APPROACH

BUILDING SKETCH (SHOW GROSS LIVING AREA ABOVE GRADE)
If for Freddie Mac or Fannie Mae, show only square foot calculations and cost approach comments in this space

ESTIMATED REPRODUCTION COST – NEW – OF IMPROVEMENTS:
- Dwelling _____ Sq. Ft. @ $ _____ = $ _____
- _____ Sq. Ft. @ $ _____ = _____
- Extras _____ = _____
- _____ = _____
- Special Energy Efficient Items _____ = _____
- Porches, Patios, etc. _____ = _____
- Garage/Carport _____ Sq. Ft. @ $ _____ = _____
- Total Estimated Cost New _____ = $ _____
- Less Depreciation: Physical | Functional | External _____ = $ _____
- Depreciated Value of Improvements _____ = $ _____
- Site Imp. "as is" (driveway, landscaping, etc.) _____ = $ _____
- ESTIMATED SITE VALUE _____ = $ _____
- (If leasehold, show only leasehold value.)
- **INDICATED VALUE BY COST APPROACH** _____ = $ _____

(Not Required by Freddie Mac and Fannie Mae)
Does property conform to applicable HUD/VA property standards? ☐ Yes ☐ No
If No, explain: _____

Construction Warranty ☐ Yes ☐ No
Name of Warranty Program _____
Warranty Coverage Expires _____

SALES COMPARISON ANALYSIS

The undersigned has recited three recent sales of properties most similar and proximate to subject and has considered these in the market analysis. The description includes a dollar adjustment, reflecting market reaction to those items of significant variation between the subject and comparable properties. If a significant item in the comparable property is superior to, or more favorable than, the subject property, a minus (−) adjustment is made, thus reducing the indicated value of subject; if a significant item in the comparable is inferior to, or less favorable than, the subject property, a plus (+) adjustment is made, thus increasing the indicated value of the subject.

ITEM	SUBJECT	COMPARABLE NO. 1		COMPARABLE NO. 2		COMPARABLE NO. 3	
Address							
Proximity to Subject							
Sales Price	$	$		$		$	
Price/Gross Liv. Area	$	$		$		$	
Data Source							
VALUE ADJUSTMENTS	DESCRIPTION	DESCRIPTION	+(−)$ Adjustment	DESCRIPTION	+(−)$ Adjustment	DESCRIPTION	+(−)$ Adjustment
Sales or Financing Concessions							
Date of Sale/Time							
Location							
Site/View							
Design and Appeal							
Quality of Construction							
Age							
Condition							
Above Grade Room Count	Total | Bdrms | Baths	Total | Bdrms | Baths		Total | Bdrms | Baths		Total | Bdrms | Baths	
Gross Living Area	Sq. Ft.	Sq. Ft.		Sq. Ft.		Sq. Ft.	
Basement & Finished Rooms Below Grade							
Functional Utility							
Heating/Cooling							
Garage/Carport							
Porches, Patio, Pools, etc.							
Special Energy Efficient Items							
Fireplace(s)							
Other (e.g. kitchen equip., remodeling)							
Net Adj. (total)		☐+ ☐−	$	☐+ ☐−	$	☐+ ☐−	$
Indicated Value of Subject			$		$		$

Comments on Sales Comparison: _____

INDICATED VALUE BY SALES COMPARISON APPROACH .... $ _____
INDICATED VALUE BY INCOME APPROACH (If Applicable) Estimated Market Rent $ _____ /Mo. x Gross Rent Multiplier _____ = $ _____

This appraisal is made ☐ "as is" ☐ subject to the repairs, alterations, inspections or conditions listed below ☐ completion per plans and specifications.
Comments and Conditions of Appraisal: _____

Final Reconciliation: _____

RECONCILIATION

This appraisal is based upon the above requirements, the certification, contingent and limiting conditions, and Market Value definition that are stated in
☐ FmHA, HUD &/or VA instructions.
☐ Freddie Mac Form 439 (Rev. 7/86)/Fannie Mae Form 1004B (Rev. 7/86) filed with client _____ 19 _____ ☐ attached.
I (WE) ESTIMATE THE MARKET VALUE, AS DEFINED, OF THE SUBJECT PROPERTY AS OF _____ 19 _____ to be $ _____

I (We) certify: that to the best of my (our) knowledge and belief the facts and data used herein are true and correct; that I (we) personally inspected the subject property, both inside and out, and have made an exterior inspection of all comparable sales cited in this report; and that I (we) have no undisclosed interest, present or prospective therein.

Appraiser(s) SIGNATURE _____ Review Appraiser SIGNATURE _____ ☐ Did ☐ Did Not
NAME _____ (if applicable) NAME _____ Inspect Property

Freddie Mac Form 70 10/86 — Fannie Mae Form 1004 10/86

Foundation's Appraisal Standards Board promotes acceptance and implementation of the Uniform Standards of Professional Appraisal Practice by industry, financial institutions, and government on both the state and federal levels. These standards, which define the process of developing an appraisal and reporting its results, are designed to elevate and establish standards for all appraisers and users of appraisals. The Foundation's Appraiser Qualifications Board works with users of appraisal services, the states, and other regulators to ensure that certified appraisers possess the educational background, knowledge, and the experience to perform their functions in a professional manner.

Among the significant professional organizations that appraisers join are the American Institute of Real Estate Appraisers (AIREA), the Society of Real Estate Appraisers (SREA) for real property appraisals, and the American Society of Appraisers (ASA) for more general appraisals including personal property assignments. There are also more specialized appraisal groups, such as the International Association of Assessing Officers (IAAO), the National Association of Independent Fee Appraisers (NAIFA), the American Society of Farm Managers and Rural Appraisers (ASFMRA), the International Right of Way Association (IR/WA), the National Society of Real Estate Appraisers (NSREA), and the National Association of Review Appraisers (NARA).

AIREA, sometimes called "the Institute," is affiliated with the NATIONAL ASSOCIATION OF REALTORS® and offers the designations of RM (Residential Member) for those members specializing in residential appraisals and the MAI (Member of the Appraisal Institute) for specialization in all real property appraisals. The SREA, sometimes called "the Society," awards the SRA (Senior Residential Appraiser), the SRPA (Senior Real Property Appraiser) and the SREA (Senior Real Estate Analyst). To attain these designations, members must demonstrate professional competence by passing difficult exams, earning experience and writing an acceptable demonstration appraisal report. In addition, there is a requirement to maintain competence through continuing education.

One characteristic of appraisal organizations is their adherence to codes of ethics designed to maintain high professional standards. For example, the AIREA code of ethics contains eight canons or articles. These articles are written in general language. Some of the actions implied by these canons include the requirement that an appraiser refrain from misconduct detrimental to the profession or the public, not base a value opinion which is calculated as a percentage of the value found or a percentage of a court judgment won, preserve confidentiality of an appraisal report and follow the Institute's Standards of Professional Practice.

Also, an appraiser could not own a secret property interest in a project being appraised, nor could the appraiser use another person to help reach a value opinion without disclosing that person's name in the appraisal report. While the wording of the canons is general, the appraiser is concerned with following the spirit of the code rather than the letter of the code. As a result, there are a number of activities that might be unethical which are not specifically spelled out.

POINTS TO REMEMBER

1. In dealing with real estate, both market conditions and the real estate itself necessitate employing a specialist for the sole purpose of estimating value. Such is the normal role assumed by the appraiser.
2. While the word *value* has different meanings to different people, two distinct meanings are used in the appraisal of real estate. First, value can be defined as the ability of a good or service to command other goods or services. Second, value is defined as the present worth of future rights to income.
3. While the terms *value, cost* and *price* are sometimes used synonymously, the three do not mean the same thing and, in fact, can be quite different.
4. Market value is normally defined as the price at which a willing buyer and willing seller will agree upon, where neither are under any undue pressure and both are negotiating at arm's length with complete knowledge of the market.
5. There are three standard approaches employed for estimating value: (1) comparable sales or market approach, (2) cost approach and (3) income or capitalization approach.
6. Each of the three standard approaches employed in estimating value is used under different circumstances and for different types of real estate.
7. Regardless of the approach used, the appraiser must follow a systematic step-by-step analysis to estimate value accurately. The appraisal process begins with the definition of the assignment and concludes with the estimate of the defined value.

KEY TERMS AND PHRASES

accrued depreciation	economic obsolescence	market approach
appreciation	effective age	market value
cost	functional obsolescence	physical deterioration
cost approach	highest and best use	physical life
curable	income approach	price
economic life	incurable	value

QUESTIONS

1. Market value is most closely related to
   I. value in exchange
   II. value in use
   A. I only
   B. II only
   C. Both I and II
   D. Neither I nor II

2. The cost approach is often more accurate when
   A. the building is old and its use is not highest and best use
   B. the building is relatively new and its use is highest and best use
   C. reproduction cost is not known
   D. the building has an income stream

3. _____ is the decreased ability of a property to provide the utility or service relative to a new property designed for similar use.
   A. Locational obsolescence
   B. Functional obsolescence
   C. Economic obsolescence
   D. Physical deterioration

4. Comparing the physical components of comparable properties is part of
   A. defining the assignment
   B. collecting data
   C. analyzing data by the market approach
   D. correlating valuation approaches

5. Which of the following best defines the term "market value"?
   I. The price at which a property will sell, assuming a knowledgeable buyer and seller both operating with reasonable knowledge and without undue pressure
   II. The worth or amount in dollars assigned a property for property taxation purposes
   A. I only
   B. II only
   C. Both I and II
   D. Neither I nor II

6. For property to decline in value as a result of changes in technology or defects in design is referred to as
   A. physical deterioration
   B. functional obsolescence
   C. locational deterioration
   D. economic obsolescence

7. If you attempt to appraise a property using the asking prices from a multiple listing service in the sales comparison approach, the derived market value would probably be
   A. too high
   B. too low
   C. approximately correct
   D. 7% greater due to the commission rate

8. Which type of depreciation is generally not curable?
   A. Economic obsolescence
   B. Functional obsolescence
   C. Physical deterioration
   D. Physical wear and tear

9. You are appraising a house which currently rents for $600 per month. Based on a GRM of 125, what value would be derived?
   A. $60,000
   B. $75,000
   C. $90,000
   D. $125,000

10. The period over which property may be profitably utilized is called its
    A. economic life
    B. amortized life
    C. physical life
    D. net life

11. You are appraising a 15-year-old apartment complex in the midst of scattered industrial property. When the apartments were built, the surrounding neighborhood was residential. This is an example of
    A. economic obsolescence
    B. functional obsolescence
    C. physical deterioration
    D. highest and best use

12. Physical deterioration results from
    I. deferred maintenance
    II. tax depreciation
    A. I only
    B. II only
    C. Both I and II
    D. Neither I nor II

13. Selling price and market value are equal
    A. never
    B. sometimes
    C. always
    D. only with residential property

14. A home constructed 20 years ago subjected to ordinary family use and maintenance in a stable neighborhood would most likely suffer more of which of the following types of depreciation?
    I. Contingent
    II. Physical
    A. I only
    B. II only
    C. Both I and II
    D. Neither I nor II

15. An income-producing piece of property rents for $1,000 per month and the GRM is 84. What is the estimated market value of the property?
    A. $1,000
    B. $12,000
    C. $84,000
    D. $142,000

16. The cost method which estimates the major functional parts of the structure is the
    A. square-foot method
    B. builder's method
    C. quantity survey method
    D. index method

17. An appraiser
    I. determines value
    II. estimates value
    A. I only
    B. II only
    C. Both I and II
    D. Neither I nor II
18. The cost approach is based upon
    I. acquisition cost
    II. reproduction cost
    A. I only
    B. II only
    C. Both I and II
    D. Neither I nor II
19. Functional obsolescence can be classified as
    I. curable
    II. incurable
    A. I only
    B. II only
    C. Both I and II
    D. Neither I nor II
20. When an appraiser estimates the value of a single-family home, the most reliance would be placed on which of the following?
    A. Cost and income
    B. Highest and best use and market
    C. Rent capitalization and market
    D. Cost and market

If you are not sure of your answers, see page 323 for correct answers and explanations.

18

Income Property Appraisal and Investment Analysis

As was discussed in the previous chapter, there are three traditional valuation approaches: (1) comparable sales approach, (2) cost approach and (3) income approach. Each of these approaches is appropriate for various types of real estate under certain economic and market conditions. Under other conditions, a particular valuation approach may be impractical. For example, in situations where there is little or no current market activity, the comparable sales approach may not be appropriate. For property that is not generating any income, the income approach is normally inapplicable. One of the responsibilities of the appraiser is to choose the approach or approaches that can best be used to estimate the value of the particular property being appraised. For property that is generating income, such as an apartment complex or a shopping center, the income approach is commonly used.

INCOME PROPERTY APPRAISAL

The *income or capitalization approach* to appraising is based on the assumption that a property's value is equal to the *present worth of future rights to income*. Or to state this assumption another way, the value of income-producing real estate is a function of the income generated by that property. If the income increases, then the value of the property increases. Likewise, as the income of property decreases, there is, in turn, a decrease in the value of that property.

The term *income*, when used in a valuation context, refers to the dollars generated by the use of a particular property. For income-producing real estate, there are two basic sources of income. First, there is the income that is earned continuously through the use of property. Such income is normally based on the collection of rent from which the payment of operating expenses is subtracted. This income is normally stated in terms of so much money per year and is referred to as *net operating income*. The second source of income is derived from the net proceeds realized when the property is sold. Whereas the net operating income is thought of as being generated on an annual basis, the income generated from selling the property is realized only once. Nevertheless, what the property is expected to sell for at the end of the holding period affects the value or worth of that property just as the annual net operating income affects value.

While there are numerous ways of estimating the value of income-producing property, all of them are based on the following steps:

A. Estimate the stabilized net operating income of the property.
B. Select an appropriate capitalization rate.
C. Apply the capitalization formula to derive the estimated value.

ESTIMATING NET OPERATING INCOME

The first step an appraiser takes is to estimate the stabilized net operating income of the subject property. Stabilized net operating income refers to an expected series of dollars that are averaged out over a number of years so that no one year materially distorts the economic life of the repairs.

To estimate net operating income, the appraiser must consider four basic stages in constructing an operating statement for the subject property. These stages are:

1. Potential Gross Income
2. Effective Gross Income
3. Expenses
4. Net Operating Income

The appraiser will ask to examine the books and receipts reflecting the previous three to five years of the project's operation. Comparison will be made with the performance of similar properties in the market and with industry-based operating ratios. In addition, the appraiser will physically inspect the property to evaluate its condition and whether any major improvements must be made in the near future. For the purposes of discussion, it will be assumed that the appraiser will be seeking to estimate the market value of the property and not the investment value of the property to a specific investor. Since depreciation and debt service of existing financing are associated with the investment value, these factors are not considered at this stage of analysis.

Table 18–1 is a reconstructed operating statement for an apartment complex. The following discussion traces the steps of an appraiser who reconstructed the statement.

RECONSTRUCTING THE OPERATING STATEMENT TO FIND NET OPERATING INCOME

Potential Gross Income

Potential gross income is that amount which would be received if the apartment project were fully leased during an entire year. If there are 200 units in the apartment project, and each unit leases for $500 per month, what is the potential gross income? Since it is conventional to report these figures on an annual basis, one must convert monthly figures to yearly figures.

POTENTIAL GROSS INCOME:
200 units × $500 per month × 12 months = $1,200,000.

Effective Gross Income

Since not every unit will be fully rented during the entire year, a reasonable vacancy allowance must be calculated. Further, some tenants may issue bad checks or leave without fully paying their bills. On the basis of past experience of the property and on the basis of performance of competitive properties in the same market, the appraiser determines that 5% is a proper allowance.

VACANCY AND BAD DEBT LOSS:
$1,200,000 × .05 = $60,000

Any additional income other than rental income will be placed in the account designated "other income." This is income from auxiliary operations such as the laundry room or soft drink machines. The appraiser calculates this sum to be $50,000.

OTHER INCOME: $50,000.

The effective gross income is calculated by taking the potential gross income and subtracting the vacancy and bad debt loss and then adding back in the other income. This is the amount that is available for meeting the necessary expenses of operating the project.

EFFECTIVE GROSS INCOME: $1,190,000.

Less Expenses

Expenses may be divided into three general categories: fixed expenses, operating expenses and a reserve for replacement.

Table 18–1. Reconstructed Operating Statement for Apartment Project

POTENTIAL GROSS INCOME			$1,200,000
Less Vacancy and Bad Debt Loss			− 60,000
Add Other Income			+ 50,000
EFFECTIVE GROSS INCOME			$1,190,000
LESS EXPENSES:			
Fixed Expenses:			
Property Taxes	$100,000		
License Fees	1,000		
Property Insurance	24,000		
		$125,000	
Operating Expenses:			
Management Fee	$ 59,500		
Maintenance	110,000		
Ground Maintenance	20,000		
Utilities	100,000		
Supplies	15,000		
Legal and Accounting	10,000		
		$314,500	
Reserve for Replacement:			
Carpeting	$ 10,000		
Appliances	15,000		
Other	5,000		
		$ 30,000	
Total Estimated Expenses:			− $ 469,500
NET OPERATING INCOME			$ 720,500

Fixed expenses are those that are set independently of the level of occupancy. These expenses can include real property taxes, license fees and property insurance. Information necessary to estimate these expenses can be obtained from the local government tax assessor's office and from insurance companies in the area.

FIXED EXPENSES: $125,000.

Operating expenses are those directly related to the level of occupancy and usage of the building. These can include management fees, maintenance, ground maintenance, utilities, supplies, legal fees, accounting fees and other such costs. It might be observed that some expenses may be a blend of fixed and operating elements. Information about these expenses can be acquired from records of the project indicating past performance. Some information can be obtained from utility companies and other providers of service. Some organizations such as the Institute of Real Estate Management (IREM) or the Building Owners and Managers Association (BOMA) may have industry expenses ratios or ratios collected on a local market basis.

OPERATING EXPENSES: $314,500.

Reserves for replacement are necessary to account for cost of short-lived items that need to be replaced every few years. For example, assume that carpeting in the apartment project must be replaced every five years at a cost of $50,000. Approximately one-fifth of the expected cost must be charged to each year's earnings. This charge can be less if the money is deposited in a bank to earn interest. The reason for this adjustment is that every year part of the value of the property is destroyed by wear and tear. Effectively, the owner is losing income every year, even though the actual expenditures may be postponed and lumped together in a single year in the future. To account for this loss of value, the expense is spread over the economic life of the item. In the apartment project, assume that such a reserve account is set up for carpeting, appliances and other items.

RESERVE FOR REPLACEMENT: $30,000.

Total estimated expenses are the accumulation of fixed expenses, operating expenses and replacement reserves.

TOTAL ESTIMATED EXPENSES:
$125,000 + $314,500 + $30,000 = $469,500.

Net Operating Income

Net operating income (NOI) is what is left over to pay the owner's profit and debt service. NOI is calculated by subtracting total estimated expenses from effective gross income.

NET OPERATING INCOME:
$1,190,000 − $469,500 = $720,500.

SELECTING AN APPROPRIATE CAPITALIZATION RATE

The second major step in estimating the value of income-producing property is the selection of an appropriate *capitalization rate*. A capitalization rate or *cap rate* is simply a rate used to convert an income stream; in the example above, the NOI of $720,500, into a lump-sum dollar value.

In real estate, the capitalization rate must include a provision for interest and, in many cases, a provision for a repayment of the original money invested. This is commonly referred to as a return "on" investment and a return "of" investment. Return "on" investment is the interest that must be paid to an investor for the use of his or her money. Return "of" investment is the recovery of the capital invested. If the original amount used to purchase real estate is returned at the end of the holding period, no capital recovery is needed in the capitalization rate. If, however, the property is expected to decline in value over time, a portion of each year's income must be used to compensate for the expected decline. For property expected to increase in value during the holding period, which does happen with real estate, the annual return "on" investment normally expected by an investor can be less since the return "of" the investment at the time of sale will be greater than the initial amount invested.

Numerous methods for deriving a capitalization rate are available. Some of these are rather straightforward, while others have been developed to allow for unique circumstances not common with all types of income property. Since it is neither appropriate nor possible to list and explain all of the various capitalization methods, a few of the more common methods are briefly illustrated below to give an idea of how this second step in the appraising of income-producing property is completed.

The *summation or build-up method* is a process by which an appraiser begins with a risk-free safe rate of interest as a foundation and upon this rate builds the necessary returns needed to compensate the investor for risk due to the project itself, a premium for a loss of liquidity and for the burden of managing the project. Using this method, the capitalization rate is different for different projects. For example, the allowance for risk associated with a warehouse rented to a AAA tenant for 15 years under a net lease is quite different than the risk associated with the income that may or may not be generated from a speculative office building built at a time when there is an oversupply of office space. Likewise, for projects requiring more management skills, as well as more of the investor's own time, a higher capitalization rate would be necessary.

Example:
Pure interest for risk-free investment	8.0%
Allowance for risk	2.0%
Allowance for nonliquidity	2.0%
Allowance for management	3.0%
Capitalization rate derived by build-up method	15.0%

In this particular instance, a cap rate of 15% has been developed. For a riskier investment, the allowance for risk could be 5% instead of 2%, and thus the overall rate would be 18%. Another point that should be made in regard to the build-up method is that the weights assigned to each of the allowances are very subjective. Thus, three different appraisers employed to estimate the same property using this approach could, and quite often do, come up with entirely different capitalization rates. That is not to say that only one of the three is correct; rather, they have each simply assigned different weights, and thus the end result, as will be noted later, will be different value estimates.

The *band of investment method* is influenced, and in turn derived, by the capital structure or financing of a particular project. Consideration is given to how much return or interest is necessary to adequately compensate each provider of funds. As was previously discussed, a real estate investment normally requires the borrowing of money. In some instances, particularly as the total dollar outlay increases, more than one lender is involved. In addition, for income-producing property, the investor has a minimum return required for the personal funds invested in the project, commonly referred to as *return on equity*. Given the amount borrowed and the interest rate charged on these borrowed funds along with the requirements of the equity participant, the owner, a weighted average is taken to develop a composite capitalization rate.

Example:

	Percentage of Total Purchase Price	Interest Required	Weighted Average
First mortgage for 75% of value	.75 ×	.12 =	.0900
Second mortgage for 15% of value	.15 ×	.15 =	.0225
Equity by investor for 10% of value	.10 ×	.17 =	.0170

Capitalization rate derived by
band of investment method: .1295 or 12.95%

What the 12.95% shows is the minimum overall rate of return necessary to satisfy the three providers of funds for this particular project. Were any of the three to increase their interest rate requirement, the weighted average would increase, and thus the capitalization rate would be higher.

The *direct or market capitalization method* is derived from information gathered from the market. Under this method, capitalization rates are extracted from recent market sales of similar properties, where both the sales price and respective net operating incomes are known by the appraiser. The rates are derived by dividing the net operating income by the sale price. Unlike the gross income multiplier approach described in the previous chapter, this approach takes into account the unique operating characteristics of each property used in the analysis.

Example:

Sales Comparable	Net Operating Income		Sales Price		Overall Rate
A	$ 324,000	÷	$ 2,700,000	=	.12
B	$ 960,500	÷	$ 8,500,000	=	.113
C	$1,180,000	÷	$10,000,000	=	.118
D	$ 827,640	÷	$ 6,840,000	=	.121
E	$1,470,600	÷	$12,900,000	=	.114

Capitalization rate derived by
direct or market method: .1172 or 11.7%

As can be seen from examining these basic capitalization methods, different rates can be derived by using different methods. The particular method chosen will, of course, influence the final capitalization rate and care should be taken by the appraiser to choose the method that best depicts the circumstances present in the subject project. As will be illustrated below, a small change in the capitalization rate has a significant effect on the final value derived under the income approach.

Providing for Capital Recovery

A special problem occurs if the real estate is expected to lose value over the investment holding period. Assume that, at the end of 40 years, the improvement will be worthless. If this is the case, the value of the improvement must be recovered out of the net operating income. This can be done by increasing the capitalization rate by an amount necessary to recover the appropriate percentage that the asset is expected to decline over each year. If the economic life of the improvement is 40 years, then, on a straight-line basis, 2½% of the value would have to be recovered each year. To determine how this would affect the capitalization rate, it is necessary to split the rate between the land and improvements. If the land represents 20% of the total value, and the basic capitalization rate is 12%, the rate adjusted for capital recovery would be derived as shown in Table 18–2.

APPLICATION OF THE CAPITALIZATION FORMULA TO ESTIMATE VALUE

The third and last step in the capitalization or income approach is to apply the capitalization formula to the information derived from the first two steps. When this is done, an estimate of value based on income can be derived.

The *capitalization formula* used in the income approach is:

Table 18–2. Capitalization Rate Adjusted for Capital Recovery

Part of Asset	Basic Rate	Adjustment	Weight	Weighted Average
LAND	.12 +	none (assume no change in value)	× .20 =	.024
IMPROVEMENTS	.12 +	.025 (100% ÷ 40 years)	× .80 =	.116
				.14 or 14%

$$V = \frac{I}{R}$$

Where
- V = Value
- I = Net Operating Income
- R = Capitalization Rate

By examining the formula, one can see that the value estimate is determined and thus affected by two things: (1) net operating income and (2) capitalization rate. By changing either or both, the value estimate also changes. Since the appraiser is responsible for estimating net operating income as well as for choosing an appropriate capitalization rate, the estimate of value is entirely dependent upon information gathered and analyzed by the appraiser.

Consider the apartment complex illustration presented earlier in this chapter. The net operating income estimate was $720,500. In the capitalization formula, above, the $720,500 represents I or the numerator. The denominator, or the rate divided *into* the net operating income, is the capitalization rate. As discussed above, this rate can vary greatly, given conditions in the marketplace and different assumptions made by the appraiser.

What is the value estimate of the apartment complex? Applying the V = I/R formula, given an income of $720,500 and the appropriate capitalization rate gives us the answers.

Using the 15% rate derived by the summation or build-up method, the estimate of value is as follows:

$$V = \left(\frac{\$720,500}{.15} \right)$$
$$= \$4,803,333$$
or $4,800,000 (rounded)

Notice what happens to the value estimate if the capitalization rate derived by the band of investment method is used:

$$V = \left(\frac{\$720,500}{.1295} \right)$$
$$= \$5,563,707$$
or $5,565,000 (rounded)

The estimate of value increases to $5,563,707 or more than $760,000 above the estimate when the income was capitalized at the lower cap rate! What happened? The net operating income did not change. What changed, and thus what caused a significant increase in the estimate of value, was the rate of capitalization. You will observe that as a result of *lowering* the cap rate from 15 to 12.95% the value was raised from less than $5 million to more than $5.5 million.

When the capitalization rate derived from the direct or market capitalization method of 11.7% is applied to the same net income, the value estimate increases even more:

$$V = \left(\frac{\$720,500}{.117} \right)$$
$$= \$6,158,120$$
or $6,160,000 (rounded)

What has happened is that by changing the capitalization rate, or R in the formula, the estimate of value has changed. Specifically, a lower cap rate resulted in a *higher* value. Had the cap rate remained the same but the net operating income increased, the result would have been a higher value. For example, assume that in our illustration total expenses were only $390,000, which would result in a NOI of $800,000. Applying the 15% capitalization rate derived from the build-up method would result in:

$$V = \left(\frac{\$800,000}{.15} \right)$$
$$= \$5,333,333$$
or $5,335,000 (rounded)

Note that by assuming a decrease in expenses of $79,500 ($469,500 − $390,000) and applying the same cap rate of 15%, the value estimate changed from $4,803,333 to $5,333,333, an increase of $530,000.

In summary, value based on the income approach is a function of two things: (1) net operating income and (2) capitalization rate. As noted in Figure 18–1, value can either be increased or decreased as either net operating income or the capitalization rate are raised or lowered.

REAL ESTATE INVESTMENT ANALYSIS

Real estate offers numerous and varied opportunities for investors. For the would-be investor, there is vacant land, houses, apartment complexes, condominiums, industrial property, office buildings, shopping centers and others. Appraisal principles provide the basic techniques for more sophisticated investment analysis.

To successfully invest in real estate, an individual must recognize how each investment opportunity compares with investment opportunities of different risk classes. An investor must be able to assess the risks of the deal offered so as to pay no more than a justified investment price.

From a financial standpoint, an investment is a commitment of present dollars or assumption of liabilities for the purpose of securing a right of reasonable expectation of future monetary benefits. The general goal or objective of the investor is to conserve the purchasing power of capital and to earn some kind of additional return on the equity invested.

Investment opportunities contain different mixes of advantages and disadvantages. Some of these advantages or disadvantages may not be immediately obvious. An investment suitable for one individual may not be suitable for another. For example, a doctor in a high tax bracket who is

Figure 18–1. Impact of Net Operating Income and Capitalization Rate on Value

Capitalization Rate Remains Constant

Net Operating Income ↑ → Value ↑
Net Operating Income ↓ → Value ↓

(direct relationship between N.O.I. and Value)

Net Operating Income Remains Constant

Capitalization Rate ↑ → Value ↓
Capitalization Rate ↓ → Value ↑

(inverse relationship between cap rate and value)

busy with a medical practice will have entirely different needs than a retired widow living on Social Security and income from investments. The doctor may need an investment which provides a tax shelter and requires little management; the widow may need an investment which provides spendable cash each month and increases in value to keep up with the increases in the cost of living. Because each investor has unique financial needs, it is necessary to weigh the various benefits and costs of holding an asset. In addition to various financial benefits, investments may also provide the owner with certain nonmonetary satisfactions, such as social status or political power. Other investments bring specific benefits to society by providing jobs, improving the physical and cultural environment and adding to the productivity of the economy.

One of the investor's most precious and irreplaceable resources is time. Once lost, time may never be regained. Benjamin Franklin constantly reminded his readers that "time is money." He pointed out that time nonproductively used was money lost. One way to use time productively is to put capital to work. money is used to earn interest. The timing of the interest is important because new funds generated may be used to earn still further interest. Understanding the relationship between time and money is the first step toward investment sophistication.

The Time Value of Money

Would an individual reasonably expect to pay $1.00 today for the promise of $1.00 a year from today? No, unless there was the intent to confer a gift of the value of using that money for the year. If the individual had placed that dollar into a bank which paid an annual interest rate of 5%, the investor would have received $1.05 at the end of that time period. That extra nickel received is interest, which is the payment for the use of the money.

If an investor owns a house which costs $10,000 and is leased for one year, the investor is entitled to receive rent for the use of the house and at the end of the lease period is entitled to receive back the possession of the house. Likewise, if an investor lets someone borrow $10,000 in cash for one year, that investor would also justifiably expect to be compensated. The money the investor lends is called the *principal*. The investor is entitled to receive both a return "on" the principal, which is the *interest* and a return "of" the principal, which is the original sum lent.

The Principle of Risk Versus Return

The reader may wonder why certain investments such as a bank account pay 5% while others such as real estate often pay 25% or more. For example, if both Investment A and Investment B are expected to pay $100 for each year in dividends, why are the two investments not selling for the same price? The answer is that investors pay a premium for certainty. If they are uncertain that Investment A will pay the promised $100 dividend but are more sure that Investment B will, Investment B will sell for a higher price. The lack of certainty on the part of the investor is based on perception of *risk* in the investment. The riskier the investment, the less the investor is willing to pay for it. Risk has two sides, the upside, which is the possibility of gain, and the downside, which is the possibility of loss. Generally, more attention is paid to the downside, i.e., loss of original investment or failure by the investor to realize the promised gain. Gamblers and speculators tend to emphasize the upside risk, i.e., the chances of gaining greater profits than expected.

As previously indicated, the general equation for valuing return from an investment is expressed as follows:

$$V = I/R$$

The greater the risk perceived the higher the capitalization rate. As the capitalization rate increases, the value of the income stream is reduced.

Example:
If an investor examines two investments, each of which pays $100 dividends annually, and determines that one is safe and should be capitalized at 6%, while the other is marginally safe and should be capitalized at 8%, how much should be offered for each?

Safe Investment $V = I/R$
                    $V = \$100/.06$
                    $V = \$1,666.67$

Marginal Investment $V = I/R$
                    $V = \$100/.08$
                    $V = \$1,250$

Return

Return is a composite of different financial benefits received from an investment. The *rate of return* is a percentage relationship between the composite returns and the investment price or equity invested (see Figure 18–2).

Benefits investors normally consider in calculating the rate of return on real estate are described below.

Cash Flow

This is the annual cash, stated as either pretax cash flow or after-tax cash flow, generated from the operation of a capital asset such as real estate. Cash flow, as will be illustrated below, is not the same thing as net operating income. For the appraiser, net operating income is the quantitative measure used to estimate value. However, for the investor the calculation of net operating income is not enough. What is needed is cash flow.

Cash flow is derived as follows:

Figure 18–2. The Capitalization Rate Equates Returns with Investments

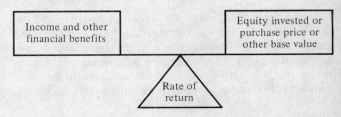

```
Net operating income
− Debt service
─────────────────────
Pretax cash flow
− Tax liability
─────────────────────
After-tax cash flow
```

As will be noted below, more information is needed to derive cash flow than is needed to calculate net operating income. First, debt service must be calculated. *Debt service* is the periodic payment, normally paid monthly but calculated on an annual basis, required by the lender to repay the money borrowed to purchase the project. The amount of debt service is a function of the amount borrowed, the interest rate charged and the time over which the debt is to be repaid.

By subtracting debt service from net operating income, pretax cash flow is determined. From the pretax cash flow, the investor's tax liability is subtracted to arrive at after-tax cash flow.

Tax liability is estimated as follows:

```
Net operating income
− Interest
− Depreciation
─────────────────────
Taxable income
× Tax rate
─────────────────────
Tax liability
```

Example:

Assume the apartment complex discussed earlier with a net operating income of $720,500. In addition, the investor borrows $3,000,000 for 15 years at an interest rate of 12% (annual debt service of $440,472). The interest on the mortgage for the first year is $360,000 ($3,000,000 × .12) and the depreciation is $200,000 (assumed). The owner is in the 28% tax bracket. What is pretax (before tax) cash flow? What is after-tax cash flow?

Calculation of pretax (before tax) cash flow:

Net operating income	$720,500
− Debt service	− 440,472
Before-tax cash flow	$280,028

Calculation of after-tax cash flow:

Net operating income	$720,500
− Interest	− 360,000
− Depreciation	− 200,000
Taxable income	160,500
× Tax rate	× .28
Taxable liability	$ 44,940
Before-tax cash flow	$280,028
− Tax liability	− 44,940
After-tax cash flow	$235,088

By capitalizing either the before-tax or after-tax cash flow, an investor can convert the cash flow into a present *investment price or value* in much the same way as the appraiser converts the net operating income into value. One reason many investors only consider cash flow in the measurement of their rate of return is that this benefit is certain, whereas other benefits are only guesses that are dependent on the state of the market at the time the asset is sold.

Tax Consequences

Certain real estate investments, in addition to cash flow, also have the ability to shelter income beyond the income generated by the project. A portion of income from an investment may be sheltered by artificial losses, whereas income from another investment may be tax free except for certain minimum tax requirements resulting from the investor's total tax situation.

Example:

In another building with the same income, the depreciation might be $270,000 instead of $200,000. Assume also that the owner/investor borrowed $4 million instead of $3 million. With these numbers, the results are as follows:

Net operating income	$720,500
− Interest	− 480,000
− Depreciation	− 270,000
Taxable income	($29,500)

Thus, in terms of this particular project, the taxable income is negative, specifically ($29,500). That does not mean the project is losing money, as the before-tax cash flow is still positive:

Net operating income	$720,500
− Debt service	− 587,296
Before-tax cash flow	$132,204

Rather, the income generated by this project has been sheltered.

Tax consequences are so important that a more detailed discussion is provided in the last section of this chapter.

Amortization

This is the periodic payback of principal owed to the lender. The effect of amortization is to build up the paper value of the investor's equity and to reduce the debt obligation. It should be noted that a portion of each payment in the debt service consists of a blend of interest and amortization of principal. The interest payment, as illustrated above, is tax deductible, whereas the amortization is not. Lenders normally use amortization schedules or tables to calculate the amount of payment necessary to amortize a certain debt, given the interest rate and the life of the loan. Table 18–3 gives the annual payment per $1,000 of loan for various interest rates over different periods of time.

Appreciation

Appreciation is an increase in the price level of an investment over a period of time. It may or may not keep up with the level of inflation. Like amortization, appreciation is a paper profit which is not realized until the asset is either refinanced, sold or traded. In order not to overstate the value of the appreciation or amortization, the investor

Table 18–3. Amortization Table
Monthly Payment per $1,000 of Loan

Interest Rate per Year	Life of the Loan			
	5 Years	15 Years	25 Years	30 Years
8%	$20.28	$ 9.56	$ 7.72	$ 7.34
10%	21.25	10.75	9.09	8.76
12%	22.24	12.00	10.53	10.29
14%	23.27	13.33	12.04	11.85
16%	24.32	14.69	13.59	13.45
18%	25.39	16.10	15.17	15.07
20%	26.50	17.56	16.79	16.71

should make an adjustment for transaction costs which include marketing fees and commissions, capital-gains taxes and various other transfer fees.

Leverage

Leverage is the use of borrowed capital to finance the purchase of real estate or other assets. To illustrate the use of leverage, consider the information presented in Table 18–4 concerning the financing and income of the apartment complex. As noted in the table, if the full $5 million is provided by the investor, with no debt, the return on equity is 14.41%. However, by borrowing $3 million of the purchase price, the return on equity is increased to 18.03%, and if $4 million is borrowed the return increases even more to 24.05%.

As this example illustrates, the investor has magnified the rate of return substantially by using leverage, or as is commonly referred to OPM—"other people's money." The result is positive leverage, which means that since the cost of the borrowed funds is lower than the overall rate of return on equity with no financing, the return on equity increases when part of the cost of investment is financed. Note, however, that leverage can be negative as well as positive. If the cost of borrowing part of the investment price exceeds the rate of return on equity, then the return on the investor's money decreases rather than increasing, as was illustrated above.

FEDERAL TAXATION

The subject of federal taxation of real estate is highly technical and ever changing. It is exposed to almost daily modification by Congress, the courts and the Internal Revenue Service. Although in most years Congress usually makes numerous minor changes in the tax law, occasionally major tax reforms take place. One major tax reform occurred in 1986. This is a subject worth studying, however, because one of the significant financial advantages of real estate is the preferred tax treatment enjoyed by certain types of real estate investments. These benefits include the tax-sheltering features of some real estate projects, allowing for creation of artificial tax losses while a project is generating a positive cash flow. In addition, real estate provides opportunities for deferral of tax gains on sale, for so-called tax-free exchanges, and for the shifting of ordinary income to capital-gains income, resulting in an overall lower tax liability.

The financial benefits that accrue from investing in real estate are directly dependent on an individual's tax bracket. Certain kinds of income and deductions are more valuable to one taxpayer than to another.

The first step in calculating a person's tax liability is to determine a person's gross income. *Gross income* is all income, from whatever source, which is not specifically excluded by law. For the sake of simplification, income may be classified into three general categories: (1) ordinary income, (2) capital-gains income and (3) nontaxable income (ordinarily referred to as exclusions).

Ordinary Income

Ordinary income includes wages and other compensation, interest and dividends, rents and royalties, alimony, pensions and proceeds from life insurance in excess of premiums paid (excluded if received because of death of the insured). Ordinary income is subject to ordinary income tax rates after all adjustments, deductions and exemptions have been applied. The 1986 tax changes took full effect in 1988. As of that year, at least in theory, there are just two tax rates of 15% and 28%. In reality, there will be a 15% rate, then a 28% rate, and finally a 33% rate for higher-income taxpayers until enough is collected to make the original 15% rate as if it were 28%, then the rate will drop back to the so-called maximum 28%. If this is confusing, do not be surprised even though Congress intended this change to be a simplification of the tax law.

Capital-gains Income

A capital gain or loss is the difference between the net sales price and the adjusted basis of a capital asset. The *net*

Table 18–4. Use of Leverage

	Situation A	Situation B	Situation C
Cost of Investment	$5,000,000	$5,000,000	$5,000,000
Amount Borrowed	0	3,000,000	4,000,000
Net Operating Income	720,500	720,500	720,500
Interest on loan (12%)	0	360,000	480,000
Return to investor (NOI—interest)	$ 720,500	360,500	240,500
Rate of return on equity	720,500 / 5,000,000 = 14.41%	360,500 / 2,000,000 = 18.03%	240,500 / 1,000,000 = 24.05%

sales price is cash, plus market value of other property received, plus the value of any liabilities such as a mortgage which will be paid off by the purchaser, minus transaction costs such as broker's commission and closing costs paid by the seller.

Adjusted basis is the original tax basis at which the property was acquired (ordinarily the purchase price), plus any capital additions (cost of major improvements), minus any depreciation taken.

Capital gains and losses may be classified as long term and short term. A long-term gain or loss results from the disposition of any capital asset which has been held at least one year. Previously, the holding period was six months, but as of 1978 it is one year. Long-term capital gains are taxed at a lower rate than are short-term gains and ordinary income. Since 1987 the maximum rate on capital gains has been 28%. Under the 1986 law, there is no longer a difference between long-term and short-term capital gains.

Exclusions

Certain income is excluded or partially excluded from gross income and not subject to taxation at ordinary or capital-gains rates. Excluded income includes interest on bonds and other obligations of states and smaller political subdivisions such as cities and counties, certain life insurance proceeds, social security, public assistance payments and other specified categories of income.

WHAT ARE ALLOWABLE DEDUCTIONS?

A *deduction* is any ordinary and necessary expense paid or incurred in a taxable year which is related to business or the production of income. Such deductions are in addition to any other deduction permitted by law and depend upon the accounting method used by the taxpayer. Except where specifically authorized by Congress, expenses for personal or family purposes are usually not deductible. A deduction has the effect of reducing the amount of taxable income and thereby reducing a taxpayer's tax liability. If a person owns a house which serves as his or her personal residence, Congress permits mortgage interest, property taxes and casualty losses as allowable deductions. In addition to these deductions, owners of real estate held for other purposes may be entitled to deductions for maintenance expenses and minor repairs, insurance premiums, and depreciation. One important change is that, under the 1986 law, you can now only deduct interest on a mortgage equal to the original cost of your house plus the costs of any improvements you have made. It is important, therefore, to keep good records any time you make improvements. Any interest on a mortgage amount above the total cost of your house cannot be deducted unless the money was used for medical or educational expenses. This change has had the effect of making so-called equity loans on the house appreciation no longer practical for tax savings purposes.

Depreciation

Care should be taken not to confuse the term "depreciation" as used for tax purposes and the same term as used for appraisal purposes. For appraisal, depreciation is any loss in utility and value in a property. For tax purposes, *depreciation* is an allowance which may be used by the taxpayer to allocate the cost of an improvement over its useful life. In order for a property to be entitled to a depreciation deduction, it must be used in trade or business or for the production of income. The concept is a bookkeeping entry and does not necessarily reflect the actual economic change in value. A depreciation deduction is often referred to as an artificial loss because it is a tax loss, not necessarily an economic loss. Because a depreciation deduction involves no actual expenditure by the taxpayer in the year that it is taken, it is a useful device for deferring taxes. Depreciation for residential rental property is 27.5 years using a straight-line method, and 31.5 years for non-residential rental. If the cost of the improvement is $100,000, what is the first year's depreciation on an apartment building? The answer is $3,636.37 ($100,000/27.5 years).

Rehabilitation Tax Credit

In order to encourage the rehabilitation of old or historic buildings, Congress has created an investment tax credit for qualified improvements. A tax credit is worth more than a deduction because it is the amount by which taxes are reduced. For example, a $1.00 deduction is worth 28 cents to a 28% taxpayer because this is how much less in taxes that must be paid. On the other hand, a $1.00 tax credit is worth $1.00 because this is how much the tax is actually reduced. Since 1986, Congress has allowed a 10% tax credit for nonhistoric buildings constructed prior to 1936, and a 20% credit for certified historic buildings.

INSTALLMENT SALES AND TAX-FREE EXCHANGES

A common way to postpone the payment of capital-gains taxes on profits made from the sale of real estate is to utilize the installment sales method. A transaction automatically qualifies under the installment sales method if payments of the gross sales price are spread over two or more years. Gross sales price includes cash received, mortgages of the seller that are assumed or taken by the buyer, and any other property or property rights given to the seller. This method permits the seller to defer paying capital-gains taxes on a pro rata basis until installments are actually received. As each installment payment is made, a portion of that payment is treated as interest, a portion as a capital gain and a portion is not subject to any kind of tax.

When real estate for investment or for production of income is exchanged for "like-kind" property, a tax-free exchange can take place. Generally, exchanges of real estate for other real estate meets the like-kind test, but any additional property included is called *boot* and is subject to taxation. Examples of boot include cash, mortgages or other liabilities assumed by one of the parties for the other or any other property such as machinery or art objects. Where a tax-free exchange takes place, the adjusted basis of each property follows the taxpayer. For example, assume that John owns Springdale with an adjusted basis of $50,000 and Ann owns Valleyview with an adjusted basis of $37,000.

Assuming they exchange properties, what will John's basis in Valleyview be? Assuming no boot passes hands, John's basis will be $50,000 in Valleyview since, in a tax-free exchange, the basis follows the taxpayer, not the property. If there is boot, the gain of the party receiving the boot will be taxed to the extent of the boot received.

Sales and Exchanges of Residences

It has been the policy of the Federal Government to encourage home ownership. Two provisions of the tax law make it less expensive to buy and sell one's home. One provision permits a rollover of deferral of capital-gains taxes on profits made on the sale of a principal residence. The second allows a forgiveness of $125,000 in capital-gains taxes for taxpayers 55 years or older who sell their principal residence.

If a taxpayer sells a principal residence, recognition of the gain can be postponed if the taxpayer purchases another principal residence of equal or greater value within 24 months of the contract date of the sale of the first principal residence. If the new house costs less than the first house, the taxpayer may be responsible for a tax on the capital gain. for example, assume that Mary Smith purchased a house in 1987 for $50,000. In 1990, she sells this house for $90,000. Within 24 months, she buys a condominium for $70,000. What is her capital gain? Answer: $20,000 ($90,000 − $70,000 = $20,000). Her basis remains $50,000, which was the purchase price of the original house. What is her capital gain if she, instead, buys a house costing $100,000? Answer: There is no capital gain because the new house cost more than she received when she sold her first house. Further, the new basis is the old basis increased by the net difference paid for the new house. What is the new basis? Answer: $60,000 ($50,000 is old basis + $10,000, which is the difference between the new purchase price of $100,000 and the old sales price of $90,000).

Taxpayers who are 55 years or older are given a once-in-a-lifetime relief of $125,000 in the gain received from the sale of their principal residence. To qualify, a taxpayer must be at least 55 years old on or before the date of the sale. The house must have been the principal residence in at least three of the five years preceding the sale. If married, only one spouse must be 55 years old, but both must join in making the election. If filing separately, each spouse is only allowed half the exclusion or $62,500. There are other, more technical, provisions which may require consultation with an attorney or tax accountant for an understanding of how the law applies in the situation of any particular individual.

SECURITIES AND SYNDICATIONS

As a result of cash flow, appreciation and the tax-shelter aspects, real estate has remained attractive to many investors. However, some of the more desirable income-producing properties are too expensive for the average investor to purchase alone. Therefore, to purchase such properties, investors commonly combine their resources and establish some form of multiple ownership arrangement such as a corporation, cooperative, condominium, tenancy in common, or partnership.

Individuals who establish and sell shares in these ownership arrangements are called *syndicators*. The shares in syndications formed by these individuals are usually classified as *securities* by federal law. Securities include stocks, bonds, certificates of interest, investment contracts, and other instruments that represent claims on ownership and future income. A very common real estate security is an *investment contract*. Investment contracts have three basic elements included in the following definition:

1. Investment by individuals in a common venture or enterprise
2. who expect to make a profit
3. from the efforts of a third person

Fitting this definition are limited partnerships and condominiums with rental pooling agreements.

The *Securities Act of 1933* is a federal statute that requires all securities not exempted to be registered with the Securities and Exchange Commission (SEC) and certain disclosures made in advance to potential investors. Further, the *1934 Securities and Exchange Act* requires all persons who sell or deal in securities to be registered also. Violations of these two laws can lead to severe penalties by the SEC and to civil lawsuits. Because real estate brokers are often put into situations where they might be considered dealing in or selling securities, it is essential to become familiar with a number of fundamental rules.

First, securities must be registered unless exempted. Because registration involves very expensive accounting, legal work and time delays, many syndicators try to qualify their offerings for one of the permitted exemptions. These include:

1. Those issued or guaranteed by federal, state, or local government.
2. *Intrastate* offerings (offerings restricted to investors of a single state as contrasted with *interstate* to investors of two or more states).
3. Some securities offered by banks, charitable organizations and short term notes of less than 9 months.
4. Certain small offerings (those, as defined by *Regulation D* of the SEC, that are less than $500,000 or offerings with no more than 35 *nonaccredited* investors; nonaccredited investors are people who have less than $1,000,000 in net worth and whose income is less than $200,000 annually).

Second, whether or not securities are exempted, the syndicator must still make required disclosures about the risks of the offering. This disclosure is made through a *prospectus* for registered securities and by *private memorandum* for exempted securities.

Third, a syndicator is always bound by the SEC *antifraud requirements;* which deal with deceptive or manipulative practices.

Fourth, even if certain securities are exempted from SEC registration, they are subject to state securities registration under each state's *blue sky laws*. These laws usually require the syndicator to make disclosures in an *offering statement*, or *offering memorandum*.

POINTS TO REMEMBER

1. To estimate the value of an income-producing property, an appraiser would estimate the stabilized net operating income of the property, select an appropriate capitalization rate and apply the capitalization formula to derive the estimated value.

2. Four common techniques for deriving a capitalization rate are: (1) the build-up method, (2) the band of investment method, (3) the comparison method and (4) direct capitalization.

3. The capitalization formula is $V = I/R$.

4. Potential gross income minus vacancy allowance equals effective gross income. Effective gross income minus operating expenses equals net operating income. Net operating income minus debt service equals before-tax cash flow. Before-tax cash flow minus tax liability equals after-tax cash flow.

5. An investor must be able to assess the risk of a deal so as not to pay more than the justified investment price.

6. An investment is a commitment of present dollars or assumption of liabilities for the purpose of securing a right to, or reasonable expectation of, future monetary benefits.

7. An investor is entitled to receive both a return "on" the investment and a return "of" the investment.

8. The riskier the investment, the less an investor should be willing to pay.

9. The rate of return is a percentage relationship between the composite returns and the investment price or equity invested.

10. Leverage is a technique of magnifying risks and returns on an investment through the use of debt financing (using other people's money).

11. The financial benefits that accrue in real estate are directly related to an individual's tax bracket.

12. Income may be classified as ordinary income, capital-gains income and nontaxable income. Ordinary income includes wages and other compensation, interest and dividends and rents and royalties. Capital-gains income is that which results from disposition of capital assets and is the difference between the net sales price and the adjusted basis. The adjusted basis is the original tax basis at which the property was acquired, plus any capital additions, minus any depreciation taken. Exclusions include all income which by law is not subject to taxation at ordinary or capital-gains rates.

13. A deduction in real estate is any ordinary and necessary expense paid or incurred in a taxable year, depending on the accounting method used by the taxpayer, which is related to business or the production of income.

14. A taxpayer may postpone the capital-gains tax on the sale of a principal residence if a new principal residence costing as much or more than the first residence is purchased within 24 months of the sales contract date.

15. A tax shelter is created by the effect of deductions attributable to interest on a mortgage note and to artificial losses generated by taking depreciation deductions.

16. Deferral of capital-gains taxes can result by selling property in an installment sale or in trading property of like-kind in a tax-free exchange. Property not of like-kind in an exchange is called boot.

KEY TERMS AND PHRASES

amortization
appreciation
basis
blue sky laws
capital gain
capitalization rate (cap rate)
depreciation (tax)

effective gross income
equity
leverage
net operating income (NOI)
operating expenses
potential gross income

present value
rate of return
securities
syndicator
tax shelter
time value of money

QUESTIONS

1. The amount to be deducted from potential gross income to allow for vacancies should be:
   A. 5% of potential gross income.
   B. 10% if the building is more than 10 years old.
   C. will range between 0 and 10%.
   D. will vary with each property.

2. As the degree of risk increases, the income generated by a piece of property will be capitalized at a:

   F. higher rate which will produce a higher value.
   G. higher rate which will produce a lower value.
   H. lower rate which will produce a higher value.
   J. lower rate which will produce a lower value.

3. A previously appraised building with a net income of $5,000 was valued at $50,000. What is the current estimate of value if the capitalization rate has increased by one percentage point?

A. $45,455 C. $50,000
B. $47,619 D. $55,555

4. The capitalization rate:
   F. goes up when the risk increases.
   G. goes down when the risk increases.
   H. goes up when the risk decreases.
   J. remains the same as long as there is net income.

5. Which of the following will result in a capitalization rate of 20%?
   A. Potential gross income $50,000; value $250,000
   B. Effective gross income $50,000; value $250,000
   C. Net income $50,000; value $250,000
   D. Cash flow $50,000; value $250,000

6. Net income is determined by deducting all operating expenses from:
   F. before-tax cash flow.
   G. potential gross income.
   H. sales price.
   J. effective gross income.

7. You are appraising a 20-year-old building with a useful remaining life of 25 years. the applicable recapture rate is:
   A. 2.5%. C. 20%.
   B. 4%.   D. 25%.

8. The period over which property may be profitably utilized is called its:
   F. economic life.   H. physical life.
   G. amortized life. J. net life.

9. Included in the capitalization rate is a return on:
   A. land and building.
   B. land and building and recapture of building.
   C. land and building and recapture of land and building.
   D. land and building and recapture of land.

10. The three components of the capitalization formula are:
    F. market, cost and income.
    G. value, rate and income.
    H. potential gross income, effective gross income and net income.
    J. economic, functional and physical.

11. When an estimate of a property's vacancy loss is subtracted from potential income, which of the following is forecast?
    A. Taxable income
    B. Net operating income
    C. Effective gross income
    D. Cash flow

12. Mortgage interest rates will differ from the capitalization rates used in appraising in that the mortgage interest rates are normally:
    A. higher   C. equal to or higher
    B. equal to   D. lower

13. An income property has a net income of $50,000 and a land value of $125,000. What is its total value using the building residual technique, assuming a 10% rate of return on investment and a 25-year building life?
    A. $267,857 C. $392,857
    B. $125,000 D. $375,000

14. The particular rate of return chosen by an investor should be used in evaluating the:
    I. land.
    II. improvements.
    III. cost of capital.
    F. I only   H. III only
    G. I and II only   J. All of the above

15. Using leverage in real estate can result in an increase in your:
    I. gain.
    II. loss.
    III. risk.
    A. I only   C. I and II only
    B. II only   D. I, II and III

19. Net operating income (NOI) minus debt service equals
    A. before-tax cash flow
    B. after-tax cash flow
    C. effective gross income
    D. potential gross income

20. Investment value is the
    A. true potential for a property to earn money
    B. tax shelter created for high-income persons
    C. worth of a property to a specific individual
    D. worth of a property as defined by the marketplace

21. If an apartment house costing $42,000 has a net income of $280 per month, what percent would it be returning on the investment?
    A. 6%   C. 9.5%
    B. 8%   D. 7.5%

22. The financial device used to maximize cash flow using other people's money is known as
    I. leverage
    II. liquidity
    A. I only   C. Both I and II
    B. II only   D. Neither I nor II

23. As risk and uncertainty increase, the expected rate of return should
    A. increase   C. remain the same
    B. decrease   D. fluctuate randomly

24. Trading on the equity is a sound policy if the property earns a rate
    I. lower than that of the borrowed funds
    II. equal to that of the borrowed funds
    A. I only   C. Both I and II
    B. II only   D. Neither I nor II

Income Property Appraisal and Investment Analysis

25. Liquidity is defined as
    A. the difference between assets and liabilities
    B. the purchasing power of an asset
    C. the ease of converting an asset into cash
    D. fluctuations in an asset's value

26. Equity build-up in real estate may be the result of a purchase for
    I. the individual's use
    II. investment property
    A. I only
    B. II only
    C. Both I and II
    D. Neither I nor II

27. After tax cash flow is derived by deducting _____ from the before-tax cash flow.
    A. tax rate
    B. debt service
    C. depreciation
    D. tax liability

28. If a person receives $40,000 each year in rental income from office space, this income is classified as
    A. capital-gains income
    B. ordinary income
    C. exclusion
    D. tax preference item

29. For the purpose of calculating capital gains or losses, the adjusted income is calculated by subtracting
    I. capital additions to the original basis
    II. any depreciation taken
    A. I only
    B. II only
    C. Both I and II
    D. Neither I nor II

30. Which of the following are allowable deductions for an improvement used as a personal residence?
    I. Interest portion of debt service on mortgage debt
    II. Cost of ordinary maintenance and repairs
    A. I only
    B. II only
    C. Both I and II
    D. Neither I nor II

31. Which is normally worth more to a taxpayer?
    A. $1.00 depreciation deduction
    B. $1.00 tax credit
    C. $1.00 capital gain
    D. $1.00 ordinary income

32. In order for a taxpayer to qualify for a $125,000 once-in-a-lifetime forgiveness of capital gain from the sale of real estate, which of the following criteria must be met?
    I. Taxpayer is at least 65 years old.
    II. The property must be the principal residence.
    A. I only
    B. II only
    C. Both I and II
    D. Neither I nor II

33. Which of the following offerings must be registered with the SEC?
    A. Intrastate offering
    B. Interstate offering
    C. Offering issued by local government
    D. Offering guaranteed by the federal government

34. Which of the following is an investment contract?
    A. Limited partnership
    B. General partnership
    C. A Hamburger Outlet Franchise to be operated by an investor
    D. An offer to purchase a rental property

35. In a tax-free exchange of real estate, which of the following would include boot?
    I. Assumption of a mortgage by one of the parties
    II. Farm land being traded for forest land
    A. I only
    B. II only
    C. Both I and II
    D. Neither I nor II

If you are not sure of your answers, see page 323 for correct answers and explanations.

19

Zoning and Taxation

Real estate is subject to many governmental restrictions at the federal, state and local levels. The government regulates private property and influences land-use decisions by proper planning and use of its *police power* and the powers of *eminent domain, taxation* and *escheat*. The police power is the inherent right of the state to regulate and promote the public welfare. Power of eminent domain is the right of government to acquire property for a public purpose after paying just compensation. The process of exercising eminent domain is *condemnation*, a court action. Taxation is the right of government to require contribution from citizens to pay for government services. Escheat is the right of government to property which is left by a deceased property owner who leaves no heirs or devisees.

The government also influences the land-use pattern by using its proprietary powers to build roads, dig canals, construct schools, provide fire protection and other services or make other capital improvements which are essential to modern urban civilization. This chapter concentrates on planning, police power and taxation. The topics of eminent domain and escheat are discussed in other chapters.

THE PLANNING PROCESS

Planning is a process for developing a guide for the future. The process is based on the scientific method and depends on collection of facts, analysis, the weighing of alternatives and the selection of goals.

Local governments receive authority to engage in land-use planning from *enabling legislation* passed by the state. Some states provide this power as part of the *home rule powers* in the municipal charter or state constitution. Most states have passed enabling legislation based on the Standard City Planning Enabling Act which was developed by the U.S. Department of Commerce in 1927. The enabling act provides for the creation of a *planning commission* or *board*. This commission is usually a board of citizens, often including real estate brokers, architects, lawyers, business people and others, who advise local government officials and legislators on planning matters. In passing a zoning ordinance, the planning commission usually recommends whether or not an ordinance should be approved by examining the proposed change and weighing its impact on the community on the basis of planning criteria. The planning commission's powers are usually limited, with the actual planning being handled by professional planners in the planning department and with final authority resting with the legislative body of the local government. Figure 19–1 illustrates the planning process.

POLICE POWER REGULATIONS

Police power is the inherent right of the state to regulate for the purpose of promoting health, safety, welfare and morality. The police power gives the state the right to impose certain restraints on human conduct which are reasonably necessary in order to safeguard the public interest. This right is the basis of zoning, the official map, building codes and subdivision regulations. When the state uses the police power, it is not required to compensate a property owner for any loss in property values as a result of the regulation. However, a police power regulation must be reasonable and must apply equally to all similar property. If a police power regulation is too restrictive or arbitrary, it may violate the due process and equal protection clauses of the U.S. Constitution. In addition, the Fifth Amendment contains a clause stating: "... nor shall private property be taken for a public use without just compensation." The U.S. Supreme Court has ruled that, while property may be regulated under the police power without requiring state compensation, if the regulation goes too far, the state must apply its powers of eminent domain and pay just compensation. It is up to the courts to decide if a regulation is too extensive in its restrictions on property rights.

Zoning

Zoning is a police power device which allows for legislative division of space into districts and imposition of

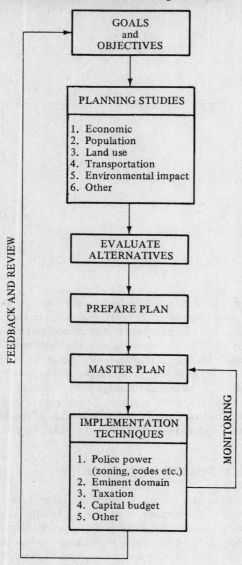

Figure 19–1. The Planning Process

regulations prescribing use and intensity of use to which land within each designated district may be put. Although rudimentary land-use regulations have existed in this country since early Colonial days, zoning is a relatively new technique. It was not until 1916 that the first comprehensive zoning ordinance was passed in the City of New York. In 1926, the U.S. Supreme Court upheld the constitutionality of zoning in the landmark case of *Village of Euclid v. Ambler Realty Co.* on the basis of police power. A local government receives the power of zoning from the state in much the same way it receives its power to plan. Ordinarily, authority is given in a state enabling act. Most zoning enabling legislation is based on the Standard State Zoning Enabling Act which was developed by the U.S. Department of Commerce in 1922 and revised in 1926.

A zoning ordinance has two major parts: (1) the text which contains various regulations and standards and (2) the map which divides an area into different districts. The zoning map is constantly updated and indicates the zoning status of each parcel of land in the community. The Standard Act indicates that zoning shall be made in accordance with a comprehensive plan, and both the text and the map are designed to help carry out the plan. A second overall purpose of zoning is to preserve property values. When zoning helps carry out a plan, it is called *directive* zoning. When it helps preserve value, it is called *protective* zoning. To carry out these two general purposes, zoning provides the following techniques to a local government:

1. Zoning establishes land-use districts and provides for different restrictions and standards within each use district. Use districts are divided into four basic categories: (1) residential, (2) commercial, (3) industrial and (4) agricultural. Each of these basic categories may be further divided. For example, the industrial uses may be divided into light and heavy industrial zones. Further, an ordinance may provide for special-use districts such as a historical district or a downtown shopping district.

    Each district is composed of uses which are relatively homogeneous or compatible. If two districts adjoin which have incompatible uses, planners normally try to place a *buffer zone* in between the two zoning districts. A buffer zone consists of uses which are compatible with uses in each adjoining district. A zoning ordinance may provide for either *exclusive-use districts* or for *cumulative districts*. If the ordinance specifies exclusive zones, only appropriate uses specified in the text may be permitted in a particular zone. For example, only industrial uses would be permitted in industrial zones. However, if the ordinance permits cumulative zoning, uses which are not specified in the text may be permitted in a particular zone. For example, in cumulative zoning a residential use might be permissible in an industrial zone. Ordinarily, cumulative zoning places all uses into a hierarchy with residential uses at the top. Uses at the top of the hierarchy may exist in lower zones but not vice versa. Thus, a residential use could be permitted in a commercial zone, but a commercial use could not be permitted in a residential zone.

2. Zoning establishes height restrictions. This is done to protect the sunlight and flow of air to adjoining properties.

3. Zoning establishes area and bulk restrictions. This is a means of regulating the intensity of development to prevent the overloading of public services and the infrastructure. Area and bulk restrictions include setback and sideyard requirements, minimum lot sizes and minimum and maximum floor area ratios (FAR). A setback or sideyard requirement specifies how far a building must be from the road and from the property line of adjoining properties. A requirement may be included for a buffer. A buffer is created by distance and barriers, such as fences or planting of bushes, and is intended to protect an adjoining property from noise, light and unsightliness of a particular land use or activity. Minimum lot sizes and minimum and maximum floor area ratios are used primarily to protect residential neighborhoods. A minimum lot size requirement might be a two-acre lot for each house. A minimum floor area might be 2,000 square feet of living space. These two

types of restrictions have been criticized for raising the cost of housing so that lower socio-economic groups are unable to afford houses in a particular neighborhood. This is referred to as *exclusionary zoning* since it tends to exclude the poor and minority groups. FAR indicates the relationship between a building area and land. For example, a 2:1 FAR means that two square feet of floor space may be constructed on one square foot of land. In other words, a two-story building covering the entire lot could be built. If only one-half of the lot were covered, a four-story building could be constructed, while if only one-quarter of the lot were covered, while if only one-quarter of the lot were covered, an eight-story building could be developed.

4. Zoning establishes other restrictions such as off-street parking requirements, open-space requirements, prohibitions against nonrelated and nonmarried persons living in a household (usually used to regulate fraternity houses, boarding houses and such), prohibitions against building in flood plains, performance standards for noise or pollution, restrictions favoring housing for the elderly, restrictions against socially offensive uses and others. Performance standards are ordinarily used in conjunction with industrial uses to ensure that the quality of the environment will be maintained.

When a zoning district is created, some uses may exist which are not consistent with the zoning ordinance. Pre-existing uses which do not conform to the zoning ordinance are called *nonconforming uses*. A nonconforming use may ordinarily remain; however, certain restrictions are usually imposed. For example, the property owner may not expand a nonconforming use. If a building which is nonconforming is destroyed or damaged to a significant degree, the owner may not replace or repair it.

If a property owner wishes to change the zoning on his or her property, the procedure is to seek an *amendment* to the map. Ordinarily, requests for re-zonings are heard by a zoning board which is appointed by a local governing board. The zoning board considers recommendations of the planners and listens to citizen groups. The zoning board makes its recommendations to the legislative body of the local government who will make the final decision. If the rezoning will create hazards or adversely affect surrounding properties, it will ordinarily be turned down. When the rezoned use is significantly different and involves only a small piece of property, the rezoning may be called a *spot* zone. Spot zoning is illegal in most states.

Example:
  Jack wishes to have his lot, which is in the middle of a residential neighborhood, rezoned so that he may build a convenience store upon it. This rezoning would be termed spot zoning.

Some properties may be adversely affected by a zoning ordinance and a unique hardship may be imposed upon them. For example, a lot may be 60 feet deep and a setback requirement may be 30 feet from the road, while a rear yard requirement may be 20 feet from the rear property line. This would leave only 10 feet upon which to place a structure. In order to seek relief from the harshness of the zoning restrictions, a property owner may seek a *variance* from the zoning board of appeals or zoning board of adjustment which may exist in the community. A variance is a type of safety valve to allow property owners who are unfairly burdened by zoning restrictions to find relief. Certain uses such as churches and child day-care centers do not fall within any zone. In order to allow these uses, zoning ordinances provide for *conditional* or *special-use permits* or *exceptions*. These permits are granted if the use meets standards specified in the ordinance. Zoning regulations are enforced by court injunctions (a building which is built in violation to the zoning ordinance can be ordered torn down), by fine (each day a structure violates the zoning ordinance may be treated as a separate violation) or by imprisonment.

Building Codes

Many local governments have passed building codes which specify minimum standards of construction for new buildings. Building codes apply to new construction and major additions to old construction. Ordinarily, a person seeking to construct a building or make major alterations must obtain a *building permit*. Many local governments have building inspectors who periodically inspect constructions to ensure that the minimum standards of the building code are being met. Before a new structure may be occupied, it is ordinarily necessary to obtain a *certificate of occupancy* indicating that the property passes a "final inspection." This certificate indicates that all local codes have been met and that the structure is suitable for occupancy. Some jurisdictions have more than one type of building code: fire codes, electrical codes, plumbing codes and others. It is important to be aware of the particular codes which exist in each locality since there is little uniformity in the nation.

Housing Codes

These are codes which specify minimum standards that a dwelling unit must meet. This type of code is designed to maintain the overall quality of housing in a community and to combat blight.

Subdivision Regulations

Subdivision regulations apply to situations in which a developer wishes to take one tract of land and break it up into smaller tracts of land for housing lots or other types of development. In order to record a subdivision plat, many local governments require that certain development standards be met. These standards relate to the size of lots, width of the streets, curbing, lighting, drainage and other improvements. If a developer wishes to turn the streets and public areas over to the local government for it to maintain, minimum construction-quality standards must be met before the local government will accept responsibility. Title to roads and other land is transferred through a process called *dedication*. Dedication involves a donation by the property owner and an acceptance by the government. Some local governments may require that the developer dedicate land for parks or school sites or pay a fee in lieu of dedication. If a subdivision exceeds 50 lots and is available for sale to persons from out of state, the sale of property may fall under the *Interstate Land Sales Full Disclosure Act*. This is a federal act which makes it unlawful to offer land for sale in interstate commerce unless certain information has been filed with HUD. In addition, certain disclosures must be made to prospective purchasers. Violation of the act may lead to fine or imprisonment.

Planned Unit Developments

Traditional zoning practices place different uses into separate districts. However, the Planned Unit Development (PUD) or Community Unit Plan (CUP) gives a developer flexibility in mixing various uses and densities. For example, a PUD could permit cluster-housing development with large open spaces. A traditional zoning ordinance would require separate housing on separate lots. A PUD is a type of exception or special use which is permitted under many modern zoning ordinances. The PUD technique allows for more efficient land-use planning and permits residents some of the advantages of condominium ownership by providing a recreational amenity package and reduced property maintenance requirements.

FUTURE TRENDS IN LAND-USE REGULATION

Several trends are occurring in land-use regulations. The first is a growing interest on the part of the federal government to become involved in land-use planning and regulations. Federal actions have included a large number of environmental laws, community development programs, interstate land sales regulations and consumer legislation including RESPA. In 1969 the U.S. Congress passed the *National Environmental Policy Act* (NEPA) which created the *Council on Environmental Quality* (CEQ) and the *Environmental Protection Agency* (EPA). The purpose of the CEQ was to advise the President on environmental policy matters, whereas the purpose of the EPA was to enforce environmental laws. NEPA was designed to require that federal agencies file an Environmental Impact Statement (EIS) in cases where a major federal action might have a significant impact on the human environment. This requirement has been instrumental in delaying or cancelling major dam and road projects which involved the expenditure of federal money. With the passage of other legislation, many large private projects such as manufacturing plants and regional shopping centers may come under the jurisdiction of the EPA.

A second trend is the increased willingness of the states to become involved with local land-use regulation. The American Law Institute has proposed the *Model Land Development Code* which calls for greater coordination on the state level of local regulations.

A third trend is the growing reluctance of local governments to accept growth for the sake of growth. Many techniques have been developed to slow growth down or to redirect growth to other communities. One technique is *timing and sequencing controls* which limit the growth of a community to the capital improvements budget. Another is *impact zoning* which assesses the costs and benefits of a particular project on the facilities of a community. Placing limitations on the number of housing units which may be constructed each year in a community, setting population ceilings for entire communities and putting moratoriums on all construction and development in a community are other techniques. Many of these have been litigated.

A fourth trend is the attitude on the part of the courts and state governments that each community has a responsibility to carry its fair share of low-income housing. Some communities are requiring that a certain percentage of each new PUD or housing development include low-income housing.

Finally, new emphasis is being given to the requirement that land-use regulations be coordinated with planning. New techniques such as *transfer development rights* (TDR) and *zoning by eminent domain* (ZED) are giving local officials more direct control over land-use decisions by private property owners. A real estate broker should strive to be familiar with the changing legal environment on the local, state and federal levels. These changes are likely to have a future impact on sales and the ability of the broker to provide a professional service to clients.

THE PROPERTY TAX PROCESS

A tax on property is referred to as an *ad valorem tax*. That is, the tax is based on the value of the property, so two different pieces of property with the same assessed value have the same ad valorem tax. Likewise, similar properties with different assessed values do not have the same property tax. The total amount of property tax due on a parcel of land and its improvements is determined only after the completion of certain steps. Whereas the property tax process varies somewhat from jurisdiction to jurisdiction, these same basic steps are followed by all jurisdictions levying a property tax.

First, the taxing jurisdiction prepares a budget which shows the expected expenditures over a period of time, normally a fiscal year. How these expenditures will be appropriated for public education, capital improvements, road maintenance, and so forth, is also shown on the budget. Once this budget is determined, the sources of revenue must be identified and estimated as to their total contribution. By subtracting sources of revenue—sales tax, income tax, federal revenue, license fees and others—from the projected total expenditures, the taxing jurisdiction knows how many dollars must be generated through the taxation of property.

The next step in the process is for the tax assessor to appraise each parcel of property and to assign an *assessed value* to the property. While various appraisal methods are used (see Chapter 17), property is normally assessed at some percentage of full market value. Full market value is the price a willing seller will accept and a willing buyer will pay at arms-length negotiating where neither are under undue pressure.

Almost all taxing jurisdictions contain certain exempt property such as property owned by federal, state and local governments and property used by certain groups such as churches, hospitals and educational institutions. The total assessed value of these exempt properties must be subtracted from the total assessed value of all property before the tax rates are determined. A *tax rate* is calculated by dividing the total amount of revenue needed by the total assessed value of all taxable property within the taxing jurisdiction. This tax rate or, in some jurisdictions, *millage rate* is then multiplied by the assessed value of each parcel to give the amount of tax due on each parcel. In order to use the millage rate to calculate taxes, it is important to remember that 1 mill is one-tenth of 1 cent or $1/$1,000 of assessed value.

LOOK THIS UP:

Does your state use millage rate _____ or tax rate? _____

Consider the following example of finding a tax rate:

Budget	$20,000,000
Revenue from other sources	−6,000,000
Property tax revenue needed	$14,000,000
Total taxable assessed value	$350,000,000

Tax rate = $14,000,000/$350,000,000 = .04
Tax rate = 4 percent
= $4 per $100 of assessed value
= 40 mills per dollar (a mill is one-tenth of 1 cent)

Residential fair market value	$60,000
Assessed at 50%	$30,000
Tax rate	$4 per $100

Tax due = $30,000/$4 per $100 = $1,200

LOOK THIS UP:

Does your state allow for any homestead exemption?

Yes _____ No _____

If yes, how much is it? _____

Once the tax bill on property is received, the owner of record has a certain period in which to challenge the assessed value. This statutory period is normally 15 days to 6 months. If a protest is filed within this period, the property owner is given the opportunity to present reasons why the assessment is incorrect. The procedure involves either meeting with the tax assessor or appearing before a local *appeals board* or *board of equalization* whose job is to listen to each complaint and then decide if indeed the property has been incorrectly assessed. If the property owner is still dissatisfied, many jurisdictions provide a tax court which periodically reviews those cases not settled by the appeals board or board of equalization.

LOOK THIS UP:

What is the appeals process in your state?

_____

_____

_____

The tax is billed and is due normally within a stated period of time. Unpaid property taxes become *specific liens* superior to private liens. Unpaid taxes beyond the grace period allowed by a jurisdiction can result in the selling of that property at *public auction* to satisfy the tax lien.

Special Assessments

From time to time, jurisdictions levy a *special assessment* on certain pieces of property for the purpose of paying for the cost of a public improvement such as a sewer or a sidewalk. Special assessments do not occur annually as do ad valorem property taxes and are not based on the value of the property. For example, a city decides to pave a previously unpaved road and agrees to pay one-third of the total. Each property owner's share is determined by front footage rather than current market value or assessed value of the property. If a city adds a playground in a certain area, those properties closest to the improvement will be assessed more than lots farther away.

Use of the Circuit-Breaker

There was a time in history when the amount of property owned and the ability to pay taxes on that property went hand in hand. Today, however, one's ability to pay taxes is more dependent on the flow of one's income than it is on asset holdings. Low- and middle-income groups have a much larger percentage of their net worth in real property than do higher income groups. This particular inequity has resulted in legislation to provide financial relief to taxpayers with heavy tax burdens. *Circuit-breaker* approaches for property tax relief, pioneered in Wisconsin over a decade ago, are being enacted throughout the United States. Under a circuit-breaker approach, a state allows a tax credit to homeowners, on the basis of age, income or disability, who meet certain qualifying conditions.

LOOK THIS UP:

Does your state have a circuit-breaker?

Yes _____ No _____

If yes, how much is it? _____

POINTS TO REMEMBER

1. Prior to the expansion of governmental police power regulations on the use of land, the most significant restriction was the law of nuisance which obligated each person to use land in such a manner as not to injure the property of another.
2. The police power is the inherent right of the state to regulate for the purpose of promoting health, safety, welfare and morality. The police power is noncompensatory and serves as the basis for zoning, the official map, building codes, housing codes and subdivision regulations.
3. Zoning is a police power device which allows for legislative division of space into districts and imposition of regulations prescribing use and intensity of use to which land within each designated district may be put.
4. Zoning establishes land-use districts and provides for different restrictions and standards within each district; establishes height restrictions; establishes area and bulk restrictions; and establishes other restrictions, such as off-street parking requirements and performance standards.
5. A pre-existing use which normally would not have been permitted in a zoning district is called a nonconforming use. Nonconforming uses are permissible until they are destroyed or materially damaged.
6. A variance is issued by a zoning board of appeals or a zoning board of adjustments to property owners who can show that a particular property is unreasonably burdened by a zoning restriction and that a hardship would result if the variance were not granted.
7. Building codes specify minimum construction standards for new buildings and major alterations of old buildings. In order to begin construction or repairs, a property owner must obtain a building permit. Before a new structure may be occupied, an occupancy permit must be obtained.
8. Subdivision regulations impose certain design and quality requirements on tracts which are divided into smaller lots by developers or property owners.
9. A Planned Unit Development (PUD) is a device which permits a mix of different uses and densities on one tract of land and gives a developer an opportunity to use the land more efficiently than is possible under conventional zoning and subdivision techniques.
10. A tax on property is referred to as an ad valorem tax since the tax is based on the value of the property.
11. In determining the tax due on a piece of property, an assessed value must be assigned to the property. Normally, this assessed value is some percentage of full market value.
12. A tax rate is normally stated in units of $100, for example, $5.99 per $100 of assessed value.
13. A mill is one-tenth of 1 cent. A tax rate of $4.00 per $100 equals 40 mills per dollar.
14. Assessed value multiplied by the tax rate or millage rate equals the amount of tax due on a parcel.

KEY TERMS AND PHRASES

assessed value
assessment
board of equalization
buffer zone
building codes
building permit
circuit-breaker

condemnation
dedication
eminent domain
housing codes
Interstate Land Sales Full Disclosure Act
millage rate

nonconforming use
Planned Unit Development (PUD)
police power
subdivision regulations
tax rate
zoning

QUESTIONS

1. The requirement that every person use his or her property in such a manner as not to injure the property of another is called
    A. escheat
    B. police power
    C. nuisance law
    D. eminent domain
2. Which right of government is based on police power?
    I. Eminent domain
    II. Zoning
    A. I only
    B. II only
    C. Both I and II
    D. Neither I nor II
3. Which of the following is the *least* correct?
    A. Zoning is based on the police power.
    B. Zoning is a compensatory regulation.
    C. Zoning power is ordinarily granted from the state through enabling legislation.
    D. Zoning may be both directive and protective.
4. Which of the following is *not* a recognized public purpose of zoning?
    A. To regulate land use
    B. To establish limitations on heights

C. To establish limitations on bulk and area
   D. To exclude low-income minorities from single-family detached housing neighborhoods
5. The police power is the inherent power of what level of government?
   I. Federal
   II. State
   A. I only C. Both I and II
   B. II only D. Neither I nor II
6. Exclusive zoning districts ordinarily segregate what kind of uses?
   I. Housing from industrial
   II. Commercial from industrial
   A. I only C. Both I and II
   B. II only D. Neither I nor II
7. If you have a FAR of 3:1, how tall could you build a building which covered one quarter of the lot?
   A. One story C. Six stories
   B. Three stories D. Twelve stories
8. A zone which separates two incompatible zoning districts from each other is called a
   A. buffer zone C. nonconforming use
   B. PUD D. variance
9. A use which existed before a zoning district was established and is not consistent with the restrictions imposed on land uses in that district is called a (an)
   A. variance
   B. nonconforming use
   C. transitional use
   D. illegal use
10. If a zoning ordinance imposes a unique hardship on a particular tract of land, the property owner should seek what kind of relief from the zoning board of adjustment?
    A. An amendment
    B. An exception
    C. A variance
    D. A special-use permit
11. In order to construct and occupy a new building, which of the following is ordinarily required in building codes?
    I. Building permit
    II. Occupancy permit
    A. I only C. Both I and II
    B. II only D. Neither I nor II
12. A process by which roads in a subdivision are turned over to local government for maintenance and control is called
    A. platting C. eminent domain
    B. dedication D. tracting
13. Which technique gives a developer flexibility to mix land uses and land-use intensities?
    I. PUD
    II. CUP
    A. I only C. Both I and II
    B. II only D. Neither I nor II
14. Upon default in payment of real estate taxes by a condominium owner,
    I. the taxing authority can levy the tax on the entire project
    II. title to the unit may be foreclosed
    A. I only C. Both I and II
    B. II only D. Neither I nor II
15. Ad valorem means
    I. according to value
    II. ability to pay
    A. I only C. Both I and II
    B. II only D. Neither I nor II
16. When property taxes are due, they become liens
    I. against the property
    II. but do not have priority over mortgages on public record
    A. I only C. Both I and II
    B. II only D. Neither I nor II
17. A parcel of property has a market value of $60,000, and the local tax rate is $3.50 per $100 of assessed value. If the property is assessed at $20,000, then
    I. the assessment ratio is one-third
    II. the tax rate is 350 mills
    A. I only C. Both I and II
    B. II only D. Neither I nor II
18. A tax assessment is intended to
    I. establish the asking price for use in listing property for sale
    II. aid in determining taxes due
    A. I only C. Both I and II
    B. II only D. Neither I nor II
19. The estimated market value of a residential property is $35,000 and the property is assessed at 60% of market value. The tax rate is $3.50 per $100 of assessed value. Which of the following is true?
    I. The assessed value is $14,000.
    II. The tax is $490.
    A. I only C. Both I and II
    B. II only D. Neither I nor II
20. The estimated market value of a residential property is $70,000. The property is assessed at 40% of market value and the tax rate is 30 mills per dollar. Which of the following is true?
    I. The tax is $840.
    II. The assessed value is $28,000.
    A. I only C. Both I and II
    B. II only D. Neither I nor II

21. A mill is a unit of value equal to
    A. .10 of a dollar   C. .001 of a dollar
    B. .01 of a dollar   D. .0001 of a dollar

22. For tax purposes, a hospital would normally be considered an
    A. exemption   C. emblement
    B. easement   D. equalization factor

23. The tax that is levied upon a property holder to pay for the paving of a road that will directly benefit the owner is called a (an)
    A. road-use tax
    B. special assessment tax
    C. highway tax
    D. ad valorem tax

24. Your annual property taxes are $750. Your taxing jurisdiction assesses property at 40% of value. If the tax rate is $5.40 per $100 of assessed value, the market value of your property is
    A. $13,889   C. $27,778
    B. $18,000   D. $34,722

25. Real property tax determinants include(s)
    I. market value
    II. assessment rate
    A. I only   C. Both I and II
    B. II only   D. Neither I nor II

26. Which of the following is *not* necessarily true about zoning?
    A. Zoning separates incompatible uses of land (in a planning sense).
    B. Zoning establishes height restrictions.
    C. Zoning establishes bulk restrictions.
    D. Zoning prevents land value decline.

27. Which regulations establish the minimum standards for roads and drainage in a large housing tract development?
    A. Building codes   C. Subdivision regulations
    B. Zoning ordinances D. FAR ordinances

28. Which of the following governmental limitations on the ownership of real estate involves the power to "take" land for a public purpose by due process of law and with just compensation?
    A. Police power
    B. Eminent domain
    C. Escheat
    D. Condemnation

29. Which amendment to the U.S. Constitution prohibits a state from using police power to unreasonably restrict private property?
    A. First Amendment
    B. Fifth Amendment
    C. Sixteenth Amendment
    D. Eighteenth Amendment

30. Budget requirements of River City from property tax levies amount to $5,080,900 and the tax rate for the coming fiscal year is determined to be $3.41/$100. What is the assessed value of taxable real property in River City?
    A. $5,080,900   C. $14,900,000
    B. $149,000,000   D. $67,114,000

If you are not sure of your answers, see page 324 for correct answers and explanations.

20

Real Estate Math

The purpose of this chapter is to identify the fundamentals necessary to understand real estate math. Upon completing this chapter, the reader will have a clearer understanding of basic arithmetic functions and the ability to apply that knowledge towards successfully solving real estate math problems.

Not everyone taking a licensing examination has the same quantitative background, nor do people use the same techniques or approaches in solving mathematical problems. Consequently, to list and explain the "right approach" that would have to be memorized and carefully adhered to would be of little help.

So rather than listing a step-by-step approach, a few simple suggestions and points are offered as aids. These should be remembered and applied in working examination questions.

These suggestions can be classified into certain things to do (1) before the examination and (2) during the examination before selecting an answer.

Before the Examination

1. Review fractions, decimals and percentages.
2. Know certain standards of measurements such as square feet per acre.
3. Know the basic formulas needed in solving real estate math problems.
4. Know the real estate math subject areas included on the examinations.

Each of the above topics is presented and explained in this chapter. The reader is advised to become thoroughly familiar with the information presented prior to working the mathematical problems.

If adequate pretest preparation has not been done, the actual selection of the correct answer will be most difficult.

During the Examination

1. Read the problem through.
   The math questions on the Uniform Examinations are given in a narrative format. As each question is read, certain "buzz words" will be recognized, e.g., commission, assessed value, per annum, square feet.
2. If appropriate, sketch the problem to observe "how it looks."
   Although it is not permissible to write on the margins of the answer sheet, it is perfectly all right to make sketches and do calculations in the test booklet. For example, if a particular problem involves lot measurements, draw a sketch of the lot and label the sides.
3. Write the formula(s) needed to solve the problem.
   In every problem, you are solving for some unknown. The unknown may be net selling price, percentage of profit, tax rate, monthly interest payment or cost per acre. Consequently, it is important to know the correct formula and how to use that formula in solving a problem.
4. Match the information given in the narrative problem with the formula chosen.
   Not every piece of information given in the narrative will necessarily be used. It might be necessary to sift through and pick out exactly what is needed. Quite often, information is given but it is not exactly what is needed and interim calculations become necessary.
5. Do any necessary interim calculations.
   For example, if the question concerns property tax, and the tax rate and assessed value are given on an annual basis, calculating the annual tax bill would not be too difficult. However, the question could ask what is the monthly tax bill, and therefore you must determine the monthly figure by first calculating the annual figure.
6. Solve for the unknown in the formula. In the previous example, the monthly tax bill is the unknown. The unknown will be clearly asked in the narrative.
7. Make sure you have solved for what is asked. In the property tax example, the annual tax bill was not the correct answer, even though it was probably among the four multiple choices. Had you chosen that as the correct answer, you would have missed the question.

8. See if your answer "looks right."
   For some problems, you may have some idea as to the answer before actually working the problem. If the answer you derive seems unusually large or small, then this should be a warning to rework the problem.
9. Choose the matching answer.
   If the other steps have been correctly done, this will be the final step. If time permits, check the answer by working the problem again. Most problems can be checked in less time than it takes to work them. Perhaps a check mark by those questions in the test question booklet (not on the exam answer sheet) you are uncertain about will serve as a reminder to rework them if time permits. If the problem is too complicated, temporarily skip it and work it after the other questions have been answered.

FRACTIONS

A fraction is defined as a portion or part of a whole. The top number of the fraction, the *numerator* or *dividend*, indicates the number of units in the partial amount and the bottom number of the fraction, the *denominator* or *divisor*, indicates the number of equal units in the whole. A fraction can be classified as either a *proper fraction* or an *improper fraction*. Proper fractions, such as $1/3$, $1/4$ or $1/2$, are those whose denominators are greater than their numerators. Improper fractions, such as $10/10$, $3/2$ or $8/3$, have a numerator either equal to or greater than their denominator. To change an improper fraction into a *mixed number* (whole number plus a fraction) simply divide the numerator by the denominator:

Examples:
$3/2$ [improper fraction] = $1\frac{1}{2}$ [mixed number]
$7/3$ [improper fraction] = $2\frac{1}{3}$ [mixed number]

Any whole number can be expressed as a fraction by making 1 the denominator:

Examples:
6 [whole number] = $6/1$ [fraction]
100 [whole number] = $100/1$ [fraction]

Reducing fractions means changing the fraction to its lowest terms. This is done by dividing both the numerator and denominator by the largest number that will divide into both evenly:

Examples:
$50/100 = 50/100 \div 50/50 = 1/2$
$12/15 = 12/15 \div 3/3 = 4/5$

Adding Fractions

In order to add fractions, each fraction must have or be changed to a common denominator. The numerators are added together and the denominator remains the same:

Examples:
$1/2 + 1/3$ converts to $3/6 + 2/6 = 5/6$
$10/15 + 1/3$ converts to $10/15 + 5/15 = 15/15 = 1$

Subtracting Fractions

The same procedure as used in adding fractions, except that the numerators are subtracted:

Examples:
$1/2 - 1/3$ converts to $3/6 - 2/6 = 1/6$
$10/15 - 1/3$ converts to $10/15 - 5/15 = 5/15 = 1/3$

Multiplying Fractions

The numerators are multiplied together, and the denominators are multiplied together. The fractions need not have common denominators:

Examples:
$3/4 \times 1/2 = 3/8$
$1/4 \times 2/6 = 2/24 = 1/12$

Dividing Fractions

The process of dividing fractions is similar to multiplying fractions, with an additional first step. The fraction you are dividing by (i.e., the *divisor*) is *inverted* and then the steps are the same as multiplying fractions:

Examples:
$3/4 \div 1/2$ inverts to $3/4 \times 2/1 = 6/4 = 1\frac{1}{2}$
$5/6 \div 1/3$ inverts to $5/6 \times 3/1 = 15/6 = 2\frac{1}{2}$

DECIMALS

Decimals are similar to fractions in that they also indicate a portion or part of a whole. The denominator is 10, 100, 1000, etc. Probably the most common use of decimals is in the exchange of money:

Example:
$\$1.65 = \$1 + 65/100$ of $\$1$

To change a fraction to its equivalent decimal form, divide the denominator into the numerator:

Example:

$1/2 = .5$ $\qquad$ $1/4 = .25$

$$2\overline{)1.00} \quad \underline{.5} \qquad 4\overline{)1.00} \quad \underline{.25}$$
$$\underline{10} \qquad\qquad \underline{8}$$
$$ \qquad\qquad 20$$
$$ \qquad\qquad \underline{20}$$

If no decimal is given, the decimal point is placed at the *end* of the whole number.

Example:
$\$1 = \$1.00$ $\qquad$ $\$10 = \$10.00$

Adding and Subtracting Decimals

Adding and subtracting decimals are done in the same way as in whole numbers except that the decimal points must be kept in line so that the decimal point in the sum will be placed correctly.

Example:

$$7 + 6.21 = \begin{array}{r} 7 \\ + 6.21 \\ \hline 13.21 \end{array}$$

If helpful, zeros can be added:

Example:

$$7 - 6.21 = \begin{array}{r} 7.00 \\ -6.21 \\ \hline .79 \end{array}$$

Multiplying Decimals

It is the same procedure as multiplying whole numbers except that the total number of decimal points in the numbers being multiplied (the *multiplicand* and the *multiplier*) is totaled and that many decimal places must appear in the answer (*product*).

Example:

$$\begin{array}{r} 6.25 \text{ (2 decimal places in multiplicand)} \\ \times \quad 3.8 \text{ (1 decimal place in multiplier)} \\ \hline 5000 \\ 1875 \\ \hline 23.750 \end{array}$$

Example:

$$\begin{array}{r} 1.91 \\ \times \quad .042 \\ \hline 382 \\ 764 \\ \hline .08022 \end{array}$$ (a zero had to be added to the front of the product to get the required number of decimal places.)

Dividing Decimals

$$\text{divisor}\overline{)\text{dividend}}^{\text{quotient}}$$

In order to divide decimals the divisor must be a whole number. This is done by moving the decimal points in the divisor and the dividend an equal number of places to the right and placing the decimal point in the quotient directly above its new position in the dividend.

Example:

$$18 \div .70 \qquad 3.14 \div 6$$

$$.70\overline{).18000}^{.257} \qquad 6\overline{)3.1400}^{.523}$$

$$\begin{array}{r} 140 \\ \hline 400 \\ 350 \\ \hline 500 \\ 490 \end{array} \qquad \begin{array}{r} 30 \\ \hline 14 \\ 12 \\ \hline 20 \\ 18 \end{array}$$

To convert decimals to fractions, the decimal is written as a fraction with a denominator equal to 1 plus the number of zeros corresponding to the number of decimal places. If necessary, the fraction is then reduced.

Examples:
$.5 = {}^5/_{10} = \frac{1}{2} \quad .77 = {}^{77}/_{100} \quad .333 = {}^{333}/_{1000}$

PERCENTAGES

Percent (%) means per hundred or parts of a hundred.

Examples:
$35\% = {}^{35}/_{100} = .35 \quad 150\% = {}^{150}/_{100} = 1.50$

To change a percent to a decimal, place a decimal point two places to the left and drop the percent sign.

Examples:
$15\% = .15 \quad 118\% = 1.18 \quad 1\% = .01$

To change decimals to percents, the procedure is reversed. Move the decimal point two places to the right and add a % sign.

Examples:
$.32 = 32\% \quad 2.15 = 215\% \quad 1 = 100\%$

To change percents to fractions, divide the percent quantity by 100, drop the percent sign and reduce the answer to the lowest terms.

Examples:
$50\% = {}^{50}/_{100} = \frac{1}{2} \quad 300\% = {}^{300}/_{100} = 3$

Working with Percentages

Many of the mathematical problems which have to be worked by people engaged in real estate activities involve percentages; consequently, it is mandatory that anyone desiring to enter the field know how to work with percentages. Percentage formulas are comprised of three variables. The basic formula can be algebraically expressed as:

P = R × B
where:
P = the part of the base
R = the number of hundredths and is followed by a "%" sign
B = the base, whole or total

Consider the following: 10 is 50% of 20
By using the basic percentage formula (P = R × B) any one of the three variables (10, 50% or 20) could be solved if the other two were known.

1. What is 50% of 20?
   P = R × B   P = .50 × 20   P = 10
2. 10 is 50% of what number?
   B = P/R   B = 10 / .5   B = 20
3. 10 is what percent of 20?
   R = P/B   R = 10 / 20   R = .5 or 50%

For people who have a difficult time solving problems algebraically, the Venn circles approach offers an alternative. The three variables in the percentage formula above can be visually expressed by the following:

Real Estate Math

By using this approach, the algebraic formula for the unknown does not have to be memorized. Rather, the unknown variable is covered and the remaining two are either multiplied or divided depending on whether the two known variables are side by side or one over the other. If they are side by side, then multiply to solve for the unknown; if one is over the other, the top variable is divided by the bottom variable. This is the basic percentage formula needed in solving real estate mathematical problems. The three components simply take on different nomenclatures when different applications are made.

BASIC FORMULAS USED IN SOLVING REAL ESTATE PROBLEMS

A number of basic mathematical calculations have to be made to successfully handle the computations necessary in real estate transactions. These calculations are much easier to perform if a few basic mathematical formulas are remembered. While not every computation can be successfully completed by using a single formula, a number of real estate math applications do involve a single basic formula. Those listed in Table 20-1 cover the broader areas of real estate applications. As a minimum, these should be remembered, and the reader should work with these until they are easy to apply in solving problems. All of the ones listed will be used in the real estate applications later in this chapter.

STANDARDS OF MEASUREMENT

Certain standards of measurement are needed in working real estate math problems. Although most of the ones listed below are commonly known, these measurements should be carefully reviewed since there are no tables or charts to refer to during the examinations. Measurements of volume are *not* included since there are currently no volume questions on the Uniform Examinations.

Linear Measurements

1 foot (ft.)	= 12 inches (in.)
1 yard (yd.)	= 3 feet (ft.)
1 mile	= 1,760 yds. = 5,280 ft.

Square Measurements

1 sq. ft.	= 144 sq. in.
1 sq. yd.	= 9 sq. ft.
1 acre	= 43,560 sq. ft.

Land Surveying Measurements

1 sq. acre	= 208.71 ft. on each side
1 section	= 1 sq. mile = 640 acres = 1/36 township
1 township	= 36 sections = 36 sq. miles = 23,040 acres
1 minute (')	= 60 seconds ('')
1 degree (°)	= 60 minutes (')
1 quadrant	= 90 degrees (°)
1 circle	= 360 degrees (°)

REAL ESTATE APPLICATIONS

The following explanations, problems and solutions are designed to help the reader become familiar with the

Table 20—1.

Problem Area	Basic Formula	Transposition	
Sales commission = selling price × rate	SC = SP × R	SP = SC/R	R = SC/SP
Selling price = cost × (1 + % profit)	SP = C × (1 + % profit)	C = SP/(1 + % profit) (1 + % Profit) = SP/C	
Selling price = cost × (1 − % loss)	SP = C × (1 − % loss)	C = SP/(1 − % loss) (1 − % Loss) = SP/C	
Present value = original value × (1 − % total depreciation)	PV = OV × (1 − % TD)	OV = PV/(1 − % TD) (1 − % TD) = PV/OV	
Present value = original value × (1 + % total depreciation	PV = OV × (1 + % TA)	OV = PV/(1 + % TA) (1 + % TA) = PV/OV	
Interest payment = principal × rate × time	I = P × R × T	P = I/R × T	R = I/P × T
Taxes = assessed value × tax rate	T = AV × R	AV = T/R	R = T/AV
Insurance premium = insured amount × rate	IP = IA × R	IA = IP/R	R = IP/IA
Income = value × rate	I = V × R	V = I/R	R = I/V
Selling price = gross rent multiplier × rent	SP = GRM × R	GRM = SP/R	R = SP/GRM
Percentage = base × rate	P = B × R	B = P/R	R = P/B
Area of rectangle = length × width	A = L × W	L = A/W	W = A/L
Area of triangle = ½ base × height	A = ½ B × H	½ B = A/H	H = A/½ B
Area of circle = π × radius square	A = 3.1416 × R^2	3.1416 = A/R^2	R^2 = A/3.1416

mathematics involved in real estate transactions. This section should be studied carefully before working the questions at the end of the chapter.

Commission and Selling Price

One of the first real estate applications for many people is the calculation of commission and selling price.

SC = SP × R

where:

SC = sales commission
SP = gross selling price
R = commission (%)

Example 1:
Bobby Broker receives an 8% commission on a house he sells for $50,000. How much sales commission did he receive?

SC = $50,000 × .08
SC = $4,000

This same formula could have been transposed to solve for one of the other unknowns.

Example 2:
Beth Broker received $4,000 in sales commission on a house she sold. What was the selling price of the house if her rate of commission was 8%?

SP = SC/R
SP = $4,000/.08
SP = $50,000

Not all commission and selling price problems are this easy; however, all of them involve the same basic formula. Consider the following:

Example 3:
Jeff the Broker lists a house for $63,000 with a commission rate of 7.5%. Jane the Salesperson, who is employed by Jeff, receives 50% of the total commission on every house she sells. If Jane sells the house for 10% less than its listing price, how much commission does she receive?

This type of problem requires some interim calculations. These necessary calculations will be much easier to recognize if note is made of certain given information.

Salesperson receives 50% of total commission paid.
House sells for 90% of list price.
Commission rate is 7.5%.

Step 1: Find the total sales commission paid:
SC = SP × R
SC = ($63,000 × .9) × .075
SC = $4,252.50

Step 2: Calculate the salesperson's commission:
P = R × B
P = .5 × $4,252.50
P = $2,126.25

Example 4:
Susan, a rental agent, receives 25% of the first month's rent and 3% of each month's rent thereafter for renting an apartment. If she rents the apartment for one year at $200 per month, what is her total commission for the year?

Step 1: First month's rental commission:
P = R × B
P = .25 × $200
P = $50
Step 2: Rental commission thereafter:
P = R × B
P = .03 × ($200 × 11) [Note: 11 months, not 12]
P = $66
Step 3: Total Commission:
$50 + $66 = $116

Example 5:
Ms. Perry is employed by Jay Realty Company on a 50-50 commission split. She sells 100 acres for $700 per acre listed with Albert Realty. The commission schedule is 7% on the first $25,000, 3% on the next $25,000, and 2% on the remainder. If the two realty firms also work on a 50-50 commission split, what is the total amount earned by Ms. Perry?

Step 1: Total sales commission paid:
Total Sales = 100 × $700 = $70,000
SC = SP × R
$25,000 × .07 $25,000 × .03 $20,000 × .02
   $1,750 $750 $400
Total commission paid = $1,750 + $750 + $400
= $2,900
Step 2: Each realty firm received 50% of the total commission paid:
$2,900 / 2 = $1,450
Step 3: Ms. Perry received 50% of her firm's total:
$1,450 / 2 = $725

Profit and Loss

Calculations dealing with profit and loss involve the same percentage formula used above. The starting point is the value before either profit (+) or loss (−). The value, which for most problems is stated as what was paid for the investment, is then multiplied by the percent of profit or loss to derive the value after either profit or loss.

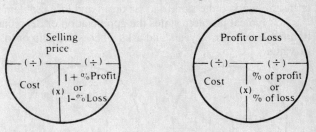

Example 6:
Ken sells his house for a 36% profit. If it cost him $42,000 what did he sell the house for?

Real Estate Math

If the house sold for a profit, he sold it for more than $42,000. How much more? 36% more.

SP = Cost × (1 + % profit)
SP = $42,000 × (1.36)
SP = $57,120

The same type of problem could be stated another way:

Example 7:
Sally pays $43,000 for a house. One year later she is transferred to another city and sells the house for $41,500. What is her percent of loss?

Percent of loss = loss / cost
Loss = $43,000 − $41,500 = $1,500
PL = $1,500 / $43,000 = .035 = 3½%

Profit and loss problems can also be stated in terms of net gain and net loss. The term *net* refers to what is left for the seller *after* any and all expenses (commission, outstanding mortgage, liens and other selling expenses). This type of problem is worked the same way as profit and loss problems.

Example 8:
Tom Seller lists his house with Holly Broker and agrees to pay her an 8% commission. Tom wants to net $5,000 on the house after paying the broker and the existing mortgage of $42,000. What must the house sell for?

Step 1: $42,000 + $5,000 = $47,000 (Gross amount received by seller which represents 92% of the selling price (100% − 8%).
Step 2: Selling Price = $47,000 / .92
SP = $51,087
Step 3: To check this problem:
$ 51,087 × .08 = $4,087 commission
− 4,087
$ 47,000   Gross to seller
−42,000   Mortgage due
$ 5,000   Net to seller

Depreciation and Appreciation

These two words have various meanings and uses in real estate. The most common use is in connection with federal income taxes (see Chapter 18). However, the use of the terms ''depreciation'' and ''appreciation'' in real estate math problems normally signals somewhat different meanings. Appreciation means an *increase in value*, whereas depreciation means a *loss in value*. Problems using these terms are worked the same way as profit and loss problems.

A typical problem states the appreciation or depreciation for X number of years and asks what is the gain or loss in value.

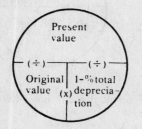
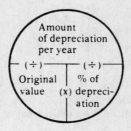

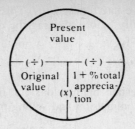
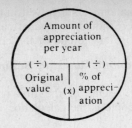

Example 9:
A parcel of land was purchased for $20,000. If it has appreciated in value 7% per year, what is its value at the end of 5 years?

Step 1: 7% per year for 5 years = 35% Total Appreciation*
Step 2: Present value = original value × (1 + % total appreciation)
PV = $20,000 × 1.35
PV = $27,000

*Note: Appreciation and depreciation problems are calculated assuming simple gain or loss rather than compound gain or loss. Example 9 *is not* worked by compounding the 7%:

Year 1 $20,000 × 1.07 = $21,400
Year 2 $21,400 × 1.07 = $22,898
Year 3 $22,898 × 1.07 = $24,501
Year 4 $24,501 × 1.07 = $26,216
Year 5 $26,216 × 1.07 = $28,051

Rather, the appreciation (7% per year) is multiplied by the number of years (5) to derive the total change (35%).

Example 10:
An eight-year-old office building has depreciated in value 6% per year. If its value today is $42,000 what was its worth new?

Step 1: .06 × 8 = .48 or 48% total loss in value
Step 2: Original value = present value / (1 − % total depreciation)
OV = $42,000 / .52
OV = $80,767

Both appreciation and depreciation can be included in the same problem.

Example 11:
Four years ago a house costing $30,000 was constructed on a lot valued at $6,000. What is the current value of the land and improvements if the land has appreciated 4% per year and the house has depreciated 3% per year?

Step 1: 4 × .03 = .12 or 12% total depreciation of house
Present value = original value × (1 − % total depreciation)
PV = $30,000 × .88
PV = $26,400
Step 2: 4 × .04 = .16 or 16% total appreciation of land
Present value = original value × (1 + % total appreciation)
PV = $6,000 × 1.16
PV = $6,960
Step 3: $26,400 + $6,960 = $33,360

Interest Rates and Mortgage Payments

As we discussed in Chapter 15, the financing of real estate is an integral part of real estate activities, and anyone employed in real estate needs to understand how to solve interest rate and mortgage problems. *Interest* is the payment made for using other people's money and is normally paid annually, semiannually, quarterly or monthly. The *interest rate* is the percent of interest charged, and unless stated otherwise, is assumed to be in *annual* terms. *Principal* is the amount borrowed.

When the time period over which interest is being calculated is exactly one year, there are three variables: (1) principal, (2) interest and (3) interest rate. For examination problems always assume *simple interest* and do not compound the interest (interest on interest) unless instructions in the problem state otherwise.

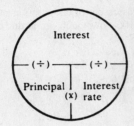

Example 12:
Clarence borrows $6,000 from University Bank for one year. If the bank charges 7% interest, how much interest is due at the end of one year?

Interest = principal × interest rate
I = $6,000 × .07
I = $420

Using the formula I = P × R gives the annual interest due, which for Example 12 is what was asked. However, not all sums of money are borrowed for exactly one year; therefore, allowance has to be made for interest periods other than those covering exactly one year. The fourth variable, *time*, is used for periods either less than or greater than one year. Time is expressed as a fraction of a year.

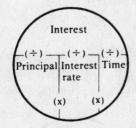

Facts to remember in calculating interest rate problems:

Annual	= once a year
Semiannual	= twice a year at six-month intervals
Biannual	= twice a year
Bimonthly	= 6 times a year (every 2 months)
Monthly	= 12 times a year
Semimonthly	= twice a month
Biennial	= once every 2 years

1 year = 12 months = 52 weeks = 360 days*
1 month = 30 days

If the time period is something other than 1 year, the formula becomes I = P × R × T where T = time. For example, if payment is monthly, T = 1/12; if payment is biennial, T = 2.

Example 13:
Consider Example 12 but assume Clarence must pay the interest monthly. How much is due the first month?

I = P × R × T
I = $6,000 × .07 × 1/12
I = $6,000 × .07 × .0833
I = $35.00

Example 14:
Katie borrows $50,000 to purchase a home. If her monthly interest payment is $364.58, what is the rate of interest?

Step 1: Annual interest payment
$364.58 × 12 = $4375
Step 2: R = I/P
R = $4375/$50,000
R = .0875 or 8¾%

Problems dealing with interest rates and mortgage payments also include *amortizing* the principal (reducing the principal by periodic payment first applied to interest on the outstanding debt and then to reducing the debt). In working this type of problem, the periodic payment or debt service will be stated in the problem so you will not need to refer to compound interest tables.

Example 15:
Lisa borrows $18,000 at an interest rate of 9%. Her monthly payment of $180 is applied first to interest and then to principal. How much is the principal reduced after the first payment?

Step 1: I = P × R × T
I = $18,000 × .09 × .08333
Monthly Interest = $135
Step 2: $180 (payment) − $135 (interest) = $45
(principal reduction)

Example 16:
Given the information in Example 15, what is the outstanding balance at the end of three months?

Step 1: 1st Month
Principal reduction = $45.00
Balance = $18,000 − $45 = $17,955
Step 2: 2nd Month
I = P × R × T
I = $17,955 × .09 × .08333
I = $134.66
$180 − $134.66 = $45.34
$17,955 − $45.34 = $17,909.66

*Unless stated otherwise, 1 year equals 360 days in calculating interest payments. This is referred to as a statutory year.

Real Estate Math

Step 3: 3rd Month
I = P × R × T
I = $17,909.66 × .09 × .08333
I = $134.32
$180 − $134.32 = $45.68
$17,909.66 − $45.68 = $17,863.98

Example 17:
The Inglewood Savings and Loan Association makes a loan to Mr. Stevens for 80% of the appraisal value of his home. The first monthly interest payment is $178.20 and the interest rate is 9%. What is the value of the house?

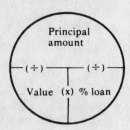

Step 1: Calculate the amount borrowed (principal)
Annual interest = $178.20 × 12 = $2,138.40
P = I/R
P = $2,138.40 / .09 = $23,760
Step 2: $23,760 principal is 80% of value
Value = $23,760 / .8
Value = $29,700

Discount Points

Discount points (see Chapter 16) are charges made at the time the loan is closed and serve to increase the effective yield to the lender. Points are calculated on the amount borrowed and in order to work this type of problem the following must be remembered:

1 discount point = 1% of the loan amount

Example 18:
In Example 17, assume that the lender informs Mr. Stevens that he will have to pay 3 points at closing. How much will this cost Mr. Stevens?

Loan amount = $23,760
3 discount points = 3% of $23,760 = $712.80

Example 19:
If in addition to the discount points, the closing cost of $1,000 will also have to be paid, how much cash will Mr. Stevens need to close the transaction? (Refer to information in Examples 17 and 18.)

Downpayment (20% of value)	$5,940.00
Closing costs	1,000.00
Discount points	712.80
Total	$7,652.80

Property Tax

The basic formula in calculating property tax problems is:

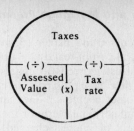

Tax bill = assessed value × tax rate

The tax rate is normally stated as per $100. The rate can also be stated as the *millage rate*. Therefore it is necesssary to remember that 1 mill = $.001 (one-tenth of one cent).

Example 20:
A vacant lot is assessed for tax purposes at $20,000. If the tax rate is $3.60/$100 how much tax is due annually?

Tax assessed value × tax rate
T = $20,000 × $3.60/$100
T = $200 × $3.60
T = $720

Example 21:
The tax rate in Plains County is 105 mills. If property is assessed at 40% of market value, what is the annual tax due on a house with a market value of $65,000?

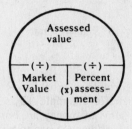

Step 1: Assessed value = market value × percent assessment
AV = $65,000 × .4 = $26,000
Step 2: Tax = assessed value × tax rate
T = $26,000 × .105
T = $2,730

Property Insurance

In solving insurance problems the same basic approach is used with other percentage problems.

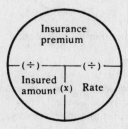

Insurance premium = insured amount × rate

Example 22:
The $65,000 house in the previous example is insured for 80% of market value. If the annual insurance bill is $171.60, what is the rate per $1,000 of coverage?

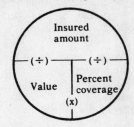

Step 1: Insured amount = value × percent coverage
IA = $65,000 × .80 = $52,000
Step 2: Insurance rate = insurance premium / insured amount
R = $171.60 / $52,000 = .0033
R = $3.30 per $1,000

Insurance problems often involve premiums paid for more than one year.

Example 23:
Mr. Skaggs wishes to insure his $70,000 house with 80% coverage. The annual insurance rate is $2.80 per $1,000 coverage; however, if he purchases a three-year policy, he can save 30% of one year's premium. What is the monthly insurance cost if he purchases a three-year policy?

Step 1: Insured amount = value × percent coverage
IA = $70,000 × .80 = $56,000
Step 2: 1 year's coverage
Insurance premium = insured amount × rate
IP = $56,000 × $2.80/$1,000
IP = $156.80
Step 3: 3 year's coverage = $156.80 × 3 = $ 470.40
Less 30% of 1 year = $156.80 × .3 = − 47.04
Total Cost $ 423.36
Step 4: Cost per month
$423.36 / 36 = $11.76

Prorations

As discussed in Chapter 16, the closing of a real estate transaction occurs on a particular date. Certain expenses incurred by buyer and seller involve charges shared by both which are divided according to contractual agreement. Other expenses, however, are ongoing and must be divided at the time of closing to cover the separate time periods over which buyer and seller actually own the property. Examples are property taxes, water bills and possibly property insurance.

To prorate, it is necessary to correctly divide these expenses (or income in certain instances) between buyer and seller. In prorating, the seller incurs these expenses *up to and including* the day of closing and likewise is credited with rents received, if applicable, up to and including the day of closing.

Example 24:
Given the information in Example 23, assume Mr. Skaggs purchased the three-year policy on June 1, 1990. If he sells the house and closing takes place September 20, 1990, how much will be credited to him if the purchaser assumes this insurance policy? (Note: there are two ways to approach this type of problem: by calculating the expired portion or by calculating the unexpired portion.)

Step 1: Year   Month   Day
        1992   17   31
        1993   6   1   June 1, 1993
        1990   9   20   September 20, 1990
           2   8   11
        2 years 8 months 11 days Unexpired

or:

Year   Month   Day
1990   9   20   September 20, 1990
1990   6   1   June 1, 1990
   0   3   19
0 years 3 months 19 days Expired

To check calculation:

Years   Months   Days
2   8   11
0   3   19
2   11   30 = 3 years

Step 2: 3 years = $423.36
        1 year = $423.36/3 = $141.12
        1 month = $141.12/12 = $11.76
        1 day = $11.76/30 = $.392
Step 3: To calculate credit due to seller
        2 years × $141.12 = $282.24
        8 months × $11.76 =   94.08
        11 days × $.392 =   4.31
        Total $380.63

Example 25:
A house is purchased and closing takes place February 17. The annual property tax bill of $324, which is due January 1 of each year, has not been paid for either the current calendar year or the previous calendar year. How much should be debited to the seller at closing?

Step 1: Previous tax year due = $324
Step 2: Current year
        Monthly tax = $324/12 = $27.00
        Daily tax = $27/30 = $.90
Step 3: January   30 days
        February 17 days
                  47 days × $.90 = 42.30
Step 4: Total tax due
        $324 + $42.30 = $366.30

Example 26:
Mr. Hubbard is selling his 12-unit apartment complex to Mr. Carn. Each unit rents for $250 per month and the rent, paid in advance, was collected for each unit by Mr. Hubbard on the first day of the month. How much of this rent will Mr. Carn be credited at closing if closing is April 21?

Step 1: Rent collected = $250 × 12 = $3,000
        Daily rent = $3,000/30 = $100

Real Estate Math

Step 2: Amount due Mr. Carn
9 days × $100 / day = $900

Investment and Capitalization

As was discussed in Chapter 18, calculating the return on investment is an important and necesssary computation for anyone investing in real estate. The process used involves the capitalization of income, which determines value by deriving the net income from the investment and a reasonable percentage of return on that investment. In order to calculate the income, investment value or capitalization rate the basic percentage formula is used where:

Value = Income/Rate of Return

If the rate of return is stated in terms other than annual, it is necessary to convert the rate to an annual return.

Example 27:
A warehouse returns $18,000 per year to its owner. If this represents a 9% return, what is the value of the investment?

Value = income / rate
V = $18,000 / .09
V = $200,000

Another measure of selling price or value of income producing property is the Gross Rent Multiplier (GRM). The formula for calculating GRM is:

GRM = sales / gross rent

Example 28:
What is the GRM for a rental duplex that sold for $60,000 and has a total rent of $570 per month?

GRM = sales price / gross rent
GRM = $60,000 / $570
GRM = 105

Sometimes it is necessary to calculate Net Operating Income (NOI) before calculating either value or return on investment. As was explained in Chapter 18, this calculation is derived as follows:

Potential Gross Income
− Vacancy Loss
Effective Gross Income
− Operating Expenses
Net Operating Income

Debt Service and depreciation are not calculated in deriving NOI. If they appear in a problem, do not include them as part of the calculation.

Example 29:
Walters owns an apartment complex that contains 20 rental units, each renting for $225 per month. If he can expect a 10% vacancy rate and if operating expenses are 45% of gross income, what is the net income of the property?

20 × $225 × 12 = $54,000 Potential gross income
$54,000 × .10 =   − 5,400 Vacancy allowance
                      $48,600 Effective gross income
$48,600 × .45 =   − 21,870 Operating expenses
                      $26,730 Net operating income

Example 30:
What return is Mr. Walters receiving on his investment if he paid $121,500 for the project?

Rate = income / value
R = $26,730 / $121,500
R = .22 or 22%

Measurements: Linear and Area

A linear measurement expresses the straight-line distance from one point to another. Such measurement can be expressed in a number of different terms, such as inches, feet, yards or miles. The Uniform Examinations do not currently use metric measurements.

A common linear measurement involves the distance across the front of a piece of property, called *front footage*. Front footage, or frontage, is always given as the first measurement when the dimensions of the parcel are given. For example, a lot 60′ × 200′ measures 60 feet wide and 200 feet deep.

Example 31:
A lot measuring 55′ × 212′ cost $5,030. What is its cost per front foot?

$5,030 / 55 = $91.45

Area measurements are used for two-dimensional flat surfaces. Common area measurements include square feet, square yards and acres.

To determine the area of a square:

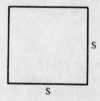

To determine the area of a rectangle:

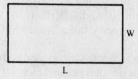

Example 32:
Bob wishes to carpet his living and dining room. The living room is 24′ × 14′ and the dining room is 13 feet square. How many sq. yards of carpeting does he need?

Step 1: LR 24′ × 14′ =   336 sq. ft.
        DR 13′ × 13′ =   169 sq. ft.
        Total   505 sq. ft.
Step 2: 505 / 9 = 56.11 sq. yds.

To determine the area of a triangle:

Area = (½ base) × height

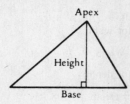

Example 33:
A triangular lot is 400' at its base and has a depth (height or altitude) of 300'. How many acres does the lot contain?

Step 1: A = ½ B × H
A = ½ × 400 × 300
A = 60,000 sq. ft.
Step 1: 1 acre contains 43,560 sq. ft.
60,000 / 43,560 = 1.38 acres

To determine the area of a trapezoid*:

Area = average of two parallel sides × height

Example 34:
The lot diagrammed below sold for $3,000. What is the price per acre?

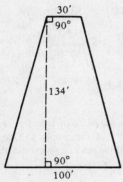

Step 1: $A = \dfrac{30' + 100'}{2} \times 134'$
A = 65' × 134' = 8,710 sq. ft.
A = 8,710 / 43,560 = .20 acres
Step 2: B = P / R
B = $3,000 / .2 = $15,000

To determine the area of a circle:

Area   = πR^2
Where: π = 3.1416
         R = radius (one-half the diameter)

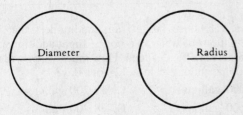

*A trapezoid is a four-sided figure (quadrilateral); two sides are parallel to each other and two are not.

Example 35:
A circular room has a diameter of 20 feet. What is the total square footage of the room?

A = 3.1416 × 10^2
A = 314.16 sq. ft.

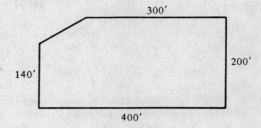

To determine the area of an odd-shaped figure, such as the one above, the figure can be broken into three geometric shapes whose separate areas can be easily calculated and then added together to give the total area.

A = L × W   A = L × W   A = ½ B × H
A = 200 × 300   A = 140 × 100   A ½(60) × 100
A = 60,000   A = 14,000   A = 3,000
Total area = 77,000 square feet

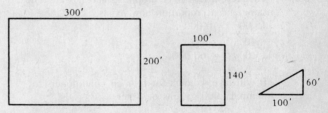

Ratio and Proportion

A ratio expresses the relationship of two numbers and is normally stated as: (1) a fraction, such as ½; (2) a single word, "to," such as 1 to 2; or (3) a colon, such as 1:2.
A proportion exists when two ratios are equal*:

½ = 2/4   or   ⅓ = 6/18

Note: by cross multiplying you get equal numbers so if three of the four numbers are known, you can solve for the fourth. For example:

5/10 = 6/x
5x = 60
x = 12
To check: 5/10 = 6/12

Example 36:
Lot A is 150' wide and Lot B is 450' wide. Both lots have the same depth. If Lot A contains 2 acres, how many acres does Lot B contain?

Step 1: Set up proportion   A   B
        Frontage   150'   450'
        Acres   2   x
Step 2: Cross multiply
        $\dfrac{150}{2} \times \dfrac{450}{x}$
        150x = 900
        x = 6 acres

Real Estate Math

Real estate proportion problems can be more complicated than Example 36, but the procedure remains the same.

Example 37:
If 2 air conditioners use 15,000 gallons of water in 10 hours, how many hours will it take 4 air conditioners to pump 12,000 gallons of water?

Step 1: Set up as in the previous problem

	Case 1	Case 2
AC	2	4
Gallons	15,000	12,000
Hours	10	x

Step 2: Since a ratio shows the relationship of any two numbers and since a proportion uses only 2 ratios, one of these three categories (AC, gallons, hours) must be eliminated. Since the number of hours is not known for Case 2, either AC or gallons must be eliminated.
This is accomplished by dividing the known variables in Case 2 by two so as to have the AC units the same for both Case 1 and Case 2. The result is:

	Case 1	Case 2
AC	2	2
Gallons	15,000	6,000
Hours	10	x

Step 3: The AC entries can be dropped since they are now the same and a proportion now exists:
$$\frac{15,000}{10} \times \frac{6,000}{x}$$
$$15,000x = 60,000$$
$$x = 4$$
It will take 4 hours for four air conditioners to pump 12,000 gallons of water.

Scale

Scale problems can be solved using the same procedure as proportion problems.

Example 38:
If the scale drawing for a lot is 6" × 8½" and the lot is actually 60' × 85', how many feet would be represented by 12¾"?

Step 1: 6" = 60' and 8½" = 85'
Either one can be used to set up a ratio.
Step 2: Scale 6"   12.75"
Actual 60'   x
Step 3: 6x = 765'
x = 127.5 feet

This type of problem can involve additional calculations.

Example 39:
What is the actual square footage of a lot that is shown on a blueprint as measuring 9.4" × 13.5" (scale: ⅛" = 1')?

Step 1: ⅛" = 1 ft., so 1" = 8 feet.
Step 2: Solving for width:
$$\frac{1}{8} \times \frac{9.4}{x} \quad \text{Width} = 75.2 \text{ feet}$$
Step 3: Solving for depth:
$$\frac{1}{8} \times \frac{13.5}{x} \quad \text{Depth} = 108 \text{ feet}$$
Step 4: 75.2 feet × 108 feet = 8,121.6 sq. feet

Miscellaneous

A few problems do not conveniently fit into the above classifications. Other problems combine two or three of the procedures discussed into a single problem.

Example 40:
According to a multiple listing agreement, Brokers A and B receive one-half of the 8% commission paid on the sale of a house. The multiple listing srevice (MLS) charges 3% of the total commission paid for its services. Salesman C, who is employed by Broker A, receives 40% of his broker's commission upon selling a house. How much will Salesman C receive if he sells a $45,000 house listed by Broker B?

Step 1: .08 × $45,000 = $3,600   Total commission paid
.03 × 3,600 = 108   MLS
$3,492   Brokers' share
Step 2: $3,492/2 = $1,746   Broker A's share
Step 3: $1,746 × .4 = $698.40   Salesman C's share

Example 41:
Five investors purchase a piece of land for $112,000. Two of the five each own 10% of the property. One owns 40% and another owns 25%. How much money did the fifth investor contribute towards the purchase?

Step 1: Investor #1   .10%
        #2   .10
        #3   .40
        #4   .25
                .85
So investor #5 owns 15%.
Step 2: P = R × B
P = .15 × $112,000
P = $16,800

PRACTICE PROBLEMS

1. A road in front of a piece of property is being widened, resulting in a 12-foot strip being taken. If the property measures 726' × 500', how many acres of land are being taken for the road?
   A. .137   C. .333
   B. .20   D. .40

2. An old warehouse has 10 air conditioners that use 12,000 gallons of water in 6 hours. Eight additional air conditioners are being added. How much water will the 8 additional units use in a 12-hour day?
   A. 4,000 gallons   C. 19,200 gallons
   B. 9,600 gallons   D. 38,400 gallons

3. Tom sells his house through a broker to whom he pays a 7% commission. If Tom nets $6,500 after paying the broker, an existing mortgage of $23,400 and a property tax lien of $512, what was the selling price of the house?
   A. $28,422
   B. $30,412
   C. $32,701
   D. $32,540

4. Greg borrowed $10,000 to buy a piece of land and agrees to pay the bank $95 per month, applied first to interest and then to principal. If the interest rate is 8½%, what will the outstanding balance be at the end of the first month?
   A. $9,905.00
   B. $9,929.17
   C. $9,975.83
   D. $10,755.00

5. Sally Salesperson receives a total commission of $1,234 from both listing and selling a house. If she received 20% of the total 7% commission for listing the house and 45% of the total commission for selling the house, how much did the house sell for?
   A. $20,314
   B. $26,432
   C. $27,121
   D. $29,085

6. Mr. Wimple sold his house for $48,500, which was 13% more than he paid for it. How much did he pay for the house?
   A. $42,250
   B. $42,920
   C. $54,805
   D. $55,747

7. David sells a piece of land for $24,450. If he netted $22,311 after paying a broker's commission, what was the rate of commission paid?
   A. 8.5%
   B. 8.75%
   C. 9.33%
   D. 9.6%

8. Dick purchased a three-year homeowner's insurance policy on January 10, 1989, for $40,000 coverage. The annual rate was $2.80 per $1000 coverage. If Louie buys the house and assumes the policy on February 17, 1990 how much should be credited to Dick at closing?
   A. $123.55
   B. $203.12
   C. $212.45
   D. $221.78

9. Property taxes have been paid for the calendar year. What amount will be credited to the seller if settlement is on March 4, the tax rate is $5.88/$100 and the assessed value is $16,400?
   A. $177.45
   B. $792.87
   C. $795.55
   D. $873.24

10. A vacant lot measures 116.25' × 281'. How many acres does it contain?
    A. .31 acre
    B. .75 acre
    C. 1.8 acre
    D. None of the answers are within .25 acre

11. Approximately what fraction is the smaller lot of the larger lot?
    A. ⅙
    B. ⅐
    C. ⅛
    D. 1/13

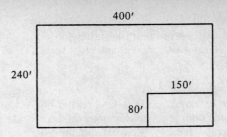

12. A five-year-old house has depreciated 6% annually each year. If the house was worth $66,500 when it was built, what is its value today?
    A. $46,550
    B. $51,154
    C. $86,450
    D. $95,000

13. Shirley purchased a one-year homeowners' insurance policy on March 7 for $188. Annual property taxes of $614.14 were paid January 1. How much should be credited to her if a purchaser assumes the insurance policy and closing takes place September 20?
    A. $191.00
    B. $255.58
    C. $257.80
    D. $544.33

14. An insurance company pays 90% of any fire damage over the $200 deductible. How much will an owner receive if he suffers an $835 fire damage?
    A. $571.50
    B. $635.00
    C. $705.55
    D. $751.50

15. A lot measures 411.4' × 900'. What is its total worth if land is valued at $6,000 per acre?
    A. $8,500
    B. $51,000
    C. $510,000
    D. $850,000

16. What is the rate of return on an investment when net operating income is $3,430 and property value is $22,000?
    A. 1.56%
    B. 6.4%
    C. 15.6%
    D. .156%

17. Ken buys a piece of land for $18,000 and then constructs a house which costs $58,000 to build. If he wishes to make a 15% profit on the lot and a 20% profit on the house, what must the total selling price be?
    A. $76,000
    B. $89,300
    C. $90,300
    D. $91,200

18. In anticipation of retirement, Clarence and Katie purchased a 10-unit apartment complex for $100,000. Each unit rents for $225 per month. If the vacancy rate is 5% and operating expenses are 50% of effective gross income, what is their rate of return?
    A. 12.8%
    B. 13.5%
    C. 27%
    D. None of these is within .5%

19. An office building is valued at $800,000 when net operating income is capitalized at a rate of 20%. If operating expenses are 40% of gross income, what is gross income?
    A. $266,667
    C. $400,000

B. $312,412   D. $507,312

20. What is the gross rent multiplier for a house that has a market value of $55,000 and rents for $500 per month?
    A. 100   C. 110
    B. 105   D. 115

21. Susan received $23,000 net after her house was sold. If her total charges at settlement were $615 and she paid a brokerage fee of 7%, what did the house sell for?
    A. $24,610   C. $25,268
    B. $24,731   D. $25,392

22. How many ¼-acre lots can a developer get out of a tract of land measuring 850′ × 900′ if he must set aside 1/10 acre for roads and parks for each lot developed?
    A. 50   C. 67
    B. 64   D. 70

23. A commercial space leases for $2,500 per month. If the dimensions of the store are 80′ × 50′, what is the annual rate per square foot?
    A. $.625   C. $8.25
    B. $7.50   D. $75.00

24. A warehouse was purchased eight years ago for $225,000. What is its value today if depreciation has been an average of 4.5% per year?
    A. $81,000   C. $166,500
    B. $144,000   D. $351,563

25. On January 1, Jack paid his annual city property taxes of $440 which were due on that date. His county property taxes of $314 were due and paid on July 1. If he sells the house and closing occurs October 9, how much will be credited to him?
    A. $271.66   C. $389.45
    B. $326.63   D. $427.34

26. A house was sold by a salesperson for $68,000. If the total commission paid was 7% and the salesperson and broker split the commission at a 40/60 ratio, how much did the salesperson receive?
    A. $1,904   C. $2,856
    B. $2,380   D. $4,760

27. Lisa earned a total of $1,850 last month from her broker. She is paid a $225 salary plus 45% of all commissions paid on real estate she sells. If the firm charges a 7% commission rate, how much real estate did she sell?
    A. $42,208   C. $51,587
    B. $48,052   D. $58,730

28. Jay borrows 80% of the appraised value of a house. If the interest on the amount borrowed is $14,025 biennial at an annual rate of 8¼%, what is the appraised value of the house?
    A. $85,000   C. $106,250
    B. $103,125   D. $425,000

29. Cathy borrows $45,000 from a bank at 7½% per annum. If the first monthly payment of $320 includes both principal and interest, what is the outstanding balance at the end of the first month?
    A. $41,625.00   C. $44,718.76
    B. $44,680.00   D. $44,961.24

30. What is the value of a building which has a monthly profit of $825 and is earning the owner a 14% annual return?
    A. $5,893   C. $82,112
    B. $70,714   D. None of the answers is within $1,000.

31. Craig would like to have a sidewalk built across the front of his property and has been quoted a price of $2.75 per sq. yd. The lot is 110 feet wide. If he wants the sidewalk to be 4 feet wide, how much will the job cost?
    A. $33.61   C. $302.50
    B. $134.44   D. $1,210

32. Don borrows 80% of the purchase price of a house from a bank at an interest rate of 9%. What is the purchase price of the house, if the interest due the first month is $254?
    A. $35,200   C. $42,240
    B. $39,111   D. $44,000

33. Debbie borrows $500 for 3 months at an interest rate of 13% per annum. If she pays both interest and loan in one payment at the end of the 3 months, how much will her payment be?
    A. $16.25   C. $516.25
    B. $65.00   D. $565.00

34. Mr. Gordon placed his house on the market for $48,500. When the house did not sell, he reduced his asking price 10% and sold it at that price. If his original asking price was 15% more than he paid for the house, then after selling it he realized a gain of
    A. $1,476   C. $5,693
    B. $2,205   D. $11,376

35. If taxes are $640.50 and the assessed value is $17,450, determine the rate.
    A. .0367/$100   C. 3.67/$100
    B. 2.72/$100   D. 4.32/$100

36. How many acres are there in a triangular lot that measures 362 feet at its base and also has an altitude of 362 feet?
    A. .75 acres   C. 3.0 acres
    B. 1.5 acres   D. None of the answers is within .25 acres

37. Helen borrows $800 for 6 months and agrees to pay both interest and principal at the end of that time. If interest due is $44, what is the annual rate of interest?
    A. 2.75%   C. 11%
    B. 5.5%   D. 22%

38. A lot measuring 80′ × 200′ sold for $88 per front foot. How much was paid for the lot?
    A. $7,040   C. $17,600

228   Chapter 20

B. $11,440 D. $1,408,000

39. A triangular lot has a frontage of one-quarter mile and is 594 feet deep. How many acres does it contain?
   A. 3 acres   C. 9 acres
   B. 6 acres   D. 12 acres

40. Two vacant lots have the same depth. Lot A is 300′ wide and Lot B is 750′ wide. If lot A is 14 acres, what is the size of Lot B?
   A. 14 acres   C. 35 acres
   B. 28 acres   D. 42 acres

41. Bob purchases a home for $55,000 and gets a commitment from a lender for an 80% loan. The lender has advised Bob that they will charge him 3 "discount points." If additional closing costs are $2,000, how much total cash must he have at closing?
   A. $1,300   C. $14,320
   B. $13,200   D. $14,650

42. Ken borrows 80% of the purchase price of a house at 9% interest. If his first month's interest payment is $330, what is the purchase price?
   A. $39,600   C. $47,520
   B. $44,000   D. $55,000

43. A store in a shopping mall is leased for $200 per month plus 1½% of gross sales over $50,000. If total rent paid for the year was $3,450, what were total gross sales for the year?
   A. $70,000   C. $160,000
   B. $120,000   D. $230,000

44. Mr. Pitt purchased a home 3 years ago for $41,000. Today he advertises it for sale at a price 40% greater than what he paid for it. If he accepts $2,000 less than the advertised price, how much profit will be net on his investment after paying a brokerage commission of 6.5%?
   A. $10,522   C. $12,669
   B. $10,799   D. $18,466

45. Jeff, a developer, bought 35 acres of land at a cost of $12,500 per acre. He spends $80,000 on roads and other improvements and builds 70 houses at an average cost of $52,000. What must Jeff sell each house for if he wants to make a 15% return on his total investment?
   A. $59,393   C. $69,874
   B. $68,302   D. $89,089

46. A property is assessed at 40% of its market value of $46,000. If the tax rate is $5.88/$100, what is the monthly property tax?
   A. $90.16   C. $225.40
   B. $135.24   D. $1,081.92

47. A room shown on a blueprint to be 6″ × 9″ is actually 18′ × 27′. If another room on the blueprint is shown as 26 square inches, how many square feet does it contain?
   A. 212 sq. ft.   C. 252 sq. ft
   B. 234 sq. ft.   D. 486 sq. ft.

48. A land developer estimates that 1/10 of the land he has is not suitable for any use, 1/5 must be used for recreation areas, streets, etc. and the remainder can be developed. If he develops 45 acres, what is the total size of his entire land holdings?
   A. 64 acres   C. 150 acres
   B. 128 acres   D. 155 acres

49. Bobby would like to completely fence his backyard which measures 60′ × 50′. If he places fence posts 10 feet apart, how many posts are needed?
   A. 20   C. 22
   B. 21   D. 23

50. Tommy can either sell his 25 acres for $5,000 per acre, or divide it into one-half acre lots at a total cost of $30,000 and sell each lot for $3,000. How much more will he make by subdividing and then selling?
   A. $5,000   C. $30,000
   B. $25,000   D. None of these; he makes less.

If you are not sure of your answers, see page 325 for correct answers and explanations.

Appendix **A**

Listing and Sales Contracts

As noted in Chapter 5, contract law is the hub of all real estate transactions. A broker and salesperson involved in real estate brokerage find themselves constantly dealing with two types of contracts, namely a listing contract and a sales contract.

The purpose of this appendix is to provide the reader the opportunity to become familiar with these two agreements. Certain topics previously discussed in the text are of paramount importance to the understanding of the listing and sales agreements, especially the discussions on the principal-agent relationship, contracts, financing and arithmetic functions used in real estate calculations.

PRACTICE PROBLEM A–1

Study Figure A–1 (Listing Contract) and Figure A–2 (Sales Contract) and then answer the 20 questions that follow. Answers are given on page 327.

QUESTIONS (PROBLEM A–1)

1. The size of the lot is approximately
   - A. one-third acre
   - B. one-half acre
   - C. two-thirds acre
   - D. one acre
2. Total annual property taxes are
   - A. $652.00
   - B. $847.60
   - C. $910.80
   - D. $988.00
3. The house contains one fireplace which is located in
   - A. living room
   - B. den
   - C. family room
   - D. kitchen
4. If Ms. Houghton receives 40% of the total commission paid, how much will she receive?
   - A. $2,432
   - B. $2,544
   - C. $3,040
   - D. $6,080
5. The seller would like to give possession
   - A. immediately
   - B. 30 days
   - C. 60 days
   - D. 90 days
6. Which of the following is not included with the house?
   - A. Side porch
   - B. Carport
   - C. Storm windows
   - D. Fenced yard
7. The listing agreement includes
   - I. built-in dishwasher
   - II. refrigerator
   - A. I only
   - B. II only
   - C. Both I and II
   - D. Neither I nor II
8. The age of the house is
   - A. new
   - B. 5 years
   - C. 10 years
   - D. 15 years
9. Had the property sold for the listed price, how much more would the commission have been compared to what it actually was?
   - A. $100
   - B. $280
   - C. $560
   - D. $810
10. How much will the principal on the purchase money mortgage be reduced by the first month's payment?
    - A. $25
    - B. $45
    - C. $70
    - D. $90
11. The house is located
    - I. within one mile of a shopping mall
    - II. on the bus line
    - A. I only
    - B. II only
    - C. Both I and II
    - D. Neither I nor II

Figure A–1

REAL ESTATE LISTING CONTRACT (EXCLUSIVE RIGHT TO SELL)

SALES PRICE $79,500	TYPE HOME one-story ranch	TOTAL BEDROOMS 3	TOTAL BATHS 2
ADDRESS 109 Blackshear Drive		JURISDICTION OF DeKalb, Texas	
AMT. OF LOAN TO BE ASSUMED $ 45,460	AS OF WHAT DATE 6/1	TAXES & INS INCLUDED yes YEARS TO GO 22 AMOUNT PAYABLE MONTHLY $ 439.16	9½% TYPE LOAN
MORTGAGE COMPANY Dundee Savings & Loan Assn.		2nd MORTGAGE	
OWNER'S NAME Dr. and Mrs. G. M. Jeffrey		PHONES (HOME)	(BUSINESS)
TENANT'S NAME		PHONES (HOME)	(BUSINESS)
POSSESSION 60 days	DATE LISTED 6/30/90	EXCLUSIVE FOR 90 days	DATE OF EXPIRATION 9/28/90
LISTING BROKER A. C. Wicker, Wicker Realty Co.		PHONE	KEY AVAILABLE AT Wicker Realty
LISTING SALESMAN Ms. Sally Houghton		HOME PHONE	HOW TO BE SHOWN Appointment only.

ENTRANCE FOYER X CENTER HALL ☐	AGE 15	AIR CONDITIONING X	TYPE KITCHEN CABINETS wooden
LIVING ROOM SIZE 18' x 12' FIREPLACE ☐	ROOFING shingle	TOOL HOUSE ☐	TYPE COUNTER TOPS formica
DINING ROOM SIZE 12' x 12'	GARAGE SIZE carport	PATIO X	EAT-IN SIZE KITCHEN X Breakfast area
BEDROOM TOTAL 3 DOWN UP	SIDE DRIVE X	CIRCULAR DRIVE ☐	TYPE STOVE X Electric
BATHS TOTAL 2 DOWN UP	PORCH X SIDE ☐ REAR ☐	SCREENED ☐	BUILT-IN OVEN & RANGE ☐
DEN SIZE FIREPLACE ☐	FENCED YARD	OUTDOOR GRILL ☐	SEPARATE STOVE INCLUDED X
FAMILY ROOM SIZE 11.5' x 20' FIREPLACE X	STORM WINDOWS X	STORM DOORS X	REFRIGERATOR INCLUDED
RECREATION ROOM SIZE FIREPLACE ☐	CURBS & GUTTERS X	SIDEWALKS	DISHWASHER INCLUDED X built-in
BASEMENT SIZE Separate rec. room	STORM SEWERS ☐	ALLEY ☐	DISPOSAL INCLUDED X
NONE ☐ 1/4 ☐ 1/3 ☐ 1/2 ☐ 3/4 X FULL ☐	WATER SUPPLY city		DOUBLE SINK X SINGLE SINK ☐
UTILITY ROOM	SEWER X city	SEPTIC ☐	STAINLESS STEEL X PORCELAIN ☐
TYPE HOT WATER SYSTEM Gas	TYPE GAS NATURAL ☐	BOTTLED ☐	WASHER INCLUDED ☐ DRYER INCLUDED ☐
TYPE HEAT Gas	WHY SELLING moving into condo		LAND ASSESSMENT $
EST. FUEL COST			IMPROVEMENTS $
ATTIC X floored	PROPERTY DESCRIPTION		TOTAL ASSESSMENT $ 26,000
PULL DOWN STAIRWAY X REGULAR STAIRWAY TRAP DOOR			TAX RATE 3.26 p/$100
NAME OF BUILDER	LOT SIZE 100 x 290'		TOTAL ANNUAL TAXES $
SQUARE FOOTAGE 1,960	LOT NO 44 BLOCK F SECTION 6		Ins.: $70,000 coverage.
EXTERIOR OF HOUSE Brick	Jamestown subdivision.		($210 annual premium)
NAME OF SCHOOLS ELEMENTARY Clairmont		JR HIGH Rockwood	
HIGH Druid Hills		PAROCHIAL	
PUBLIC TRANSPORTATION one block			
NEAREST SHOPPING AREA North DeKalb Shopping Mall - within one mile			

REMARKS Sliding door to concrete patio off DR; washer/dryer connections in kitchen; newly refinished hardwood floors in BR's; includes: carpeting (LR, DR, FR), st. windows, st. doors, shades, curtain rods, elec. stove, TV antenna. Not incl. tagged azalea by porch.

Date: June 30, 1990

In consideration of the services of **A. C. Wicker** (herein called "Broker") to be rendered to the undersigned (herein called "Owner"), and of the promise of Broker to make reasonable efforts to obtain a Purchaser therefor, Owner hereby lists with Broker the real estate and all improvements thereon which are described above (all herein called "the property"), and Owner hereby grants to Broker the exclusive and irrevocable right to sell such property from 12:00 Noon on **June 30**, 19**90** until 12:00 Midnight on **September 28**, 19**90** (herein called "period of time"), for the price of **Seventy-Nine Thousand Five Hundred** Dollars ($**79,500**) or for such other price and upon such other terms (including exchange) as Owner may subsequently authorize during the period of time.

It is understood by Owner that the above sum or any other price subsequently authorized by Owner shall include a cash fee of **8** per cent of such price or other price which shall be payable by Owner to Broker upon consummation by any Purchaser or Purchasers of a valid contract of sale of the property during the period of time and whether or not Broker was a procuring cause of any such contract of sale.

If the property is sold or exchanged by Owner, or by Broker or by any other person to any Purchaser to whom the property was shown by Broker or any representative of Broker within sixty (60) days after the expiration of the period of time mentioned above, Owner agrees to pay to Broker a cash fee which shall be the same percentage of the purchase price as the percentage mentioned above.

Broker is hereby authorized by Owner to place a "For Sale" sign on the property and to remove all signs of other brokers or salesmen during the period of time, and Owner hereby agrees to make the property available to Broker at all reasonable hours for the purpose of showing it to prospective Purchasers.

Owner agrees to convey the property to the Purchaser by deed with the usual covenants of title and free and clear from all encumbrances, tenancies, liens (for taxes or otherwise), but subject to applicable restrictive covenants of record. Owner acknowledges receipt of a copy of this agreement.

WITNESS the following signature(s) and seal(s):

Date Signed June 30, 1990

Listing Agent X

Address 1154 Larch Lane Telephone

(Owner)

(Owner)

Listing and Sales Contracts

Figure A-2

REAL ESTATE SALES CONTRACT (OFFER TO PURCHASE AGREEMENT)

This AGREEMENT made as of _____ July 15 _____, 19 90.

among __Mr. and Mrs. Robert Harrison__ (herein called "Purchaser"),

and __Dr. and Mrs. G. M. Jeffery__ (herein called "Seller"),

and __A. C. Wicker__ (herein called "Broker"),

provides that Purchaser agrees to buy through Broker as agent for Seller, and Seller agrees to sell the following described real estate, and all improvements thereon, located in the jurisdiction of __DeKalb, Mississippi__,

(all herein called "the property"): __Lot 44, Block F, Section 6, Jamestown Subdivision. Included in sale: all carpeting (LR, DR, FR), storm windows, st. doors, shades, curtain rods, elec. stove, TV antenna. Not incl: azalea by porch__ (street address): __109 Blackshear Drive__

1. The purchase price of the property is __Seventy-Six Thousand__ Dollars ($ __76,000.00__), and such purchase price shall be paid as follows: __$5,000 deposit acknowledged in Paragraph 2, $45,325.78 assumption of existing mortgage (as of August 1), $12,000 purchase money mortgage, & $13,674.22 additional cash at settlement.__

2. Purchaser has made a deposit of __Five Thousand__ Dollars ($ __5,000.00__) with Broker, receipt of which is hereby acknowledged, and such deposit shall be held by Broker in escrow until the date of settlement and then applied to the purchase price, or returned to Purchaser if the title to the property is not marketable.

3. Seller agrees to convey the property to Purchaser by Deed with the usual covenants of title and free and clear from all monetary encumbrances, tenancies, liens (for taxes or otherwise), except as may be otherwise provided above, but subject to applicable restrictive covenants of record. Seller further agrees to deliver possession of the property to Purchaser on the date of settlement and to pay the expense of preparing the deed of conveyance.

4. Settlement shall be made at __Hipp and Hipp, Attorney at Law__ on or before __August 20__, 19 __90__, or as soon thereafter as title can be examined and necessary documents prepared, with allowance of a reasonable time for Seller to correct any defects reported by the title examiner.

5. All taxes, interest, rent, and impound escrow deposits, if any, shall be prorated as of the date of settlement.

6. All risk of loss or damage to the property by fire, windstorm, casualty, or other cause is assumed by Seller until the date of settlement.

7. Purchaser and Seller agree that Broker was the sole procuring cause of this Contract of Purchase, and Seller agrees to pay Broker for services rendered a cash fee of __8__ per cent of the purchase price. If either Purchaser or Seller defaults under such Contract, such defaulting party shall be liable for the cash fee of Broker and any expenses incurred by the non-defaulting party in connection with this transaction.

Subject to: __Buyer assuming existing mortgage of $45,325.78 as of August 1, 1990, int. rate of .095 per annum. Seller taking back a $12,000 purchase money mortgage, of .10 per annum, $125 per month remaining balance due in 6 years. Seller to provide a certificate of termite inspection from approved exterminator.__

8. Purchaser represents that an inspection satisfactory to Purchaser has been made of the property, and Purchaser agrees to accept the property in its present condition except as may be otherwise provided in the description of the property above.

9. This Contract of Purchase constitutes the entire agreement among the parties and may not be modified or changed except by written instrument executed by all of the parties, including Broker.

10. This Contract of Purchase shall be construed, interpreted, and applied according to the law of the jurisdiction of __Mississippi__ and shall be binding upon and shall inure to the benefit of the heirs, personal representatives, successors, and assigns of the parties.

All parties to this agreement acknowledge receipt of a certified copy.

WITNESS the following signatures:

X Seller	X Purchaser
X Seller	X Purchaser
X Broker	

Deposit Rec'd $ __5,000.00__

Personal Check   Cash

(Cashier's Check)   Company Check

Sales Agent:

12. The size of the basement is approximately how many square feet?
    A. 980
    B. 1,470
    C. 1,960
    D. There is no basement
13. If a 14′ × 21′ den is added to the house, the square footage will increase by what percent?
    A. Less than 10%
    B. 10%
    C. 15%
    D. More than 20%
14. The purchaser made a deposit of
    I. $5,000
    II. .063 of the listing price
    A. I only
    B. II only
    C. Both I and II
    D. Neither I nor II
15. The loan-to-value ratio on the purchase money mortgage is
    A. 10%
    B. 16%
    C. 22%
    D. 80%
16. The annual property insurance rate is
    A. $3.33/$100
    B. $3.67/$100
    C. $4.44/$100
    D. Cannot determine from information provided
17. The sales contract contains a contingency clause(s) for the buyer
    I. assuming the existing mortgage
    II. providing a certificate of termite inspection
    A. I only
    B. II only
    C. Both I and II
    D. Neither I nor II
18. If the property is reassessed at 40% of the sales price, what will the annual property tax be?
    A. $666
    B. $991
    C. $848
    D. $1,239
19. If after a title search the title to the property proves to be not marketable, the deposit money belongs to
    A. Houghton
    B. Jeffery
    C. Wicker
    D. Harrison
20. As of July 15 the sales contract is
    A. void
    B. exculpatory
    C. executed
    D. executory

PRACTICE PROBLEM A–2

Study Figure A–3 (Listing Contract) and Figure A–4 (Sales Contract) and then answer the 20 questions that follow. Answers are given on page 328.

QUESTIONS (PROBLEM A–2)

1. The listing is acquired
    A. March 7
    B. March 21
    C. March 22
    D. March 23
2. The lot size is approximately
    A. one-fifth acre
    B. one-fourth acre
    C. one-third acre
    D. one-half acre
3. The attic is accessible by
    A. pulldown stairway
    B. regular stairway
    C. trap door
    D. there is no attic
4. The house contains one fireplace which is located in the
    A. living room
    B. recreation room
    C. den
    D. master bedroom
5. The basement in the house contains how many square feet?
    A. 510
    B. 1,020
    C. 2,040
    D. The house does not have a basement.
6. The property tax rate is
    A. $1.44/$100
    B. $2.88/$100
    C. $3.46/$100
    D. $1.73/$100
7. The source of the water supply is
    A. city
    B. county
    C. drilled well
    D. dug well
8. The roof of the house is
    A. slate
    B. asphalt
    C. shingle
    D. tile
9. If Helen Pitt receives 50% of the total commission paid, she will receive
    A. $1,225.00
    B. $1,312.25
    C. $1,470.00
    D. $2,625.00
10. If total transfer tax and document stamp fees amount to $937.50, the Chapmans will pay
    A. $0
    B. $312.47
    C. $468.75
    D. $937.50
11. The existing mortgage is
    A. conventional
    B. FHA
    C. VA
    D. balloon
12. If the Chapmans escrowed their property taxes each month, the total monthly payment to First Savings and Loan of Martinsville would be
    A. $147.76
    B. $190.96
    C. $666.16
    D. $206.84
13. According to the listing agreement, the exterior of the house is in what condition?
    A. Poor
    B. Fair
    C. Good
    D. Excellent
14. The purchaser made a deposit of
    I. $1,500

Figure A–3

REAL ESTATE LISTING CONTRACT (EXCLUSIVE RIGHT TO SELL)

SALES PRICE $42,000.00   TYPE HOME Ranch   TOTAL BEDROOMS 3   TOTAL BATHS 1½
ADDRESS Summit View Drive   JURISDICTION OF Martin County, Mississippi
AMT. OF LOAN TO BE ASSUMED $ 18,450.00   AS OF WHAT DATE 3/1/90   TAXES & INS INCLUDED No   YEARS TO GO ___   AMOUNT PAYABLE MONTHLY $ 147.76   11 % TYPE LOAN FHA
MORTGAGE COMPANY First Savings & Loan, Martinsville   2ND MORTGAGE ____
OWNER'S NAME Robert & Evalyn Chapman   PHONES (HOME) ____ (BUSINESS) ____
TENANT'S NAME ____   PHONES (HOME) ____ (BUSINESS) ____
POSSESSION within 90 days   DATE LISTED 3/7/90   EXCLUSIVE FOR 60 days   DATE OF EXPIRATION 5/6/90
LISTING BROKER Greg Sanderfur & Assoc. Realty   PHONE ____   KEY AVAILABLE AT ____
LISTING SALESMAN Helen Pitt   HOME PHONE ____   HOW TO BE SHOWN call first

ENTRANCE FOYER ☐ CENTER HALL ☐	AGE 12	AIR CONDITIONING ☒	TYPE KITCHEN CABINETS
LIVING ROOM SIZE 14' x 15' FIREPLACE ☐	ROOFING Comp. Shingle TOOL HOUSE ☐		TYPE COUNTER TOPS
DINING ROOM SIZE 12' x 10'	~~GARAGE~~ Carport PATIO ☐		EAT-IN SIZE KITCHEN ☐
BEDROOM TOTAL 3 DOWN UP	SIDE DRIVE ☒ paved CIRCULAR DRIVE ☐		TYPE STOVE ☒ Gas
BATHS TOTAL 1½ DOWN UP	PORCH ☐ SIDE ☐ REAR ☐ SCREENED ☐		BUILT-IN OVEN & RANGE ☐
DEN SIZE FIREPLACE ☐	FENCED YARD OUTDOOR GRILL ☐		SEPARATE STOVE INCLUDED ☒
FAMILY ROOM SIZE FIREPLACE ☐	STORM WINDOWS ☐ STORM DOORS ☐		REFRIGERATOR INCLUDED ☐
RECREATION ROOM SIZE 30' x 17' FIREPLACE ☒	CURBS & GUTTERS ☐ SIDEWALKS ☐		DISHWASHER INCLUDED ☒ portable
BASEMENT SIZE 30' x 34'	STORM SEWERS ☐ ALLEY ☐		DISPOSAL INCLUDED ☐
NONE ☐ 1/4 ☐ 1/3 ☐ 1/2 ☐ 3/4 ☐ FULL ☒	WATER SUPPLY City		DOUBLE SINK ☐ SINGLE SINK ☐
UTILITY ROOM	SEWER ☒ City SEPTIC ☐		STAINLESS STEEL ☐ PORCELAIN ☐
TYPE HOT WATER SYSTEM 40 gal. elec.	TYPE GAS NATURAL ☐ BOTTLED ☐		WASHER INCLUDED ☐ DRYER INCLUDED ☐
TYPE HEAT FHA	WHY SELLING Moving to another city.		LAND ASSESSMENT $ 3,000.00
EST. FUEL COST $68 per month			IMPROVEMENTS $ 15,000.00
ATTIC ☒ 12" insulation	PROPERTY DESCRIPTION		TOTAL ASSESSMENT $
PULL DOWN STAIRWAY ☐ REGULAR STAIRWAY ☐ TRAP DOOR ☒	(1½ mi. outside city limits)		TAX RATE
NAME OF BUILDER	LOT SIZE 80' x 110'		TOTAL ANNUAL TAXES $ 518.40
SQUARE FOOTAGE	LOT NO 17 BLOCK A SECTION Mountain View subdivision.		
EXTERIOR OF HOUSE Brick & Frame construction - good condition.			

NAME OF SCHOOLS   ELEMENTARY Conway   JR HIGH Pleasant View
HIGH Martin County   PAROCHIAL ____
PUBLIC TRANSPORTATION None
NEAREST SHOPPING AREA Madison Square - ½ mile
REMARKS Included in sale: A/C in bedroom, portable dishwasher, gas stove.
Not included in sale: Refrigerator, gas grill, tagged bushes.

Date: March 7, 1990

In consideration of the services of Greg Sanderfur & Assoc. (herein called "Broker") to be rendered to the undersigned (herein called "Owner"), and of the promise of Broker to make reasonable efforts to obtain a Purchaser therefor, Owner hereby lists with Broker the real estate and all improvements thereon which are described above (all herein called "the property"), and Owner hereby grants to Broker the exclusive and irrevocable right to sell such property from 12:00 Noon on March 7, 19 90 until 12:00 Midnight on May 6, 19 90 (herein called "period of time"), for the price of Forty-Two Thousand-------------------- Dollars ($ 42,000.00) or for such other price and upon such other terms (including exchange) as Owner may subsequently authorize during the period of time.

It is understood by Owner that the above sum or any other price subsequently authorized by Owner shall include a cash fee of 7 per cent of such price or other price which shall be payable by Owner to Broker upon consummation by any Purchaser or Purchasers of a valid contract of sale of the property during the period of time and whether or not Broker was a procuring cause of any such contract of sale.

If the property is sold or exchanged by Owner, or by Broker or by any other person to any Purchaser to whom the property was shown by Broker or any representative of Broker within sixty (60) days after the expiration of the period of time mentioned above, Owner agrees to pay to Broker a cash fee which shall be the same percentage of the purchase price as the percentage mentioned above.

Broker is hereby authorized by Owner to place a "For Sale" sign on the property and to remove all signs of other brokers or salesmen during the period of time, and Owner hereby agrees to make the property available to Broker at all reasonable hours for the purpose of showing it to prospective Purchasers.

Owner agrees to convey the property to the Purchaser by deed with the usual covenants of title and free and clear from all encumbrances, tenancies, liens (for taxes or otherwise), but subject to applicable restrictive covenants of record. Owner acknowledges receipt of a copy of this agreement.

WITNESS the following signature(s) and seal(s):

Date Signed March 7, 1990   X _____ (Owner)

Listing Agent _____ X

Address _____ Telephone _____   X _____ (Owner)

Figure A-4

REAL ESTATE SALES CONTRACT (OFFER TO PURCHASE AGREEMENT)

This AGREEMENT made as of _____ March 22, 19 90,

among Donald and Shirley Skaggs _____ (herein called "Purchaser"),

and Robert and Evalyn Chapman _____ (herein called "Seller"),

and Greg Sanderfur _____ (herein called "Broker"),

provides that Purchaser agrees to buy through Broker as agent for Seller, and Seller agrees to sell the following described real estate, and all improvements thereon, located in the jurisdiction of Martin County, Mississippi,
(all herein called "the property"): Lot 17, Block A, Mountain View Subdivision. Included in sale: all shrubs & bushes, gas grill, A/C in bedroom, portable dishwasher, gas stove. Not incl: refrigerator. _____ (street address): Summit View Drive

1. The purchase price of the property is Thirty-Seven Thousand Five Hundred----------------------- Dollars ($ 37,500.00), and such purchase price shall be paid as follows: $1,500.00 deposit acknowledged in Paragraph 2, $28,000 new mortgage, $8,000 additional cash at closing.

2. Purchaser has made a deposit of One Thousand Five Hundred---------------- Dollars ($ 1,500.00) with Broker, receipt of which is hereby acknowledged, and such deposit shall be held by Broker in escrow until the date of settlement and then applied to the purchase price, or returned to Purchaser if the title to the property is not marketable.

3. Seller agrees to convey the property to Purchaser by Deed with the usual covenants of title and free and clear from all monetary encumbrances, tenancies, liens (for taxes or otherwise), except as may be otherwise provided above, but subject to applicable restrictive covenants of record. Seller further agrees to deliver possession of the property to Purchaser on the date of settlement and to pay the expense of preparing the deed of conveyance.

4. Settlement shall be made at Martinsville Building and Loan Association on or before August 1, 19 90, or as soon thereafter as title can be examined and necessary documents prepared, with allowance of a reasonable time for Seller to correct any defects reported by the title examiner.

5. All taxes, interest, rent, and impound escrow deposits, if any, shall be prorated as of the date of settlement.

6. All risk of loss or damage to the property by fire, windstorm, casualty, or other cause is assumed by Seller until the date of settlement.

7. Purchaser and Seller agree that Broker was the sole procuring cause of this Contract of Purchase, and Seller agrees to pay Broker for services rendered a cash fee of 7 per cent of the purchase price. If either Purchaser or Seller defaults under such Contract, such defaulting party shall be liable for the cash fee of Broker and any expenses incurred by the non-defaulting party in connection with this transaction.

Subject to: Buyer acquiring new conventional mortgage of $28,000, interest rate not to exceed 12% 30-year life. Seller to provide a certificate of termite inspection from licensed termite inspection company. Cost of transfer tax and document stamps to be divided equally between buyer and seller.

8. Purchaser represents that an inspection satisfactory to Purchaser has been made of the property, and Purchaser agrees to accept the property in its present condition except as may be otherwise provided in the description of the property above.

9. This Contract of Purchase constitutes the entire agreement among the parties and may not be modified or changed except by written instrument executed by all of the parties, including Broker.

10. This Contract of Purchase shall be construed, interpreted, and applied according to the law of the jurisdiction of Mississippi and shall be binding upon and shall inure to the benefit of the heirs, personal representatives, successors, and assigns of the parties.

All parties to this agreement acknowledge receipt of a certified copy.

WITNESS the following signatures:

X _____ Seller   X _____ Purchaser

X _____ Seller   X _____ Purchaser

X _____ Broker

Deposit Rec'd $ 1,500.00

(Personal Check)   Cash

Cashier's Check   Company Check

Sales Agent:

Listing and Sales Contracts

II. .04 of the purchase price
A. I only C. Both I and II
B. II only D. Neither I nor II
15. The sellers would like to give possession
A. immediately C. within 90 days
B. within 30 days D. do not care
16. The house includes a
A. garage C. fenced yard
B. carport D. circular drive
17. The offer to purchase agreement includes
I. A portable dishwasher
II. gas grill on patio
A. I only C. Both I and II
B. II only D. Neither I nor II
18. The hot-water system is
A. 30-gallon electric C. 30-gallon oil
B. 40-gallon electric D. 40-gallon gas
19. In addition to the deposit, how much cash will the buyers need for the purchase price?
A. $8,000 C. $28,000
B. $9,500 D. $36,000
20. The house contains
I. forced-hot-air heating system
II. circular drive
A. I only C. Both I and II
B. II only D. Neither I nor II

PRACTICE PROBLEM A–3

Study Figure A–5 (Listing Contract) and Figure A–6 (Sales Contract) and then answer the 20 questions that follow. Answers are given on page 328.

QUESTIONS (PROBLEM A–3)

1. The architectural style of the house is
A. ranch C. modern colonial
B. southern colonial D. Cape Cod colonial
2. The age of the house is
A. 10 years C. 30 years
B. 20 years D. More than 30 years
3. The exterior of the house is
A. brick C. wood
B. shingles D. clapboard
4. The lot size is approximately
A. 1/8 acre C. 1/2 acre
B. 1/4 acre D. more than 1/2 acre
5. If the property sells for the listed price, the broker's commission will be
A. $1,995
B. $2,660
C. $3,040
D. none of these are within $100
6. The interest payable to Mr. Hipp on the purchase money mortgage the first month is
A. $62.50 C. $100.00
B. $75.00 D. $750.00
7. If the buyer's total investment is $2,000 and the expenses incurred the first year in renting the property are $1,000, what is the return on his investment the first year?
A. 55% C. 82%
B. 73% D. 123%
8. The house is located
I. on the bus line
II. two miles from LaGrange Plaza
A. I only C. Both I and II
B. II only D. Neither I nor II
9. The total assessed value of the property for computing annual property tax is
A. $344 C. $19,000
B. $16,226 D. $38,000
10. The listing agreement expires
A. January 10 C. April 9
B. March 9 D. April 10
11. The size of the basement is
A. one-fourth C. one-half
B. one-third D. full
12. A fireplace is located in the
A. living room C. family room
B. den D. recreation room
13. The current lessee is
A. P. Seale Hipp C. Ronald J. deValinger
B. Richard T. Walters D. E. C. Stevens, Jr.
14. If a bedroom 12.5' × 10' was added to the back of the house, the square footage of the house would be increased by
A. 5% C. 15%
B. 10% D. greater than 15%
15. The terms of the purchase money mortgage include
A. $28,500; 25 years; 12%
B. $38,000; 25 years; 12%
C. $7,500; 5 years; 10%
D. $7,500; 5 years; 9%
16. The first offer made on the house by Mr. Stevens was for

Figure A–5

REAL ESTATE LISTING CONTRACT (EXCLUSIVE RIGHT TO SELL)

SALES PRICE $38,000.00   TYPE HOME Cape Cod Colonial   TOTAL BEDROOMS 2   TOTAL BATHS 1
ADDRESS 506 Park Avenue   JURISDICTION OF LaGrange, Mississippi
AMT OF LOAN TO BE ASSUMED $ ___   AS OF WHAT DATE ___   TAXES & INS INCLUDED ___   YEARS TO GO ___   AMOUNT PAYABLE MONTHLY $ ___ @ ___   TYPE LOAN ___
MORTGAGE COMPANY ___   2nd MORTGAGE ___
OWNER'S NAME Mr. P. Seale Hipp   PHONES (HOME) ___ (BUSINESS) ___
TENANT'S NAME Mr. Ronald J. deValinger   PHONES (HOME) ___ (BUSINESS) ___
POSSESSION ASAP   DATE LISTED 1/10/90   EXCLUSIVE FOR 90 days   DATE OF EXPIRATION 4/10/90
LISTING BROKER Mr. Richard T. Walters   PHONE ___   KEY AVAILABLE AT ___
LISTING SALESMAN ___   HOME PHONE ___   HOW TO BE SHOWN ___

ENTRANCE FOYER ☐   CENTER HALL ☒   AGE 30   AIR CONDITIONING ☐   TYPE KITCHEN CABINETS wooden
LIVING ROOM SIZE 12' x 15'   FIREPLACE x br   ROOFING shingles   TOOL HOUSE ☐   TYPE COUNTER TOPS tempered hardwood
DINING ROOM SIZE 12' x 11'   GARAGE SIZE ___   PATIO ☐   EAT-IN SIZE KITCHEN x
BEDROOM TOTAL 2   DOWN ___ UP ___   SIDE DRIVE ☒   CIRCULAR DRIVE ☐   TYPE STOVE ☐
BATHS TOTAL 1   DOWN ___ UP ___   PORCH ☐ SIDE ☐ REAR ☐   SCREENED ☒   BUILT-IN OVEN & RANGE ☒
DEN SIZE ___   FIREPLACE ☐   FENCED YARD picket   OUTDOOR GRILL ☐   SEPARATE STOVE INCLUDED ☐
FAMILY ROOM SIZE ___   FIREPLACE ☐   STORM WINDOWS xscreens   STORM DOORS ☐   REFRIGERATOR INCLUDED ☐
RECREATION ROOM SIZE ___   FIREPLACE ☐   CURBS & GUTTERS x   SIDEWALKS x   DISHWASHER INCLUDED x
BASEMENT SIZE ___   STORM SEWERS ☒   ALLEY ☐   DISPOSAL INCLUDED ☒
NONE ☐ 1/4 ☐ 1/3 ☐ 1/2 ☐ 3/4 ☒ FULL ☐   WATER SUPPLY city   DOUBLE SINK ☒   SINGLE SINK ☐
UTILITY ROOM ___   SEWER x city   SEPTIC ☐   STAINLESS STEEL x   PORCELAIN ☐
TYPE HOT WATER SYSTEM 40 gal. gas   TYPE GAS NATURAL x   BOTTLED ___   WASHER INCLUDED ☐ DRYER INCLUDED ☐
TYPE HEAT Gas forced air furnace   WHY SELLING Disposing of invest.   LAND ASSESSMENT $ 4,056
EST. FUEL COST ___   IMPROVEMENTS $ 12,170
ATTIC x Bath roughed in.   PROPERTY DESCRIPTION ___   TOTAL ASSESSMENT $ 16,226
PULL DOWN STAIRWAY ☐   REGULAR STAIRWAY ☒   TRAP DOOR ☐   TAX RATE $2.12 p/$100
NAME OF BUILDER ___   LOT SIZE 55' x 100'   TOTAL ANNUAL TAXES $ 344
SQUARE FOOTAGE 1,250   LOT NO 6   BLOCK A   SECTION College View Estates
EXTERIOR OF HOUSE Natural shingles, shutters, gutters - good condition.
NAME OF SCHOOLS ELEMENTARY Park Avenue - ½ block   JR HIGH Broad Street - 2 blocks
HIGH LaGrange City - 1 mile   PAROCHIAL ___
PUBLIC TRANSPORTATION Not on bus line
NEAREST SHOPPING AREA LaGrange Plaza - 1 mile
REMARKS New vinyl floors in kitchen. Both bedrooms carpeted w/window air conditioners. Tile bath. Seller will take back purchase money mortgage. Rent - $175 per mo. Lease expires 3/31/90

Date: January 10, 1990

consideration of the services of Richard T. Walters (herein called "Broker") to be rendered to the undersigned (herein called "Owner"), and of the promise of Broker to make reasonable efforts to obtain a Purchaser therefor, Owner hereby lists with Broker the real estate and all improvements thereon which are described above (all herein called "the property"), and Owner hereby grants to Broker the exclusive and irrevocable right to sell such property from 12:00 Noon on January 10, 19 90 until 12:00 Midnight on April 10, 19 90 (herein called "period of time"), for the price of Thirty-Eight Thousand-------------- Dollars ($ 38,000.00) or for such other price and upon such other terms (including exchange) as Owner may subsequently authorize during the period of time.

It is understood by Owner that the above sum or any other price subsequently authorized by Owner shall include a cash fee of 7 per cent of such price or other price which shall be payable by Owner to Broker upon consummation by any Purchaser or Purchasers of a valid contract of sale of the property during the period of time and whether or not Broker was a procuring cause of any such contract of sale.

If the property is sold or exchanged by Owner, or by Broker or by any other person to any Purchaser to whom the property was shown by Broker or any representative of Broker within sixty (60) days after the expiration of the period of time mentioned above, Owner agrees to pay to Broker a cash fee which shall be the same percentage of the purchase price as the percentage mentioned above.

Broker is hereby authorized by Owner to place a "For Sale" sign on the property and to remove all signs of other brokers or salesmen during the period of time, and Owner hereby agrees to make the property available to Broker at all reasonable hours for the purpose of showing it to prospective Purchasers.

Owner agrees to convey the property to the Purchaser by deed with the usual covenants of title and free and clear from all encumbrances, tenancies, liens (for taxes or otherwise), but subject to applicable restrictive covenants of record. Owner acknowledges receipt of a copy of this agreement.

WITNESS the following signature(s) and seal(s):

Date Signed January 10, 1990   X _____ (Owner)

Listing Agent _____ X

Address _____ Telephone _____   _____ (Owner)

Listing and Sales Contracts

Figure A–6

REAL ESTATE SALES CONTRACT (OFFER TO PURCHASE AGREEMENT)

This AGREEMENT made as of __February 7__, 19 __90__,

among __E. C. Stevens, Jr.__ (herein called "Purchaser"),

and __P. Seale Hipp__ (herein called "Seller"),

and __Richard T. Walters__ (herein called "Broker"),

provides that Purchaser agrees to buy through Broker as agent for Seller, and Seller agrees to sell the following described real estate, and all improvements thereon, located in the jurisdiction of __LaGrange, Mississippi__,

(all herein called "the property"): __Lot 6, Block A, College View Estates. Included in sale: carpeting, 2 window air conditioners, dishwasher, disposal, storm windows, screens, picket fence.__

(street address).: __506 Park Avenue__

1. The purchase price of the property is __Thirty-Eight Thousand--------------------------------------__ Dollars ($ __38,000.00__), and such purchase price shall be paid as follows: __New mortgage $28,500; deposit $2,000 as acknowledged in Paragraph 2 below; $7,500 purchase money mortgage.__

2. Purchaser has made a deposit of __Two Thousand--------------------------------__ Dollars ($ __2,000.00__) with Broker, receipt of which is hereby acknowledged, and such deposit shall be held by Broker in escrow until the date of settlement and then applied to the purchase price, or returned to Purchaser if the title to the property is not marketable.

3. Seller agrees to convey the property to Purchaser by Deed with the usual covenants of title and free and clear from all monetary encumbrances, tenancies, liens (for taxes or otherwise), except as may be otherwise provided above, but subject to applicable restrictive covenants of record. Seller further agrees to deliver possession of the property to Purchaser on the date of settlement and to pay the expense of preparing the deed of conveyance.

4. Settlement shall be made at __LaGrange Bank & Trust__ on or before __March 1__, 19 __90__, or as soon thereafter as title can be examined and necessary documents prepared, with allowance of a reasonable time for Seller to correct any defects reported by the title examiner.

5. All taxes, interest, rent, and impound escrow deposits, if any, shall be prorated as of the date of settlement.

6. All risk of loss or damage to the property by fire, windstorm, casualty, or other cause is assumed by Seller until the date of settlement.

7. Purchaser and Seller agree that Broker was the sole procuring cause of this Contract of Purchase, and Seller agrees to pay Broker for services rendered a cash fee of __7__ per cent of the purchase price. If either Purchaser or Seller defaults under such Contract, such defaulting party shall be liable for the cash fee of Broker and any expenses incurred by the non-defaulting party in connection with this transaction.

Subject to: __(1) Buyer acquiring first mortgage $28,500 from LaGrange Bank & Trust, 25 years amortization, interest rate not to exceed 12 percent. (2) Seller taking $7,500 purchase money mortgage, 10 percent, $100 per month, balance due in 5 years from date of closing. (3) Tenant signing new 1 year lease for $205 per month.__

8. Purchaser represents that an inspection satisfactory to Purchaser has been made of the property, and Purchaser agrees to accept the property in its present condition except as may be otherwise provided in the description of the property above.

9. This Contract of Purchase constitutes the entire agreement among the parties and may not be modified or changed except by written instrument executed by all of the parties, including Broker.

10. This Contract of Purchase shall be construed, interpreted, and applied according to the law of the jurisdiction of __Mississippi__ and shall be binding upon and shall inure to the benefit of the heirs, personal representatives, successors, and assigns of the parties.

All parties to this agreement acknowledge receipt of a certified copy.

WITNESS the following signatures:

X_____	X_____
Seller	Purchaser
_____	_____
Seller	Purchaser
X_____	
Broker	

Deposit Rec'd $ __2,000.00__

(Personal Check)   Cash

Cashier's Check   Company Check

Sales Agent:

    A. $28,500   C. $38,000
    B. $36,000   D. $38,500

17. Included with the property is a (an)
    A. tool house   C. outdoor grill
    B. patio   D. screened porch

18. Mr. Hipp is selling the house because
    I. he wishes to dispose of the investment
    II. he is moving to another city
    A. I only   C. Both I and II
    B. II only   D. Neither I nor II

19. The house contains a
    I. gas forced-air heater
    II. 40-gallon electric hot-water system
    A. I only   C. Both I and II
    B. II only   D. Neither I nor II

20. Included as items in the sale is a (an)
    I. separate electric stove
    II. outdoor grill
    A. I only   C. Both I and II
    B. II only   D. Neither I nor II

Appendix ***B***

Preparation of Settlement Statement Worksheet

An important and necessary part of any real estate sales transaction is the closing or settlement. While the paperwork is normally completed by an escrow agent, closing attorney or title company, a professional real estate broker or salesperson should have a clear understanding of how a settlement statement worksheet is completed.

The purpose of this appendix is to provide the reader with the opportunity to practice completing the worksheet. Prior to preparing a settlement statement worksheet the reader should review Chapter 16, which explains exactly what happens at a typical real estate closing.

COMPLETING THE WORKSHEET

The accounting approach generally used in completing a settlement statement worksheet is a relatively simple procedure of double entry bookkeeping. The worksheet consists of a *buyer's statement* and a *seller's statement*. Both of these in turn are divided into a *debit column and a credit column*. A *debit* is something that is owed. For the buyer, a debit entry will be entered for anything charged against or subtracted from his or her account. Likewise, a debit to the seller means a charge against the seller's account. A *credit* is something that is received. For the buyer, a credit entry will be entered for anything received or added to his or her account. Likewise, a credit to the seller means a receivable to the seller's account.

In some instances, a double entry is made, that is, a credit to one of the two parties and a debit to the other, or vice versa. This occurs as, for example, with the purchase price when there is direct transfer of equity from one of the two parties to the other.

The order in which the different line items are listed need not follow any particular pattern, although in most instances the first entry is the purchase price. The last entries are the *amount due from/to buyer to close* the transaction and the *amount due to/from seller to close*.

For some of the line entries, practices vary from jurisdiction to jurisdiction as to who pays what. Exactly who is to pay a particular expense should have been included in the sales agreement and, of course, any discrepancies or misunderstandings will need to be corrected prior to the actual time of closing.

The entries listed and briefly discussed below include those typically found in conjunction with various real estate closings. Not every one of these will appear on any one closing worksheet, and certain ones will vary from jurisdiction to jurisdiction.

Typical Entries

1. *Purchase or Selling Price*. This is the buyer's principal expense. The full amount is entered as a debit to the buyer and as a credit to the seller.

2. *Deposit or Earnest Money*. This is what the buyer has already put up and is a portion of the purchase price. It will be credited to the buyer since the full purchase price was debited to the buyer. This entry does not appear on the seller's statement unless the seller has received the payment from either the broker or buyer.

3. *New Mortgage*. If the property is being partially or entirely financed with a new mortgage, the amount of that mortgage is credited to the buyer. The amount borrowed is the means by which the buyer will pay for part or all of the purchase price.

4. *Assumed Mortgage*. A credit to the buyer and a debit to the seller. The assumption of an existing mortgage means less cash received by the seller than if the property were free and clear of any debt.

5. *Purchase Money Mortgage*. This is treated the same way as an assumed mortgage: a credit to the buyer (an obligation for future payment) and a debit to the seller (since he or she does not receive it in cash at closing).

6. *Mortgage Interest-New Mortgage*. A debit to the buyer. Quite possibly the closing date and the day of the month when the mortgage is due, typically the first day of the month, will not be the same. Therefore, the buyer will need to pay interest on the amount borrowed from the date of closing until the beginning of the next loan payment period (typically the first day of the following month).

7. *Mortgage Interest-Assumed Mortgage*. Interest on an

assumed mortgage must be prorated over the month with the seller paying up to and including the day of closing. If the interest for the particular month was previously paid in advance by the seller, the prorated amount would be debited to the buyer and credited to the seller. For interest payments made in arrears, which is much more often the case, the entry would be a credit to the buyer and a debit to the seller.

8. *Mortgage Interest-Purchase Money Mortgage.* Interest on a purchase money mortgage or any other second mortgage is entered the same as for a new mortgage, namely, debit buyer, credit seller.

9. *Sales Commission.* Typically a debit to the seller; however, if the broker is working for the buyer or for both buyer and seller, a debit entry would also be made to the buyer or both buyer and seller.

10. *Property Tax.* Property taxes are also prorated with the seller paying for the day of closing. If paid in advance by the seller, this entry is a credit to the seller and a debit to the buyer. For taxes paid in arrears, the amount is credited to the buyer and debited to the seller.

11. *Property Insurance.* For the buyer assuming a seller's insurance policy, the prorated amount is credited to the seller and debited to the buyer. If the buyer is purchasing a new policy, the amount is debited to the buyer unless the new policy was paid for prior to closing, in which case no entry for insurance would be made.

12. *Legal Fees.* Various expenses for such things as preparation of the deed, recording of the deed, notary fees, release of existing mortgages and other legal fees are incurred in any conveyance of real estate. Who pays these legal fees varies from jurisdiction to jurisdiction and should be clearly stated in the sales agreement.

13. *Title Examination.* The expense of searching the title and rendering an opinion or abstract of title is normally debited to the purchaser.

14. *Title Insurance.* Often a lender will require the borrower to purchase a title insurance policy. If so, this entry is a debit to the buyer.

15. *Survey.* If the lender requires a survey of the subject property to be conducted as a condition of making the loan, this expense is debited to the borrower.

16. *Appraisal.* Like the survey, an appraisal is often required by the lender and is debited to the buyer.

17. *Credit Report.* This expense of investigating the credit of the borrower is debited to the buyer.

18. *Loan Discount Fee or Placement Fee (Points).* While the amount of this fee varies from jurisdiction to jurisdiction and lender to lender, it is normally paid by the borrower on a conventional loan. However, who is to pay it will be stated in the sales contract.

19. *Document Stamps.* For those jurisdictions requiring the purchase of document stamps before the instrument of conveyance is recorded, the contract should state the person(s) responsible for paying this fee. This debit entry can be to either or both buyer and seller.

20. *Transfer Tax.* As is the case with document stamps, the payment of the transfer tax, if it exists, can be a debit to either or both buyer and seller.

21. *Termite Inspection.* It is quite common for the seller to pay for an inspection for termites or termite damage. This entry is normally debited to the seller.

22. *Water.* If the meter is not read on the day of closing, this expense will be prorated between buyer and seller. If paid in advance, buyer is debited and seller is credited. If paid in arrears, buyer is credited and seller is debited.

23. *Rental Property.* If the subject property is rental property, then any rent or security deposit collected or due must be prorated between buyer and seller. Rent collected in advance is credited to the buyer and debited to the seller. The seller receives prorated rent for the day of closing.

24. *Escrow Accounts.* If the seller has money on deposit with the lender to cover property taxes, hazard insurance or mortgage insurance, this amount is credited to the seller. Likewise, if the lender requires the borrower to establish an escrow account, this amount is debited to the buyer. For an assumed loan where the buyer is "taking over" the escrow account of the seller, the procedure would be to debit the buyer and credit the seller.

25. *Sale of Personal Property (Chattels).* Personal items such as rugs, draperies or yard equipment will be conveyed under a separate bill of sale. However, as an entry on the worksheet, this appears as a debit to the buyer and a credit to the seller.

Subtotals

Once all of the necessary entries have been made each of the four columns is totaled separately.

Balance due to/from Seller

This amount is the difference between the seller's debits and credits. If the credits are greater than the debits (as is almost always the case) the *balance due to seller* is the amount the seller will receive in cash at closing. Debits greater than credits means the seller owes cash in order to close the transaction.

Balance due from/to Buyer

This is the difference between the buyer's debits and credits. If the debits are greater than the credits (as is almost always the case) the *balance due from buyer* is the amount of cash the buyer must have to close the transaction. Credits greater than debits means the buyer will receive cash at closing.

Totals

Once the balance due to/from entry has been made for each of the two parties, the buyer's debits and credits will be equal and the seller's debits and credits will be equal.

Problem B-1

In order to see how various debit and credit entries are made for a typical real estate transaction, the following problem is given as an example. (Note: The completed

Figure B-1

REAL ESTATE LISTING CONTRACT (EXCLUSIVE RIGHT TO SELL)

SALES PRICE **$79,500**   TYPE HOME **one-story ranch**   TOTAL BEDROOMS **3**   TOTAL BATHS **2**
ADDRESS **109 Blackshear Drive**   JURISDICTION OF **DeKalb, Mississippi**
AMT. OF LOAN TO BE ASSUMED $ **45,460**   AS OF WHAT DATE **6/1**   TAXES & INS INCLUDED **yes**   YEARS TO GO **22**   AMOUNT PAYABLE MONTHLY $ **439.16**   TYPE LOAN **9½%**
MORTGAGE COMPANY **Dundee Savings & Loan Assn.**   2nd MORTGAGE
OWNER'S NAME **Dr. and Mrs. G. M. Jeffrey**   PHONES (HOME) _____ (BUSINESS) _____
TENANT'S NAME _____   PHONES (HOME) _____ (BUSINESS) _____
POSSESSION **60 days**   DATE LISTED **6/30/90**   EXCLUSIVE FOR **90 days**   DATE OF EXPIRATION **9/28/90**
LISTING BROKER **A. C. Wicker, Wicker Realty Co.**   PHONE _____   KEY AVAILABLE AT **Wicker Realty**
LISTING SALESMAN **Ms. Sally Houghton**   HOME PHONE _____   HOW TO BE SHOWN **Appointment only.**

ENTRANCE FOYER ☒ CENTER HALL ☐	AGE **15**	AIR CONDITIONING ☒	TYPE KITCHEN CABINETS **wooden**
LIVING ROOM SIZE **18' x 12'** FIREPLACE ☐	ROOFING **shingle**	TOOL HOUSE ☐	TYPE COUNTER TOPS **formica**
DINING ROOM SIZE **12' x 12'**	GARAGE SIZE **carport**	PATIO ☒	EAT-IN SIZE KITCHEN ☒ **Breakfast area**
BEDROOM TOTAL **3** DOWN UP	SIDE DRIVE ☒	CIRCULAR DRIVE ☐	TYPE STOVE ☒ **Electric**
BATHS TOTAL **2** DOWN UP	PORCH ☒ SIDE ☐ REAR ☐	SCREENED ☐	BUILT-IN OVEN & RANGE ☐
DEN SIZE FIREPLACE ☐	FENCED YARD ☐	OUTDOOR GRILL ☐	SEPARATE STOVE INCLUDED ☒
FAMILY ROOM SIZE **11.5' x 20'** FIREPLACE ☒	STORM WINDOWS ☒	STORM DOORS ☒	REFRIGERATOR INCLUDED ☐
RECREATION ROOM SIZE FIREPLACE ☐	CURBS & GUTTERS ☒	SIDEWALKS ☐	DISHWASHER INCLUDED **x built-in**
BASEMENT SIZE **Separate rec. room**	STORM SEWERS ☐	ALLEY ☐	DISPOSAL INCLUDED ☒
NONE ☐ 1/4 ☐ 1/3 ☐ 1/2 ☐ 3/4 ☒ FULL ☐	WATER SUPPLY **city**		DOUBLE SINK ☒ SINGLE SINK ☐
UTILITY ROOM	SEWER ☒ **city**	SEPTIC ☐	STAINLESS STEEL **x** PORCELAIN ☐
TYPE HOT WATER SYSTEM **Gas**	TYPE GAS NATURAL ☒	BOTTLED ☐	WASHER INCLUDED ☐ DRYER INCLUDED ☐
TYPE HEAT **Gas**	WHY SELLING **moving into condo**		LAND ASSESSMENT $
EST. FUEL COST			IMPROVEMENTS $
ATTIC ☒ **floored**	PROPERTY DESCRIPTION		TOTAL ASSESSMENT $ **26,000**
PULL DOWN STAIRWAY ☒ REGULAR STAIRWAY ☐ TRAP DOOR ☐			TAX RATE **3.26 p/$100**
NAME OF BUILDER	LOT SIZE **100 x 290'**		TOTAL ANNUAL TAXES $
SQUARE FOOTAGE **1,960**	LOT NO **44** BLOCK **F** SECTION **6**		Ins.: **$70,000 coverage.**
EXTERIOR OF HOUSE **Brick**	**Jamestown subdivision.**		**($210 annual premium)**

NAME OF SCHOOLS   ELEMENTARY **Clairmont**   JR HIGH **Rockwood**
HIGH **Druid Hills**   PAROCHIAL _____
PUBLIC TRANSPORTATION **one block**
NEAREST SHOPPING AREA **North Dekalb Shopping Mall - within one mile**
REMARKS **Sliding door to concrete patio off DR; washer/dryer connections in kitchen; newly refinished hardwood floors in BR's; includes: carpeting (LR, DR, FR), st. windows, st. doors, shades, curtain rods, elec. stove, TV antenna. Not incl. tagged azalea by porch.**

Date: **June 30, 1990**

In consideration of the services of **A. C. Wicker** (herein called "Broker") to be rendered to the undersigned (herein called "Owner"), and of the promise of Broker to make reasonable efforts to obtain a Purchaser therefor, Owner hereby lists with Broker the real estate and all improvements thereon which are described above (all herein called "the property"), and Owner hereby grants to Broker the exclusive and irrevocable right to sell such property from 12:00 Noon on **June 30**, 19**90** until 12:00 Midnight on **September 28**, 19**90** (herein called "period of time"), for the price of **Seventy-Nine Thousand Five Hundred** Dollars ($ **79,500**) or for such other price and upon such other terms (including exchange) as Owner may subsequently authorize during the period of time.

It is understood by Owner that the above sum or any other price subsequently authorized by Owner shall include a cash fee of **8** per cent of such price or other price which shall be payable by Owner to Broker upon consummation by any Purchaser or Purchasers of a valid contract of sale of the property during the period of time and whether or not Broker was a procuring cause of any such contract of sale.

If the property is sold or exchanged by Owner, or by Broker or by any other person to any Purchaser to whom the property was shown by Broker or any representative of Broker within sixty (60) days after the expiration of the period of time mentioned above, Owner agrees to pay to Broker a cash fee which shall be the same percentage of the purchase price as the percentage mentioned above.

Broker is hereby authorized by Owner to place a "For Sale" sign on the property and to remove all signs of other brokers or salesmen during the period of time, and Owner hereby agrees to make the property available to Broker at all reasonable hours for the purpose of showing it to prospective Purchasers.

Owner agrees to convey the property to the Purchaser by deed with the usual covenants of title and free and clear from all encumbrances, tenancies, liens (for taxes or otherwise), but subject to applicable restrictive covenants of record. Owner acknowledges receipt of a copy of this agreement.

WITNESS the following signature(s) and seal(s):

Date Signed **June 30, 1990**   _____ (Owner)
Listing Agent **X**
Address **1154 Larch Lane**   Telephone _____   _____ (Owner)

Figure B–2

REAL ESTATE SALES CONTRACT (OFFER TO PURCHASE AGREEMENT)

This AGREEMENT made as of _____ July 15 _____, 19 90 .

among ____Mr. and Mrs. Robert Harrison_____ (herein called "Purchaser").

and ____Dr. and Mrs. G. M. Jeffery_____ (herein called "Seller").

and ____A. C. Wicker_____ (herein called "Broker").

provides that Purchaser agrees to buy through Broker as agent for Seller, and Seller agrees to sell the following described real estate, and all improvements thereon, located in the jurisdiction of ____Dekalb, Texas_____.

(all herein called "the property"): ___Lot 44, Block F, Section 6, Jamestown Subdivision. Included in sale: all carpeting (LR, DR, FR), storm windows, st. doors, shades, curtain rods, elec. stove, TV antenna. Not incl: azalea by porch___ (street address): 109 Blackshear Drive

1. The purchase price of the property is ___Seventy-Six Thousand--------------------------------
Dollars ($ __76,000.00__), and such purchase price shall be paid as follows: $5,000 deposit acknowledged in Paragraph 2, $45,325.78 assumption of existing mortgage (as of August 1), $12,000 purchase money mortgage, & $13,674.22 additional cash at settlement.

2. Purchaser has made a deposit of ___Five Thousand-----------------------------------___ Dollars ($ __5,000.00__) with Broker, receipt of which is hereby acknowledged, and such deposit shall be held by Broker in escrow until the date of settlement and then applied to the purchase price, or returned to Purchaser if the title to the property is not marketable.

3. Seller agrees to convey the property to Purchaser by Deed with the usual covenants of title and free and clear from all monetary encumbrances, tenancies, liens (for taxes or otherwise), except as may be otherwise provided above, but subject to applicable restrictive covenants of record. Seller further agrees to deliver possession of the property to Purchaser on the date of settlement and to pay the expense of preparing the deed of conveyance.

4. Settlement shall be made at ___Hipp and Hipp, Attorney at Law_____ on or before ___August 20___, 19 90 , or as soon thereafter as title can be examined and necessary documents prepared, with allowance of a reasonable time for Seller to correct any defects reported by the title examiner.

5. All taxes, interest, rent, and impound escrow deposits, if any, shall be prorated as of the date of settlement.

6. All risk of loss or damage to the property by fire, windstorm, casualty, or other cause is assumed by Seller until the date of settlement.

7. Purchaser and Seller agree that Broker was the sole procuring cause of this Contract of Purchase, and Seller agrees to pay Broker for services rendered a cash fee of ___8___ per cent of the purchase price. If either Purchaser or Seller defaults under such Contract, such defaulting party shall be liable for the cash fee of Broker and any expenses incurred by the non-defaulting party in connection with this transaction.

Subject to: ___Buyer assuming existing mortgage of $45,325.78 as of August 1, 1990, int. rate of .095 per annum. Seller taking back a $12,000 purchase money mortgage, of .10 per annum, $125 per month remaining balance due in 6 years. Seller to provide a certificate of termite inspection from approved exterminator.___

8. Purchaser represents that an inspection satisfactory to Purchaser has been made of the property, and Purchaser agrees to accept the property in its present condition except as may be otherwise provided in the description of the property above.

9. This Contract of Purchase constitutes the entire agreement among the parties and may not be modified or changed except by written instrument executed by all of the parties, including Broker.

10. This Contract of Purchase shall be construed, interpreted, and applied according to the law of the jurisdiction of ___Texas___ and shall be binding upon and shall inure to the benefit of the heirs, personal representatives, successors, and assigns of the parties.

All parties to this agreement acknowledge receipt of a certified copy.

WITNESS the following signatures:

X_____ Seller	X_____ Purchaser
X_____ Seller	X_____ Purchaser
X_____ Broker	

Deposit Rec'd $ __5,000.00__

Personal Check   Cash

(Cashier's Check)   Company Check

Sales Agent:

Preparation of Settlement Statement Worksheet

Figure B–3

SETTLEMENT STATEMENT WORKSHEET

Property Address _____   Date of Contract _____

Buyer _____   Broker _____

Seller _____   _____

SETTLEMENT DATE:	BUYER'S STATEMENT		SELLER'S STATEMENT	
	DEBIT	CREDIT	DEBIT	CREDIT

244   Appendix B

Figure B–4. Settlement Statement Worksheet

SETTLEMENT STATEMENT WORKSHEET

Property Address 109 Blackshear Drive   **Date of Contract** July 15, 1990

Buyer Mr. & Mrs. Robert Harrison   **Broker** Mr. A. C. Wicker

Seller Dr. & Mrs. G. M. Jeffery

SETTLEMENT DATE: August 20, 1990	BUYER'S STATEMENT		SELLER'S STATEMENT	
	DEBIT	CREDIT	DEBIT	CREDIT
Purchase Price	76,000.00			76,000.00
Earnest Money Deposit		5,000.00		
Assumed Mortgage Balance		45,325.78	45,325.78	
Mortgage Interest (8/1–8/20)		239.22	239.22	
Purchase Money Mortgage		12,000.00	12,000.00	
PMM Interest (8/21–8/30)	33.33			33.33
Sales Commission			6,080.00	
Property Taxes		117.71	117.71	
Property Insurance	457.45			457.45
Termite Inspection			30.00	
Water		10.00	10.00	
Attorney Fees	200.00			
Sale of Personal Property	335.00			335.00
SUBTOTALS	77,025.78	62,692.71	63,802.71	76,825.78
Due From Buyer To Close		14,333.07		
Due To Seller To Close			13,023.07	
TOTALS	$77,025.78	$77,025.78	$76,825.78	$76,825.78

Preparation of Settlement Statement Worksheet

listing agreement and sales agreement are those used in Problem A–1, Appendix A.) Besides the information provided in the listing agreement (Figure B–1) and the sales agreement (Figure B–2) the following information is given:

Closing took place on August 20, 1990. Property taxes due July 1, 1990, for the next twelve months were not paid. A three-year insurance policy on the property which expires August 16, 1992, and costs $690 will be assumed by the Harrisons. The first monthly payment on the purchase money mortgage is due October 1 and the first day of each month thereafter. Interest on the PMM until September 1 is due at closing. Attorney Hipp is charging the Harrisons $200 to close the transaction, and the termite inspection is $30. The quarterly water bill is $18 paid in arrears, and the June 30 bill was paid. A separate bill of sale covering the following personal property has been prepared: pool table ($100), table ($50), 8 chairs ($20 per chair) and lawn furniture ($25).

Use the blank settlement statement worksheet (Figure B–3) to complete this problem. Assume 30 day months and complete the worksheet on the basis of the information given, even if some of that information is different from common procedures in your jurisdiction.

Solution and Comments

If you correctly interpreted the information given, the completed worksheet should contain the information shown in Figure B–4. If yours does not contain the same information, perhaps you should work the problem again.

The following entries and calculations were made:

1. *Purchase Price.* $76,000 as per offer to purchase agreement. The full amount was debited to the buyer and credited to the seller.
2. *Earnest Money Deposit.* $5,000 as per offer to purchase agreement. Note Paragraph 2 on the sales agreement.
3. *Mortgage Balance.* $45,325.78 as per offer to purchase agreement. Note that this is as of August 1, 1990.
4. *Mortgage Interest.* $239.22
   August 1 Outstanding Balance $45,325.78
   September 1 Next Payment
   Seller owes 20 days interest on $45,325.78 at .095 interest
   $45,325.78 × .095 ÷ 12 = $358.83 per month
   $358.83 ÷ 30 = $11.961 per day
   20 days (August 1–August 20) = $11.961 × 20 = $239.22
5. *Purchase Money Mortgage.* $12,000 as per offer to purchase agreement
6. *PMM Interest.* $33.33
   First monthly payment is due October 1
   At closing interest up to September 1 is due
   $12,000 × .10 ÷ 12 = $100.00 interest per month
   $100 ÷ 30 = $3.333 interest per day
   10 days (August 21–August 30) = $3.333 × 10 = $33.33
7. *Sales Commission.* $6,080
   $76,000 × .08 = $6,080

8. *Property Tax.* $117.71
   Annual tax due July 1, 1990, was not paid
   Annual tax = $26,000 × $3.26 / $100 = $847.60
   Monthly tax = $847.60 ÷ 12 = $70.633
   Daily tax = $70.633 ÷ 30 = $2.354
   Time Expired 1 month 20 days = $117.71
9. *Property Insurance.* $457.45
   Three-year policy $690 expires August 16, 1992
   Yearly $230 Monthly $19.166 Daily $.6388
   Unexpired Period 1 Year 11 Months 26 Days = $457.45
10. *Termite Inspection.* $30
11. *Water.* $10
    $18 for 3 months
    June 30 paid
    September 30 will be paid again
    1 Month 20 Days used by seller
    Monthly $6.00 Daily $.20 = $10
12. *Attorney Fees.* $200
13. *Sale of Personal Property.* $335
    $100 Pool table
     50 Table
    160 Eight chairs
     25 Lawn furniture
    $335
    Due from Buyer to Close: $14,333.07
    Due to Seller to Close: $13,023.07

PRACTICE PROBLEM (PROBLEM B–2)

Complete the settlement statement worksheet (Figure B–5) and then answer the 25 questions dealing with the problem. The necessary information for answering these questions can be found in the listing agreement (Figure B–6), the sales agreement (Figure B–7) and the following additional information:

The Skaggs obtained the necessary financing, and closing was August 1, 1990. Since the first monthly payment on the new mortgage is not due until October 1, 1990, the buyer must pay 29 days interest on the new mortgage at closing for the month of August. The lender is also requiring the Skaggs to place three months' property tax in escrow. Property taxes for the fiscal year beginning July 1, 1990, were paid by the Chapmans who also have a two-year insurance policy purchased June 14, 1989 for $280, which is to be assumed by the Skaggs.

Other Expenses:

Termite Inspection, $25

Document Stamps, $.55 per $500 of purchase price or fraction thereof

Transfer Tax, ½% of purchase price

Title Exam and Insurance, $200 plus ½% of purchase price

Survey, $60

Appraisal, $70

Credit Report, $15

Other Legal Fees For Buyer, $35

(Answers on page 328.)

Figure B–5

SETTLEMENT STATEMENT WORKSHEET

Property Address _____   Date of Contract _____

Buyer _____   Broker _____

Seller _____   _____

SETTLEMENT DATE:	BUYER'S STATEMENT		SELLER'S STATEMENT	
	DEBIT	CREDIT	DEBIT	CREDIT

Preparation of Settlement Statement Worksheet

Figure B-6

REAL ESTATE LISTING CONTRACT (EXCLUSIVE RIGHT TO SELL)

SALES PRICE $42,000.00   TYPE HOME Ranch   TOTAL BEDROOMS 3   TOTAL BATHS 1½
ADDRESS Summit View Drive   JURISDICTION OF Martin County, Mississippi
AMT. OF LOAN TO BE ASSUMED $ 18,450.00   AS OF WHAT DATE 3/1/90   TAXES & INS. INCLUDED No   YEARS TO GO ___   AMOUNT PAYABLE MONTHLY $ 147.76   11% TYPE LOAN FHA
MORTGAGE COMPANY First Savings & Loan, Martinsville
OWNER'S NAME Robert & Evalyn Chapman   PHONES (HOME) ___ (BUSINESS) ___
TENANT'S NAME ___   PHONES (HOME) ___ (BUSINESS) ___
POSSESSION within 90 days   DATE LISTED 3/7/90   EXCLUSIVE FOR 60 days   DATE OF EXPIRATION 5/6/90
LISTING BROKER Greg Sanderfur & Assoc. Realty   PHONE ___   KEY AVAILABLE AT ___
LISTING SALESMAN Helen Pitt   HOME PHONE ___   HOW TO BE SHOWN call first

ENTRANCE FOYER ☐	CENTER HALL ☐	AGE 12	AIR CONDITIONING ☐	TYPE KITCHEN CABINETS
LIVING ROOM SIZE 14' x 15'	FIREPLACE ☐	ROOFING Comp. Shingle	TOOL HOUSE ☐	TYPE COUNTER TOPS
DINING ROOM SIZE 12' x 10'		~~CARPORT~~ x Carport	PATIO ☐	EAT-IN SIZE KITCHEN ☐
BEDROOM TOTAL 3 DOWN	UP	SIDE DRIVE x paved	CIRCULAR DRIVE ☐	TYPE STOVE x Gas
BATHS TOTAL 1½ DOWN	UP	PORCH ☐ SIDE ☐ REAR ☐	SCREENED ☐	BUILT-IN OVEN & RANGE ☐
DEN SIZE	FIREPLACE ☐	FENCED YARD	OUTDOOR GRILL ☐	SEPARATE STOVE INCLUDED x
FAMILY ROOM SIZE	FIREPLACE ☐	STORM WINDOWS ☐	STORM DOORS ☐	REFRIGERATOR INCLUDED
RECREATION ROOM SIZE 30' x 17'	FIREPLACE x	CURBS & GUTTERS ☐	SIDEWALKS	DISHWASHER INCLUDED x portable
BASEMENT SIZE 30' x 34'		STORM SEWERS ☐	ALLEY ☐	DISPOSAL INCLUDED ☐
NONE ☐ 1/4 ☐ 1/3 ☐ 1/2 ☐ 3/4 ☐ FULL x		WATER SUPPLY City		DOUBLE SINK ☐ SINGLE SINK ☐
UTILITY ROOM		SEWER x City	SEPTIC ☐	STAINLESS STEEL ☐ PORCELAIN ☐
TYPE HOT WATER SYSTEM 40 gal. elec.		TYPE GAS Natural	BOTTLED ☐	WASHER INCLUDED ☐ DRYER INCLUDED ☐
TYPE HEAT FHA		WHY SELLING Moving to another		LAND ASSESSMENT $ 3,000.00
EST. FUEL COST $68 per month		city.		IMPROVEMENTS $ 15,000.00
ATTIC x 12" insulation		PROPERTY DESCRIPTION		TOTAL ASSESSMENT $
PULL DOWN STAIRWAY ☐ REGULAR STAIRWAY ☐ TRAP DOOR x		(1½ mi. outside city limits)		TAX RATE
NAME OF BUILDER		LOT SIZE 80' x 110'		TOTAL ANNUAL TAXES $ 518.40
SQUARE FOOTAGE		LOT NO 17 BLOCK A SECTION Mountain View subdivision.
EXTERIOR OF HOUSE Brick & Frame construction - good condition.

NAME OF SCHOOLS   ELEMENTARY Conway   JR HIGH Pleasant View
HIGH Martin County   PAROCHIAL ___
PUBLIC TRANSPORTATION None
NEAREST SHOPPING AREA Madison Square - ½ mile
REMARKS Included in sale: A/C in bedroom, portable dishwasher, gas stove.
Not included in sale: Refrigerator, gas grill, tagged bushes.

Date: March 7, 1990

In consideration of the services of Greg Sanderfur & Assoc. (herein called "Broker") to be rendered to the undersigned (herein called "Owner"), and of the promise of Broker to make reasonable efforts to obtain a Purchaser therefor, Owner hereby lists with Broker the real estate and all improvements thereon which are described above (all herein called "the property"), and Owner hereby grants to Broker the exclusive and irrevocable right to sell such property from 12:00 Noon on March 7, 1990 until 12:00 Midnight on May 6, 19 90 (herein called "period of time"), for the price of Forty-Two Thousand------------------ Dollars ($ 42,000.00) or for such other price and upon such other terms (including exchange) as Owner may subsequently authorize during the period of time.

It is understood by Owner that the above sum or any other price subsequently authorized by Owner shall include a cash fee of 7 per cent of such price or other price which shall be payable by Owner to Broker upon consummation by any Purchaser or Purchasers of a valid contract of sale of the property during the period of time and whether or not Broker was a procuring cause of any such contract of sale.

If the property is sold or exchanged by Owner, or by Broker or by any other person to any Purchaser to whom the property was shown by Broker or any representative of Broker within sixty (60) days after the expiration of the period of time mentioned above, Owner agrees to pay to Broker a cash fee which shall be the same percentage of the purchase price as the percentage mentioned above.

Broker is hereby authorized by Owner to place a "For Sale" sign on the property and to remove all signs of other brokers or salesmen during the period of time, and Owner hereby agrees to make the property available to Broker at all reasonable hours for the purpose of showing it to prospective Purchasers.

Owner agrees to convey the property to the Purchaser by deed with the usual covenants of title and free and clear from all encumbrances, tenancies, liens (for taxes or otherwise), but subject to applicable restrictive covenants of record. Owner acknowledges receipt of a copy of this agreement.

WITNESS the following signature(s) and seal(s):

Date Signed March 7, 1990   X _____ (Owner)
Listing Agent _____ X
Address _____ Telephone _____   X _____ (Owner)

Figure B–7

REAL ESTATE SALES CONTRACT (OFFER TO PURCHASE AGREEMENT)

This AGREEMENT made as of _____ March 22 _____, 19 90 .

among   Donald and Shirley Skaggs _____ (herein called "Purchaser"),

and   Robert and Evalyn Chapman _____ (herein called "Seller"),

and   Greg Sanderfur _____ (herein called "Broker"),

provides that Purchaser agrees to buy through Broker as agent for Seller, and Seller agrees to sell the following described real estate, and all improvements thereon, located in the jurisdiction of   Martin County, Kentucky

(all herein called "the property"): Lot 17, Block A, Mountain View Subdivision. Included in sale: all shrubs & bushes, gas grill, A/C in bedroom, portable dishwasher, gas stove. Not incl: refrigerator. _____ (street address); Summit View Drive

1. The purchase price of the property is Thirty-Seven Thousand Five Hundred----------------------- Dollars ($ 37,500.00), and such purchase price shall be paid as follows: $1,500.00 deposit acknowledged in Paragraph 2, $28,000 new mortgage, $8,000 additional cash at closing.

2. Purchaser has made a deposit of One Thousand Five Hundred---------------- Dollars ($ 1,500.00) with Broker, receipt of which is hereby acknowledged, and such deposit shall be held by Broker in escrow until the date of settlement and then applied to the purchase price, or returned to Purchaser if the title to the property is not marketable.

3. Seller agrees to convey the property to Purchaser by Deed with the usual covenants of title and free and clear from all monetary encumbrances, tenancies, liens (for taxes or otherwise), except as may be otherwise provided above, but subject to applicable restrictive covenants of record. Seller further agrees to deliver possession of the property to Purchaser on the date of settlement and to pay the expense of preparing the deed of conveyance.

4. Settlement shall be made at   Martinsville Building and Loan Association   on or before August 1 _____, 19 90 , or as soon thereafter as title can be examined and necessary documents prepared, with allowance of a reasonable time for Seller to correct any defects reported by the title examiner.

5. All taxes, interest, rent, and impound escrow deposits, if any, shall be prorated as of the date of settlement.

6. All risk of loss or damage to the property by fire, windstorm, casualty, or other cause is assumed by Seller until the date of settlement.

7. Purchaser and Seller agree that Broker was the sole procuring cause of this Contract of Purchase, and Seller agrees to pay Broker for services rendered a cash fee of ___7___ per cent of the purchase price. If either Purchaser or Seller defaults under such Contract, such defaulting party shall be liable for the cash fee of Broker and any expenses incurred by the non-defaulting party in connection with this transaction.

Subject to: Buyer acquiring new conventional mortgage of $28,000, interest rate not to exceed 12% 30-year life. Seller to provide a certificate of termite inspection from licensed termite inspection company. Cost of transfer tax and document stamps to be divided equally between buyer and seller.

8. Purchaser represents that an inspection satisfactory to Purchaser has been made of the property, and Purchaser agrees to accept the property in its present condition except as may be otherwise provided in the description of the property above.

9. This Contract of Purchase constitutes the entire agreement among the parties and may not be modified or changed except by written instrument executed by all of the parties, including Broker.

10. This Contract of Purchase shall be construed, interpreted, and applied according to the law of the jurisdiction of   Kentucky   and shall be binding upon and shall inure to the benefit of the heirs, personal representatives, successors, and assigns of the parties.

All parties to this agreement acknowledge receipt of a certified copy.

WITNESS the following signatures:

_____ X   Seller   _____ X   Purchaser

_____ X   Seller   _____ X   Purchaser

_____ X   Broker

Deposit Rec'd $ 1,500.00

(Personal Check)   Cash

Cashier's Check   Company Check

Sales Agent:

Preparation of Settlement Statement Worksheet

QUESTIONS (PROBLEM B-2)

1. The property tax rate is
   A. $1.44/$100
   B. $2.88/$100
   C. $3.46/$100
   D. $1.73/$100

2. If Greg Sanderfur receives 50% of the total commission, he will receive
   A. $1,225.00
   B. $1,312.25
   C. $1,470.00
   D. $2,625.00

3. The lot size is approximately
   A. one-fifth acre
   B. one-fourth acre
   C. one-third acre
   D. one-half acre

4. The existing mortgage is
   A. conventional
   B. VA
   C. FHA
   D. past due

5. If the Chapmans escrowed their property taxes each month, the total monthly payment to First Federal Savings and Loan of Martinsville would be
   A. $147.76
   B. $160.86
   C. $190.96
   D. $206.84

6. The purchaser made a deposit of
   I. $1,500
   II. 4% of the asking price
   A. I only
   B. II only
   C. Both I and II
   D. Neither I nor II

7. The offer to purchase agreement includes
   I. a portable dishwasher
   II. a gas grill on the patio
   A. I only
   B. II only
   C. Both I and II
   D. Neither I nor II

8. In order to fully carpet the living room and dining room, how many square yards of carpeting would be needed?
   A. 110
   B. 36
   C. 330
   D. 37

9. How much cash is due from the buyer at closing to close the transaction?
   A. $8,000.00
   B. $9,677.62
   C. $10,113.12
   D. None of these is within $30.00

10. The total debit to the seller for transfer tax and document stamps is
    A. $93.75
    B. $114.38
    C. $118.00
    D. $228.76

11. The cost of examining the title and insuring the title is
    A. credited to the seller
    B. debited to the seller
    C. credited to the buyer
    D. debited to the buyer

12. Had the property sold for the asking price, the total debit to the Chapmans for transfer tax and document stamps would have been
    A. $46.20
    B. $114.39
    C. $128.10
    D. $256.20

13. When the Chapmans listed the house, they wanted to give possession by
    A. June 1
    B. July 1
    C. August 1
    D. September 1

14. The house includes a
    A. garage
    B. carport
    C. fenced yard
    D. circular drive

15. The loan-to-value ratio on the Skaggs' mortgage is
    A. 134%
    B. 66%
    C. 80%
    D. 75%

16. What is the outstanding balance owed First Savings and Loan of Martinsville by the Chapmans on August 1?
    A. $18,450.00
    B. $18,387.12
    C. $18,305.13
    D. $18,106.16

17. Had property taxes for the current fiscal year not been paid, what entry would have been made at closing?
    A. Debit buyer $473.76; credit seller $473.76
    B. Credit buyer $473.76; debit seller $473.76
    C. Credit buyer $44.64; debit seller $44.64
    D. Debit buyer $44.64; credit seller $44.64

18. If the annual property insurance rate is $3.50 per $1000, how much coverage is presently carried?
    A. $40,000
    B. $37,500
    C. $42,000
    D. $80,000

19. The total amount of cash the seller will leave closing with is
    A. $9,609.85
    B. $16,412.19
    C. $33,331.09
    D. $17,025.96

20. Total credits to the seller are
    A. $38,095.47
    B. $21,069.51
    C. $29,500.00
    D. $39,109.85

21. The mortgage interest due on the new mortgage October 1 is
    A. $95
    B. $180
    C. $280
    D. $305

22. The listing obtained by Helen Pitt was
    A. open
    B. net
    C. exclusive agency
    D. exclusive right to sell

23. The earnest money deposit of $1,500 was
    I. held by the broker
    II. debited to the seller
    A. I only
    B. II only
    C. Both I and II
    D. Neither I nor II

Appendix B

24. Had the Skaggs not been able to acquire a new 30-year conventional mortgage of $28,000, interest rate not to exceed 12%
    I. they could void the contract
    II. the broker would still be due a commission
    A. I only   C. Both I and II
    B. II only   D. Neither I nor II
25. There is a contingency clause for
    I. seller obtaining a 30-year, $28,000, 12% mortgage
    II. seller providing a certificate of termite inspection
    A. I only   C. Both I and II
    B. II only   D. Neither I nor II

PRACTICE PROBLEM (PROBLEM B–3)

Complete the settlement statement worksheet (Figure B–8) and then answer the 25 questions dealing with the problem. The necessary information for answering these questions can be found in the listing agreement (Figure B–9), the sales agreement (Figure B–10) and the following:

Mr. deValinger signed a new one-year lease on February 7 and closing took place March 1, 1990. Mr. Stevens obtains a 25-year, $28,500 loan at 12% interest, and since the first payment is not due until May 1, LaGrange Bank and Trust charges him 29 days' interest at closing to cover the month of March. The bank requires him to establish an escrow account beginning with 4 months' insurance premiums and 10 months' property tax. Taxes for the fiscal year beginning July 1, 1988, were not paid, nor have the taxes for the current fiscal year been paid. Mr. deValinger made a $200 security deposit when he rented the house, and Mr. Hipp has agreed to pay the transfer tax. A one-year home insurance policy purchased November 10, 1989, for $144 will be assumed, and the city water charge is $16 per quarter paid in arrears with the last payment occurring at the end of 1989.

Also:

Transfer Tax, $20 plus 1% of purchase price
Title Exam and Insurance, $225 plus ½% of purchase price
Survey, $70
Personal Property Sold To Mr. Stevens by Mr. Hipp, $250

(Answers on page 328.)

QUESTIONS (PROBLEM B–3)

1. The annual property tax is
   A. $86   C. $344
   B. $258   D. $360
2. If the property sold for the listed price, the total commission would be
   A. $3,040   C. $2,328
   B. $2,660   D. $2,280
3. The amount of principal reduced by the first month's payment on the purchase money mortgage is
   A. $27.50   C. $37.50
   B. $32.50   D. $65.00
4. The property tax is prorated on the closing statement worksheet as a
   I. debit to the buyer
   II. credit to the seller
   A. I only   C. Both I and II
   B. II only   D. Neither I nor II
5. The property insurance is prorated as a
   I. debit to the buyer
   II. credit to the seller
   A. I only   C. Both I and II
   B. II only   D. Neither I nor II
6. The first mortgage of $28,500 is shown as a
   I. credit to the buyer
   II. debit to the seller
   A. I only   C. Both I and II
   B. II only   D. Neither I nor II
7. The balance due from the buyer to close is
   A. $0   C. $2,000.00
   B. $659.64   D. $2,136.42
8. The total of the seller's credits is
   A. $38,000.00   C. $39,375.89
   B. $38,349.60   D. $39,616.14
9. If the tax rate was increased by 50%, the monthly escrow necessary to pay the annual tax would be
   A. $28.67   C. $43.00
   B. $42.18   D. $57.33
10. The unpaid property tax mentioned in the narrative is a
    I. credit to the buyer
    II. debit to the buyer
    A. I only   C. Both I and II
    B. II only   D. Neither I nor II
11. Should the property suffer a casualty loss on February 28, the loss would be borne by the
    I. buyer
    II. seller
    A. I only   C. Both I and II
    B. II only   D. Neither I nor II
12. The amount due to the seller to close is
    A. $39,375.89   C. $29,103.14
    B. $36,616.14   D. $27,004.48
13. The amount of the property tax proration is
    A. $344.00   C. $545.62
    B. $457.70   D. $574.28

Preparation of Settlement Statement Worksheet 251

Solution to Problem B-2

SETTLEMENT STATEMENT WORKSHEET

Property Address __Summit View Drive__ Date of Contract __March 22, 1990__

Buyer __Donald & Shirley Skaggs__ Broker __Greg Sanderfur__

Seller __Robert & Evalyn Chapman__

SETTLEMENT DATE: August 1, 1990	BUYER'S STATEMENT		SELLER'S STATEMENT	
	DEBIT	CREDIT	DEBIT	CREDIT
Purchase Price	37,500.00			37,500.00
Earnest Money Deposit		1,500.00		
New Mortgage		28,000.00		
Mortgage Interest (8/2-8/30)	270.67			
Loan Balance			18,305.13	
Sales Commission			2,625.00	
Property Tax	473.76			473.76
Property Insurance	121.71			121.71
Termite Inspection			25.00	
Transfer Tax	93.75		93.75	
Document Stamps	20.63		20.63	
Title Exam and Title Insurance	387.50			
Survey	60.00			
Appraisal	70.00			
Credit Report	15.00			
Tax Escrow	129.60			
Legal Fees	35.00			
SUBTOTALS	$39,177.62	29,500.00	21,069.51	38,095.47
Due From Buyer To Close		$9,677.62		
Due To Seller To Close			17,025.96	
TOTALS	$39,177.62	$39,177.62	$38,095.47	$38,095.47

Figure B–8

SETTLEMENT STATEMENT WORKSHEET

Property Address _____   Date of Contract _____

Buyer _____   Broker _____

Seller _____   _____

SETTLEMENT DATE:	BUYER'S STATEMENT		SELLER'S STATEMENT	
	DEBIT	CREDIT	DEBIT	CREDIT

Preparation of Settlement Statement Worksheet

Figure B-9

REAL ESTATE LISTING CONTRACT (EXCLUSIVE RIGHT TO SELL)

SALES PRICE $38,000.00   TYPE HOME Cape Cod Colonial   TOTAL BEDROOMS 2   TOTAL BATHS 1
ADDRESS 506 Park Avenue   JURISDICTION OF LaGrange, Indiana
AMT. OF LOAN TO BE ASSUMED $ _____   AS OF WHAT DATE _____   TAXES & INS INCLUDED _____   YEARS TO GO _____   AMOUNT PAYABLE MONTHLY $ _____ @ _____   TYPE LOAN _____
MORTGAGE COMPANY _____   2nd MORTGAGE _____
OWNER'S NAME Mr. P. Seale Hipp   PHONES (HOME) _____ (BUSINESS) _____
TENANT'S NAME Mr. Ronald J. deValinger   PHONES (HOME) _____ (BUSINESS) _____
POSSESSION ASAP   DATE LISTED 1/10/90   EXCLUSIVE FOR 90 days   DATE OF EXPIRATION 4/10/90
LISTING BROKER Mr. Richard T. Walters   PHONE _____   KEY AVAILABLE AT _____
LISTING SALESMAN _____   HOME PHONE _____   HOW TO BE SHOWN _____

ENTRANCE FOYER ☐   CENTER HALL ☒   AGE 30   AIR CONDITIONING ☐   TYPE KITCHEN CABINETS wooden
LIVING ROOM SIZE 12' x 15'   FIREPLACE ☒ br   ROOFING shingles   TOOL HOUSE ☐   TYPE COUNTER TOPS tempered hardwood
DINING ROOM SIZE 12' x 11'   GARAGE SIZE _____   PATIO ☐   EAT-IN SIZE KITCHEN ☒
BEDROOM TOTAL 2 DOWN _____ UP   SIDE DRIVE ☒   CIRCULAR DRIVE ☐   TYPE STOVE ☐
BATHS TOTAL 1 DOWN _____ UP   PORCH ☐ SIDE ☐ REAR ☐   SCREENED ☒   BUILT-IN OVEN & RANGE ☒
DEN SIZE _____   FIREPLACE ☐   FENCED YARD picket   OUTDOOR GRILL ☐   SEPARATE STOVE INCLUDED ☐
FAMILY ROOM SIZE _____   FIREPLACE ☐   STORM WINDOWS ☒ screens   STORM DOORS ☐   REFRIGERATOR INCLUDED ☐
RECREATION ROOM SIZE _____   FIREPLACE ☐   CURBS & GUTTERS ☒   SIDEWALKS ☒   DISHWASHER INCLUDED ☒
BASEMENT SIZE _____   STORM SEWERS ☒   ALLEY ☐   DISPOSAL INCLUDED ☒
NONE ☐ 1/4 ☐ 1/3 ☐ 1/2 ☒ 3/4 ☐ FULL ☐   WATER SUPPLY city   DOUBLE SINK ☒   SINGLE SINK ☐
UTILITY ROOM _____   SEWER ☒ city   SEPTIC ☐   STAINLESS STEEL ☒   PORCELAIN ☐
TYPE HOT WATER SYSTEM 40 gal. gas   TYPE GAS NATURAL ☒   BOTTLED ☐   WASHER INCLUDED ☐ DRYER INCLUDED ☐
TYPE HEAT Gas forced air furnace   WHY SELLING Disposing of invest.   LAND ASSESSMENT $ 4,056
EST. FUEL COST _____   IMPROVEMENTS $ 12,170
ATTIC ☒ Bath roughed in.   PROPERTY DESCRIPTION _____   TOTAL ASSESSMENT $ 16,226
PULL DOWN STAIRWAY ☐   REGULAR STAIRWAY ☒   TRAP DOOR ☐   TAX RATE $2.12 p/$100
NAME OF BUILDER _____   LOT SIZE 55' x 100'   TOTAL ANNUAL TAXES $ 344
SQUARE FOOTAGE 1,250   LOT NO 6   BLOCK A   SECTION College View Estates
EXTERIOR OF HOUSE Natural shingles, shutters, gutters - good condition.
NAME OF SCHOOLS ELEMENTARY Park Avenue - ½ block   JR HIGH Broad Street - 2 blocks
HIGH LaGrange City - 1 mile   PAROCHIAL _____
PUBLIC TRANSPORTATION Not on bus line
NEAREST SHOPPING AREA LaGrange Plaza - 1 mile
REMARKS New vinyl floors in kitchen. Both bedrooms carpeted w/window air conditioners. Tile bath. Seller will take back purchase money mortgage. Rent - $175 per mo. Lease expires 3/31/90

Date: January 10, 1990

In consideration of the services of Richard T. Walters (herein called "Broker") to be rendered to the undersigned (herein called "Owner"), and of the promise of Broker to make reasonable efforts to obtain a Purchaser therefor, Owner hereby lists with Broker the real estate and all improvements thereon which are described above (all herein called "the property"), and Owner hereby grants to Broker the exclusive and irrevocable right to sell such property from 12:00 Noon on January 10, 19 90 until 12:00 Midnight on April 10, 19 90 (herein called "period of time"), for the price of Thirty-Eight Thousand-------------- Dollars ($ 38,000.00) or for such other price and upon such other terms (including exchange) as Owner may subsequently authorize during the period of time.

It is understood by Owner that the above sum or any other price subsequently authorized by Owner shall include a cash fee of 7 per cent of such price or other price which shall be payable by Owner to Broker upon consummation by any Purchaser or Purchasers of a valid contract of sale of the property during the period of time and whether or not Broker was a procuring cause of any such contract of sale.

If the property is sold or exchanged by Owner, or by Broker or by any other person to any Purchaser to whom the property was shown by Broker or any representative of Broker within sixty (60) days after the expiration of the period of time mentioned above, Owner agrees to pay to Broker a cash fee which shall be the same percentage of the purchase price as the percentage mentioned above.

Broker is hereby authorized by Owner to place a "For Sale" sign on the property and to remove all signs of other brokers or salesmen during the period of time, and Owner hereby agrees to make the property available to Broker at all reasonable hours for the purpose of showing it to prospective Purchasers.

Owner agrees to convey the property to the Purchaser by deed with the usual covenants of title and free and clear from all encumbrances, tenancies, liens (for taxes or otherwise), but subject to applicable restrictive covenants of record. Owner acknowledges receipt of a copy of this agreement.

WITNESS the following signature(s) and seal(s):

Date Signed January 10, 1990   X _____ (Owner)
Listing Agent _____ X
Address _____ Telephone _____   _____ (Owner)

Figure B–10

REAL ESTATE SALES CONTRACT (OFFER TO PURCHASE AGREEMENT)

This AGREEMENT made as of _____ February 7 _____, 19 90 ,

among E. C. Stevens, Jr. _____ (herein called "Purchaser"),

and P. Seale Hipp _____ (herein called "Seller"),

and Richard T. Walters _____ (herein called "Broker"),

provides that Purchaser agrees to buy through Broker as agent for Seller, and Seller agrees to sell the following described real estate, and all improvements thereon, located in the jurisdiction of LaGrange, Mississippi _____ ,

(all herein called "the property"): Lot 6, Block A, College View Estates. Included in sale: carpeting, 2 window air conditioners, dishwasher, disposal, storm windows, screens, picket fence. _____ (street address). : 506 Park Avenue

1. The purchase price of the property is Thirty-Eight Thousand-- Dollars ($ 38,000.00), and such purchase price shall be paid as follows: New mortgage $28,500; deposit $2,000 as acknowledged in Paragraph 2 below; $7,500 purchase money mortgage.

2. Purchaser has made a deposit of Two Thousand-------------------------------Dollars ($ 2,000.00) with Broker, receipt of which is hereby acknowledged, and such deposit shall be held by Broker in escrow until the date of settlement and then applied to the purchase price, or returned to Purchaser if the title to the property is not marketable.

3. Seller agrees to convey the property to Purchaser by Deed with the usual covenants of title and free and clear from all monetary encumbrances, tenancies, liens (for taxes or otherwise), except as may be otherwise provided above, but subject to applicable restrictive covenants of record. Seller further agrees to deliver possession of the property to Purchaser on the date of settlement and to pay the expense of preparing the deed of conveyance.

4. Settlement shall be made at LaGrange Bank & Trust _____ on or before March 1 _____, 19 90 , or as soon thereafter as title can be examined and necessary documents prepared, with allowance of a reasonable time for Seller to correct any defects reported by the title examiner.

5. All taxes, interest, rent, and impound escrow deposits, if any, shall be prorated as of the date of settlement.

6. All risk of loss or damage to the property by fire, windstorm, casualty, or other cause is assumed by Seller until the date of settlement.

7. Purchaser and Seller agree that Broker was the sole procuring cause of this Contract of Purchase, and Seller agrees to pay Broker for services rendered a cash fee of ____7____ per cent of the purchase price. If either Purchaser or Seller defaults under such Contract, such defaulting party shall be liable for the cash fee of Broker and any expenses incurred by the non-defaulting party in connection with this transaction.

Subject to: (1) Buyer acquiring first mortgage $28,500 from LaGrange Bank & Trust, 25 years amortization, interest rate not to exceed 12 percent. (2) Seller taking $7,500 purchase money mortgage, 10 percent, $100 per month, balance due in 5 years from date of closing. (3) Tenant signing new 1 year lease for $205 per month.

8. Purchaser represents that an inspection satisfactory to Purchaser has been made of the property, and Purchaser agrees to accept the property in its present condition except as may be otherwise provided in the description of the property above.

9. This Contract of Purchase constitutes the entire agreement among the parties and may not be modified or changed except by written instrument executed by all of the parties, including Broker.

10. This Contract of Purchase shall be construed, interpreted, and applied according to the law of the jurisdiction of Mississippi and shall be binding upon and shall inure to the benefit of the heirs, personal representatives, successors, and assigns of the parties.

All parties to this agreement acknowledge receipt of a certified copy.

WITNESS the following signatures:

_____ X   _____ X
                 Seller   Purchaser

_____   _____
                 Seller   Purchaser
                               X
_____
                 Broker

Deposit Rec'd $ 2,000.00

(Personal Check)   Cash

Cashier's Check   Company Check

Sales Agent:

Preparation of Settlement Statement Worksheet

Solution to Problem B–3

SETTLEMENT STATEMENT WORKSHEET

Property Address __506 Park Avenue__   Date of Contract __February 7, 1990__

Buyer __E. C. Stevens, Jr.__   Broker __Richard T. Walters__

Seller __P. Seale Hipp__

SETTLEMENT DATE: March 1, 1990	BUYER'S STATEMENT		SELLER'S STATEMENT	
	DEBIT	CREDIT	DEBIT	CREDIT
Purchase Price	38,000.00			38,000.00
Earnest Money Deposit		2,000.00		
New Mortgage		28,500.00		
Mortgage Interest (3/2–3/30)	275.50			
Purchase Money Mortgage		7,500.00	7,500.00	
Sales Commission			2,660.00	
Property Tax		574.28	574.28	
Property Insurance	99.60			99.60
Security Deposit		200.00	200.00	
Water		10.84	10.84	
Transfer Tax			400.00	
Title Exam & Title Insurance	415.00			
Survey	70.00			
Tax Escrow	286.66			
Insurance Escrow	48.00			
Sale of Personal Property	250.00			250.00
SUBTOTALS	39,444.76	38,785.12	11,345.12	38,349.60
Due From Buyer To Close		659.64		
Due To Seller To Close			27,004.48	
TOTALS	$39,444.76	$39,444.76	$38,349.60	$38,349.60

14. The amount of the insurance proration is
    A. $44.40   C. $99.60
    B. $87.60   D. $111.60
15. The total of the buyer's credits is
    A. $38,000.00   C. $39,444.76
    B. $38,349.60   D. $39,616.14
16. There is a contingency clause in the contract for the
    I. seller taking a $7,500 purchase money mortgage
    II. tenant signing a new one-year lease for $215 per month
    A. I only   C. Both I and II
    B. II only   D. Neither I nor II
17. The lot size is approximately
    A. one-eighth acre
    B. one-fourth acre
    C. one-half acre
    D. more than one-half acre
18. The purchaser made a deposit of
    I. $3,000
    II. more than 5% of the asking price
    A. I only   C. Both I and II
    B. II only   D. Neither I nor II
19. The house includes a (an)
    A. outdoor grill   C. assumable mortgage
    B. utility room   D. side drive

20. The loan-to-value ratio on the new mortgage is
    A. 60%   C. 80%
    B. 75%   D. 90%
21. The security deposit is
    I. debited to the buyer
    II. credited to the seller
    A. I only   C. Both I and II
    B. II only   D. Neither I nor II
22. The total cost of examining and insuring the title is
    A. $225.00   C. $415.00
    B. $367.50   D. $605.00
23. The total property tax and insurance escrow Mr. Stevens must establish at closing is
    I. $286.66
    II. debited to buyer at closing
    A. I only   C. Both I and II
    B. II only   D. Neither I nor II
24. The transfer tax is
    I. debited to the buyer
    II. $380
    A. I only   C. Both I and II
    B. II only   D. Neither I nor II
25. The water expense is
    A. $10.84   C. $18.00
    B. $16.00   D. $24.16

Preparation of Settlement Statement Worksheet

Appendix C

Diagnostic Examination

For most people using this textbook, the ultimate objective is to pass a real estate licensing examination. How successful one is depends upon a number of things. Certainly one of the necessary ingredients is how well real estate terminology and principles are understood.

Regardless of background or experience, each reader would like to have some idea as to his or her understanding of the subject material. The following diagnostic examination is offered for that purpose. Ordinarily, the diagnostic examination should be taken after studying the textbook. The diagnostic sections will show the reader his or her weak areas. A person who already has a background in real estate may take the examination before reading the textbook to also discover areas needing more study.

The questions presented below follow the same basic format as that used on the Uniform Examinations. The questions are divided into 11 groups. Each group covers one broad subject area of real estate. Separating these questions into groups allows the reader to identify easily both weak and strong areas. After answering the questions, complete Table C–1 to find out which areas and chapters need to be studied. While the passing score on the examinations differs from state to state, a score of less than 80% correct on any diagnostic section means that careful review is needed.

GROUP I
PRINCIPAL-AGENT

1. When an agent acts beyond the scope of authority, the agent can be sued by a third party for a breach of an
   I. ostensible authority
   II. implied warranty of authority
   A. I only   C. Both I and II
   B. II only   D. Neither I nor II

2. An agency relationship which is legally binding on the principal may be created by
   I. estoppel
   II. ratification
   A. I only   C. Both I and II
   B. II only   D. Neither I nor II

3. Implied agency is created
   A. voluntarily by conduct and acts of principal and agent which reflect intent to create an agency relationship
   B. voluntarily through contractual agreement between principal and agent
   C. by force of law when circumstances make such an agency necessary
   D. by force of law to prevent the principal from denying its existence

4. A prospect is told by a broker that a house does not have termites. The broker produces an affidavit from the owner which attests to this fact. A sale is made. Before closing, termites are discovered and damage indicates that they have been there for several months. Which of the following is true?
   I. The prospect may collect damages from the broker for misrepresentation.
   II. There was no misrepresentation on the part of the broker.
   A. I only   C. Both I and II
   B. II only   D. Neither I nor II

5. When a third party relies in good faith upon a principal's express, implied or negligent representation that an agency exists, this is an
   A. actual agency
   B. ostensible agency
   C. agency by ratification
   D. agency by necessity

Table C–1

Question Group	Subject	Number of Questions	Suggested Passing Score (80%)	Number Answered Correctly	Percentage Correct	Chapter(s)
1.	Principal—Agent	20	16	—	—	6
2.	Contracts	15	12	—	—	5
3.	Conveyance	10	8	—	—	13
4.	Settlement procedure	10	8	—	—	16
5.	Interest and ownership	15	12	—	—	2, 8, 9
6.	Government	15	12	—	—	12, 19
7.	Finance	25	20	—	—	14, 15
8.	Appraisal and property management	15	12	—	—	10, 17, 18
9.	Property description	5	4	—	—	7
10.	Arithmetic functions	25	20	—	—	20
11.	License law	25	20	—	—	1
				Total Correct	Percentage Correct	

6. A person becomes an attorney-in-fact by
   A. operation of law
   B. being sworn in before the Superior Court
   C. being given a power of attorney
   D. passing a state bar examination

7. John, a broker, lends Jerry $100,000. In consideration for the loan, John is given a 20% equity interest in Jerry's 50-unit condominium project and an exclusive right to sell the units for one year for which he will receive a 6% commission. The proceeds of the sale will be used to pay off the loan. Later Jerry is hit on the head and adjudged insane. Which of the following is true?
   A. John's authority is terminated.
   B. John has an agency coupled with an interest and may sell the condominiums.
   C. Jerry's debt of $100,000 is discharged by operation of law.
   D. John must wait until Jerry is adjudged sane before he is permitted to sell the condominiums.

8. Mary Ann has been employed by Al to buy a specific warehouse for $100,000. The owner will not sell the property for less than $125,000. Without disclosing anything to Al, Mary Ann buys it for herself. Which of the following is true?
   I. Mary Ann may have to sell the warehouse to Al if he wants it.
   II. Mary Ann may lose her commission even if Al pays $125,000 for the warehouse.
   A. I only   C. Both I and II
   B. II only   D. Neither I nor II

9. A broker has a house listed for $60,000 which is the fair market value. He is able to negotiate a sale of this house to his son-in-law for $60,000. The principal has not been advised of the family relationship. Which of the following is true?
   I. The broker may lose his commission.
   II. The sale is fraudulent.
   A. I only   C. Both I and II
   B. II only   D. Neither I nor II

10. Under the law of agency, a broker will have difficulty collecting a commission if he or she
    I. represented two parties without disclosure
    II. failed to be licensed
    A. I only   C. Both I and II
    B. II only   D. Neither I nor II

11. The agency relationship between a broker and the principal means that
    A. it cannot be terminated during the listing period
    B. the agent is required to always act for the benefit of the principal
    C. the agent is always responsible to the seller
    D. the broker's compensation will come from both parties involved in the transaction

12. What is the maximum commission rate that a broker may charge on the sale of improved property?
    A. A rate determined by the Multiple Listing Service
    B. A rate set by the local real estate board
    C. A rate set by the State Licensing Commission
    D. A rate agreed upon by principal and agent

13. A broker has a listing for $75,000. The broker receives an offer for $100,000 and an offer for $60,000. Which of the following is true?
    A. The broker must sell the house for $100,000 and receive a $25,000 commission.
    B. The broker must turn the offer for $100,000 over to the principal and may reject the offer for $60,000.
    C. The broker must turn both offers over to the principal.
    D. The broker may sell the house for $100,000 but will receive only the agreed-to compensation.

14. In an open listing, the agency authority of all brokers is terminated

Diagnostic Examination

I. when the house is sold by any broker or the owner
 II. only when the owner of the house notifies each broker that the house has been sold
 A. I only   C. Both I and II
 B. II only D. Neither I nor II

15. Termination of the agency by acts of the parties include all except
 A. breach by agent
 B. performance
 C. discharge by bankruptcy
 D. mutual agreement

16. Which of the following is *not* a type of agency?
 A. Ostensible   C. By necessity
 B. Implied   D. Overt

17. A real estate broker authorized by an owner to completely manage a rental property and to make all necessary management decisions is a (an)
 A. general agent   C. universal agent
 B. special agent   D. implied agent

18. A listing real estate broker is a (an)
 I. fiduciary
 II. agent
 A. I only   C. Both I and II
 B. II only D. Neither I nor II

19. An agent assumes liability for
 A. negotiable instruments bearing the name of the principal
 B. torts of third parties against the principal
 C. monies owed by third parties to the principal
 D. contracts of undisclosed principal

20. Donald, a licensed broker, is engaged by Bob, a prospect, to locate a house. Donald locates a property owned by Shirley. A contract results between Bob and Shirley. Bob pays Donald a commission. Which of the following is true?
 I. Shirley is the principal and Donald is the agent.
 II. Bob is the principal and Donald is the agent.
 A. I only   C. Both I and II
 B. II only D. Neither I nor II

GROUP 2
CONTRACTS

21. At what point in time is a contract formed?
 A. At the time constructive communication of the acceptance is given by an authorized means of communication
 B. Upon actual receipt of the acceptance by the offeror or the offeror's agent
 C. Upon notice to the offeree of receipt of the acceptance
 D. At the moment the offeree decides to accept

22. An oral agreement for the sale of real estate may be legally enforced through specific performance where the
 A. price of the real estate is less than $500
 B. seller and buyer explicitly agree to be bound by the oral agreement in front of witnesses
 C. down payment exceeds 29% of the purchase price
 D. buyer has taken possession, made improvements and made part payment

23. All contracts for the sale of real estate must be in writing to be
 A. bilateral   C. unilateral
 B. executed   D. enforceable

24. Generally, unless there are certain provisions to the contrary in the contract, the terms of a sales contract are
 I. enforceable after closing
 II. not binding after closing because of the doctrine of merger
 A. I only   C. Both I and II
 B. II only D. Neither I nor II

25. An owner's agreement to sell at a stipulated price for a specific time in return for a consideration from a potential buyer is a (an)
 A. receipt and binder
 B. escrow agreement
 C. option
 D. trust agreement

26. Earnest money is
 A. a deposit on contract paid by the purchaser to the seller
 B. the money financed by the mortgage company
 C. the real estate broker's commission
 D. the difference between the selling price and the existing debt on the property

27. In most states, under an installment contract title passes to the buyer upon
 A. signing the real estate contract
 B. recording the real estate contract
 C. making the initial down payment
 D. payment in full of the obligation

28. One of the prerequisites of an informal contract is consideration, which may be defined as
 A. the offer made by one party and an acceptance made by the other party
 B. the fiduciary relationship between the buyer and the seller

C. a promise made to induce someone to do something that he or she would not otherwise do

D. an agreement where the seller gives the buyer the right to purchase a property within a set period of time

29. When the sales contract specifies that time is "of the essence"
   A. either party is entitled to an adjournment for a reasonable time
   B. the contract is voidable if the closing does not occur on the stated date
   C. the contract is valid for only 90 days
   D. the time of closing must be determined within 30 days

30. In order to protect a buyer's interest in real property from destruction due to fire or harsh weather one may
   I. include a clause in the contract specifying the seller's liability for loss until the transfer of title
   II. stipulate that damage in excess of a certain amount shall make the contract null and void
   A. I only   C. Both I and II
   B. II only   D. Neither I nor II

31. In most states, if the actions of a landlord result in construction eviction, you as a tenant
   I. do not have to pay your rent but you may remain in the apartment
   II. can pack and leave and you have no further obligation
   A. I only   C. Both I and II
   B. II only   D. Neither I nor II

32. The right of a landlord to re-enter or regain possession of the premises upon expiration of a lease is known as
   A. dispossession   C. eviction
   B. reversion   D. remainder

33. An estate from period to period
   I. may be from month to month
   II. has a definite termination date
   A. I only   C. Both I and II
   B. II only   D. Neither I nor II

34. Under common law, if the lease makes no provisions as to who shall make necessary repairs to the premises, who is responsible?
   I. Lessor
   II. Lessee
   A. I only   C. Both I and II
   B. II only   D. Neither I nor II

35. In the absence of provisions to the contrary, sale of the leased premises by the landlord generally
   A. terminates the lease by operation of law
   B. terminates a tenancy at will
   C. does not terminate the lease
   D. makes the lease voidable at the option of the tenant

GROUP 3
CONVEYANCE

36. A type of notice involving recordation, persons in possession and physical circumstances is
   A. constructive   C. specific
   B. actual   D. accretion

37. The requirement for stating consideration in the deed is that
   A. the exact amount must be specified in most states
   B. in most states it is only necessary to state a nominal amount
   C. it is not necessary to state any consideration in the deed
   D. consideration must only be stated in a warranty deed

38. Which of the following is *not* required by law to be contained in a deed?
   A. Consideration
   B. Name of parties
   C. Conditions of payment
   D. Description of premises

39. In reference to deeds, the grantee is the
   I. seller
   II. purchaser
   A. I only   C. Both I and II
   B. II only   D. Neither I nor II

40. A deed which in effect states that a person transfers his or her present rights, if any, to the property is a
   A. bargain-and-sale deed
   B. general warranty deed
   C. special warranty deed
   D. quitclaim deed

41. A bargain-and-sale deed
   I. does not transfer full title to the property
   II. implies that the grantor has possession or title of property
   A. I only   C. Both I and II
   B. II only   D. Neither I nor II

42. The primary purpose of the acknowledgment is to
   I. transfer title
   II. permit recordation
   A. I only   C. Both I and II
   B. II only   D. Neither I nor II

43. The legal effect of properly recording a deed is to
    I. establish priority
    II. give constructive notice
    A. I only
    B. II only
    C. Both I and II
    D. Neither I nor II

44. An agreement between two or more persons, entered into by deed, whereby one of the parties promises the performance of certain acts, is called a (an)
    A. condition
    B. covenant
    C. usufructuary right
    D. estoppel

45. Special warranty deeds are ordinarily recommended when
    A. the seller wishes to restrict liability to title defects occurring after the seller acquired title
    B. title is not sufficiently secure to qualify for a general warranty deed
    C. the seller wishes to transfer special interest in real estate to a grantee
    D. the grantor merely wishes to convey quiet title

GROUP 4
SETTLEMENT PROCEDURE

46. Title insurance premiums are paid
    A. by the mortgagee at closing
    B. monthly with each mortgage payment
    C. annually
    D. once at the time the policy is issued

47. If a seller refused to pay an earned commission at closing the broker may file a
    I. lien against the property
    II. suit against the seller
    A. I only
    B. II only
    C. Both I and II
    D. Neither I nor II

48. Under the Torrens System, transfer of title occurs when
    A. the deed is accepted by the grantee
    B. title insurance is issued
    C. a new certificate is registered with the registrar of title
    D. the deed is recorded with the county clerk

49. In a closing statement, apportionments are set forth in the form of
    A. credits and charges
    B. profit and loss
    C. income and expenses
    D. revenues and deductions

50. After a claim is settled by a title insurance company, how does the company acquire all rights and claims of the insured against any other person who is responsible for the loss?
    A. Subrogation
    B. Subordination
    C. Distraint
    D. Substitution

51. Any outstanding claim or encumbrance which impairs an owner's title to real estate is known as a (an)
    A. lien on the title
    B. cloud on the title
    C. color of title
    D. impairment of title

52. Abstract of title is a
    A. covenant of warranty
    B. condensed history of title
    C. guarantee of title
    D. Torrens Certificate

53. Which of the following is prohibited by RESPA?
    A. Discount points
    B. Required title insurance for mortgagee
    C. Excessive escrow accounts for payment of property taxes, insurance and other charges
    D. Loan origination fees

54. When the title search indicates a marketable title
    I. the seller owns the property free and clear of encumbrances
    II. the seller cannot be assured of the insurability of the property
    A. I only
    B. II only
    C. Both I and II
    D. Neither I nor II

55. Which of the following statements is most accurate?
    I. The escrow agent is directed only by the instructions of the seller.
    II. The escrow agent is bound by written instructions and is neutral between the buyer and the seller.
    A. I only
    B. II only
    C. Both I and II
    D. Neither I nor II

GROUP 5
INTEREST AND OWNERSHIP

56. The overhang of a porch or balcony beyond the established boundary line of a parcel of land is known as a (an)
    A. encroachment
    B. easement
    C. right-of-way
    D. license

57. Which is *not* true regarding joint tenancy?
    A. A new tenant to the estate is a tenant in common.
    B. Right of survivorship exists.
    C. Tenancy is for the entire and undivided part of the estate.
    D. It can be passed on to heirs.

58. The life estate that a wife has in fee simple real property owned by her husband during marriage is known as
    A. curtesy   C. community property
    B. remainder   D. dower

59. "A" and "B" own land which is in undivided ownership. If "A" dies the land goes to his heirs. This is an example of a
    A. joint tenancy
    B. life estate
    C. tenancy in common
    D. tenancy by the entirety

60. An easement by prescription is defined as an easement
    A. expressly granted in a deed conveying property
    B. acquired through the open, continuous and adverse use of real property for a specified time period
    C. created by operation of the law where the easement is necessary
    D. granted in a prescribed or specific location

61. The addition to one's land by the gradual deposit of soil through natural causes is
    A. eminent domain
    B. avulsion
    C. accretion
    D. adverse possession

62. A condominium can be
    I. commercial property
    II. residential property
    A. I only   C. Both I and II
    B. II only   D. Neither I nor II

63. Luke gave Matthew an estate for the life of John. Matthew dies. Which of the following is true?
    A. Matthew's heirs keep the property until John dies.
    B. Luke gets the property back.
    C. John gets the property.
    D. Luke's heirs keep the property.

64. Ownership of private property by an individual is described as
    I. personalty
    II. severalty
    A. I only   C. Both I and II
    B. II only   D. Neither I nor II

65. Rights of a condominium owner are defined by which group of legal laws or documents?
    A. The declaration, the management agreement and the landlord-tenant laws of the municipality
    B. The bylaws, the declaration and the management agreement
    C. The bylaws, the declaration and the corporate charter
    D. The bylaws, the homestead exemption and the landlord-tenant laws of the municipality

66. A consideration in determining whether or not an object is a fixture includes
    I. what was the intent of the party affixing the object
    II. how was the object annexed
    A. I only   C. Both I and II
    B. II only   D. Neither I nor II

67. If Ann conveys property to Betty "*so long as* the property is not used to sell liquor" and Betty sells liquor on the property,
    A. Betty has breached the obligation not to commit waste
    B. title to the property automatically reverts to Ann or her heirs
    C. Betty is not affected unless she is violating a local ordinance
    D. Ann or her heirs have the right of termination

68. If there is a dominant and servient estate, the estate is subject to an
    I. easement appurtenant
    II. easement in gross
    A. I only   C. Both I and II
    B. II only   D. Neither I nor II

69. How should tenants in common proceed to divide their interest?
    A. Foreclosure suit
    B. Partition suit
    C. Suit to quiet title
    D. Suit in detachment

70. In most eastern states, the right of an owner of land next to a stream to use the water is called
    A. riparian rights
    B. easement rights
    C. meander rights
    D. accretion rights

Diagnostic Examination

GROUP 6
GOVERNMENT

71. If a broker is showing homes to a minority prospect and the prospect does not ask to see homes in white neighborhoods the broker
    I. should inquire as to why the prospect does not want to live in white neighborhoods
    II. never has the right to control the selection of homes by prospects
    A. I only
    B. II only
    C. Both I and II
    D. Neither I nor II

72. To aid in accomplishing equal opportunity in housing the broker should
    I. attempt to replace white residents with minority residents
    II. avoid any action which results in excluding someone from owning a home because of race
    A. I only
    B. II only
    C. Both I and II
    D. Neither I nor II

73. Under an affirmative fair housing marketing plan
    I. an effort is made to attract minority homebuyers and renters to majority neighborhoods
    II. federal funds are provided for real estate commissions
    A. I only
    B. II only
    C. Both I and II
    D. Neither I nor II

74. If a prospect should ask, the real estate broker or salesperson is required to provide which of the following?
    I. Location of minority neighborhoods
    II. Location of "white only" neighborhoods
    A. I only
    B. II only
    C. Both I and II
    D. Neither I nor II

75. Local government can require industry to conform to certain air, noise and pollution requirements. Such police power regulations are referred to as
    A. performance standards
    B. nonconforming uses
    C. variances
    D. planned unit developments

76. Property taxes levied on a piece of property depend upon the
    I. assessed value
    II. tax rate or millage rate
    A. I only
    B. II only
    C. Both I and II
    D. Neither I nor II

77. If a property owner does not pay the property taxes levied on the property
    I. the due taxes are a lien on the property
    II. the jurisdiction can take action to have the property sold to pay the past due taxes
    A. I only
    B. II only
    C. Both I and II
    D. Neither I nor II

78. A homeowner receives a tax bill of $800. Property in the jurisdiction is assessed at one-fourth market value. What is the estimated market value of the property if the tax rate is $3.50/$100 of assessed value?
    A. $22,857
    B. $32,000
    C. $45,714
    D. $91,428

79. A mechanic's lien is a (an)
    A. general lien
    B. specific lien
    C. encroachment
    D. fixture

80. How are liens usually ranked in priority?
    A. The last filed has first priority
    B. The bank has first priority
    C. The first filed has priority
    D. The largest money claim on the property has priority

81. Which of the following is an example of a general lien?
    A. Vendor's lien
    B. Decedent's debts
    C. Attachments
    D. Mechanic's lien

82. Which best defines a lien?
    A. An intentional relinquishment of some right or interest
    B. A privilege to pass or cross the property of another
    C. A hold or claim upon the property of another as security for some debt or charge
    D. A slanting structure placed against and attached to the primary building on a property

83. Transfer of Development Rights (TDRs) is a method of
    A. inverse condemnation
    B. zoning property for public use without compensating the private property owner
    C. preventing unwanted social groups from migrating to the community
    D. separating the rights to use the land from the land itself

84. The urban land-use pattern is a result of
    I. decisions regarding the sale, purchase and improvement of real estate
    II. zoning and other land-use control measures
    A. I only
    B. II only
    C. Both I and II
    D. Neither I nor II

85. The extent of which of the following activities is to maintain the quality of housing in a community?
    A. Rent controls
    B. Enforcement of housing codes
    C. High property taxes
    D. Enforcement of fair housing laws

GROUP 7
FINANCE

86. An FHA mortgage is secured through which of the following?
    A. A qualified lending institution
    B. HUD
    C. FDIC
    D. FSLIC

87. The main difference between a straight-term mortgage and a fully amortized mortgage is in the
    I. method of repaying the principal
    II. term of the loan
    A. I only
    B. II only
    C. Both I and II
    D. Neither I nor II

88. When property fails to sell at court foreclosure for the amount sufficient to satisfy a mortgage debt, the mortgagee may sue for a
    I. satisfaction of mortgage debt
    II. deficiency judgment
    A. I only
    B. II only
    C. Both I and II
    D. Neither I nor II

89. States where the borrower keeps title to real estate upon executing a mortgage are called
    A. redemption theory states
    B. title theory states
    C. lien theory states
    D. trust theory states

90. The interest which an owner has in real estate over and above the claims against it is referred to as
    A. equity
    B. estate
    C. leverage
    D. value

91. The mortgagee has certain remedies to pursue if the mortgagor fails to pay the loan when due. Which of the following is *not* a remedy?
    A. Mortgagee in possession
    B. Legal foreclosure
    C. Strict foreclosure
    D. Subordination agreement

92. Federally chartered savings and loan associations are organized under the
    A. Federal Housing Administration
    B. Federal Home Loan Bank System
    C. Federal Reserve System
    D. Federal Deposit Insurance Corporation

93. When the buyer takes title to property "subject to" existing financing, the
    I. buyer is not personally liable for the debt
    II. seller is not personally liable for the debt
    A. I only
    B. II only
    C. Both I and II
    D. Neither I nor II

94. The three parties involved in a trust deed are the
    A. benefactor, trustor and principal
    B. beneficiary, trustee and principal
    C. benefactor, trustee and trustor
    D. beneficiary, trustee and trustor

95. A release schedule clause would most likely be included in which of the following types of mortgages?
    A. Package
    B. Open-end
    C. Purchase money
    D. Blanket

96. Amortization refers to the
    A. depreciation of real estate
    B. appreciation of real estate
    C. debt service constant
    D. periodic payment of debt

97. If a piece of property is foreclosed and the price paid at the foreclosure sale does not satisfy the debt secured by the mortgage, what clause protects the mortgagor from being sued personally for the deficiency?
    A. Novation clause
    B. Parol evidence clause
    C. No payment clause
    D. Exculpatory clause

98. Regulation Z was issued by the
    A. Department of Housing and Urban Development
    B. Securities and Exchange Commission
    C. Federal Reserve System
    D. Federal Trade Commission

99. Regulation Z does *not* apply to which of the following credit transactions?
    I. Where the loan is repayable in three installments
    II. Where the amount of the loan is greater than $25,000
    A. I only
    B. II only
    C. Both I and II
    D. Neither I nor II

100. The acknowledgment of an earnest money deposit is called a (an)
    A. escrow contract
    B. receipt and binder
    C. exchange contract
    D. estoppel certificate

101. Which of the following statements is true regarding FHA and VA financing?
    I. In order to qualify for an FHA loan, the property must meet certain minimum standards.
    II. A nonveteran or a veteran who has lost his or her eligibility may not assume a VA mortgage.
    A. I only
    B. II only
    C. Both I and II
    D. Neither I nor II

102. The number of discount points charged on mortgages is determined primarily by the

Diagnostic Examination

A. Federal Reserve System
B. Federal National Mortgage Association
C. money market
D. Federal Housing Administration

103. Regulation Z deals with
    A. truth-in-lending
    B. maximum credit charges
    C. minimum credit charges
    D. closing costs

104. The purpose of an estoppel certificate is to
    A. stop payment on the mortgage
    B. establish a new mortgage
    C. identify the mortgagee
    D. state the amount owed on the mortgage

105. If there are several borrowers on a mortgage note, the lender may insert the words "jointly and severally" following the names of the borrowers. This wording
    I. enables the lender to collect from any one or all of the borrowers
    II. makes each borrower personally liable to pay the entire indebtedness
    A. I only   C. Both I and II
    B. II only   D. Neither I nor II

106. Conventional mortgage loans are
    A. guaranteed by VA
    B. insured by FHA
    C. sometimes insured in part by private mortgage insurance companies
    D. guaranteed by FHA

107. A mortgage is a pledge
    I. of real property for security of a debt
    II. given by a mortgagee
    A. I only   C. Both I and II
    B. II only   D. Neither I nor II

108. When property is put up as collateral for a loan, the borrower is known as the _____ and the lender is known as the _____
    A. mortgagor, mortgagee
    B. seller, lender
    C. mortgagee, mortgagor
    D. mortgagee, financial intermediary

109. The higher the loan-to-value ratio the
    I. lower the equity required of the borrower
    II. more leverage for the borrower
    A. I only   C. Both I and II
    B. II only   D. Neither I nor II

110. A written transfer of ownership of a mortgage loan from one lender to another is called a
    A. mortgage release
    B. mortgage assumption
    C. mortgage spreading
    D. mortgage assignment

GROUP 8
APPRAISAL AND PROPERTY MANAGEMENT

111. When employing the cost approach to value, it is necessary to estimate
    I. land value
    II. depreciation
    A. I only   C. Both I and II
    B. II only   D. Neither I nor II

112. The valuation approach that always will result in the highest estimate of value is the
    I. market approach
    II. income approach
    A. I only   C. Both I and II
    B. II only   D. Neither I nor II

113. Market value is most clearly defined in terms of
    A. value in exchange
    B. value in use
    C. investment value
    D. loan value

114. The market approach would normally be used in estimating the value of a (an)
    A. church   C. hotel
    B. oil refinery   D. vacant land

115. In the market comparison approach, physical units of comparison are used in adjusting for
    A. scenic view   C. location
    B. size   D. age

116. Market value and selling price are equal
    A. sometimes
    B. never
    C. always
    D. only when there is no government financing

117. In order to be a Certified Property Manager, a person must fulfill requirements established by a (an)
    A. Board of REALTORS®
    B. Institute of the NATIONAL ASSOCIATION OF REALTORS®

C. State Real Estate Board
D. state-accredited licensing school

118. For an object or service to have value, it must be characterized by
   I. demand and scarcity
   II. utility and transferability
   A. I only   C. Both I and II
   B. II only   D. Neither I nor II

119. Compensation for professionally managing property is usually in the form of a (an)
   A. straight salary
   B. percentage of appraised value
   C. assessment fee charged to the tenants
   D. percentage of gross income

120. A church would normally be best appraised through the
   A. cost approach
   B. income approach
   C. market comparison approach
   D. gross rent multiplier approach

121. Replacement cost new is used when
   I. the subject property is new
   II. there is a great deal of functional obsolescence in the subject property
   A. I only   C. Both I and II
   B. II only   D. Neither I nor II

122. Which of the following is *not* a principal function of a property manager?
   A. Collecting rents
   B. Keeping the property insured
   C. Physical maintenance of the property
   D. Investing to enlarge the property

123. Loss in real property value can be a result of
   I. economic obsolescence
   II. functional obsolescence
   A. I only   C. Both I and II
   B. II only   D. Neither I nor II

124. The technique of capitalization is employed by the appraiser in the
   I. cost approach
   II. income approach
   A. I only   C. Both I and II
   B. II only   D. Neither I nor II

125. Value is measured in the income approach by determining the present worth of the
   I. reversion
   II. net operating income
   A. I only   C. Both I and II
   B. II only   D. Neither I nor II

Figure C–1. Subdivision Plat to Be Used for Group 9, Property Description on Page 268

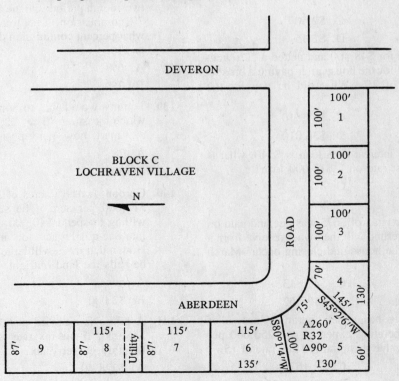

Diagnostic Examination

GROUP 9
PROPERTY DESCRIPTION

Questions 126-130 refer to the subdivision plat shown on page 267.

126. According to the plat, how many lots have easements?
    A. none
    B. 1
    C. 2
    D. 3

127. A house built on Lot 6 will face what direction?
    A. North
    B. South
    C. East
    D. West

128. The average size lot is less than
    I. 10,000 square feet
    II. one-third acre
    A. I only
    B. II only
    C. Both I and II
    D. Neither I nor II

129. Which lot(s) is described by the following: "Beginning at a point 370' from the southwest intersection of Deveron and Aberdeen Road; thence southwesterly for 145'; thence east for 130'; thence north for 100'; thence 70' in a westerly direction following the curvature of Aberdeen Road to the point of beginning"?
    A. Lots 1, 2, 3, 4
    B. Lots 4, 5, 6
    C. Lot 1
    D. Lot 4

130. The delta of 90° describes the angle between
    I. the northern boundary of Lot 6 and the eastern boundary of Lot 4
    II. the northern boundary of Lot 4 and the western boundary of Lot 6
    A. I only
    B. II only
    C. Both I and II
    D. Neither I nor II

GROUP 10
ARITHMETIC FUNCTIONS

131. If 16 air conditioners discharge 8,000 gallons of water in 4 hours, how many air conditioners will discharge 6,000 gallons in 2 hours?
    A. 12
    B. 18
    C. 24
    D. 32

132. A lot 92' × 90' sold for $24,840. What was its price per square foot?
    A. $3.50
    B. $3.00
    C. $2.50
    D. $2.15

133. Jack sold a house for $48,400 and netted a 20% gain over what he paid for the house after paying a brokerage commission of 7%. What did he pay for the house?
    A. $45,012
    B. $35,332
    C. $37,510
    D. $36,010

134. If the semiannual interest on a loan is $540, what is the annual interest rate on a $12,000 loan?
    A. 4.5%
    B. 7%
    C. 8%
    D. 9%

135. The annual property tax of $675 was due and paid on January 1. What refund will the owner receive from a buyer if he sells the house and closing occurs March 7?
    A. $605.63
    B. $549.38
    C. $493.13
    D. $125.62

136. An office building has a net operating income of $325,000 after operating expenses of $250,000 per year. What is its value if capitalized at a rate of 15%?
    A. $500,000
    B. $575,000
    C. $2,167,000
    D. $3,250,000

137. A warehouse has depreciated 8% per year. If it was worth $175,000 four years ago, what is its value today?
    A. $119,000
    B. $132,576
    C. $133,000
    D. $231,000

138. Sally Salesperson sold $250,000 in real estate over a two-month period. On the first $100,000 she received 7% commission. If her total commission was $19,000 what percent commission did she receive on the other part?
    A. 6%
    B. 7%
    C. 8%
    D. 9%

139. Tommy would like to completely fence in his yard which measures 80' × 220'. If he places fence posts 20' apart, how many posts are needed?
    A. 28
    B. 30
    C. 31
    D. 32

140. Gordon owns 15 acres of land. He has been offered $12,000 per acre if he sells all 15 acres. If he is willing to spend $40,000, he can subdivide his land into one-quarter acre lots and sell each lot for $3,700. How much more will he make by subdividing than if he sells the land outright?
    A. none
    B. $2,000
    C. $42,000
    D. He actually loses

141. A house is assessed at 60% of its market value of $88,000. If the tax rate is $3.12/$100, what is the monthly property tax?
    A. $228.80
    B. $93.28
    C. $114.40
    D. $137.28

142. A 12′ × 16′ room is shown on a blueprint as 3″ × 4″. If another room on the blueprint is shown as 9 square inches, how many square feet does it contain?
   A. 108
   B. 144
   C. 164
   D. 192

143. Mr. Johnson has advertised his house for sale at a price 30% more than the $46,000 he paid for it three years ago. If he accepts $3,000 less for it than the advertised price, how much profit will he realize after paying a brokerage commission of 7%?
   A. $10,800
   B. $9,614
   C. $7,084
   D. $6,824

144. Two parcels of land have the same width. Lot A is 400′ deep and Lot B is 700′ deep. If Lot A is 3 acres, what is the size of Lot B?
   A. 21 acres
   B. 5.25 acres
   C. 3 acres
   D. 1.71 acres

145. A one-half acre triangular lot has a frontage of 150 feet. What is its depth?
   A. 72.6′
   B. 145.2′
   C. 290.4′
   D. 580.8′

146. Evalyn borrowed $3,000 three months ago. If today she owes $63.75 interest, what is the annual rate of interest?
   A. 2.125%
   B. 4.25%
   C. 7.0%
   D. 8.5%

147. What is the value of a building which has a monthly profit of $1,220 and is earning the owner a return of 16%?
   A. $14,640
   B. $122,000
   C. $7,625
   D. $91,500

148. Brian borrowed three-fourths of the purchase price of a house from a bank at an interest rate of 8½%. What did he pay for the house if the interest due the first month is $224?
   A. $42,165
   B. $39,529
   C. $31,624
   D. $40,000

149. A commercial building leases for $2,000 per month. If the dimensions of the space are 45′ × 60′, what is the annual rate per square foot?
   A. $1.35
   B. $8.88
   C. $6.35
   D. $3.50

150. What is the gross rent multiplier for a house with a market value of $64,520 renting for $595 per month?
   A. 6
   B. 7.5
   C. 8
   D. 9

151. Which of the following sales would net the brokerage firm making the sale a profit of $2,440?

	Sales Price	Commission Rate	Selling Expense
A.	$40,572	6%	$400
B.	$34,857	7%	$610
C.	$35,533	7.5%	$225
D.	$42,950	8%	$916

152. The building below cost $9.50 per square foot to build five years ago. If the cost of building it today is $20,416, the cost per square foot has increased by how much?

   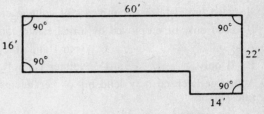

   A. 42%
   B. 75%
   C. 175%
   D. 200%

153. Kathy purchased a two-year homeowner's insurance policy on February 7, 1989, for $388. How much should be credited to her at closing on June 2, 1990, if a buyer assumes her policy?
   A. $132.02
   B. $255.98
   C. $148.19
   D. $115.85

154. Gene sells his house and nets $8,540 after paying a brokerage fee of 7%, an existing mortgage of $22,243 and a tax lien of $425. What is the selling price of his house?
   A. $24,374
   B. $31,208
   C. $33,392
   D. $33,557

155. A building with walls one foot thick measures 90′ × 70′ around the exterior. Inside there are 20 support columns, each one foot square. What is the useable floor area of the building?
   A. 5,964 sq. ft.
   B. 5,984 sq. ft.
   C. 6,121 sq. ft.
   D. 6,280 sq. ft.

GROUP 11
LICENSE LAW

156. Elmer, a broker, can acquire an interest in property listed with him if
   I. the price he pays is based on a value determined by an outside appraiser
   II. he discloses his true position to his client and his client consents
   A. I only
   B. II only
   C. Both I and II
   D. Neither I nor II

157. Normally, an unlicensed person attempting to collect a real estate commission has been guilty of a
   A. misdemeanor
   B. felony
   C. duress
   D. nothing

158. A licensee can have a license suspended or revoked for

Diagnostic Examination

I. failing to appear at a hearing of the Real Estate Commission to which he or she has been subpoenaed

II. borrowing a broker's license

A. I only
B. II only
C. Both I and II
D. Neither I nor II

159. If an unlicensed person attempted to file suit in a court of law for an unpaid real estate commission,

I. permission would have to be received from the state licensing agency

II. the suit would be dismissed by a court

A. I only
B. II only
C. Both I and II
D. Neither I nor II

160. To become a real estate salesperson in most states, a person

I. must have at least four years of college credits

II. need only be employed by a real estate company

A. I only
B. II only
C. Both I and II
D. Neither I nor II

161. A broker licensee may lend his or her license to a salesperson

I. for just and reasonable cause

II. only for emergencies

A. I only
B. II only
C. Both I and II
D. Neither I nor II

162. If a buyer defaults and forfeits an earnest money deposit being held by the broker, the broker

I. is not entitled to any of the commission unless the sales agreement states to the contrary

II. should keep all of the earnest money deposit to assure a claim on the commission

A. I only
B. II only
C. Both I and II
D. Neither I nor II

163. Real estate licensing laws

A. vary from state to state
B. are uniform throughout the country
C. usually allow one to split a fee or commission with someone not licensed as a broker or salesperson
D. are regulated by the NATIONAL ASSOCIATION OF REALTORS®

164. A licensed salesperson can receive a sales commission from any broker licensed in

I. the same state
II. any state

A. I only
B. II only
C. Both I and II
D. Neither I nor II

165. Members of real estate commissions in most states are

A. elected by the public
B. appointed by local real estate boards
C. appointed by the governor
D. appointed by the executive director

166. An unlicensed real estate salesperson negotiates the sale of vacant land. The commission is payable to

A. the salesperson
B. the real estate commission
C. the broker
D. no one

167. A licensed salesperson may

I. act as an agent for the seller of a home
II. change from one broker to another without reporting the change to the real estate commission

A. I only
B. II only
C. Both I and II
D. Neither I nor II

168. Reciprocity in real estate refers to

A. the agreement between brokerage firms to split commissions
B. the ability of an owner to collect the commission if he or she finds the buyer
C. an agreement between states recognizing the license of a nonresident broker
D. an agreement between brokers of one firm and salespersons of another firm

169. The licensing of brokers is regulated by the

A. planning commissions
B. police power of the state
C. NATIONAL ASSOCIATION OF REALTORS®
D. local real estate boards

170. Wording common to the definition of a broker in all jurisdictions is

I. "who for compensation"
II. "acting on behalf of another"

A. I only
B. II only
C. Both I and II
D. Neither I nor II

171. The purpose of the real estate licensing law is to protect the

A. broker
B. salesperson
C. public
D. real estate commission

172. For a broker to commingle funds means to

A. place the broker's savings account and checking account together
B. mix the broker's own funds with those of his or her salespersons
C. divide any down payment into sales commission and escrow account
D. mix personal funds with client funds

173. In most states a broker's license may be suspended for

I. failing to work full time
II. splitting commissions with unlicensed brokers

A. I only
B. II only
C. Both I and II
D. Neither I nor II

174. Which of the following may carry out real estate transactions without the necessity of obtaining a license as a real estate salesperson or broker?
   I. A person selling his or her own property
   II. An attorney-at-law in the normal course of practicing law
   A. I only
   B. II only
   C. Both I and II
   D. Neither I nor II

175. Which of the following would normally be reason for suspending a broker's license?
   I. Charging more than a 10% commission
   II. Ignoring an owner's instructions not to show property to a minority prospect
   A. I only
   B. II only
   C. Both I and II
   D. Neither I nor II

176. A real estate broker
   I. must maintain a separate baking account for each client's escrow money
   II. can pay a commission to any licensed broker or salesperson
   A. I only
   B. II only
   C. Both I and II
   D. Neither I nor II

177. Which of the following organizations requires a real estate broker to maintain a separate real estate escrow account?
   A. Local real estate board
   B. State broker's association
   C. Multiple listing association
   D. State licensing agency

178. A licensed broker can pay a commission to any
   I. broker licensed in his state
   II. salesperson licensed in his state
   A. I only
   B. II only
   C. Both I and II
   D. Neither I nor II

179. A licensed salesperson can receive a commission from
   I. individuals he or she successfully represents
   II. builders he or she successfully represents
   A. I only
   B. II only
   C. Both I and II
   D. Neither I nor II

180. The authority to license salespersons and brokers is
   I. derived from the police power of the state
   II. has been held by the courts in some states as violating the Fifth Amendment
   A. I only
   B. II only
   C. Both I and II
   D. Neither I nor II

SOLUTIONS

Question	Correct Answer	Question	Correct Answer	Question	Correct Answer	Question	Correct Answer
#1	B	#33	A	#65	B	#97	D
#2	C	#34	B	#66	C	#98	C
#3	A	#35	C	#67	B	#99	C
#4	D	#36	A	#68	A	#100	B
#5	B	#37	B	#69	B	#101	A
#6	C	#38	C	#70	A	#102	C
#7	B	#39	B	#71	B	#103	A
#8	C	#40	D	#72	B	#104	D
#9	A	#41	B	#73	A	#105	C
#10	C	#42	B	#74	D	#106	C
#11	B	#43	C	#75	A	#107	A
#12	D	#44	B	#76	C	#108	A
#13	C	#45	A	#77	C	#109	C
#14	A	#46	D	#78	D	#110	D
#15	C	#47	B	#79	B	#111	C
#16	D	#48	C	#80	C	#112	D
#17	A	#49	A	#81	B	#113	A
#18	C	#50	A	#82	C	#114	D
#19	D	#51	B	#83	D	#115	B
#20	B	#52	B	#84	C	#116	A
#21	A	#53	C	#85	B	#117	B
#22	D	#54	B	#86	A	#118	C
#23	D	#55	B	#87	A	#119	D
#24	B	#56	A	#88	B	#120	A
#25	C	#57	D	#89	C	#121	B
#26	A	#58	D	#90	A	#122	D
#27	D	#59	C	#91	D	#123	C
#28	C	#60	B	#92	B	#124	B
#29	B	#61	C	#93	A	#125	C
#30	C	#62	C	#94	D	#126	B
#31	B	#63	A	#95	D	#127	C
#32	B	#64	B	#96	D	#128	B

Question	Correct Answer	Question	Correct Answer	Question	Correct Answer	Question	Correct Answer
#129	D	#142	B	#155	A	#168	C
#130	A	#143	D	#156	B	#169	B
#131	C	#144	B	#157	A	#170	C
#132	B	#145	C	#158	C	#171	C
#133	C	#146	D	#159	B	#172	D
#134	D	#147	D	#160	D	#173	B
#135	B	#148	A	#161	D	#174	C
#136	C	#149	B	#162	A	#175	D
#137	A	#150	D	#163	A	#176	D
#138	C	#151	C	#164	D	#177	D
#139	B	#152	B	#165	C	#178	A
#140	B	#153	A	#166	D	#179	D
#141	D	#154	D	#167	D	#180	A

Appendix D

Practice Salesperson's Examination

QUESTIONS

1. A broker employed to sell a house is normally what type of agent?
   I. General agent
   II. Special agent
   A. I only
   B. II only
   C. Both I and II
   D. Neither I nor II

2. Generally, the highest priority lien is
   A. a general lien
   B. a special lien
   C. the first lien recorded
   D. a property tax lien

3. Regulation Z affects what kind of loans?
   I. Loans to consumers
   II. Loans to corporations
   A. I only
   B. II only
   C. Both I and II
   D. Neither I nor II

4. If the lender advances $960 and the borrower must repay $1,000, the discount rate is
   A. 4%
   B. 96%
   C. 100%
   D. 104%

5. Why will an effective property manager continue to advertise when property is 100% rented?
   A. The expense is tax deductible.
   B. To dispose of excess revenue
   C. It is cheaper to maintain a continuous advertising campaign than to advertise only when a vacancy occurs.
   D. To maintain public awareness and prestige of the project.

6. To an innocent purchaser, a prior sale recorded by deed in the land records gives
   A. actual notice
   B. constructive notice
   C. no notice
   D. equitable estoppel

7. A proper escrow, once established, should be
   A. held by the seller only
   B. held by the broker only
   C. beyond the control of any one party who has an interest in the transaction.
   D. held by the purchaser

8. Which of the following will *not* terminate an agent's authority?
   I. Death of either principal or agent
   II. Appointment of a subagent
   A. I only
   B. II only
   C. Both I and II
   D. Neither I nor II

9. A net income of $10,000 capitalized at a rate of 8% indicates a value _____ the value indicated by capitalizing a net income of $5,000 at a rate of 4%.
   I. less than
   II. equal to
   A. I only
   B. II only
   C. Both I and II
   D. Neither I nor II

10. VA financing requires that a borrower
    I. be married
    II. sign a statement that he or she intends to live on the property
    A. I only
    B. II only
    C. Both I and II
    D. Neither I nor II

11. When financing an office building, a lender is required to

I. use discount points
  II. adhere to Regulation Z
  A. I only   C. Both I and II
  B. II only   D. Neither I nor II

12. _____ eviction occurs when the leased property has deteriorated, due to the fault of the landlord, so that the tenant is unable to occupy the premises for the purpose intended.
  A. Constructive   C. Eminent domain
  B. Actual   D. Distressed

13. If an infant sells realty, after reaching the age of majority receives and spends the purchase price, then disaffirms the contract, the courts will
  A. bind the infant to the contract
  B. restore the infant's property to the infant
  C. bind the infant's parents to the contract
  D. sentence the infant to juvenile court for fraud

14. An acre contains _____ square feet.
  A. 45,360   C. 43,650
  B. 43,560   D. 46,350

15. Title insurance does not cover
  I. hidden defects of record
  II. defects occurring after the policy is written
  A. I only   C. Both I and II
  B. II only   D. Neither I nor II

16. All those rights that go with the land are called
  A. habendums   C. cessions
  B. seizins   D. appurtenances

17. Mrs. Perry has listed her property with Broker Albert. Mr. Jay sells the property. Who is the principal?
  A. Mr. Jay
  B. Mrs. Perry
  C. Mr. Albert
  D. There is no principal.

18. Which of the following clauses protects the mortgagee from waste during the foreclosure process?
  A. Stop payment clause
  B. Receiver clause
  C. Collector clause
  D. Acceleration clause

19. A decrease in value as a result of deferred maintenance is referred to as
  A. economic obsolescence
  B. functional obsolescence
  C. physical deterioration
  D. accelerated depreciation

20. An executory contract is one which is
  I. entered into by the executor of an estate
  II. for the performance of an action in the future
  A. I only   C. Both I and II
  B. II only   D. Neither I nor II

21. In most states the final requirement for a valid deed to transfer title is the
  A. signature of the grantor(s)
  B. signature of the grantee(s)
  C. delivery and acceptance
  D. acknowledgment

22. Which agency is created when a principal gives the false impression that another is the agent, and a third person, relying on that information, deals with the agent and thereby is damaged as a result of that reliance?
  A. Agency by stature
  B. Agency by necessity
  C. Agency by estoppel
  D. Implied agency

23. A form of concurrent ownership based upon the common law precept that husband and wife are one is
  A. tenancy in partnership
  B. tenancy by the entirety
  C. joint tenancy
  D. tenancy in common

24. A mortgage covering mechanical equipment and appliances as well as real property is a (an)
  A. overall mortgage
  B. package mortgage
  C. blanket mortgage
  D. purchase money mortgage

25. A second mortgage may become a first or prior mortgage by which of the following means?
  A. Subordination agreement
  B. Execution clause
  C. Estoppel certificate
  D. Novation

26. A broker takes a listing from a seller who tells the broker that the house should not be shown to minority groups. The broker should
  A. explain that this violates federal law
  B. report the incident to HUD and accept the listing
  C. place this restriction on the listing
  D. show the house only to minority groups

27. If an area were changed to residential zoning, a drug store in the zone may be permitted as a (an)
  A. variance
  B. nonconforming use
  C. spot-zoning variance
  D. exception

28. A listing real estate broker ordinarily has the authority to
  I. make representations as to the subject matter of the agency contract
  II. accept a promissory note from a purchaser as an earnest money deposit

A. I only   C. Both I and II
B. II only   D. Neither I nor II

29. The purpose of the Real Estate Settlement Procedures Act is to
   A. reduce legal expenses of closing
   B. regulate the activities of real estate brokers at closing
   C. reduce the amount of paperwork at closing
   D. provide mortgage borrowers accurate information on the nature and cost of the settlement process before the time of closing

30. If John, a broker, sells a listed house, he will receive a 7% commission. A purchaser hires John to find a home for which he will pay the broker a 3% finder's fee. In order to keep the transaction at arm's length, John negotiates the sale without disclosing either agency contract. Which of the following is true?
   I. John may receive 7% from the seller.
   II. John may receive 3% from the buyer.
   A. I only   C. Both I and II
   B. II only   D. Neither I nor II

31. A contract made with an insane person under guardianship is
   A. void
   B. voidable
   C. valid
   D. enforceable

32. Under which of the following is the lender referred to as the beneficiary?
   A. Land contract
   B. Mortgage
   C. Estoppel certificate
   D. Deed of trust

33. If the seller finances part of the purchase price and wishes to maintain priority of lien, the borrower should give a
   A. purchase money mortgage
   B. subordination agreement
   C. escrow loan
   D. chattel loan

34. Suzie Salesperson is showing a prospect a house listed with her broker for $50,000. The principal is a weak-willed spinster. Suzie states to the prospect, "Offer her $35,000. We can both work on her to sell at the reduced price." A sale is made at $35,000.
   I. Suzie and her broker are entitled to no commission.
   II. Suzie's broker may have to pay actual damages which are proven in court.
   A. I only   C. Both I and II
   B. II only   D. Neither I nor II

35. A real estate broker
   A. may act for only one party in a transaction
   B. may act for both parties if licensed for a minimum of one year
   C. is a fiduciary and has the duty to remain neutral
   D. may act for both parties with the knowledge and consent of both

36. Lee Hall, a broker, has 100 acres listed for $2,000 per acre. One day after the listing is acquired coal is discovered on the land causing the value of the land to double. The seller did not know about the coal. Lee Hall finds a ready, willing and able buyer at $2,000 per acre.
   I. Lee is entitled to a commission.
   II. Lee's duty to sell is at $4,000 per acre by operation of law.
   A. I only   C. Both I and II
   B. II only   D. Neither I nor II

37. David purchased a two-year homeowner's insurance policy on September 22, 1989, for $296. How much should be credited to him at closing on June 30, 1990?
   A. $181.71
   B. $169.38
   C. $126.62
   D. $114.29

38. A real estate salesperson is a (an)
   I. agent of the broker's principal
   II. subagent of the broker's principal
   A. I only   C. Both I and II
   B. II only   D. Neither I nor II

39. State-chartered savings and loan associations
   I. cannot hold membership in the Federal Savings and Loan Insurance Corporation
   II. can be a member of the Federal Deposit Insurance Corporation
   A. I only   C. Both I and II
   B. II only   D. Neither I nor II

40. Which of the following is *not* required of a legal offer?
   A. State definite and certain terms
   B. Be communicated to the offeree
   C. Exhibit present contractual intent
   D. State a specific termination date

41. Where it is not specified otherwise, normally a tenant is liable for
   A. ordinary wear and tear, but not liable for waste
   B. waste, but not liable for ordinary wear and tear
   C. all damage occurring while the leasehold is in the tenant's possession
   D. damage in the leasehold if the tenant has an insurable interest

42. The best kind of deed for the grantee is a
   A. quitclaim
   B. bargain and sale
   C. general warranty
   D. special warranty

43. A title insurance policy offers protection against all of the following except
   A. forged signatures
   B. conveyance by minors
   C. hidden easements
   D. eminent domain

Practice Salesperson's Examination

44. Severalty ownership is ownership
    A. by several persons
    B. by title passing to the survivors upon death of a person
    C. of an undivided interest in property
    D. by one person only

45. If a prospective buyer needs financing to consummate a purchase, an offer may be made with a clause stating that the
    I. contract is contingent upon obtaining a mortgage at a particular rate of interest, term and amount
    II. seller agrees to accept a purchase money mortgage from the buyer for a specified amount, term and interest rate
    A. I only   C. Both I and II
    B. II only   D. Neither I nor II

46. Property ownership in the United States is described as a (an)
    A. feudal system
    B. allodial system
    C. Roman system
    D. government survey system

47. Which of the following statements is correct regarding condominiums?
    A. The percentage of operating expenses levied on each individual owner is based on personal income.
    B. Operating expenses incurred for upkeep of the common areas are prorated based on the number of occupants per unit.
    C. Operating expenses charged each individual owner are based on each owner's individual share of the common elements.
    D. Operating expenses include the debt service on each individual unit.

48. "Blockbusting" occurs when
    I. the broker induces a homeowner to list property by indicating that persons of a minority group are moving into the area and causing prices to drop
    II. a member of a minority group purchases a home in a previously homogeneous neighborhood
    A. I only   C. Both I and II
    B. II only   D. Neither I nor II

49. A clause in a mortgage which causes the entire principal to become due upon default is called a (an)
    A. receiver   C. brundage
    B. defeasance   D. acceleration

50. The appropriate time adjustment to make for a comparable sale which sold three years ago for $50,000 and has increased at a 5% compound rate is
    A. less than $7500.00
    B. $7500.00
    C. less than $7881.25
    D. $7881.25

51. The following property description is an example of which method of land description?
    All that parcel of land in Land Lot 119 of the 13th District of Henry County, Iowa, and being Lot 8, Block B of the Valley View Subdivision recorded in Plat Book 374, Page 66.
    A. Monument   C. Metes and bounds
    B. Lot and block   D. Government survey

52. If a loan is assumed,
    I. the person assuming the loan becomes a co-guarantor
    II. the original mortgagor is released from the mortgage
    A. I only   C. Both I and II
    B. II only   D. Neither I nor II

53. "A" offers to sell his farm to "B" for $26,000. "B" makes a counteroffer to buy the farm at $25,000, provided "A" takes back a mortgage for $15,000 at 8% interest for 15 years. "A" refuses the offer and the next day sells the farm to "C" for $25,000 with a mortgage for $15,000 at 8% interest, payable in 15 years. The next day "B" accepts the original offer. Which of the following is true?
    A. "B" can compel "A" to sell to "B."
    B. "B" cannot compel "A" to sell to "B."
    C. "B" can record the agreement which would be a cloud on the title.
    D. "B" can compel "C" to assign the agreement to "B."

54. Regarding an owner's standard policy of title insurance, which of the following statements is correct?
    I. An owner's equity resulting from an increase in value is covered.
    II. An owner's equity resulting from amortization of the loan is not covered.
    A. I only   C. Both I and II
    B. II only   D. Neither I nor II

55. Which of the following affects the level of debt service?
    I. Interest rate
    II. Repayment term of the loan
    A. I only   C. Both I and II
    B. II only   D. Neither I nor II

56. The market comparison approach is ordinarily most applicable to which type of land use?
    A. Single-family houses
    B. Office buildings
    C. Theaters
    D. Mobile homes

57. Which of the following statements regarding financing is (are) true?
    I. A first mortgage is always larger than a second mortgage.

II. A second mortgage cannot be foreclosed without the consent of the first mortgagee.
   A. I only
   B. II only
   C. Both I and II
   D. Neither I nor II

58. Under common law, if there is no provision in the lease stating when the rent is due, it is ordinarily due on the
   A. first day of each month
   B. last day of each month
   C. last day of the lease term
   D. first day of the lease term

59. Which of the following in regard to a real estate sales contract is most accurate?
   I. A sales agreement is a written instrument which conveys legal title to, or an interest in, realty.
   II. The contract for purchase and sale merges in the deed which, when properly delivered and accepted, evidences the transfer of title or interest in the realty.
   A. I only
   B. II only
   C. Both I and II
   D. Neither I nor II

60. Which of the following will terminate an easement?
   I. Nonuse over the statutory period
   II. Where the purpose or necessity ceases to exist
   A. I only
   B. II only
   C. Both I and II
   D. Neither I nor II

61. A 20-year-old office building has a remaining life of 20 years. The applicable straight-line depreciation rate an appraiser would use is
   A. 20%
   B. 100%
   C. 5%
   D. The appraiser is not concerned with recapture rates

62. Loan discount points on VA loans are legally paid by the
   A. lender
   B. purchaser
   C. seller
   D. broker

63. A term mortgage provides for no _____ over the term of the mortgage.
   I. amortization of the principal
   II. interest payments
   A. I only
   B. II only
   C. Both I and II
   D. Neither I nor II

64. Under common law, the risk of loss or damage due to fire or other hazards before delivery of the deed but after the signing of the contract is assumed by the
   I. buyer
   II. seller
   A. I only
   B. II only
   C. Both I and II
   D. Neither I nor II

65. Under the Federal Fair Housing Act of 1968, complaints may be filed
   I. with the Department of Housing and Urban Development, state or local agency
   II. by civil suit to the local federal district court
   A. I only
   B. II only
   C. Both I and II
   D. Neither I nor II

66. Before a newly constructed dwelling unit can be used by people, the appropriate governmental agency must issue a
   A. notice of inspection
   B. building permit
   C. certificate of occupancy
   D. health permit

67. A _____ states that the lender's rights and interests in the property cease if the principal and interest are paid according to the agreement.
   A. defeasance clause
   B. lien release
   C. title transfer
   D. deed assignment

68. In property description, the term "bounds" refers to
   I. distance
   II. direction
   A. I only
   B. II only
   C. Both I and II
   D. Neither I nor II

69. The cost approach in appraisal is based on
   A. value in exchange
   B. cost of acquisition
   C. cost of production
   D. value in use

70. Regulation Z is based on the authority of the
   I. Consumer Credit Protection Act
   II. Truth-in-Lending Act
   A. I only
   B. II only
   C. Both I and II
   D. Neither I nor II

71. Title insurance protects
   A. all previous owners against claims
   B. only future heirs of the policyholder
   C. against forged deeds and documents
   D. future owners other than heirs if the property is sold

72. In preparation for closing the property transaction, which of the following would normally be the obligation of the seller?
   A. Tax receipt and lien clearances
   B. Property survey
   C. Appraisal report
   D. Fire and hazard insurance

73. An easement in gross is the right to use the land of another. It requires
   A. no adjacent or dominant estate
   B. an adjacent property

Practice Salesperson's Examination

C. recordation in the public land records
   D. an annual licensing fee
74. Regarding condominium ownership,
   I. mortgage interest and property taxes paid by individual owners are deductible on their personal income tax return
   II. periodic maintenance fees are levied on individual unit owners for the purpose of maintaining the common areas
   A. I only
   B. II only
   C. Both I and II
   D. Neither I nor II
75. In states where a mortgage is given and title to the property does not pass to the mortgagee, the theory explaining this is
   A. lien theory
   B. title theory
   C. mortgage theory
   D. trust deed theory
76. The river running between my estate and that of my neighbor suddenly changed its course and removed some of my land to my neighbor's side. This action is known as
   I. accretion
   II. reliction
   A. I only
   B. II only
   C. Both I and II
   D. Neither I nor II
77. Under common law, the following unities are necessary to create a joint tenancy
   I. title
   II. interest
   A. I only
   B. II only
   C. Both I and II
   D. Neither I nor II
78. Members of a planning board or zoning commission are generally appointed by
   A. local REALTORS®
   B. the grand jury
   C. city council, city manager with the consent or confirmation of the city council or by the mayor
   D. the state legislature
79. Which of the following mortgages allows for future advances of funds to the borrower?
   A. Blanket mortgage
   B. Package mortgage
   C. Open-end mortgage
   D. Purchase money mortgage
80. Covenants of title may be
   I. implied by law
   II. expressly stated in the deed
   A. I only
   B. II only
   C. Both I and II
   D. Neither I nor II

SOLUTIONS

Question	Correct Answer	Question	Correct Answer	Question	Correct Answer	Question	Correct Answer
#1	B	#21	C	#41	B	#61	C
#2	D	#22	C	#42	C	#62	C
#3	A	#23	B	#43	D	#63	A
#4	A	#24	B	#44	D	#64	A
#5	D	#25	A	#45	C	#65	C
#6	B	#26	A	#46	B	#66	C
#7	C	#27	B	#47	C	#67	A
#8	B	#28	A	#48	A	#68	B
#9	B	#29	D	#49	D	#69	C
#10	B	#30	D	#50	D	#70	C
#11	D	#31	A	#51	B	#71	C
#12	A	#32	D	#52	A	#72	A
#13	B	#33	A	#53	B	#73	A
#14	B	#34	C	#54	D	#74	C
#15	B	#35	D	#55	C	#75	A
#16	D	#36	D	#56	A	#76	D
#17	B	#37	A	#57	D	#77	C
#18	B	#38	D	#58	C	#78	C
#19	C	#39	D	#59	B	#79	C
#20	B	#40	D	#60	C	#80	C

Appendix E

Practice Broker's Examination

QUESTIONS

1. Which of the following is (are) true in regard to mortgage financing?
   I. Except under unusual circumstances, most lenders normally do not bring foreclosure proceedings until the loan is 60 days or more in arrears.
   II. By including an acceleration clause in the mortgage contract, the lender is entitled to the remaining mortgage balance if the conditions of the contract are not met.
   A. I only
   B. II only
   C. Both I and II
   D. Neither I nor II

2. A licensed broker accepts an earnest money deposit in cash for the principal, as authorized, after finding a ready, willing and able buyer. The next day the buyer is transferred out of town and the seller releases the buyer from the contract. The seller agrees to return the deposit. Assuming the listing contract is silent on this issue, which of the following is true?
   A. The broker is entitled to keep the earnest money as a commission.
   B. Since no sale actually resulted, the broker did not earn a commission.
   C. The broker must turn the earnest money into court through an interpleader.
   D. The broker must obey the seller's instructions as to the disposition of the deposit.

3. In the market comparison approach to value, comparable sales are adjusted to the
   A. most comparable sales property
   B. subject property
   C. standards of the market
   D. "ideal" standard of comparison

4. Ginnie Mae can be described as a (an)

   A. government-sponsored, privately owned corporation that supplements private mortgage market operations
   B. agency of the federal government that insures mortgage loans
   C. federal government corporation designed to handle special assistance functions for certain FHA and VA loans and to guarantee certain securities backed by mortgage loans
   D. agency of the federal government that regulates interest rates charged by federally chartered financial institutions

5. When is the doctrine of constructive notice applied?
   I. A legal advertisement in the newspaper
   II. Knowledge based upon the existence of recorded documents
   A. I only
   B. II only
   C. Both I and II
   D. Neither I nor II

6. Nancy Salesperson receives $200 salary each month plus 40% of the total commission on every house she sells. Tom, the broker, lists a house for $62,500 with a commission rate of 7%. If Nancy sells that house for 10% less than the listing price and that is her only sale this month, her total compensation for the month will be
   A. $1,575.00
   B. $1,775.00
   C. $2,362.50
   D. $2,562.50

7. A covenant in a deed where the grantor guarantees that he or she owns and is in possession of property and has the right to sell is known as
   A. quitclaim
   B. warranty
   C. grant
   D. seizin

8. The Parol Evidence Rule states that

A. a written contract cannot be modified by evidence of prior oral agreements

B. improvements added to property usually pass with it when sold

C. the life of a term loan can be extended without prepayment in the interim

D. an interest in real property is less than a tenancy in severalty.

9. A landlord may assign all or part of his or her rights under a lease contract only if

   I. the tenant agrees

   II. state law permits

   A. I only   C. Both I and II
   B. II only   D. Neither I nor II

10. Dick paid $44,600 for his house last year. What must he sell the house for if he wants to net $15,000 after paying an 8% sales commission and an outstanding mortgage of $37,600?

    A. $48,168   C. $56,808
    B. $48,392   D. $57,175

11. Robert sold his farm for a 43% profit. If it cost him $84,000, what did he sell if for?

    A. $112,560   C. $120,120
    B. $116,660   D. $127,000

12. To hypothecate means to

    A. enter into a participation agreement with other lenders

    B. borrow money at below-market interest rates

    C. mortgage out

    D. pledge something as security but retain possession of it

13. If a certain property has a high degree of risk associated with its ability to generate income, the capitalization rate used in the income approach value will be

    A. higher, thus producing a higher value

    B. higher, thus producing a lower value

    C. lower, thus producing a lower value

    D. lower, thus producing a higher value

14. How much simple interest is due on a $38,000 loan at 9½% per annum at the end of 6 years and 3 months?

    A. $21,375.00   C. $22,743.00
    B. $22,562.50   D. $38,000.00

15. The covenant in a deed promising the grantee that no one with title paramount to the grantor's will disturb possession is the covenant

    A. of further assurances

    B. against encumbrances

    C. of quiet enjoyment

    D. of seizin

16. If an offer to purchase contains a clause that a more formal agreement will be drawn up within five days after the seller signs the agreement, the

    I. person making the offer has five days to withdraw the offer

    II. agreement is a valid contract if it provides that the final price will be negotiated within five days

    A. I only   C. Both I and II
    B. II only   D. Neither I nor II

17. The type of agreement known as a sandwich leasehold comes into being when

    A. the original tenant sublets the premise to subtenants

    B. the lease is signed with the property manager rather than the owner

    C. the property is sold and the lease is transferred to the new owner

    D. a sale-leaseback transaction occurs

18. Which of the following is generally not a function of the property manager?

    A. Keeping the property insured

    B. Marketing space and advertising

    C. Long-term property management decisions

    D. Physical care of the premises

19. In valuation theory the concept which considers the usefulness of a property is its

    A. situs   C. functional utility
    B. cost   D. location

20. Mr. Wicker purchased an apartment complex containing 12 units each renting for $250 per month. His annual total expenses are $14,400. If he paid $135,000 for the apartments, what is his return on the investment?

    A. 16%   C. 22%
    B. 18%   D. 27%

21. A family room is shown on a blueprint as being 3½" by 4½". The scale is given as one-fourth inch equals one foot. In order to fully carpet the room, how many square yards of carpeting will be needed?

    A. 26   C. 28
    B. 27   D. 29

22. The determination as to whether mortgages will sell at a discount or at a premium will be influenced by

    A. escrow and other closing costs

    B. the credit of the mortgagor

    C. interest rates of competing demands for funds

    D. the time of the year the mortgage is closed

23. The advertising of the sale of real property in the newspaper is a (an)

    A. option

    B. offer

    C. counteroffer

    D. invitation seeking an offer

24. A rectangular lot measuring 300' by 726' is purchased by a developer for $64,000. He uses 20% of the land for streets and dedicated areas at a total cost of $20,000

and subdivides the remainder into one-half acre lots. How much must each lot sell for in order for him to realize a 20% return on his total investment?

A. $7,680   C. $10,500
B. $10,080   D. $12,600

25. Mr. Ellis paid $265.48 interest one month on a loan he secured at 9¼% per annum. What is the loan balance?

A. $2,870   C. $35,397
B. $34,440   D. $36,614

26. The fundamental valuation principal underlying the market comparison approach is

A. anticipation   C. competition
B. substitution   D. conformity

27. In determining potential tenants, the property manager should

A. consider the racial and ethnic background
B. avoid probing into the person's past credit record
C. try to obtain the best qualified tenant so as to maintain a high occupancy rate
D. select any tenant as long as they have the necessary security deposit

28. The current tax rate of $3.16/$100 of assessed value is applied to a house assessed at 60% market value. If the annual tax bill is $1,403.04, what is the market value of the house?

A. $44,400   C. $74,000
B. $62,160   D. $110,000

29. Jack expects to lease a house for $200 per month when it is finished. A building contractor agrees to forfeit $100 per day if the construction is not completed by June 2. Which of the following is true?

A. The clause is unenforceable and the injured party can collect nothing because it is a penalty.
B. The clause will be enforced because it is a provision for liquidated damages.
C. The court will allow the injured party to recover nominal damages.
D. This is a valid clause for compensatory damages and is enforceable.

30. Which of the following generally cannot be used by the buyer as an excuse to cancel the sales contract?

A. Fraudulent representation
B. Latent defects
C. Undue influence
D. Patent defects

31. Two pumps discharge 8,000 gallons of water in 3 hours. How many pumps would it take to discharge 30,000 gallons in 1 hour?

A. 20   C. 26
B. 23   D. 30

32. When lawful letting or permission has ended and the tenant continues in possession, this is known as

A. tenancy at sufferance
B. monthly tenancy
C. tenancy at will
D. trespass

33. If a deed of trust is used, the lender is known as whom?

A. Mortgagee   C. Trustee
B. Beneficiary   D. Trustor

34. The annual taxes of $686 on a home were due and paid on July 1. What refund will the owner receive if he sells the house and closing is March 7?

A. $470.67   C. $215.33
B. $272.49   D. $158.16

35. Functional obsolescence can be

I. curable
II. incurable

A. I only   C. Both I and II
B. II only   D. Neither I nor II

36. In a warranty deed the seller makes covenants to the buyer that includes the covenant

A. of seizin and equal protection
B. of quiet enjoyment and nondiscrimination
C. against encumbrances and the covenant against further mortgages
D. of further assurance and warranty of title

37. Ordinarily a management agreement for a new condominium in its initial phase provides that

A. each unit owner manages his or her own unit
B. the sponsor manages the project until the last unit is sold
C. the sponsor executes the management agreement with the association until control is turned over to unit owners
D. management immediately rests with the association

38. In which type of capitalization method is it necessary to know how much to compensate each provider of funds in the money market?

A. Build-up method
B. Band of investment method
C. Comparison method
D. Property residual method

39. On which of the following properties would the broker realize a net commission of $3,000?

	Sale Price	Commission Percentage	Selling Expense
A.	$55,500	6%	$200
B.	$57,833	7%	$440
C.	$53,385	7%	$700
D.	$52,250	8%	$1,180

40. If a certificate of title indicates defects or otherwise shows clouds on the title the

A. seller must pay damages for the defects
B. sales contract is void and title will not be conveyed

Practice Broker's Examination

C. title company will intercede and remedy all defects of the title

D. parties to the contract are directed back to the sales agreement for clarification

41. A real estate closing which does not require the actual presence of the seller or the purchaser is known as what type of closing?
    A. Apportionment
    B. Broker's
    C. Escrow
    D. Exchange

42. Mr. Maronick purchased a two-year homeowner's insurance policy on September 22, 1989, for $48,000 coverage. The annual rate was $3.05 per $1,000 coverage. If Mr. Milburn buys the house and assumes the policy on October 9, 1990, how much should be credited to Mr. Maronick at closing?
    A. $153.71
    B. $146.40
    C. $139.49
    D. $127.29

43. What is calculated after operating expenses have been subtracted on an income statement?
    A. Effective gross income
    B. Net operating income
    C. Net cash flow
    D. Gross scheduled income

44. At the end of a lease, generally all improvements and repairs to the leased property become the possession of the
    I. lessor
    II. lessee
    A. I only
    B. II only
    C. Both I and II
    D. Neither I nor II

45. When a broker is asked questions about the condition of a property of which he or she is not certain, the broker should
    I. direct the buyer to the owner for the answer(s)
    II. if a sale is imminent the broker should use his or her experience to make an educated guess
    A. I only
    B. II only
    C. Both I and II
    D. Neither I nor II

46. The landlord may recover possession of the property by going into court and obtaining a (an)
    A. eviction subpoena
    B. unlawful detainer
    C. repossession notice
    D. distraint warrant

47. Bobby Chapman borrows $30,000 from a bank and agrees to pay them $315 per month applied first to interest and then to principal. If the interest rate is 9%, what will the outstanding balance be after the second payment?
    A. $30,000.00
    B. $29,819.33
    C. $29,910.00
    D. $29,886.21

48. An item of accrued depreciation is curable if the
    A. cost to cure is no greater than the expected increase in value
    B. cost to cure is no greater than the reproduction cost new
    C. cost to cure is no greater than the replacement cost new
    D. item can be physically replaced or repaired

49. With a variable rate mortgage the
    I. term of the loan might increase
    II. interest rate charged may decrease
    A. I only
    B. II only
    C. Both I and II
    D. Neither I nor II

50. All deeds should be
    I. signed by the grantee
    II. recorded
    A. I only
    B. II only
    C. Both I and II
    D. Neither I nor II

51. A novation agreement
    A. releases the mortgagor from any liability to the mortgagee
    B. allows prepayment of a mortgage without penalty
    C. releases a mechanic's lien
    D. is related to the receiver covenant in a mortgage

52. A lot measures 613' by 812'. What is its total worth if land is valued at $12,000 per acre?
    A. $137,123
    B. $134,046
    C. $131,681
    D. $114,261

53. When a property tax is not paid the
    I. delinquent tax may become a lien on the property
    II. property may be sold to pay the delinquent tax
    A. I only
    B. II only
    C. Both I and II
    D. Neither I nor II

54. A Planned Unit Development is a
    A. method of developing large tracts of land in stages
    B. growth model used to determine if a community's planning program is being carried out properly
    C. type of zoning that permits design flexibility from rigid zoning standards
    D. method of obtaining variances from land development standards because of hardships not self-imposed

55. A payment of $100,000 per year on a million dollar mortgage converts to a
    A. 10% mortgage constant
    B. mortgage constant of 100,000
    C. need to know length of mortgage to determine answer
    D. need to know interest rate to determine answer

56. The Truth-in-Lending Act (Regulation Z)
    I. regulates interest rates on VA and FHA mortgages

II. requires disclosure of finance charges on residential mortgages

A. I only
B. II only
C. Both I and II
D. Neither I nor II

57. A prospect requests racial information from a broker regarding a particular neighborhood. May the broker answer the request?
   I. No
   II. Yes, if you also direct the prospect's attention to the Equal Housing Opportunity poster.

   A. I only
   B. II only
   C. Both I and II
   D. Neither I nor II

58. When a purchaser assumes an existing mortgage the
   A. mortgagor is released from any liability to the mortgagee
   B. purchaser is obligated for the value of the realty alone
   C. purchaser assumes personal liability for a deficiency
   D. purchaser releases the mortgagor from any liability to any government guarantee agency such as VA

59. What is the gross rent multiplier for a house that has a market value of $48,500 and rents for $475 per month?
   A. 100
   B. 102
   C. 106
   D. 110

60. In a net lease
   A. the landlord pays all expenses and the tenant pays some fixed rate
   B. the tenant pays everything
   C. who pays what expense is negotiable
   D. the landlord always nets the same amount of income each year

61. The secondary mortgage market participant which is a subsidiary of the Federal Home Loan Bank System is the
   A. Federal National Mortgage Association
   B. Government National Mortgage Corporation
   C. Federal Home Loan Mortgage Corporation
   D. Mortgage Guaranty Insurance Corporation

62. The building below cost $14.00 per square foot to build in 1968. If the total cost today to build the same building is $27,000, the cost per square foot has increased approximately

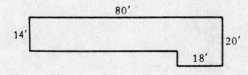

   A. 46%
   B. 77%
   C. 85%
   D. 116%

63. The borrower should incorporate a prepayment clause into the promissory note since such omission may

   I. interfere with the sale of the property
   II. prevent the owner from refinancing

   A. I only
   B. II only
   C. Both I and II
   D. Neither I nor II

64. Advantages to the seller of a sale and leaseback transaction include all of the following except
   A. if the property increases in value through the course of the leaseback, the seller automatically benefits through reduced rental rates
   B. the seller obtains the full cash value of the property which is usually much greater than that obtainable under mortgage financing
   C. the seller is able to reinvest cash gained from the sale
   D. the seller secures a substantial tax advantage when the entire amount of the rent becomes tax deductible instead of only the interest portion of the debt and accrued depreciation

65. Which form of ownership is recognized by the courts only when the instrument makes it clear that survivorship is intended by the use of appropriate words such as "to the grantees, their survivors, survivor's heirs and assigns"?
   A. Tenancy in severalty
   B. Joint tenancy
   C. Tenancy by entirety
   D. Tenancy in common

66. Tigger owns a large shopping center for which he is renegotiating leases. An economic forecast indicates that inflation will continue to increase. What type of lease would you recommend?
   A. Net
   B. Percentage
   C. Flat
   D. Gross

67. What is the rate of return on an investment when net operating income is $6,612 and the property is valued at $84,500?
   A. 7.8%
   B. 8.9%
   C. 10%
   D. 12.8%

68. Federal Fair Housing Laws prohibit
   I. refusing to show a house to a particular person on the basis of race
   II. quoting different prices to different people on the basis of religion

   A. I only
   B. II only
   C. Both I and II
   D. Neither I nor II

69. A mortgagee's policy of title insurance is purchased by the
   A. mortgagee
   B. mortgagor
   C. seller
   D. lender

70. A commercial building rents for $1,500 per month. If the dimensions of the store are 60' by 45', what is the annual rate per square foot?
   A. $2.25
   B. $6.67
   C. $4.80
   D. $7.25

Practice Broker's Examination

71. A release of mortgage instrument is normally used to release property secured by a (an)
    A. open-end mortgage
    B. purchase money mortgage
    C. package mortgage
    D. blanket mortgage

72. Some of the economic attributes of land are
    A. scarcity, modification, immobility
    B. fixity of investment, indestructibility
    C. situs, nonhomogeneity
    D. fixity of investment, situs

73. A chain of title refers to a
    A. continuous title insurance
    B. certificate of title
    C. listing of all recorded instruments affecting title of the subject property
    D. measurement used in surveying land

74. Fran offered to purchase a house contingent on obtaining a mortgage at 9% interest for 30 years. Which of the following is true?
    I. The agreement is a binding contract when a lending institution makes a formal commitment.
    II. The sale of the house becomes an absolute duty only when a promissory note is signed and a mortgage is issued.
    A. I only
    B. II only
    C. Both I and II
    D. Neither I nor II

75. Discount points are used by the lender
    A. to attract borrowers
    B. to increase effective yields
    C. in figuring monthly installments on a level payment plan
    D. to pay for the appraisal and title examination

76. What estate comes into possession upon the expiration of a life estate?
    A. escheat
    B. reversionary interest
    C. remainderment
    D. easement

77. The city took 20% of Mr. Jeffery's front property. The lot is 200' by 300'. How many acres did Mr. Jeffery lose?
    A. 5
    B. 28
    C. .28
    D. .5

78. The down payment requirement is generally the highest under which type of loan?
    A. VA
    B. FHA
    C. Conventional
    D. Conventional-insured

79. The term *menace* in contracts refers to
    A. use of force
    B. threat of violence
    C. undue influence
    D. the failure to act

80. A clause giving the mortgagee the right to call the loan balance due and payable if the mortgagor sells the property is referred to as a (an) _____ clause.
    A. condemnation
    B. mortgage transfer
    C. reversal
    D. due on sale

SOLUTIONS

Question	Correct Answer	Question	Correct Answer	Question	Correct Answer	Question	Correct Answer
#1	C	#21	C	#41	C	#61	C
#2	D	#22	C	#42	C	#62	C
#3	B	#23	D	#43	B	#63	C
#4	C	#24	D	#44	A	#64	A
#5	C	#25	B	#45	A	#65	B
#6	B	#26	B	#46	B	#66	B
#7	D	#27	C	#47	B	#67	A
#8	A	#28	C	#48	A	#68	C
#9	D	#29	A	#49	C	#69	B
#10	D	#30	D	#50	B	#70	B
#11	C	#31	B	#51	A	#71	D
#12	D	#32	A	#52	A	#72	D
#13	B	#33	B	#53	C	#73	C
#14	B	#34	C	#54	C	#74	A
#15	C	#35	C	#55	A	#75	B
#16	D	#36	D	#56	B	#76	B
#17	A	#37	C	#57	A	#77	C
#18	C	#38	B	#58	C	#78	C
#19	C	#39	D	#59	B	#79	B
#20	A	#40	D	#60	C	#80	D

Glossary of Real Estate Terms

Many questions on the Real Estate Licensing Examinations are based on word recognition. This glossary is a tool that can help you become skillful in answering such questions. At the end of each chapter is a section called "Key Terms And Phrases." If after having read the chapter you do not recognize some of the terms and phrases, you should write them down on an index card. On the other side of the index card, write down the definition of that term or phrase, which appears in this glossary. When you have some spare time, take out some of the cards you have prepared and see if you remember the definition before you look on the other side. This glossary includes additional terms and phrases which may help you. Each definition is followed by the chapter number in which the word most prominently appeared. Following the "Glossary of Real Estate Terms" is a specialized glossary which deals with housing and construction terms

TRICK WORDS

Make sure that you know the difference between the following pairs of words. These are so-called trick words which appear frequently to trap the unwary or unprepared examinee.

Devise	Demise
Encroachment	Encumbrance
Eviction	Ejectment
Executor	Executory Contract
Installment Sale	Installment Land Contract
Leasehold	Leased Fee
Mortgagor	Mortgagee
Open Mortgage	Open End Mortgage
Principal	Principle
Second Mortgage	Second Mortgage Market
Severalty	Joint Tenancy
Subordination	Subrogation
Testate	Intestate

AAA Tenants: the most credit-worthy tenants as determined by national credit rating service, 10

Abandonment: the release of a claim or right in a piece of property with the intention of terminating ownership and without giving it to anyone else, 10

Abatement: a reduction in amount, 18

Able: in the phrase "ready, willing and able" this term refers to the financial capability of a purchaser, 6

Abnormal Sale: A sale that is not typical within the context of the market. This can occur because of undue pressure on either the buyer or seller or for some other reason, 17

Abode: a home or place of residence, 11

Abrogate: to repeal, 5

Absentee Ownership: the owner(s) of property does not physically reside on the property, 10

Absorption Rate: the percent of total real estate space of a particular type that can be sold or leased in a local market, 18

Abstract of Title: a history of the ownership of a parcel of land which lists transfers of title, rights and liabilities, 16

Abut: to border on or to share a common boundary, 7

Accelerated Depreciation: the methods of depreciation for income tax purposes which increase the write-off at a rate higher than under straight-line depreciation, 18

Acceleration Clause: states that upon default all of the principal installments come due immediately, 14

Acceptance: a voluntary expression of unconditional and absolute assent by the offereee to be bound by the terms of the offer in the manner requested or authorized by the offeror, 5

Access: the right to enter upon and leave property, 8

Accessibility: the ease with which one can enter and leave a property, 19

Accession: the idea that the owner of land is entitled to all that the soil produces or all that is added to the land either intentionally or by mistake, 13

Accord and Satisfaction: an agreed-to substitution of a different performance for the original obligation, 5

Account Stated: an agreement that parties who have had a series of money transactions agree that after off-setting the various debits and credits, the new balance remaining is the true sum owed by one of the parties, 5

Accretion: refers to land which is accumulated by the gradual washing or motion of water, 13

Accrue: an accumulation, 18

Accrued Depreciation: any diminishment of utility or value from the reproduction cost new of an improvement on land, 18

Acknowledgment: a formal declaration to a public official, by a person who has executed an instrument which states that the execution was voluntary, 13

Acquisition: the process by which property ownership is achieved, 8

Acquisition Cost: total cost of purchasing an asset which includes closing costs and other transaction expenses added to the selling price, 18

Acre: a measure of land equal to 43,560 square feet, 20

Acreage Property: unimproved property, 2

Action to Quiet Title: the lawsuit filed by a person to remove or clear the claims of others against property, 16

Actual Age: the historical age of a building, 17

Actual Authority: a power that a principal has expressly conferred upon an agent or any power that is incidental or necessary to carry out the express power, 6

Actual Eviction: the violation of any material breach of covenants by the landlord or any other act which wrongfully deprives the tenant of the possession of the premises, 10

Actual Notice: the actual knowledge that a person has about the existence of a particular fact, 14

Actual Possession: refers to the physical occupancy of real estate as distinguished from constructive possession which refers to the legal right to assume occupancy, 10

Adequate Public Facilities Ordinance: a local government ordinance that requires that certain public facilities such as roads, utilities and so forth are completed or soon to be completed before new real estate development can be permitted, 19

Adjacent: next to or bordering on, 19

Adjunction: the process of adding a parcel of land to a larger parcel, 19

Adjusted Cost Basis: the value of property for accounting purposes, equal to the original costs plus costs of any improvements less depreciation, 18

Adjustments: in the market data approach to value, these are the additions and subtractions which are made to account for differences between market comparable properties and the subject property being appraised, 17

Administrator, Administratrix: a person appointed by a court to settle the estate of a deceased person, 13

Administrator's Deed: issued to grantee who purchases property from an estate, 13

Ad Valorem: a prefix meaning "based on value." Most local governments levy an ad valorem tax on property, 19

Advance: used in construction financing to provide the builder with working capital, 15

Adverse Possession: a method of acquiring original title to property by open, notorious and hostile possession for a statutory period of time; also referred to as prescription, 13

Affiant: a person who has made an affidavit, 5

Affidavit: a written statement sworn to before a public official or other authorized person, 16

Affidavit of Title: a sworn statement by seller that no defects other than those stated in a contract or deed exist in the title being conveyed, 13

Affirm: to verify, 16

Affirmation: a solemn and formal declaration which is a substitute for an oath attesting to the truth of some manner, 16

Affirmative Fair Housing Marketing Plan: a requirement by HUD for all subdivisions, multi-family projects and mobile home parks of five or more units before these projects are eligible for participation in various federal programs, including home mortgage programs, 19

After-Tax Cash Flow: cash throw-off plus tax savings or minus tax liability of a project, 18

Agency: a relationship in which one party (the principal) authorizes another party (the agent) to act as the principal's representative in dealing with third parties, 6

Agency by Estoppel: occurs when the principal leads a third person to believe that somebody is his or her agent, 6

Agency by Necessity: authority created by operation of law in an emergency, 6

Agency by Ratification: occurs when a principal agrees to be bound by the acts of a person purporting to act as an agent, even though the person was not in fact an agent, 6

Agent: one who acts for and in place of a principal for the purpose of affecting the principal's legal relations with third persons, 6

Agreement: an expression of mutual assent by two or more parties, 5

Agreement of Sale: a contract between a purchaser and seller in which they agree on the terms and conditions of a sale. Also called sales contract, 5

Agricultural Property: an unimproved property available for farming activities, 2

Air Rights: the right to use, control and occupy the space above a particular parcel of land, 2

Alienation: a term which means the transfer of title from one person to another, 8

Alienation Clause: a provision in a mortgage requiring full payment of the debt upon the transfer of title to the property, 14

Allodial: the system of property ownership in America today; the term means free from the tenurial rights of a feudal overlord, 8

Alluvion: the deposit of soil upon land due to the natural flow of a river, 13

A.L.T.A. Title Policy: a standard title insurance policy with expanded coverage, 16

Alteration: an unauthorized modification of the contract by one of the parties, 5

Amenities: benefits received from a particular location or improvement of property, 17

Amortization: the repayment of a financial obligation over a period of time in a series of periodic installments. In a level-payment mortgage, this is the portion of the debt service that reduces the principal, 15

Amortized Loan: a financial debt that is paid off over a period of time by a series of periodic payments. A loan can be fully amortized or partially amortized requiring a balloon payment to satisfy the debt at the end of the term, 15

Anchor Tenant: a well-known commercial business such as a chain store or department store used as the primary tenant in a shopping center, 10

Annexation: (1) the addition of personal property to real property, 2; (2) in local government law, the addition of a surrounding area to the corporate jurisdiction of a city, 19

Annual: yearly, 20

Annual Percentage Rate (APR): the yearly cost of credit, 15

Annuity: a series of payments either made or received at even intervals over a period of time. An example is the series of payments made to satisfy a mortgage debt, 15

Anticipation, Principle of: value changes in expectation of some future benefit or detriment affecting the property, 17

Apparent Authority: authority in which the principal allows third persons to believe that an agent exists, 6

Appeals Board: Many jurisdictions provide a means by which a property owner can protest a tax bill. The procedure may involve meeting with the tax assessor or appearing before a local appeals board or board of equalization, 19

Apportionment: a division of expenses and charges between buyer and seller at the date of closing. Normally, the seller pays expenses up to and including the day of closing, 16

Appraisal: an opinion or estimate of value, 17

Appraisal Process: a systematic procedure of collecting and analyzing data to reach an opinion of value, 17

Appraisal Report: submitted by the appraiser to support the opinion of value, 17

Appreciation: an increase in value, 17

Appurtenance: any right or privilege which belongs to and passes with land, 8

Arc: used in the metes and bounds method of land description to denote curved boundary lines, 7

Arms-length Transaction: occurs between willing buyer and willing seller with each party completely knowledgeable about the market, 17

Arrears: not on time; late in making payments or completing work, 14

Arterial Street: a major road designed to be a through street and to handle a large volume of traffic, 19

Artificial Person: an entity recognized by law as having legal rights such as a corporation, 4

As is: a phrase which disclaims any promises or warranties. A person purchasing real estate "as is" takes it in exactly the condition in which it is found, 6

Asking Price: the listed price of property, 6

Assemblage: bringing two or more lots together under one ownership, 17

Assessed Value: the value placed on property by the tax assessor for the purpose of determining the property tax, 19

Assessment: placing a value on property for the purpose of levying a property tax, 19

Assessor: a tax official who determines the assessed value of property, 19

Assets: the real and personal property one possesses; assets minus liabilities equal net worth, 18

Assignee: the person receiving a contractual benefit or right, 5

Assignment: (1) the means by which a person transfers contract rights, 5; (2) occurs when the lessee parts with the entire estate, retaining no interest, 10

Assignor: the person transferring a contractual right or benefit, 5

Associate Broker: an individual who is licensed as a broker but who works in conjunction with another broker, 4

Assumption Fee: a charge levied by a lender to a purchaser who takes title to property by assuming an existing mortgage, 16

Assumption of Mortgage: a transfer of mortgage obligation to the purchaser who becomes personally liable on any deficiencies occurring in a foreclosure sale with the original borrower being secondarily liable, 14

Attachment: the process of taking a person's property into legal custody by a court order called a writ of attachment, 12

Attestation: the process of witnessing, 13

Attorney-at-law: a person authorized to practice law under state licensing requirements, 2

Attorney in Fact: a person given the authority to act on behalf of another under a power of attorney, 8

Attorney's Opinion of Title: a statement issued by an attorney after analyzing an abstract as to quality of title, 16

Attractive Nuisance: a potentially hazardous object or condition located on a parcel that is attractive to young children. Ordinarily, the owner is liable for any injuries incurred, 11

Auction: the selling of property to the highest bidder, 5

Authority: the power of an agent to affect the principal's legal relations for lawful purposes, 6

Authorization to Sell: another name for the listing agreement entered into by seller and broker determining the rights and responsibilities of both, 6

Avulsion: occurs in cases where there is a sudden change in the bed of a river which had been used as a boundary by property owners. Such a sudden change conveys no new land, 13

Bad Title: title with defects making it unmarketable, 16

Bailment: occurs when one person, called the bailor, gives possession and control of personal property, but not ownership, to a person called a bailee, 6

Balance, Principle of: an appraisal valuation principle which states that there is an ideal equilibrium in assembling the four

Glossary of Real Estate Terms

factors of production. If too few, the property is underimproved; if too many, the property is overimproved, 19

Balloon Payment: the remaining balance at maturity on a loan that has not been completely repaid through periodic payments. Once paid, the outstanding balance is zero, 15

Band of Investment Method: a technique for deriving a capitalization rate related to the typical capital structure of a particular project and to how much would be necessary to compensate each provider of funds, 18

Bargain and Sale Deed: an instrument conveying title which recites a valuable consideration and commonly uses the words "bargain and sale" or words of similar import, 13

Base Lines: imaginary lines running east-west which intersect with meridian lines to form the starting points in the rectangular survey method of land description, 7

Base Rent: in percentage leases, this is the minimum due to the landlord, 10

Basic Industry: an industry which attracts income from outside the community, 19

Basis: the value of property for income tax purposes. Calculated as original cost plus all capital improvements, minus accrued depreciation, 18

Basis Point: There are 100 basis points in one percentage point, 15

Bearing: in legal descriptions, the bearing is identified with reference to the quadrants on a compass and is expressed in terms of degrees, minutes and seconds, 7

Beltway: a circumferential highway around a major city, 19

Bench mark: a bronze disk permanently placed and precisely identified by government survey teams, 7

Beneficial Interest: an equitable title in property, 8

Beneficiary: (1) the lender under a deed of trust, 14; (2) the investor in an REIT, 8

Bequeath: to leave or hand down personal property by will, 13

Biennial: once every two years, 20

Bilateral Contract: a contract in which a promise is given for the promise of another. It becomes binding when mutual promises are communicated, 5

Bill of Sale: a document used to transfer ownership of personal property, 5

Binding Arbitration: a procedure of private adjudication of disputes. Each party agrees to be bound by a decision reached by a panel of arbitrators, 5

Bird Dog: a colloquial expression describing a salesperson specializing in obtaining new listings for a brokerage firm, 6

Blanket Mortgage: a mortgage which covers more than one piece of real estate. Often used by a developer in the financing of undeveloped lots, 15

Blight: in city planning, decay in a neighborhood, 19

Block: a means of subdividing large tracts of land into smaller sections, each of which is numbered. For example, Lot 4, Block 8; 7

Blockbusting: any activity which attempts to drive prices down for the purpose of causing transition from one ethnic group to another. This is a violation of federal fair housing laws, 12

Blue Sky Laws: state regulations over the sale of securities, 18

Board of Equalization: located at both the state and local levels, this board hears formal tax assessment complaints and has the power and authority to adjust inequities, 19

Bona Fide: in good faith, 5

Bond: (1) in finance, similar to a promissory note; an interest-bearing certificate of indebtedness, 14; (2) in law, the amount put up to secure the performance of some obligation, 4

Book Value: the worth of property as carried on the owner's books. Calculated as cost plus capital improvements minus accrued depreciation, 18

Boot: in federal taxation, cash or something else of value given in the exchange of two properties when the value of one is less than the value of the other, 18

Borrower: the person obtaining funds from the lender with the understanding that the funds will be paid back, 15

Boundary: the border of a parcel of land, 7

Bounds: refers to boundaries; used with the word "metes" in the metes and bounds method of land description, 7

Breach of Contract: a failure to perform as promised at the time the performance was due, 5

Breakeven Point: in finance, this point is reached when total income is equal to total expenses, 18

Broker: a person acting as an intermediary for another and who, for a fee, offers to perform certain functions such as those done by real estate brokers or mortgage brokers, 4

Budget Mortgage: a type of loan in which each monthly payment covers, in addition to principal and interest, one-twelfth of annual expenses such as property taxes and property insurance, 15

Buffer Zone: a means by which planners use space to separate two adjoining districts which have incompatible uses. A buffer zone consists of uses which are compatible with uses in each adjoining district, 19

Building Code: ordinances passed by local governments which specify minimum standards of construction for new buildings. They also apply to major additions to old construction, 19

Building Permit: a permit which is required by local governments before a building can be constructed or remodeled, 19

Building Residual Technique: a method of capitalizing income which allows for the recapture of the building investment over the building's remaining life, 17

Building Restrictions: public regulations requiring certain construction standards for the health and safety of the public, 19

Build-up Method: a technique for deriving a capitalization rate, 18

Bulk Zoning: zoning regulating the intensity of development on land, 19

Bundle of Rights: the rights of an owner to possess, control, enjoy and dispose of property, 8

Business Cycle: a recurring change of highs and lows in the economy, 15

Buyer's Market: a situation where there exists an oversupply of certain kinds of real estate. This results in greater opportunities for buyers to find properties on favorable terms and prices, 11

Bylaws: legal documentation in a condominium regime which provides the establishment of the homeowner's association, provides the powers and authority given to the board of directors and indicates various rights and responsibilities of the unit owners, 9

Canadian Roll-over Mortgage: *see* Renegotiable Rate Mortgage

Cancellation Clause: a clause containing rights for one or more of the parties to a lease to terminate the contract, 10

Canons of Ethics: *see* Code of Ethics, 4

Capacity: the ability to perform certain acts such as entering into a contract, 5

Capital: (1) in economics, a factor of production which includes all physical resources except for land, 2; (2) in finance, a sum of money, 15

Capital Gains: the tax profit realized from the sale of property, 18

Capital-gains Tax: a tax on profits of a qualified capital asset, 18

Capitalization: used in the income approach to value. To capitalize income means to convert future income into present (current) value, 17

Capitalization Rate: the rate of interest considered to be a reasonable return on investment given the risk, 17

Capital Recovery: a return "of" capital, 18

Cap. Rate: an abbreviation of capitalization rate, 17

Carryover Clause: *see* Extender Clause, 10

Cash Flow: the sum of money generated from income-producing property after all operating expenses and mortage payments have been made, 18

Cash Throw-off: before-tax cash flow, 18

Caveat Emptor: means "Let the buyer beware," 5

CBD: the abbreviation for central business district, 19

Certificate of Eligibility: certificate given to veterans bearing evidence of their qualifications for a VA mortgage loan, 15

Certificate of Estoppel: instrument signed by mortgagor or mortgagee stating unpaid amount on the principal of the mortgage when the mortgage is being assigned, 14

Certificate of No Defense: *see* Certificate of Estoppel, 14

Certificate of Occupancy: local governments require the owner of a new structure to obtain this certificate before the structure may be occupied, 19

Certificate of Reasonable Value (CPR): issued by the Veterans Administration to certify the value of property secured by a VA mortgage, 15

Certificate of Title: a document given by the title examiner stating the quality of title the seller possesses, 16

Cession Deed: used to transfer a portion of an individual's property to a local government for streets or sidewalks, 13

Chain: a unit of land measurement equal to 66 feet, 20

Chain of Title: a history of the conveyances and encumbrances affecting title to a parcel of land, 16

Change, Principle of: an appraisal principle which holds that the environment is constantly changing and these changes affect the value of a particular site, 17

Chattel Mortgage: one in which personal property is pledged to secure a note, 14

Chattel Real: (1) an object which has become annexed to real property. Also referred to as a fixture, 2; (2) all interests, such as leaseholds, which in reality are of less dignity than a freehold estate, 8

Checks: the name given to the 24-by-24 mile areas formed by the intersection of guide meridians and parallels in the rectangular survey method of land description, 7

Circuit-breaker: an approach for property tax relief in which a state allows a tax credit to homeowners on the basis of age and disability who meet certain qualifying conditions, 19

City Planning: the effort on the part of the city to coordinate, direct and control the type of development taking place so as to ensure maximum benefits to the populace, 19

Civil Action: a lawsuit between private parties, 5

Civil Rights Act of 1866: a law which prohibits discrimination in all real estate transactions based on race, 12

Clerk of County Court: in most states, this is the public official with whom legal instruments are recorded, 13

Closed Mortgage: a mortgage that cannot be prepaid before maturity, 15

Closing: this is the time that title normally passes and at which prorations are made between buyer and seller in a real estate transaction. Also called settlement, 16

Closing Costs: the expenses incurred and paid at the time of settlement in the transferring of property, 16

Closing Date: date for transferring title, 16

Closing Statement: a statement prepared indicating debits and credits due on closing, 16

Cloud on Title: any claim affecting title to property, 16

Code of Ethics: (1) included in the license laws of most states, this is regarded as the standard of conduct required by the commission of all persons licensed in that state, 3; (2) codes of responsibility adopted by professional groups such as the NATIONAL ASSOCIATION OF REALTORS®, the American Institute of Appraisers and others, 2

Codicil: a formal amendment to a will, 13

Cognovit Note: authorizes confession of a judgment, 14

Coinsurance Clause: requires the insured to carry a certain amount of coverage in order to recover the total amount of a loss, 11

Collateral: pledged property as security for a loan, 14

Color of Title: any claim to title which for some reason is defective, 13

Commercial Banks: the largest financial intermediary directly involved in the financing of real estate. Their primary real estate activity involves short-term loans, 15

Commercial Frustration: occurs if the purpose of a lease or contract cannot be effectuated, 10

Commercial Property: income property zoned for such uses as office buildings or service facilities, 19

Commingling: illegally mixing deposits or monies collected from a client with one's personal account, 24

Commission: (1) amount due as fee for broker's performance, usually a percentage of sales price, 6; (2) in government, a board empowered to do something, 19

Commissioners: members of the real estate commission or other similar body, such as a county commission, who act as the governing of policymaking body of the commission, 4

Commissioner's Deed: given to foreclose a deed of trust in lieu of a trustee's sale, 13

Commitment: a pledge or promise, 15

Commitment Letter: a promise received from a lender to supply financing if certain conditions are met, 15

Committee Deed: issued by a group of people who are appointed by the court to administer the property of someone who has been adjudged legally incompetent, 13

Common Elements: property jointly owned on a pro rata basis with other unit owners in a condominium regime, 9

Common Law: (1) a body of legal rules derived from accepted customs and procedures in England. Serves as the foundation for most laws in every state except Louisiana, 2; (2) system of court-made law in this country, 5

Communicated: the receiving of either an offer or an acceptance by the offeror or offeree, 5

Community Property: any property acquired in certain states by purchase or as compensation by either spouse during the period of marriage is considered to be owned in an undivided half interest by each, 8

Community Reinvestment Act: a provision of the Housing and Community Development Act of 1977 intended to prevent the practice of redlining and disinvestment by lenders in central city areas, 15

Comparable: comparable property recently sold which is used in the market data approach, 17

Comparable Sales Approach: *see* Market Data Approach, 17

Comparative Analysis: a method of appraising property in which the selling prices of similar properties are used as the basis for estimating the value of the subject property, 17

Comparative Square Foot Method: a technique to estimate reproduction or replacement cost which measures the total square footage or cubic footage and multiplies this total by the current cost per square foot, 17

Comparison Method: a technique for deriving a capitalization rate based on determining how much more an investor has to be compensated for a particular real estate investment in comparison to an "ideal" real estate investment, 17

Competent Parties: those who are legally capable of entering into contracts, 5

Component Depreciation: breaking down a depreciable capital asset into components and depreciating each component separately, 18

Compound Interest: interest paid on interest, in addition to being paid on the original principal, 20

Concession: a service offered by the owner to a tenant that results in the actual rent paid being less than the rent specified in the lease, 10

Condemnation: the process of exercising eminent domain through court action, 19

Conditional Commitment: a commitment by a lender to make a loan on the fulfillment of specified conditions, 15

Conditional Fee Estate: an interest in real estate which exists as long as a specified condition exists, 8

Conditional Sale Contract: a contract for the sale of personal property in which title is retained by the seller until the conditions of the contract have been met, 13

Condition Concurrent: a condition which requires mutual performance of parties, 5

Condition Precedent: one which requires something to occur before a duty becomes absolute and enforceable, 5

Condition Subsequent: something which extinguishes a duty to perform, 5

Condominium: a legal form of ownership which involves a separation of property into individual ownership elements and common ownership elements, 9

Condominium Declaration: the document which legally establishes the condominium regime. Also referred to as the master deed, 9

Condominium Plan: a graphic three-dimensional description of the various units and common areas in the condominium regime, 9

Confirmation of Sale: the court's approval of the price, terms and conditions of a sale ordered by the court, 14

Confiscation: a taking of property without just compensation, 19

Conformity, Principle of: according to this economic principle a piece of land must be used in such a way as to conform to surrounding land uses if maximum value is to be achieved, 17

Consent: agreement or approval, 5

Conservator: a guardian, 13

Consideration: anything of value offered to induce someone to enter into a contractual agreement, 5

Construction Loan: a mortgage loan which provides the funds necessary for the building or construction of a real estate project, 15

Constructive Eviction: occurs when the tenant's use of the premises is substantially disturbed or interfered with by the landlord's actions or failure to act where there is a duty to act, 10

Constructive Notice: the knowledge that the law presumes a person has about a particular fact irrespective of whether the person knows about the fact or not, 14

Constructive Possession: the legal right to occupy property without actual physical occupancy, 8

Consumer Price Index (CPI): an index prepared by the Bureau of Labor Statistics to measure changes in price levels of a predetermined mix of consumer goods and services. This index is often used as a means of changing lease payments, 10

Contiguous: adjoining or touching, 8

Contingency: a condition upon which the enforceability of a contract is often dependent, 5

Contract: an agreement resulting from the objective expression of mutual assent by competent parties which the law recognizes in some way as a duty and the breach of which the law gives a remedy, 5

Contract for a Deed: a means by which the seller passes possession but retains title to the property until the total or a substantial portion of the purchase price is paid, 14

Contract Rent: the amount of rent due as stated in the lease agreement, 10

Contractual Lien: a lien created by agreement of parties, for example, a mortgage given to secure the debt represented by a promissory note, 14

Contribution, Principle of: the value of a component part of a piece of property is equal to what that component part adds to total value, less any costs incurred, 17

Conventional Mortgage: a loan made without any government agency guaranteeing or insuring the mortgage, 15

Conversion: (1) occurs when a building originally under one form of ownership is changed into a different form of ownership, 9; (2) change in use of building, 2

Conveyance: the transfer of title to land from one party to another, 13

Cooperative: a form of property ownership in which a corporation is established to hold title in property and to lease the property to shareholders in the corporation, 9

Cooperative Sale: a sale involving two separate brokers sharing a commission, 6

Corporate Veil: the buffer which protects a shareholder of a corporation from personal liability stemming from any transactions undertaken by the corporation, 8

Corporation: a legal entity organized to have perpetual legal existence and to have legal power to carry on certain activities such as owning real estate, 8

Corporeal Property: involves possessory interests in land, including fee simple ownership, life estates and others, 8

Correction Deed: an instrument that corrects a mistake in a previous deed given by the same grantor; also known as deed of confirmation, 13

Correction Lines: used in the rectangular survey method of land description to adjust for the curvature of the earth's surface, 7

Cost Approach: a method of estimating value based on the economic principle of substitution; the value of a building cannot be greater than the cost of purchasing a similar site and constructing a building of equal utility, 17

Cost Basis: the value of property for accounting purposes. Equal to the original price plus all acquisition expenses, 18

Co-tenants: a co-owner of a property interest or estate, 8

Counteroffer: an implied rejection of the original offer by proposing a new offer or by making conditional acceptance, 5

Covenant: a contractual promise on the part of one person to another, for example, a grantee agreeing to restrict the use of the granted property in some manner, 13

Covenant Against Encumbrances: the assurance that no encumbrances other than those specified in the deed exist, 13

Covenant of Further Assurance: a promise that the grantor will perform further acts reasonably necessary to correct any defects in the title or in the deed instrument, 13

Covenant of Quiet Enjoyment: a promise that no one has superior or paramount title to that of the grantor, assures the grantee of peaceful possession without fear of being ousted by a person with a superior claim to the property, 13

Covenant of Right to Convey: the assurance that the grantor has the right, power and authority to convey the title being granted, 13

Covenant of Seizin: gives the assurance that the grantor has the exact estate in the quantity and quality which in fact is being conveyed, 13

Covenant of Trust: makes the seller a trustee of the purchase price funds for the benefit of the buyer until the time for recording mechanic's and materialman's liens has expired, 13

Covenant of Warranty of Title: the assurance that the grantor will underwrite the legal expenses if any person establishes a claim superior to the title given by the grantor, 13

Credit: (1) the ability to secure financing, 15; (2) something payable or to be received, 16

Creditor: the person to whom a debt is owed, 15

Cross Index: a means of indexing title records by which each party in the conveyance instrument is listed. Also referred to as grantor-grantee index, 16

Cul-de-sac: a dead end street with a turn-around at the end, 7

Curable Depreciation: depreciation is considered curable if the cost of the repair is less than what the repair adds to the value of property, 17

Curtesy: the rights that a husband acquires in his wife's property upon her death, 8

Curtilage: enclosed area surrounding a house, 11

Damages: the court-ordered monetary payment people receive when either their personal or property rights have been violated, 5

Date of Appraisal: the date as of which the opinion of value is based, 17

Debit: money owed, 16

Debt Coverage Ratio: ratio which is calculated by dividing the annual net operating income by the annual debt service of a mortgage loan, 18

Debt Financing: the use of borrowed funds to make a real estate purchase, 15

Debt Service: an installment payment which includes both interest and amortization of principal, 15

Decedent: a deceased person, 5

Declaration of Homestead: in those states which provide for a homestead exemption, this is the document which must be filed by the head of the household, 8

Declining-balance Depreciation: an accelerated depreciation method in which, after the depreciation is taken, the remaining depreciable balance is the base for calculating the subsequent year's depreciation, 18

Decree: court order, 5

Decree of Foreclosure: a court order making a foreclosure effective, 14

Dedication: a process by which title to roads and other land is transferred by a property owner to the government, 19

Deduction: a legal adjustment to reduce taxable income, 18

Deed: a written instrument, usually under seal, which contains an agreement to transfer some property interest from a grantor to a grantee, 13

Deed Books: part of the public records in which copies of deeds are recorded; also called libers, 13

Deed in Lieu of Foreclosure: used by the mortgagor who is in default to convey the property to the mortgagee in order to eliminate the need for a foreclosure, 13

Deed in Trust: used to convey property to a trustee in a land trust, 13

Deed of Release: given by lienholders, remaindermen or mortgagees to relinquish their claims on the property, 13

Deed of Surrender: used to merge a life estate with a reversion or remainder, 13

Deed of Trust: a deed to real property, which serves the same purpose as a mortgage, involving three parties instead of two. The third party holds title for the benefit of the lender, 14

Deed Poll: deed signed only by the grantor, 13

Deed Restriction: *see* Restrictive Covenant, 13

Default: the failure to perform a contractual obligation or duty, 5

Defeasance Clause: a necessary mortgage clause in title theory states. When the debt is satisfied, this clause causes title to pass automatically back to the borrower, 14

Defeasible: fee ownership with conditional restrictions which, if broken, can result in title to the property reverting back to the grantor or his heirs, 8

Defect in Title: any lien, claim or encumbrance on a particular piece of real estate that has been properly recorded in the public records. Recorded defects impair clear title and may result in the title being unmarketable, 16

Deferred Interest Mortgage: under this mortgage, a lower interest rate and thus a lower monthly mortgage payment is charged. Upon selling the house, the lender receives the deferred interest plus a fee for postponing the interest that would normally have been paid each month, 15

Deferred Maintenance: needed repairs which have not been made, 10

Deficiency Judgment: a personal claim based on a judicial order against the debtor. This occurs when the property fails to bring in a price at the foreclosure sale which covers the mortgage amount, 13

Delivery: the formal transfer of the deed or other instrument to the new owner, 13

Delta: the angle between the two intersecting lines; used in the metes and bounds land description method, 7

Demand: a basic economic term which denotes a qualified buyer who is ready, willing and able to make a purchase, 2

Demise: to transfer an estate to another by means of a lease, 10

Density: in planning, this is the number of households or buildings per each acre of land, 19

Dependency, Principle of: the use, and thus the value of a parcel of land can change as a result of modifications of other parcels or other changes in the land-use pattern or environment, 2

Depreciation: a decrease in value due to physical deterioration, functional or economic obsolescence, 17

Depreciation (Tax): deduction, based on some percentage of the building value, that is used to reduce the tax liability of an owner of qualified property, 18

Depth Table: a rule of thumb used by appraisers to adjust for differences in lot size, 17

Descent: refers to any passage of title to property upon intestacy to those heirs, related by blood or marriage, whom the law designates, 13

Deterioration: a loss in value due to wear and tear, by action of the natural elements or use, 17

Devise: transferring title to real property by means of a will, 13

Direct Capitalization: a method of capitalizing income based on dividing net operating income by a rate of return derived by analyzing similar properties and comparing their income to their selling price, 17

Direct Sales Comparison Approach: *see* Market Data Approach, 17

Disclaimer: a denial of legal responsibility, 5

Disclosed Principal: one whose identity is known to the third person before the third person enters into contractual relationships negotiated by the agent, 6

Disclosure Statement: a written statement required under the National Consumer Credit Protection Act, to be given by a lender to individual borrowers for certain types of consumer loans, 16

Discounting: the process of adjusting a sum to take into account the time value of money, 18

Discount Points: a fee charged by the lender at settlement that results in increasing the lender's effective yield on the money borrowed. One discount point equals one percent of the loan amount, 5

Disintermediation: a term used to refer to the withdrawing of funds from financial institutions and lending it directly to money users, resulting in less mortgage money available for loans, 15

Dispossession: the removal of someone from real estate through legal process, 8

Distraint: taking personal property of defaulting tenant to satisfy rent due, 10

Distress: *see* Distraint, 10

Document: an official paper establishing facts or giving instructions, 8

Documentary Stamps: a charge levied by some local and state governments at the time that legal documents such as deed are entered into the public records, 16

Domicile: the legal residence of a person, 4

Dominant Estate: the tract of land in an easement appurtenant which benefits from the easement, 8

Donee: the recipient of a gift, 13

Donor: the giver of a gift, 13

Dower: the rights that a wife acquires in her husband's fee simple property, 8

Down Payment: the amount paid by the purchaser which when added to the mortgage amount equals the total sales price. At time of closing this is referred to as equity, 15

Downzoning: action by a local government to reduce the allowable density for a parcel of land, 19

Due-on-Sale Clause: a clause included in many mortgages permitting the lender to require the borrower to repay the outstanding balance when the property is sold, 14

Durability: a physical characteristic of real estate that describes the relative permanence of buildings and the indestructibility of land, 2

Duress: involves the use of force or improper actions against a person or property in order to induce a party to enter into a contract, 5

Earnest Money: a sum of money given to bind an offer or agreement, 5

Easement: a right to limited use or enjoyment by one or more persons in the land of another, 8

Easement Appurtenant: an easement created to benefit a particular tract of land, 8

Easement by Implication: occurs because of necessity, such as the conveyance of a land-locked property, 8

Easement in Gross: a personal right to use the land of another, 8

Economic Base Analysis: a technique by which a relationship is determined between basic and nonbasic industries to forecast future economic growth in the community, 19

Economic Life: the time period over which an improvement to land earns more income than the cost incurred in generating the income, 17

Economic Obsolescence: a loss in value due to factors outside the subject property, such as changes in competition or surrounding land use. Also referred to as locational obsolescence, 17

Economic Rent: the amount of rental which a building would receive if set by the market as opposed to contract rent set by the lease, 17

Effecting a Sale: completing the negotiation of a sales transaction, 16

Effective Age: the difference between the theoretical economic life of a structure and its actual remaining economic life, 17

Effective Gross Income: income received from property before the deductions for operating expenses; also called gross income, 17

Effective Interest Rate: the percentage rate of interest actually being paid by a borrower, 16

Ejectment: taking legal action to regain possession of real property with damages for its unlawful retention, 8

Emblements: refers to crops which require annual planting, 8

Eminent Domain: the right of government to acquire property for a public purpose after paying just compensation, 19

Enabling Legislation: statutes which confer powers to municipal corporations or private corporations, 19

Encroachment: the extension of some improvement or object across the boundary of an adjoining tract, 8

Encumbrance: any interest in or claim on the land of another which in some manner burdens or diminishes the value of the property, 18

Enforceable: any agreement in which the parties to it can be compelled to perform, 5

Environmental Impact Statement (EIS): a study analyzing how a proposed property will affect the ecology and environment, 19

Environmental Protection Agency (EPA): the federal agency that oversees and enforces federally enacted minimum standards dealing with environmental protection, 19

Equal Credit Opportunity Act (ECOA): a federal act which prohibits discrimination by lenders on the basis of sex or marital status in any aspect of a credit transaction, 15

Equal Dignities Rule: if the principal wishes to empower the agent to enter into a contract on the principal's behalf and the contract falls within the requirements of the statute of frauds, the appointment must also be in writing, 5

Equalization Board: a board established to hear property owners' complaints regarding the assessment of property for tax purposes, 19

Equitable Conversion: occurs under common law when a real estate sales contract is signed which is not subject to any unfulfilled contingencies, 5

Equitable Lien: created when justice and fairness would require a court of equity to declare such a lien exists or when conduct of parties would imply that a lien was intended, 14

Equitable Redemption: the process by which a borrower (mortgagor) redeems his or her property upon full payment of the outstanding debt, 14

Equity: (1) the value of real estate less any liens against it, 15; (2) the principle of fairness and legal jurisprudence, 14

Equity of Redemption: the right of the mortgagor to get back the property by paying the debt owed, interest and court costs, 14

Escalation Clause: (1) in finance, permits the lender to raise the interest rate upon the occurrence of certain stipulated conditions, 14; (2) in leasing, permits the lessor to raise lease payments upon the occurrence of certain stipulated conditions, 10

Escape Clause: a provision in a contract which under specified circumstances frees a party from certain responsibilities, 5

Escheat: the right of government to ownership of property which is left by a deceased property owner who leaves no will and dies without descendants, 13

Escrow: the deposit of funds with a neutral third party who is instructed to carry out the provisions of an agreement, 16

Escrow Agent: an independent third party bound to carry out the written provisions of an escrow agreement, 16

Estate: a legally recognized interest in the use, possession, control and disposition that a person has in land and defines the nature, degree, extent and duration of a person's ownership in land, 8

Estate at Sufferance: retention of possession without the consent of the landlord after the lease has expired; also referred to as tenancy at sufferance, 10

Estate at Will: an occupation of space for an indefinite period which can be terminated by either the lessor or lessee at any time. Also referred to as tenancy at will, 10

Estate for Years: a conveyance of realty for a definite stated period of time. The term may be one month, one week or even one day, 10

Estate from Year to Year: a leasehold which is automatically renewed for the same term as in the original lease; also referred to as a periodic tenancy or an estate from period to period, 20

Estate in Fee: represents the highest quantum of ownership recognized by the law. Same as fee simple estate, 8

Estoppel: the prevention of a person's denying or alleging a fact because it is contrary to a previous denial or affirmation, 5

Estoppel Certificate: *see* Certificate of Estoppel, 14

Et al.: abbreviation for *et alius* which means "and another," 15

Eviction: any action by the landlord which interferes with the tenant's possession or use of the leased premises in whole or in part, 10

Exception: a clause withdrawing some interest from grant in a deed, 13

Exclusionary Zoning: in zoning ordinances certain area and bulk restrictions such as minimum lot sizes regulate the intensity of development to prevent the overloading of public services; these restrictions may also tend to exclude the poor and minority groups in these areas, 19

Exclusive Agency Listing: the owner employs only one broker but retains the right to personally sell the property and thereby not pay a commission. However, if anyone other than the owner makes the sale the listing broker is still entitled to the commission stipulated, 6

Exclusive Right to Sell Listing: under this listing arrangement the broker employed is entitled to a commission no matter who sells the property during the listing period, 6

Exculpatory Clause: a clause in a contract which frees a party from liability, for example, a section in a lease releasing the landlord from any liability for personal or property damages to the tenants, 10

Execute: to make a complete action such as performing a contract, 5

Executed Contract: one in which the obligations have been performed on both sides of the contract and nothing is left to be completed, 5

Execution Sale: the selling of a judgment debtor's property, 14

Executor: a person appointed in the will to carry out the instructions of the testator, pay the debts of the estate and dispose of the property as instructed, 13

Executor's Deed: quitclaim deed given by executor selling property pursuant to carrying out the obligations in a will, 13

Executory Contract: one in which obligation to perform exists on one or both sides of a contract, 5

Executory Interest: either an interest which exists for future possession without any lesser estate preceding it or which occurs upon the happening or nonhappening of a specified event, 8

Exempt: to relieve from liability, 4

Express Contract: an agreement formed through the oral or written words of the parties, 5

Extender Clause: a clause in the listing contract which provides that the broker will be entitled for specified period after expiration date of listing to receive a commission if the property is sold to any prospect whom the broker showed the property to during the listing period, 6

Extension Agreement: a formal agreement entered into between mortgagor and mortgagee lengthening the amortization period on a loan, 14

Factors of Production: inputs necessary to create a productive asset. Consists of land, labor, capital and management, 2

Fair Credit Reporting Act: a federal act which attempts to regulate the actions of credit bureaus that give out erroneous information regarding consumers, 15

Fair Market Value: the price negotiated for a parcel of real estate in a competitive market where both buyer and seller are free to act and under no undue pressure, 17

Fannie Mae: Federal National Mortgage Association, 15

Federal Deposit Insurance Corporation (FDIC): a federal agency established to insure the deposits in member commercial banks, 15

Federal Fair Housing Act of 1968: an act prohibiting discrimination in the sale or rental of housing on the basis of race, color, religion or national origin and as amended, sex. Passed as Title VIII of the Civil Rights Act of 1968, 12

Federal Home Loan Bank System (FHLBS): a federal agency which oversees and regulates all federally chartered savings and loan associations, 15

Federal Home Loan Mortgage Corporation (FHLMC): "Freddie Mac" is a wholly owned subsidiary of the Federal Home Loan Bank System which serves as a secondary mortgage market for savings and loan associations who are members of the FHLBS, also referred to as The Mortgage Corporation, 15

Federal Housing Administration (FHA): a federal agency established in 1934 to increase home ownership by providing an insurance program to safeguard the lender against the risk of nonpayment. Currently part of HUD, 15

Federal Land Bank: a part of the Farm Credit Administration which is a source of long-term, first mortgages to farmers, 15

Federal National Mortgage Association (FNMA): commonly known as "Fannie Mae," this quasi-private corporation is the largest buyer of existing mortgages in the secondary mortgage market, 15

Federal Reserve System (FRS): a federal agency which oversees and regulates monetary policy which in turn affects the availability of credit and interest rates. All federally chartered commercial banks must be members, 15

Federal Savings and Loan Insurance Corporation (FSLIC): an agency of the federal government which insures the deposits in member savings and loan associations, 15

Fee Simple Absolute: represents the highest quantum of ownership recognized by the law; also referred to as fee simple or fee, 8

Fee Simple Determinable: an estate which has been created to exist only until the occurrence or nonoccurrence of a particular event, 8

Fee Simple Subject to a Condition Subsequent: an estate which is subject to a power in the original grantor or the grantor's heirs to terminate the estate upon the happening of an event, 8

Fee Simple Subject to an Executory Limitation: an estate which will automatically pass on to a third person upon the occurrence or nonoccurrence of a stated event, 8

Fee Tail: an estate which was designed to restrict the conveyance of title to the descendants of the grantee, 8

Feudal System: established in England after the Norman Conquest of 1066; all property theoretically resided in the king, 8

FHA Insurance: insurance protecting lenders from loss due to default. The borrower is charged an insurance fee of ½% on the unpaid balance, 15

Fiduciary: a person who essentially holds the character of trustee. A fiduciary must carry out the duties in a manner which best serves the interest of the party for whom the fiduciary relationship is established, 6

Financing: acquisition of borrowed capital, 15

Finder's Fee: a payment made by one party to another for locating a prospect. Often used in financing when a mortgage broker locates available capital for a borrower, 15

First Lien: claim with highest priority against property; also known as a senior lien, 14

First Mortgage: a mortgage on real estate in which the lender's rights are superior to the rights of subsequent lenders, 14

First Right of Refusal: a provision requiring an owner to allow a specified person or group the first chance to purchase property at a fair market price before it can be offered to a third party. Commonly used in condominiums and cooperatives, 9

Fixed Gross Lease: *see* Gross Lease, 10

Fixity of Location: a physical characteristic of land which makes it subject to the influence of surrounding land uses, 2

Fixture: broadly defined as personalty which has become realty. Examples include built-in cabinets or bathtubs. Also referred to as chattel real, 2

Flat Lease: one where the rent payment remains the same throughout the term of the lease, 10

Flexible Loan Insurance Program (FLIP): a financing technique in which cash is deposited in a pledged, interest-bearing savings account where it serves as both a cash collateral for the lender and as a source of supplemental payments for the borrower during the first few years of the loan, 15

Floor Area Ratio (FAR): indicates the relationship between a building area and land. For example, a 2:1 FAR means that two square feet of floor space may be constructed on one square foot of land, 19

Foreclosure: a legal procedure to levy on pledged property used to secure a debt under a mortgage or other lien, 14

Forfeiture: loss of property for some specified reason, 13

Formal Contract: contracts under seal, recognizances or negotiable instruments. Formal contracts are enforceable because of the way they are written and do not depend upon sufficiency of consideration, 5

4-3-2-1 Rule: a rule of thumb used by appraisers in estimating value of land. States that, in a standard sized lot, 40% of the value is allocated to the front quarter of the lot, 30% to the second quarter, 20% to the third quarter and 10% to the back quarter, 17

Fraud: a misrepresentation of a material fact which is made with knowledge of its falsity and with intent to deceive a party who in fact relies on the misrepresentation to his or her detriment and injury, 5

Freehold Estate: one which continues for an indefinite period of time, 8

Free Market System Auction: the mortgage purchase procedure used by FNMA, 15

Front Foot: a property measurement for purposes of valuation which is measured by the front footage on the street line, 20

Full Covenant and Warranty Deed: *see* Warranty Deed, 13

Fully Amortized Mortgage: a method of loan repayment in which the dollar amount of each payment is the same. The first part of each payment is interest and the remainder reduces the principal. Over the life of the mortgage, the outstanding balance is reduced to zero, 15

Functional Obsolescence: a loss in value due to conditions within the structure which make the building outdated when compared with a new building, 17

Future Interest: present estate with right of possession postponed into the future, for example, a remainder following a life estate, 8

Gap Financing: a loan covering the time period between when the construction loan is due and the conditions set by the permanent lender have not been met, 15

General Agent: one authorized to transact all of the principal's affairs within the context of a broad commercial or other kind of endeavor, 6

General Lien: a lien that attaches to all property owned by an individual, 14

General Warranty Deed: contains covenants in which the grantor formally guarantees that good and marketable title is being conveyed, 13

Gift Deed: used to convey property which is given without valuable consideration, 13

GI Loan: *see* VA mortgage, 15

Good Consideration: consideration based on love and affection, 5

Good Faith: refers to reasonable and fair dealing with other individuals, 16

Good Title: one which is free from encumbrances such as liens, pending litigation and other such defects, 13

Government National Mortgage Association (GNMA): commonly known as "Ginnie Mae," this agency of HUD operates in the secondary mortgage market. It is involved with special government financing programs, 15

Government Survey: a method of land description based on townships and sections, 7

Grace Period: a period between the time and obligation is due and the time default actually occurs, 14

Graduated Lease: provisions in this lease provide for periodic step increases in the rental payments, 10

Graduated Payment Mortgage (GPM): a new financing technique for residential real estate in which monthly payments start at a lower rate and increase periodically over the life of the mortgage, 15

Grandfather Clause: creating an exemption from application of a new law due to previously existing circumstances, 4

Grant: transferring real estate by means of a deed, 13

Grant Deed: limits the responsibility of the grantor to the period of time that the grantor actually possessed the property, 13

Grantee: purchaser or donee receiving title to property, 13

Glossary of Real Estate Terms

Grantor: owner making conveyance of title or interest in property, 13

Grantor-Grantee Index: a means of indexing title records by which each party in the conveyance instrument is listed, 16

Gross Income: the actual income received from property before the deduction for any expenses, 17

Gross Income Multiplier (GIM): a method of appraising income-producing property based on a multiple of the annual gross income; also called gross rent multiplier, 17

Gross Leasable Area: total area on which rent is paid by tenants, 10

Gross Lease: a lease in which the landlord, not the tenant, is responsible for property tax, maintenance, repairs and other operating costs, 10

Gross Rent Multiplier (GRM): *see* Gross Income Multiplier, 17

Ground Lease: a lease of land, usually for a long term, 15

Ground Rent: a payment made by the tenant under a ground lease, 15

Growth Management: the process of controlling the size, timing and direction of growth in a community, 19

Guaranty Fund: *see* Recovery Fund, 4

Guide Meridians: a surveying measurement used in the government survey method denoting imaginary lines located every 24 miles east and west of a principal meridian, 7

Habendum Clause: the part of the deed defining the extent of the estate granted, 13

Habitable: whether housing is suitable for occupancy, 19

Heterogeneous: diverse or unique, (nonhomogeneous), 2

Highest and Best Use: the legal use of a parcel of land which, when capitalized, will generate the greatest net present value of income, 17

Hoffman Rule: a rule of thumb used by appraisers in estimating the value of land. States that the front half of a 100-foot-deep lot is worth two-thirds of that lot's value, 17

Hold Harmless Clause: an exculpatory clause freeing one from personal liability, 5

Holding Over: the retention by the tenant of possession after expiration of term of the lease, 10

Holographic Will: entirely handwritten will which fails to be properly witnessed, 13

Homeowner's Association: has the authority and responsibility to manage the common elements of a condominium project after the original owner gives up control, 9

Homeowner's Policy: a package insurance policy available to anyone who owns and occupies either a one- or two-family residence, 11

Homeowner's Warranty (HOW): a 10-year warranty program for new homes administered by a subsidiary of the National Association of Home Builders, 11

Home Rule: the power of local self government given either by the state constitution or legislation to a municipal corporation, 19

Homestead Exemption: (1) a statutory or constitutional right which gives a person who is defined as the head of a household protection from creditors for property known as the homestead, 8; (2) in some states this is a reduction of the tax-assessed value of a primary residence, 19

Homogeneous: similar in type, 2

Horizontal Property Act: the name for legislation in some states allowing for the creation of the condominium form of ownership, 9

Housing and Urban Development (HUD): an agency of the federal government which oversees many federal housing programs, 12

Housing Codes: local government codes which specify minimum standards that a dwelling unit must meet, 19

Hundred Percent Location: the location which generates the highest per square foot revenues for a particular type of use in a geographic area, 17

Hypothecate: the process of pledging something as security but retaining possession of it, 14

Illiquidity: when an asset cannot readily be converted into cash, 18

Illusory Offer: one which does not bind the offeror to any real commitment, 5

Immobility: incapable of being moved, fixed in location, such as land, 2

Implied Authority: authority which is created by the actions or conduct of the principal, giving to the agent the reasonable impression that the scope of authority is broadened from that actually expressed in words, 6

Implied Contract: a contract formed through the acts or conduct of the parties involved, 5

Implied Warranties: (1) guarantees in a deed assumed by law to exist although they are not specifically stated, 13; (2) courts will find unstated promises in a transaction when circumstances and justice require it, 5

Implied Warranty of Authority: when an agent acts on behalf of a principal, the agent implies to a third party that there is authority to act, 6

Improved Land: any land to which improvements such as roads or buildings have been made, 2

Inactive Status: a provision included in state licensing law providing for a person's license to be inactive, 4

Inchoate: pending, possibly occurring in the future, 8

Inchoate Interest: someone's possible future right to property, 8

Income Approach: a traditional means of appraising property based on the assumption that value is equal to the present worth of future rights to income, 17

Income Property: property that generates income for its owner, for example, an office building or apartment complex, 17

Income Tax Liability: based on a taxpayer's taxable income multiplied by the tax rate in each marginal tax bracket, 18

Incompetent: one who is legally unable to take care of himself, 5

Incorporeal Property: intangible property which is not visible but exists as a legal right, 2

Increasing and Decreasing Returns: this economic principle states that the addition of more factors of production will add higher and higher amounts to net income up to a certain point, which is the point where the maximum value of the asset has been reached; any further addition of factors of production will do nothing to increase the value, 17

Incremental Condominiums: projects in which the developer reserves the right to add additional units to the project and to change the pro rata interest of each unit owner in the common elements, 9

Incumbrance: *see* Encumbrance, 8

Incurable Depreciation: elements of a structure which are neither physically possible nor economically feasible to correct, 17

Indemnify: reimburse, 11

Independent Contractor: one whose time and effort are regulated by the individual and is not under the direction or control of others, 6

Index Lease: the rental is tied to some commonly agreed to price index such as the Consumer Price Index or the Wholesale Price Index, 10

Index method: a technique available to estimate reproduction or replacement cost which takes the original cost of construction and multiplies that figure by a price index to allow for price changes, 17

Individual Unit Elements: that part of a condominium complex owned by the individual, 9

Inflation: a general price level increase for goods and services in the economy, 17

Ingress: entrance to land, 19

Inhabit: to occupy, 19

Inheritable: an interest in land which can be passed to a relative upon the death of the owner, 8

Inheritance Tax: a tax levied by the state on the estate of a deceased resident, 13

Injunction: a court order prohibiting or compelling a certain act, 14

In Personam: legal proceeding against a person, 14

In Rem: legal proceeding against a specific object, 14

Installment Land Contract: *see* Land Contract, 15

Installment Sale: a means of deferring the paying of capital gains taxes until the installment payments are actually received, 18

Institutional Lenders: savings and loan associations, commercial banks and mutual savings banks, 15

Instrument: a written legal document setting forth the rights and liabilities of the parties, 5

Insurable Interest: the relationship to the object or the person to be insured that one must show in order to take out an insurance policy, 11

Insurance: a means by which one party shifts and spreads the risk of a certain loss or disastrous event to a whole group of other individuals, 11

Insurance Coverage: the total amount of insurance protection carried, 11

Insurance Rate: the ratio of the insurance premium to the amount of insurance coverage, 11

Intangible Property: involves personal property rights which are rights the law recognizes such as patents and trademarks, contractual rights and legal claims, 2

Intensity of Development: the amount of floorspace over a given area of land, 19

Interest: (1) the sum paid for the use of money, 15; (2) the degree of rights in the ownership of land, 8

Interest Rate: the cost of using money expressed as a percent per period, 15

Interim Financing: financing obtained during the time of construction, 15

Intermediate Theory States: similar to title theory states in that title is said to pass to the mortgagee upon default, 14

Internal Rate of Return: equating the worth of future benefits to the present worth of the investment; also referred to as discounted cash flow, 18

Interpleader: action by a third party to determine rights that exist between two or more other parties, 6

Interstate Land Sales Full Disclosure Act: a federal act which makes it unlawful to offer land in a subdivision meeting statutory qualifications for sale in interstate commerce unless certain information has been filed with HUD, 19

Intestate: dying without a will, 13

Intrinsic Value: actual underlying worth, 17

Invalid: without legal force, 10

Involuntary Lien: an encumbrance against property without the owner's consent, 14

Inwood: a technique to estimate current value based on a series of periodic payments of principal and interest of one dollar, 17

Irrevocable: not capable of being changed, 5

Joint Tenancy: a form of concurrent ownership which occurs when two or more persons own a single estate in land with right of survivorship, 8

Joint Venture: an agreement by two or more individuals or entities to engage in a single project or undertaking, 8

Judgment: the final legal determination of rights between disputants by a court of competent jurisdiction, 14

Judgment Foreclosure: the selling of property through a court procedure to satisfy a lien, 14

Judgment Lien: the charge upon the land of a debtor resulting from the decree of a court entered in the judgment docket, 14

Junior Lien: an encumbrance second in priority to a previously recorded lien or to a lien to which the encumbrance has been subordinated, 14

Junior Mortgage: one which has a lower priority or lien position than a first mortgage; also called a second mortgage, 15

Jurisdiction: the extent of authority of a court to render legal decisions over persons or subject matter, 6

Just Compensation: a term ordinarily used when land is taken through condemnation which means fair and reasonable compensation for direct economic loss resulting at the date of the taking, 19

Land Capacity: the ability of land to economically absorb inputs of capital and labor, 2

Land Contract: the seller accepts a down payment on a parcel of land but title to the property does not pass until the last principal payment has been received. This is referred to as an installment sales contract, 15

Glossary of Real Estate Terms

Land Economics: a social science which studies the relation of people to the utilization and distribution of land and to the creation of real estate products, 2

Land Efficiency: a qualitative measure which refers to how factors of production will be combined with land, 2

Land Grant: a gift of land by the government, 13

Land Lease: in certain parts of the country, the land under residential real estate is leased through a long-term lease agreement whereby the owner of the land receives periodic rent for the use of the land, 15

Land-use Map: a map showing types and intensities of land use, 19

Land-use Regulations: police power regulations over the use of land, 19

Landed Homes Association: a concept of ownership which allows for fee ownership in a single-family detached house and the land surrounding the house. In addition, the owner owns an interest called a participation in an association which owns a package of amenities such as a swimming pool or a golf course, 9

Landlocked: completely shut in by adjoining parcels of land with no access to public roads, 8

Landlord: the owner or lessor of property, 10

Landmark: a fixed object used as a boundary mark in describing a parcel of land, 7

Land Residual Technique: a method of capitalizing income that is used when the value of the land is not known and when the building can be valued based on its replacement cost, 17

Land Trust: a device whereby property is transferred to a trustee under a trust agreement, 8

Latent Defect: a defect which cannot be discovered by ordinary inspection, 13

Law Day: the day payment is due on a mortgage note or the mortgage defaults, 14

Law of Nuisance: a property owner may not use his or her property in such a manner as to interfere with reasonable and ordinary use of an adjoining property owner, 2

Lawful Object: contractual obligations not prohibited by law, 5

Lease: an agreement by which a landlord gives the right to a tenant to use and to have exclusive possession but not ownership of realty for a specified period of time in consideration for the payment of rent, 10

Leased Fee: the landlord's interest in leased property, 10

Leasehold: the interest that the tenant has created by a lease, 10

Lease Purchase Agreement: an arrangement whereby part of the rent payment is applied to the purchase price and when the prearranged total amount has been paid, title is transferred, 10

Legal Benefit: consideration which occurs when one receives a promise, act or forbearance to act to which a person is not legally entitled, 5

Legal Capacity: the recognition which the law gives that a person has the ability to incur legal liability or acquire legal rights, 5

Legal Description: a written description of a parcel of land which locates it precisely, 7

Legal Detriment: the consideration which occurs when a person does something that one is not obligated to do or gives up a legal right, 5

Legal Entity: any person, proprietorship, partnership, copartnership or corporation which has the legal capacity to enter into an agreement or contract, 5

Legality of Form: *see* Statute of Frauds, 5

Legality of Object: a requirement for a valid and enforceable contract which states that the subject matter of the contract must be legal, 5

Legally Sufficient Consideration: a necessary requirement for a valid informal contract, 5

Legally Sufficient Description: a proper description of land such that a competent surveyor could locate its precise boundaries, 7

Legal Rate of Interest: the maximum interest rate which may be charged under state law, 15

Less than Freehold Estate: estates in possession generally referred to as leaseholds. Considered to exist for a definite period of time or successive periods of time until terminated by notice; also known as nonfreehold estates, 8

Lessee: tenant, 10

Lessor: landlord, 10

Level-payment Mortgage: a method of loan repayment in which the dollar amount of each payment is the same, 15

Leverage: using borrowed capital to finance the purchase of real estate or other assets, 18

Levy: (1) imposition of property tax, 19; (2) in executing on a lien, obtaining money by the sale of property, 14

License: a personal privilege to go upon the land of another; not considered an interest in land, 8

Licensee: anyone, either a broker or salesperson, licensed to broker real estate, 4

Lien: a legally recognized right to enforce a claim or charge on the property of another for payment of some debt, duty or obligation, 14

Lienee: the person whose property is burdened by the lien, 14

Lienor: the person who owns the lien, 14

Lien Theory State: the mortgage merely creates a lien right in the mortgagee with the mortgagor retaining the title, 14

Life Estate: an interest which lasts only for the term of a life or lives of one or more persons, 8

Life Estate Pur Autre Vie: a life estate in one person with another person serving as the measuring life, 8

Life Tenant: the holder of a life estate, 8

Like-kind Property: property which qualifies for a tax-free exchange, 18

Limited Common Elements: those portions of a condominium jointly owned by all unit owners but under the exclusive control or possession of only some of the owners, 9

Limited Partnership: an entity with a general partner and one or more passive investors, called limited partners, 8

Line of Credit: the extent that an individual may borrow from a bank without further need of approval, 16

Linkage: the proximity of a parcel of land to a supporting land use; refers to the time and distance cost necessary to access the supporting facility, 2

Liquidated Damages: an agreed-to sum which will be paid if the contract is breached, 5

Liquidity: the ease with which an asset may be converted into cash, 18

Lis Pendens: a notice filed for the purpose of serving constructive notice that title or some matter involving particular real property is in litigation, 14

Listing Contract: an employment agreement between an owner and broker defining the duties and rights of both parties, 6

Livery of Seizin: the process of title transfer under common law, 13

Loan Closing: when all conditions have been met, the loan officer disburses funds and authorizes the recording of the mortgage, 16

Loan Commitment: a contractual agreement from a lender to finance a certain amount of the purchase price, 15

Loan Correspondent: a person who negotiates and services loans for out-of-state lenders, 15

Loan Origination Fee: a charged incurred by a borrower to cover the administrative costs of the lender in making a loan, 16

Loan Processing: steps taken by a lender to complete a loan transaction, 15

Loan-to-Value Ratio: the relationship between the amount borrowed and the appraised value of the property, 15

Location: (1) a particular surface on the earth which is defined by legal description, 7; (2) how a particular site relates to a surrounding land-use pattern, 2

Locational Obsolescence: see Economic Obsolescence, 17

Long-term Capital Gain: the gain realized from the sale or exchange of an asset held for more than one year, 18

Lot: a small parcel of land having frontage on a street, 17

Lot and Block: a method of land description frequently used after land has been subdivided into building lots; also referred to as the recorded plat method, 17

Loyalty: the duty owed by an agent to avoid conflicts of interest or any activity which is detrimental to a principal, 6

L.S.: an abbreviation for "locus sigilli" meaning in place of a seal, 13

Maintenance Fee: payment made by the unit owner of a condominium to the homeowner's association for expenses incurred in upkeep of the common areas, 19

Management Agreement: an employment contract between the owner of real estate and a property management firm that agrees to oversee the management of the property, 9

Market: the economic function of bringing buyers and sellers together through the price mechanism, 2

Marketable Title: one which is free from reasonable doubts or objections and which the courts would compel a purchaser to accept under the terms of a sales contract. Also referred to as merchantable title, 13

Market Data Approach: a means of estimating value by comparing similar properties. Used when there is an active market and where comparables can be identified. Also called comparable sales approach, 17

Market Value: the price at which a willing buyer and a willing seller will agree upon where neither is under any undue pressure and both are negotiating at arms length with complete knowledge of the market, 17

Master Deed: see Condominium Declaration, 9

Master Plan: a program for the future development of a community which serves as the guideline for capital expenditures, 19

Material Fact: a fact which, if known, would affect the judgment of one or more of the parties to a transaction, 16

Maturity: the date when a note or negotiable instrument is due and payable, 14

Mechanic's Lien: a statutory lien levied on property by a person who is wrongfully not compensated after providing labor (mechanic) or material (materialman) for the improvement to land, 14

Menace: involves the threat of duress, 5

Merchantable Title: see Marketable Title, 13

Merger: the absorption of one thing into another. In contract laws, for example, the oral discussion that takes place between a potential buyer and seller merge into the written sales contract, and thus the sales contract takes precedence over previous oral discussions, 13

Meridians: imaginary lines running north-south which intersect with base lines to form reference points in the rectangular survey method of land description, 7

Metes and Bounds: a method of land description which involves identifying distances and directions which makes use of both the physical boundaries and measurements of the land, 7

Mill: a mill is equal to one-tenth of one cent and is used to state the property tax rate, 19

Millage Rate: a tax rate stated in tenths of a cent. For example, a millage rate of 150 mills on property assessed at $100,000 would result in a property tax of $1,500 ($100,000 × .150), 19

Mineral Deed: only conveys the mineral rights while reserving the surface and air rights to the grantor, 13

Minor: an infant; one who has not attained majority in a state and does not have legal capacity to be bound by most contracts, 5

Misrepresentation: an innocent or negligent misstatement of a material fact detrimentally relied upon by the other party, 5

Mobile Home Mortgage: security for a loan financing a mobile home. The amortization period of the loan is normally 7 to 10 years, 15

Month-to-Month Tenancy: a lease which has a term of one month but renewable for successive months at the option of both parties, 10

Monument: physical evidence of a point of beginning established by surveyors for use in locating parcels of land, 7

Mortgage: the secondary financing obligation in which the borrower or mortgagor agrees to pledge property to secure the debt represented by the promissory note or bond, 14

Mortgage Banker: a financial middleman who, in addition to bringing borrower and lender together, makes loans, packages them and sells the packages to both primary and secondary investors, 15

Glossary of Real Estate Terms

Mortgage Broker: a person who brings together the user of capital (borrower) and the supplier of capital (lender). For this service a finder's fee is usually paid by the borrower, 15

Mortgage Correspondent: a person authorized to represent a financial institution in a particular geographic area for the purpose of placing loans, 15

Mortgagee: a lender who receives a pledge of property to secure a debt, 14

Mortgagee-in-Possession: lender who has taken over property after default for the purpose of collecting rents and conserving the property until foreclosure, 14

Mortgagee's Title Policy: *see* Title Insurance, 16

Mortgagor: a borrower who pledges property through a mortgage to secure a debt, 14

Multiple Listing: marketing service in which many brokers pool all of their listings and establish procedures for sharing commissions, 6

Municipal Corporation: a city, 19

Mutual Assent: an offer and acceptance which together form the terms of a contract, 5

Mutual Mistake: occurrence in a contract when both parties are mistaken as to the same material fact, 5

Mutual Rescission: a mutual release in which each party agrees to release the other party in exchange for one's own release, 5

Mutual Savings Banks: located primarily in the northeastern states, this financial intermediary is a primary source of real estate financing for residential real estate, 15

Narrative Appraisal: the report compiled by an appraiser stating an opinion of value based on data and the appraisal methods used in deriving the estimate of value, 17

National Association of Real Estate License Law Officials (NARELLO): a group of real estate license law officials from the United States, Canada, the Virgin Islands and Guam who regulate the more than 2 million real estate licensees, 4

NATIONAL ASSOCIATION OF REALTORS®: the largest trade organization in the real estate profession, 2

National Environmental Policy Act: passed by Congress in 1969, this act created the Council on Environmental Quality and the Environmental Protection Agency and established the requirement for Environmental Impact Statements, 19

National Flood Insurance Program: a federal program enacted by Congress in 1968 intended to provide insurance coverage for those people suffering both real and personal property losses as a result of floods, 15

Negative Covenants: limitations or restrictions placed on the use of land which run with the land; also called restrictive covenants, 8

Negative Easements: an easement in which the use of the land is restricted, 8

Neighborhood: a homogeneous grouping of residential buildings within customarily accepted geographic boundaries, 19

Neighborhood Life Cycle: the growth, maturity, decline and possible renewal phases of the life of a neighborhood, 17

Net Income (Net Operating Income or NOI): gross income less all operating expenses. NOI is used in the income approach to value, 17

Net Leasable Area: the part of total area leased that is exclusively used by a tenant, normally excluding such areas as hallways, washrooms, etc., 10

Net Lease: imposes on the lessee an obligation to pay such costs as property taxes, special assessments and insurance premiums as agreed to between the parties, 10

Net Listing: the broker agrees to sell the property in order to achieve a net price to the owner and anything which is received above the net price is the broker's commission. A net listing is prohibited by the licensing law in many states, 6

Nominal Interest Rate: the rate of interest stated in the contract, 16

Nonassumption Clause: if included in a mortgage, this clause prohibits an assumption without consent of the lender, 14

Nonbasic Industry: a service or support industry in economic base analysis, 19

Nonconforming Use: a pre-existing use of land which does not conform to the zoning ordinance but which may legally remain, 19

Noncorporeal Property: property which does not entitle the owner to possession, although it may include certain use rights, 8

Nonrecourse Loan: the sole security for such a loan is the property pledged and, on the basis of agreement, the borrower cannot be held personally responsible, 14

Nonresident: one whose primary residence is in another state, 4

Notary Public: a person with the authority to take oaths and acknowledgments, 5

Note: a signed instrument acknowledging the existence of a debt and the promise to pay, 14

Notice of Pendency: a filing to give constructive notice to the world that a piece of property is in litigation, 14

Novation: occurs when the person in a contract to whom the duty was owed expressly agrees to substitute the delegatee or new obligor for a consideration and agrees to discharge the old obligor from the obligations under the contract, 5

Nuisance: any use of property which is harmful or injurious to a person or another property, 2

Null and Void: invalid and unenforceable, 5

Nuncupative Will: an oral will in front of witnesses; recognized in some states, 13

Obligee: a person entitled to the performance of a duty such as the lender or mortgagee, 14

Obligor: a person who owes a duty such as the borrower or mortgagor, 14

Obsolescence: a loss in value because of a decrease in the usefulness of property due to decay, changes in technology or people's behavior patterns and taste, 17

Occupancy: physical possession of real estate, 2

Occupancy Rate: the ratio of the space rented to the total amount of space available for rent, 17

Offer: a promise conditioned upon some requested for act or promise, 5

Offer and Acceptance: the necessary elements of mutual assent, for example, an agreement of one party to buy and another party to sell, 5

Official Map: a land-use control used to designate and reserve private land for street widenings, new streets, parks and other public improvements, 19

One-third, Two-thirds Rule: an appraisal rule of thumb stating that the first one-third of a standard lot nearest the street contains half the value while the rear two-thirds of the lot contains the other half of the value, 18

On or About: designation of approximate date without a commitment to a precise date, 16

Open-end Mortgage: a loan containing a clause which allows the mortgagor to borrow additional money without rewriting the mortgage, 15

Open Listing: an agreement between an owner and a broker giving the broker the nonexclusive right to sell the property, 6

Open Mortgage: a mortgage without a prepayment clause, 19

Operating Expenses: expenses incurred in the day-to-day operation of property which are subtracted from gross income to derive net income, 17

Operation of Law: the application of established rules of law upon a particular fact situation, 5, 6, 7, 9, 10

Opinion of Title: *see* Attorney's Opinion of Title, 11

Option: a right which is given for consideration to a party (optionee) by property owner (optionor) to purchase or lease property within a specified time at a specified price and terms. An option is irrevocable by the optionee and will not be extinguished by death or insanity of either party, 5

Optionee: the holder of the option, 5

Optioner: the seller of the option, 5

Ordinance: a statute enacted by the legislative branch of a local government, 19

Ordinary Life Estate: *see* Life Estate, 8

Origination Fee: the charge made for arranging a mortgage loan, 15

Ostensible Authority: authority which a third person can reasonably assume that an agent has on the basis of actions or inactions of the principal; also called apparent authority, 6

Outbuilding: an accessory structure other than the main structure on land, 13

Overimproved Land: occurs when the owner combines more factors of production inputs with the land than can be profitably absorbed, 2

Ownership: the right to hold, possess, control and dispose of property, 8

Ownership in Severalty: individual ownership, 8

Owner's Title Policy: a policy insuring the owner of real estate against certain defects of title, 11

Package Mortgage: a mortgage used in the purchase of new residential property which in addition to real property covers certain personal property items and equipment, 15

Parol: verbal, not in writing, 5

Parol Evidence Rule: states that testimony will be inadmissible to show oral agreements which modify the subject matter of a written contract which is objectively intended to be a complete integration of the agreement of the parties, 5

Partial Eviction: occurs when the landlord interferes with part of the tenant's right of possession to the premises, 10

Partially Amortized Mortgage: a method of loan repayment in which the balance of the outstanding loan is not zero at maturity, and thus a balloon payment is due at that time, 15

Partially Disclosed Principal: one whose identity is not known to the third person, but the third person knows that he or she is dealing with an agent of an unknown principal, 16

Partial Release Clause: a part of a mortgage which provides for the release of part of the property used as security in the loan upon payment of a certain amount of the mortgage, 14

Participation Mortgage: an agreement between a mortgagee and a mortgagor which provides the lender with a certain percentage of ownership in the project once the lender makes the loan, 15

Partition: the dividing of real estate held by two or more people which results in each of the parties holding individual or severalty ownership, 8

Patent: a government grant of land, 13

Patent Defect: a defect which can be discovered by ordinary inspection, 13

Payback Period: the time necessary for the cash flow generated from a project to equal the initial amount invested, 18

Percentage Lease: the lessor receives a percentage of the gross sales or net profits as the rental payment for the lease of the property, 10

Perch: a rod (16.5 feet in length), 7

Percolation: ability of soil to absorb water, 19

Perfecting Title: the process of removing title defects, 11

Performance Bond: a bond issued to guarantee the completion of construction or other undertaking, 4

Perils: the hazard or risk insured against by an insurance policy, 11

Periodic Tenancy: a lease which has the original terms automatically renewed for successive periods until proper notice to terminate is given by either the landlord or tenant, 10

Permanent Mortgage: a long-term loan, 15

Permissive Waste: occurs if the tenant or mortgagor fails to properly maintain and repair the premises, thus allowing the improvements to deteriorate beyond normal wear and tear in a manner which impairs rights of owners having future interests in the land, 10

Personal Property: moveables which are not annexed to or part of the land, also referred to as chattels, 2

Physical Deterioration: the loss in value due to wear and tear of the structure, 17

Physical Life: the normal or expected time over which an asset such as a building should last, 17

PITI: an abbreviation which means "principal, interest, taxes and insurance." In residential financing, it is common for the monthly mortgage to include these four payments, 15

Planned Unit Development (PUD): a type of exception or special use permitted under many modern zoning ordinances allowing a mixture of different land uses or densities; also referred to as community unit plan (CUP), 19

Planning Commission: a local government agency which determines plans for the physical growth of a community, 19

Plat: a map showing the division of land into lots and blocks, 7

Plat Books: located in the public records, these books identify parcels of property that have been subdivided into blocks and lots, 7

Platted Land: land that has been subdivided and recorded as a subdivision, 7

Pledge: putting up property as security for a loan or performance of some duty, 14

Plottage: occurs when two or more sites are combined with the result that the value of the assembled site is worth more than the value of the sum of each of the individual sites, 17

PMI: private mortgage insurance, 15

Points: see Discount Points, 16

Police Power: the inherent power of the state to regulate in order to promote public health, safety, morality or welfare, 19

Policy: in insurance, the name given to the contractual agreement entered into between the insurance company and the insured, 11

Population Density: the number of people in a given area, 19

Possession: the physical control of real property, 8

Possibility of Reverter: the right retained when a fee simple determinable is granted, 8

Potential Income: the maximum income possible from a piece of property if all the space is fully rented, 17

Power of Attorney: a written instrument giving a person the authority to act on behalf of another person, 5

Preliminary Binder: a report issued by a title company which indicates the company's willingness to insure subject to stated exceptions, 16

Premises: the introductory section of a deed, 13

Premium: payment made by the insured to the insurance company, 11

Prepaid Expenses: payments made by the purchaser at settlement to provide for future charges such as property taxes and mortgage insurance, 16

Prepayment Clause: a section in a mortgage note which permits the borrower to pay without penalty the outstanding balance before the due date, 14

Prepayment Penalty: the charge levied by the lender for paying off a mortgage prior to its maturity date, 14

Prescription: a means of acquiring title to property through open and continuous use, 13

Prescriptive Easement: an easement obtained by the open, notorious, hostile and continuous use of the property belonging to someone else for a statutory period of time, 8

Prescriptive Title: see Adverse Possession, 8

Present Value: the worth in today's dollars of a future income stream and/or reversion at a given discount rate, 18

Price: an amount usually expressed in terms of money, paid for property, 17

Prima Facie: all the necessary proof in a lawsuit to justify a legal decision unless rebutted, 6

Primary Financing: the loan that has first priority, 15

Primary Mortgage Market: the financial market where loans are made directly from the lender to the borrower, 15

Prime Contractor: the contractor hired directly by owner, 11

Prime Rate: the interest rate charged to a lender's AAA customers. This is normally the base from which other interest rates are derived, 15

Principal: (1) one who employs an agent, 6; (2) money or capital, 15

Principle: a fundamental idea upon which other ideas are based, 2

Prior Appropriation System: a system of water law used in most of the western states. Under this system a water right is a separate property right apart from the ownership of land, 8

Private Mortgage Insurance: a private insurance program which insures the lender for the loan amounts in excess of 80% of value, 15

Private Property: real estate owned by individuals in contrast to public property which is owned by the government, 2

Privity of Estate: the lessor and lessee share a property interest in the land and owe reciprocal obligations as a result, 10

Probate: the process of proving a will before a duly authorized court or person, 13

Procuring Cause: the actions by a broker which result in the owner being able to make a sale, 6

Profit á Prendre (Profit): the right to remove something such as gravel or minerals from the land of another, 8

Promissory Note: the primary legal financing obligation in which the borrower promises to pay back a sum of money borrowed, 14

Promulgate: to declare, 6

Property: anything in which there may be ownership, 2

Property Manager: a person employed by the owner to collect rents, negotiate leases, maintain the property and other such services, 10

Property Residual Technique: a method of capitalizing income which requires both the income stream and the value of the site at the end of the income stream to be discounted to the present to estimate property value, 17

Proprietary Lease: used in cooperative apartment in which the tenant makes a capital contribution to the corporation and receives a lease for an apartment, 10

Pro Rata: in proportion, 16

Proration: dividing property taxes, hazard insurance and other expenses or income between the buyer and seller as of date of settlement, 16

Public Offering Statement: in many states the developer of a condominium project must file this document intended to protect the public by disclosing pertinent facts to the potential purchaser, 9

Public Records: records which give constructive notice of information relating to land, 14

Public Sale: sale open to everybody, 14

Public Utility Easement: the taking of an interest of land under government authority by a public utility in order to install power lines, pipes, etc., 8

Puffing: to exaggerate, for example, to refer to a house as having "the most gorgeous view in the city," 6

Purchase and Leaseback: the simultaneous buying of property and leasing it back to the seller, 15

Purchase Money Mortgage: a mortgage given by the seller to the buyer to cover all or part of the sales price, 15

Qualified Fee: a legal interest in land which is subject to a limitation(s) placed on the estate by the owner, 8

Quantity Survey Method: a technique available to estimate reproduction or replacement cost which requires calculating the quantity and cost of each material item plus the total cost of installation, 17

Quarter Section: twenty-five percent of one section; it measures 2640 feet by 2640 feet and has an area of 160 acres, 7

Quasi Contract: refers to a contract implied in law, 5

Quiet Enjoyment: the right of an owner to use property without interference of possession by someone with a superior title, 13

Quiet Title: court action to remove a cloud on the title, 16

Quitclaim Deed: only conveys what present interest a person may have in a particular property but makes no representations or warranties of title, 13

Quotient: an answer in division problems resulting from dividing numerator by denominator, 20

Radius: the distance from the center of the circle to its perimeter, used in the metes and bounds land description method, 7

Range: a strip of land located every 6 miles east and west of each principal meridian in the rectangular survey method of land description, 7

Rate of Return: a percentage relationship between the investment price or equity invested and the composite returns, 18

Ratification: approval of a previously unauthorized act performed on behalf of a person which gives the act validity and legally binding effect, 5

Ready, Willing and Able: someone fully qualified to enter into a transaction, 6

Real Estate: land and all man-made improvements both on and to the land, plus all tangible interest in the real property, 2

Real Estate Board: an organization in a geographic area whose membership consists primarily of real estate brokers and salespersons, 4

Real Estate Bond: a negotiable instrument issued by a person or an entity such as Real Estate Investment Trust in denominations of $500 or $1,000 and which is secured by a collective mortgage on all or a specified portion of the issuer's property, 14

Real Estate Commission: the state regulatory body whose duty it is to carry out the real estate license laws in a particular state, 4

Real Estate Investment Trust (REIT): an association whereby individual investors pool their funds and which, if certain tax requirements are met, a pass through of income without double taxation is possible, 8

Real Estate Market: the mechanism by which rights and interests in real estate are sold, prices set, supply adjusted to demand, space allocated among competing alternate uses and land-use patterns set, 2

Real Estate Settlement Procedure Act (RESPA): a law which covers mortgage loans made for one- to four-unit residential property. It requires the lender to provide the loan applicant with pertinent information so that the borrower can make informed decisions as to which lender will be used to finance the purchase, 16

Reality of Consent: for a contract to be valid and enforceable there must be the fulfillment of reasonable expectations based on the free will of the contracting parties, 5

Real Property: refers to land and improvements both on and to the land and also to the physical aspects of real estate, including surface, air and subsurface rights, 2

Realtist: a member of the National Association of Real Estate Brokers, 2

REALTOR®: a registered trademark of the NATIONAL ASSOCIATION OF REALTORS®. It is used by brokers and salespersons who hold active membership in the association, 2

Realty: a term used to refer to land and the improvements on and to the land, 2

Reappraisal Lease: includes a provision that periodically the property will be revalued and the rent will be set at a percentage of the appraised market value, 20

Recapture: difference between total accelerated depreciation taken and total straight-line depreciation over the entire holding period of the asset, 18

Receipt: an acknowledgment that money or something else of value has been received, 5

Receiver: a court-appointed person who is charged with preserving a property, collecting rents and doing anything necessary to maintain the property's condition, 14

Receiver Clause: a clause in a mortgage which permits the appointment of a receiver upon default, 14

Reciprocity: the recognition that states give whereby a licensee of one state can be involved in real estate transactions in other states, 4

Reconveyance Deed: a deed by a trustee to reconvey the property of the trust back to the trustor, 13

Recordation: filing a document in the public land records thereby giving constructive notice to the world of the existence of the document and its contents, 16

Record(ed) Plat: a map located in the public land records showing the subdivision of land, 16

Recovery Fund: a fund established in some states for payment to persons who have suffered loss as a result of wrongful actions by licensed brokers and salespersons, 4

Rectangular Survey: a method of land description used in about 30 states based on imaginary lines of longitude (meridians) and latitude (base lines); also referred to as the U.S. government survey system, 7

Redemption Period: the right of a mortgagor to make good on the default within a specified time and receive the property back, 13

Redlining: a practice of refusing to provide services such as loans or insurance in certain geographic areas because of the feeling that the area is a high risk, 15

Reduction of Mortgage Certificate: given by the mortgagee stating the balance due on a mortgage, 14

Re-entry: the right of the landlord to repossess leased property following the violation of the terms in the lease, 10

Refinancing: a description of an extension of the existing financing either through the same lender or through a new financial arrangement, 15

Regulation B: passed by the Federal Reserve Board to define obligations and procedures under the Equal Credit Opportunity Act, 15

Regulation Q: the regulation which establishes the maximum interest payments that can be paid on savings accounts by commercial banks and thrift institutions, 15

Regulation Z: issued by the Federal Reserve System to implement the Truth-in-Lending Law (National Consumer Credit Protection Act), 15

Rejection: a refusal of an offer by the offeree which has the legal effect of extinguishing the offer, 5

Release Clause: a stipulation that, upon the payment of a certain percentage of a loan, certain lots will be removed from the blanket lien held by the lender, 14

Reliction: an increase in the amount of land due to the permanent withdrawal of a river or sea, 8

Remainder: a future interest which is created simultaneously with the granting of an estate of limited or potentially limited duration, 8

Remainderman: the person who has a future interest in a life estate once the present estate terminates, 8

Remise: to quitclaim or release, 13

Renegotiable Rate Mortgage: a renegotiated loan where the maturity is fixed (for example, 30 years) but the interest rate, and hence the monthly payment, is renegotiated periodically (for example, every 3 or 5 years), 15

Rent: the payment made for the use of land, 2

Rent Concession: a discount lowering the actual cost of a lease to a tenant, 10

Rent Control: in certain geographic locations laws have been passed which impose limitations on how much rent can be charged and what percentage increase can be levied by the landlord, 10

Rent-up: period required to reach necessary occupancy levels of newly opened real estate project, 18

Renunciation: the action by one of the parties to a contract surrendering a right or interest, 5

Replacement Cost: the cost of substituting a similar structure with utility equivalent to the subject property but constructed with modern materials, 17

Repossess: to regain legal possession of property as a result of the nonpayment of rent or breach of some condition or covenant, 10

Reproduction Cost: the cost of exactly duplicating a structure using the same material and design, 17

Rescission: repealing a contract either by mutual consent of the parties to the contract or by one party when the other party is in breach of the contract, 5

Resident Manager: an employee of the property management firm and its representative on the premises, 10

Residual: real estate is said to be residual in that its value is dependent on how much compensation is left after the other factors of production have been compensated, 2

Restriction: a limitation on the use of real estate, 8

Restrictive Covenant: a clause in a deed which restricts use of property for a specified time, 11

Revenue Stamps: *see* Documentary Stamps, 13

Reverse Annuity Mortgage (RAM): a financing arrangement in which the lender pays the borrower a fixed annuity based on a percentage of the property's value. The loan is not repaid until the death of the borrower and then it is settled through normal probate procedures, 15

Reversion: a future interest in the grantor which occurs whenever the owner of real estate conveys an estate of lesser duration than the owner has, 8

Reversionary Interest: a future interest a person has in property after present possession is terminated, 8

Revocation: the nullification of an offer to contract by the original offeror, 8

Right of Redemption: the legal ability to buy back one's property within the time specified in each state after a judicial sale by paying the debt, interest and certain costs, 14

Right of Re-entry: the right retained when a fee simple on condition subsequent exists; also referred to as the power of termination, 8

Right of Survivorship: upon the death of a joint tenant or tenant by the entirety the interest does not pass to the tenant's heirs but to the other joint tenant(s); also referred to as the grand incident of joint tenancy, 8

Right of Way: an easement allowing someone to cross over a parcel of land, 8

Right to Use: in time-share condominiums, the legal means by which the purchaser can occupy the property for a stated period of time, 9

Riparian Rights: a legal right of a landowner who owns land next to a natural watercourse to reasonable use of whatever water flows past the property, 8

Risk: the chance of loss or gain ordinarily used in the sense of exposure to hazard or peril, 11

Run with the land: certain restrictions, easements and covenants are part of the ownership of land and thus are terminated when title is transferred but remain in effect from owner to owner, 8

"R" Value: a measurement of insulation's resistance to heat transfer, 11

Sale-leaseback: a technique used by owners of property as a means of raising capital. The process involves the simultaneous selling and leasing back of the property usually through a net lease, 15

Sales Contract: an agreement in which the buyer and seller agree to the terms and conditions of the sale of property, 5

Salesperson: a natural person licensed to perform on behalf of any licensed real estate broker any act or acts authorized to be performed by the broker, 4

Salvage Value: the expected worth of a piece of property at the end of its economic life, 18

Satisfaction of Mortgage: an instrument issued by the mortgagee when the mortgage has been paid in full, 14

Satisfaction Piece: an instrument issued by a person holding a lien to indicate lien is discharged, 14

Savings and Loan Associations: an important source of funds for financing residential real estate, 15

Scarcity: the scarcity of real estate refers to the limited supply of certain types of real estate at particular locations, 2

Scenic Easement: a negative easement which prevents the impairment of a scenic view or prevents any construction, 8

Seal: an impression in wax or paper to signify the formality of an execution of an instrument, 5

Secondary Financing: a loan secured by a junior mortgage on real property, 14

Secondary Mortgage Market: the means by which existing mortgages are bought and sold. Provides a lender an opportunity to sell a loan prior to its maturity date, 15

Second Mortgage: a mortgage subordinate to a first mortgage; also referred to as a junior mortgage, 14

Section: a tract of land one mile square containing 640 acres. It is used in the rectangular survey method of land description, 7

Securities: property interests whereby one commits money or accepts liability for the purpose of making a profit from the efforts of another, 8

Security Deed: a security instrument used in place of a mortgage in Georgia, 14

Security Deposit: a sum of money given to assure the performance of an obligation, 10

Seisin (Seizin): the possession of land by someone holding a freehold estate, 8

Servient Estate: the tract of land burdened by an easement, 8

Setback Lines: a requirement in zoning ordinances in which all structures are to be a minimum distance from property lines, 19

Settlement: the closing of a real estate transaction where prorations between buyer and seller are made; also referred to as closing, 16

Severalty Ownership: ownership by one person, 8

Sheriff's Deed: a deed given when property is sold by a court order to satisfy a judgment for money or for foreclosure of a mortgage, 13

Sinking Fund: a sum of money set aside periodically which with its accrued interest will pay for the replacement of assets, 18

Site: a lot ready for development, 2

Situs: refers to the economic location of real estate, 5

Special Agent: one limited in authority to transact a single business affair or a specific series of business affairs or to perform restricted acts for the principal, 6

Special Assessment: from time to time jurisdictions levy a charge on certain pieces of property for the purpose of paying for the cost of a public improvement such as sewers or sidewalks which particularly benefit properties being assessed as opposed to those improvements benefiting the public at large, 19

Special Warranty Deed: the grantor warrants against defects that have occurred after the grantor acquired title, 13

Specific Lien: one that attaches to a particular property, 14

Specific Performance: an equitable remedy in which the court orders the contract to be performed as agreed to by the parties, 5

Spot Zoning: a rezoned use which is significantly different from adjoining properties and involves only a small piece of property, 19

Spreading Agreement: an agreement by a mortgagor to place additional property under the provisions of an existing mortgage, 14

Standby Commitment: an agreement between a lender and a builder whereby, for a fee, the lender stands ready to make a certain loan amount for a specific period of time, 15

Statute: a law passed by a state legislature, 4

Statute of Frauds: every state has some form of laws which require that certain contracts must be in writing in order to be enforceable, 5

Statute of Limitations: state laws limiting the time within certain court actions may be brought, 5

Statutory Lien: a lien which is created by legislation establishing requirements that must be fulfilled before the lien may be levied, 14

Statutory Period of Redemption: the time within which property may be redeemed after foreclosure sale, 14

Steering: the channeling of prospective home purchasers or renters by real estate broker or salesperson into racially homogeneous neighborhoods and actively discouraging them away from neighborhoods of different racial or ethnic composition, 12

Straight-line Depreciation: a method of computing depreciation for income tax purposes in which the difference between the original cost and the salvage value is deducted in installments evenly over the depreciable life of the asset, 18

Straight-term Mortgage: see Term Mortgage, 15

Straw Man: someone who buys property for another so as to conceal the identity of the true owner; sometimes referred to as a nominee, 8

Strict Foreclosure: when a purchaser defaults under a mortgage, the seller acquires title to land and wipes out the mortgagor's equity, 14

Subcontractor: a person employed by the prime contractor to carry out part of a contractual agreement as in the construction of a building, 2

Subdivision: a tract of land that has been divided into smaller lots, 2

Subdivision Regulations: before a subdivision plat can be recorded many local governments require that certain development standards be met, 19

Subject to Mortgage: when a person purchases property and takes over the mortgage payments, no personal liability is undertaken by the purchaser, 14

Sublease: the transfer when the original lessee retains a reversion, 10

Subordination Clause: in insurance law, agreement that the first lienholder will agree to take a junior position to another lienholder, 14

Subrogation: the substitution of one person into another person's legal position in reference to a third person, 14

Subscription and Purchase Agreement: the sales contract for each condominium unit, 9

Substitution, Principle of: the value of a parcel of real estate is normally equal to the cost of acquiring an equally desirable substitute, 17

Glossary of Real Estate Terms

Sufficient Consideration: value which the law finds necessary in order to support the creation of a binding contract, 5

Suit: a court action to enforce a legal claim or right, 5

Sum-of-the-year's digits: an accelerated method for calculating depreciation for income tax purposes, 18

Superadequacy: a feature of a building which is not fully valued by the market. It is measured as part of functional obsolescence, 17

Support Deed: a deed conveyed by a grantor to another in consideration for an agreement to take care of the grantor for life, 13

Surety: a guarantee, 6

Surplus Funds: the money obtained at a foreclosure sale over and above the amount necessary to pay the liens on the property, 14

Surrender and Acceptance: a mutual agreement between landlord and tenant to terminate a lease prior to the expiration date, 10

Survey: the process by which a parcel of land is measured, 7

Survivorship: the rights one has as the survivor under a joint tenancy or tenancy by the entirety, 8

Syndicate: an arrangement to raise equity capital for real estate purchases or for other types of investments, 8

Tacking: process of putting additional amounts of money owed to a lender under a senior lien giving this lender a priority lien position for new money lent over existing junior lien holders, 14

Take Back a Mortgage: describes what happens when a seller provides the financing for the sold property and is given a purchase money mortgage by the buyer, 15

Take-out Commitment: an agreement by a permanent lender to provide the permanent financing for a real estate project when a certain event occurs, normally the completion of the project, 15

Tangible Property: objects and other physical things, 2

Taxation: the right of government to require contribution from citizens to pay for government services, 19

Tax Base: the total tax-assessed value of all real property in a particular jurisdiction, 19

Tax Certificate: a document given to the purchaser at a tax sale auction which entitles the holder to a tax deed or a treasurer's deed at the end of the tax redemption period, 14

Tax Deed: a deed issued when property is sold to satisfy delinquent taxes, 13

Tax-free Exchange: a method of deferring capital-gains taxes by exchanging one qualified property for another qualified property, 18

Tax Rate: the rate, normally stated in units of $100, multiplied by the assessed value of property to determine the amount of the property tax due, 16

Tax Roll: located in the public records, this identifies each parcel of land, the owner of record and the assessed value of the property, 19

Tax Sale: foreclosure of an unpaid tax lien in a public sale, 14

Tax Shelter: shielding income or gains from income tax liability, 18

Tenancy: the possession of an estate, 8

Tenancy at Sufferance: a tenancy which is created when one is in wrongful possession of realty, even though the original possession may have been legal, 10

Tenancy at Will: an occupation of space for an indefinite period which can be terminated by either the lessor or lessee at any time, 10

Tenancy by the Entireties (Entirety): a form of concurrent ownership which may only be created in cases of a husband and wife, 8

Tenancy from Period to Period: a leasehold which is automatically renewed for the same term as in the original lease; also referred to as a periodic tenancy or an estate from year to year, 10

Tenancy in Common: a form of concurrent ownership where two or more persons hold separate titles in the same estate, 8

Tenancy in Partnership: a multiple form of ownership where the property is held in a lawful business venture, 8

Tenant: one who has the legal right to occupy the property of another under an agreement to pay rent, 10

Tenement: property held by a tenant, 10

Termite Clause: a standard clause in many states used in sales contracts in which it provides that the property is free of termites, 5

Term Mortgage (Straight Term): a method of financing in which interest only is paid during the time of the loan. At maturity, generally five years or less, the entire principal is due, 15

Testate: to die having left a will, 13

Testator: a person who has made a will, 13

Testimonium: the last part of the deed containing the execution, attestation and acknowledgment, 13

Tier: a row of townships running east and west and comprising an area six miles wide. Used in the rectangular survey method, 7

Time Is of the Essence: a phrase included in contracts to require punctual performance of all obligations, 5

Time Sharing: a form of condominium ownership in which the buyer owns the property for a certain specified time interval, 9

Time Value of Money: based on the idea that since money is assumed to earn interest, a dollar today is considered to be more valuable than a dollar a year from today, 18

Timing and Sequencing Controls: a technique developed by local governments which limits the growth of a community to the capital improvements budget, 19

Title: the legally recognized evidence of a person's right to possess property, 13

Title Company: a company which examines the public records to determine the marketability of an owner's title, 16

Title Insurance: a policy that protects the insured against loss or damage due to defects in title, 16

Title Theory States: states in which a mortgage actually conveys title subject to a condition, 14

Topo: shortened form of the term *topography*, 19

Topographic Map: map showing changes in elevation through contour lines, 19

Topography: a description of surface features of land, 2

Torrens System: a method of registering title to land, 16

Tort: a civil wrong for which the law allows an injured party to recover damages from a wrongdoer, 6

Township: a 6-by-6 mile area containing 36 sections, each 1 mile square. A division of land in the rectangular survey method of land description, 7

Tract: an area of land, 7

Tract Index: a means of indexing title to property in which a separate page is kept for each tract of land in a particular jurisdiction, 16

Trade Fixtures: personal property used in business which has been annexed to real property and is removable by the owner, 2

Trading on the Equity: increasing the rate of return on the owner's equity by borrowing part or all of the purchase price at a rate of interest less than the expected rate of return generated on the net income of the property, 18

Transcript: a copy of any kind, 5

Transferability: the ability to exchange goods and services. In real estate legal rights are transferred, 2

Transfer of Title: the conveyance of the legal right to land from one party to another, 13

Transfer Tax: a charge levied on property when ownership is transferred from one party to another, 16

Trespass: illegal entry upon the property belonging to someone else, 8

Trust: a legal relationship under which title to property is transferred to a person, called a trustee, who has control over the property and must manage it for some other person, called a beneficiary, 8

Trust Deed: *see* Deed of Trust, 14

Trustee: a person who holds title and control over property and manages it for another person called a beneficiary, 14

Trustee's Deed: a conveyance of property by a trustee of property under his or her trust, 14

Trustee's Sale: a sale conducted by a trustee once a default of a trust deed occurs foreclosing the borrower's interest in the property, 14

Trust Fund: money or anything of value received by the broker to be held in escrow, 16

Trustor: the person who creates a trust and gives the instructions to the trustee; also called a settlor, 14

Truth-in-Lending Law: common name given to the National Consumer Credit Protection Act. Requires lender to make credit disclosures to individual borrowers for certain types of loans, 15

Underimproved Land: when a parcel of land can profitably absorb more units than are currently being employed, 2

Undisclosed Principal: when a third person is not advised of the existence of an agency relationship, the unknown person for whom the agent is acting is called an undisclosed principal, 6

Undivided Interest: the interest of co-owners in which individual interest is indistinguishable, 8

Undue Influence: occurs when a person in a fiduciary capacity or in a position of authority misuses the trust or power in order to unfairly induce a party to enter into a contract, 6

Unencumbered Property: property that is free and clear of any liens, 14

Unenforceable Contract: an agreement in which something prevents courts from hearing disputes regarding the enforceability of the agreement, 5

Uniformity: equal treatment in tax assessments, 19

Unilateral Contract: one for which a promise is given for the act or performance of another, 5

Unilateral Mistake: a mistake of a material fact involving the contract which is made by just one of the parties, 8

Uninsurable Title: one a title insurance company refuses to insure due to some present claim or encumbrance, 16

Unit: that portion of the condominium intended for the exclusive use and possession of the unit owner, 9

Unit Deed: the instrument of conveyance used to transfer title to an individual unit in a condominium development, 9

Unities: joined in one; for example, in order for a joint tenancy to exist four unities are necessary: (1) time, (2) title, (3) interest and (4) possession, 8

Unit-in-Place Method: a technique available to estimate reproduction or replacement cost where the cost is grouped by stages of construction, 17

Unity of Interest: states that each joint tenant must have the same estate and an equal fractional share in the property, 8

Unity of Person: in order for a tenancy by the entireties to exist there must be a husband and wife, 8

Unity of Possession: the right of each tenant to the possession and use of the whole property, 8

Unity of Time: states that all interests of the joint tenants must have been acquired at the same moment, 8

Unity of Title: states that the joint tenancy interests were created in a single conveying instrument, 8

Universal Agent: has the authority to do all acts that can be lawfully delegated to a representative, 6

Unlawful Detainer: when a tenant unjustifiably retains possession of land, 10

Unrecorded Instrument: any legal document that has not been placed in the public records, 13

Unsecured Loan: a loan made on the signature and credit of the borrower, not secured by collateral, 15

Up Rent Potential: the forecasted amount that rental rates can be increased in a real estate market, 10

Urban Renewal: the acquisition of certain areas by government action for the purpose of redevelopment, 19

Useful Life: the time period over which property is expected to have utility, 17

Usufructuary Right: a personal right to make reasonable use of another's property, 8

Usury: charging more than the legal rate of interest for the use of money, 15

Utility: (1) the usefulness or satisfaction received from a good service, 2; (2) various services such as electricity, water and gas, 19

VA Mortgage (GI Mortgage): mortgage guaranteed by Veterans Administration, 15

Vacancy Allowance (Vacancy Rate): the percentage of a building's space which is not rented due to oversupply, tenant turnover, etc. Potential income minus vacancy allowance equals gross income, 17

Vacate: to give up possession, 10

Valid Contract: a binding agreement containing all of the essential legal elements, 5

Valuable Consideration: anything of value offered as an inducement, 5

Value: the ability of a good or service to command other goods or services; the present worth of future rights to income, 17

Variable Interest Rate Mortgage (VRM): the interest rate charged by the lender varies according to some index not controlled by the lender, 15

Variance: a type of safety valve to allow a property owner who is unfairly burdened by zoning restrictions to find relief, 19

Vendee: purchaser, 13

Vendee's Lien: held by the purchaser for the purchase price paid if the seller defaults on the delivery of the deed, 14

Vendor: seller, 13

Vendor's Lien: the amount of the purchase price still due to the seller, 14

Vested Interest: a fixed or determined interest in property, 8

Vested Right: one where the owner is identified and has a present right to future possession, 8

Veterans Administration (VA): an agency of the federal government created to provide a loan guaranty program which enables qualified veterans to finance real estate purchases with a higher loan-to-value ratio than is normally possible with conventional financing, 15

Voidable Contract: an agreement in which one or more of the parties may elect to avoid or to ratify the legal obligations created by the contract, 6

Void Contract: a contract which has no legal effect, 5

Voluntary Alienation: the transfer of title by a deed, 13

Voluntary Lien: an encumbrance placed on property through some willful act of the owner, 14

Voluntary Waste: impairment of the rights of a person owning a future interest and which occurs when the tenant abuses the realty, for example, cuts down trees or demolishes improvements, 10

Waiver: the renunciation of a claim or privilege, 8

Warranty: an assurance that defects do not exist, 13

Warranty Deed: a deed in which the grantor makes formal assurance as to quality of title, 13

Waste: the impairment of property by a tenant, 8

Water Rights: the right of a landowner to water adjoining or passing through property, 8

Water Table: the distance from ground level to natural groundwater, 19

Wear and Tear: the lessening in value of an asset due to ordinary and normal use, 17

Will: a legal declaration in which a person disposes of property to take effect upon his or her death, 13

Wraparound Mortgage: a junior mortgage which provides an owner additional capital without refinancing the first mortgage, 15

Writ of Execution: a court order to an officer to carry out a judicial decree, 14

Written Release: occurs when one party agrees to discharge an obligation of the other party, 5

Yield: the interest earned by an investor on the investment, 18

Yield to Maturity: the total return to an investor if the investment is held to total term, 18

Zoning: a police power device which allows for legislative division of space into districts and imposition of regulations prescribing use and intensity of use to which land within each designated district may be put, 19

Zoning Ordinance: a zoning law passed by a local government which consists of a text of regulations and a map, 19

Glossary of Construction Terminology and Illustrations

The following are definitions and illustrations relating to housing construction. They are included in this glossary specifically for use in those states where construction questions are included on the State Test. The reader is advised to check with his or her real estate commission to ascertain whether or not construction questions are included on a particular State Test. The following definitions are taken from *Homeowner's Glossary of Building Terms*, U.S. Department of Housing and Urban Development, Washington, D.C.

Acoustical Tile: special tile for walls and ceilings made of mineral, wood, vegetable fibers, cork or metal. Its purpose is to control sound volume while providing cover.

Air Duct: pipes that carry warm air and cold air to rooms and back to furnace or air-conditioning system.

Ampere: the rate of flow of electricity through electric wires.

Apron: a paved area, such as the juncture of a driveway with the street or with a garage entrance.

Backfill: the gravel or earth replaced in the space around a building wall after foundations are in place.

Balusters: upright supports of a balustrade rail.

Balustrade: a row of balusters topped by a rail, edging a balcony or a staircase.

Baseboard: a board along the floor against walls and partitions to hide gaps.

Batt: insulation in the form of a blanket rather than loose filling.

Batten: small, thin strips covering joints between wider boards on exterior building surfaces.

Beam: one of the principal horizontal wood or steel members of a building.

Bearing Wall: a wall that supports a floor or roof of a building.

Bib or Bibcock: a water faucet to which a hose may be attached; also called a hose bib or sill cock.

Bleeding: seeping of resin or gum from lumber. This term is also used in referring to the process of drawing air from water pipes.

Brace: a piece of wood or other material used to form a triangle and stiffen some part of a structure.

Braced Framing: construction technique using posts and cross-bracing for greater rigidity.

Brick Veneer: brick used as the outer surface of a framed wall.

Bridging: small wood or metal pieces placed diagonally between floor joists.

Building Paper: heavy paper used in walls or roofs to dampproof.

Built-Up Roof: a roofing material applied in sealed, waterproof layers, where there is only a slight slope to the roof.

Butt Joint: joining point of two pieces of wood or molding.

Bx Cable: electrical cable wrapped in rubber with a flexible steel outer covering.

Cantilever: a projecting beam or joist, nor supported at one end, used to support an extension of a structure.

Carriage: the member which supports the steps or treads of a stair.

Casement: a window sash that opens on hinges at the vertical edge.

Casing: door and window framing.

Cavity Wall: a hollow wall formed by firmly linked masonry walls, providing an insulating air space between.

Chimney Cap: concrete capping around the top of chimney bricks and around the floors to protect the masonry from the elements.

Chair Rail: wooden molding on a wall around a room at the level of a chair back.

Chamfered Edge: molding with pared-off corners.

Chase: a groove in a masonry wall or through a floor to accommodate pipes or ducts.

Chimney Breast: the horizontal projection—usually inside a building—of a chimney from the wall in which it is built.

Circuit Breaker: a safety device that opens (breaks) an electrical circuit automatically when it becomes overloaded.

Cistern: a tank to catch and store rain water.

Clapboard: a long, thin board, thicker on one edge, overlapped and nailed on for exterior siding.

Collar Beam: a horizontal beam fastened above the lower ends of rafters to add rigidity.

Coping: tile or brick used to cap or cover the top of a masonry wall.

Corbel: a horizontal projection from a wall, forming a ledge or supporting a structure above it.

Corner Bead: a strip of wood or metal for protecting the external corners of plastered walls.

Cornice: horizontal projection at the top of a wall or under the overhanging part of the roof.

Course: a horizontal row of bricks, cinder blocks or other masonry materials.

Cove Lighting: concealed light sources behind a cornice or horizontal recess which direct the light upon a reflecting ceiling.

Crawl Space: a shallow, unfinished space beneath the first floor of a house that has no basement, used for visual inspection and access to pipes and ducts. Also, a shallow space in the attic, immediately under the roof.

Cripples: Cut-off framing members above and below windows.

Door Buck: the rough frame of a door.

Dormer: the projecting frame of a recess in a sloping roof.

Double Glazing: an insulating windowpane formed of two thicknesses of glass with a sealed air space between them.

Double Hung Windows: windows with an upper and lower sash, each supported by cords and weights.

Downspout: a spout or pipe to carry rainwater down from a roof or gutters.

Downspout Leader: a pipe for conducting rainwater from the roof to a cistern or to the ground by way of a downspout.

Downspout Strap: a piece of metal that secures the downspout to the eaves or wall of a building.

Drip: the projecting part of a cornice which sheds rainwater.

Dry Wall: a wall surface of plasterboard or material other than plaster.

Eaves: the extension of a roof beyond house walls.

Efflorescence: white powder that forms on the surface of brick.

Effluent: treated sewage from a septic tank or sewage treatment plant.

Fascia: a flat, horizontal member of a cornice placed in a vertical position.

Fill-Type Insulation: loose insulating material which is applied by hand or blown into wall spaces mechanically.

Flashing: noncorrosive metal used around angles or junctions in roofs and exterior walls to prevent leaks.

Floor Joists: framing pieces which rest on outer foundation walls and interior beams or girders.

Flue: a passageway in a chimney for conveying smoke, gases or fumes to the outside air.

Footing: concrete base on which a foundation sits.

Foundation: lower parts of walls on which the structure is built.

Application of Insulation
A: wall section with blanket type; B: wall section with "press-fit" insulation; C: ceiling with full insulation

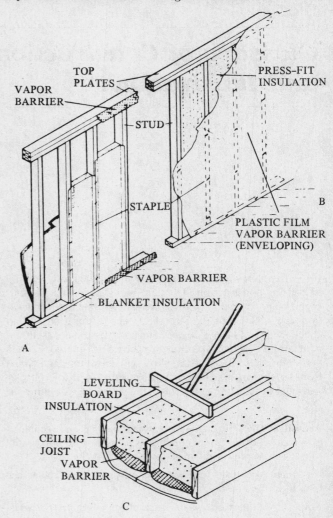

Combined Slab and Foundation
(thickened edge slab)

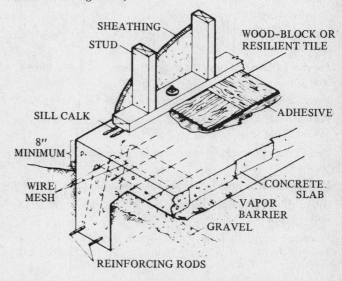

Glossary of Construction Terminology and Illustrations

Floor Framing

1. nailing bridging to joists; 2. nailing board subfloor to joists; 3. nailing header to joists; 4. toenailing header to sill.

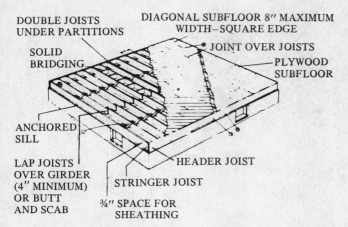

Wall Framing Used with Platform Construction

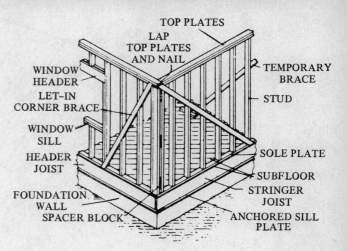

Foundation walls of masonry or concrete are mainly below ground level.

Framing: the rough lumber of a house—joists, studs, rafters and beams.

Furring: thin wood or metal applied to a wall to level the surface for lathing, boarding or plastering, to create an insulating air space and to dampproof the wall.

Fuse: a short plug in an electric panel box which opens (breaks) an electrical circuit when it becomes overloaded.

Gable: the triangular part of a wall under the inverted "v" of the roof line.

Gambrel Roof: a roof with two pitches, designed to provide more space on upper floors. The roof is steeper on its lower slope and flatter toward the ridge.

Girder: a main member in a framed floor supporting the joists which carry the flooring boards. It carries the weight of a floor of partition.

Glazing: fitting glass into windows or doors.

Grade Line: the point at which the ground rests against the foundation wall.

Basement Details

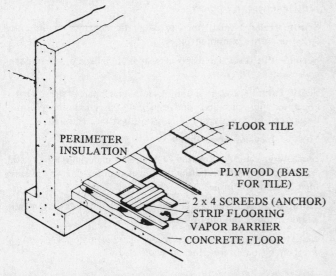

Green Lumber: lumber which has been inadequately dried and which tends to warp or "bleed" resin.

Gounds: pieces of wood embedded in plaster of walls to which skirtings are attached. Also, wood pieces used to stop the plaster work around doors and windows.

Gusset: a brace or bracket used to strengthen a structure.

Gutter: a channel at the eaves for conveying away rainwater.

Hardwood: the close-grained wood from broad-leaved trees such as oak or maple.

Headers: double wood pieces supporting joists in a floor or double wood members placed on edge over windows and doors to transfer the roof and floor weight to the studs.

Heel: the end of a rafter that rests on the wall plate.

Hip: the external angle formed by the juncture of two slopes of a roof.

Hip Roof: a roof that slants upward on three or four sides.

Jalousies: windows with movable, horizontal glass slats angled to admit ventilation and keep out rain. this term is also used for outside shutters of wood constructed in this way.

Jamb: an upright surface that lines an opening for a door or window.

Joist: a small rectangular sectional member arranged parallel from wall to wall in a building or resting on beams or girders. They support a floor or the laths or furring strips of a ceiling.

Kiln-Dried: artificial drying of lumber, superior to most lumber that is air dried.

King-Post: the middle post of a truss.

Lag-Screws or Coach-Screws: large, heavy screws, used where great strength is required, as in heavy framing or when attaching ironwork to wood.

Lally Column: a steel tube sometimes filled with concrete. It is used to support girders or other floor beams.

Lath: one of a number of thin, narrow strips of wood nailed to rafters, ceiling joists, wall studs, etc., to make a groundwork or key for slates, tiles or plastering.

Leaching Bed: tiles in the trenches carrying treated wastes from septic tanks.

Glossary of Construction Terminology and Illustrations

Ceiling and Roof Framing

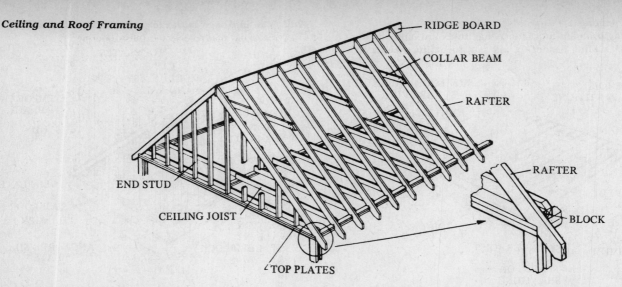

Ledger: a piece of wood which is attached to a beam to support joists.

Lintel: the top piece over a door or window which supports walls above the opening.

Load-Bearing Wall: a strong wall capable of supporting weight.

Louver: an opening with horizontal slats which permit passage of air but exclude rain, sunlight and view.

Masonry: walls built by a mason using brick, stone, tile or similar materials.

Moisture Barrier: treated paper or metal that retards or bars water vapor; used to keep moisture from passing into walls or floors.

Molding: a strip of decorative material having a plane or curved narrow surface prepared for ornamental application. These strips are often used to hide gaps at wall junctures.

Mullion: slender framing which divides the lights or panes of windows.

Newel: the upright post or the upright formed by the inner or smaller ends of steps about which steps of a circular staircase wind. In a straight flight staircase, the principal post at the foot or the secondary post at a landing.

Nosing: the rounded edge of a stair tread.

Parging: a rough coat of mortar applied over a masonry wall as protection or finish; may also serve as a base for an asphaltic waterproofing compound below grade.

Pilaster: a projection of the foundation wall used to support a floor girder or stiffen the wall.

Pitch: the angle of slope of a roof.

Plasterboard: gypsum board; used instead of plaster. (*See* Dry Wall)

Plates: pieces of wood placed on wall surfaces as fastening devices. The bottom member of the wall is the sole plate, and the top member is the rafter plate.

Plenum: a chamber which can serve as a distribution area for heating or cooling systems, generally between a false ceiling and the actual ceiling.

Pointing: treatment of joints in masonry by filling with mortar to improve appearance or protect against weather.

Post-and-Beam Construction: wall construction in which beams are supported by heavy posts rather than by many smaller studs.

Prefabrication: construction of components such as walls, trusses, or doors, before delivery to the building site.

Rabbet: a groove cut in a board to receive another board.

Radiant Heat: coils of electricity, hot water or steam pipes embedded in floors, ceilings, or walls to heat rooms.

Rafter: one of a series of structural roof members spanning from an exterior wall to a center ridge beam or ridge board.

Reinforced Concrete: concrete strengthened with wire or metal bars.

Ridge Pole: a thick longitudinal plank to which the ridge rafters of a roof are attached.

Riser: the upright piece of a stair step, from tread to tread.

Roof Sheathing: sheets, usually of plywood, which are nailed to the top edges of trusses or rafters to tie the roof together and support the roofing material.

Sandwich Panel: a panel with plastic, paper or other material enclosed between two layers of a different material.

Sash: the movable part of a window—the frame in which panes of glass are set in a window or door.

Scotia: a concave molding.

Scuttle Hole: a small opening either to the attic, to the crawl space or to the plumbing pipes.

Seepage Pit: a sewage disposal system composed of a septic tank and a connected cesspool.

Septic Tank: a sewage settling tank in which part of the sewage is converted into gas and sludge before the remaining waste is discharged by gravity into a leaching bed underground.

Shakes: handcut wood shingles.

Sheathing: the first covering of boards or material on the outside wall or roof prior to installing the finished siding or roof covering. (*See* Wall Sheathing)

Shim: thin, tapered piece of wood used for leveling or tightening a stair or other building element.

Shingles: pieces of wood, asbestos or other material used as an overlapping outer covering on walls or roofs.

Application of Asphalt Shingles

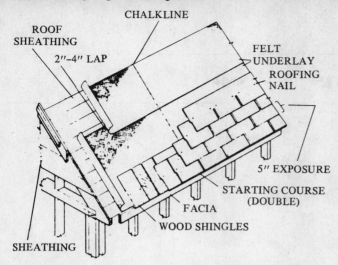

Shiplap: boards with rabbeted edges overlapping.

Siding: boards of special design nailed horizontally to vertical studs with or without intervening sheathing to form the exposed surface of outside walls of frame buildings.

Sill Plate: the lowest member of the house framing resting on top of the foundation wall. Also called the mud sill.

Skirtings: narrow boards around the margin of a floor; baseboards.

Slab: concrete floor placed directly on earth or a gravel base and usually about four inches thick.

Sleeper: strip of wood laid over concrete floor to which the finished wood floor is nailed or glued.

Soffit: the visible underside of structural members such as staircases, cornices, beams, a roof overhang or eave.

Softwood: easily worked wood or wood from a cone-bearing tree.

Soil Stack: vertical plumbing pipe for waste water.

Stringer: a long, horizontal member which connects uprights in a frame or supports a floor or the like. One of the enclosed sides of a stair supporting the treads and risers.

Studs: in wall framing, the vertical members to which horizontal pieces are nailed. Studs are spaced either 16 inches or 24 inches apart.

Subfloor: usually, plywood sheets that are nailed directly to the floor joists and that receive the finish flooring.

Sump: a pit in the basement in which water collects to be pumped out with a sump pump.

Swale: a wide, shallow depression in the ground to form a channel for storm water drainage.

Tie: a wood member which binds a pair of principal rafters at the bottom.

Tile Field: open-joint drain tiles laid to distribute septic tank effluent over an absorption area or to provide subsoil drainage in wet areas.

Toenail: driving nails at an angle into corners or other joints.

Tongue-and-Groove: carpentry joint in which the jutting edge of one board fits into the grooved end of a similar board.

Trap: a bend in a water pipe to hold water so gases will not escape from the plumbing system into the house.

Tread: the horizontal part of a stair step.

Truss: a combination of structural members usually arranged in triangular units to form a rigid framework for spanning between load-bearing walls.

Valley: the depression at the meeting point of two roof slopes.

Vapor Barrier: material such as paper, metal or paint which is used to prevent vapor from passing from rooms into the outside walls.

Venetian Window: a window with one large fixed central pane and smaller panes at each side.

Vent Pipe: a pipe that allows gas to escape from plumbing systems.

Verge: the edge of tiles, slates or shingles, projecting over the gable of a roof.

Wainscoting: the lower three or four feet of an interior wall when lined with paneling, tile or other material different from the rest of the wall.

Wall Sheathing: sheets of plywood, gypsum board or other material nailed to the outside face of studs as a base for exterior siding.

Weather Stripping: metal, wood, plastic or other material installed around door and window openings to prevent air infiltration.

Weep Hole: a small hole in a wall that permits water to drain off.

Solutions and Explanations

CHAPTER 2

1. (A) The "bundle of rights" is a legal concept, while three-dimensional space is a physical concept.
2. (B) Heterogeneity is the only correct physical characteristic related to real estate given in the question.
3. (A) Since land and improvements are immobile, the local environment has a significant impact on the utility of real estate.
4. (C) See definition of *highest and best use*.
5. (C) The law permits various interests to be severed from the land itself, such as leases, easements, conditional fees, air rights and mineral rights. Each of these interests may be separately sold or retained, thus magnifying the economic utility of the land.
6. (B) See definition of *situs*.
7. (C) Since real estate is fixed in location and thus highly dependent on local changes in the environment. Real estate people tend to specialize because local market is unique.
8. (C) See limitation on ownership rights.
9. (B) A fixture is treated as realty. Technically, it is a chattel real or personalty which has become realty.
10. (A) By definition, a tree is realty unless it is severed from the land for a sufficient period of time.
11. (D) Definition of intangible property includes contract rights.
12. (C) Both are important in determining whether or not an article is a fixture.
13. (D) See definition of *highest and best use*.
14. (C) No two parcels of land are exactly the same.
15. (C) Situs is an economic characteristic.

CHAPTER 3

1. (B) NAR is the NATIONAL ASSOCIATION OF REALTORS®.
2. (B) See definition of a *market*.
3. (A) Because real estate purchases usually require the use of borrowed funds, real estate markets have become very dependent on fluctuations in the money supply.
4. (D) See definition of a *syndicator*.
5. (C) CPM means "Certified Property Manager" and is awarded by the Institute of Real Estate Management (IREM).
6. (A) The real estate industry accounts for approximately 10% of the national employment
7. (D) Article 14 of the NAR Code of Ethics requires REALTORS® to submit disputes with other REALTORS® to arbitration.
8. (B) Article 6 of the NAR Code of Ethics urges the use of exclusive listings.
9. (C) Article 22 of the NAR Code of Ethics requires a REALTOR® to work through a listing broker and not directly with the owner.
10. (D) Article 8 of the NAR Code of Ethics requires full disclosure in situations when a REALTOR® is representing two parties to a transaction.

CHAPTER 4

1. (B) Licensing laws are based on the police power of the state. The justification for the police power is to protect the public.
2. (D) No one would be entitled to a commission in such a case. A valid license must be effective at the time the service was performed.
3. (C) A trustee is normally exempt by state licensing law requirements.
4. (D) License expirations vary from state to state. See your state's licensing law.
5. (C) This is grounds for suspension of license or other disciplinary action because the broker is violating ethical standards and fiduciary duties of an agent.
6. (B) The salesperson is a legal extension of the broker, and the salesperson's license is issued directly to the broker to hold while the salesperson is in the broker's employment.
7. (C) It should be noted that the escrow money was collected by the salesperson and not the broker. The escrow account is under the name of the broker, and thus the money should be turned over to the broker for deposit.
8. (C) State licensing law requires that a natural person be named in the license of a corporation.
9. (A) Since a salesperson is not entitled to hold his or her own license, the license must be returned to the real estate commission and will not be operative until a new broker is found.
10. (D) Anyone working for consideration, whether salary or commission, must be licensed unless specifically exempt.
11. (C) A salesperson must be a natural person.
12. (A) Only executors are exempt from among the choices given.
13. (D) When a broker's license is suspended, the licenses of salespersons employed by the broker may be transferred to another broker. A commission does not have the final word because a person may always appeal an administrative decision to the appropriate court.
14. (B) A salesperson's license is not operative if the holding broker's license is revoked, unless the license is transferred to another licensed broker.
15. (B) Ordinarily, under state law a broker may only share a commission with a salesperson employed by that broker or with another licensed broker.
16. (C) State law provides for fine, imprisonment, and other disciplinary actions for violating rules and regulations of the real estate commission.
17. (A) Most state laws require minimum experience for a *broker's* license, but a salesperson must ordinarily meet only certain minimum educational requirements.
18. (A) Answer is merely a restatement of definition of an "associate broker."
19. (D) A salesperson can only receive a commission from the broker holding the salesperson's license.
20. (C) Violation of licensing laws could result in either suspension or revocation of a license. A person selling his or her own home does not need to be licensed.
21. (C) Both are grounds for revocation.
22. (D) The real estate commission must be notified of any change in employment. The broker is the seller's agent.
23. (B) Only one escrow account which contains all clients' money must be maintained.
24. (B) Generally you are guilty of a misdemeanor.
25. (A) See definition of *police power*.

CHAPTER 5

1. (D) Neither witnesses nor a closing date are required for a valid real estate contract. If there is no stated date of closing, the law will presume a reasonable closing date. Witnesses are normally required only for more formal documents such as deeds.
2. (D) A contract exists because this is a unilateral mistake of which Tom did not have notice.
3. (B) See definition of *parol evidence rule*.
4. (D) Neither statement is true because, unless otherwise stated, an auction is considered to be "with reserve," meaning the auctioneer can withdraw the property anytime before accepting the bid.
5. (C) A requirement of a valid contract is an offer and acceptance. In this instance there were two offers.
6. (B) The contract is void because there are no objective criteria in determining what is acceptable financing.
7. (A) A counter offer exists only if there is a new condition or deviation from the original offer in the acceptance. Good title is always presumed.
8. (B) Under common law, the only way to accept a unilateral contract is by completion of the act. Modern law does not favor this strict interpretation and will often permit a partial completion to serve as acceptance.
9. (D) A contract for the sale of real estate must be in writing to be enforceable (statute of frauds). Pam is entitled to all of her money back.
10. (A) An acceptance is effective when properly dispatched in an authorized means of communication.
11. (C) An exculpatory clause is one that frees a person from liability. The law will not as a matter of public policy enforce exculpatory clauses that attempt to free an individual from his or her own negligence or wrongdoing.
12. (A) If a contract is illegal at the time it is made, the contract is void, even though a law is passed which would have made the same act legal.

Solutions and Explanations

13. (D) Even if an offer is said to be irrevocable, the offer may be revoked at will unless it is an option.
14. (C) A counter offer is an implied rejection of the original offer. Thus, the original offer is terminated.
15. (B) In order for consideration to exist, both parties to a contract must give up a right that they did not have to give up. The contractor gave nothing in this transaction since he was obligated to perform the contract at the original price.
16. (C) The $400 was considered to be legally sufficient consideration, even though it may have been a poor business judgment. A remedy for a breach of a contract involving the transfer of real estate is specific performance.
17. (C) This is a valid contract.
18. (D) A contract with a minor for other than the reasonable value of necessities is voidable at the option of the minor. She may therefore back out of the deal.
19. (C) Ordinarily, self-induced intoxication is not a defense against the contract.
20. (B) Under common law, equitable conversion occurs upon the signing of an absolute and unconditional sales contract of real estate, absent provisions to the contrary in the agreement itself.
21. (D) Contractual provisions can modify presumptions under either common law or statutes as to who bears the risk of loss.
22. (C) "Time is of the essence" are magic words that have been judicially interpreted to mean the contract time provisions will be strictly adhered to. Absent these words, the law will presume reasonable latitude.
23. (D) Unlike an offer, once a contract is created, it is enforceable upon the estate of the decedent unless it is a contract for personal services or one that could not be assigned because it was based on the personal credit of the purchaser.
24. (D) Statute of frauds applies only to certain executory contracts and merely affects the enforceability of the contract in a court of law. Once a contract has been executed, the statute no longer applies. Fraud and perjury are not forbidden by the statute of frauds, although they are illegal for other reasons.
25. (C) Definition of *rescission*.
26. (C) A covenant is not a condition; therefore, she can only sue for damages.
27. (C) See definition of *equitable conversion*.
28. (C) Death of a party to a contract is not cause for nonperformance.
29. (C) See definition of *bilateral contract*.
30. (B) See definition of *express contract*.

CHAPTER 6

1. (C) Ordinarily, the broker has earned his commission the moment a qualified buyer is found. The listing contract may contain provisions to the contrary.
2. (A) State licensing law prohibits paying finder's fee or kickbacks. It is irrelevant whether the kickback is money or an expensive ring.
3. (A) The public is entitled to expect fair dealing with professional agents such as real estate brokers, even though no formal principal-agent relationship exists.
4. (D) Neither client owes you a commission because you have breached the fiduciary duty of disclosing a dual agency relationship.
5. (D) The broker is a gratuitous volunteer and is not entitled to a commission since he can show no employment contract, either expressly or by implication by either party.
6. (B) Normally, unless the broker was the efficient and procuring cause of the sale, he is not entitled to a commission under an open listing contract. In this instance, the owner of the house, acting in good faith, sold the house not knowing of the fraud on the part of the purchaser. Since the purchaser intentionally acted to defraud the broker of his right to a commission, the courts would make the wrongdoer personally liable as the measure of damages.
7. (D) The license of a salesperson must be operative at the time the service is performed for either the salesperson or the broker to be entitled to the commission.
8. (D) The broker has violated several of his fiduciary duties as an agent. First, he has failed to give notice of a material fact that the house has termites. Second, he has violated his duty of due care to make sure that no misrepresentations appeared in the contract. For either of these two reasons, he would not be entitled to a commission. Note that the question said which of the following is *not* true.
9. (A) The general rule is that you are entitled to a commission when you find a ready, willing and able buyer. Generally, your right to a commission is not defeated merely because a seller is unable to convey good title.
10. (C) This is nothing more than sales puffery or sales talk. It is not a misrepresentation because it is not a material fact that can *reasonably* be relied upon by a purchaser, since you are merely stating an opinion.
11. (C) Since a real estate broker's authority is generally limited to bringing buyer and seller together, he would by definition be a special agent.
12. (C) A broker has an absolute duty to account for money in his care.
13. (B) James Spence is a minor and therefore enters into voidable contracts except for reasonable necessities. If he avoids the contract, Kathy is not entitled to a commission.
14. (B) Wedgworth is entitled to a commission since he found a ready, willing and able buyer, and his right is not defeated by a mutual agreement of buyer and seller to rescind the sales contract. He must return the earnest deposit and bring a separate suit for the commission in a court of law.
15. (C) The definition of a net listing contract is a set net price to

the seller with *everything* above that amount going to the broker. This is *not* a net listing.

16. (B) By failing to disclose his relationship with the purchasers, the broker has breached his agency relationship of fidelity. Even if the house had sold at the fair market value, the broker would have not been entitled to the commission.

17. (C) In general, a broker must give notice of all material facts to his principal.

18. (A) A principal can bind himself to a contract entered into by an agent acting beyond the agent's scope of authority if the principal ratifies the contract. Ratification does not involve dismissing or punishing the agent.

19. (A) By definition, an agent for an undisclosed principal is personally liable for any contract entered into by the undisclosed principal.

20. (B) Brown has apparent authority to sell the store to Roe. Thus, Bennett can not rescind the contract. Brown was given legitimate instructions, which he violated, and he can be sued for breaching his fiduciary duty.

21. (B) The broker has breached his duty of loyalty when he decides to buy the mansion for himself. A broker may not compete with his principal without disclosure and permission.

22. (C) An ostensible agency is created when a third party is told by the principal that someone is an agent of the principal.

23. (B) When an agent tells a third party that he has certain authority that he in fact does not have, this is a breach of an implied warranty of authority.

24. (B) Bryan has an agency obligation to advise his principal of any material facts affecting the subject matter of the agency. His authority has, by operation of law, been terminated because of a material change in circumstances.

25. (A) All of the elements necessary for an agency coupled with an interest are present in the fact situation. Death does not terminate an agency coupled with an interest.

26. (C) Brokers have a duty to submit all offers to their principals.

27. (C) See explanation of classification of agencies.

28. (C) See discussion of subagency and multiple listing service.

29. (B) In a listing agreement, the seller is the principal and the broker is the agent.

30. (C) See definition of *universal agent*.

CHAPTER 7

1. (D) The monuments method of land description relies on the use of both natural and artificial landmarks.

2. (B) Each township is divided into 36 sections.

3. (C) The rectangular survey method is another name for the U.S. government survey system.

4. (D) The monuments method of land description is quite common in older descriptions in rural areas and is less precise than lot and block, recorded plat or metes and bounds.

5. (A) The lot and block method is also referred to as the recorded plat method and is used in recording lots and blocks in subdivisions.

6. (A) ½ × ¼ × 640 acres = 20 acres
   20 × $2,000 = $40,000

7. (B) See definition of *township*.

8. (A) Since the earth's surface is not flat, correction lines are added to allow for the earth's curvature.

9. (D) Any reference point can be used as the starting point, and monuments can be used in the description.

10. (C) See definition of a *range*.

11. (C) R3W means the township is to the west of R2W; thus it would be immediately to the left.

12. (C) Note the direction of the arrow, which is towards the left of the page rather than towards the top.

13. (D) A dotted line represents an easement. There are three lots with dotted lines.

14. (C) The total area of Lots 6 and 7 is 15,750 square feet.
    15,750/43,560 = .3615
    $3,000/.3615 = $8,300

15. (A) See Figure in text.

16. (B) Lot 9 is NE ¼ of NW ¼ of NW ¼, s.18 ¼ × ¼ × ¼ × 640 = 10

17. (D) See Figure in text.

18. (B) ½ × ¼ × ¼ × 640 = 20

19. (C) A check or quadrangle is a 24 × 24 mile area. It contains 576 square miles and 576 sections.

20. (B) The bearing may be in either a clockwise or a counter-clockwise direction.

21. (A) An acre contains 43,560 square feet.

22. (A) See definition of a *plat*.

23. (D) See definition of a *check*.

24. (B) See definition of *delta*.

25. (D) See explanation of the *lot and block method* of land description.

Solutions and Explanations 317

CHAPTER 8

1. (C) The estate concept permits different interests to be severed from the land itself and separately sold to different users.
2. (C) A fee tail is a freehold estate.
3. (A) The key to this question is the "automatic" termination, which is charateristic of fee simple determinable.
4. (C) By definition, the "power of termination" is associated with the fee simple subject to a condition subsequent.
5. (C) Fee, fee simple and fee simple absolute refer to the same concept.
6. (C) Since the life estate and the future interest have come under a single ownership, no one else has any claim or interest on or in the property.
7. (C) A life estate is a type of freehold estate.
8. (B) A life estate is not inheritable.
9. (C) The definition of waste is any action or inaction that unreasonably impairs or injures the interests of the remainderman.
10. (D) See definition of *curtesy*.
11. (C) A future interest is an estate in land.
12. (C) Both estates may be followed by a reversion.
13. (D) See definition of *profit*.
14. (D) A dominant estate is one benefited by an easement, while a servient estate is one burdened by an easement.
15. (B) By definition, an easement appurtenant runs with the land of the dominant estate.
16. (C) Ownership in severalty merely refers to individual ownership. By definition, Betty also has a life estate.
17. (B) Since there is no indication of marriage and no indication of a trustee or beneficiary, the only logical answer is a tenancy in common.
18. (A) Under a tenancy in common there is no right of survivorship. Thus, when Betty dies her interest goes to her heirs.
19. (A) In community property states, property owned by an individual before the marriage remains that individual's property in severalty.
20. (A) Joint tenancy normally simplifies probate. However, under federal tax law, inheritance taxes are still owed.
21. (B) Unity of person refers to the marriage status. Only married persons can own property by the entirety.
22. (B) This is essentially the same as question 21.
23. (C) This is the only unity in a tenancy in common.
24. (A) Since four unities must be present to create a joint tenancy, Jenny can only be a tenant in common. The other two tenants, in regard to their relationship to each other, are not affected by Charlene's transfer and thus remain joint tenants in a two-thirds undivided interest in the property.
25. (D) In community property states, property owned by the individuals before marriage remains property in severalty.
26. (C) Only the tenancy in common will give the tax loss flowthroughs that the three are seeking and also avoid double taxation.
27. (B) See definition of *severalty ownership*.
28. (A) The only true statement is that Jan and Carol must be husband and wife.
29. (C) A corporation is ordinarily subject to taxation, and any dividends distributed are also taxed as part of the individual's income. If an REIT distributes less than 95% of its net income, it is treated as a taxable entity.
30. (D) See definition of *joint tenancy*.
31. (B) The nature of a trust is to separate legal ownership, which is held by the trustee, from equitable or beneficial ownership, which is held by the beneficiary.
32. (D) An REIT is a separate legal entity and shields investors from personal liability.
33. (B) One of the requirements of an REIT is that there must be at least 100 owners.
34. (B) A characteristic of a limited partnership is that the general partner or partners have the right to manage the business and are subject to personal liability.
35. (D) Since partition is not permitted and arbitration or petition would not be legally effective, one method to divide the property is for both the wife and husband to voluntarily transfer title to a third person, known as a straw man or nominee, and have the land subdivided and transferred back to the separate individuals.
36. (A) See definition of *easement in gross*.
37. (A) See definition of *easement appurtenant*.
38. (C) "X" had a life estate for the life of another. When "X" dies the property is inherited by "X's" heirs. The life estate continues as long as "Y" is alive.
39. (D) See explanation of *homesteading*.
40. (C) See explanation of *tenancy in common*.
41. (B) An easement does not have to be in writing.
42. (B) See definition of *syndication*.
43. (D) See discussion of *riparian system*.
44. (D) Joint tenancy has the right of survivorship.
45. (A) See discussion of *allodial*.

CHAPTER 9

1. (A) A unit is the individual ownership right in the condominium, while everything else is in pro rata common ownership.
2. (C) A master deed is the same instrument as the declaration or the enabling declaration.
3. (B) Since each individual owns a pro rata share of the com-

mon elements as part of the unit, the individual would be separately assessed for the property taxes. The package insurance policy, however, is taken out by the homeowner's association, and the association is responsible for paying the premiums.

4. (A) When a rental pooling arrangement is included as part of the package that the purchaser of a condominium receives, this is treated as a security, requiring SEC registration unless it meets the requirements of an exemption.

5. (A) If a condominium owner fails to pay insurance premiums, the policy will be cancelled. Failure to pay special assessments imposed either by the homeowner's association to make major improvements or failure to pay special assessments imposed by local government can lead to a special lien being imposed on the unit.

6. (A) State law ordinarily requires 100% vote to modify a condominium declaration unless the declaration provides otherwise.

7. (D) Each individual unit owner owns a pro rata share of the common areas.

8. (B) A purchaser's share in a landed homes association is called a "participation."

9. (A) Normally, replacement reserves are an account to accumulate funds for making major repairs such as the replacement of roofs. If insufficient funds have been accumulated when the replacement must be made, an extra fee called a special assessment is imposed on the unit owners on a pro rata basis.

10. (A) To protect consumers from high pressure sales talks or impulsive purchases, many states permit a cooling-off period to allow purchasers to change their minds.

11. (C) A condominium form of ownership is not limited to residential property.

12. (A) Nonpayment of maintenance fees can result in a lien being placed on the delinquent units.

13. (B) See definition of *master deed*.

14. (A) See definition of *bylaws*.

15. (A) Condominiums are a legal form of property ownership.

CHAPTER 10

1. (D) Ann has an estate for years, which is a prior legal interest in the property. A subsequent purchaser will take the property subject to the lease.

2. (A) Fred has exclusive right to possession of his leased premises. Since the rug was negligently placed on the floor, Fred may be sued by John.

3. (C) Periodic tenancies for more than one year are automatically renewed for a period of one year, unless appropriate notice to terminate is given.

4. (D) Gene has no legal basis since, in order to argue constructive eviction, the tenant must vacate.

5. (B) A leasehold estate is inheritable.

6. (A) Under common law, the tenant is responsible for maintaining and repairing the property.

7. (B) Under common law, absent agreement to the contrary, rent is due at the end of the term.

8. (A) See definition of *leased fee interest*.

9. (C) See explanation of *tenancy pur autre vie*.

10. (C) See definition of *partial eviction*. Herman's duty to pay rent is temporarily suspended.

11. (B) See definition of *sublease*.

12. (C) Death of either party will terminate a tenancy at will.

13. (A) See definition of *surrender and acceptance*.

14. (A) The lessee is the tenant and his interest is called a leasehold.

15. (A) See definition of *emblements*.

16. (B) See definition of *distress* or *distraint*.

17. (B) Using leased premises for illegal purposes is grounds for terminating the lease.

18. (B) Since the lease has been signed prior to the mortgage, the lease is not affected by the foreclosure of the mortgage.

If the lease had been signed after a mortgage had been given, foreclosure would terminate the lease.

19. (C) A leasehold is a nonfreehold estate and is considered to be personal property (chattel real).

20. (B) See definition of *sublease*.

21. (C) See explanation of *management plan*.

22. (B) See definition of *sublease*.

23. (D) See definition of *flat lease*.

24. (C) Ordinarily, any property interest can be mortgaged.

25. (C) Ordinarily, any interest in which the person is subject to monetary loss should be insured.

26. (A) See definition of *subordination clause*.

27. (C) See definition of *percentage lease*.

28. (D) See definition of *net lease*.

29. (C) See definition of *reappraisal lease*.

30. (A) $150 \times 70 \times \$5.75 \times 2.75 / 36 = \$4,612$.

31. (A) See explanation of *sandwich lease*.

32. (D) See definition of *concession*.

33. (B) Compensation for a property manager is normally a percent of gross income.

34. (D) See definition of *index lease*.

35. (A) A net lease does not ordinarily include payment by the lessee for mortgage debt service.

36. (B) See definition of *demise*.

37. (D) See definition of *tenancy*.

38. (D) The lessor has the reversionary interest.

39. (B) See definition of gross lease

40. (A) $(60 \times 100) + (48 \times 100) = 10,800$
$10,800 \times \$5.50 = \$59,400$.

Solutions and Explanations

CHAPTER 11

1. (C) Homeownership may offer advantages of protection against inflation and tax deductions.
2. (B) The lender's rules of thumb are based on gross income rather than net income.
3. (A) Housing needs are usually tied to phases in the family life cycle.
4. (B) A high percentage of owner-occupied houses is indicative of neighborhood stability.
5. (C) Buffers and building and health code enforcement can protect a neighborhood from nuisances and hazards.
6. (A) A worn trail may be a sign of an unrecorded easement.
7. (D) HOW is a warranty program sponsored by a subsidiary of the National Association of Home Builders.
8. (B) The only thing under the HOW program covered for 10 years is major structural defects.
9. (A) See definition of *coinsurance*.
10. (A) Capital improvements can result in special tax assessments.
11. (A) See definition of *apportionment* or *pro rata clause*.
12. (C) $\dfrac{\$90,000}{\$120,000} \times \$40,000 = \$30,000$.
13. (D) See definition of *subrogation clause*.
14. (A) $\$400,000 / \$900,000 = .444$
    $.444 \times \$300,000 = \$133,000$
15. (A) See specific perils not covered under HO-2 Form.

CHAPTER 12

1. (D) Students as such are not protected by either the Federal Fair Housing Act of 1968 or the Civil Rights Act of 1866.
2. (B) The Civil Rights Act of 1866 prohibits discrimination based on race in all instances. The Federal Fair Housing Act of 1968 allows for some exemptions.
3. (C) See remedies under the 1968 Federal Fair Housing Act.
4. (B) See remedies under the Civil Rights Act of 1866.
5. (B) Occupation is not a protective classification under either act.
6. (B) Since the apartment project was built for the church's membership, the church may discriminate on the basis of religion but may not discriminate on the basis of race.
7. (A) See remedies under the 1968 Federal Fair Housing Act.
8. (B) If the owner uses the services of a real estate broker, the 1968 Federal Fair Housing Act must be strictly adhered to.
9. (A) The Civil Rights Act of 1866 places no restrictions on the amount of punitive damages if one is discriminated against on the basis of race.
10. (C) Discrimination on the basis of sex is prohibited by a 1974 amendment to the 1968 Federal Fair Housing Act. Discrimination based on extending credit was prohibited under the original act.
11. (B) See definition of *steering*.
12. (C) HUD administers federal fair housing laws.
13. (B) Discrimination on the basis of sex was prohibited by an amendment in the Housing and Community Development Act or 1974.
14. (A) The 1968 Act prohibits steering.
15. (A) To be exempt, the dwellings must be for four or fewer families, including the one occupied by the owner.

CHAPTER 13

1. (B) In order to give constructive notice to third parties, a deed must be recorded. Title is ordinarily conveyed when delivered *and* accepted.
2. (C) The doctrine of merger states that, when a deed is accepted, all prior agreements are extinguished unless specific provisions are included that the obligations will survive the issuance of the deed.
3. (A) A general warranty deed guarantees that good and marketable title is being conveyed. A quitclaim deed conveys whatever present title a grantor has but makes no warranties or representations.
4. (A) A general warranty deed contains the most guarantees that a grantor can give to a grantee.
5. (A) The covenant of seizin or the covenant of right to convey, which is normally included as part of the covenant of seizin, would be violated.
6. (D) The covenant of quiet enjoyment refers to the fact that no one has title superior or paramount to that of the grantor.
7. (D) In some states such as New York, a covenant of trust has been established by state law to make a seller a trustee for purchase price funds to insure that unrecorded mechanic's liens will be paid off.
8. (C) A special warranty deed and a grant deed warrant title only against defects that have occurred after the grantor obtained title.
9. (A) In a quitclaim deed, a grantor conveys only what present interest he has in the property. A special warranty deed will convey any subsequently acquired title by operation of law.
10. (B) In most states, actual consideration does not need to be recited if the consideration that is recited is clearly nominal.

11. (A) When a person dies testate, he has died with a will. The will provides for the appointment of an executor.
12. (C) "Good" consideration refers to love and affection and is distinguished from valuable consideration, which is something of monetary worth. A gift deed is given for good consideration.
13. (C) A deed of surrender is used to merge a life estate with a reversion or remainder.
14. (D) A deed of confirmation, also known as a correction deed, is used to correct a previously delivered defective deed.
15. (A) A grantee must be an existing legal entity. Since an unincorporated association has no recognized legal existence, a deed to such a grantee is void.
16. (C) In most states, title passes when the deed is delivered and accepted.
17. (B) Executing and delivering a deed after death is not effective because both the grantor and grantee must be alive at the time of delivery and acceptance.
18. (A) A breach of a *condition* leads to forfeiture. A breach of covenant merely leads to a suit for damages.
19. (A) So as not to be liable to the grantee for unpaid taxes, it is common for the grantor to grant the property subject to the tax assessments.
20. (B) By definition, *habendum* means "to have and to hold."
21. (B) By definition, *attestation* means "to witness."
22. (B) By definition, *devise* is a testamentary disposition of real property.
23. (C) See definition of *escheat*.
24. (A) See definition of *adverse possession*.
25. (C) See definition of *patent*.
26. (D) See definition of *prescriptive easement*.
27. (D) See definition of *constructive notice*.
28. (C) See definition of *quiet enjoyment*.
29. (D) A quitclaim deed conveys only present interest.
30. (B) See definition of *covenant of warranty forever*.
31. (B) See definition of *descent*.
32. (C) See definition of *avulsion*.
33. (B) See explanation of *severance damages*.
34. (A) See definition of *partition*.
35. (A) See definition of *premises*.

CHAPTER 14

1. (C) A lender is the obligee in a promissory note and a mortgagee under a mortgage.
2. (A) In a deed of trust, the trustor or grantor pledges property as security for a debt.
3. (D) The promissory note or bond represents the primary obligation to repay a debt in a real estate financing transaction.
4. (D) See definition of *acceleration clause*.
5. (A) See definition of *statutory redemption*.
6. (A) See definition of *strict foreclosure*.
7. (B) See definition of *confirmation*.
8. (B) Unlike a foreclosure in which all junior liens are extinguished, taking a deed in lieu of foreclosure has the same effect as purchasing the property subject to all junior liens. The lender would not be entitled to a deficiency judgment in such a case.
9. (C) See definition of *reconveyance deed*.
10. (B) See definition of *land contract*.
11. (D) See definition of *satisfaction piece*.
12. (D) See definition of *hypothecation*.
13. (C) Waste is anything that impairs the security of the lender. A promise to keep property repaired would be a covenant against waste.
14. (A) See definition of *partial release clause*.
15. (C) When a purchaser assumes a mortgage, the original mortgagor remains liable. When a mortgagee agrees to substitute the new purchaser and expressly releases the original mortgagor from personal liability, a novation is said to have occurred.
16. (C) See explanation of *certificate of reduction of mortgage* and *estoppel certificate*.
17. (B) See definition of *participation mortgage*.
18. (A) See definition of *mortgagee-in-possession*.
19. (A) See explanation of *judgment in rem*.
20. (A) Both a lien and an easement are encumbrances.
21. (A) See definition of *mechanic's lien*.
22. (B) Normally, a person is not entitled to a tax deed until the redemption period has expired. Thus, a tax certificate is issued.
23. (D) See definition of *special assessment*.
24. (B) Constructive notice includes recorded instruments, public notices in official newspapers, and any information a person would have from physically inspecting the property.
26. (A) See definition of *mortgagor*.
27. (A) See definition of *due on sale*.
28. (A) The borrower is the obligor.
29. (C) See definition of *subordination clause*.
30. (C) Generally, the mortgage recorded first has top priority.
31. (B) See definition of *lien*.
32. (D) See definition of *vendor's lien*.
33. (D) See explanation of *power of sale*.
34. (C) See definition of *chattel mortgage*.
35. (D) See definition of *satisfaction of mortgage*.

Solutions and Explanations

CHAPTER 15

1. (C) FHA financing can be used for both single-family homes and mobile homes.
2. (A) See definition of *purchase money mortgage*.
3. (C) See definition of *package mortgage*.
4. (D) Private mortgage insurance has an annual insurance premium of ¼%.
5. (B) FHA requires a ½% annual insurance premium.
6. (D) See definition of *open mortgage*.
7. (B) RESPA requires disclosure of closing costs. Regulation Z requires disclosure of APR and finance charges and is referred to as the Truth-in-Lending Act.
8. (C) See definition of *participation mortgage*.
9. (A) Federally chartered savings and loan associations must be members of the Federal Savings and Loan Insurance Corporation.
10. (D) Of the four choices, FNMA is the only buyer in the secondary mortgage market.
11. (D) VA guarantees mortgages and FHA insures mortgages.
12. (C) See discussion of *finder's fee*.
13. (A) The appraisal fee is paid by the mortgagor or borrower as part of the loan origination fee.
14. (C) Regulation Z requires disclosure of APR and finance charges.
15. (D) "FRS" denotes the Federal Reserve System.
16. (C) An equity participation mortgage gives the lender a share in the ownership of the mortgaged property.
17. (C) In order to assure the lender of his security interest, the loan is advanced only as stages of the project are completed.
18. (A) See definition of *partial release of mortgage*.
19. (D) A lender may make a VA mortgage for any amount; however, VA only guarantees $27,500.
20. (C) See definition of *Free Market System Auction*.
21. (B) Regulation Z covers all real estate transactions involving consumers and credit *not* in excess of $25,000 in nonreal estate transactions.
22. (A) See definition of *usury*.
23. (C) See definition of *equity*.
24. (C) Loans are based on the appraised value or sales price, whichever is less.
25. (B) See definition of *blanket mortgage*.
26. (A) See definition of *open-end mortgage*.
27. (C) See definition of *fully amortized level payment mortgage*.
28. (A) Businesses, governments and lenders are not protected by Regulation Z.
29. (A) Historically savings and loan associations have made approximately one-half of all single-family real estate mortgages.
30. (D) FHA prohibits prepayment penalties on FHA mortgages.
31. (A) See definition of *takeout commitment*.
32. (C) See definition of *redlining*.
33. (A) Title examination fees, appraisal fees and survey fees are not considered to be finance charges and do not have to be disclosed under Regulation Z.
34. (A) $40,000 × .8 × .03 = $960.
35. (C) $960 + $8,000 + $1,000 = $9,960.
36. (B) See discussion of *Truth-in-Lending Act*.
37. (B) See definition of *usury*.
38. (C) Lenders set interest rates on conventional loans.
39. (D) See definition of *budget mortgage*.
40. (C) See discussion of *loan underwriting*.
41. (D) MGIC insures conventional loans.
42. (C) See discussion of discount points.
43. (C) See definition of *loan-to-value ratio*.
44. (C) Private lenders provide the funds for FHA loans.
45. (A) See discussion of FHA.

CHAPTER 16

1. (C) Constructive notice consists of more than just recorded instruments. See definition of *constructive notice*.
2. (D) See definition of *tract index*.
3. (A) See definition of *abstract of title*.
4. (A) Any defect in title is referred to as a cloud on title. This includes unexpired breaks or gaps in the chain of title.
5. (A) See definition of *lis pendens*.
6. (B) In most states, a title insurance policy will only indemnify the named insured. A mortgagee's policy will not insure an owner but rather the mortgagee alone. Title insurance only indemnifies for defects that existed at the time the policy was issued and were not excepted in the title insurance policy.
7. (B) See definition of *subrogation*.
8. (B) Title insurance will indemnify for the cost of defending a lawsuit brought about because of an alleged defect existing at the time the policy was issued.
9. (B) When title is registered under the Torrens System, future title transfers must go through the system and new certificates must be issued.
10. (B) Only title insurance will indemnify an owner for the cost of defending title defects.
11. (B) RESPA requires certain financial disclosures in title closing.
12. (C) If the closing date is not specified in the sales contract, the closing date will ocur in a reasonable period of time.

13. (D) An escrow agent acts on behalf of whomever is specified in the written instructions establishing the escrow arrangement.
14. (D) Recording gives constructive notice to the world.
15. (D) Closing costs are normally set by negotiation or custom. RESPA deals with disclosure information and not fee setting.
16. (C) Prorations are calculations to allocate each person's share of an ongoing expense such as property taxes or an assumed insurance policy.
17. (B) No meeting is required under an escrow settlement, and the procedure can be conducted by mail.
18. (A) Normally, a deed is a deed poll, which means that only the grantor signs the deed. If both parties sign the deed, such a deed is called an indenture deed.
19. (A) Under an escrow closing, buyer and seller do not have to meet; however, this does not eliminate the necessity for an attorney to represent either buyer or seller.
20. (B) Kickbacks are prohibited under RESPA.
21. (A) Since the financing is often a condition to the sales contract, normally the financial commitment is made after the sales contract is signed.
22. (D) RESPA only involves institutional-made first mortgage loans for single-family residential real estate.
23. (C) See definition of *good-faith estimate*.
24. (D) RESPA does not require a lender to use a particular settlement service provider; however, those providers used by the lender must be made known to the borrower.
25. (C) $\$60,000 \times .02 = \$1,200$.
26. (C) See discussion of *title insurance*.
27. (B) $\$60,000 \times .8 \times .01 = \$480$.
28. (D) RESPA deals with disclosure information.
29. (B) Title examination expenses are normally paid by the buyer and are not prorated.
30. (D) See definition of *escrow agent*.

CHAPTER 17

1. (A) Market value is a type of value in exchange.
2. (B) The larger the accrued depreciation, the less accurate the cost approach tends to be.
3. (B) See definition of *functional obsolescence*.
4. (C) A necessary step in the market approach is the adjustment process, which involves comparing the physical components of comparable properties with the subject property.
5. (A) See definition of *market value*.
6. (B) See definition of *functional obsolescence*.
7. (A) Normally, property is listed at a price somewhat higher than the actual selling price.
8. (A) Economic obsolescence is based on changes in the surrounding land-use patterns and thus is not generally curable.
9. (B) Value as derived by a gross rent multiplier is calculated by multiplying monthly rent by the GRM. $\$600 \times 125 = \$75,000$.
10. (A) See definition of *economic life*.
11. (A) See definition of *economic* or *locational obsolescence*.
12. (A) Physical deterioration is not related to tax depreciation. Failure to maintain a property can lead to physical deterioration.
13. (B) See definition of *market value*. If the selling price is based on the factors included in the definition of market value, the two will be equal; however, this is not generally the case.
14. (B) If the neighborhood is stable, there has been no economic obsolescence; however, a house that is 20 years old is subject to natural wear and tear leading to physical deterioration.
15. (C) $\$1,000 \times 84 = \$84,000$.
16. (B) See explanation of *builder's method*.
17. (B) An appraisal is an opinion or estimate of value and not a determination or prediction of value.
18. (B) The cost of acquisition is not used in deriving value via the cost approach.
19. (C) Functional obsolescence can be either curable or incurable.
20. (D) The cost and market approaches are normally used in appraising residential real estate.

CHAPTER 18

1. (D) Vacancies are related to the market and to the particular location and thus will vary with each property.
2. (B) As risk increases, the appraiser capitalizes income at a higher rate which results in a lower value.
3. (A) $R = I/V$
    $R = \$5,000 / \$50,000 = .10$
    $R = .10 + .01 = .11$
    $V = \$5,000 / .11 = \$45,455$
4. (A) As risk increases, the capitalization rate is increased.
5. (C) In the formula $V = I/R$, I refers to net operating income $R = \$50,000 / \$250,000 = .20$
6. (D) Gross income (effective gross income) minus operating expenses equals net income (net operating income).
7. (B) Recapture is based on the remaining economic life of a building. Each year, $1/25$ or 4% of the building must be recaptured.

Solutions and Explanations

8. (A) See definition of *economic life*.
9. (B) See definition of *capitalization rate*.
10. (B) The formula for the capitalization rate is Value = Income / Rate.
11. (C) See definition of *effective gross income*.
12. (D) Capitalization rate includes the cost of capital (mortgage rate) plus management, premium for illiquidity and compensation for risk.
13. (C) NOI before recapture $50,000
    Income to land
       ($125,000 × .10   − 12,500
       Building income $37,500
    Return of investment ($1/25 = 4\%$)
    Return on investment (10%)
    Overall building cap. rate = 14%
    $37,500 / .14 = $267,857
    Land value $125,000
    Building value   267,857
    Total value $392,857
14. (C) A capitalization rate includes a return on land and a return on and of the improvements.
15. (C) Leverage can be positive or negative.
16. (B) $85,000 × .12 = $10,200
17. (C) $52,000 / $300,000 = 17.3%
18. (A) ROI = Return / Investment Price
19. (A) See explanation of *before-tax cash flow*.
20. (C) Investment value is defined from the perspective of an individual investor.
21. (B) $280 × 12 / $42,000 = 8%.
22. (A) See definition of *leverage*.
23. (A) As risk increases, the rate of return increases.
24. (D) Money should be borrowed when the return on the investment is greater than the cost of borrowing the money.
25. (C) See definition of *liquidity*.
26. (C) See definition of *equity*.
27. (D) Before-tax cash flow minus tax liability equals after-tax cash flow.
28. (B) Rental income is treated as ordinary income.
29. (B) Capital improvements are added to the original basis, not subtracted.
30. (A) Of the choices provided, only interest on debt service is deductible.
31. (B) Only the tax credit is worth $1.00. All other items are worth less than $1.00.
32. (B) The taxpayer must be at least 55 years old.
33. (B) See explanation of an *interstate offering*.
34. (A) See definition of an *investment contract*.
35. (A) See definition of *boot*.

CHAPTER 19

1. (C) See definition of *nuisance law*.
2. (B) Zoning is based on police power. Eminent domain is a separate power in itself.
3. (B) Zoning is noncompensatory.
4. (D) Excluding low-income minorities is not a public purpose of zoning.
5. (B) Police power is the inherent power of the state government.
6. (C) See definition of *exclusionary zoning*.
7. (D) FAR of 3:1 means 3 square feet of floor space can be constructed on 1 square foot of land. If only one quarter of the lot is covered, the building can be 12 stories tall.
8. (A) See definition of *buffer zone*.
9. (B) See definition of *nonconforming use*.
10. (C) See definition of *variance*.
11. (C) Before a building can be constructed, building codes require issuance of a building permit. An occupancy permit is issued after the building is completed and found to have complied with the building code.
12. (B) See definition of *dedication*.
13. (C) PUD and CUP are names for the same technique.
14. (B) Each owner in a condominium project holds separate title, which can be separately foreclosed.
15. (A) See definition of *ad valorem*.
16. (A) See explanation of *property tax lien*.
17. (A) The property is assessed at one-third of market value. One mill equals one-tenth of one percent.
18. (B) See explanation of *tax assessment*.
19. (D) The assessed value is $21,000, and the tax is $735.
20. (C) The tax is $840, and the assessed value is $28,000.
21. (C) A mill is .001 of a dollar.
22. (A) See explanation of an *exemption*.
23. (B) See definition of *special assessment tax*.
24. (D) $750 / .0540 = $13,888
    $13,888 / .4 = $34,722
25. (C) Both are needed to determine the amount of property tax.
26. (D) Zoning does not necessarily prevent land value decline.
27. (C) See definition of *subdivision regulations*.
28. (B) See definition of *eminent domain*.
29. (B) See discussion of *Fifth Amendment*.
30. (B) AV = T/R
    $5,080,900 / $3.41 × $100 = $149,000,000

CHAPTER 20

1. $A = L \times W$
   $A = 726 \times 12 = 8,712$ sq. ft.
   $8,712 / 43,560 = .20$ acres
           Correct Answer B

2. Proportion problem
   Step 1: AC   10 8
      Gallons 12,000 X
      Hours   6 12
   Step 2: Eliminate hours so as to have a ratio:
      AC   10 8
      Gallons 24,000 X
      Hours   12 12
   Step 3: $\dfrac{10}{24,000} \times \dfrac{8}{X}$
      $10x = 192,000$
      $x = 19,200$
           Correct Answer C

3. Step 1: $\$23,400 + \$512 + \$6,500 = \$30,412$
   Step 2: $\$30,412$ is 93% of selling price
      Selling price = $\$30,412 / .93$
      SP = $\$32,701$
           Correct Answer C

4. Step 1: $\$10,000 \times .085 = \$850$ annual interest
      $\$850 / 12 = \$70.83$ first month's interest
   Step 2: $\$95.00 - \$70.83 = \$24.17$ principal reduction
   Step 3: $\$10,000 - \$24.17 = \$9,975.83$
           Correct Answer C

5. Step 1: She receives 65% of total commission
      Sales commission = total commission / percent received
      SC = $\$1,234 / .65 = \$1,898.46$
   Step 2: Sales commission = selling price × rate
      SP = $\$1,898.46/.07 = \$27,121$ Correct Answer C

6. Cost = selling price / (1 + % profit)
   Cost = $\$48,500 / 1.13$
   Cost = $\$42,920$
           Correct Answer B

7. Step 1: Selling price − net = sales commission
      SC = $\$24,450 - \$22,311$
      SC = $\$2,139$
   Step 2: Rate = sales commission/selling price
      R = $\$2,139 / \$24,450$
      R = $.08748 = 8.75\%$ Correct Answer B

8. Step 1: Insurance premium = insurance value × rate
      IP = $\$40,000 \times \$2.80/\$1,000$
      IP = $\$112.00$/year
   Step 2: 1991 12 40 Policy Expires
      1990 2 17 Settlement
         1 10 23 Unexpired portion
   Step 3: Cost per year: $\$112$
      Cost per month: $\$112 / 12 = \$9.33$
      Cost per day: $\$9.33 / 30 = \$.311$
   Step 4: 1 year × $\$112.00 = \$112.00$
      10 months × $\$9.33 = 93.30$
      23 days × $\$.311 = \underline{7.15}$
            $\$212.45$
           Correct Answer C

9. Step 1: Tax bill = assessed value × tax rate
      T = $\$16,400 \times \$5.88/\$100$
      T = $\$964.32$
   Step 2: Unexpired portion = 9 months 26 days
      Monthly tax = $\$964.32 / 12 = \$80.36$
      Daily tax = $\$80.36 / 30 = \$2.678$
   Step 3: 9 months × $\$80.36 = \$723.24$
      26 days × $\$2.678 = \underline{69.63}$
      Total $\$792.87$
           Correct Answer B

10. Step 1: $A = L \times W$
       $A = 116.25 \times 281 = 32,666$ sq. ft.
    Step 2: 1 acre = 43,560 sq. ft.
       $32,666 / 43,560 = .7499$ acre
            Correct Answer B

11. Step 1: Smaller lot
       $A = L \times W$
       $A = 150' \times 80' = 12,000$ sq. ft.
    Step 2: Larger lot
       $A = L \times W$
       $A = 400' \times 240' = 96,000$ sq. ft.
            $\underline{-12,000}$ sq. ft.
            $84,000$ sq. ft.
    Step 3: $12,000 / 84,000 = 1/7$
            Correct Answer B

12. Step 1: 5 yrs. × .06 = .30 total depreciation
    Step 2: Present value = original value × (1 − % depreciation)
       PV = $\$66,500 \times .70$
       PV = $\$46,550$ Correct Answer A

13. Step 1: Property tax
       Sept 20 to Jan 1 = 3 months 10 days
       $\$614.14 / 12 = \$51.178$ per month
       $\$51.178 / 30 = \$1.706$ per day
    Step 2: $\$51.178 \times 3 = \$153.535$
       $\$1.706 \times 10 = \underline{17.059}$
             $\$170.594$
    Step 3: Insurance
       Sept 20 to March 7 = 5 months 17 days
       $\$188.00 / 12 = \$15.666$ per month
       $\$15.666 / 30 = \$.522$ per day
    Step 4: $\$15.666 \times 5 = \$78.333$
       $\$.522 \times 17 = \underline{8.877}$
       $\$87.210 + \$170.594 = \$257.80$
            Correct Answer C

14. $\$835$ Loss
    $\underline{-200}$ Deductible
    $\$635 \times .9 = \$571.50$ Correct Answer A

15. $A = L \times W$
    $A = 411.4 \times 900 = 370,260$ sq. ft.
    $370,260 / 43,560 = 8.5$ acres
    $8.5 \times \$6,000 = \$51,000$ Correct Answer B

16. Rate = Income / Value
    R = $\$3,430 / \$22,000$
    R = $.1559 = 15.6\%$ Correct Answer C

Solutions and Explanations

17. Land $18,000 × 1.15 = $20,700
    House $58,000 × 1.20 = $69,600
    Total $90,300
    Correct Answer C

18. Step 1:
    $225 × 10 × 12 = $27,000 Potential income
                     − 1,350 Vacancy
                      25,650 Effective Gross income
                     −12,825 Operating expenses
                     $12,825 NOI
    Step 2: Rate = income / value
            R = $12,825 / $100,000
            R = .12825 = 12.8%   Correct Answer A

19. Income = value × rate
    I = $800,000 × .2
    I = $160,000
    NOI = 60% of gross income
    Gross income = $160,000 / .6 = $266,667
    Correct Answer A

20. GRM = Selling price / rent
    GRM = $55,000 / $500
    GRM = 110   Correct Answer C

21. $23,000 + $615 = 93% of selling price
    Selling price = cost / (1 − % loss)
    SP = $23,615 / .93
    SP = $25,392   Correct Answer D

22. Step 1: (43,560 × .25) + (43,560 × .10) × 15,246 sq. ft. per lot
    Step 2: 850′ × 900′ = 765,000 sq. ft.
            765,000 / 15,246 = 50 lots   Correct Answer A

23. $2,500 × 12 = $30,000 annual rent
    80′ × 50′ = 4,000 sq. ft.
    $30,000 / 4,000 sq. ft. = $7.50 per sq. ft. Correct Answer B

24. 8 years × 0.45 = .36 total depreciation
    Present value = original value × (1 − % depreciation)
    PV = $225,000 × (1 − .36)
    PV = $225,000 × .64
    PV = $144,000   Correct Answer B

25. Step 1:   City taxes
               12 months   0 days (total for year)
             − 9 months   9 days (October 9)
                2 months 21 days (time remaining)
    Step 2:   County taxes
               12 months   0 days
             − 9 months   9 days
                2 months 21 days (time remaining this year)
             + 6 months   (time remaining this year)
                8 months 21 days (total time remaining)
    Step 3: City taxes
            $440.00 / 12 = $36.666/month
            $440.00 / 360 = $1.222/day
            2 months × $36.666 = $73.332
            21 days × $1.222 =   25.662
                                 $98.994
    Step 4: County taxes
            $314.00 / 12 = $26.166/month

    $314.00 /360 = $.872/day
    8 months × $26.166 = $209.328
    21 days × $.872 =   18.312
                         $227.640
    $98.99 + $227.64 = $326.63
    Correct Answer B

26. Total commission = selling price × commission rate
    TC = $68,000 × .07 = $4,760
    Salesperson's share = $4,760 × .40 = $1,904
    Correct Answer A

27. Step 1: Commission = $1,850 − $225 = $1,625
            Total commission paid = $1,625 / .45 = $3,611.11
    Step 2: Selling price = sales commission / rate
            SP = $3,611.11 / .07 = $51,587
    Correct Answer C

28. Step 1: Principal = Interest / Rate × Time
            P = $14,025 / (.0825 × 2)
            P = $85,000
    Step 2: Value = principal / percent loan
            V = $85,000 / .8 = $106,250   Correct Answer C

29. Interest = principal × rate × time
    I = $45,000 × .075 × .08333
    I = $281.24
    $320 − $281.24 = $38.76
    $45,000 − $38.76 = $44,961.24
    Correct Answer D

30. $825 × 12 = $9,900 annual income
    Value = income / rate
    V = $9,900 / .14 = $70,714   Correct Answer B

31. A = L × W
    A = 110 × 4 = 440 sq. ft.
    440 / 9 = 48.888 sq. yd.
    48.888 × $2.75 = $134.44   Correct Answer B

32. Step 1: Annual interest = $264.00 × 12 = $3,168
            Principal = interest / interest rate
            P = $3,168 / .09 = $35,200
    Step 2: Value = principal / percent loan
            V = $35,200 / .80 = $44,000
    Correct Answer D

33. Step 1: Interest = principal × rate × time
            I = $500 × .13 × .25
            I = $16.25
            $500.00 + $16.25 = $516.25
    Correct Answer C

34. Selling price = $48,500 × .9 = $43,650
    Cost = asking price / (1 + % profit)
    C = $48,500 / 1.15 = $42,174
    $43,650 (selling price) − $42,174 (cost) = $1,476
    (gain)   Correct Answer A

35. Tax rate = tax bill / assessed value
    TR = $640.50 / $17,450
    TR = .0367 = $3.67/$100   Correct Answer C

36. A = ½ BH
    A = .5(362) × 362
    A = 65,522 sq. ft.
    65,522 / 43,560 = 1.5 acres   Correct Answer B

37. Rate = interest / principal × time
    R = $44 / ($800 × .5)
    R = .11 = 11%   Correct Answer C
38. 80 × $88 = 7,040   Correct Answer A
39. Step 1: A = ½ BH
            A = .5(1,320) × 594
            A = 392,040 sq. ft.
    Step 2: 392,040 / 43,560 = 9 acres
                            Correct Answer C
40. $\frac{300'}{14} \times \frac{750'}{x}$ (Cross Multiply)
    300x = 10,500
    x = 35 acres   Correct Answer C
41. Step 1: Loan amount = $55,000 × .8 = $44,000
            1 discount point = 1% of the loan
            3 discount points = $1,320
    Step 2: $1,320 discount points
            11,000 equity
             2,000 closing cost
            $14,320 necessary to close
                            Correct Answer C
42. Principal = interest / rate × time
    P = $330 / (.09 × .0833)
    P = $44,000
    Value = principal / percent loan
    V = $44,000 / .8 = $55,000   Correct Answer D
43. Step 1: $200 × 12 = $2,400 minimum rent
            $3,450 (total rent) − $2,400 (minimum rent)
            = $1,050 (rent based on excess sales)
    Step 2: Excess rent / percent charge over excess = excess sales
            $1,050 / .015 = $70,000 (excess sales)
            $50,000 + $70,000 = $120,000 total sales
                            Correct Answer B
44. Step 1: $41,000 × 1.4 = $57,400 asking price
                           − 2,000 reduction in price
                            $55,400 selling price
    Step 2: Selling price × commission rate = net to seller
            $55,400 × .935 = $51,799

Step 3: Selling price − net to seller = net profit on investment
        $51,799 − $41,000 = $10,799
                            Correct Answer B
45. Step 1: Total cost
            35 acres × $12,500 = $ 437,500
            Roads   80,000
            70 × $52,000   3,640,000
            Total Cost $4,157,500
    Step 2: Selling price = cost × (1 + % profit)
            SP = $4,157,500 × 1.15 = $4,781,128
            $4,781,128 / 70 = $68,302 price per house
                            Correct Answer B
46. Step 1: Assessed value = market value × tax rate
            AV = $46,000 × .40 = $18,400
    Step 2: Tax = assessed value × tax rate
            T = $18,400 × $5.88 / $100
            T = $1,081.92
            $1,081.92/12 = $90.16 per month
                            Correct Answer A
47. Step 1: 6″ = 18′ and 9″ = 27′
            Therefore, 1″ = 3′ and 1 sq. in. = 9 sq. ft.
    Step 2: Sq. inches 1   26
            Sq. ft.   9   x
            x = 234 sq. ft.   Correct Answer B
48. Step 1: 1/10 + 1/5 = 3/10 or 30% that cannot be developed
            The remaining 70% developed totals 45 acres
    Step 2: B = P / R
            B = 45 / .7 = 64 acres
                            Correct Answer A
49. A lot 60′ × 50′ is 220′ all the way around
    220 / 10 = 22 fence posts   Correct Answer C
50. Step 1: Alt. 1: 25 acres × $5,000 = $125,000 selling
    Step 2: Alt. 2: 50 lots × $3,000 = $150,000
                    $30,000 costs   − 30,000
                    subdividing $120,000
            He will make $5,000 less by subdividing
                            Correct Answer D

PROBLEM A-1

Question	Correct Answer	Question	Correct Answer	Question	Correct Answer	Question	Correct Answer
#1	C	#6	D	#11	A	#16	A
#2	B	#7	A	#12	B	#17	A
#3	C	#8	D	#13	C	#18	B
#4	A	#9	B	#14	C	#19	D
#5	C	#10	A	#15	B	#20	D

Solutions and Explanations

PROBLEM A-2

Question	Correct Answer	Question	Correct Answer	Question	Correct Answer	Question	Correct Answer
#1	A	#6	B	#11	B	#16	B
#2	A	#7	A	#12	B	#17	C
#3	C	#8	C	#13	C	#18	B
#4	B	#9	B	#14	C	#19	A
#5	B	#10	C	#15	C	#20	A

PROBLEM A-3

Question	Correct Answer	Question	Correct Answer	Question	Correct Answer	Question	Correct Answer
#1	D	#6	A	#11	C	#16	C
#2	C	#7	B	#12	A	#17	D
#3	B	#8	D	#13	C	#18	A
#4	A	#9	B	#14	B	#19	A
#5	B	#10	D	#15	C	#20	D

PROBLEM B-2

Question	Correct Answer	Question	Correct Answer	Question	Correct Answer	Question	Correct Answer
#1	B	#7	C	#13	A	#19	D
#2	B	#8	D	#14	B	#20	A
#3	A	#9	B	#15	D	#21	C
#4	C	#10	B	#16	C	#22	D
#5	C	#11	D	#17	C	#23	A
#6	A	#12	C	#18	A	#24	A
						#25	B

PROBLEM B-3

Question	Correct Answer	Question	Correct Answer	Question	Correct Answer	Question	Correct Answer
#1	C	#7	B	#13	D	#19	D
#2	B	#8	B	#14	C	#20	B
#3	A	#9	C	#15	C	#21	D
#4	D	#10	A	#16	A	#22	C
#5	C	#11	B	#17	A	#23	B
#6	A	#12	D	#18	B	#24	D
						#25	A

Selected Bibliography

Brokerage and Law

Case, Frederick E. *Real Estate Brokerage: A Systems Approach.* Englewood Cliffs, New Jersey: Prentice-Hall, Inc., 1982.

Henszey, Benjamin N., and Friedman, Ronald M. *Real Estate Law.* Boston: Warren, Gorham & Lamont, 1979.

Jennings, Marianne M. *Real Estate Law.* New York: Kent Publishing Company, 1985.

Kratovil, Robert, and Werner, Raymond J. *Real Estate Law.* 9th ed., Englewood Cliffs, New Jersey: Prentice-Hall, Inc., 1988.

Lindeman, Bruce. *Real Estate Brokerage Management.* 2nd ed. Englewood Cliffs, New Jersey: Prentice-Hall, 1988.

Semenow, Robert W. *Questions and Answers on Real Estate.* 9th ed., Englewood Cliffs, New Jersey: Prentice-Hall, Inc., 1978.

Finance and Math

Brueggeman, William B., Fisher, Jeffrey D., and Stone, Leo D. *Real Estate Finance.* 8th ed., Homewood, Illinois: Richard D. Irwin, Inc., 1989.

Dasso, Jerome, and Kuhn, Gerald. *Real Estate Finance.* Englewood Cliffs, New Jersey: Prentice-Hall, Inc., 1981.

Ordway, Nicholas; Ordway, Kathy; and Tosh, Dennis S. *Real Estate Math Made Easy.* 2nd ed. Reston, Virginia: Reston Publishing Company, Inc., 1986.

Wiedemer, John P. *Real Estate Finance*, 6th ed. Englewood Cliffs, NJ: Prentice Hall, 1990.

Appraisal and Investment Analysis

American Institute of Real Estate Appraisers. *The Appraisal of Real Estate.* 9th ed., Chicago: American Institute of Real Estate Appraisers, 1987.

Bloom, George F., and Harrison, Henry S. *Appraising the Single Family Residence.* Chicago: American Institute of Real Estate Appraisers, 1978.

Friedman, Jack P., and Ordway, Nicholas. *Income Property Appraisal and Analysis*, 2nd ed. Englewood Cliffs, NJ: Prentice Hall, 1987.

Jaffe, Austin J., and Sirmans, C. F. *Real Estate Investment Decision Making.* Englewood Cliffs, New Jersey: Prentice-Hall, Inc., 1982.

Pyhrr, Stephen A., and Cooper, James R. *Real Estate Investment.* 2nd ed. Boston: Warren, Gorham & Lamont, 1989.

Society of Real Estate Appraisers. *Appraising Real Property.* Chicago: Society of Real Estate Appraisers, 1984.

Journals and Periodicals

Journal of Property Management. Published by the Institute of Real Estate Management. 430 North Michigan Avenue, Chicago, Illinois, 60611.

Real Estate Review. Published by Warren, Gorham & Lamont, Inc. 210 South Street, Boston, Massachusetts, 02111.

Real Estate Today. Published by the NATIONAL ASSOCIATION OF REALTORS.® 430 North Michigan Avenue, Chicago, Illinois, 60611.

The Appraisal Journal. Published by the American Institute of Real Estate Appraisers. 430 North Michigan Avenue, Chicago, Illinois, 60611.

The Mortgage Banker. Published by the Mortgage Bankers Association of America. 1125 Fifteenth Street, N.W., Washington, D.C., 20005.

The Real Estate Appraiser and Analyst. Published by the Society of Real Estate Appraisers. 645 North Michigan Avenue, Chicago, Illinois, 60611.

General Interest

Badzinski, Stanley. *Home Construction and Estimating.* Englewood Cliffs, New Jersey: Prentice-Hall, Inc., 1979.

Committee on Professional Standards. *Interpretation of the Code of Ethics*, 6th ed., Chicago: NATIONAL ASSOCIATION OF REALTORS,® 1990.

Downs, James C., Jr. *Principles of Real Estate Management*. 12th ed., Chicago: Institute of Real Estate Management, 1980.

Harrison, Henry S. *Houses*. Chicago: NATIONAL ASSOCIATION OF REALTORS,® 1973.

Harwood, Bruce and Jacobus, Charles. *Real Estate Principles*. 4th ed., Reston, Virginia: Reston Publishing Company, Inc., 1986.

Hinds, Dudley S., and Ordway, Nicholas. *International Real Estate Investment*. Chicago: Real Estate Education Company, 1983.

Hinds, Dudley S.; Carn, Neil G.; and Ordway, Nicholas. *Winning at Zoning*. New York: McGraw-Hill Book Company, 1979.

National Association of Real Estate License Law Officials. *Annual Report of the Interstate Cooperation Committee*. Omaha, Nebraska: National Association of Real Estate License Law Officials. 1989.

————. *Guide To Examinations and Careers In Real Estate*. Reston, Virginia: Reston Publishing Company, Inc., 1980.

Ring, Alfred A., and Dasso, Jerome. *Real Estate Principles and Practices*. 11th ed., Englewood Cliffs, New Jersey: Prentice-Hall, Inc., 1985.

U.S. Department of Housing and Urban Development. *Settlement Costs and You: A Guide for Homebuyers*. Washington, D.C.: U.S. Government Printing Office, 1977.

Wofford, E. Larry. *Real Estate*. 2nd ed. New York: John Wiley & Sons, 1986.

Your Housing Rights (HUD-177-EO(4), June 1976). Copies of the Federal Fair Housing Act may be obtained by writing to: Office of Public Information, Department of Housing and Urban Development, 451 7th Street, S.W., Washington, D.C. 20024.

State real estate commissions publish copies of the rules and regulations applicable in their particular state.

Real Estate Commissions

Alabama
Real Estate Commission
State Capitol
Montgomery, Alabama 36130
(202) 261—5544

Alaska
Division of Occupational Licensing
Economic Development Suite 722
3601 C. Street
Anchorage, Alaska, 99503
(903) 563—2169

Alberta
Deputy Superintendent of Real Estate
Department of Consumer and Corporate Affairs
19th Floor
10025 Jasper Avenue
Edmonton, Alberta, Canada T5J 3ZB
(403) 422—1588

Arizona
Commissioner
Department of Real Estate
202 E. Earll Drive
Phoenix, Arizona 85012
(602) 255—4670

Arkansas
Executive Secretary
Real Estate Commission
One Riverfront Place
Suite 660
North Little Rock, Arkansas 72114
(501) 371—1247

British Columbia
Secretary
Real Estate Council
626 West Pender Street
Vancouver, British Columbia V6B 1V9
(604) 683—9664

California
Commissioner
Department of Real Estate
2201 Broadway
P.O. Box 187000
Sacramento, California 95818
(916) 739—3600

Colorado
Director
Real Estate Commission
1776 Logan Street
Denver, Colorado 80203
(303) 894—2166

Connecticut
Director
Real Estate Division
165 Capital Avenue
Hartford, Connecticut 06106
(203) 566—5130

Delaware
Administrative Assistant
Real Estate Commission
P.O. Box 1401
Margaret O'Neill Building
Dover, Delaware 19903
(302) 736—4522

District of Columbia
Commission Support Officer
Real Estate Commission
614 H Street, NW
P.O. Box 37200
Washington, D.C. 20013
(202) 727—7468

Florida
Director
Real Estate Commission
P.O. Box 1900
Orlando, Florida 32802
(305) 423—6053

Georgia
Commissioner
Real Estate Commission
40 Pryor Street, SW
Atlanta, Georgia 30303
(404) 656—3916

Guam
Administrator
Real Estate Agency
Department of Revenue and Taxation
855 West Marine Dr.
Agana, Guam 96910
(671) 477—1040

Hawaii
Executive Secretary
Real Estate Commission
Professional & Vocational
Licensing Division
P.O. Box 3469
Honolulu, Hawaii 96801
(808) 548—7464

Idaho
Executive Director
Real Estate Commission
State Capitol Building
Boise, Idaho 83720
(202) 334—3285

Illinois
Commissioner
Department of Professional Regulation
320 West Washington
Springfield, Illinois 62786
(217) 785—0800

Indiana
Deputy Director
Real Estate Commission
1021 State Office Building
100 North Senate Avenue
Indianapolis, Indiana 46204
(317) 232—2980

Iowa
Executive Secretary
Real Estate Commission
Department of Commerce
1918 S.E. Hulsizer
Ankeny, Iowa 50021
(515) 281—3183

Kansas
Director
Real Estate Commission
900 Jackson Street
Room 501
Topeka, Kansas 66612
(913) 296—3411

Kentucky
Executive Director
Real Estate Commission
222 S. First Street
Suite 300
Louisville, Kentucky 40202
(502) 588—4462

Louisiana
Executive Director
Real Estate Commission
P.O. Box 14785
Capital Station
Baton Rouge, Louisiana 70898
(504) 925—4771

Maine
Director
Real Estate Commission
4th Floor, State Office Building
Augusta, Maine 04333
(207) 289—3735

Maryland
Executive Director
Real Estate Commission
501 St. Paul Place
Suite 804
Baltimore, Maryland 21202
(301) 333—6230

Massachusetts
Executive Secretary
Board of Registration of Real Estate
Brokers & Salesmen
100 Cambridge Street
Room 1518
Boston, Massachusetts 02202
(617) 727—7376

Michigan
Administrative Secretary
Department of Licensing & Regulation
Real Estate Division
P.O. Box 30018
Lansing, Michigan 48909
(517) 373—0490

Minnesota
Director of Licensing
Department of Commerce
500 Metro Square Building
St. Paul, Minnesota 55101
(612) 297—4630

Mississippi
Administrator
Real Estate Commission
1920 Dunbarton Street
Jackson, Mississippi 39216
(601) 987—3969

Missouri
Executive director
Real Estate Commission
P.O. Box 1339
Jefferson City, Missouri 65102
(314) 751—2334

Montana
Administrator
Board of Realty Regulation
1424 Ninth Avenue
Helena, Montana 59620
(406) 444—2961

Nebraska
Director
Real Estate Commission
301 South Centennial Mall
Lincoln, Nebraska 68508
(402) 471—2004

Nevada
Administrator
Real Estate Division
201 South Fall Street
Carson City, Nevada 89710
(702) 885—4280

New Brunswick
Licensing Supervisor
Real Estate Council
P.O. Box 785
Fredericton, New Brunswick E3B 5B4
(506) 455—9733

New Hampshire
Executive director
Real Estate Commission
3rd Floor, Johnson Hall
107 Pleasant St.
Concord, New Hampshire 03301
(603) 271—2701

New Jersey
Executive Director
Real Estate Commission
20 West State Street
Trenton, New Jersey 08625
(609) 987—2010

New Mexico
Executive Secretary
Real Estate Commission
4125 Carlisle Blvd.
Albuquerque, New Mexico 87107
(505) 841—6524

New York
Director
Department of State
Division of Licensing Services
162 Washington Avenue
Albany, New York 12231
(518) 473—2419

North Carolina
Executive Director
Real Estate Commission
1313 Navaho Drive
Raleigh, North Carolina 27619
(919) 733—9580

North Dakota
Secretary-Treasurer
Real Estate Commission
314 East Thayer Avenue
P.O. Box 727
Bismarck, North Dakota 58502
(701) 224—2749

Nova Scotia
Superintendent
Consumer Services Division
P.O. Box 998
Halifax, Nova Scotia B3J 2X3
(902) 424—4690

Ohio
Superintendent
Division of Real Estate
Two Nationwide Plaza
Columbus, Ohio 43266
(614) 466—4100

Oklahoma
Executive Director
Real Estate Commission
4040 North Lincoln Blvd.
Suite 100
Oklahoma City, Oklahoma 73105
(405) 521—3387

Ontario
Registrar
Ministry of Consumer and Commercial
Relations
Business Practices Division
555 Yonge Street
Toronto, Canada M7A 2H6
(416) 963—0406

Oregon
Commissioner
Real Estate Agency
158 12th Street, NE
Salem, Oregon 97310
(503) 378—4170

Pennsylvania
Administrative Secretary
Department of State
Professional & Occupational Affairs
Real Estate Commission
P.O. Box 2649
Harrisburg, Pennsylvania 17105
(717) 783—3658

Quebec
Superintendent
Service de Courtage Immobilier du Quebec
Ministere de la Justice
220 Grande Allee Est
Quebec, Canada G1R 2J1
(418) 643—4597

Rhode Island
Deputy Administrator
Real Estate Division
100 North Main Street
Providence, Rhode Island 02903
(401) 277—2255

Saskatchewan
Superintendent of Insurance,
Consumer and Commercial Affairs
1871 Smith Street
Regina, Saskatchewan, Canada S4P 3V7
(306) 787—2958

South Carolina
Commissioner

Real Estate Commission
1201 Main Street
Suite 1500
Columbia, South Carolina 29201
(803) 737—0700

South Dakota
Executive Secretary
Real Estate Commission
P.O. Box 490
Pierre, South Dakota 57501
(605) 773—3600

Tennessee
Executive Director
Real Estate Commission
1808 West End Building
Nashville, Tennessee 37219
(615) 741—2273

Texas
Administrator
Real Estate Commission
P.O. Box 12188, Capital Station
Austin, Texas 78711
(512) 459—6544

Utah
Director
Real Estate Division
160 East 300 South
Salt Lake City, Utah 84145
(801) 530—6747

Vermont
Executive Director
Real Estate Commission
Pavilion Office Building
Montpelier, Vermont 05602
(802) 828—3228

Virginia
Director
Department of Commerce
Real Estate Commission
3600 W. Broad St.
Richmond, Virginia 23230
(804) 367—8552

Virgin Islands
Director
Real Estate Commission
Property and Procurement Building
St. Thomas, Virgin Islands 00802
(809) 774—3130

Washington
Executive Secretary
Real Estate Division
P.O. Box 9012
Olympia, Washington 98504
(206) 753—0775

West Virginia
Executive Secretary
Real Estate Commission
1033 Quarrier Street
Suite 400
Charleston, West Virginia 25301
(304) 348—3555

Wisconsin
Bureau Director
Department of Regulation & Licensing
Real Estate Examining Board
1400 East Washington Avenue
Madison, Wisconsin 53708
(608) 266—5450

Wyoming
Executive Director
Real Estate Commission
4301 Herschler Building
Cheyenne, Wyoming 82002
(307) 777—7141

Index

A

Abandonment 100
Abstract of title 171
Acceleration clause 135
Acceptance 37
Accession 130
Accord and satisfaction 44
Accretion 130
Acknowledgment 129
Actual communication 38
Actual damages 43
Actual notice 144
Adjusted basis 202
Adjusted sales price 186
Administrator 129
Ad valorem tax 210
Adverse possession 130
Affirmative Fair Housing Marketing Plan 120
Agency 48
   capacity of parties 50
   creation 50
   purpose 51
   termination 57
Agent 48
   authority 54
   broker as 51
   duties to principal 55
   kinds of 49
   relation to third parties 57
Agreement to insure 172
Air rights 5
Alienation 76
Allodial system 74
Alteration 44
American Institute of Real Estate Appraisers 18
American Society of Real Estate Counselors 18
Amortization 158
Amortization loans 158

Annual percentage rate 152
Anticipation 184
Appeals board 211
Apportionment clause 113
Appraisal 183
Appraisal Foundation 188
Appraisal process 184
Appraisal report 188
Appreciation 200
Appurtenant 128
APR 152
Arbitration 100
Assessed value 210
Assignment 43
Associate broker 27
Assumption of mortgage 140
Attachment 143
Attestation 128
Attorney-in-fact 128
Authority 48
Avulsion 130

B

Balloon payments 159
Band of investment method 197
Base lines 67
Basis 202
Bench mark 64
Beneficiary 138
Bilateral contract 37
Binder 42
Blanket mortgages 163
Block 69
Blockbusting 117
Board of equalization 211
Boot 202
Breach of contract 43
Broker 27

Broker examination   2
Brundage clause   140
Budget mortgages   159
Buffer zone   208
Build-up method   196
Builders method   186
Building manager   95
Building permit   209

C

Capital-gains income   201
Capitalization approach   197
Capitalization rate   196
Cash flow   199
Caveat emptor   40
Certificate of eligibility   161
Certificate of occupancy   209
Certificate of reasonable value   161
Certificate of title   171
Chain of title   170
Change   184
Chattel real   9
Circuit-breaker   211
Civil Rights Act of 1866   116
Closed mortgage   161
Closing   173
Clustering   210
Cluster zoning   210
Code of ethics   19
Coinsurance clause   112
Color of title   130
Commercial banks   154
Commercial frustration   100
Commingling   33
Commission   27
Common elements   88
Community property   82
Community Reinvestment Act   153
Community Unit Plan (CUP)   210
Comparable sales approach   185
Comparative unit method   186
Competition   183
Concessions   96
Concurrent owners   80
Condemnation   131
Condition   42
Condominium law   88
Conformity   183
Consequential damages   43
Consideration   38
Construction loans   159
Constructive eviction   101
Constructive notice   144
Contracts   36
   Breach and remedies   43
   Conditions and contingency clauses   42
   Definition   36
   Discharge   43
   Factors affecting validity   39
   Formation   36
   Rights of third persons   43

Contribution   184
Conventional life estates   76
Conventional mortgages   160
Cooperative ownership   92
Corporations   82
Correction lines   67
Cost approach   186
Council on Environmental Quality (CEQ)   210
Counteroffer   37
Covenants   42
Credit union   156
Crops   79
Cross index   170
Cumulative districts   208
Curable deterioration   187
Curtesy   77

D

Dedication   131
Deduction   202
Deeds   123
   Contents   126
   Covenants   124
   Requirements   126
   Types   123
Deed restrictions   127
Defeasance clause   137
Deferred interest mortgages   165
Deficiency judgment   137
Delivery and acceptance   126
Demand   6
Demise   97
Deposit receipt   42
Depreciable basis   202
Determinable fee estate   76
Descent   129
Devise   129
Direct capitalization method   197
Directive zoning   208
Discount points   177
Disintermediation   151
Divisibility of land   8
Dominant estate   78
Dower   77
Due on sale clause   140
Durability of land   6
Duress   41

E

Earnest money deposit   56
Easement   78
Economic life   187
Economic obsolescence   187
Effective age   187
Effective gross income   195
Emblements   79
Eminent domain   207
Encroachment   79
Environmental Impact Statement (EIS)   210
Environmental Protection Agency (EPA)   210

Equal Credit Opportunity Act   152
Equal dignities rule   51
Equal opportunity in housing   116
Equitable conversion   42
Equitable lien   141
Equitable redemption   136
Equitable title   42
Escheat   130
Escrow account   173
Escrow agent   173
Estates   74
Estate for years   97
Estate from year to year   97
Eviction   101
Exception   127
Exchanges   202
Exclusions   202
Exclusive agency listing   53
Exclusive right to sell listing   53
Exclusive use districts   208
Executed contract   39
Execution   126
Executory contract   39
Express contract   38

F

Factors of production   7
Fair Credit Reporting Act   153
Fannie Mae   157
Federal Deposit Insurance Corporation (FDIC)   154
Federal Fair Housing Law of 1968   116
Federal Home Loan Bank System (FHLBS)   154
Federal Home Loan Mortgage Corporation (FHLMC)   158
Federal Housing Administration (FHA)   161
Federal National Mortgage Association (FNMA)   157
Federal Reserve System (FRS)   154
Federal Savings and Loan Insurance Corporation (FSLIC)   154
Federal taxation   201
Federal Truth-In-Lending Act   151
Fee simple absolute   74
Fee simple determinable   76
Fee simple estate   74
Fee simple subject to a condition subsequent   76
Fee tail   76
Feudal system   74
FHA   161
FHLBS   154
Fiduciary relationship   55
Finance companies   156
Financing real estate   148
Finder's fee   155
Fire and hazard insurance   111
First mortgages   160
First right of refusal   91
Fixed gross lease   98
Fixtures   9
Flexible loan insurance program (FLIP)   164
FLIP   164
Floor area ratios   208
FNMA   157
Foreclosure   139

Foreign funds   156
Fraud   40
Freddie Mac   158
Free Market System Auction   158
Freehold estates   74
Frustration of purpose   44
FSLIC   154
Full replacement coverage   113
Fully amortized mortgages   158
Functional obsolescence   187
Future covenants   124
Future interest   77

G

General liens   143
General partnership   82
General warranty deed   123
Ginnie Mae   158
GNMA   158
Good consideration   127
Good faith estimate   174
Government National Mortgage Association (GNMA)   158
Graduate lease   100
Graduated payment mortgage (GPM)   163
Grant deed   125
Grantee   123
Granting clause   127
Grantor   123
Grantor-grantee index   170
Gridiron pattern   69
GRM   187
Gross lease   98
Gross rent multiplier (GRM)   187
Guaranteed loans   161

H

Habendum clause   128
Heirs   129
Hereditaments   128
Heterogeneity of land   6
Highest and best use   7
Hold-harmless clause   140
Holding over   98
Home improvement loans   162
Home rule powers   207
Homeowner's association   88
Homeowner's insurance policy   111
Home Owners Warranty (HOW)   108
Homestead   77
Horizontal property act   88
Housing and Community Development Act of 1974   116
Hypothecate   137

I

Illusory offer   36
Immobility of land   5
Impact zoning   208
Improvements   5
Income approach   194

Increasing and decreasing returns 184
Incurable deterioration 187
Indestructibility of land 6
Index lease 100
Individual ownership 80
Infant 39
Inheritable estates 74
Insane persons 40
Installment land contract 138
Installment sales 202
Institute of Real Estate Management (IREM) 18
Insurable interest 111
Insurance 111
Insurance companies 154
Intangible property 10
Interim financing 159
Interstate Land Sales Full Disclosure Act 210
Intestate 129
Intoxicated persons 40
Investment syndicates 83
Investment Tax Credit 202

J

Joint tenancy 80
Joint ventures 83
Jones v. Alfred H. Mayer Co. 116
Judgment 143
Judicial foreclosure 137

L

Land 5
Land contracts 163
Land descriptions 64
Land leases 163
Land sales contract 138
Land surveying measurements 218
Land trusts 83
Landed homes association 92
Late payment clause 139
Lateral and subjacent support 79
Law of nuisance 8
Leases 98
Legal benefit 39
Legal capacity 39
Legal description 64
Legal detriment 39
Legal rights, bundle of 8
Legality of form 41
Legality of object 41
Lending laws 151
Less than freehold estates 74
Lessee 97
Lessor 97
Leverage 201
License 79
License law and statutes 26
Lienholder 141
Liens 141
Lien theory 137
Life estate 76

Life estate pur autre vie 76
Life insurance companies 154
Life tenant 76
Limited common elements 88
Limited partnership 82
Linear measurements 218
Liquidated damages 43
Lis pendens 143
Listing contract 173
Loan commitment 155
Loan guaranty program 161
Loan-to-value ratio 160
Lot and block 69
Loyalty 55

M

Maintenance 96
Maintenance fee 88
Management plan 96
Management agreement 96
Marketable title 170
Market comparison approach 185
Market price 184
Market value 184
Master-servant relationship 48
Materialman's lien 142
Mechanic's lien 142
Menace 41
Merger 44
Metes and bounds 64
MGIC 161
Mill 211
Mileage rate 211
Mineral rights 5
Minor 39
Misrepresentation 40
Mistakes 40
MLS 53
Mobile home mortgages 163
Model Land Development Code 210
Modification of land 7
Monuments 66
Mortgage banking companies 155
Mortgage brokers 155
Mortgagee 135
Mortgage Guaranty Insurance Corporation (MGIC) 161
Mortgages 135
Mortgagor 135
Multiple listing service 53
Multiple ownership 82
Mutual assent 36
Mutual rescission 44
Mutual savings banks 154

N

National Association of Home Builders (NAHB) 108
National Association of Real Estate Brokers (NAREB) 17
National Association of Real Estate License Law Officials (NARELLO) 26

NATIONAL ASSOCIATION OF REALTORS® (NAR) 17
National banks 154
National Consumer Credit Protection Act 151
National Environmental Policy Act (NEPA) 210
National Flood Insurance Program 153
National Housing Act of 1934 161
National Housing Act of 1961 89
Negative cash flow 199
NEPA 210
Net lease 99
Net listing 53
Net operating income 196
Net sales price 202
N.O.I. 196
Nonconforming use 209
Nonfreehold estates 74
Nonhomogeneity 6
Noninheritable freehold estates 76
Note 135
Notice statutes 144
Novation 43

O

Obligee 135
Obligor 135
Offer and acceptance 36
Open listing 52
Open mortgage 161
Operating expenses 196
Opinion of title 171
Option 38
Optionee 38
Optionor 38
Ordinary income 201
Ordinary life estate 76
Ownership 80

P

Package mortgages 163
Parol evidence rule 42
Partial eviction 101
Partial release clause 140
Partially amortized mortgage 159
Participation mortgage 165
Partnership 82
Patent 131
Pension funds 156
Percentage lease 99
Perfecting title 171
Permanent loans 160
Personal property 9
Physical deterioration 186
Planned unit development (PUD) 210
Planning 207
Plat of the condominium subdivision 90
Plat of subdivision 69
PMI 161
Point of beginning (POB) 65
Points 177
Police power 207

Possibility of reverter 77
Potential gross income 195
Power of attorney 49
Power-of-sale clause 137
Power of termination 77
Preliminary binder 172
Prepaid items 178
Prepayment privilege clause 135
Present contractual intent 36
Present covenants 124
Prime rate 160
Principal 48
    duties to agent 56
    kinds of 49
    relations to third parties 57
Principal meridians 67
Principle of dependency 7
Prior appropriation system 80
Priority of lien 144
Private mortgage insurance 161
Procuring cause 52
Profits 79
Promissory note 135
Property insurance 111
Property management 95
Property ownership 80
Pro rata clause 113
Prorations 223
Protective zoning 208
Public offering statement 89
PUDs 210
Pur autre vie 76
Purchase money mortgages 162

Q

Quadrangles 67
Quadrants 65
Quantity survey method 186

R

Ranges 67
Rate of return 199
Ratios 225
Ready, willing and able 54
Real estate 5
Real estate commission 27
Real estate investment trust (REIT) 83
Real Estate Licensing Examinations (RELE) 1
Real estate markets 18
Real Estate Securities and Syndication Institute (RESSI) 18
Real estate recovery fund 30
Real Estate Settlement Procedures Act (RESPA) 174
Reality of consent 40
Realtist 17
REALTOR® 17
Realtors National Marketing Institute (RNMI) 18
Reappraisal lease 100
Reasonable time 37
Receiver 137
Reciprocity 32

Recorded plat 67
Recording 179
Rectangular survey system 67
Redlining 153
Regulation Z 151
REIT 83
Reliction 130
Remainder 78
Remaining economic life 187
Renegotiable rate mortgage (RRM) 164
Replacement cost 186
Reproduction cost 186
Rescission 43
Reservation 127
Resident manager 95
RESPA 174
Respondeat superior 48
Restrictive covenant 127
Return 199
Reverse annuity mortgages 164
Revocation of offer 38
Rights and interests 74
Right of survivorship 81
Riparian rights 79
RRM 164
R value 111

S

Sale-leaseback 165
Salesperson 27
Salesperson examination 2
Savings and loan associations 154
Scarcity 8
Seal 128
Second mortgages 162
Secondary mortgage market 157
Sections 68
Servicing a loan 156
Servient estate 78
Settlement 177
Severalty 80
Shared appreciation mortgage (SAM) 165
Short rates 113
Situs 8
Sleeper clause 139
Society of Industrial and Office Realtors (SIOR) 18
Source of funds 153
Special assessments 142
Special purpose deeds 125
Special-use permits 209
Special warranty deeds 124
Specific liens 142
Specific performance 43
Spillover effect 8
Spot zoning 209
Standard City Planning Enabling Act 207
Standby commitment 160
Statute of frauds 41
Standard State Zoning Enabling Act 208
Standards of measurement 218

Statutes of descent and distribution 129
Statutory lien 141
Statutory redemption 136
Steering 117
Straight-line depreciation 202
Straight-term mortgages 158
Straw man 81
Street address 64
Strict foreclosure 136
Subdivision regulations 209
Subject to 140
Subletting 98
Subordination clause 140
Subrogation 113
Substitution 183
Summation method 196
Superadequacy 187
Supervening illegality 44
Surrender and acceptance 100
Surveys 64
Survivorship 81
Syndication 83

T

Take-out commitment 160
Tangible property 10
Tax certificate 142
Tax-free exchange 202
Tax levy 210
Tax liens 142
Tax rate 211
Tax sales 211
Tenancy at sufferance 98
Tenancy at will 98
Tenancy by the entirety 81
Tenancy in common 80
Tenancy in partnership 82
Tenement 128
Term mortgages 158
Testate 129
Testimonium 128
Time sharing 91
Time value of money 199
Timing and sequencing controls 210
Title 123
Title insurance 171
Title theory 137
Torrens System 173
Tort liability 48
Townships 67
Tract index 170
Transfer development rights (TDR) 210
Transfer tax stamps 129
Transferability 7
Trust 83
Trust deeds 138
Trustee 138
Trustor 138
Truth-In-Lending Act 151

U

Undivided interest 80
Undue influence 41
Unenforceable contract 39
Uniform Landlord-Tenant Act 101
Uniform Partnership Act 82
Uniform Settlement Statement 174
Uniform Vendor and Purchaser Risk Act 42
Unilateral contract 37
Unilateral mistake 40
Unit deed 90
U.S. government survey system 67
Unit-in-place method 186
Unities of ownership 81
Usury 151
Utility 6

V

VA mortgages 161
Vacancy allowance 195
Valid contract 39
Value 183
Valuable consideration 127
Variable rate mortgages (VRM) 164
Variance 209
Vendee 143
Vendor 143
Vested 77
Veterans Administration (VA) 161
Vicarious liability 48
Village of Euclid v. Amber Realty Co. 208
Void contract 39
Voidable contract 39
Voluntary conveyance 123
Voluntary lien 141
VRM 164

W

Warranty deed 123
Waste 76
Water rights 79
Wills 129
Wraparound mortgages 162
Writ of attachment 143
Written release 44

Z

Zoning 207